Popular Music Since 1955

Popular Music
Since 1955

A critical guide to the literature

Paul Taylor

G.K.HALL & CO.

70 LINCOLN STREET, BOSTON, MASS.

Published 1985 in the United States of America and
Canada by G. K. Hall & Co., 70 Lincoln Street,
Boston, Massachusetts 02111, U.S.A.

First published 1985 by Mansell Publishing Limited
(A subsidiary of The H. W. Wilson Company)
6 All Saints Street, London N1 9RL, England

Library of Congress Cataloging in Publication Data

Taylor, Paul.
    Popular music since 1955.

    Includes index.
    1. Music, Popular (Songs, etc.)—Bibliography.
I. Title.
ML128.P63T39   1985b   016.78'042'0904   85-8732
ISBN 0-8161-8784-3

Printed and bound in Great Britain by Robert Hartnoll (1985 Ltd)
Bodmin, Cornwall

Contents

Preface

In 1955 rock'n'roll emerged as an important new musical force which was to capture the popular imagination, become the catalyst of a powerful youth culture, revolutionize the popular-music industry and deeply influence all other forms of music.

As popular music became vitalized by this new injection, literature began to appear on the subject. From mainly pictorial collections, patronizing biographies and fan magazines in the early years, by the late sixties a serious approach had begun to evolve and by the late seventies a vast range and volume of material had been produced. To date there has been no serious attempt to bring together, organize and assess this substantial body of literature.

The aim of this work is to provide a critical, bibliographical guide to the literature of contemporary popular music published in English since 1955.

Introduction

DEFINITION

The concise Oxford dictionary defines the word 'popular', as related to music, as: 'not seeking to appeal to a refined or classical taste' and 'adapted to the understanding, taste or means of the people'. *Webster's new international dictionary* adds: 'beloved or approved by the people, pleasing to the people in general' and includes the concepts: 'easy to understand' and 'adapted to mean: inferior or cheap'.

Each of these notions may be applied to the subject of this book, but the term 'popular' when applied to music is an ill-defined and problematical one. It is regarded here as describing a collection of musical forms, types or styles which are followed by mass audiences of record buyers and concert goers. It excludes serious, classical or art music, which is created by the musically educated for a refined audience.

Folk music is excluded as, by definition, its traditions are historical, although some contemporary folk artists, in the American sense, are included as their music is really modern, comprising recently written songs.

Jazz is regarded as a fringe subject, partly because of its current position as a sophisticated form of music which has evolved far from its historical, popular roots, but mainly because it has been an aim from the outset that this current work should complement *The literature of jazz: a critical guide*, by Don Kennington and Danny L. Read (2nd ed. – London: The Library Association, 1980.). Some overlap has of course been unavoidable when dealing with such closely related subjects and, indeed, is desirable to ensure that this work stands alone in its own right. 1955 is the year in which coverage begins because it was in that year that rock'n'roll was established as a potent force and it is the influence of rock'n'roll that has created modern popular music.

THE MUSIC

Contemporary popular music evolved in the United States of America. It is a fusion of musical styles combining influences from white country music, itself a popular form which had evolved from traditional white folk music; black rhythm & blues, which had evolved from the black country blues into the urban blues forms; and the commercial popular music of Tin Pan Alley, the music hall, vaudeville and light music forms.

By the early fifties the power of the cinema as the focus of popular fantasy was waning largely because of the post-war boom in television throughout the USA and by the mid fifties this was also true of the United Kingdom.

Jazz, the dance music followed by young people in the pre-war period, had on the one hand developed into dance-band music, losing its spontaneity and excitement and, on the other hand, evolved into its sophisticated modern styles. A need for a new, exciting form of music, accessible to a mass, youthful audience, was strongly evident.

The war years had somewhat retarded the development of music during the forties, partly because of the emphasis on things military but also because of the reduction in recording activity owing to a shortage of shellac. Beneath the surface, however, were latent forces. The increasing urbanization in America was bringing both white country music and black country blues to the cities. In addition, musical instruments were developing. Les Paul and Leo Fender were among those producing electric instruments and amplification which gave increased power and a pulsating beat to these mixing musical styles.

On both sides of the Atlantic young people were becoming more affluent than ever before. There were more of them with a new economic power, more leisure time and a view that respect for one's elders was an outmoded concept. This 'generation gap' was seen as an inevitable and unavoidable cultural feature; the condemnation from adults only exacerbated the condition and rock'n'roll offered a rallying point of common identity.

The music-industry machine and the mass media, naturally ready to capital-ize on a new, long-awaited phenomenon, rolled into action to launch the biggest entertainment revolution since the silent film.

Exactly which was the first rock'n'roll recording is a matter for some debate and the truth is that there was a large degree of parallel development.

Sh'boom by the Chords, a hit in early 1954, is frequently cited as the first rock'n'roll record. It is not white rock'n'roll, in fact, but the first success of the Doo-wop style, which was a diluted rhythm & blues form aimed at the commercial market.

Bill Haley and the Comets' efforts in 1953 were an extension of the country swing, showband style but his recording of Rock around the Clock, on April 12th 1954, is probably a more definite starting point. The use of the record in the soundtrack of the film Blackboard Jungle, 1955, was certainly a significant factor in the establishment of the music in the public consciousness.

It was Elvis Presley, however, who became the first rock'n'roll star. When he entered Sam Phillips' Sun studios on July 6th 1954 for his first professional recording session, he fused the black rhythm & blues of Memphis with his own hillbilly, country tradition and symbolized a new musical form to the awaiting mass audience.

Since 1956 the pervasive influence of rock'n'roll has dominated popular music. It generated experimentation leading to the evolution of other forms, stimulating and effecting diversification of country music and black music and transforming the tradition of Tin Pan Alley which has, perhaps, performed a refining role and added its own commercialism.

Before 1956, Tin Pan Alley was dominated by songs from Broadway and Hollywood musicals, ballad-singing crooners and swing singers, like Sinatra who fringed, but could not be truly defined as jazz. Black music and country music had their audiences as did the embryonic folk, protest movement. With the new music emerged a young, white audience who were beginning to listen to black music. Country music stayed, for a time, as a separate entity with a few artists performing in both the rockabilly and mainstream country styles in Nashville.

In the United Kingdom, skiffle appeared in 1955. Born in the rhythm sections of traditional jazz bands, it was influenced notably by the blues of Leadbelly and the protest songs of Woody Guthrie but also by the English music-hall tradition.

Rock'n'roll in its early, pure form was over by 1960 and a period of diluted pop music prevailed which created the surfing sound in California. This lull was broken in 1963 by the Beatles' breakthrough and the invasion of America by British Beat. The Beatles were to dominate popular music for the next five years and with Bob Dylan, who had come from the folk movement and established the singer-songwriter trend, they brought a sense of respectability. For the first time this new music was being allowed a degree of serious appreciation.

Since 1967 rock music in all its many manifestations has evolved into the eighties through West Coast rock, progressive rock and heavy metal to the new wave, co-existing with the pop and cabaret styles which have been modified but are strictly, traditionally, from Tin Pan Alley. Black music, in the meantime, has produced its own immensely successful stages from Phil Spector's Wall of Sound and Tamla Motown in the early and mid sixties to Phillie, disco and funk in the seventies with the rougher soul music keeping its roots very much in the gospel struggle.

By the mid seventies country music had gained a wide, general audience, and had been influenced lyrically by the singer-songwriters and musically by rock music.

Thus the evolution continues, ever spurred on by the relentless commercial need to find something new.

THE LITERATURE

During the fifties and early sixties popular music was written about in the few existing music papers with occasional publications appearing in the form of fan magazines or collections of photographs. The limited number of biographies which did begin to appear were patronizing in style and poor in production. Clearly, this reflected the view of publishers that those interested in such music would be unlikely to desire to read about it.

Indeed, as Simon Frith points out (*The sociology of rock*. – London: Constable, 1978.), it would not be until the late sixties that it was becoming evident, or at least socially acceptable, that such music could deserve the interest of other than the uneducated teenager.

In fact, it was during the late sixties that serious writings began to appear in *Rolling Stone* magazine which was soon followed by the likes of *Crawdaddy*, *Cream* and *Zigzag*. In addition, the effect of such a new approach to the subject created an atmosphere in which more books began to appear, including a few serious historical analyses.

Frank Hoffman (*The literature of rock, 1954–1978.* – Metuchen, New Jersey; London: Scarecrow Press, 1981.) makes an interesting comparison of numbers of articles cited in the *Readers' guide to periodical literature* between 1959 and 1979. Taking into account that this index covers few specialist, popular-music publications, there were twenty-seven articles cited in 1959, fifty-two in 1963 and two hundred and thirty-three in 1979.

As can be seen, the expansion over recent years has been dramatic and there have certainly been more publications in all areas of popular music since 1977 than in the previous twenty-two years covered here. Indeed the books which have appeared since work began on this project have greatly increased the original estimated extent of the work, amounting to some 300 titles.

The simplest interpretation of the explosion in the literature is that, despite what we are often told, young people are more literate and wish to read about their interests. In addition, there is now a generation approaching middle age who have been brought up with rock'n'roll, its descendants and associates, who permeate society and retain an interest in some popular-musical form and wish to read about it in an educated, informal way, thereby creating a demand which is on the whole yet to be fulfilled.

The literature of modern popular music reflects closely the characteristics of its subject: it is an emerging art form struggling to be taken seriously. It is brash, self-conscious, usually superficial, frequently pretentious but occasionally it is beginning to show sparks of genuine thought and creativity.

AIMS AND SCOPE

The purpose of this book is to provide a critical, bibliographical guide to this extensive body of literature. It has been the aim to include:

1. A comprehensive guide to English-language monographs. These have virtually all been published in North America or the United Kingdom. There is a degree of interchange of publications between the USA and the United Kingdom but it is by no means a complete process. Many works appear in a variety of editions with North American and British imprints whereas others may only find their way across the Atlantic because of the vigilance of specialist bookshops and libraries. Because a title appears here with full annotation, having been examined, it means that, on the whole, copies exist in the United Kingdom. It does not mean that they are or ever have been widely available.

2. Major, current periodicals, magazines, trade and music papers available in the United Kingdom and North America are included in detail. There is a brief listing of defunct United Kingdom publications and a detailed section on fan magazines devoted to individual artists.

3. Fiction focussing on the subject has been reviewed in detail.

4. General books on films concerned with the subject or featuring artists, are included with synopses of the films.

5. A wide range of related subjects have emerged during this study and have naturally found their place around the nucleus of works concerned directly with forms of music and artists and their work. Social aspects, related subcultures, business economics, politics and associated visual arts are a few.

6. The period covered is 1955 to 1982 inclusive with, in addition, the significant books published during 1983 and 1984 to make this work as contemporary as possible. \

7. Forms of printed material regarded as outside the scope of this work but worth noting are:

Record sleeves. Genuine biographical or critical information is, in general, rare but there are exceptions and sleeves often do provide excellent illustrative material and song lyrics.

Sheet music collections. High-quality portraits and good biographical essays are more frequently available in this form. A guide to contemporary sheet music is a challenge awaiting another stoic researcher.

Tutors. Not a good information source, but in some cases styles of playing instruments are well examined using particular artists as examples and in a few cases well-known musicians have given their names to tutors.

Concert programmes. As a souvenir of an evening's entertainment, programmes have been a form of ephemeral literature for many years. Usually of use as a source of illustrative material; very occasionally they may also contain a useful essay or interview. No large collection of these exists and one may only track them down in private collections and fan club offices.

Publicity materials. The most fugitive source of all. These will include duplicated fact sheets, glossy pamphlets, posters, handbills, T-shirts, badges, hats and even paper underwear. Apart from collectors and a very few, record-company office archives, access to these materials is problematical. Occasionally, however, fan club and record collecting magazines do include advertisements as does *Exchange and Mart*.

EXTENT

Included are over 1,600 entries for monographs which cite over 2,000 editions. (Paperback editions with an identical imprint but different ISBN are not counted separately.) In addition details of over 200 periodicals are given.

ARRANGEMENT

The table of contents shows clearly the classified arrangement that has been adopted. It has been the aim to provide a logical organization of material, relating associated subjects in clear, well-defined chapters.

The specific arrangements within chapters and sections is outlined in the appropriate introductions.

Within classified sections and subsections headings are arranged alphabetically in strict word-by-word sequences.

Entries have been prepared using the *Anglo-American cataloguing rules*. – Second edition. – London: Library Association, 1978.

There are frequent *see* and *see also* references. Where reference is made between chapters, brackets appear; within a chapter they do not.

Capitals have been used for the names of people, groups and films where they are subjects. This is for ease of consultation of the Name Index and as an aid to consulting the extensive Chapter 6 in particular.

It has been a principle to cite with full bibliographical details and description the most recent edition of a work, published in the United Kingdom, in the hope that this is the most likely to be available. The only exception is where a later edition is by a publisher specializing in reprints (for example, White Lion). All other editions are carefully noted within the entry.

TERMINOLOGY

Terminology is a particular problem when approaching the organization of material in this field. The cross fertilization of musical influences and sudden appearance of new musical styles has resulted in widespread confusion in precise classification and description. Titles usually fail to describe accurately their subject matter and are frequently misleading.

The use of the terms 'pop' and 'rock' is a major problem. Their usage has evolved to communicate quite different meanings: 'rock' now refers to the more serious, album-orientated end of the white, contemporary, popular-music spectrum, whereas 'pop' is the more ephemeral, lighter, singles-orientated form. During the sixties, however, pop was used to refer to all forms of contemporary popular styles and rock meant specifically the rock'n'roll of the fifties.

Confusion does not end here. *The illustrated encyclopedia of rock*, by Nick Logan and Bob Woffinden (London: Salamander, 1982. *See* section 1.1) represents the problem well. Included is information on black music and musicians from rhythm & blues, soul, reggae and disco styles as well as country music, contemporary folk and pop artists. The term 'rock', therefore, is used here to describe modern popular music, excluding the area of cabaret.

New rock record, by Terry Hounsome and Tim Chambre (Poole, Dorset: Blandford Press, 1981. *See* section 1.8) again offers confusion by including a wide range of black artists, some country, folk and much pop music, but becoming terribly confused over what to exclude: Barry Manilow, for example, is omitted.

The soul book, edited by Ian Hoare (London: Eyre Methuen, 1975. *See* Chapter 5) is a collection of excellent essays on a far wider range of black music than the narrow term 'soul' implies, emphasizing that this problem in terminology is pervasive.

Material has, of course, been arranged by what it actually covers. Hence, at first sight, some placings within the arrangement may appear contradictory. As a general rule a more specific term will frequently have been used in a title to describe a work concerning a wider area and will, therefore, appear in a more general section. For example, *The sound of the city: the rise of rock'n'roll*, by Charlie Gillett (London: Souvenir Press, 1972. *See* Chapter 1.) is not an isolated study of rock'n'roll but a complex history of the interrelationship of black and white popular music throughout the fifties and sixties. It therefore appears in the general histories section.

For specific definitions of musical and technical terms *see* the introductory notes to the relevant section and the glossary (pp. 479–496).

SOURCES

On embarking on the project it was clear that one of the major characteristics of the literature of the subject was its fugitive nature. Much appears only in paperback form and most publishers avoid legal deposit and subsequent bibliographical control.

After the *BLAISE* on-line system had been used to search exhaustively the current and retrospective data bases of the British Library and Library of Congress, a nucleus of material was supplemented by the extensive searching of manual bibliographies: *Cumulative Book Index*, *Library of Congress Catalog*, *American Books in Print* and so on.

My own library provided me with a variety of brief bibliographies in a few of the more serious works and, indeed, gave a basis on which to begin the accumulation of information, its examination and the writing of annotations, biographies and so on. The subsequent tracking down and discovery of material was then by improvisation and the following of leads as they arose.

The librarian of the English Folk Dance and Song Society, Malcolm Taylor, provided me with a great deal of material from his own collection and much useful advice. Westminster's Central Music Library has a very good collection of works on all forms of popular music. Many days were spent there in which the staff made countless trips to the basement without complaint.

The university libraries of Keele, Essex, Sussex and Nottingham were also used. The special collection of American material at Exeter University was particularly useful and the help and interest of David Horn is most appreciated. The library and bookshop of the Pompidou Centre in Paris also provided many rare American publications.

The national inter-library loans network provided hundreds of books from unlikely public, college and university libraries throughout the country and the British Library, Lending Division proved to have a remarkable collection of rare American material.

Publishers in the United Kingdom and the USA supplied information in a most generous way. Hundreds were contacted, many of whom produced out-of-print items and happily sent them to me, even across the Atlantic. Bookshops were another surprising source. Compendium in Camden High Street, Magic Bus in Richmond (which has now unfortunately closed), Books Bits and Bobs in Kingston, all bookshops specializing in the subject, were very useful sources. In addition many other London bookshops were used and many hours were spent, over three years, scribbling notes, particularly in Foyles of Charing Cross Road, the shelf stock of which has now greatly improved on the subject thanks to some well-directed advice on American publications.

The staff of the *New Musical Express*, *Melody Maker*, *Sounds* and *Record Mirror* as well as editors of dozens of fanzines and other magazines have all been most helpful, many of them on a number of occasions supplying facts, tracing material, providing me with access to their archives or introductions to friends and colleagues.

Finally, friends, acquaintances and colleagues have been the sources of a remarkable volume of rare publications and facts. I am truly grateful for the interest and enthusiasm that has been shown in the project by so many people, in particular Joy Taylor for her encouragement, constant reminders to ensure my obsession was kept in reasonable perspective, and almost perfect spelling.

And, not forgetting, for their inspiration: my long-time music tutor and friend Brian Redfern, Mr Mojo Risin' and, latterly, Nesta Marley.

CHAPTER ONE

General works

The variety of general works has increased dramatically in recent years. As well as the common approaches, such as encyclopedias, directories, histories and collected essays, which are to be found with the majority of subjects, and the obvious specific forms, such as discographical works, which one would naturally associate with a musical subject, there are also some types of publication which are unique to this field or are applied in a unique way.

The statistical data, notably of record charts and other ranking lists, is a particular specific form which is currently greatly expanding. Almanacs dealing with the trivia and microscopic details of artists' lives point towards a demand for tabulated facts otherwise difficult to retrieve. Perhaps the most extraordinary form to have appeared, however, is the collection of genealogical tables plotting the evolution and interrelationships of rock groups. The remarkable number of quizbooks is an indication of the ever-growing enquiry, albeit mainly superficial, which exists on the subject.

The variety of these publications is matched by the variation in the quality of their writing, accuracy and scholarship, which means one must approach them with a degree of discrimination and care.

Nevertheless, here is a body of informational and reference sources which provide a wealth of facts on the subject and a background and introduction to the literature as a whole.

1.1 ENCYCLOPEDIAS

Although when used in conjunction with other general sources or as an introduction to specific subject works the following encyclopedic offerings form a basis to work from, there is a real need for a regularly updated, authoritative work. The inherent contemporary and dynamic nature of modern popular music makes this both essential and difficult.

When *Lillian Roxon's Rock encyclopedia* appeared in 1969, it promised to be such a work but the author's death prevented the fulfilment of that promise, and Irwin Stambler's two excellent encyclopedias have never been revised. The most recent disappointment has been the publication of *The illustrated encyclopedia of rock* by Nick Logan and Bob Woffinden. Its early potential to provide the much demanded, regular revision was wasted in the most recent update, which fails to be a cohesively organized reference source.

1

The strong emphasis on the performer, which pervades popular music, is very much reflected in these works, which consist mainly of entries for artists while record companies, forms of music, instruments, writers, venues and so on take very much a secondary place.

Dachs, David
  Encyclopedia of pop/rock / David Dachs. – New York: Scholastic Press, 1972. – 138p.: ill., ports; 20cm. (pbk.)

Alphabetically arranged, although largely biographical, with entries for musical styles, record companies, songwriters and a few producers. A brief but informative little source, particularly for its date of publication, there are some very good photographs and a well-written text which only occasionally betrays an aim at the American high schools market. It is surprisingly good on its coverage of British groups of the sixties and the then contemporary West Coast movement.

The encyclopedia of rock / edited by Phil Hardy and Dave Laing. – St.
  Albans: Panther.
  In 3 vols.

  Volume 1: The age of rock'n'roll. – 1976. – 352p.; 18cm. Includes index.
  ISBN 0-586-04267-9 (pbk.)

  Volume 2: From Liverpool to San Francisco. – 1976. – 398p.; 18cm.
  Includes index. ISBN 0-586-04268-7 (pbk.)

  Volume 3: The sounds of the seventies. – 1976. – 320p.; 18cm. Includes
  index. ISBN 0-586-04269-5 (pbk.)

  Also published in one volume:

Encyclopedia of rock 1955–75 / edited by Phil Hardy and Dave Laing. –
  London: Aquarius; in association with Panther Books, 1977. – 287p.;
  23cm. Includes index. ISBN 0-90461-905-2

Forty-two of the best-known authorities from all areas of popular music were the contributors to this well-edited encyclopedia. Originally published as three separate volumes, the arrangement of the single-volume edition is alphabetical in the three chronological sections of the originals. There are sadly no illustrations or discographies, but there is a great deal of information here, written with scholarship and authority. Coverage is particularly detailed for the growth of rock'n'roll in Britain and there is some excellent analysis of its roots. It is a pity that the single-volume edition has no cohesive sequence and that no update has appeared.

Logan, Nick
  The illustrated encyclopedia of rock / Nick Logan and Bob Woffinden. – 3rd ed. – London: Salamander Books, 1982. – 288p.: ill. (chiefly col.), facsims (chiefly col.), ports (chiefly col.); 30cm. Includes discographies and index. ISBN 0-86101-116-3 (cased). ISBN 0-86101-141-4 (pbk.)
  Originally published as '*The illustrated New Musical Express encyclopedia of rock*': London: Hamlyn; Salamander Books, 1976.

Also published: New York: Harmony Books, 1977.

Previous edition: London: Hamlyn; Salamander Books, 1978.

When it first appeared in 1976, this beautifully designed encyclopedia was by far the most informative work of its kind to have been published in Britain. Alphabetically arranged by artists and musical forms, there are concise, well-written notes, portraits, album covers and discographies for each entry. The second edition proved to be an excellent work of revision. The third, long-awaited 1982 edition, however, is a disappointing effort comprising a briefly updated version of the second edition with an additional thirty-two pages devoted to a chapter on artists of the eighties. There are striking omissions. Gary Numan, for example, appears in neither section. Nevertheless, this is currently the best reference source and an essential work for most libraries and enthusiasts.

Logan, Nick
The New Musical Express book of rock / edited by Nick Logan and Bob Woffinden. – Rev. ed. – London: Star Books, 1977. – 553p.; 18cm.
Includes discographies. ISBN 0-352-39715-2 (pbk.)
Previous edition: London: Star Books, 1975.

Basically with the same text as the first edition of *The illustrated New Musical Express book of rock*, but without illustrations, this is packed with information and discographies but has not been further revised because of the success of the illustrated version. The editors were always the main writers of the text.

Nite, Norm N.
Rock on: the illustrated encyclopedia of rock'n'roll; the modern years /
Norm N. Nite; special introduction by Wolfman Jack. – New York: T. Y.
Crowell, 1978. – 448p.: ill., ports; 23cm. Includes discographies.
ISBN 0-6900-1196-2

This second volume of the author's encyclopedia is alphabetically arranged and includes artists from the early sixties to the mid seventies. There are hundreds of illustrations and selective discographies. Although the most successful British performers are included, there is a distinct American bias. The coverage is far wider than simply rock'n'roll and as with the first volume there is a lack of both musical analysis and any indication of the relative importance of artists. This second volume is of far less value including little information not widely available.

Nite, Norm N.
Rock on: the illustrated encylopedia of rock'n'roll; the solid gold years /
Norm N. Nite; special introduction by Dick Clark. – New York: Harper &
Row, 1982. –x, 722p.: ill., ports; 23cm. Includes discographies and index.
ISBN 0-06-181642-6
Originally published: New York: T. Y. Crowell, 1974.
Also published: New York: Popular Library, 1977.

A basic encyclopedia covering the period from 1954 to the early sixties with an alphabetically arranged series of over a thousand biographies. Discographies are included, many of which extend into the seventies for those artists who survived. There is a complete American bias and no British artists are included. There are in excess of 350 illustrations and entries include not only artists from the field of rock'n'roll but country, folk and curiosity acts of the period. The information is clearly presented and there is a great deal of information here not available elsewhere but a general lack of both musical criticism and indication of commercial importance.

The Rolling Stone encyclopedia of rock & roll / edited by Jon Pareles and
    Patricia Romanowski. – London: Rolling Stone Press/Michael Joseph,
    1983. – xv, 615p. ill., ports; 26cm. Includes discographies.
    ISBN 0-7181-2384-0 (cased). ISBN 0-7181-2400-6 (pbk.)
    Also published: New York: Rolling Stone Press, 1983.
Although displaying an understandable American bias (the discographies, for example, include American release dates and album titles), this is an extremely useful source of information. It is arranged alphabetically by artist, and its contributors include many of the best-known rock writers. It is an essential addition to any library wishing to cover popular music.

Roxon, Lillian
    Lillian Roxon's Rock encyclopedia: the classic and definitive book on rock –
    now including all the stars and groups of the 70s / compiled by Ed Naha. –
    Rev. ed. – London: Angus & Robertson, 1980. – 565p, 16p. of plates: ill.,
    ports; 23cm. Includes discographies and index. ISBN 0-207-14186-X
    (cased). ISBN 0-207-14026-X (pbk.)
    Previous edition: New York: Grosset & Dunlap, 1969.
    Also published: New York: Grosset & Dunlap, 1978.
An updated, revised and extended new edition of the original work of Lillian Roxon, who died in 1973. This is very much an American encyclopedia. Arranged in an alphabetical sequence of artists and topic, there are brief essays followed by a very full discography which lists not only the names of albums but each track and also singles with their B sides. All discographical information is American and only major British artists who have achieved success in the USA are included. The other weakness is a poor coverage of fifties rock'n'roll. Nevertheless this is a rich reference source, well written and accessible.

Stambler, Irwin
    Encyclopedia of pop, rock and soul / by Irwin Stambler. – New York: St.
    Martin's Press; London: St. James' Press, 1974. – 609p. 30p. of plates: ill.,
    ports; 25cm. Includes bibliography. ISBN 0-900997-24-9
A successor to the author's *Encyclopedia of popular music*; although the best-known British artists are included, this is primarily the most complete and detailed source of information on American popular music up until 1974. The extensive notes and valuable collection of portraits complement the excellent and detailed sections on performers, writers, producers, forms of music and so on. There are in all over 500 entries with appendices including a list of American gold records awarded since 1965, a list of Grammy songwriters'

awards and a list of award nominations for film music of the Academy of Motion Pictures Arts and Sciences. The bibliography is of his sources of information in periodicals. This is the fullest single source of information on modern American popular music of all kinds and it is a real loss that no revision has since appeared.

Stambler, Irwin
  Encyclopedia of popular music / by Irwin Stambler. – New York: St.
  Martin's Press, 1965. – 359p.: ill., ports; 25cm.
In all there are over 600 entries of a predominantly biographical nature with a few for terms and musicals. The intelligent, informative style and excellent selection of illustrations give good background to modern popular music. It includes the early part of the period covered with information on many singers of the fifties not in his later work. There are useful lists of award-winning records in various categories, by year from 1958 to 1964. Awards for shows, film music, nominations for Academy awards 1934–64 and a list of gold records are all included.

GLOSSARIES

Hibbert, Tom
  Rockspeak!: the dictionary of rock terms / compiled by Tom Hibbert. –
  London: Omnibus Press, 1983. – 176p: ill.; 19cm. ISBN 0-7119-0093-0
  (pbk.)
A glossary of over 1,000 words and phrases with definitions of musical and slang terms associated with rock culture. Weak as a guide to musical terminology, it is unique as a glossary published as a monograph.

1.2 HISTORIES

Works included offer the background from which popular music has evolved since 1955 as well as giving accounts and analyses of its progress since that date. Often subjective, impressionistic views, they vary from serious, almost academic studies to chiefly pictorial works.

   The surveys look at the music as it existed at the time of writing without historical interpretation.

American music: from Storyville to Woodstock / edited by Charles Nanry;
  with a foreword by Irving Louis Horowitz. – New Brunswick, New Jersey:
  Transaction Books; Rutgers University, 1972. – 290p.: ill., ports; 25cm.
  ISBN 0-87855-007-0 (cased). ISBN 0-87855-506-4 (pbk.)
With essays by authorities on periods and styles of music, the history of the development of American popular music is well traced. The growth of rock'n'roll from its folk base is rather sketched over, but its importance in the wider cultural context fully appreciated.

Andersson, Muff
Music in the mix: the story of South African popular music / Muff
Andersson. – Johannesburg, South Africa: Ravan Press, 1981. – 189p.: ill.,
ports; 30cm. Includes index. ISBN 0-86975-218-9 (pbk.)
A very good survey of music in South Africa with an historical analysis and
discussion of the propaganda element. The fusion of white rock, black
African, soul and West Indian forms is particularly well discussed. Many
of the artists covered will be totally unknown to European and American
audiences.

Bane, Michael
White boy singin' the blues: the black roots of white rock / by Michael Bane.
– Harmondsworth: Penguin Books, 1982. – 269p.; 20cm. Includes index.
ISBN 0-1400-6045-6 (pbk.)
Starting with the African and sacred roots of the blues and its evolution into
the Memphis jazz of Beale Street, the promising beginning of the author's
history continues to meander through each form of modern popular music,
underlining these roots but drawing few exciting conclusions and making no
interesting observations. The chapter on Limey rock discusses the ironic
recycling of black music by British rhythm & blues and pop groups such as the
Rolling Stones, Beatles and Yardbirds, and the new wave is seen as a white
reaction against the packaged sound of black disco. In general an unsatisfactory history, unoriginal and uncohesive.

Barnes, Ken
Twenty years of pop / by Ken Barnes. – Havant, Hampshire: Kenneth
Mason, 1973. – 96p.; ill., ports; 21cm. ISBN 0-859-37024-0 (pbk.)
An outline history of popular music from 1950 to 1973. The author takes the
most successful seven singles from each year from 1950 to 1970 and briefly
describes them. He then lists all records that entered the top ten of the charts
in Britain in the years 1971 to 1973 with some brief comments on the evolution of the industry. A very brief outline of the period but in highlighting the
notable records of each year the evolution of popular music in the period is
well signposted. This is particularly useful as a classroom book because of its
clear layout and simple style.

Belz, Carl
The story of rock / Carl Belz. – 2nd ed. – New York: Oxford University
Press, 1972. – 286p.: ill., ports; 22cm. Includes bibliography, discography
and index. ISBN 0-19-501554-1
Previous edition: New York: Oxford University Press, 1969.
Written by the Director of the Rose Art Museum who teaches fine art at
Brandeis University, this is an outline history from a purely artistic stand-
point. The discussion opens with a definition of folk, popular and rock music,
suggesting that folk and rock can exist without a commercial motivation

whereas the sole aim of popular or pop music is financial success. Whether this is a sound thesis and rock can be considered as folk is questionable. Nevertheless, this is a thoughtful study with countless examples and excellent discography and bibliography.

Boeckman, Charles
    And the beat goes on: a survey of pop music in America / by Charles
    Boeckman. – Washington: R. B. Luce, 1972. – 224p.: ill., ports; 23cm.
    Includes index
A sketchy overview of the development of popular music in America up to the early seventies is followed by the state of the art at that time. Although black music is covered, the bias is towards white rock and pop artists and, although commercial country music is briefly included, there is no hint of its imminent gain in popularity in the seventies. There are some good illustrations but on the whole this is an unsatisfactory work.

Burnett, Michael
    Pop music / Michael Burnett. – London: Oxford University Press, 1980. – 48p.: ill., ports, music; 19cm. Includes discography. ISBN 0-19-321327-3 (pbk.)
Written for British schools, this informative outline includes definitions of musical styles, music exercises, questions, projects and an excellent chronology of major events. There is a remarkable amount of detail for such a short book, giving an excellent starting point for the study of the subject. The author's analyses, although for young people, are astute and not at all patronizing.

Byrne, John
    The story of pop / John Byrne. – London: Heinemann Educational, 1975. – vi, 88p.: ill., ports; 18cm. Includes index. ISBN 0-435-27025-7 (pbk.)
This brief history of popular music since the advent of rock'n'roll is aimed at British schools. The vocabulary is carefully controlled for a reading age of about ten with a detailed glossary and comprehension questions. The rock'n'roll era is well described as are the work of the Beatles and Bob Dylan and there is a good section on black music. There has, unfortunately, been no revision since the new wave and therefore much of the contents will seem remote to the age group at which it is aimed.

Cash, Tony
    Anatomy of pop / edited by Tony Cash. – London: British Broadcasting Corporation, 1970. – 132p.: ill., ports; 21cm. Includes bibliography and index. ISBN 0-563-10261-6 (pbk.)
Written by a team of music journalists to accompany a series of television programmes broadcast in 1970, this collection of essays includes some interesting musical analysis. As a brief outline of the subject, however, it now appears naive and dated.

Cohn, Nik
Awopbopaloobop alopbamboom: pop from the beginning / Nik Cohn. –
Rev. ed. – London: Paladin, 1972. – 256p., 12p. of plates: ill., ports; 20cm.
Includes index. ISBN 0-586-08014-7 (pbk.)
Originally published as '*Rock from the beginning*': New York: Stein & Day,
1969.
Previous edition: London: Paladin, 1970.

The author, who is a journalist and novelist, gives a witty, personal, impressionistic history of popular music from the emergence of rock'n'roll up to the late sixties. The revised edition includes footnotes and additions which update his views on particular artists and are often dramatic changes of opinion. Although this is not an academically written, documented history, the author's knowledge and love of the subject more than compensate for any personal biases or omissions. For example, he believes that the Beatles were the most disastrous thing that ever happened to rock'n'roll because their sophistication took away its essential rawness, and thinks Bob Dylan is completely overrated. His interest lies in the late fifties and in the continuation of rhythm & blues through people like the Rolling Stones. His views, although often against general opinion, are well thought out, well argued and very well written. This is an essential contribution to the subject and begs an updating to include the seventies.

Ewen, David
All the years of American popular music / David Ewen. – Englewood Cliffs,
New Jersey: Prentice-Hall, 1977. – xviii, 850p.; 25cm. Includes index.
ISBN 0-13-022442-1

The most detailed history of popular music yet written by the well-known music historian. He makes a thorough survey of his subject up to 1976 with possibly greater emphasis on folk traditions, minstrels, vaudeville and jazz than on more contemporary forms. The major modern artists are included but there is no analysis of their specific influences. The index is well constructed, making this an excellent reference source for background information.

Ewen, David
American popular songs from the Revolutionary War to the present / David
Ewen. – New York: Random House, 1966. – xiii, 507p; 24cm. Includes
index

Entries are included under performers, composers, musicals and some topics as well as the lyrics and background information to 3,600 songs. There is a list of bestselling records from 1919–66 which includes over 1,000 titles and a chronological listing entitled 'all-time hit parade' 1765–1966. There is an index of performers and the songs associated with them. Here is background to contemporary popular song as well as some current information.

Ewen, David
Great men of American popular song: the history of the American popular

*song told through the lives, careers, achievements and personalities of its
foremost composers and lyricists from William Billings of the Revolutionary
War through Bob Dylan, Johnny Cash, Burt Bacharach* / by David Ewen. –
Englewood Cliffs, New Jersey: Prentice-Hall, 1972. – x, 404p.; 25cm.
Includes index. ISBN 0-13-364182-1
A comprehensive history of American popular music in the form of a series of
essays on its composers and songwriters. This is a good background volume.
Included are biographies of all the major names as well as many who have
faded into obscurity. Stronger historically than on more recent writers, there
is no musical analysis but impressions of the relative artistic contribution of
those included.

Ewen, David
History of popular music / by David Ewen. – London: Constable, 1961. –
229p.; 21cm. Includes bibliography and index
Originally published: New York: Barnes & Noble, 1961.
A well-written history of the development of popular music in America. Only
the end section mentions rock'n'roll but there is a good background to
modern jazz and light music styles.

Gabree, John
The world of rock / John Gabree. – Greenwich, Connecticut: Fawcett
Publications, 1968. – 176p: ill., ports; 18cm. (pbk.)
An account of the important groups active during the late sixties as well as a
history of the earlier rock'n'roll and rhythm & blues artists and the development of the music. Seeing rock as a political force Gabree regards the Beatles'
success as being due to their musical and lyrical safeness. He does not develop
this idea systematically, however, and the book fails to be cohesive, being
neither sociological, nor really political, nor an aesthetic appreciation nor
popular in its approach.

Gillett, Charlie
The sound of the city: the rise of rock and roll / Charlie Gillett. Rev. ed. –
London: Souvenir Press, 1983. – 8, x, 516p.; 22cm. Includes bibliography,
discography and index. ISBN 0-285-62567-5 (cased). ISBN 0-285-62619-1
(pbk.)
Originally published: New York: Outerbridge & Dienstfrey, 1970.
Previously published: London: Souvenir Press; Sphere, 1971.
Written by one of the leading authorities on the subject, this is a detailed
survey and analysis of the evolution of contemporary popular music. Its
constituent influences are meticulously discussed and the detail in which
individual songs are documented is remarkable. One of Charlie Gillett's
particular areas of emphasis is the development and influence of the independent record companies, but he does not ignore the importance of individual
artists and he is particularly strong on the contribution of black rhythm &
blues. The late sixties are rather sketched over and some of his conclusions,
reached in 1969, about the direction of the music and the relative significance
of certain artists are, with hindsight, rather adrift. This is, however, one of the

most significant histories in the field, packed with detail, with appendices of facts and a superb bibliography and discography. The new edition is a good revision, retaining the author's original emphasis.

The History of Rock. – London: Orbis, 1982–. Weekly. 1st issue. – 36p.: ill. (chiefly col.), facsims (chiefly col.), ports (chiefly col.); 30cm. Projected to be in 120 parts.
A colourful history of popular music since 1955, essays are included by most of the leading writers in the field. The projected work will reach approaching 4,000 pages and, although well produced and certainly useful, it will have cost the subscriber £80, a somewhat expensive historical source.

Hopkins, Jerry
   The rock story / by Jerry Hopkins. – New York: Signet, 1970. – 191p.: ill., ports; 18cm. (pbk.)
Rather than attempting to cover the whole evolution of rock music, Hopkins offers a picture of the rock world by focussing on selected details. For example, he describes the atmosphere of the late fifties by looking at disc jockey Dick Clark; record production is covered by describing the making of Aretha Franklin's record, I Never Loved a Man; there is an essay on groupies, and the rise and demise of a group is documented in the context of the Buffalo Springfield. Well-written, sensitive and serious, this is a good example of an author respecting the subject and his reader.

Jahn, Mike
   Rock from Elvis Presley to the Rolling Stones / by Mike Jahn. – New York: Quadrangle, 1973. – x, 326p.: ill., ports; 23cm. Includes discography and index. ISBN 0-8129-0314-5
A personal history of the development of rock'n'roll from 1955 to the seventies. The music of the major stars is examined, their contributions discussed and the evolution of the music outlined. Discographical information is lacking but the illustrations are good and the text lively.

Laing, Dave
   The sound of our time / by Dave Laing. – London: Sheed and Ward, 1969. – 198p.; 21cm. Includes bibliography. ISBN 0-7220-0593-8
A concise, analytical history with a definitely sociological style which places popular music within its historical context. The social structure of the music business is followed by a brief history and a personal view of the major creative forces of recent times. A conclusion sees popular music as a conflict between the pure commercialism of the industry and the self-expression of aspiring youth. Laing places this argument in the tradition of Charlie Chaplin and develops a medium and message theme à la McLuhan which was far more contemporary at the time of writing. Although now a little self-conscious and dated, some of Laing's analysis is still very interesting.

Palmer, Tony
   All you need is love: the story of popular music / Tony Palmer; edited by

Paul Medlicott. – London: Futura Publications, 1977. – xii, 323p.: ill., facsims (some col.), ports; 29cm. Includes index. ISBN 0-8600-75176 (pbk.)
Originally published: London: Weidenfeld and Nicolson; Chappell, 1976
Also published: New York: Grossman Publishers, 1976.

Based on a sixteen-part television series written and directed by Palmer, this is a personal view of the evolution of contemporary popular music from its roots in folk traditions and music hall. It includes the mainstream of show-business as well as jazz, musicals and country music. Attempting to cover the whole spectrum has often forced the author into oversimplifying influences and into following through the evolutionary process on too straight a course, often omitting quite obvious digressions. Nevertheless, if one accepts this as a personal account, it is informative and illustrated with an unusual selection of photographs, well arranged with an excellent index.

Pascall, Jeremy
The illustrated history of rock music / Jeremy Pascall. – London: Hamlyn, 1978. – 222p.: ill. (chiefly col.), facsims (chiefly col.), ports (chiefly col.); 30cm. Includes bibliography and index. ISBN 0-600-37605-2

A brief but well-written and beautifully illustrated introductory history of rock music from 1954 to the late seventies. The twenty-five years are divided into five periods: the images and energy of each comes through in the well-chosen illustrations. It is remarkable that the author has managed to include a portrait of all major artists and also to include a cohesive, poignant narrative. The bibliography is brief but sound.

The Radio One story of pop: the first encyclopedia of pop. – London: Phoebus, 1973–1974. Weekly. 1st issue. – 34p.: ill. (chiefly col.), facsims (chiefly col.), ports (chiefly col.); 30cm. In 26 parts.

Published to coincide with the excellent twenty-six-part BBC radio series, this is a well written, beautifully illustrated and surprisingly comprehensive chronological outline of the development of popular music since 1955. The complete work is over 900 pages long and Phoebus subsequently published edited groupings of the magazine in hardback form.

Robinson, Richard
Electric rock / by Richard Robinson. – New York: Pyramid, 1971. – 126p.: ill., ports; 18cm. (pbk.)

With some good illustrations but a poorly written, superficial text, the author attempts to outline the development of rock from its early forms into the heavily produced and staged manifestation which had begun to appear at the turn of the decade. Included are the major artists but the comment is uncritical.

The Rolling Stone illustrated history of rock & roll / edited by Jim Miller. – Rev. ed. – London: Picador, – 1981. – 474p.: ill., ports; 27cm. Includes discography and index. ISBN 0-330-26568-7 (pbk.)
Also published: New York; Toronto: Random House, 1981.

Previous edition: New York: Rolling Stone Press, 1976.
Some of the best-known writers on popular music have contributed a total of eighty-four essays on styles, eras and specific artists. The collection of essays, arranged broadly chronologically, is well written, intelligent and includes most of the major names. There are, however, some notable omissions and an obvious American bias. The illustrations are superb and the discographies useful, including record numbers but only American releases. The 1976 edition was produced in an unusually large format of some 37cm, making the illustrations even more spectacular. The revised edition, however, includes the innovations of the late seventies, the new wave, disco and Bruce Springsteen, updating the original's content well and including proportionately more British artists.

Shaw, Arnold
   The rock revolution / Arnold Shaw. – New York: Crowell-Collier Press; London: Collier Macmillan, 1969. – 215p., 32p. of plates: ill., ports; 22cm.
   Includes discography and index. ISBN 0-02-782400-4
Arnold Shaw was one of the general professional managers of Hill and Range Songs (a major music publisher in the fifties) and later manager of the Marks Music Corporation. He therefore approaches his survey of the changes in popular music between 1955 and 1969 with a wealth of first-hand experience. He lists the major elements of change, as he sees them, with a sociological slant but surprisingly concentrates on the sixties with considerable detail, not neglecting British artists. He attempts to investigate such topics as the sexual content of popular music, relationships between the generations and alienation. It is a pity that the author did not approach his subject from the business standpoint but his effort is useful, with a good discography.

Soul, pop, rock, stars, superstars. – London: Octopus Books, 1974. – 255p.:
   ill. (chiefly col.), ports (chiefly col.); 31cm. ISBN 0-7064-0409-2 (pbk.)
A brief outline history, the text offers sparse information but there is a fine selection of illustrations.

Tobler, John
   25 years of rock / John Tobler and Pete Frame. – London: W. H. Smith; Hamlyn, 1980. – 252p.: ill., ports; 30cm. ISBN 0-600-37638-9
An outline of the period between 1955 and 1980 published to accompany a BBC twenty-five-part radio series. There is a chapter for each year. The illustrations are rare, or at least never before published, and the text by these two reputable journalists is good but necessarily brief. The aim, to put the music into the historic context of world events, is interesting but an impossible task in a single volume.

25 years of rock & roll. – Tulsa, Oklahoma: Harrison House, 1979. – 96p.: ill.
   (some col.), ports (some col.); 27cm. ISBN 0-517-30391-4 (pbk.)
A sketchy history, it culminates in a collection of coloured portraits of the stars of the late seventies, including Kiss, Elvis Costello, Blondie and Springsteen. Written from an American viewpoint, it is a reasonable attempt which fairly reflects Britain's role in the evolution of modern popular music.

Uslan, Michael
  Dick Clark's The first twenty five years of rock & roll / Michael Uslan and
  Bruce Solomon; introduction by Dick Clark. – New York: Dell, 1981. –
  352p.: ill., ports; 20cm. ISBN 0-440-51763-X (pbk.)
After Dick Clark's introductory summary of the changes in music during his
career, the author offers a chronological survey of the twenty-five years since
rock'n'roll emerged. Concise, with some good illustrations, there is no
attempt at analysis but little is missed up to the new-wave era.

Whitcomb, Ian
  After the ball: pop music from rag to rock / Ian Whitcomb. –
  Harmondsworth: Penguin, 1973. – 8, 312p.; 18cm. Includes index.
  ISBN 0-14-00-3450-1 (pbk.)
  Originally published: London: Allen Lane, 1972.
  Also published: New York: Simon and Schuster, 1973.
While still a history student at Trinity College Dublin, Ian Whitcomb wrote
and recorded a song which became a big hit in the USA. After this solitary
taste of the musical world, he began writing and researching the history of
popular music. This history begins in 1892 with the song After the Ball, the
first to sell one million copies of the sheet music. The account continues
through early jazz to the influences of radio and the beginnings and growth of
the record industry. The invasion of Britain by American music is then
described and analysed particularly well. Finally, the birth of rock'n'roll, its
influences and its growth in Britain is followed by Whitcomb's autobiographical account of his own experience as a writer and recording artist.
Although very sketchy in its coverage of the last twenty-five years, the book
does place music of this recent time firmly in the context of the musical styles
from which it has evolved and offers thoughtful, though sometimes naive,
analysis.

Yorke, Ritchie
  Axes, chops & hot licks: the Canadian rock music scene / Ritchie Yorke. –
  Edmonton: M. G. Hurtig, 1971. – xii, 224p.: ill., ports; 22cm. Includes
  index. ISBN 0-8883-0052-2
Canada has always made its small but significant contribution to popular
music generally via the success of its artists in the USA. This tendency
reached a peak in the early seventies when the singer-songwriters Neil
Young, Joni Mitchell and Gordon Lightfoot were achieving massive world
successes which have been proven to be artistically of great significance. The
author looks at all the major Canadian artists between 1950 and 1970. He
includes many obscure artists and all of the major ones: the Band, Ronnie
Hawkins, Bachman–Turner Overdrive and the Guess Who as well as the
three quoted above. There are extensive quotes from interviews and a glossary of musical jargon relevant to the narrative. The illustrations are well
produced and many are unique.

Yorke, Ritchie
  The history of rock'n'roll / Ritchie Yorke; prepared in association with

CHUM Ltd. – London: Eyre Methuen, 1976. – 174p.: ill. (some col.), facsims (some col.), ports (some col.); 28cm. ISBN 0-413-37640-0 (pbk.) Also published: Toronto: Methuen, 1976; New York: Methuen / Two Continents, 1976.

An attractive and surprisingly informative outline history by a notable music journalist who was commissioned by the Canadian radio station CHUM Ltd. to write for a series of 48-hour programmes, the History of Rock'n'Roll. It was published to coincide with the broadcast of the series in North America. It is brief and chronologically arranged, covering the period from 1955 to 1975. Brief essays surveying the significant developments and personalities of each year are combined with well-selected portraits and lists of notable records not mentioned in the text.

SURVEYS

The fifties

Gammond, Peter
  A guide to popular music / by Peter Gammond. – London: Phoenix, 1960. – 274p.: ill., ports; 20cm.

Written at the end of the fifties by someone who knows the business from the inside, this interesting survey of the popular-music scene covers the whole spectrum of popular music. Particularly interesting is the emphasis placed on the various contemporary styles. Dance music, musicals and cabaret artists, fringing on jazz, are still more important than the pop and rock'n'roll artists who are still seen as only for teenagers. This is, therefore, useful in the understanding of the attitudes towards the music which by the end of the decade will have transformed the music industry. There are some interesting photographs.

Millar, Gavin
  Pop / Gavin Millar. – Bromley, Kent: Axle Publications, 1963. – 12p.: 21cm. (pbk.)

A curious little pamphlet which comprises an unanalytical essay on the British music business at the time.

The sixties

Silver, Caroline
  The pop mainstream / by Caroline Silver. – New York: Scholastic Book Service, 1966. – 136p.: ill., ports; 18cm.(pbk.)

Writing at a crucial time when in America at least pop music was starting to be viewed with some seriousness, the author surveys the various forms and offers a brief analysis on historical development, but mainly describes the work of the leading artists of the time. The Beatles, the Rolling Stones and lesser groups of the British invasion are featured as well as American folk rock artists and the Beach Boys.

The seventies

Hodenfield, Chris
Rock '70 / Chris Hodenfield. – New York: Pyramid Books, 1970. – 140p.:
ill., ports; 18cm. (pbk.)
A survey of rock and pop music at the turn of the decade with portraits of the
major stars. Predominantly American in viewpoint, the text gives brief
analyses of the contemporary musical styles.

Jasper, Tony
The 70s: a book of records / Tony Jasper. – London: Macdonald Futura
Publications, 1980. – 416p.; 18cm. Includes bibliography, discographies
and filmography. ISBN 0-7088-1944-3 (pbk.)
A survey of popular music of the seventies which includes a series of essays on
the developments during the decade as well as detailed listings of successful
records, a chronology of events and quizzes. There are biographies of new
artists, a filmography, a good survey of the music press and a bibliography of
music books published in the decade. Packed with information, but its usefulness would be greatly improved by an index.

Jasper, Tony
Simply pop / by Tony Jasper. – London: Queen Anne Press, 1975. – 80p.:
ill., ports; 23cm. ISBN 0-362-00247-9 (pbk.)
A look at pop in the mid seventies for the young fan with an emphasis on the
teenage idols of the time. There are quizzes and a good deal of information
for the age range.

Pop today / editor and designer Gavin Petrie. – London: Hamlyn, 1974. –
128p.; ill. (some col.), ports (some col.); 29cm. ISBN 0-600-37080-1
A collection of photographs, many full page and beautifully coloured, of the
leading artists of the early seventies with a young teenage following. Slade,
David Essex, Marc Bolan, Suzi Quatro, Sweet and Gary Glitter are all
included. Well produced and suitably written; the teenybop phenomenon is
well depicted with some interesting observations.

Rees-Parnall, Hilary
Tune in: pop music in Britain today / Hilary Rees-Parnall. – London:
Harrap, 1981. – 48p.: ill., ports; 22cm. ISBN 0-245-531716-3 (pbk.)
A survey of the recent British music scene for non-English-speaking students.
Well illustrated, the text is interestingly written with some useful observations
on the period.

Robinson, Richard
Pop, rock and soul / by Richard Robinson. – New York: Pyramid, 1972. –
146p.: ill., ports; 18cm. (pbk.)
In an attempt to survey the whole of popular music in the early seventies,
including black music, the author provides us with an inferior collection of
writings. Poorly produced, badly written and uncritical, this book is of little
informational value.

Robinson, Richard
   The rock scene / by Richard Robinson and Andy Zwerling. – New York:
   Pyramid, 1971. – 147p.: ill., ports; 18cm. (pbk.)
A superficial survey of the most popular groups and individuals around at the
beginning of the decade. Included are the Jefferson Airplane, Grand Funk
Railroad, Led Zeppelin, Joe Cocker, the Who, Sly and the Family Stone and
Elton John. It is not a critical survey and the authors do try to cover a wide
variety of styles in a short book. They do, without conclusion, seem to be
looking for signs of the future evolution of rock music but the overall result is
a self-conscious, superficial attempt.

Scoppa, Bud
   The rock people / Bud Scoppa. – New York: Scholastic Book Service, 1973.
   – 108p.: ill., ports; 18cm. ISBN 0-590-09080-7 (pbk.)
A survey of the American rock scene in the early seventies for American
schools with a noticeable lack of information on British artists.

Van der Kiste, John
   Roxeventies: popular music in Britain 1970–79 / John Van der Kiste. –
   Torpoint, Cornwall: Kawabata Press, 1982. – 41p.; 21cm. Includes discography. ISBN 0-906110-34-3 (pbk.)
Surveying the changing trends in Britain during the seventies, this is an
intelligently observed essay quoting all the major records within the text with
the author's view of the top one hundred singles of the decade in an appended
discography. There is a brief section on the media of the period and a well-
observed postscript. The production is, unfortunately, poor.

1.3 WHO'S WHOS

Alphabeat: who's who in pop. – London: Century 21 Publishing, 1969. –
   126p., Chiefly ill. (some col.), chiefly ports (some col.); 27cm.
   ISBN 0-8509-4005-2
A simple biographical dictionary for the young fan. The text gives the briefest
of details of the artists covered – predominantly those successful at the time of
publication with a few earlier, influential individuals.

Bane, Michael
   Who's who in rock / by Michael Bane; researcher Kenny Kertok. – Oxford:
   Clio Press, 1981. – x, 259p.: ill., ports; 29cm. Includes index.
   ISBN 0-87196-465-1
   Originally published: New York: Facts on File, 1981.
With a definite American bias, this collection of biographical notes from Facts
on File includes 1,200 entries for solo performers and members of groups as
well as entries under group names. The list is selective, however, and
although the index is an aid to the main sequence, the result is unsatisfactory.
The 200 illustrations are not well reproduced.

York, William
Who's who in rock: an A–Z of groups, performers, producers, session men engineers . . . / compiled and edited by William York. – Rev. ed. – London: Omnibus Press, 1979. – 237p.; 26cm. ISBN 0-86001-608-0 (pbk.)
Originally published: Seattle: Atomic Press, 1978.

This information was largely taken from record sleeves and supplemented by sources from the American music press. It is a straightforward alphabetical list of people involved in the popular-music industry. In addition, it includes names of groups, listing in full their personnel. The information has a distinct American slant and includes lists of records the cited person was involved with, their function and significant dates. The value of this work as a reference source is that it includes not only the major names in the industry but also the people behind the scenes who play such important, but outwardly secondary, roles. The fact that it is full of inaccuracies unfortunately lessens its value.

York, William
Who's who in rock music / William York. – London: Arthur Barker, 1982. – 413p.; 28cm. ISBN 0-213-16820-2 (pbk.)
Originally published: New York: Scribner, 1982.

A much-improved, corrected and updated version of this author's earlier work. Over 13,000 entries are included in a single alphabetical sequence. Artists, producers, engineers, groups and session musicians are all included with full career details concisely described. In his introduction the author explains that he has included artists who consider their music to be rock, but there are notable omissions and some odd inclusions. This is by far the most complete source of biographical information in the field.

GENEALOGICAL CHARTS

Frame, Pete
Pete Frame's Rock family trees. – London: Omnibus Press, 1980. – 36p.: ill., geneal. tables; 33cm. Includes index. ISBN 0-86001-414-2 (pbk.)

A well-known journalist and editor of *Zigzag* magazine, Pete Frame has drawn up a collection of thirty fold-out genealogical tables illustrating the evolution, associations and relationships between groups of musicians from a wide range of popular music. Packed with remarkable detail, the information, of which this is often the only source, is difficult to access. Nevertheless, this is an important information source and, although not comprehensive, it covers the genealogies of many of the most significant groups and musicians.

Frame, Pete
Peter Frame's Rock family trees 2. – London: Omnibus Press, 1983. – 32p.: ill., geneal. tables; 33cm. Includes index. ISBN 0-7119-0172-4 (pbk.)

An excellent second collection to bring us up-to-date with the complex relationships of the new wave.

COLLECTED LIVES AND WORKS

Balliett, Whitney
  American singers / Whitney Balliett. – New York: Oxford University Press,
  1979. – 178p.; 22cm. ISBN 0-19-502524-9
A collection of well-written short essays on the lives, work and significance of
a wide range of popular singers from the past fifty years. Some, such as Mabel
Mercer, Bobby Short and Blossom Dearie, come from the worlds of jazz and
cabaret, but also included are Ray Charles, Joe Turner and Tony Bennett.
Some of the profiles include lengthy quotes from interviews.

Barnes, Ken
  Sinatra and the great song stylists / Ken Barnes; with contributions from
  Stan Britt, Arthur Jackson, Fred Dellar and Chris Ellis. – London: Ian
  Allan, 1972. – 192p., 48p. of plates: ill., ports; 24cm. Includes disco-
  graphies and index. ISBN 0-7110-0400-5
This collection of biographies includes all the most influential popular vocal-
ists since the twenties. Well-arranged and written in an informative style, the
major current middle-of-the-road artists such as Sinatra, Perry Como, Andy
Williams and Tony Bennett are here.

Bowman, Robyn
  Book of rock secrets / by Robyn Bowman; designed by Ferry Zayadi (VIZ
  & Co.). – London: Virgin Books, 1982. – 78p.: ill., facsims, ports; 24cm.
  ISBN 0-90708-54-5 (pbk.)
In the form of a collection of questionnaires completed by contemporary pop
and rock performers, the information is brief and trivial. Included are the
vital statistics, likes and dislikes, and a portrait of the artist. Adam Ant,
Annabella of Bow Wow Wow, Lemmy of Motorhead, Gary Glitter, Paul
Weller of the Jam, Buster Bloodvessel of Bad Manners are all here.

The boys who rock / text by Phil Byford. – Ae Hendrik ido Anbacht, The
  Netherlands: Dragon's Dream; distributed by WHS Distributors, 1982. –
  92p.: chiefly col. ill., col. ports; 30cm. ISBN 90-6332-921-0 (pbk.)
With scant information, this is a collection of coloured illustrations of the
leading male performers of pop, rock and soul music in action. The text is in
English.

Busnar, Gene
  The superstars of rock: their lives and their music / Gene Busnar. – New
  York: Messner, 1980. – 223p.: ill., ports; 26cm. ISBN 0-671-32967-7 (pbk.)
Aimed at the early teenager, this is a collection of brief biographies of the
stars of the late seventies. Well illustrated, it is an adequate survey.

Charlesworth, Chris
  A–Z of rock guitarists / by Chris Charlesworth. – London; New York:
  Proteus, 1982. – 128p.: ill. (some col.), ports (some col.); 27cm.
  ISBN 0-86276-081-X (cased). ISBN 0-86276-080-1 (pbk.)

Included are over two hundred brief biographies, the majority with a portrait, of the leading guitar players. The author comments with authority on techniques and performing styles.

Clews, Frank
  The golden disc / by Frank Clews. – London: Brown, Watson, 1963. –
  155p., 32p. of plates: ill., ports; 18cm. (pbk.)
With two concluding chapters outlining the history of the presentation of gold discs for million-selling records, this is basically a collection of biographies. Written in the pre-Beatle era when it was still exceptional for a British artist to win a gold disc, there is the usual naive, patronizing style of the period but a great deal of information. Eddie Calvert, Cliff Richard, Kenny Ball, Emile Ford, Duane Eddy, Pat Boone and the Everly Brothers are among those included. There is an amusing selection of contemporary posed portraits.

Clews, Frank
  Teenage idols / by Frank Clews. – London: Brown, Watson, 1963. – 159p.,
  32p. of plates: ill., ports; 18cm. (pbk.)
Written before the Liverpool groups had revolutionized the British pop music scene, this is a look at the stars of the early sixties. Elvis Presley, Cliff Richard, the Shadows, Rick Nelson, the Everly Brothers, Bobby Vee, Marty Wilde and John Leyton are some of those included. It is written in the style of the period, patronizing the reader at every turn, although including much contemporary information and interviews. It often makes hilarious reading. The illustrations are an interesting collection reflecting the period well.

Dalton, David
  Rock 100 / David Dalton and Lenny Kaye. – New York: Grosset &
  Dunlap, 1977. – 280p.: ill., ports; 28cm. Includes index. ISBN 0-448-12228-6
  (cased). ISBN 0-448-12240-5 (pbk.)
The brief biographies of the top one hundred artists of rock music, in the view of the authors, are arranged chronologically in groupings of the style and period of their music. All the major artists are included with excellent illustrations. An American bias is evident but is not a negative feature as both the relative significance of British artists in the USA and the significant American artists who made no impact in Britain are well covered.

David, Andrew
  Rock stars: people at the top of the charts / Andrew David. – New York:
  Exeter Books, 1979. – 96p.: ill., ports; 29cm. Includes discographies.
  ISBN 0-89673-034-4
Brief biographical notes on the major stars of the mid seventies and each artist or band has a full-page portrait. There are brief, selective discographies of American releases. Although superficial, this does include accurate, basic information.

Ellis, Robert
  The pictorial album of rock / by Robert Ellis; with a foreword by Phil

Collins. – London: Salamander Books, 1981. – 224p.: col. ill., col. ports; 30cm. Includes index. ISBN 0-86101-125-2 (pbk.)
A beautifully produced collection of over five hundred coloured photographs of artists from all areas of popular music performing in concert, with brief biographical notes. The book attempts to cover the current major artists, including those of the sixties and seventies who still maintain their popularity, but there is an emphasis on stars who have emerged more recently.

Elson, Howard
Whatever happened to . . . ? / Howard Elson and John Brunton. – London; New York: Proteus, 1981. – 160p.: ill., ports; 27cm. ISBN 0-906071-46-1 (cased). ISBN 0-906071-40-2 (pbk.)
This collection of biographies of two hundred stars of the last twenty-five years is fascinating in that their single similar characteristic is that since their success they have faded into obscurity. Included are the fates of such artists as Tiny Tim, the Bay City Rollers, the Monkees, Mary Hopkin, Dion and Alvin Stardust. Ironically the latter has since reappeared. Each text is matched with a portrait to aid the memory.

Gambaccini, Paul
Masters of rock / Paul Gambaccini. – London: British Broadcasting Corporation; Omnibus Press, 1982. – 223p.: ill., ports; 24cm.
ISBN 0-563-20068-5 (BBC) (cased). ISBN 0-711-96081-7 (Omnibus) (pbk.)
Originally written as a twenty-five-part series for BBC radio, here is a collection of well-written, perceptive essays on some of the greats of pop, rock and black music. Included are Smokey Robinson, Bruce Springsteen, Sam Cooke, Rod Stewart, Joni Mitchell, Led Zeppelin, Isaac Hayes, Dusty Springfield, Chuck Berry, the Rolling Stones, Diana Ross, Billy Joel, Otis Redding, the Beach Boys, Stevie Wonder, Eric Clapton, the Drifters, Bob Dylan, David Bowie, Eric Burden, Paul Simon, the Temptations, Carole King, the Beatles and Elvis Presley. Each essay is accompanied by a portrait of the artist.

Grove, Martin A.
Teen idols / Martin A. Grove. – New York: Manor Books, 1979. – 136p.: ill., ports; 18cm. ISBN 0-532-19258-3 (pbk.)
A collection of brief biographies of the major pop stars from Elvis Presley and Bill Haley to David Cassidy and the Beatles. Poorly illustrated and superficial.

Guralnick, Peter
Feel like going home: portraits in blues & rock'n'roll / Peter Guralnick. – London: Omnibus Press, 1978. – 256p.: ill., ports; 23cm.
ISBN 0-860-01493-2 (pbk.)
Originally published: New York: Fusion Book; Sunrise Books; Dutton, 1971.
A collection of essays on seminal artists important in the creation of modern popular music including blues singers Muddy Waters and Howlin' Wolf and

rock'n'roller Jerry Lee Lewis. The essay on country singer Charlie Rich, however, is one of the best insights into the disappointments and failures of a successful artist almost, but not quite, at the top. This is a highly regarded work, strangely lacking in cohesion.

Jacobs, David
  Pick of the pop stars / David Jacobs. – Nottingham: Palmer, 1962. – 112p.:
  ill., ports; 25cm.
David Jacobs was a leading disc jockey of the late fifties and sixties. He was the introducer of one of the early teenage-orientated television shows, Juke Box Jury, which continued throughout the sixties. This is, nominally, his view of the music scene of the period featuring the artists appearing in the record charts. Interestingly illustrated, it is a typically condescending period piece.

Leach, Robert
  How the planets rule the superstars / Robert Leach. – London: Everest,
  1975. – 173p.: ill.; 18cm. ISBN 0-9039-2539-7 (pbk.)
Nothing about music, but here is one is one of the extremes in trivial litera-ture on the major pop stars of the early seventies. Simple astrological charts are included.

Lydon, Michael
  Rock folk: portraits from the rock'n'roll pantheon / Michael Lydon. – New
  York: Dell, 1973. – 199p.: ill., ports; 22cm. ISBN 0-7402-2145-X (pbk.)
  Originally published: New York: Dial, 1971.
A collection of profiles, which were originally published in various American magazines, of important artists including Janis Joplin, Chuck Berry and the Grateful Dead. Although the author occasionally becomes a little obscure, it is generally revealing and well reported.

The Official Radio Luxembourg book of record stars / edited by Jack
  Fishman. – London: Souvenir Press; Manchester: World Distributors,
  1962. – 160p.: ill., ports; 27cm.
Beginning before the Second World War, Radio Luxembourg was the earliest of the commercial radio stations broadcasting to Britain. Before the pirate stations emerged in the sixties, followed by the legal commercial stations in the seventies, Luxembourg was a major influence on record-buying in Britain, introducing mainly American artists. This collection of short bio-graphies and accompanying portraits gives a very good indication of taste at the time in all areas of popular music.

Pleasants, Henry
  The great American popular singers / Henry Pleasants. – London: Victor
  Gollancz, 1974. – 384p.: ill., ports; 24cm. Includes index.
  ISBN 0-575-01774-0
  Originally published: New York: Simon and Schuster, 1974.
A collection of twenty-two biographies of popular singers with an introduc-tory essay and references to and illustrations of many more, this covers the

period from Al Jolson to Barbra Streisand. All areas of popular music are represented from country music to soul. There is a fine index and a useful glossary.

Rickard, Graham
   Famous names in popular music / Graham Rickard. – Hove, Sussex: Wayland, 1980. – 48p.: ill., ports; 24cm. Includes bibliography and index. ISBN 0-85340-760-6
A collection of brief biographies with portraits of twenty-one of the most influential performers of popular music this century. Written as part of an educational series, this is a good collection for the early teenager.

Robinson, Richard
   Rock superstars / by Richard Robinson. – New York: Pyramid, 1973. – 159p.: ill., ports; 18cm. (pbk.)
A collection of brief biographical sketches focussing on the lifestyle of the major stars of the period. There is a clear appreciation of popular music of all kinds and the essay on Stevie Wonder is a particularly interesting study.

Rock guitarists: from the pages of Guitar Player Magazine. – New York: Guitar Player Books, 1975. – 171p.: ill., ports; 27cm. Includes index. ISBN 0-8256-9505-8 (pbk.)
The magazine *Guitar Player* was first published in the USA in 1967. Aimed at anyone interested in any aspect of the instrument, it includes interviews, criticism and discussions on guitarists and their styles. This is a good collection of seventy articles in their entirety on guitarists from a wide range of styles. Authoritatively written, the articles are critical and intelligent.

Rock guitarists: from the pages of Guitar Player Magazine. – New York: Guitar Player Books, 1978. – 214p.: ill., ports; 27cm. Includes index. ISBN 0-8256-9506-6 (pbk.)
A second collection of sixty slightly longer articles. Well chosen and well illustrated.

Rock life / editor and designer Gavin Petrie. – London: Hamlyn, 1974. – 128p.: ill. (some col.), ports (some col.); 29cm. ISBN 0-600-38708-9
A selection of twenty-two essays from a series called Rock Giants which appeared in *Melody Maker*. Written by some of Britain's best-known music journalists of the period, it is well illustrated and also includes the transcript of a conversation between a group of English performers: Dave Dee, Alvin Stardust, Marty Wilde and a promoter, Hal Carter. Often revealing, their answers to questions posed by *Melody Maker* journalist Chris Welch reflect their varied experiences from the fifties, sixties and early seventies. This is a well-selected collection of intelligent biographical essays which have not dated.

Shapiro, Harry
   A–Z of rock drummers / by Harry Shapiro. – London: New York: Proteus,
   1982. – 128p.: ill. (some col.), ports (some col.); 27cm. ISBN 0-86276-085-2
   (cased). ISBN 0-86276-084-4 (pbk.)
Over two hundred entries are included, together with a good collection of
portraits of the most influential drummers of the last twenty-five years. The
biographies are brief but informative.

Simon, George Thomas
   The best of the music makers: from Acuff to Ellington to Presley to Sinatra
   to Zappa and 279 more of the most popular performers of the last fifty years /
   by George T. Simon and friends; foreword by Dinah Shore. – Garden City,
   New York: Doubleday, 1979. – xvi, 365p.: ill., ports; 25cm. Includes index.
   ISBN 0-3851-4380-X
Covering the whole range of popular music, jazz, folk and country music, the
author gives brief but informative accounts of the lives of the major stars. He
is, perhaps, stronger on artists of the thirties, forties and fifties than those of
the more recent decades of the rock'n'roll era, but as a general, well-
illustrated, biographical guide, this is a fine attempt.

Superstars / compiled by the editors of *Tiger Beat* magazine. – New York:
   New American Library, 1972. – 143p.: ill., ports; 18cm. (pbk.)
A brief look at the major artists of the early seventies published by the
teenage monthly magazine *Tiger Beat*. The majority of artists and groups
included are American. The illustrations are poorly reproduced and in
general the biographies are very badly written.

Superstars of the 70's. – London: Octopus Books; Phoebus, 1976. – 92p.: ill.
   (chiefly col.), col. facsim, ports (chiefly col.); 31cm. ISBN 0-7064-0447-5
This collection of coloured portraits of the major stars of the early seventies,
with brief biographical notes on each of the included artists, represents a
colourful survey of the period. Emphasis is on the idols of teenybop with their
glittering costumes and big smiles. Each artist or group has a summary and
chronology of their career.

Tobler, John
   The guitar greats / John Tobler & Stuart Grundy. – London: British
   Broadcasting Coropration, 1983. – 248p.: ill., ports; 30cm. Includes
   discographies and index. ISBN 0-563-17957-0 (pbk.)
Published as a tie-in with the BBC radio series of the same title, the careers of
the world's most successful guitarists are described. B. B. King, James
Burton, Scotty Moore, Hank Marvin, Eric Clapton, Jeff Beck, Pete Townshend, Jimmy Page, Ry Cooder, Ritchie Blackmore, Steve Miller, Joe Walsh,
Brian May and Carlos Santana are all here. The list is lacking Mark Knopfler
of Dire Straits and Andy Summers of Police but this is, nevertheless, a very
good series of essays, with good illustrations and brief discographies.

Tobler, John
   Guitar heroes / John Tobler. – London: Marshall Cavendish, 1978. – 88p.:
   ill., ports; 23cm. Includes discographies. ISBN 0-85685-438-7
The electric guitar has from the beginning been the most important instrument of rock music. By the late sixties the guitar hero had become the main
focus of rock fans' adulation. This very well illustrated book includes the
biography of thirty-two guitarists from the pioneers of the electric guitar style
of the forties and early fifties, such as Les Paul and B. B. King, to the
superstars of the late sixties, such as Eric Clapton and Jimi Hendrix, without
ignoring some of the less well known but technically innovative musicians.
Each biography includes a brief discography of representative albums.

COLLECTED INTERVIEWS

Elmlark, Walli
   Rock raps of the 70's / by Walli Elmlark and Timothy Beckley. – New York:
   Drake, 1972. – 125p.: ill., ports; 28cm. ISBN 0-8774-9285-9 (pbk.)
A collection of interviews with some leading figures of the early seventies.
There are some good portraits but the interviews vary greatly in their quality
and in the interest of their content. Some of the subjects now seem a little
obscure.

Giants of rock music / edited by Pauline Rivelli and Robert Levin. – New
   York: Da Capo, 1981. – 125p.: ill., ports; 22cm. ISBN 0-306-80148-5
   Previously published as '*The rock giants*': New York: World Publishing,
   1970.
A collection of interviews and articles originally appearing in the defunct
American magazine *Jazz and Pop*. Mostly the subjects are American stars of
the late sixties, such as the Jefferson Airplane, Frank Zappa, John and Yoko
Lennon, Randy Newman, the Creedence Clearwater Revival, Canned Heat
and Cream.

James, Sally
   Sally James' almost legendary pop interviews. – London: Eel Pie, 1981. –
   96p.: ill., ports; 20cm. ISBN 0-906008-28-X (pbk.)
Sally James has been a presenter of British pop-music television programmes
for children for some years and has recently become well known as the
presenter of Tiswas, a Saturday morning children's programme. She has
always included a spot where she interviews current pop stars and this is a
collection of these interviews. Her subjects include Adam Ant, Sheena
Easton, Motorhead, Spandau Ballet, Bad Manners, the Stray Cats, Toyah,
Dave Edmunds and Phil Collins. The quality varies widely from serious
dialogues to those in which the interviewer is not being taken at all seriously.

Leigh, Spencer
   Stars in my eyes: personal interviews with top music stars / by Spencer Leigh.
   – Liverpool: Raven Books (Music), 1980. – 160p.: ill., facsims, ports;
   30cm. ISBN 0-85977-016-8 (pbk.)

Written by a freelance journalist who conducted twenty-three interviews with stars from the whole spectrum of popular music. The artists included are Charles Aznavour, Marc Bolan, Victor Borge, Bo Diddley, Tom Paxton, Cliff Richard and Don Williams. The interviews vary in their depth and their revelations but are, on the whole, readable, with some good portraits.

The road to rock: a Zigzag book of interviews / edited by Pete Frame. –
London: Charisma Books, 1974. – 224p.: ill., ports; 19cm.
ISBN 0-85947-014-8 (pbk.)
A collection of eight interviews which appeared originally in the monthly magazine *Zigzag*. The subjects include Pete Townshend, Jimmy Page, Rod Stewart, Elton John and other influential artists whose comments can be set in the context of the early seventies and whose circumstances have now changed. Although the book is poorly produced, this is a fascinating collection.

The Rolling Stone interviews / compiled by the editors of *Rolling Stone*. – New
York: Paperback Library, 1971. – 465p.: ill., ports; 18cm. (pbk.)
The Rolling Stone interviews: volume 2 / compiled by the editors of *Rolling
Stone*. – New York: Warner Books, 1973. – 365p.: ill., ports; 18cm. ISBN
0-446-59866-6 (pbk.)
From its beginning *Rolling Stone* has always included lengthy interviews with the leading musical names of the time. Its editor, Jann Wenner, is a leading figure in this form of journalism and has provided many important pieces. The first volume includes the best interviews between late 1967 and the first months of 1971; the second covers the next period up to late 1973. The interviews are detailed, incisive and provide a picture of the innovation of the period. The first volume is probably the better. The remarkable amount of information here is unfortunately often inaccessible owing to the lack of indexes.

The Rolling Stone interviews 1967–1980: talking with the legends of rock & roll
/ edited by Peter Herbst; introduction by Ben Fong-Torres. – London:
Arthur Barker, 1981. – 426p.: ill., ports; 24cm. ISBN 0-213-16818-9 (pbk.)
Originally published: New York: St. Martin's Press, 1981.
An updating of the previous *Rolling Stone* collections of interviews, here are twenty-five of the most significant artists in popular music during *Rolling Stone's* existence. Some of the interviews are abridged, but it is a fine collection and well produced. The subjects include John Lennon, Eric Clapton, Mick Jagger, Bob Dylan, Stevie Wonder, Chuck Berry, Billy Joel, Van Morrison and Neil Young. There is an excellent collection of portraits and an appendix of brief biographies of the journalists.

Sander, Ellen
Trips: rock life in the sixties / by Ellen Sander. – New York: Charles
Scribner's Sons, 1973. – xi, 272p.: ill., ports; 24cm. Includes discographies
and index. ISBN 0-684-12752-0
The evolution of popular music into a major cultural force which occurred in

the late sixties, is sketched in the form of recollections and anecdotes. The author extensively interviewed many of the leading American figures, mainly from the late sixties, who offer a wide range of views from the honest to the pretentious. There are rare illustrations and an appendix which classifies the major artists, giving a brief biography and a selective discography. Well indexed, this is an American view which is entertaining but adds little.

Saporita, Jay
    Pourin' it all out / Jay Saporita. – Secaucus, New Jersey: Citadel Press,
    1980. – 204p.: ill., ports; 24cm. ISBN 0-8065-0696-2 (cased).
    ISBN 0-8065-0729-2 (pbk.)
A collection of interviews and conversations with a wide range of people involved in rock at the end of the seventies. There is no cohesive theme or attempted conclusion.

Wale, Michael
    Voxpop: profiles of the pop process / by Michael Wale, – London: Harrap,
    1972. – 220p.; 22cm. ISBN 0-245-50904-6 (cased). ISBN 0-245-51083-4
    (pbk.)
An investigation of the popular-music business by this British journalist and television presenter who interviewed thirty-two prominent people from all areas of the industry. Managers, record-company executives, producers, promoters, session musicians as well as some major stars, including Marc Bolan, were encouraged to give their views. The result is an outdated but fascinating collection of conflicting, subjective accounts of the relative importance of each of the subjects' roles, of exploitation and self-importance. Wale's conclusions and statistical tables are concise and informative.

COLLECTED QUOTATIONS

The book of rock quotes / compiled by Jonathan Green. – Rev. ed. – London:
    Omnibus Press, 1981. – 128p.: ill., ports; 25cm. ISBN 0-86001-943-8 (pbk.)
    Previous edition: London: Omnibus Press, 1977.
Classified into sections by subject, this is a collection of quotations extracted from interviews, songs and writings, reflecting the views of hundreds of people from all areas of the music business. Generally amusing, the brief quotes are often hopelessly out of context and the use of lyrics as an expression of an artist's view on a subject is very dubious.

Loose talk: the book of quotes from the pages of the Rolling Stone Magazine /
    compiled by Linda Botts. – London: Omnibus Press; Rolling Stone Press,
    1980. – 222p.: ill., ports; 24cm. Includes index. ISBN 0-86001-774-5 (pbk.)
Loose Talk was a column of quotations from celebrities, politicians and musicians which appeared in the *Rolling Stone* magazine. Often amusing, sometimes revealing, this is a well-chosen selection which is augmented by notable extracts from other sections of *Rolling Stone* over the years. The quotations are presented in a random way, but there is a simple index to the makers of the remarks.

The superstars in their own words / photographed and edited by Douglas Kent
 Hall; from interviews by Sue C. Clark. – New York: Music Sales Corpora-
 tion; London: Music Sales, 1979. – 192p.: ill., ports; 29cm. Includes index.
 ISBN 0-8256-6020-3 (pbk.)
 Originally published as '*Rock: world bold as love*': New York: Cowles, 1970.
A pretentious work 'designed to reflect the vitality, the integrity and simple
purity of the rock world', this is a collection of quotes from the leading artists
of the late sixties. A wide range of black and white American stars are
included: Sly Stone, Jimi Hendrix, the Jefferson Airplane, John Fogerty of
Creedence Clearwater, Tina Turner, Jim Morrison, David Ruffin and Country Joe Macdonald all offer their pearls to us. The optimism of the period is
evident here, always with the naivety, excess and a false sense of permanence.

1.4 COLLECTED ARTICLES, ESSAYS

There is a great deal of useful information and enjoyable reading in some of
the following collections of writings, many of which would originally have
been lost amidst the contemporary gossip and illustrations in their original
magazines and musicpapers.

The age of rock: sounds of the American cultural revolution, a reader / edited
 by Jonathan Eisen. – New York: Vintage Books, 1969. – 388p., 16p. of
 plates: ill., ports; 22cm. ISBN 0-394-70535-1 (pbk.)
 Also published: New York: Random House, 1969.
A large collection of articles from various American publications from the
late sixties. Included are the major journalists of popular music from the
period, writing on many of the stars, and contemporary topics from biographical essays to musicological analyses. Although the Beatles feature
strongly, there is an American bias and a wide variation in the quality of the
writing.

The age of rock 2: sights and sounds of the American cultural revolution /
 edited by Jonathan Eisen. – New York: Vintage Books, 1970. – 339p.;
 20cm. ISBN 0-394-70879-2 (pbk.)
 Also published: New York: Random House, 1970.
A collection of pieces by notable writers of the time which include essays on
aspects of popular-music culture as well as analyses of the work of particular
artists. The Woodstock festival and Altamont are very much on people's
minds. Not such a good collection as the first volume edited by Eisen, it still
has some good moments. The viewpoint is very much an American one.

Christgau, Robert
 Any old way you choose it: rock and other pop music 1967–1973 / by Robert
 Christgau. – Baltimore, Maryland: Penguin Books, 1973. – 330p.; 18cm.
 Includes index. ISBN 0-1400-3762-4 (pbk.)

Written by the music critic of the American magazines *Newsday, Village Voice* and *Esquire*, this collection of essays which appeared in these magazines deals with the whole spectrum of popular music. The author has the ability to cope with white rock and pop music as well as black music, with equal clarity and depth of understanding. He is occasionally wrong in his assessments; for example, he was unimpressed by Jimi Hendrix at the legendary Monterey Festival: the festival established Hendrix as a major performer. On the other hand, he sings the praises of soul singer Al Green long before the latter had even signed a recording contract. Overall, the essays are mostly interesting and always provocative; for example, his support of Creedence Clearwater in comparison with the Doors was an unfashionable view but well argued and persuasive.

Goldman, Albert
Freakshow: the rocksoulbluesjazzsickjewblackhumorsexpoppsych gig and other scenes from the counter-culture / Albert Goldman. – New York: Atheneum, 1971. – xix, 387p.; 22cm.
A collection of articles on a wide range of musical subjects from Elvis Presley and Colonel Parker to a study of Tamla Motown. The only real cohesion in the collection is a cynical viewpoint. In the Motown piece Goldman analyses the ways in which Motown expresses the true modern black feeling in America; he rejects the blues revival as superficial nostalgia; and, always looking for a new standpoint, he expands a review of a Rolling Stones concert into a debate of rock as fascism. He pursues the concept that in their pursuit of evil, the Stones have attained beauty. In general, mostly pretentious nonsense.

Goldstein, Richard
Goldstein's greatest hits: a book mostly about rock'n'roll / by Richard Goldstein. – Englewood Cliffs, New Jersey: Prentice-Hall, 1970. – 228p.: ill., ports; 24cm. Includes index. ISBN 0-13-357913-1
A good selection of essays on a wide range of major artists. The emphasis is on the stars of the late sixties, notably the Doors, Jefferson Airplane and Bob Dylan. The author analyses musical and writing styles but is often pretentious.

The Guitar Player book / by editors of the *Guitar Player* magazine. – Saratoga, California: Guitar Player Books; New York: Grove Press, 1979. – 403p.: ill., ports; 29cm. Includes index. ISBN 0-8021-4167-6 (Grove Press) (cased). ISBN 0-394-17045-8 (Guitar Player Books) (pbk.)
Composed of articles which originally appeared in the *Guitar Player* magazine, the book includes essays on types of instruments, styles of playing and repairing guitars, as well as interviews and biographies of the world's leading guitarists. A fine collection of writings on all types of music, including jazz, classical and folk, here are some fascinating details on the technique and the development in style of contemporary music's most important instrument.

Jewell, Derek
   The popular voice: a musical record of the 60s and 70s / Derek Jewell. –
   London: Sphere, 1980. – 256p., 12p. of plates: ill., ports; 20cm. Includes
   index. ISBN 0-7221-5099-7 (pbk.)
   Originally published: London: Deutsch, 1980.
As jazz and popular-music critic of *The Sunday Times* the author has covered
two decades of all aspects of popular music. This is a collection of his writings
which ranges from in-depth, searching analyses to short, snappy reviews. His
subjects vary from reviews of films and books to the jazz establishment and
punk rock. Each piece is well argued and well written. The collection gives a
good outline of the music of the period with a jazz bias. It is never patronizing
and always poignant.

Kaufman, Murray
   Murray the K tells it like it is baby / Murray Kaufman; with forewords by
   Tony Bennett, George Harrison and others. – New York: Holt, Rinehart &
   Winston, 1966. – 127p.: ill., ports; 25cm.
Murray Kaufman, or Murray the K, was a notable American disc jockey and
publicist in the Beatles' invasion of the USA from the beginning. George
Harrison's introduction is poor and a little embarrassing, and these anecdotes
about the stars are occasionally revealing but generally dull and self-centred.

Landau, Jon
   It's too late to stop now; a rock and roll journal / by Jon Landau. – San
   Francisco: Straight Arrow Books, 1972. – 227p.; 22cm. Includes discography. ISBN 0-8793-2016-8 (cased). ISBN 0-8793-2015-X (pbk.)
   Also published: New York: Simon & Schuster, 1972.
A selection of essays by one of popular music's leading journalists who is also
a record producer and now manages Bruce Springsteen. His work, which
transplants many of the ideas of auteur film criticism to rock music, sometimes fails by being too complex in its analysis of a simple subject. Nevertheless his writings on Otis Redding, Bob Dylan and artists from many different
styles of music are literate and intuitive. After a long essay on the state of the
art in 1970 his collection of pieces includes many record reviews. The discography is of records reviewed or mentioned in the text.

Norman, Philip
   The road goes on forever: portraits from a journey in contemporary music /
   Philip Norman. – London: Elm Tree Press, 1982. – 206p., 16p. of plates:
   ill., ports; 24cm. ISBN 0-241-10862-4 (pbk.)
As a popular-music critic for *The Times* and *The Sunday Times*, Philip
Norman has interviewed, reviewed and criticized the whole spectrum of the
music over almost fifteen years. This is a collection of thirty-six examples of
his writings which include pieces on Bill Haley, Suzi Quatro, Barry White,
Alice Cooper, Stevie Wonder, Fleetwood Mac, Blondie, the Everly Brothers,
the Rolling Stones, Elvis Presley, Chuck Berry, Fats Domino and so on.
Included is the first interview given by Yoko Ono after Lennon's death: Life
without John. A readable but patchy collection with some interesting quotations but poor critical appraisals.

Playboy's music scene. – Chicago: Playboy Press, 1972. – 189p.: col. ill., col.
    ports; 18cm. (pbk.)
Reviews and interviews originally appearing in *Playboy* magazine and including subjects from jazz, rock and country music.

Race, Steve
    Dear music lover . . . / Steve Race. – London: Robson Books, 1981. –
    117p.: ill., facsim., music; 23cm. ISBN 0-86051-134-0
Written in the form of twenty lengthy letters, the author covers a wide range
of topics from various areas of music including modern popular forms. One
chapter discusses the validity of untrained composers such as Paul McCartney
and untrained singers such as Bob Dylan and Louis Armstrong. He strongly
believes they have a valid place and professes to oppose the snobbery of the
classically trained. The musical examples are very interesting.

Rock and roll will stand / edited by Greil Marcus. – Boston, Massachusetts:
    Beacon Press, 1969. – viii, 182p.; 22cm.
A collection of late-sixties writings on West Coast music and its associated
culture, in which the major groups of the period are all discussed. In general,
it is a sensible collection from a chaotic, drug-orientated period. The quality
of writing is variable, however, with Marcus's own essays being very good.

The Rolling Stone record review / by the editors of *Rolling Stone*. – New York:
    Pocket Books, 1971. – 566p.; 18cm. ISBN 0-671-78531-1 (pbk.)
The Rolling Stone record review: the authoritative guide to contemporary
    records, volume 2 / by the editors of *Rolling Stone*. – New York: Pocket
    Books, 1974. – 599p.; 18cm. ISBN 0-671-75894-X (pbk.)
These haphazard collections of reviews, some of which have been abridged,
originally appeared in *Rolling Stone*. They are particularly well written,
expressing a wide range of knowledge and understanding of a variety of
musical forms. The insight displayed is, with hindsight, remarkable.

The Rolling Stone rock'n'roll reader / edited by Ben Fong-Torres. – New
    York: Bantam Books, 1974. – 783p.; 18cm. ISBN 0-553-07483-5 (pbk.)
A collection of articles originally published in *Rolling Stone* from its inception
in November 1967 until the end of 1973. It reflects in a literate, although
occasionally pretentious way, the development of popular music over this
period. The collection includes many interviews with rock stars, articles on
performances and critical comment on significant records and innovations in
style.

The Sixties: the decade remembered now, by the people who lived in it then /
    edited by Lynda Rosen Obst; designed by Robert Kingsbury. – New York:
    Random House; Rolling Stone Press, 1977. – 317p.: ill., ports; 37cm. ISBN
    0-394-40687-1 (cased). ISBN 0-394-73239-1 (pbk.)
Published in a large format, this collection of seventy-one essays on the
decade includes pieces by some of the best-known writers on popular culture.
The subjects include all the major events, particularly relevant to the Ameri-

can scene, from the assassinations of the Kennedys and Martin Luther King to an essay by Carl Bernstein, of Watergate fame, on the New York blackout of 1965, as well as a fine collection of essays on major musical topics. To name but a few of the contributors, Michael Bloomfield has a superb piece on Bob Dylan's change to electric music at the Newport Festival in 1965; Greil Marcus writes on the Altamont Festival; Myra Friedman on Janis Joplin; Lou Adler on the Monterey Pop Festival of 1967; Wavy Gravy on Woodstock; and Tony Fawcett on the Beatles. To set the music in the context of its time this is an excellent collection of essays and is matched by the complementary collection of photographs.

Stranded: rock and roll for a desert island / edited by Greil Marcus. – New
York: Alfred A. Knopf, 1979. – xii, 305p.; 22cm. Includes discography.
ISBN 0-394-50828-9 (cased) ISBN 0-394-73827-6 (pbk.)
Twenty of the best American rock writers were posed the question: what one rock'n'roll album would you take to a desert island? The result is a collection of essays supporting their selections. The choices are diverse in period, style and in the reasons for their selection. The pieces are more than simple criticisms and, because of the quality of writing and depth of knowledge, they present a wide, intelligent view of the music. The writers include Dave Marsh, Lester Bangs, John Rockwell and solitary emigré Englishman Simon Frith. The subjects include Van Morrison, the Eagles, Bruce Springsteen and the Ronettes. There is an appendix by Greil Marcus in which he offers an annotated discography of his view of the best in rock from its beginnings to date. The selection, which has a strong American bias and includes singles as well as albums, is a useful personal guide to significant developments over twenty-five years.

Twenty-minute fandangoes and forever changes / edited by Jonathan Eisen. –
New York: Vintage Books, 1971. – 324p.; 20cm. ISBN 0-394-71120-3
(pbk.)
Also published: New York: Random House, 1971.
A third collection of essays and articles on the period of the late sixties, Forever Changes comes from the title of the West Coast group Love's most successful album, in many ways encapsulating the feeling of the time. It complements well the editor's *The age of rock.*

*What's that sound?: the contemporary music scene from the pages of Rolling
Stone* / edited by Ben Fong-Torres. – New York: Anchor Press; Double-
day, 1976. – 426p.; 18cm. ISBN 0-385-11482-6 (pbk.)
A well-selected collection of features which previously appeared in *Rolling Stone*. Many of the pieces update interviews and articles in previous collections. For example, there are excellent features on Bob Dylan and Led Zeppelin which discuss their respective careers in the mid seventies, as well as an excellent essay on the importance of the jazz–rock fusion.

Williams, Paul
    Outlaw blues: book of rock music / Paul Williams. – New York: E. P.
    Dutton, 1969. – 191p.: ill., ports; 21cm. (pbk.)
A collection of essays written betweeen 1966 and 1968 and originally published in *Crawdaddy* magazine. Williams founded the magazine and his essays
are largely record reviews with some interviews. The most notable is between
Williams and David Anderle, a business advisor of the Beach Boys during
1966 and 1967. This offers a sensitive insight into the personality of Brian
Wilson. Other notable pieces include excellent essays on Bob Dylan's work,
the Doors and the Byrds. Williams' writing is some of the most lucid, intelligent and authoritative that rock journalism has produced.

1.5 YEARBOOKS AND DIRECTORIES

Yearbooks and directories are serious attempts to survey the work of the
music industry over the year and/or to impart hard information. They vary
from *Kemps international music & recording industry yearbook*, a solidly
produced commercial directory, to *The rock yearbook*, published by Virgin
Books, which includes a great deal of information about the industry but is
certainly for the mass market.

Attwood, Tony
    British songwriters' guide / prepared for R. S. Productions by Tony
    Attwood. – Totnes, Devon: R. S. Productions, 1981. 10 leaves; 30cm.
    Includes bibliography. ISBN 0-906888-06-9 (unbound)
The addresses of record companies, music publishers and recording studios
are arranged alphabetically. There are brief introductory notes on what to do
with your new composition.

British record company & music industry index. – Totnes, Devon: R. S. Publi-
    cations, 1979. – 12p.; 30cm. (unbound)
Divided into record companies, orchestras, art centres, schools and industrial
organizations, this alphabetically arranged listing of names and addresses is
aimed at anyone approaching the industry for information. There is a brief
introduction offering advice on sources of specific information within organizations.

Contemporary music almanac. – New York: Schirmer Books; London:
    Collier Macmillan, 1980. – Annual. 1980/81/Ronald Zalkind. – 1980. –
    944p.: ill., ports; 24cm. ISBN 0-02-87297-6. ISSN 0196-6200
An extensive yearbook and directory, this includes a summary of the musical
events of 1979, top film, album and singles charts, a calendar for 1980 and
1981, and a series of feature articles. A 'who's who' section of major performers, list of films, gold records back to 1958 and directory of radio
stations, professional organizations, music publishers, promoters, agents and

record companies all make this book a mine of information. It is naturally concerned primarily with the American music industry but is the fullest directory to date.

Glassman, Judith
  The year in music 1978 / Judith Glassman. – New York: Columbia House, 1978. – 320p.: ill. (some col.), ports (some col.); 29cm. ISBN 0-930748-08-4
A survey of the musical year in the USA in which the author looks at the main activities and successes in each style: rock, rhythm & blues, country and western, jazz, classical, disco, theatre and easy listening. The major trends are discussed with lists of top sellers and major awards. There is a section devoted to biographies of the major artists of the year, newcomers and a section listing fan clubs, music publishers, periodicals, record companies and a calendar of the events of the year. In general, a good survey which is yet to reappear for successive years. The index is particularly well constructed, giving easy access to a wealth of information.

Kemps international music & recording industry yearbook. – London: Kemps, 1965–. Annual. 1981. – 1980. – 132p.: ill.; 21cm. ISBN 0-905255-68-2. ISSN 0305-7100
This comprehensive yearbook and directory surveys the previous year in the industry, discusses current trends and gives exhaustive details of organizations involved in all aspects of music. This is an indispensable reference source.

Melody Maker desk diary and yearbook 1956–. – London: IPC Specialist and Professional Press, 1955–. Annual. 1983. – 1982. – 204p.: ill.; 22cm.
  Originally published as '*Melody Maker Yearbook*': London: Longacre Press.
The nucleus of this work is a desk diary for use in the office of music-associated businesses. In addition it includes selected directory information.

Music & Video Week directory. – London: Music Week, 1968–. Annual. 1983. – 1982. – 130p.: ill.; 21cm.
  Originally published as '*Music Week directory*'.
Issued as part of the trade paper's subscription, this is an excellent directory to a wide range of sources associated with the music and video industries. Artist management, agents, concert promoters, musical-equipment hire, record companies, studios, video distributors and music publishers are all comprehensively included, as well as many other categories.

Music business yearbook: musicfax for the eighties published annually. – London: Eccentric Music, 1981–. Annual. No. 1 / written and compiled by Gary Gee; illustrations Pudsey. – 1981. – 104p.: ill.; 21cm. ISBN 0-9507421-0-4 (pbk.)
With the aim of providing information on a 'comprehensive network of music services' in the United Kingdom, the arrangement is first by topic, for example music publishers, merchandising, agencies, small labels, and then by

region. The names and addresses are accurate, featuring the smaller companies, more appropriate for the independent musician at the beginning of his career. Certainly far from comprehensive, this is a useful directory with just a slight flavour of the anti-establishment which will, one hopes, continue.

Rock and roll yearbook. – Bolton: Dalrow Publications, 1956–. 1957/Barry
E. Cummings, executive editor; Fred Wagner, editor. – 1956. – 100p.: ill.,
ports; 27cm. (pbk.)
Originally published: New York: Filosa Publications, 1956.
Including only American performers, this is a rare document profusely illustrated with rare portraits of the innovators of rock'n'roll. The text does not have the patronizing air of British writing of the period and reflects well the early American attitude to the music, which stems from its, even then, commercial potential.

The rock yearbook 1981–. – London: Virgin Books, 1980–. Annual. 1983. –
1982. – 240p.: ill. (some col.), facsims (some col.), ports (some col.); 30cm.
ISBN 0-907080-57-X (pbk.)
This book maintains the same format for its first three years of existence: after a chronological survey of the preceding year, September to August, there are reviews of the current situation in all styles of popular music: reggae, rock, soul/disco, folk, blues, electronic and rockabilly. There are reviews of albums of the year, a section on books and films, record charts and statistics on bestselling records and most successful artists. Essays by leading journalists on leading artists and a collection of high-quality photographs make this an excellent source and summary of the changes in all areas of popular music. As usual, the title 'rock' is narrow and misleading.

The year in rock. – Farncombe, Surrey: LSP Books, 1981–. Annual. 1981 –
1982 / edited by John Swenson; art direction Ed Caraeff. – 271p.: ill.,
facsims, ports; 23cm. ISBN 0-85321-083-7 (pbk.)
Originally published: New York: Amordian Press; Delilah
Communications, 1981.
Including the Billboard top-forty album charts for the year beginning August 1980 and ending August 1981, this is a retrospective survey of the whole music scene for that period from an American viewpoint. Included are reviews of the major albums, interviews and essays on leading artists and a fine selection of photographs. The writing is very good throughout and if this publication continues, it will become a useful reference source.

ALMANACS

Formento, Dan
Rock chronicle: a 365 day-by-day journal of significant events in rock history
/ by Dan Formento. – London: Sidgwick & Jackson, 1982. – 367p.: ill.,
ports; 24cm. ISBN 0-283-98960-2 (pbk.)
Originally published: New York: Delilah Communications, 1982.

A daily list of significant events in the fields of pop, rock, country and black music. Births, deaths, record release and recording dates and notable performances are all included. It is briefer and less satisfactory than the other two similar works, by Marchbank and Silverton. There is space to add one's own events of interest to each day.

Lowe, Leslie
Directory of popular music 1900–1965 / by Leslie Lowe. – Droitwich, Worcestershire: Peterson, 1975. – 1034p. Includes index
A remarkable source of information, this is a chronological listing of songs published since 1900 by month, with full credits, as well as similar lists of stage shows, musical films and other historical information.

Marchbank, Pearce
The illustrated rock almanac / compiled, written and edited by Pearce Marchbank and Miles. – New York; London: Paddington Press, 1977. – 191p.: ill., ports; 28cm. ISBN 0-448-22675-8 (pbk.)
A daily calendar with explanatory notes of events, births, deaths, record releases, performances and so on, relating to the world of popular music. Often items are listed which relate to popular culture generally or even significant political events. As a reference source, however, its single chronological sequence lacks a name index.

Silverton, Pete
Rock diary 1983 / by Pete Silverton and Dave Fudger. – London; New York: Proteus, 1982. – 128p.: ill., ports; 27cm. ISBN 0-86276-020-8
A daily calendar of events involving the music business. The release dates of significant records, births and deaths of artists and anniversaries of important events are all included. There is no index, making it an interesting but poor information source. It is not as reliable or as full as the similar, earlier attempt by Pearce Marchbank.

ANNUALS

Annuals, as defined here, are aimed at the Christmas gift market. They are colourfully presented, profusely illustrated and many also include games and puzzles to occupy the preteenager over the Christmas holiday.

It's rock scene. – Maidenhead: Purnell, 1964–1979. Annual. 1979. – 61p.: ill. (some col.), ports (some col.); 27cm. ISBN 0-361-04558-1
Formerly titled '*Top pop stars*'; '*Top 20*'; '*Top pop scene*'.
A Christmas gift packed with pictures of the current stars, it includes interviews, articles, puzzles and quizzes. After a company reorganization in 1980, Purnell reduced its output of children's annuals and this ceased publication after a long, sustained life.

Look In pop annual. – London: ITV Books, 1977–. Annual. 1982. – 76p.: ill.
　(some col.), ports (some col.); 28cm. ISBN 0-90796-505-9
Look In is a weekly children's magazine based on an ITV television programme. This annual includes quizzes, puzzles, strip cartoons and short
features on the current stars. A well-designed Christmas gift.

The Melody Maker file 1974 / editor Ray Coleman. – London: IPC Specialist
　and Professional Press, 1973. – 127p.: ill., ports; 28cm. ISBN 0-6170-0093-X
　(pbk.)
Appearing only once, this well-produced publication surveyed the year's
activity in the music business with a fine selection of articles and photographs
which had appeared in the music paper.

Mirabelle Sunshine pop book. – London: IPC Magazines 1973–1975.
　Annual. 1976. – 1975. – 79p.: ill. (some col.), ports (some col.); 28cm.
　ISBN 0-8503-7264-X
Mirabelle is a preteenage weekly comic for girls. This annual of puzzles,
games, stories and photographs of the stars appeared for three years only.

Music Star annual: 1974–1977. – London: IPC Magazines, 1973–1976.
　Annual. 1977. – 1976. – 76p., 16p. of plates: ill. (some col.), ports (some
　col.); 28cm. ISBN 0-8503-7145-5
A Christmas gift with some good coloured portraits and interesting text for
the early teenager.

New Musical Express Annual: 1955–1973. – London: IPC Magazines,
　1955–1972. Annual. 1973 / edited by Jack Scott. – 1972. – 95p.: ill. (some
　col.), ports (some col.); 28cm. ISBN 0-85037-039-6
New Musical Express hot rock guide: 1974 / edited by Jack Scott. – London:
　IPC Magazines, 1973. – 95p.: ill. (some col.), ports (some col.); 28cm. ISBN
　0-85037-112-0
New Musical Express greatest hits: the very best of NME 1975 / edited by Jack
　Scott. – London: IPC Magazines, 1974. – 95p.: ill. (some col.), ports (some
　col.); 28cm. ISBN 0-85037-147-0
Beginning not long after the birth of the *NME* in 1952, the annual was a
collection of photographs and articles, not all of which had appeared during
the previous year. As the years went by the format became exclusively a
selection of articles chronicling the development of music during the year. In
1973 and 1974 the two later manifestations were essentially attempts to
revitalize interest, but failed, and an annual has not appeared since. During
the early sixties it occasionally appeared twice a year. Always interesting, it
well represents the changing face of music if one is fortunate enough to scan
through a selection of editions.

Pelham pop annual. – London: Pelham, 1970. Annual. 1970 / edited by Peter
　Douglas and Peter Oakes. – 120p.: ill. (some col.), ports (some col.); 27cm.
A survey of the year's pop scene for young fans with some good illustrations,
this only appeared once.

Rock on! annual. – London: IPC Magazines, 1978–1979. Annual. 1980. –
1979. – 78p.: ill. (some col.), ports (some col.); 28cm. ISBN 0-85037-490-1
The annual of the monthly magazine, this included features on the leading
performers of the year and a good selection of coloured portraits. Aimed at
the Christmas gift market, it was for a mid-teenage audience.

Smash Hits yearbook. – London: EMAP National Publications, 1982–.
Annual. 1983. – 1982. – 68p.: ill. (some col.), ports (some col.); 28cm.
(pbk.)
The first appearance of this annual with features on current artists, a pop
calendar for the year, quizzes, puzzles and other entertaining items. The
illustrations and level of writing offer considerably more than most Christmas
giftbooks of this kind.

Supersonic annual. – London: IPC Magazines, 1977–. Annual. 1977. – 1978. –
78p.: ill. (some col.), ports (some col.); 28cm. ISBN 0-8503-7356-5
Supersonic was a BBC children's television programme featuring music popular with the early teenage and preteenage audience. This appeared only once,
aimed at the Christmas gift market, and included short articles, quizzes and a
good collection of portraits. There was also a short-lived tie-in magazine of
the same title.

Top of the Pops annual 1976 – . Manchester: World International
Publications, 1975–. Annual. 1983 / edited by Ken Irwin. – 1982. – 62p.: ill.
(some col.), ports (some col.); 25cm. ISBN 0-7235-6656-2
Published for the Christmas gift market, this is a survey of the year's successful artists who have appeared on the BBC television programme Top of the
Pops, a weekly survey of the singles charts. It includes quizzes, puzzles and a
very good selection of illustrations.

Top twenty / edited by Phil Buckle. – London: New English Library, 1963. –
126p., 22p. of plates: ill., ports; 18cm. (pbk.)
A survey of the year's successful artists, it gives brief biographies with some
comments on contemporary styles and trends in music. As a guide to music of
the time it is superficial but as a reflection of the period, interesting.

Valentine pop. – London: IPC Magazines, 1959–1970. Annual. 1970. – 81p.:
chiefly ill. (some col.), ports (some col.); 25cm. ISBN 0-9003-7653-8 (pbk.)
Originally published by Amalgamated Press, Fleetway Publications and later
IPC Magazines, *Valentine* was a weekly comic for teenage and preteenage
girls. Its annual covered the pop scene with very brief notes but a good
collection of portraits of pop stars. It faded out in 1970.

The year's top twenty / edited by Philip Buckle. – London: Mayflower, 1964. –
125p., 16p. of plates: ill., ports; 19cm. (pbk.)
A survey of the year's successful chart acts with brief biographies and
comments.

ACADEMIC YEARBOOKS

Popular music. – Cambridge: Cambridge University Press, 1981–. Annual.
  1: Folk or popular? distinctions, influences, continuities / edited by Richard
  Middleton and David Horn. – 1981. – vii, 222p.: ill., ports; 24cm.
  2: Theory and method / edited by Richard Middleton and David Horn. – x,
  341p.: ill., facsims, music; 24cm. Includes bibliography. ISSN 0261-1430
Focussing on a particular theme each year, this unique serial offers a serious
approach to the subject. Its scope, and thereby definition of 'popular', is very
wide including historical essays, folk music, jazz, music hall, rock and so on.
Number 1 included such topics as the Tyneside Concert hall, by David
Harker, popular music in Afghanistan, and God, modality and meaning in
some recent songs of Bob Dylan, by Wilfrid Mellers. Number 2 looks at the
aesthetics of rock music, by Peter Wicke, the blues and aspects of African
music. There are record and book reviews, tending to be somewhat self-
consciously academic and, in number 2, there is a lengthy bibliography of
currently published material which attempts, but fails, to be comprehensive. In
all, a fascinating work for the enthusiast which suffers badly from a dull,
textbook appearance and subscription basis which will deprive it of a wider
audience.

GAZETTEERS

Wootton, Richard
  Honky tonkin': a travel guide to American music / by Richard Wootton. –
  3rd ed. – London: Travelaid Publishing, 1980. – 180p.: ill., maps; 22cm.
  ISBN 0-902743-16-3 (pbk.)
  Previous edition: London: Richard Wootton, 1978.
  Also published: Charlotte, North Carolina: East Woods Press, 1980.
The author is a British freelance writer who has regularly visited America,
dropping in on nightspots, record shops, local record companies and talking
to artists, writers and disc jockeys. He has compiled a guide, arranged
alphabetically by state, which reviews the entertainment offered in the major
towns and cities. Items included are naturally selective but the most famous
clubs and venues are given. The guide to local radio is more comprehensive
and there is a list of currently available music periodicals. When a particular
style of music is discussed in its regional context, the author includes a good,
brief essay. The book underlines the fact that the USA is a collection of very
different states with their own local cultures. The range of entertainment is
remarkable and the depth of Richard Wootton's research impressive. The
improvement in the quality of the book throughout its editions has been
considerable.

1.6 STATISTICAL INFORMATION, CHARTS, LISTS

The most obvious manifestation of the overt commercialism of modern popular music is the constant emphasis on record sales.

The ranking of records by sales figures has been an important function of the American trade papers, *Cash Box* and *Billboard*, since the forties but by the fifties the concept of the top ten or the hit parade was of real significance to the fan and a major feature of the music press, *Melody Maker, New Musical Express* and so on. Certainly this trend was encouraged by the record companies for as soon as a record appeared on the chart its plays on the radio increased, more sales were generated and hence the snowball grew.

The importance of chart data, although in essence ephemeral, has created a subculture of its own and a growing literature.

The same basic data are presented either in the original chart form, reproduced from the music press, or reorganized by artist to offer information to be absorbed and no doubt regurgitated when confronted with quizbooks.

Secondary listings have more recently been generated offering a wide range of additional, often subjective, data. Other works have appeared on gold discs and hit records containing greater detail but still firmly based on the concepts of sales and the charts.

Edwards, Joseph
Top 10's and trivia of rock & roll and rhythm & blues, 1950–1973 / Joseph Edwards. – St. Louis, Missouri: Blueberry Hill, 1974. – 632p.; 24cm.
Packed with information unavailable elsewhere, this compilation of American charts includes rare early examples taken from the American trade paper *Billboard*. The categories popular, rock'n'roll and rhythm & blues are divided into singles and albums. The songs which reached number one in the ratings are marked. Indexes are by artist and title and there is a section of questions and answers.

Edwards, Joseph
Top 10's and trivia of rock & roll and rhythm & blues: 1974 supplement /
Joseph Edwards. – St. Louis, Missouri: Blueberry Hill, 1974. – 35p.; 24cm.
An updating supplement in the same format as the main volume, but with no question-and-answer section.

Goldstein, Stewart
Oldies but goodies: the rock'n'roll years / by Stewart Goldstein and Alan Jacobson. – New York: Van Nostrand Reinhold, 1978. – 328p.: ill., ports; 24cm. Includes indexes. ISBN 0-4428-0365-6 (cased). ISBN 0-4428-0431-8 (pbk.)
Originally published: New York: Mason-Chater, 1977
With an introduction by former teenage idol Paul Anka, this has a wider coverage than rock'n'roll music of the fifties: in fact, it covers the period from 1954 to 1965. After an introduction, each year is broken down month by month and the significant singles, according to the authors, listed. This main

sequence is followed by lists which include the artists with most number-one hits, artists with the most songs of the year according to the authors' choice, most songs reaching the top forty, the most successful artists of instrumentals and so on. A quiz and a list of song titles including a name, a title and an artist index, make this not a comprehensive but a useful source of information, if rather subjective in approach.

The Guinness book of British hit albums: the British hit albums 1958–82 / Jo
  and Tim Rice, Paul Gambaccini and Mike Read; editorial associate Steve
  Smith. – Enfield: GRRR Books; Guinnes Books, 1983. – 216p.: ill.,
  facsims, ports; 21cm. ISBN 0-85112-246-9 (pbk.)
In the compilation of this book of album chart data the compilers experienced problems in the consistency of chart information, problems of obtaining charts and the problem of the longevity of albums as compared with singles. Nevertheless, this is an excellent source of information, arranged alphabetically by artist with portraits, humorous little comments and full lists of albums, highest position reached and length of time on the charts. There are appendices of number-one albums, biggest sellers, most successful artists and so on. An indispensable reference book.

The Guinness book of British hit singles: the Guinness book of records
  / Jo and Tim Rice, Paul Gambaccini and Mike Read. – Rev. ed. – Enfield:
  Guinness Superlatives, 1981. – 352p.: ill., ports; 21cm. Includes indexes.
  ISBN 0-85112-224-8 (pbk.)
  Previous editions: Enfield: Guinness Superlatives, 1977; 1979.
Covering the period 1952–80, this is a complete guide to the records that appeared in the top-fifty charts of the *New Musical Express* and *Music Week*, compiled by an authoritative group of writers involved in the music business as broadcasters and journalists, including Tim Rice, the notable lyricist. Arranged alphabetically by artists, information on their successful records is listed chronologically with full information of the dates of entry into the charts, positions reached, the label and record number. There are portraits with humorous notes, an alphabetical index by title and an appendix of analyses of the most successful records, most successful artists, lists of number-one records and other statistical breakdowns. This is by far the best source of information on successful singles in Britain with its excellent arrangement and indexes.

The Guinness book of hits of the 70's / Jo and Tim Rice, Paul Gambaccini and
  Mike Read. – Enfield: Guinness Superlatives, 1980. – 239p.: ill., ports;
  21cm. Includes indexes. ISBN 0-85112-217-5 (cased). ISBN 0-85112-205-1
  (pbk.)
In an identical format to *British hit singles*, this covers the single decade of the seventies with far more illustrations and appendices of statistical facts. It is the aim of the editors to produce editions for the fifties and sixties as complete volumes as well as to produce the accumulating versions biennially.

The illustrated book of rock records: a book of lists / compiled by Barry Lazell
and Dafydd Rees. – London: Virgin Books, 1982. – 191p.: ill., facsims,
ports; 20cm. ISBN 0-907080-32-4 (pbk.)
A wide variety of lists of information including the twenty bestselling singles
in the USA in the sixties, the twenty bestselling singles in Britain in the
sixties, the ten bestselling singles in the seventies, the twenty bestselling
singles in Britain in the seventies, the singles that stayed longest in the charts,
groups with over ten members, the first singles of the Beatles, the Shadows,
the Who, the Rolling Stones, the most ridiculous song titles and many more.
Although it includes some interesting illustrations, this is not a comprehensive information source but a selective, entertaining collection.

Jasper, Tony
   British record charts 1955–1982 / compiled by Tony Jasper in association with
   Music Week. – Poole, Dorset: Blandford Press, 1982. – 320p.; 22cm.
   ISBN 0-7137-1332-1 (cased). ISBN 0-7137-1332-X (pbk.)
   Previous editions: London: Queen Anne Press, 1975; London: Macdonald
   and Janes, 1978; London: Macdonald; Futura, 1979.
A complete compilation of the British singles record charts from 1955 to 1979
as published by the *Record Mirror, Record Retailer* and *Music Week*. The
placings were originally compiled independently by the *Record Mirror* with
the help of the American music paper, *Billboard*. The charts up to 1968 tend
to have discrepancies with those of the BBC, which made up its own. Since
1968, however, the British Market Research Bureau has been the organizer
of the information for *Record Mirror, Music Week* and the BBC. There are
no indexes to these charts but there are annual summaries of successful
records and lists of the most successful artists. This is an essential reference
source for information on the British singles charts from a chronological
angle.

Jones, Alan
   Chart file 1982 / Alan Jones with Barry Lazell and Dafydd Rees. – London:
   Virgin Books, 1982. – 188p.: ill., ports; 18cm. ISBN 0-907080-49-9 (pbk.)
Barry Lazell and Dafydd Rees are directors of the Media Research and
Information Bureau (MRIB) and Alan Jones contributes the weekly chart-file
column to the *Record Mirror*. Basically a successor to Dafydd Rees's
attempted *Star-file annual*, this book covers the year 1981. Arranged by artist,
the singles and albums which entered the British and American charts are
listed in separate sections with details of the highest position reached and
dates. This is followed by lists analysing the 200 top-selling albums and singles
for the year in both countries and a range of other information such as top
male soloists, top female soloists, top groups, top movie songs, most weeks
on the charts and gold and platinum records. In all an excellent information
source.

Jones, Alan
   Chart file 1983 / Alan Jones with Barry Lazell and Dafydd Rees. – London:
   Virgin Books, 1983. – 184p.: ill., ports; 18cm. ISBN 0-907080-73-1 (pbk.)

With some changes in detail from the previous year's version, this includes
UK and American top hundred singles and albums with a range of analytical
charts showing the most successful artists. If this continues to be produced as
an annual it will be a real asset.

Marsh, Dave
> *The book of rock lists* / by Dave Marsh and Kevin Stein. – London:
> Sidgwick & Jackson, 1981. – 643p.: ill., facsims, ports; 20cm. Includes
> bibliographies and discographies. ISBN 0-283-98837-1 (pbk.)
> Originally published: New York: Dell, 1981.

Arranged in thirty-four sections, this vast collection of information about a
wide range of music lacks only a theme. It lists a mass of unconnected facts;
for example, biographical information such as the fifteen great recording
engineers, rock songs based on literature, most profound rock lyrics, which
includes the most unintelligible, the twenty-five best rock books, the ten best
liner notes, ten legendary and influential concert promoters, the ten worst
instruments and fifteen rock songs based on classical concepts – a remarkable
collection of facts which attempts to be entertaining first and informative
second. The lists of the 'best' and 'worst' variety simply represent the subjective views of the authors or other well-known artists and writers in the field.

Miron, Charles
> *Rock gold: all the hit charts from 1955 to 1976* / Charles Miron. – New York:
> Drake Publishers, 1977. – 160p.: ill., ports; 21cm. Includes indexes.
> ISBN 0-8473-1467-7

The top-thirty charts gleaned from the American trade papers *Billboard* and
Cashbox over twenty-one years. The book includes portraits of leading artists
and indexes by title and performer.

Rees, Dafydd
> *Star-file annual: incorporating the year's record information from Music
> Week and Billboard* / compiled by Dafydd Rees; foreword by Derek
> Taylor; introduction by John Tobler. – London: Star Books, 1977. – 395p.;
> 18cm. ISBN 0-352-39573-7 (pbk.)

Rees, Dafydd
> *Star-file annual: incorporating the year's record information from Music
> Week and Billboard* / compiled by Dafydd Rees; introduction by John
> Tobler. – Feltham, Middlesex: Hamlyn, 1978. – 439p.; 18cm.
> ISBN 0-660-38333-4 (pbk.)

An attempt to provide up-to-date annual chart information, this was the
predecessor of Alan Jones' *Chart file*. It appeared for only two consecutive
years (1977 covering the year 1976 and 1978 covering the year 1977) and
contains the details of record releases which entered the *Music Week* charts in
Britain for the top-fifty singles and top-sixty albums and the *Billboard* charts
in the USA for the top-hundred singles and top-two-hundred albums. Information is arranged by title, artists, record label, writer and producer. There
are supplementary lists of top-selling records, gold records and overall top
records of the year. In general, an excellent information source.

Rock almanac: top 20 American and British singles and albums of the Fifties,
   Sixties and Seventies / edited by Stephen Nugent and Charlie Gillett. – New
   York: Anchor Books, 1978. – 485p.; 21cm. ISBN 0-385-11204-1 (pbk.)
   Originally published: New York: Doubleday, 1976.
Much of the information had already appeared in the British *Rock file* series
when the first edition of the *Rock almanac* appeared in 1976. This paperback
edition was published four years after compilation and therefore lacked the
contemporary feel of *Rock file*. The comparison of British and American
charts is interesting but probably the most valuable feature is an essay by Paul
Gambaccini on British and American popular radio practice.

The *Rock file* series were not yearbooks in the conventional sense but a
mixture of contemporary surveys of the British scene at the time of their
publication and some excellent essays, as well as a variety of charts and other
statistical data which were the nucleus of each volume. The rather confused,
unconnected contents are described below.

Rock file / edited by Charlie Gillett. – London: Pictorial Presentations
   Limited; New English Library, 1972. – 156p., 12p. of plates: ill., geneal.
   table, ports; 18cm. ISBN 0-450-01430-4 (pbk.)
Included is Charlie Gillett's outline essay of the music of 1971, the hundred
bestselling records up to then, an essay by Simon Frith on the contemporary
recording business and an essay by Dave Laing on the British element in
popular lyrics and the influence of the music-hall tradition. There is a list
arranged by artist of entries into the top-twenty British charts between 1955
and 1969, including number of weeks, best position and label.

Rock file 2 / edited by Charlie Gillett. – St. Albans, Hertfordshire: Panther,
   1974. – 169p., 16p. of plates: ill., ports; 18cm. ISBN 0-586-04087-0 (pbk.)
Simon Frith surveys the year's singles in Britain, there is an essay on reggae,
Pete Wingfield writes on the Philadelphia sound and *Rock file 2* incorporates
a wealth of statistical information. This includes the most successful record
labels, British album chart-toppers, top album artists as well as, again, the full
list of British entries into the singles chart between 1970 and 1973 and a full
list of album chart entries between 1960 and 1973.

Rock file 3 / edited by Charlie Gillett and Simon Frith. – St. Albans,
   Hertfordshire: Panther, 1975. – 224p., 16p. of plates: ill., ports; 18cm.
   ISBN 0-586-04261-X (pbk.)
Included is a chronological list of the suggested best singles, one hundred
essential rock albums and the usual contemporary essays. There is also a log
of British hit songs and their sources and an index of the most successful
songwriters. Of particular interest is the information on the American and
original versions of every British top-twenty hit since 1955.

Rock file 4 / edited by Charlie Gillett and Simon Frith. – St. Albans,
   Hertfordshire: Panther, 1976. – 400p.; 18cm. ISBN 0-586-04370-5 (pbk.)

The fourth edition includes much of the material first published in the original, 1972, edition, plus lists of all American and British chart-toppers from 1955 to 1974. The essays include one on American radio and its influence and A & R (Artist and Repertoire) men and their power in recording companies.

Rock file 5 / edited by Charlie Gillett and Simon Frith. – St. Albans, Hertfordshire: Panther, 1978. – 286p.; 18cm. ISBN 0-586-04680-1 (pbk.)
After an interesting sociological essay by Simon Frith on youth culture and its cults, there is a series of lists including the chart entries from 1967 to 1977, and lists of the most successful producers and album chart-toppers. The new element is the influence of the producer and this is the single best source of information on these major contributors to record making.

Rohde, H. Kandy
    The gold of rock and roll, 1955–1967 / edited with special appreciations by
    H. Kandy Rohde; with research assistance by Laing Ned Kandel. – New
    York: Arbor House, 1970. – 352p.: ill., ports; 23cm.
The American top-ten charts are arranged chronologically with brief surveys of the musical and non-musical events of the year. Well illustrated, but with no additional analysis.

Solomon, Clive
    Record hits: the British top 50 charts, 1952–1977 plus U.S. chart positions /
    Compiled by Clive Solomon, Howard Pizzey and Martin Watson. – Rev.
    ed. – London: Omnibus Press, 1979. – 270p.; 25cm. Includes indexes.
    ISBN 0-86001-565-3 (pbk.)
    Previous edition: London: Omnibus Press, 1977.
A meticulously compiled work listing all records to enter the top-fifty charts on both sides of the Atlantic, with information on record labels, dates of entry into the charts, highest position and weeks surviving there. These lists, arranged by artist, are complemented by a title index and appendices of most successful records. An excellent, comprehensive work but not attractively produced.

Tobler, John
    The rock lists album / John Tobler, Alan Jones. – London: Plexus, 1982. –
    256p.: ill., ports; 23cm. ISBN 0-85965-049-9 (cased). ISBN 0-85965-048-0
    (pbk.)
An arbitrary collection of lists of facts including biggest-selling records, gold discs and greatest hits, as well as more intriguing lists such as longest singles and shortest tracks, famous bootlegs, child recording stars, unproven Phil Spector productions, a year of rock stars' birthdays and so on. With a suitably unusual collection of photographs, this is very amusing.

Whitburn, Joel
    The Billboard book of US top 40 hits 1955 to present / by Joel Whitburn. –
    Enfield: Guinness Superlatives, 1983. – 509p.: ill., ports; 25cm.
    ISBN 0-815112-245-0 (pbk.)

The first publication of a Joel Whitburn book in the United Kingdom; there is a title index and a complete summary of number-one records, by year.

Whitburn, Joel
  Bubbling under the hot hundred 1959–1981 / compiled by Joel Whitburn. – Menomonee Falls, Wisconsin: Record Research, 1982. – 234p.: 25cm. Includes index. ISBN 0-89820-046-6 (pbk.)
The most recent addition to the author's series of chart information publications, this lists singles which just failed to make the *Billboard* Hot 100. These unfortunates are listed weekly in *Billboard*. Information is arranged alphabetically by artist with date of releases and date of appearance in the listing. There is also a title index.

Whitburn, Joel
  Top country & western records 1948–1971 / compiled by Joel Whitburn. – Menomonee Falls, Wisconsin: Record Research, 1972. – 184p.; 25cm. Includes index. ISBN 0-89820-015-6 (pbk.)
The country chart of *Billboard* is used as a basis for the information here. The range of country-flavoured styles included is surprisingly wide. Alphabetically arranged by artist; date of entry, highest position and length of time on the chart are well presented. There is a title index and a list of top-selling records.

Whitburn, Joel
  Top country & western records 1972–1973 / compiled by Joel Whitburn. – Menomonee Falls, Wisconsin: Record Research, 1974. – 68p.; 25cm. ISBN 0-89820-016-4 (pbk.)
An initial supplement to the previous title, including two years' chart information.

Whitburn, Joel
  Top country & western records 1974– / compiled by Joel Whitburn. – Menomonee Falls, Wisconsin: Record Research, 1975. – Annual. 1980. – 1981. – 49p.; 25cm. ISBN 0-89820-45-8 (pbk.)
An annual supplement to the previous title, with one year's chart information.

Whitburn, Joel
  Top easy listening records 1962–1974 / compiled by Joel Whitburn. – Menomonee Falls, Wisconsin: Record Research, 1975. – 1975. – 198p.; 25cm. Includes index. ISBN 0-89820-022-9 (pbk.)
Billboard's easy-listening chart appears to be a very arbitrary collection of music ranging from country-music ballads, songs from musicals and light instrumentals to middle-of-the-road pop. Nevertheless, records which have appeared are listed in alphabetical order of artist with full information on date of entry, highest position and length of time on the charts. There is a title index.

Whitburn, Joel
  Top easy listening records 1975– / compiled by Joel Whitburn. –
  Menomonee Falls, Wisconsin: Record Research, 1976. – Annual. 1978. –
  1979. – 24p.; 25cm. ISBN 0-89820-034-2 (pbk.)
An annual supplement to the previous title including one year's chart
information.

Whitburn, Joel
  Top LPs 1949–1972 / compiled by Joel Whitburn. – Menomonee Falls,
  Wisconsin: Record Research, 1973. – 224p.; ill., ports; 25cm. Includes
  index. ISBN 0-89820-009-1 (pbk.)
Using information from the *Billboard* top-hundred album charts, this is a
listing of the successful albums of the period arranged alphabetically by artist.
Date of entry, highest chart position and length of time on the charts are all
included. There is a title index and list of top-selling albums.

Whitburn, Joel
  Top LPs 1973– / compiled by Joel Whitburn. – Menomonee Falls,
  Wisconsin: Record Research, 1974. – Annual. 1978. – 1979. – 32p.; 25cm.
  ISBN 0-89820-032-6 (pbk.)
An annual supplement to the previous title with one year's chart information.

Whitburn, Joel
  Top pop artists and records 1952–1978 / compiled by Joel Whitburn. – Rev.
  ed. – Menomonee Falls, Wisconsin: Record Research, 1979. – 662p.: ill.,
  ports; 25cm. Includes index. ISBN 0-89820-039-3 (cased).
  ISBN 0-89820-037-7 (pbk.)
  Originally published as '*Top pop records 1955–1972*': Menomonee Falls,
  Wisconsin: Record Research, 1973.
  Previous edition published as '*Joel Whitburn's pop annual 1955–1977*':
  Menomonee Falls, Wisconsin: Record Research, 1978.
Arranged alphabetically by artist, every record to enter the *Billboard* Hot 100
chart during the period is listed with details of date of entry, highest position,
total number of weeks on the chart, most successful month and full discographical information. Well presented, this is a comprehensive source of
information on nationwide American hits with a title index and chronological
listing of records reaching the number-one position.

Whitburn, Joel
  Top pop records 1978–. Menomonee Falls, Wisconsin: Record Research,
  1979–. Annual. 1981. – 1982 / compiled by Joel Whitburn. – 52p.; 25cm.
  ISBN 0-89820-047-4 (pbk.)
An annual supplement to the author's work derived from the Hot 100 charts
which updates the accumulations.

Whitburn, Joel
  Top rhythm & blues records 1949–1971 / compiled by Joel Whitburn. –
  Menomonee Falls, Wisconsin: Record Research, 1972. – 184p.; 25cm.

Includes index. ISBN 0-89820-026-1 (pbk.)
Dealing with a far wider range of music than basic rhythm & blues, this
includes information on singles which entered the *Billboard* charts devoted to
black music. The title changed its name over the years. Arranged alphabetically by artist, there is full information on date of entry, highest position and a
title index.

Whitburn, Joel
    Top rhythm & blues records 1972–1973 / compiled by Joel Whitburn. –
    Menomonee Falls, Wisconsin: Record Research, 1974. – 62p.; 25cm. ISBN
    0-89820-026-1 (pbk.)
An initial supplement to the previous title including two years' chart
information.

Whitburn, Joel
    Top rhythm & blues records 1974– / compiled by Joel Whitburn. –
    Menomonee Falls, Wisconsin: Record Research, 1975–. Annual. 1978. –
    1979 – 44p.; 25cm. ISBN 0-89820-035-0 (pbk.)
An annual supplement to the previous title including one year's chart
information.

Worth, Fred L.
    Thirty years of rock'n'roll trivia / Fred L. Worth. – New York: Warner
    Books, 1980. – 352p.; 18cm. ISBN 0-446-91494-0 (pbk.)
This is a pot-pourri of facts with no cohesive structure, concentrating on the
trivial and ignoring hard information. Lists of unlikely-named groups; the real
names of stars; an ad hoc list of little-known performers and their associated
backing groups is the closest one comes to finding useful facts. Poorly produced and sadly lacking in illustrations, it is occasionally entertaining in the
obscurity of its coverage.

GOLD RECORDS, HIT RECORDS

Emerson, Lucy
    The gold record / Lucy Emerson. – New York: Fountain Publications, 1978.
    – 136p.: ill., ports; 18cm. ISBN 0-9161-8404-8 (pbk.)
A history of million-selling recordings from Caruso to the mid seventies. The
qualifications for gold records, anecdotes, biographical sketches of exceptional artists and a listing of winners to date are all briefly included.

The Guinness book of 500 number one hits / Jo & Tim Rice, Paul Gambaccini
    and Mike Read. – Enfield: Guinness Superlatives, 1982. – 263p.: ill., ports;
    24cm. Includes indexes. ISBN 0-85112-250-7 (pbk.)
Covering the period from 1952 to 1982, the 500 records which topped the
British singles charts during that period are listed in a chronological sequence
with detailed historical notes, descriptions and suggestions of the reason for
their success. There are indexes to song titles and artists and an appendix of
statistical information.

Murrells, Joseph
  The book of golden discs / compiled by Joseph Murrells. – Rev. ed. –
  London: Barrie and Jenkins, 1978. – 413p.: ill., ports; 31cm. Includes
  indexes. ISBN 0-214-20480-4
  Originally published as '*Daily Mail book of golden discs*': London:
  McWhirter Twins Ltd, 1966.
  Previous edition: London: Barrie and Jenkins, 1974.
A complete list of all recordings since 1903 which have been certified as
having sold at least one million copies, with biographical notes on the artists.
The arrangement is chronological with the biographies and description of the
records arranged by artist within each year. An appendix includes a fascinating collection of statistics and indexes give access to the information by artist
and title. The main sequence of complete biographies and notes covers the
period up to the end of 1975 with an appendix of million-selling releases
briefly listed up to the end of 1977. The latest edition is in a larger, more
accessible format than the previous versions.

Savile, Jimmy
  Nostalgia book of hit singles / Jimmy Savile and Tony Jasper. – London:
  Frederick Muller, 1982. – 320p.: ill., ports; 27cm. ISBN 0-584-11037-5
  (pbk.)
Taking twenty hit songs from each year between 1954 and 1982, the authors
describe the song, its activities in the charts, its artists, significant facts and
importance. Unashamedly subjective, the only criterion for inclusion is that
the record appeared in the British top-twenty charts and has, to some extent,
maintained its popularity. Jimmy Savile, the well-known disc jockey, would
appear to have contributed his considerable experience of hit records to
Jasper's writing.

1.7 BIBLIOGRAPHIES

The need for a full bibliography of modern music is well reflected by the lack
of work so far published.
  A few works include brief listings and detailed bibliographies have been
produced for the artists below.

(*See also* Chapter 6, BAEZ, JOAN: BIBLIOGRAPHIES:
DISCOGRAPHIES; THE BEATLES: BIBLIOGRAPHIES; PRESLEY,
ELVIS: BIBLIOGRAPHIES: DISCOGRAPHIES; THE ROLLING
STONES: BIBLIOGRAPHIES; SINATRA, FRANK:
BIBLIOGRAPHIES: DISCOGRAPHIES: FILMOGRAPHIES)

Hanel, Ed
  The essential guide to rock books / compiled by Ed Hanel. – London:
  Omnibus Press, 1983. – 94p.: ill.; 25cm. ISBN 0-7119-0109-0 (pbk.)

With illustrations of some book jackets, this is a good attempt to offer a brief guide. Annotations, where they are included, are very brief and uncritical and there is certainly a hint that not all the titles included have been seen by the author. It is far from comprehensive.

Hoffman, Frank
The literature of rock, 1954–1978 / by Frank Hoffman. – Metuchen, New Jersey; London: Scarecrow Press, 1981. – xi, 337p.: ill.; 22cm. Includes indexes. ISBN 0-8108-1371-8

After a brief introductory essay analysing the explosion in the literature of popular music since 1954, the contents are minutely classified by style of music and aspects of the industry. The majority of citations are from periodicals or extracts from a few encyclopedias, notably Stambler's *Encyclopedia of pop, rock and soul*. The annotations are very brief, offering no background details about the subject. There is an index by subject and author and a brief bibliography of sources, listing only sixty books. The major criticism of the work is its coverage, which is very selective, arbitrarily citing articles and omitting major monographs, even biographies. Interesting, it is unreliable and erratic.

Horn, David
The literature of American music in books and folk music collections: a fully annotated bibliography / David Horn. – Metuchen, New Jersey; London: Scarecrow Press, 1977. – 507p.; 22cm. Includes indexes. ISBN 0-8108-0996-6

David Horn is a librarian at Exeter University, which has a special collection of books on American music. In addition to using this collection, he spent some time in the USA tracking down fugitive material. He covers jazz, folk music, old-time country music and popular music in this excellent bibliography. It deals exclusively with 'America' with an historical emphasis but does include a few books relating to the post-1955 period. This is therefore, a source of historical, background reading, very useful and particularly thorough.

Mecklenburg, Carl Gregor Herzog zu
1971/72/73 supplement to international jazz bibliography (ijb) & selective bibliography of some jazz background literature & bibliography of two subjects previously excluded / Carl Gregor Herzog zu Mecklenburg. – Graz: Friedrich Korner and Dieter Glawischnig, 1975. – 246p.; 24cm. ISBN 3-7024-0075-3 (pbk.)

Published at the Institute for Jazz Research in co-operation with the International Society for Jazz Research. Included for the first time are sections on popular music. The section on the period since the fifties includes nearly 250 entries but many are duplicated, often lacking basic details such as publishers and pagination. There are, however, some interesting citations of foreign-language material. Basically a poor piece of work, possibly because popular music is treated as an appendage.

1.8 DISCOGRAPHIES AND COLLECTORS' GUIDES

The major record companies have produced annual listings of their available recordings for many years. The EMI, CBS, Decca and RCA listings were the mainstay of discographical information for the trade in Britain until the establishment of *Music Master* during the late seventies.

Discographies devoted to popular music are relatively few and it is only recently that they have begun to appear. Guides for record collecting are the major form. These fall into two types: price guides and critical guides listing selected, classic recordings that no collection should be without. The *Rolling Stone record guide* is by far the best of this subjective variety. The bootleg listings are by definition incomplete efforts.

Paul Pelletier and his Record Information Service supply the only serious attempt to provide academically produced label discographies up to the standard found in the field of jazz. These are listed under specific record companies (Chapter 4, Record companies).

Other specific discographies are under major artists and forms of music.

Anderson, Ian
    Rock record collectors guide / by Ian Anderson. – London: MRP Books,
    1977. – 177p., 32p. of plates: ill., ports; 20cm. Includes bibliography. ISBN
    0-905590-04-X (pbk.)
Written by a disc jockey with wide experience in local radio throughout Britain, this is a guide to the best rock and pop records available in the United Kingdom divided into classic albums, greatest-hits albums, compilation albums as well as a few spoken-word albums. The author grades the chosen records with one to three stars. The annotations are brief but informative, and the illustrations very good. There are notes on record buying, care of records, a list of magazines and a brief bibliography. This is a useful guide not because of its comprehensiveness but because it includes almost exclusively only records released on British record labels.

The bootleg bible. – Manchester: Babylon Books, 1981. – 272p.: ill., facsims;
    20cm. (pbk.)
A much improved and updated discography which is a great improvement on Babylon Books' earlier *The complete bootlegs checklist & discography*. A straightforward alphabetical sequence of artists and full details of recordings are given with location of the performance and songs included. It is difficult to assess the coverage of such unofficial, even illegal, productions but this is the most impressive source of information available.

Christgau, Robert
    Christgau's guide: rock albums of the 70s / Robert Christgau. – London:
    Vermilion, 1982. – 471p.; 24cm. ISBN 0-09-147891-X (pbk.)
    Originally published: New Haven, Connecticut: Ticknor & Fields, 1981.
A well-known record critic here gives brief criticisms of over 3,000 albums

released during the seventies. Arranged alphabetically by artists, they are rated A+ to E−. In many ways it is an odd collection. Included are certainly the best albums, but it is the way in which the bad examples are selected that is dubious, and simply mediocre records are avoided.

Collectable EPs: part 1 A–F, January 1950 to December 1975. – London: Vintage Record Centre, 1982. – 130p.: ill., facsims; 20cm.
ISBN 0-907744-02-8 (pbk.)
Collectable 45s: price reference guide to singles; part 1 A–K, January 1950– December 1964. – London: Vintage Record Centre, 1981. – 128p.: ill., facsims; 20cm. ISBN 0-907744-00-1 (pbk.)
Collectable 45s: price reference guide to singles; part 2 L–Z, January 1950– December 1964. – London: Vintage Record Centre, 1981. – 136p.: ill., facsims; 20cm. ISBN 0-907744-01-X (pbk.)
The beginning of a promising series, these listings are arranged by artist giving estimated current values of each disc, ranked from A – £1.25, B – £2.25 to L – £100. As with most price guides, there is a great deal of over-estimation, but these are surprisingly comprehensive with label illustrations.

Collis, John
The rock primer / edited by John Collis. – Harmondsworth: Penguin Books, 1980. – 335p.; 20cm. Includes index. ISBN 0-14-046-465-4 (pbk.)
This is an historical outline of popular music since the Second World War as reflected by its record releases. It reviews 220 albums in detail and included are examples of the earlier roots in folk and blues. Divided into eleven chapters, written by seven well-known authorities, each section is preceded by an essay on the period. The reviews of the most representative albums, which constitute the bulk of the text, are followed by a list of significant singles in the particular style. Well indexed, the guide offers a series of subjective views which give a very distorted interpretation resulting in what overall is a poor guide for the selection of a basic collection.

The complete bootlegs checklist & discography. – Manchester: Babylon Books, 1980. – 112p.: ill., facsims, ports; 25cm. (pbk.)
A poorly organized discography of illicit records available by the major artists from all styles of contemporary popular music. There is an essay on those of Bob Dylan. There are two confusing sequences and poor reproductions of record sleeves.

Dellar, Fred
The Omnibus rock discography / by Fred Dellar and Barry Lazell. – London: Omnibus Press, 1982. – 192p.: ill., ports; 20cm.
ISBN 0-7119-0108-2 (pbk.)
A selective listing with full discographical details of the albums, extended players and singles of over 400 artists. The major artists are all here. The result is a very good personal choice, not comprehensive but a good selection tool.

Docks, L. R.
American premium record guide: identification & values (1915–1965) 78s,
45s & LPs / by L. R. Docks. – 2nd ed. – New York: Crown Publications,
1981. – 750p.: ill., facsims; 22cm. Includes bibliography.
ISBN 0-517-54404-0 (pbk.)
Previous edition: New York: Wallace-Homestead, 1979.
This includes 45,000 recordings representing over 6,200 artists from a wide
range of popular music, and valuations which relate to the American
collectors' market. Reproductions of record sleeves, an extensive bibliography and essays on trends in collecting and hints on finding bargains are
very informative but specifically for the American collector.

Gambaccini, Paul
Critics choice top 200 albums / compiled by Paul Gambaccini, with Susan
Ready. – London: Omnibus Press, 1978. – 96p.: ill., facsims, ports; 26cm.
ISBN 0-86001-494-0 (pbk.)
Forty-eight of the most informed and best-known writers, critics and disc
jockeys in various fields of popular music were invited to compile a list of
their all-time top-ten albums. The results of this crude survey were analysed
and the resulting 200 cited albums were graded by their number of citations.
Hardly a scientific analysis, but a very interesting and informative list which
does serve as a good guide to the most highly regarded albums and thus a
basis for a standard collection. Included are portraits of prominent artists as
well as illustrations of the album-cover designs of these 200 albums.

Helander, Brock
The rock who's who: a biographical dictionary and critical discography
including rhythm-and-blues, soul, rockabilly, folk country, easy listening,
punk and new wave / Brock Helander. – New York: Schirmer Books, 1982.
– 686p.; 24cm. Includes bibliography, discographies and index.
ISBN 0-02-871250-1 (cased). ISBN 0-02-871920-4 (pbk.)
Not a biographical dictionary but strictly aimed at being a critical discography, this is arranged in a strict alphabetical sequence with brief factual
notes on the careers of artists followed by full, detailed discographies. The
criticisms of albums are linked in the narrative but vary in length and value.
The work is sadly lacking in illustrations and, although a good attempt, the
bibliography omits many well-known books and is bulked out by periodical-
article citations.

Hibbert, Tom
Rare records: wax trash & vinyl treasures / Tom Hibbert. – London; New
York: Proteus, 1982. – 128p.: ill. (some col.), facsims (some col.), ports
(some col.); 28cm. ISBN 0-86276-048-8 (cased). ISBN 0-86276-047-X
(pbk.)
Focussing on British releases, the author divides the period from the late
fifties to the late sixties into ten convenient groupings including such sections
as The twang's the than, Merseybeat & R'n'B, From Mods to Manson,
Everybody's in showbiz and The beat goes on. Within each section unusual or

rare records of the period are discussed. Often contentious, the author chooses obscure recordings by obscure or faded artists. There are reproductions of album sleeves and many very rare photographs. At the end of each chapter there is a listing of collectable singles and albums graded from A to E. Unfortunately there is no index to artists or songs; a pity, as this is a source of much exceptional and useful information.

Hounsome, Terry
New rock record: a collector's directory of rock albums and musicians /
Terry Hounsome & Tim Chambre. – Poole, Dorset: Blandford Press, 1981.
– ix, 526p.; 24cm. Includes indexes. ISBN 0-7137-1117-5 (pbk.)
Originally published as '*Rockmaster*': Southampton, Hampshire: Terry Hounsome, 1978.
Previous edition published as '*Rock Record*': Southampton, Hampshire: Terry Hounsome, 1979.
Originally privately published with a very poor production, this expanded edition includes over 4,500 groups and individual artists with details of approximately 30,000 long-playing record albums on which they appear. Some 25,000 musicians are listed and indexed. The aim of this discography is to identify the musicians who performed on each of the albums. It thus provides a unique and detailed analysis of working musicians within its scope. The problem is that the authors fail to define their understanding of the word 'rock' and the coverage is therefore often debatable. For example they include pop groups like Abba, but not Barry Manilow or Bette Midler and yet they include Irish folk musicians Planxty and the Chieftains and British traditional folk singer Martin Carthy. Their selection is, therefore, confusing and one may be disappointed by such omissions. Nevertheless, this is a valuable reference source and the result of an immense amount of research.

Jack Jackson's record round-up / edited by Don Nicholl. – London: Parrish, 1955. – 128p.: ill., ports; 25cm.
Jack Jackson was one of the leading disc jockeys on British radio in the fifties. He was early in using sound effects, jingles and the complex cutting of tapes to make his shows more than just a sequence of records. This publication, using his name, survey the popular-music scene at the point of the emergence of rock'n'roll, listing recordings by the major artists of the period.

Music Master. / Hastings, Sussex: John Humphries, 1974–. Annual with monthly supplements. 1981 / edited by John Humphries. – 1981. – 987p.; 31cm. ISBN 0-904520-11-0. ISSN 0308-9347
An essential reference tool for retailers as well as librarians, *Music Master* is a listing of available recordings. Published as an annual volume with monthly, accumulating supplements, divided into sections for singles, albums, cassettes and video, with a labels list and who's who section, it is well guided with excellent instructions. There is a section of statistical data on releases of the year. Each section has access by artist as well as title. Classical releases are not ignored but naturally are given only a small section. Singles have been included in the one volume since 1977.

Osborne, Jerry
A guide to record collecting / by Jerry Osborne and Bruce Hamilton. –
Phoenix, Arizona: O'Sullivan Woodside, 1979. – 142p.: ill., facsims; 20cm.
ISBN 0-89019-068-2 (pbk.)
Broadly classified into styles – for example, country and soul and rock – and
then alphabetically by artist, this is a selective guide. Current prices are
included for the American collector, dependent on condition. There are
useful articles offering hints on record collecting.

Osborne, Jerry
*Osborne & Hamilton's original record collectors' price guide: soundtrack &
original cast* / by Jerry Osborne and Bruce Hamilton. – Phoenix, Arizona:
O'Sullivan Woodside, 1981. – 156p.: ill., facsims; 28cm. ISBN 0-89019-077-1
(pbk.)
Soundtrack albums from films and recordings from musicals are arranged in
alphabetical order of title. Current, estimated value, dependent on condition,
is tabulated. There is an essay on collecting such discs.

Osborne, Jerry
Popular and rock price guide for forty-fives: the little record with the big hole
/ by Jerry Osborne and Bruce Hamilton. – 3rd ed. – Phoenix, Arizona:
O'Sullivan Woodside, 1981. – 254p.: ill., facsims; 28cm. Includes index.
ISBN 0-89019-075-5 (pbk.)
Previous edition: Phoenix, Arizona: O'Sullivan Woodside, 1979.
A guide for collectors of singles, arranged alphabetically by artist and includ-
ing full discographical details and estimated value in America. There is a title
index.

Osborne, Jerry
Popular and rock records 1948–1978 / by Jerry Osborne; edited by Bruce
Hamilton. – 2nd ed. – Phoenix, Arizona: O'Sullivan Woodside, 1978. –
252p.: ill., facsims; 28cm. Includes index. ISBN 0-89019-075-5 (pbk.)
Previous edition: Phoenix, Arizona: O'Sullivan Woodside, 1976.
Arranged alphabetically by artist or group, this book lists album and singles
releases in the USA. There are full discographical details, a song-title index
and guide to current value in America. Scope is wide but does not include
jazz, folk and country.

Osborne, Jerry
Record albums, 1948–1978 / by Jerry Osborne; edited by Bruce Hamilton. –
2nd ed. – Phoenix, Arizona: O'Sullivan Woodside, 1978. – vii, 256p.: ill.,
facsims; 28cm. Includes index. ISBN 0-89019-066-6 (pbk.)
Previous edition: Phoenix, Arizona: O'Sullivan Woodside, 1977.
After a useful introduction on the second-hand record market, there is an
alphabetical arrangement by artist listing full discographical details of album
releases. Scope is wide, including all popular, folk and jazz forms. The index
is by album title.

Osborne, Jerry
 Records collectors' price guide / by Jerry Osborne; edited by Bruce
 Hamilton. – Phoenix, Arizona: O'Sullivan Woodside, 1976. – 196p.: ill.,
 facsims; 28cm. Includes index. ISBN 0-89019-053-4 (pbk.)
A price guide to American releases arranged alphabetically by artist. There
are full discographical details and an index by song title and album name.
Included are jazz, folk and country.

The perfect collection / edited by Tom Hibbert. – London; New York:
 Proteus, 1982. – 128p.: ill.; 27cm. ISBN 0-86276-106-9 (cased).
 ISBN 0-86276-105-0 (pbk.)
Arranged chronologically from the fifties to date, here is a list of records,
regarded by the contributors to this work as the most perfect, well-balanced
collection of popular music albums. Those included have not all been commercially successful and some are obscure, but this is an interesting selection
with intelligent notes justifying choice.

Preston, Mike
 Tele-tunes 2: the second book of TV and film music / compiled by Mike
 Preston. – 2nd rev. ed. – Kidderminster, Worcestershire: Record
 Information Centre, 1979. – 152p.; 22cm. ISBN 0-906655-01-3 (pbk.)
 Previous edition: Kidderminster, Worcestershire: Record Information
 Centre, 1979.
This is a unique reference source providing indexes to the titles of the theme
tunes of television programmes and films. Access is by name of the pro-
gramme or film. There is full discographical information and separate lists of
compilation albums. Other information includes lists of award-winning
themes, advertising jingles, albums advertised on television and a list of
advertisements with voice-overs with the names of the appropriate actors.
This will become a useful source if regularly revised.

Propes, Steve
 *Golden goodies: a guide to 50's and 60's popular rock & roll record
 collecting* / Steve Propes. – Radnor, Pennsylvania: Chilton Book Company,
 1975. – 185p.; 21cm. ISBN 0-8019-6220-X (cased). ISBN 0-8019-6221-8
 (pbk.).
A short introduction summarizes the variety of styles of music of the period.
Each category is then taken in turn and, after brief introductory comments,
its major artists are listed with their most important recordings. Details are of
American releases but this selection gives an excellent guide and is more
concisely presented in this shorter edition.

Propes, Steve
 Golden oldies: a guide to 60's record collecting / Steve Propes. – Radnor,
 Pennsylvania: Chilton Book Company, 1974. – xii, 240p.; 21cm.
 ISBN 0-8019-6062-2 (cased). ISBN 0-8019-6076-2 (pbk.)
A companion to the same author's guide to the fifties. After a good analysis of
the styles of popular music during the decade, the author takes each category

and describes the major artists and their significance, listing their American singles releases with full discographical information. This is an excellent guide.

Propes, Steve
Those oldies but goodies: a guide to 50's record collecting / Steve Propes. – New York: Macmillan, 1973. – viii, 192p.; 21cm.
After an introduction which emphasizes the significance of the fifties in the development of modern popular music, the author goes on to analyse the styles of the period. The major artists within each style and their relative significance are discussed with a listing of their American singles releases including full discographical details. This is an excellent guide to the music of the period.

Record business: indie catalogue 1981–82 / compilers Patricia Thomas and Dafydd Rees. – London: Record Business, 1981. – 63p.; 22cm. (pbk.)
Previous edition: London: Record Business, 1979.
An alphabetical list of artists and their recordings released by small, independent record companies. Few well-known artists are included, giving a unique source of information for many of the lesser-known. There is an index to the companies included.

The Rolling Stone record guide: reviews and ratings of almost 10,000 currently available rock, pop, soul, country, blues, jazz and gospel albums / edited by Dave Marsh; with John Swenson. – London: Virgin Books, 1980. – 631p.: ill., facsims; 24cm. Includes bibliography. ISBN 0-907080-00-6 (pbk.)
Originally published: New York: Random House, 1979.
By far the most comprehensive guide to popular music albums, this is a collection of record reviews written by some of the most authoritative critics and journalists today, including Bob Blumenthal, Ira Mayer, Chet Flippo, Martha Hume, Joe McEwen and Kit Rachlis, as well as Dave Marsh and John Swenson, the editors. The predominant section covers rock, soul, country and pop and is alphabetically arranged by artist. There is a listing of their significant albums, each given a star rating up to five. This is followed by a brief criticism of the artist's work in general and comment on specific albums. Then there are separate blues, jazz, gospel, anthologies and soundtrack sections in the same format. There is a listing of five-star records, an excellent glossary and a selective but well-annotated bibliography. The only confusing aspects are that reproductions of album sleeves appear arbitrarily throughout the text, not related to artists, and often American titles are cited which do not coincide with British releases. This is an indispensable work for any library or serious record collector.

Singles Master. – London: John Humphries, 1976. – 30cm. Weekly, monthly summaries and yearly master catalogue 1976. –
Published for only one year listing available singles by title and artist, it was amalgamated into the *Music Master* in 1977.

Tudor, Dean
Contemporary popular music / Dean Tudor and Nancy Tudor. – Littleton,
Colorado: Libraries Unlimited, 1979. – 313p.; 24cm. (American popular
music on Elpee). Includes bibliography. ISBN 0-87287-191-6
Part of a four-volume series (the others are *Jazz*, *Black music* and *Grassroots
music*); after an excellent introduction outlining the development of popular
music, this volume is divided into two sections: Mainstream Popular Music
and Rock. The authors' stated aim is to group significant recordings, rather
than artists, into genres. This arrangement certainly avoids the problem
encountered with artists who have recorded various styles of music, but is
often confusing. With the objective of including 'the best and most enduring'
albums, each entry has an annotation of around three hundred words. Stage
and film music and cabaret artists are included in this volume as well as
rockabilly, rock'n'roll, heavy metal, acid rock and most other classifications.
In general this is a very good, thoughtful, guide, the result of a great deal of
work, with an excellent bibliography.

1.9 QUIZBOOKS

Reflecting the interest in the growing body of information about the music
and its artists, quizbooks vary greatly in their level and obscurity.

(*See also* section 5.4, COUNTRY MUSIC: QUIZBOOKS; Chapter 6,
THE BEATLES: QUIZBOOKS; PRESLEY, ELVIS: QUIZBOOKS; THE
ROLLING STONES: QUIZBOOKS)

Allan, Jon
The rock trivia quizbook / Jon Allan. – New York: Drake Publishers, 1976.
– vii, 182p.: ill., ports; 26cm. ISBN 0-8473-1193-7 (pbk.)
A good collection of questions and answers with picture quizzes. It ranges
from the difficult to the completely obscure.

Billington, Jonathan
The great rock pop & soul quiz / Jonathan Billington; edited by Susan
Lurie; designed by Irva Mandelbaum. – New York: Prestige Books, 1981. –
255p.: ill., ports; 30cm. (pbk.)
A poorly produced publication in the form of a workbook with line drawing
picture quizzes, this is a simple collection of questions and answers. There is a
distinct American bias.

Burt, Rob
The illustrated rock quiz / Rob Burt. – London: Marshall Cavendish, 1979.
– 96p.: ill., ports; 29cm. ISBN 0-85685-762-9 (pbk.)
Well arranged by style and individual artist, this is not a quizbook for the
casual listener but for the expert. The whole range of popular music, apart

from cabaret, is included with questions, answers and picture quizzes. This is a genuinely searching but entertaining and well-thought-out book.

Dachs, David
Pop-rock question and answer book / David Dachs. – New York: School
Book Service, 1972. – 86p.: ill., ports; 20cm. (pbk.)
Aimed at American high schools, here is a good range of exercises, quizzes and picture quizzes on a wide spectrum of popular music.

Eldin, Peter
Top of the pops quiz / compiled by Peter Eldin; illustrated by Alan Case. –
London: Armada, 1980. – 128p.: ill.; 18cm. ISBN 0-00-691565-5 (pbk.)
A quiz and games book with answers for the young teenager. There are mazes, picture quizzes, crosswords and anagrams as well as straightforward questions.

Hale, Tony
Quiz kid / compiled by Tony Hale. – London: British Broadcasting
Corporation, 1977. – 123p.: ill., facsims; 18cm. ISBN 0-563-17213-4 (pbk.)
Based on a BBC Radio One series, this is a good selection of questions, answers and puzzles which are not for the real expert, but are above the level of the average teenage fan.

Hewitt, Graham
The quiz book of music / Graham Hewitt. – London: Futura Publications,
1979. – 189p.; 18cm. ISBN 0-7088-1623-1 (pbk.)
A collection of 1,366 questions and answers about all types of music, predominantly focussing on serious music, though popular music and jazz are not entirely neglected. The questions vary from the very simple to the technical.

Kinn, Maurice
The Armada pop quiz book / Maurice Kinn; illustrations by David Kemps;
crosswords compiled by Derek Johnson. – London: Armada Books, 1975.
– 124p., 4p. of plates: ill., ports; 18cm. ISBN 0-0069-0953-1 (pbk.)
Compiled by the former owner of the *New Musical Express*, who has wide experience in music journalism, this is a collection of questions and answers, games and puzzles for children. This particular collection was one of the bestselling children's paperbacks of the year.

Kinn, Maurice
Daily Mirror pop club quiz book / editor Maurice Kinn; illustrations by
Andrew Perrin and David Kemp; crosswords compiled by Derek Johnson.
– London: Maurice Kinn Productions, 1976. – 94p.; 18cm.
ISBN 0-905568-00-1 (pbk.)
A second entertaining quizbook by this author with questions and answers, games and crosswords for children.

Pollock, Bruce
 The rock & roll fun book / Bruce Pollock. – New York: Scholastic Book
 Services, 1981. – 64p.: ill., ports; 20cm. ISBN 0-590-31616-8 (pbk.)
Quizzes, picture quizzes and a variety of puzzles for the young enthusiast.
There is a strong American bias.

Read, Mike
 Mike Read's rock and pop quiz book. – London: Elm Tree Books; Sphere
 Books, 1981. – 91.: ill., ports; 20cm. ISBN 0-7221-7252-4 (pbk.)
A relatively easy collection of questions and picture quizzes, this is for the
young fan rather than the expert. Published as a tie-in with the television
programme of the same title, which is presented by the author.

Rider, David
 Johnnie Walker's 'Pop the question' / compiled by David Rider; with
 cartoons by Trevor Chrismas. – London: Everest Books, 1975. – 137p.,
 16p. of plates: ill., ports; 18cm. ISBN 0-9039-2533-9 (pbk.)
A collection of questions and answers under the title of the BBC Radio One
quiz programme. Entertaining, but not searching enough for the enthusiast.

Schaffner, Nicholas
 505 rock'n'roll questions your friends can't answer / Nicholas Schaffner and
 Elizabeth Schaffner. – New York: Walker, 1980. – 128p.; 19cm. Includes
 index. ISBN 0-8027-7171-8 (pbk.)
A good collection of questions and answers contrived by the expert on the
Beatles. Not as obscure as some of the questions in the quizbooks devoted to
particular artists, but difficult.

Sinclair, Jill
 Pop quiz: from the BBC television programme / questions compiled by Jill
 Sinclair and Frances Whitaker. – London: British Broadcasting
 Corporation, 1982. – 64p.: ill., maps, ports; 20cm. ISBN 0-563-20085-5
 (pbk.)
Questions and answers from BBC Television's Pop Quiz show are presented
in nine chapters, enabling the game to be reproduced by the reader. A good
collection of questions which include a few to test the expert.

Sotkin, Marc
 The official rock'n'roll trivia quiz book / by Marc Sotkin. – New York:
 Signet, 1977. – 154p., 8p. of plates: ill., facsims, ports; 18cm.
 ISBN 0-451-08485-3 (pbk.)
Almost a thousand questions and answers on the whole range of rock, pop
and soul music with a good picture quiz. The questions range from the simple
to completely obscure trivia.

Sotkin, Marc
 The official rock'n'roll trivia quiz book: 2 / by Marc Sotkin. – New York:
 Signet, 1978. – 154p., 8p. of plates: ill., facsims, ports; 18cm.
 ISBN 0-451-08299-0 (pbk.)
A second volume of well-chosen questions.

Tobler, John
  Pop Quest: so you think you know all about rock'n'pop / John Tobler &
  Cathy McKnight. – London: Independent Television Books; Arrow Books,
  1978. – 125p.: ill., facsims, ports; 18cm. ISBN 0-09-917570-3 (pbk.)
A collection of questions and answers, classified by style of music, divided by
short essays on collecting records, pop and rock on television, and types of
music. Pop Quest was a series broadcast on the ITV network – a quiz
programme including features and news elements aimed at teenagers.

Uslan, Michael
  The rock'n'roll trivia quiz book / by Michael Uslan and Bruce Solomon;
  designed by Joel Avirom. – New York: Simon and Schuster, 1978. – 127p.:
  ill., ports; 28cm. ISBN 0-6712-4264-4 (pbk)
An entertaining, searching quizbook which will stretch the enthusiast. There
is obviously an American bias, but this does not detract from its being a fine
collection of questions, picture quizzes and answers.

CHAPTER TWO

Social aspects of popular music

The significance of popular music, its context in society in general, its associated fashions and the relationship between the artists and the audience, are all aspects which have been the constant concern of the popular press since the fifties. Occasionally a more serious approach has been adopted, as with the essays by Colin MacInnes: *England, half English.* Since 1965, starting with Peter Leslie's *Fab*, there have been a number of attempts to analyse these wider cultural points.

The outstanding work, because of the author's deep understanding both of the music and its social and political essence coupled with an authoritative prose style and genuine enthusiasm, is Greil Marcus's *Mystery train.*

Jasper, Tony
    Understanding pop / Tony Jasper. – London: S.C.M. Press, 1972. – 192p.:
    ill., facsims, ports; 22cm. Includes bibliography. ISBN 0-334-01728-9 (pbk.)
The author's aim is to offer an analysis of popular music – its types, the industry and its social aspects – in a simple but informative style. His standpoint is often a defensive one, rejecting the idea that evil is inherent in the music and suggesting that such cultural associations are created by the media. Jasper's usual Christian viewpoint only appears in a final chapter which explains that there is nothing irreligious about listening to pop music and indeed the vitality is to be encouraged. The bibliography is brief.

Leslie, Peter
    FAB: the anatomy of a phenomenon / Peter Leslie. – London: MacGibbon & Kee, 1965. – 187p., 8p. of plates: ill., ports; 22cm.
An early serious examination of the relationship between pop music, fashion and teenage culture which still offers considerable information and insight. There is a series of case histories including Lonnie Donegan, Tommy Steele, Adam Faith, Cliff Richard and the Beatles. The information about the industry at this stage of its development is particularly useful as it is reported in an unusually factual way for the time. The research into the youth subcultures is especially revealing.

Mabey, Richard
    The pop process / Richard Mabey. – London: Hutchinson Educational, 1969.
    – 190p.; 22cm. Includes bibliography. ISBN 0-09-098870-1

The social, cultural and musical importance of popular music is analysed in a historical context. Of particular interest is the section on the sources of fashion which is an analysis, in considerable depth, of the evolution and spread of musical trends. The influence of the media is discussed and the style of 'protest music' is taken as a case study. The careers of Bob Dylan and the Beatles are looked at with special emphasis. Obviously dated, this is an intelligent, well-written piece of work with a good bibliography and plenty of references.

MacInnes, Colin
England, half English / Colin MacInnes. – London: MacGibbon & Kee, 1961. – 208p; 22cm.
This collection of essays which appeared in various British cultural journals in the late fifties, including *Encounter*, *New Left Review*, *Saltire Review* and the *Twentieth Century*, includes an unusual essay on Tommy Steele and another on pop songs and teenagers. Superior in tone, reflecting the attitude of the cultural establishment at the time, the author describes the stage performance of Steele and his songs in the context of its blatant imitation of American singers, hence the title of the book. The essay on pop songs defines the 'new' musical style dismissively. MacInnes then analyses the economic power of the teenage market and discusses the musical style of singers like Paul Anka and concludes that this teenage culture is producing a mindless generation, 'the dullest society in western Europe'. It all seems irrelevant now in the context of general acceptance of popular music as at least a minor art form, but historically it is a worthy reference.

Marcus, Greil
Mystery train: images of America in rock'n'roll music / Greil Marcus. – London: Omnibus Press, 1977. – xiii, 279p.; 20cm. Includes index and discographies. ISBN 0-86001-311-1 (pbk.)
Originally published: New York: E. P. Dutton, 1975.
Journalist and former university lecturer Greil Marcus analyses the work of six performers including Elvis Presley, Randy Newman, Sly Stone and Robert Johnson, and sets them in the currents of traditional American culture and thought in a work considered by many to be the best single volume so far on the subject of contemporary popular music. The author goes beyond simple analysis, adding a level of scholarship and genuine intuition that are unique in this subject. His analysis of the relationship between the performer and the audience, which he calls the 'promise', is an original conception, beautifully described. His notes and discographies are excellent.

Melly, George
Revolt into style: the pop arts in Britain / George Melly. – Harmondsworth: Penguin Books, 1972. – 253p.; 18cm. Includes index. ISBN 0-14-00-3394-7 (pbk.)
Originally published: London: Allen Lane, 1970.
An account of the evolution of popular culture in Britain from the beginning of the fifties until the late sixties. George Melly, himself a jazz performer as well as a journalist and critic, makes an informed and sensitive analysis. His views

on the development of popular music are perceptive and incisive and his speculations on the future have been proven remarkably accurate. This is a notable work not only because it is well written and informative, but also because the author fuses a perceptive, artistic approach with a strong sense of the historical and social context of the art forms.

Palmer, Tony
    Born under a bad sign / Tony Palmer; illustrated by Ralph Steadman. –
    London: William Kimber, 1970. – 192p.: ill., facsims, ports; 24cm.
    ISBN 0-7183-0301-6
Published soon after the author's television film on pop music, All My Loving, this is a collection of observations and analyses of the influence of the phenomenon as it existed in the late sixties. The use of the word 'pop' is particularly significant as the author refers to the distinct differences in the styles within the music and the various degrees of value and significance. If writing later he would have referred to his subject as 'rock'. He outlines the development of the music, discusses the main artists, reproduces transcripts from interviews with managers, press agents, writers and performers and concludes by summing up the social and political mood of the time. He suggests that pop music has an important function for young people in communicating their deeper feelings. With the optimism of the late sixties, Palmer takes the music very seriously, comparing it favourably with classical music as a socially important medium and frequently overstating his case.

Pichaske, David
    A generation in motion: popular music and culture in the sixties / David
    Pichaske. – New York: Schirmer Books, 1979. – xxi, 248p., 23 leaves of
    plates: ill., ports; 25cm. Includes discography and index. ISBN 0-02-871860-7
    (cased). ISBN 0-02-871850-X (pbk.)
Written by the associate professor of English at Bradley University, Peoria, Illinois, this book, very literary in its approach, traces the growth of the significance of popular music as a cultural influence from the beatniks of the fifties to the disillusionment of the seventies. The central theme is the concept of motion, change and the search of youth to find an idealistic, alternative lifestyle which culminated in the flower-power movement. The author illustrates his arguments with hundreds of extracts from song lyrics. There is a good discography and index.

Sandford, Jeremy
    Synthetic fun: a short soft glance / By Jeremy Sandford. – Harmondsworth:
    Penguin Books, 1967. – 172p.: ill., ports; 18cm. (pbk.)
Published at the same time as Sandford's famous television play, Cathy Come Home, this is an analysis of popular culture generally with several sections relating to music. It is curious, in the light of his sensitive, almost idealistic book on festivals, *Tomorrow's people*, that Sandford's early attitude was rigidly anti-pop. He has very much the traditional view of teenage audiences as 'hysterical morons'. Prejudiced and ill-informed, the book does reflect a view which still pervaded the late sixties.

2.1 SOCIOLOGY

Frith, Simon
Sound effects: youth, leisure, and the politics of rock / Simon Frith. – Rev. ed.
– London: Constable, 1983. – 294p.; 22cm. Includes bibliography and index.
ISBN 0-09-464940-5 (cased). ISBN 0-09-464950-2 (pbk.)
Previous edition published as '*The sociology of rock*': London: Constable,
1978.
Simon Frith is a lecturer in sociology at Warwick University as well as being one
of the most respected rock-music journalists. This is a sociological analysis
specifically related to Britain. Frith looks at the consumption of popular music
by examining youth culture and youth leisure in the context of sociological
theory and media image. The business itself, how the industry functions, its
structure and its economics is then scrutinized with great detail. In the final
section the author looks at the ideologies, the culture of those within the
industry, particularly the musicians, and the importance of the music as a mass
medium. The roles of the music press and radio are discussed in depth, as are
the roots of rock from a cultural standpoint. There is an excellent bibliography
and notes section. This is an important contribution to the subject and the only
complete sociological analysis published. The second edition is a full revision
into the eighties with much re-worked text.

Grossman, Loyd
A social history of rock music: from greasers to glitter rock / Loyd Grossman.
– New York: David McKay Company, 1976. – ix, 150p.; 21cm. Includes
index. ISBN 0-679-50610-1
An attempt to give a survey of the development and social importance of rock
and pop music and then to explode many of the myths, this book tends to be too
sketchy in its analysis of particular albums and artists. Although often offering
interesting views of the social significance of the music, it makes the sweeping
statement that rock has created generations who refuse to look beyond their
own individual passions and pleasures. In all, it is a patchy analysis which is not
a scholarly examination but a series of personal views, often with little
substance to support them.

2.2 SUBCULTURES

The works included here are concerned with the relationship between styles of
music and their related youth subcultures. They vary from superficial glances to
sociological analyses but each adds to the understanding of the music itself.

Brake, Mike
*The sociology of youth culture and youth subcultures: sex and drugs and
rock'n'roll?* / Mike Brake. – London: Routledge & Kegan Paul, 1980. – viii,
206p.; 23cm. Includes bibliography and index. ISBN 0-7100-0363-3
(cased). ISBN 0-7100-0364-1 (pbk.)

Written as a doctoral thesis and full of academic cross-references and unintelligible jargon. The author's main theme is that youth subcultures with their styles of dress, behaviour and music should be seen as collectively adopted cultural solutions to the problems faced by contemporary youth. He points out that as a solution the membership of such groups is essentially 'magical' as it fails to come to terms with the socio-economic aspects of the society in which such subcultures develop. This conclusion is an obvious truism. Interesting, however, are the detailed studies of the wide variety of youth subcultures which sprang up during the sixties and seventies. These are classified into the British working-class culture, the bohemian and radical middle-class cultures of Britain and, to a lesser extent, America, and the developing West Indian and Asian youth cultures in Britain. The emphasis is not musical but nevertheless relevant to the serious student although hardly to the casual reader. The bibliography is extensive.

Chipman, Bruce L.
Hardening rock: an organic anthology of the adolescence of rock'n'roll /
edited and with an introduction by Bruce L. Chipman; with an appreciative
essay by X. J. Kennedy. – Boston: Little, Brown, 1972. – xviii, 154p.: ill.,
ports; 26cm.
Mainly a collection of photographs from the mid fifties to the early seventies mixed with song lyrics which attempts to create the mood and show the development of rock culture. The illustrations include pictures of performers but mainly cover the whole panoply of the teenage subculture in the USA. The notes and essays give an interesting, though not profound, introduction and the bulk of the text consists of song lyrics.

Doney, Malcolm
Summer in the city: rock music and way of life / Malcolm Doney. –
Berkhamsted: Lion Publishing, 1978. – x, 133p.: ill., ports; 20cm.
ISBN 0-85648-085-1 (pbk.)
Written by a journalist who writes for the Christian news magazine *Crusade*, this is a survey of the evolution of rock music and the growth of its influence which relates each changing phase to its period and related youth cultures. It is not an in-depth sociological study but it does include some interesting analysis and does not fail to comment on any significant movements. Although written from a Christian viewpoint it contains few moralizing undertones and Malcolm Doney's central theme is to underline the importance of the music as a reflection of the changes in society.

Hebdige, Dick
Subculture: the meaning of style / Dick Hebdige. – London: Methuen, 1979. –
195p.: ill.; 19cm. Includes bibliography and index. ISBN 0-416-70850-1
(cased). ISBN 0-416-70860-9 (pbk.)
The author is a research worker at the Faculty of Art and Design of the Polytechnic of Wolverhampton. He analyses the emergence of youth subcultures in post-war Britain. He goes beyond simply describing the appearance, tastes and music of the Teddy Boys, Mods, Skinheads, Punks and so on,

and looks at how a subculture is created and how its general acceptance leads to its end. He is especially interested in the symbolic styles of the cults and he adopts a number of approaches derived from semiotics. He particularly refers to the works of Genet in this investigation of images. His study of the white subcultures which have grown up around West Indian ska and reggae music in relation to the Rastafarians is particularly poignant. This is a perceptive study for those who wish to know why styles of music became identified with particular subcultures.

Popular song & youth today / edited by Louis M. Savary. – New York:
    Association Press, 1971. – 160p.: ill., ports; 21cm. ISBN 0-8096-1800-1
A superficial sociological analysis of popular music and its subcultures in America in the late sixties. The author sees popular music as a continuation of a traditional heritage manifesting itself in a commercial world. It is seen as a force of manipulation and producer of trends rather than a reflection. The drug culture of the late sixties is cited as an example of the mass communication of an undesirable trait through the medium of rock.

Willis, Paul E.
    Profane culture / Paul E. Willis. – London: Routledge & Kegan Paul, 1978. –
    x, 212p.; 23cm. Includes index. ISBN 0-7100-8789-6
An excellent sociological analysis of youth subcultures and their associated music and lifestyles which displays not only the academic background of the author but also a real knowledge of the music. The emphasis is on British subcultures of the sixties and early seventies; not as comprehensive as Mike Brake's work but more approachable.

Working class youth culture / edited by Geoff Mungham and Geoff Pearson. –
    London: Routledge and Kegan Paul, 1976. – vii, 167p.: ill.; 24cm. Includes
    bibliography and index. ISBN 0-7100-8374-2 (pbk.)
An interesting study which goes back to the fifties and looks at dozens of British movements. Musical aspects are brought into some, but not all of the cults. Where music is discussed, however, as in the case of Hippies, it is accurately described and integrated into the subculture as a cohesive element.

TEDDY BOYS – THE FIFTIES

Teddy Boys first appeared in the mid fifties. A British phenomenon, they wore their hair in elaborate quiffs, heavily dressed with grease. Their dress included long, pseudo-Edwardian drape jackets (which gave rise to their name), thick crêpe-soled shoes known as 'brothel creepers' and thin string ties. Their activities centred around rock'n'roll music, cafés with juke boxes and public houses. In the sixties the cult evolved into the 'Rockers' with the added obligatory motorcycle. By the late seventies there was a considerable revival of interest in rock'n'roll and rockabilly styles and the cult seems to have been given a new lease of life. It is ironic that many new 'Teds' are the sons of the original generation.

Baker, Chuck
   The rockin' fifties: a rock and roll scrapbook; a fast encounter with the generation that spawned rock and roll and student unrest, Howdy Doody and revolution, Elvis Presley and flights in space! / Chuck Baker. – Woodland Hills, California: Avanco, 1973. – 175p.: chiefly ill., ports; 28cm. Includes bibliography and discography
Including many images which will be totally foreign to the British reader, this collection of photographs of America in the fifties is, nevertheless, a valuable collage of the period. The text is brief but the mood of the period is successfully conveyed.

Steele-Perkins, Chris
   The Teds / Chris Steele-Perkins & Richard Smith. – London: Travelling Light/Exit, 1979. – 120p.: chiefly ill.; 28cm. ISBN 0-906333-05-9 (pbk.)
With only a brief text, this collection of photographs depicts the Teddy Boy revival and includes some 'Teds' who have remained such since the fifties. Their world of tattoos and grease is shown in all its seediness, giving overall a pathetic picture demanding the analysis which is unfortunately lacking.

Vollmer, Jurgen
   Rock'n'roll times / photographed and designed by Jurgen Vollmer. – Paris: Editions de Neste, 1980. – 82p.: chiefly ill.; 28cm. ISBN 2-86396-056-3 (pbk.)
Evoking the feeling of the fifties, this is a collection of contemporary photographs of leather- and drape-jacketed youths and their young ladies. Each photograph is captioned simply with the name of a song from the rock'n'roll era. As a bonus there are some early photographs of the Beatles in their Hamburg days dressed in similar leather style with greasy hair. The introduction is in both French and English.

MODS AND ROCKERS

The Mod cult began in London around 1963 and was basically a working-class movement with a highly stylized form of dress, the fashions of which changed very frequently, and an interest in rhythm & blues music. Mods wore their hair short and well-cut in a series of changing styles and their transport was the motor-scooter. They would either wear casual clothes and a Parka to ride their scooters or expensive suits with a specific length of sidevent and the latest Italian shoes. The Mods were noted for taking pep pills and particularly 'purple hearts'. The Who and Small Faces groups became the home-grown musical idols of the Mods and the Who's rock opera Quadrophenia recalls the Mod days. There was a revival of the cult in the late seventies and the two-tone groups used a combination of Mod dress with ska and bluebeat rhythms, which were later musical styles followed by Mods in the mid to late sixties.

Rockers were the sworn enemies of the Mods. A later manifestation of Teddy Boys, they wore leather jackets, had greased hair and rode motorcycles.

Their music was fifties rock'n'roll. During the bank holiday weekends of 1963 and 1964 Mods and Rockers fought violent battles in the resorts of southern England.

Barnes, Richard
  Mods / compiled by Richard Barnes. – London: Eel Pie Publishing, 1979. –
  128p.: chiefly ill., facsims, ports; 26cm. ISBN 0-906008-14-X (pbk.)
After an essay describing the Mod subculture, this is a fascinating collection of photographs, press cuttings and advertisements, mainly from 1964, which gives a real insight into their image and style. Their musical tastes are not neglected with illustrations of their idols, black American as well as British, and also detailed frozen frames of dances. The more violent aspects of the Mods and Rockers conflicts are well illustrated. This is a well-conceived and carefully designed work.

Cohen, Stanley
  Folk devils and moral panics: the creation of mods and rockers / Stanley
  Cohen. – London: MacGibbon and Kee, 1972. – 224p.: ill; 23cm.
  ISBN 0-261-10021-1
  Also published: London: Paladin, 1973.
A sociological study which does accurately describe the rocker's identification with rock'n'roll and analyses this, then anachronistic, association. The more eclectic music of the Mods is described less accurately, largely overlooking their association with black soul music. More useful for its sociological analysis than musical content.

HIPPIES

San Francisco had been an important centre of alternative American culture since the late forties. Cool jazz, Jack Kerouac and the writers of the beat generation were the direct antecedents of the Hippie movement. Associated with the use of the, so-called, soft drugs, cannabis and LSD, the Haight Ashbury district of San Francisco became the centre of the flower-power movement which came into international focus during 1967. Long hair, love-ins, peace, flowers and acid rock were the words which appeared in the popular press; a reaction to the horrors of the Vietnam war and oppressive Western governments, was the echo from the underground press. Hippies, who lived in communes, believed in free love and were generally from comfortable, middle-class backgrounds, appeared throughout the world and still survive in small numbers engaged in peaceful, usually artistic pursuits; most became disillusioned by 1968. The Grateful Dead and the Jefferson Airplane are the notably important bands but in Britain, the Hippies' acid-rock taste was represented by the Pink Floyd, Tomorrow, Soft Machine and even Procul Harum.

Anthony, Gene
The summer of love: Haight Ashbury at its highest / written and photo-
graphed by Gene Anthony. – Millbrae, California: Celestial Arts, 1980. –
134p.: chiefly ill. (some col.), ports (some col.); 24cm. Includes index.
ISBN 0-89087-250-3 (pbk.)
A pictorial impression of the area of San Francisco which was the nucleus of the
Hippie community around 1967. Illustrations include musicians such as Janis
Joplin and the Grateful Dead as well as unknown exotic people of the time.
Published for the sake of pure nostalgia, the real feeling of optimism and the
naivety of the time are lost within the bizarre clothes and drugs.

SKINHEADS

First appearing in Britain in the late sixties, Skinheads were a working-class
reaction to the flower power of middle-class hippiedom. Hair cropped to the
scalp, enormous cherry-red boots, working shirts and ludicrously short jeans
supported by superfluous braces was, and remains, the standard uniform.
Always violent, the skinhead subculture survived the seventies, becoming
increasingly racist. Often skinheads have played a major role in attacks and
riots against Asians in the English Midlands as well as in east London and
Southall (west London). Originally they were followers of ska and reggae,
itself a contradiction, but more recently Oi! music – violent, ugly, unintelligent
– has been the genre for skinheads.

Knight, Nick
Skinhead / Nick Knight. – London: Omnibus Press, 1982. – 96p.: chiefly ill.,
ports; 29cm. ISBN 0-7119-0052-2 (pbk.)
A collection of photographs of skinheads from the East End of London.
Grotesque images with brief notes depict well but, on the whole, explain
nothing about the cult.

RASTAFARIANS

In some ways a curious cult, the Rastafarian movement sprang up in the ghettos
of Kingston, Jamaica. Bred by unemployment and squalor and fed by easily
obtainable marijuana or ganga, this deeply-religious cult preaches that Haile
Selassie of Ethiopia, the Lion of Judah, was the reincarnation of Jesus Christ
and refuses to accept his death. Men grow their hair in long, plaited dreadlocks
while women cover their heads, use no cosmetics and wear long, modest
dresses. Rastas in Britain may be seen with their hair hidden under woollen
caps coloured green, for the land of Ethopia, red, for the blood of their
brothers, yellow, for the sun and black, for their skin. Their belief in the return
of black people to Africa, focussed on Ethiopia, may not be a realistic aim but
Rastafarianism possesses a distinctive, innocent dignity which is as rare as it is
naive. The music of reggae plays an important role in communicating the ideals
of the movement. The late Bob Marley was its leading musician and writer.

(*See also* the section on Reggae in Chapter 5.)

Barrett, Leonard Emanuel
The Rastafarians: the dreadlocks of Jamaica / by Leonard Emanuel Barrett. –
Kingston, Jamaica: Sangster's Book Stores Ltd; London: Heinemann Educational, 1977. – xiv, 257p.: ill.; 23cm. Includes bibliography and index.
ISBN 0-435-89457-9 (cased). ISBN 0-435-89458-7 (pbk.)
Basically a social history of the evolution of Rastafarianism, there is useful information on the influence of reggae in the development of the movement. The description of the religion is particularly comprehensive with detailed references and bibliographical notes.

Boot, Adrian
Jamaica: Babylon on thin wire / Adrian Boot, Michael Thomas. – London:
Thames and Hudson, 1976. – 96p.: ill., facsims, ports; 24cm.
ISBN 0-500-2081-3 (pbk.)
A serious, very readable study of Jamaican culture. After a history of the island and its ethnic and cultural heritage, the authors focus on its politics, social make-up and economics. The extremes of wealth and poverty turn the focus to deprivation and the background of Rastafarianism and evolution of reggae. Highly regarded, this is an excellent study.

Cashmore, Ernest
Rastaman: the Rastafarian movement in England / Ernest Cashmore. –
London: Allen & Unwin, 1980. – 272p.; 22cm. Includes bibliography and index. ISBN 0-04-301116-0 (pbk.)
Originally published: London: Allen & Unwin, 1979.
A detailed sociological analysis of the Rastafarian movement, its development in England and its associated youth subculture. The author pays great attention to the importance of reggae music, the message associated with it and its leading artists being discussed in depth. For the serious student, this book nevertheless is certainly accessible to the layperson seeking background to the music.

Owens, Joseph
Dread: the Rastafarians of Jamaica / Joseph Owens; introduction by Rex
Nettleford. – London; Kingston, Jamaica; Port of Spain, Jamaica:
Heinemann, 1979. – 282p.; 20cm. Includes index. ISBN 0-435-98650-3
(pbk.)
Originally published: Kingston, Jamaica: Sangster's Book Stores, 1976.
Written by an American social worker who worked in West Kingston from 1970 to 1972, this is an academic treatise on Rastafarianism. It is not for the casual reader but gives excellent background to reggae and its associated cult.

Thomas, Michael
Jah revenge: Babylon revisited / by Michael Thomas and Adrian Boot. –
London: Eel Pie, 1982. – 96p.: ill., ports; 30cm. ISBN 0-906008-59-X (pbk.)

With a selection of excellent illustrations, this is more than a revised edition of these authors' previous work, *Jamaica: Babylon on thin wire*, listed above under Boot, Adrian. Since the previous, optimistic book, there has been Bob Marley's death and a shift to the right in Jamaican politics. In this book the music and Rastafarianism are again important themes, but so is the violence of the society and the growing despair.

2.3 STARDOM

The mythology of stardom, its lifestyle, pressures, rewards and disasters is as much a source of the fascination and attraction of the stars as is their music.

Bennett, H. Stith
   On becoming a rock musician / H. Stith Bennett. – Amherst,
   Massachusetts: University of Massachusetts Press, 1980. – 235p.; 24cm.
   Includes index. ISBN 0-87023-311-4
Using examples of specific artists and information gathered from extensive interviews, this is a serious attempt to study the rise of rock performers from a sociological standpoint. The rock performer's environment, the influence of the media, the effect of exposure to wealth and the relationship with management and record companies, are all well examined. An interesting attempt, but the result is rather dull.

Dallas, Karl
   Singers of an empty day: last sacraments for the superstars / Karl Dallas;
   illustrated by Gloria Dallas. – London: Kahn & Averill, 1971. – 208p.: ill.,
   ports; 21cm. Includes index. ISBN 0-900707-12-7
The superstars of popular music are seen by the author as folk heroes. His examples include Mick Jagger, Frank Sinatra, Elvis Presley, John Lennon, Bob Dylan, Jimi Hendrix, Brian Jones and Janis Joplin. He examines what he describes as the 'autodestruct mechanism' of the star and states that the modern superstar has the choice between death and obscurity. Although his themes tend to become confused, his analysis of the decline of, for example, the Beatles, Janis Joplin and the Rolling Stones, is interesting and thoughtful but, in retrospect, in error.

Fox-Sheinwold, Patricia
   Too young to die / by Patricia Fox-Sheinwold. – London: Cathay Books,
   1980. – 353p.: ill., ports; 27cm. Includes discographies and filmographies.
   ISBN 0-86178-051-5 (pbk.)
This collection of victims of stardom covers the twentieth century from Rudolph Valentino to Elvis Presley and includes Brian Jones, Buddy Holly, Janis Joplin, Jim Croce, Duane Allman and Cass Elliot. The collection of essays is well written and informative, avoiding sentimentality but certainly ghoulish.

Herman, Gary
Rock'n'roll Babylon / Gary Herman. – London: Plexus, 1982. – 190p.: ill., ports; 29cm. Includes index. ISBN 0-85965-040-5 (cased). ISBN 0-85965-041-3 (pbk.)

This is an embittered account of the corruption, hypocrisy and destruction wrought on its stars by a ruthless, greedy industry. The opening chapter describes the Monterey Pop Festival, 1967, as the encapsulation of a false hope and continues with a description of the decay of the early stars: Elvis Presley, Johnny Cash, Jerry Lee Lewis and Chuck Berry. Themes such as drug abuse, stage-door sex, debauchery on the road, conversion to various forms of religious mysticism and finally the destructive effect of the mass media, continue throughout the book. Few of the major stars escape, and as well as the usual decadents, one may find the likes of the Beatles and Bob Marley. A sad but fascinating collection of lurid facts, it is in general accurate and obviously sensational.

No one waved goodbye: casualty report on rock and roll / edited by Robert Somma; designed by Ronn Campisi. – New York: Outerbridge & Dienstfrey, 1971. – 121p.: ill., ports; 23cm. ISBN 0-8769-0029-5

A collection of essays on the lives and deaths of the casualties of stardom, it includes pieces by well-known authors in the field. The usual subjects are included, Janis Joplin, Jim Morrison and so on, but there are also lesser-known artists from the sixties. There is no attempt at general analysis.

Sinclair, Marianne
Those who died young: cult heroes of the twentieth century / Marianne Sinclair. – London: Plexus, 1979. – 192p.: ill., ports; 30cm. ISBN 0-85965-029-4 (cased). ISBN 0-85965-023-5 (pbk.)

A range of cult figures from the twentieth century are interestingly juxtaposed, with intelligent biographical notes and well-chosen illustrations. Edith Piaf, Brian Jones, Jim Morrison, Jimi Hendrix and Janis Joplin are, naturally included.

Taylor, Ken
Rock generation: the inside exclusive / Ken Taylor. – Melbourne: Sun Books, 1970. – 149p.: ill., ports; 19cm. ISBN 0-7251-0116-4 (pbk.)

Written by a former Australian disc jockey and record producer for the biggest Australian record company, Festival, this book is full of lurid facts about totally obscure artists and groups. Written to be sensational, to expose the horrific, destructive influence of the popular-music lifestyle on so many young innocents, this reads like a pastiche but is quite serious. Rock'n'roll in Australia may have been like this but it is doubtful. 'Sex, blackmail, animalistic orgies, violence' reads the cover notes; this must be the worst book on the subject yet to be published.

Too fast to live, too young to die. – London: Plexus, 1982. 176p.: ill., ports; 30cm. ISBN 0-85965-059-6 (cased). ISBN 0-85965-058-8 (pbk.)

A collection of short biographies, with portraits, of a wide variety of artists who have suffered untimely deaths, not all from over-indulgence. They include John Lennon, Jim Morrison, Eddie Cochran, Sam Cooke, Hank Williams and Sid Vicious as well as lesser-known people such as Gram Parsons of the Byrds and Sandy Denny of the Fairport Convention. A good collection, it examines the growth of popular mythology.

2.4 WOMEN

The position of women in popular music changed dramatically during the seventies. Traditionally female vocalists had been decorative, frivolous creatures manipulated in a male-dominated business. Grace Slick of the Jefferson Airplane was to demonstrate in the late sixties that women could assume dominant roles in bands and write powerful rock songs. She was followed by singer-songwriters, such as Joni Mitchell, Carole King and Carly Simon, who dominated the album charts.

Patti Smith showed an aggressive, decadent face to early American punk rock which was followed by an explosion of women artists during the British new wave from Gaye Advert to Toyah with Blondie's Debbie Harry somehow combining the toughness of a rock star with the visual image of a contemporary Marilyn Monroe. In short, the sight of a woman playing in a band is no longer a source of amusement or even novelty.

This changing position is the context in which these works have been written, taking as examples the careers of leading women artists.

Katz, Susan
   Superwomen of rock / by Susan Katz. – New York: Tempo Books, 1978. –
   134p., 12p. of plates: ill., ports; 18cm. ISBN 0-448-16254-7 (pbk.)
Using the examples of Linda Ronstadt, Rita Coolidge, Olivia Newton-John, Carly Simon and Stevie Nicks of Fleetwood Mac, all of very different musical styles and backgrounds, the author looks at their successful but contrasting careers. The theme is one concerned with the problems of women being taken seriously in the music business, but to the author the retention of femininity is the real achievement of these particular singers. The overall effect is unsatisfactory.

New women in rock / edited by Liz Thomson. – London: Omnibus Press, 1982.
   – 96p.: ill. (some col.), facsims, ports (some col.); 29cm. Includes
   discography. ISBN 0-7119-0054-X (pbk.)
Focussing on the women who have come to prominence since 1977, this book includes not only notes on new-wave singers such as Nina Hagen, Poly Styrene and the Slits, but also singer-songwriters such as Kate Bush and Joan Armatrading, pop singers such as Toyah and Kim Wilde and disco star Grace Jones. The brief notes are written by journalists including Rosalind Russell, Robert Shelton, Deanne Pearson, Giovanni Dadomo and Joan Komlosy. The

photographs are well produced and each artist or group has an associated discography. The implicit message is the number of new women involved in rock music and their new, aggressive and creative role.

Orloff, Katherine
  Rock'n'roll woman / by Katherine Orloff. – Los Angeles: Nash Publishing, 1974. – 199p.: ill., ports; 28cm. ISBN 0-8402-8077-7 (pbk.)
This is a rare collection of twelve interviews with some of the best-known women rock performers including Maria Muldaur, Bonnie Raitt, Toni Brown, Linda Ronstadt, Grace Slick, Carly Simon, Nicole Barclay and Rita Coolidge. Katherine Orloff's questions aim to bring out the obvious difficulties of women in a man's world. The backgrounds of the artists, their influences and problems are described as well as their attitudes in areas of politics, sex, drugs and music. The portraits are very good.

Pavletich, Aida
  Sirens of song: the popular female vocalist in America / Aida Pavletich. – New York: Da Capo, 1982. – 281p.: ill., ports; 22cm. ISBN 0-306-80162-0 (pbk.)
  Originally published as '*Rock-a-bye baby*': Garden City, New York: Doubleday, 1980.
An excellent survey, divided into musical styles, of the evolution of the place of women in contemporary American popular music. Country, folk, singer-songwriters, rock and black singers are all well covered in equal depth and with great sensitivity. The author takes no political viewpoint, for example, in the conventional stance of Tammy Wynette compared to the radical one of Grace Slick, but she presents her subjects in their context. The theme is certainly one of tenacity in a male-dominated business but there is no overtly feminist slant. In general, this is a good study with some interesting portraits.

Shevey, Sandra
  Ladies of pop-rock / by Sandra Shevey. – New York: Scholastic Book Service, 1972. – 147p.: ill., ports; 20cm. (pbk.)
Aimed partially as a reader for American high schools, this is a well-written, informative and often-cited little collection of biographies and interviews with women stars of the late sixties and early seventies. The Janis Joplin, Carole King and Grace Slick sections are good but particularly revealing is the section on Joni Mitchell.

2.5 IN POLITICS

Popular music with its roots in folk music has always reflected the attitudes of society and has occasionally been explicitly satirical. The protest movement of the early sixties was such an overt expression of political comment but throughout its history rock music has often been a medium through which anti-establishment attitudes have been voiced. Such attitudes can be seen in the work of Chuck Berry, the Beatles and the Kinks, through to the likes of Tom Robinson and the Clash.

Works on this aspect tend to concern the protesting influence of rock music and the attitudes of the musicians. In general the content and the real significance of the music is greatly overestimated.

(*See also* the 'Protest' section in Chapter 5.)

Harker, Dave
   One for the money: politics and popular song / Dave Harker. – London:
   Hutchinson, 1980. – 301p.; 22cm. Includes index and bibliography.
   ISBN 0-09-140730-3 (cased). ISBN 0-09-140731-1 (pbk.)
Dave Harker lectures on courses for trade unionists at Manchester Polytechnic as well as writing widely on subjects associated with folk music. This analysis is an attempt to explain the development of post-war popular song in terms of the structure of the music industry in Britain and the USA. Beginning with an interesting suggestion that the very statement 'popular song' is rooted deeply in assumptions of class, the political theme is developed using Bob Dylan's career, with extensive examples of lyrics, to show the way in which a politically aware protest singer's work becomes eroded by the industry. He then uses some of his folk music sources to show, as an alternative, developments in that field. There are extensive notes and a good bibliography as well as detailed appendices of statistical tables relating to successful artists and records. The author's theme of the inevitable corruption of the popular artist by the evils of capitalism is pursued in depth but the arguments continually fail to be persuasive although the research and scholarship are undisputed.

McGregor, Craig
   Up against the wall, America / by Craig McGregor. – Sydney: Angus &
   Robertson, 1973. – 72p.: ill., ports; 24cm.
The author, an Australian, spent two years living in America in the late sixties. This collection of essays is his reflections on the social disintegration of America during the time. He attempts to persuade the reader that the nation's spirit is reflected in its most important art form: rock music. There is much interesting thought here but it is hidden among a confused mass of random impressions.

Sinclair, John
   Guitar army: street writings / *Prison writings* / by John Sinclair; designed by
   Gary Grimshaw. – New York: Douglas Book Corporation, 1972. – 364p.:
   ill., ports; 21cm. ISBN 0-8820-9000-3 (cased). ISBN 0-8820-9014-3 (pbk.)
The role of popular music as a weapon of cultural change is the author's central theme. He takes examples from blues and folk tradition as well as contemporary writers such as Bob Dylan and Jim Morrison. Often the narrative degenerates into political rhetoric, which detracts from an otherwise significant subject.

Sinclair, John
   Music and politics / by John Sinclair and Robert Levin. – New York: World
   Publishers, 1971. – 133p.: ill.; 23cm.

The author's own writings as well as extracts from art reviews, interviews and political manifestos published in jazz and underground magazines are brought together to demonstrate the political undercurrent in contemporary music. The roots of protest in folk music and the blues are explored but the general effect is confusing.

The sounds of social change: studies in popular culture / edited by R. Serge
  Denisoff and Richard A. Peterson. – Chicago: Rand McNally, 1972. – xi,
  332p.; 23cm. Includes index
A collection of essays on various aspects of popular music which reflect the changing attitudes of society. Songs of political protest movements, songs reflecting changing moral attitudes and songs about drugs are all examined. Not a work for the casual reader; much of the text analyses sociological surveys and is highly technical in its language.

2.6 In religion

Gospel music was certainly one of the seeds from which rock'n'roll grew and many white and many more black artists began their singing in church choirs and gospel groups.

Pop gospel, the use of light pop songs with simple Christian messages, has existed since the sixties with the likes of Cliff Richard and continues as a growing form. During the late sixties Jesus rock even appeared for a brief period and was taken up by the Byrds but quickly faded.

The works included are generally of a light nature, drawing Christian attitudes from pop themes. Johannes Riedel's *Soul music, black and white* is the exception, being a serious, analytical treatise.

Garner, Peter
  Pop goes the Gospel / by Peter Garner. – Gerrards Cross, Buckinghamshire:
  W E C Youth, 1978. – 12p.; 14cm. – (Camp talk; no. 10). (pbk.)
An unusual little pamphlet: the author supports the energy and happiness produced in young people by pop music but condemns the lifestyle, drugs and promiscuity. There is a brief, but informative, introduction to pop gospel.

Jasper, Tony
  Jesus in a pop culture / Tony Jasper. – London: Fontana. 1975. – 189p.; 19cm.
  ISBN 0-0021-5371-8 (pbk.)
A serious attempt to reconcile modern popular music and its lifestyle with a Christian stance. The author, always a defender of the music, uses modern pop gospel singers, and notably Cliff Richard, to demonstrate pop's good side.

Jasper, Tony
  Pop / Tony Jasper. – London: S. C. M. Press, 1970. – 32p.: ill., ports; 23cm.
  (pbk.)

This is a Christian survey of popular music at the end of the sixties with a message that pop and rock is not all bad. Not moralizing in tone, it is a superficial glance with some historical perspective.

Lawhead, Steve
  Rock reconsidered; a Christian looks at contemporary music / Steve
  Lawhead. – Downes Grove, Illinois: Inter-Varsity Press, 1981. – 156p.;
  20cm. ISBN 0-87784-812-2 (pbk.)
A moralistic condemnation of the influence of contemporary music on young people: permissive sex, drugs, violence, the breakdown of the family and all other imaginable social ills are certainly created or exacerbated by it. Nonsense.

Riedel, Johannes
  Soul music, black and white: the influence of black music on the churches /
  Johannes Riedel. – Minneapolis, Minnesota: Augsberg Publishing House,
  1975. – 159p.: music; 20cm. Includes discography and index.
  ISBN 0-8066-1414-5
The author examines both the influence of gospel music on the format of worship and the influence of the church in inspiring singing and in assimilating blues forms into an acceptable style. This is a study of authority and scholarship.

2.7 IN EDUCATION

The use of pop, rock and folk in schools to encourage children to express themselves artistically is a recent and refreshing development.
  The published audiovisual materials are surprisingly few in number, considering the potential of such learning media.

Attwood, Tony
  Pop workbook / Tony Attwood and Paul Farmer. – London: Edward
  Arnold, 1978. – 96p.: ill., ports; 24cm. Includes discography and index.
  ISBN 0-7131-0155-5 (pbk.)
Writing for British schools, the authors provide a wide range of exercises which attempt to engender an interest in music generally as well as develop learning skills in an area of teenage interest. The text is informative with some good illustrations and a useful discography of significant records.

Pop music in school / edited by Graham Vulliamy and Ed Lee. – New ed. –
  Cambridge: Cambridge University Press, 1980. – ix, 229p.: ill., music; 24cm.
  Includes bibliography, discography and index. ISBN 0-521-22930-8 (cased).
  ISBN 0-521-29727-3 (pbk.)
  Previous edition: Cambridge: Cambridge University Press, 1976.
Consisting of eight lengthy essays making the case for using pop music in the

classroom, this is a well-constructed and informative work. Edited by lecturers in education, it has an excellent section defining and describing the various styles within popular music before suggesting its educational applications. There are numerous musical examples, a fine bibliography and a discography. The new edition fully revises the 1976 edition with the inclusion of notes on punk and disco music.

Pop, rock and ethnic music in school/ edited by Graham Vulliamy and Ed Lee.
– New ed. – Cambridge: Cambridge University Press, 1982. – 256p.: ill.,
music; 24cm. Includes bibliography, discography and index.
ISBN 0-521-23341-0 (cased).   ISBN 0-521-29927-6 (pbk.)
Following these editors' previous publication, *Pop music in school*, they extend their theme to include the various forms of ethnic music which have become associated with Britain's ethnic minorities. There is much additional, practical material including a case study of work done with the Inner London Education Authority. There are many musical examples and an excellent bibliography.

Vulliamy, Graham
Popular music: a teacher's guide / Graham Vulliamy and Edward Lee. –
London: Routledge and Kegan Paul, 1982. – viii, 127p.: music; 24cm.
Includes bibliography. ISBN 0-7100-0595-3
A good guide to a series of books on various forms of popular music. The authors offer an excellent introduction. They develop their frequent theme of the importance of using music in the classroom. The bibliography is lengthy and there are profuse musical examples.

AUDIO-VISUAL MATERIALS

Jewell, Derek
Enjoying pop / commentary by Derek Jewell. – London: Times Cassettes;
Wakefield: Educational Productions, 1975. 1 sound cassette (90 min.):
1⅞ips, stereo, Dolby processed
A brief history of popular music from ragtime to the progressive rock of the seventies. Well-written and narrated, the analysis is simple but intelligent, with a good selection of musical examples.

Pollock, Bruce
Rock / by Bruce Pollock. – Pleasantville, New York; London: Educational
Audio Visual, 1975. – 11p.; 28cm. 3 filmstrips: col.: 35mm. 1 sound tape reel
(58 min.): 3¾ips, mono; 5in.
There is some quite good musical criticism and an attempt to convey an introduction to basic musical theory in a rock music context, with an emphasis on contemporary rock and pop music of the mid seventies. Pulsed with audible or inaudible frame-change signals, the recording is also available on cassette and disc.

Spencer, Piers
  The influence of pop on creative music in the classroom / by Piers Spencer. –
  York: University of York, Department of Music, 1974. – 12p.: ill.; 30cm. 1
  sound tape reel; 3¾ips, mono; 4in.
An attempt to reproduce the atmosphere of a classroom in which pop music
structures are used in simple musical composition. There are lengthy musical
examples illustrating techniques of developing particular themes.

CHAPTER THREE

Artistic aspects of popular music

Whether the disciplines of criticism and analysis applied to classical music should be used in the discussion of popular music is a debate that continues. The works which have attempted such analysis are joined here by collections of song lyrics which attempt to stand alone as poetry, indexes to songs, a thematic catalogue and the visual arts which the music has curiously spawned.

Until the emergence of television, cinema was certainly the most significant art form that had appeared this century and its reciprocal interaction with popular music has been considerable.

Record sleeves have become an important secondary art form being a significant element in the marketing of albums. The collections of album sleeves listed below along with collections of photographs, many of which were used for album sleeves as well as publicity and in the press, make an interesting body of work.

Peellaert's *Rock Dreams* has become a classic work in this visual field and as a collection of brilliantly conceived images, which both add to the understanding of the music and have their own place as very original works of art, it is remarkable.

3.1 AESTHETICS

Fletcher, Peter
   Roll over rock: a study of music in contemporary culture / by Peter Fletcher. – London: Stainer & Bell, 1981. – 175p.; 22cm. ISBN 0-8524-9576-5
The popular music of the past 150 years is examined, including folk influences and the growth of jazz. The author examines pop and what he calls élite music (classical forms) in the context of their worth and depth in both artistic and social terms. Although his thesis would appear to be one of rejecting the élitism of high culture, his conclusions are ambivalent.

Meltzer, R.
   The aesthetics of rock / By R. Meltzer. – New York: Something Else Press, 1970. – 346p.: ill., ports; 20cm. Includes index. ISBN 0-87110-037-1 (cased). ISBN 0-87110-069-X (pbk.)
A rambling treatise examining rock music as art and analysing the criteria of such an examination. This is a difficult work to assess: the style crosses over

between being a pseudo-philosophical text and avant-garde journalism. There are copious footnotes and a detailed index but neither help one's comprehension.

3.2 MUSICAL CRITICISM AND ANALYSIS

Bobbitt, Richard
Harmonic technique in the rock idiom: the theory & practice of rock harmony / Richard Bobbitt. – Belmont, California: Wadsworth, 1976. – 246p.: ill., music; 25cm. Includes bibliography and index. Also available in the format of a workbook. ISBN 0-5340-0474-1. ISBN 0-5340-0478-4 (workbook)
Whether or not rock music should be taught using the same techniques as for classical music is debatable, but that is the aim of the author. Based around numerous musical examples, over six hundred compositions are analysed. Examples are from well-known songs with a general theme of the harmonic styles being evolved from the music of entire periods. Not for the general reader, but a genuine attempt to offer an academic approach.

Lee, Ed
Music of the people: a study of popular music in Great Britain / by Edward Lee. – London: Barrie & Jenkins, 1970. – xiv, 274p., 25p. of plates: ill., facsim, music, ports; 25cm. Includes bibliography and index. ISBN 0-2146-6067-2
The two aims of this book are to offer a concise history of popular music in Britain from before the Norman Conquest to 1970, and to discuss modern popular music from both the technical and aesthetic viewpoints. It is the second part which is of particular interest and analyses include the work of Bob Dylan and the Beatles. The Beatles' melodic style is analysed in some depth. The attitudes of musicians and their audiences are looked at and their influences on each other. There are extensive examples of music and lyrics used to illustrate points within the text. The bibliography for modern popular music is very brief. There are indexes to musical examples, first lines of songs and a general index to the text. Although musical terminology is frequently used, it is clearly explained. The author avoids appearing to be condescending and generally gives an illuminating approach to the subject.

Mellers, Wilfrid
Caliban reborn: renewal in twentieth-century music / Wilfrid Mellers. – London: Victor Gollancz, 1968. – xi, 195p.: ill.; 23cm. Includes index. ISBN 0-575-00046-5
Mainly concerned with serious music, Professor Mellers traces the revolutionary strands in music from Wagner to Schoenberg, Webern to Stockhausen and from Debussy through Satie, Messiaen, Boulez and Varese. He looks at what he calls a new primitivism in Orff and Stravinsky, hence The Tempest and the title of the book. A fascinating chapter is devoted to modern music and the developments in jazz and popular music. The Beatles and Bob Dylan are

discussed at the period around 1966, before their major achievements had been seen. Nevertheless, this places the development of popular music in the mid sixties in the context of music in general and it makes *Caliban reborn* a unique work.

Mellers, Wilfrid
    Twilight of the Gods: the Beatles in retrospect / Wilfrid Mellers. – London:
    Faber, 1976. – 215p.: music; 20cm. Includes discography.
    ISBN 0-571-10998-5 (pbk.)
    Originally published: London: Faber, 1973.
    Also published: New York: Viking Press, 1974.
This is a unique musicological analysis of each of the songs composed by the four Beatles when they were together, as well as their early solo efforts. It is the only book to attempt analysis and criticism of modern pop music in an academic, serious way. Mellers is not patronizing and his appreciation of the group's music is clearly evident. There are copious musical examples and readable notes which make this a fascinating work both for the lay reader and the musician. The author's style does attract criticism, however, as, although full of information on the simple backgound to lyrical ideas and the situations in which songs were composed or inspired, he is often extravagant in language and appears pretentious.

Middleton, Richard
    Pop music and the blues: a study of the relationship and its significance / by
    Richard Middleton. – London: Gollancz, 1972. – 271p.: music; 23cm.
    Includes bibliography, discography and index. ISBN 0-575-01442-3
Richard Middleton, a lecturer in music at the Open University, uses the term 'pop music' in the same context as 'pop art'. This problem of precise definition is at first confusing for he includes such forms as rock'n'roll, Merseybeat and black soul music as subdivisions of pop: such a definition is not generally accepted. Nevertheless, as an analysis of the evolution of rock music and soul music from the blues, this is a detailed study. His thesis is that the evolution of this music stems from the gradual emancipation of Negroes and the development of Negro culture and music in the context of the changing relationship of Western and non-Western cultures. He sees this coupled with the growth of a non-conformist adolescent group attracted to the seemingly more liberated non-Western traditions and particularly Negro music. The various forms of blues are discussed and their influences on popular music styles. He pays detailed attention to the Beatles' and Bob Dylan's work, which he analyses in depth. Given the author's background, his musical analyses are from an academic standpoint but are clear and untechnical. The bibliography includes useful references to background sociological works as well as books on the blues. The glossary of musical terms is useful.

Ricigliano, Daniel Anthony
    Melody and harmony in contemporary songwriting / Daniel A.
    Ricigliano. – New York: Donato Music Publishing 1978. – viii, 280p.: music;
    28cm. Includes index

The book is profusely illustrated with musical examples of well-known popular songs. The author describes in technical detail the development in melody and harmony in various styles.

Schafer, William John
Rock music: where it's been, what it means, where it's going / William J. Schafer. – Minneapolis, Minnesota: Augsberg Publishing House, 1972. – 128p.: ill., music; 20cm. ISBN 0-8066-1234-7
A serious study of the rock-music form with musical examples, which examines its musical evolution and speculates on its likely development. Lyrical themes are not ignored and the change in the themes of songs and their presentation is also briefly discussed.

Stewart, Dave
Introducing the dots / Dave Stewart. – Poole, Dorset: Blandford Press, 1982. – 128p.: ill., music; 25cm. ISBN 0-7137-1125-6 (pbk.)
Dave Stewart is one of the most highly regarded British keyboard players. He has played with the bands Egg, Khan, National Health and Bruford and in addition he has had some hit singles since the early eighties, recorded with other notable artists including Colin Blunstone. Basing the book on a series of articles written for the magazine *Sound International*, he explains the application of conventional musical notation to rock music and offers a readable guide to its use and interpretation. There are some 425 musical examples.

3.3 SONGS AS POETRY

Damsker, Matt
Rock voices: the best lyrics of an era / edited and text by Matt Damsker. – London: Arthur Barker, 1981. – 139p.; 21cm. ISBN 0-213-16809-X (pbk.)
Originally published: New York: St Martin's Press, 1980.
This is a well-chosen collection of lyrics from the late sixties to the late seventies by the major songwriters. Selected from a wide range of musical styles, but omitting any songs from the new wave, included are lyrics by Bob Dylan, Billy Joel, Bruce Springsteen, the Grateful Dead, Paul Simon and many others. Each writer is given a brief, but informative, biographical sketch and there are detailed notes to each selected lyric setting its time and context. An introductory essay pretentiously discussing rock lyrics in the terms of poetry appreciation mars an otherwise well-selected, well-criticized collection.

Jasper, Tony
Sound seventies / Tony Jasper. – Great Yarmouth, Norfolk: Galliard, 1972. – 60p.: ill., ports; 24cm. ISBN 0-85249-117-4 (pbk.)
This book is aimed as a basis for using pop music in the classroom, particularly in a religious context. The author looks at a random selection of albums from the early seventies and then chooses a varied collection of songs. The lyrics are grouped by theme and there are brief notes on the message of each song.

The poetry of rock / edited by Richard Goldstein. – New York: Bantam Books, 1969. – 147p., 16p. of plates: ill., ports; 18cm. Includes index. (pbk.)
This is a collection of lyrics dating from the mid fifties to the late sixties. The editor does not claim the lyrics to be poetry but claims that their use of language, sense of rhythm and power show 'poetic qualities'. Choosing seventy-five of the best-known songs, Goldstein shows the way in which lyrics have broadened in scope and become increasingly socially aware and sophisticated. His comments are interesting and the introduction intelligent. When it was published, the question of popular lyrics aspiring to be poetry was an issue of some importance. It now seems largely irrelevant.

The poetry of soul / edited by A. X. Nicholas. – New York: Bantam Books, 1971. – 103p.; 18cm. Includes index. ISBN 0-553-06521-0 (pbk.)
Divided into four sections: black world as passion; black world as pain; black world as protest and black world as celebration. Many of the best-known songs from a wide range of black artists and styles have been well chosen. B. B. King, Otis Redding, James Browne, Sam Cooke, Curtis Mayfield and Marvin Gaye are well represented, in addition to most other major writers. There is a brief note on each artist's style, significance and content.

Pollock, Bruce
    In their own words: lyrics and lyricists 1955–1974 / Bruce Pollock. – New York: Macmillan; London: Collier Macmillan, 1975. – xx, 231p.: ill., ports; 22cm. Includes index. ISBN 0-02-597950-7
The work of the leading songwriters from the whole spectrum of popular music is discussed and analysed with profuse, well-selected examples. There are quotations from interviews with most of the writers with some fascinating insights into their methods of working and inspirations, as well as outlines of their careers.

3.4 Song indexes

80 years of American song hits, 1892–1972: a comprehensive yearly reference book listing America's major hit songs and their writers. – New York: Chappell, 1973. – 106p.; 27cm. Includes index. (pbk.)
An index to American songs arranged by year with details of their writers and the performers who made them successful. Well designed, with a useful title index, this admirably covers the period from 1955 to the early seventies.

Havlice, Patricia P.
    Popular song index / Patricia Pate Havlice. – Metuchen, New Jersey: Scarecrow Press, 1975. – 933p.; 22cm. Includes indexes. ISBN 0-8108-0820-X
Havlice, Patricia P.
    Popular song index: first supplement / Patricia Pate Havlice. – Metuchen, New Jersey: Scarecrow Press, 1978. – 368p.; 22cm. Includes indexes. ISBN 0-8108-1099-0

Well organized with access by first line, first line of chorus, song title, best-known singer, composer and lyricist, this well-produced reference source includes popular songs of a wide range of styles and eras. There are certainly omissions but many are rectified by the first supplement. The basis of the index is some 301 collections published between 1940 and 1972. All but thirteen of these were American. Over 30,000 songs are included.

Shapiro, Nat
   Popular music: an annotated index to American popular songs / edited by Nat Shapiro. – New York: Adrian Press. 6 vols. so far
   Volume 1: 1950–1959. – 2nd ed. – 1967. – xiii, 347p.: 24cm. Includes index
   Previous edition: 1964.
   Volume 2: 1940–1949. – 1965. – xiii, 347p.: 24cm. Includes index
   Volume 3: 1960–1964. – 1967. – xiii, 335p.: 24cm. Includes index
   Volume 4: 1930–1939. – 1968. – xiii, 335p.: 24cm. Includes index
   Volume 5: 1920–1929. – 1969. – 331p.: 24cm. Includes index
   Volume 6: 1965–1969. – 1973. – xiii, 385p.: 24cm. Includes index
This includes the significant songs arranged by year of popularity in the USA, which usually coincides with the year of publishing. Information under each entry covers writer, publisher and source, if the song is from a musical or film. There is an index of publishers, index of titles and a supplement of significant songs published before a particular period and becoming popular later. Each volume includes an introductory essay to songs of the period and a list of best-selling records as well as miscellaneous facts.

Whitter, John
   Song index: popular songs and where to find them / compiled by John Whitter and Ruth Watts. – London: Association of Assistant Librarians, 1981. – 111p.: 21cm. ISBN 0-900092-36-X
Including just under 5,000 songs, this is an index based on seventy-six volumes of song collections from pop songs to traditional folk. It is, therefore extremely limited, failing to include some of the most popular songs. The arrangement is an alphabetical song list including coded sources, a key to the codes and a list of collections indexed. Well produced but of little value.

3.5 THEMATIC CATALOGUES

Macken, Bob
   The rock music source book / Bob Macken, Peter Fornatele and Bill Ayres. – Garden City, New York: Anchor Press; Doubleday, 1980. – 645p.; 21cm. Includes bibliography, discographies and filmography. ISBN 0–385–14139–4 (pbk.)
Compiled by three American broadcasters and journalists, this is a unique work which after an introductory section analyses the major themes of lyrics from all styles of popular songs over the last twenty-five years. The themes are arranged alphabetically with the songs then classified as classics, definitive and reference songs. The song title, artist and record label are given. Although the

information here is vast, the value is debatable and certainly the groupings are odd and subjective. There are also many omissions. The bibliography is useful and there are also discographies of important albums, the authors' opinions on their top-forty albums as well as the important dates in rock, rock deaths and a list of record companies. An interesting idea but neither as useful nor as extensive as it promises to be.

3.6 FILMS

The musical film has proved itself an exciting and popular form of entertainment since Al Jolson's The Jazz Singer in 1927. It survived and evolved through the elegance of Fred Astaire and spectacle of Busby Berkeley in the thirties on to Gene Kelly's choreography and Sinatra's slick singing of the forties and early fifties. On the way jazz had been introduced to a wider audience through the cinema.

Since Sinatra's success on film in the forties and Bing Crosby's a decade before, it had been established that the progression from recording artist to film star was a logical, if not an easy, step. As soon as rock'n'roll emerged, therefore, its early stars soon appeared in films. Bill Haley in Rock Around the Clock, in 1956, was the first many British people ever heard of rock'n'roll. It was banned in several towns because of the hysterical effect it was claimed to produce on its young audience. In 1956 Elvis Presley followed with Love Me Tender, the first of his thirty-three films.

Two formats emerged of which these two early films were clear examples. On the one hand a thin storyline was broken by the appearance of the artists performing their hit recordings, as in Rock Around the Clock. In the other the star would act in a leading role, occasionally breaking into song. These patterns continued as the main forms until the seventies.

In Britain Cliff Richard made a series of musical films in the Elvis mould whereas the Beatles avoided similar disasters only by the skilful direction of Richard Lester.

In 1970 Woodstock was a revolutionary approach, being the filmed, beautifully edited record of the live performance of leading artists. This was followed by the likes of the Rolling Stones' Gimme Shelter, 1970, Pink Floyd at Pompeii, 1971, and more recently the Last Waltz, 1978, and No Nukes, 1980.

In addition, rock, pop and black music have increasingly been used as film scores. Easy Rider, 1969, was an early successful example but contemporary country, outlaw music, was used in the Electric Horseman, 1980, and films establishing a place in time such as Coming Home, 1978, which set itself firmly in 1968 with an inspired choice of soundtrack.

The so-called rock operas: Jesus Christ Superstar, 1973, Godspell, 1973, Hair, 1979, and, of course, Tommy, 1975, have also been produced with generally unsatisfactory results. Pink Floyd's The Wall, 1982, is a theatrical representation of an album; a new concept again. That'll Be the Day, 1973, and Stardust, 1974, the story of the rise and fall of a rock star, have included the performance of a pop star, David Essex, his singing, a story about the music and a pop-music score. Similarly The Rose, 1979, and A Star is Born, 1976, included well-known artists who performed in the role of the actors in tragic stories involved with stardom and its consequences.

During the late seventies the disco film appeared with Saturday Night Fever, 1977, Grease, 1978, Music Machine, 1979, Can't Stop the Music, 1980 and a host of even poorer offerings, all having glitter, dancing, disco music and romance. The fashion has now passed.

As for the literature, included here are the reference sources which have so far appeared on this important subject. Books written about specific films appear under the featured artist in Chapter 6, or, where a novelization has been produced and the subject matter concerns popular music, in Chapter 7.

Dellar, Fred
The NME guide to rock cinema / Fred Dellar; with a foreword by Monty Smith. – Feltham, Middlesex: Hamlyn Paperbacks, 1981. – 191p., 16p. of plates: ill., facsims; 18cm. ISBN 0-600-20367-0 (pbk.)
Well written in a humorous style and never afraid of being critical. After an essay on the development of rock-music-related cinema from the fifties and speculation into the eighties, this is a directory, alphabetically arranged by film title. Full credits, the plot and a list of the music in the soundtrack with related artists are included. The scope is wide – for example, Brando's film The Wild One and James Dean's Rebel Without a Cause are both included – but neither film incorporates any significant music nor are the central figures or the actors musicians. The justification is that the films embody the atmosphere out of which rock'n'roll grew. With some good, though very selective stills, this is an excellent reference source. The introduction concludes that apart from a very few good films in the genre the quality has failed to improve over twenty-five years and the attitude is still 'give 'em what they want – give 'em garbage'. A sad reflection.

Ehrenstein, David
Rock on film / David Ehrenstein & Bill Reed; art direction by Ed Caraeff. – London: Virgin Books, 1982. – 293p.: ill., facsims; 23cm. Includes index. ISBN 0-907080-31-6 (pbk.)
Originally published: New York: Delilah Communications, 1982.
After a rambling, uninspired introductory essay, this is arranged alphabetically with full credits and brief critical synopses. A wide range of films are included in which rock, pop, black and country music are used as the soundtrack or in which music is the theme. It has definite American bias; for example, many of the early-sixties beach movies not included in the *NME guide* are included, whereas some second-feature British pop films of the same period have been missed. There are some other surprising omissions: for example, The Beatles at Shea Stadium, Cliff Richard's film, Serious Charge and Kris Kristofferson's Alice Doesn't Live Here Anymore. Not as comprehensive or as informative as the *NME guide*, it is well designed, but disappointing.

Hirschhorn, Clive
   The Hollywood musical / Clive Hirschhorn. – London: Octopus Books,
   1981. – 456p.: ill. (some col.); 33cm. Includes index. ISBN 0-7064-1280-X
   Also published: New York: Crown, 1981.
Beginning with Jolson's The Jazz Singer, 1927, and concluding with Neil
Diamond's version, 1980, this is a beautifully illustrated and well-written
introduction to 1,344 musical films. Each year has a headed section listing
Academy Awards followed by a survey of the year's output. The term 'musical'
is used to describe a wide range of films and included are Elvis's efforts, Arlo
Guthrie's Alice's Restaurant and Robert Altman's Nashville. Appendices
include listings of pop musicals and documentaries such as Woodstock and
Monterey Pop. There are indexes to film titles, songs, performers, composers
and lyricists. In all, this is a good reference source which lacks musical analysis
but provides the basic facts in a popular and accessible format.

Jenkinson, Philip
   Celluloid rock: twenty years of movie rock / Philip Jenkinson and Alan
   Warner. – London: Lorrimer, 1974. – 136p.: ill. (some col.) facsims, (some
   col.), ports (some col.); 26cm. Includes filmography and index.
   ISBN 0-85647-046-5 (pbk.)
Written by a well-known film critic and television presenter, this covers the
period from 1953 to 1974. Included is information and commentary on films
about rock, pop and black music, films with a background of the music or
teenage culture, films with well-known artists in acting roles and films with
significant musical soundtracks. The author notes that there is a real problem in
quoting definite release and production dates as these data are particularly
unreliable. In addition, titles tend to change and credits are often sketchy.
There is a good selection of stills and although not an exhaustive study, this is a
good reference source. Unfortunately both the index and filmography include
errors and the text mentions films and artists not indexed.

3.7 PHOTOGRAPHS

Davies, Chalkie
   Pointed portraits / by Chalkie Davies. – London: Eel Pie, 1981. – 112p. of ill.,
   ports; 26cm. ISBN 0-906008-33-67 (pbk.)
A collection of photographs of some of the most important musicians of recent
years with an emphasis on the British stars from the new wave. The main
interest lies in the innovative composition of the photographs as well as the
choice of artists. The book describes itself as a 'coffee table book for people
who don't own coffee tables'.

Gray, Andy
   Great popstars / Andy Gray. – London: Hamlyn, 1973. – 160p. of ill. (some
   col.), chiefly ports (some col.); 31cm. ISBN 0-600-38696-1
A good collection of portraits of the most successful recording artists from 1955
to 1973. All the major performers are here with lists of their successful records.

Hammond, Harry
Hit parade: a thirty five year perspective of the pop scene through the photographs of / Harry Hammond and Gered Mankowitz. – London: Eel Pie, 1982. – 160p.: ill. (some col.), ports (some col.); 27cm.
ISBN 0-906008-70-0 (pbk.)
Harry Hammond began photographing popular performers in 1947 and continued throughout the fifties until 1962. Gered Mankowitz began his career at sixteen and in 1969 was given his first album-sleeve assignment. Since then he has produced over 500 including artists such as Toyah, Elton John, the Rolling Stones and Duran Duran as well as working freelance for *The Observer*, the *Sunday Express* and *Face*. In 1981 they shared an exhibition at the Photographers Gallery and the resulting success prompted this publication of their work. It includes a fine selection of excellent studies.

Hasebe, Koh
Music life rock photo gallery / Koh Hasebe. – New York: Sire Books; Chappell Music, 1976. – 156p.: chiefly ill., ports; 30cm. (pbk.)
A fine collection of photographs many of which have previously appeared in American magazines. It includes mainly leading artists of the seventies with a few from the previous decade. Stevie Wonder, Alice Cooper, Chicago, Santana, Carly Simon, Led Zeppelin, the Who, the Beatles, James Brown and Rod Stewart are all represented.

Hirsch, Abby
The photography of rock / edited by Abby Hirsch; designed by George Delmerico. – Henley-on-Thames: Aidan Ellis Publishing, 1973. – 241p.: chiefly ill., chiefly ports; 28cm. ISBN 0-85628-006-2 (pbk.)
Originally published: New York: Bobbs-Merrill, 1972
This collection of pictures covering the period between 1965 and 1972 was compiled by an American journalist with a particular interest in popular culture. Nine of the best-known and most prolific photographers have their work included. They are Nicholas De Sciose, Wendi Lombardi, Bob Green, Amalie Rothchild, Bob Cato, Jim Hamilton, KLN, Elliot Landy and Lee Marshall. There is a brief biography of each photographer and a list of the precise occasion of each of the following photographs. Occasionally notes of particular interest or comment are included. This is a superb collection offering the images of the development of rock and the projection of its performers during this significant period. The locations are all American although there is a good share of British performers. There is no index as emphasis is on the art of the photographer and not the stars themselves.

Leibovitz, Annie
Shooting stars / edited by Annie Leibovitz; designed by Tony Lane. – San Francisco: Straight Arrow Books, 1973. – 152p.: chiefly ill., chiefly ports; 35cm. ISBN 0-8793-2036-2
An excellent collection of portraits from *Rolling Stone* magazine of some of the major artists of the late sixties and early seventies. Some British artists are

included but the collection is mainly of American stars. Brief notes by each of the twenty-one photographers precede their work which has been well chosen to provide a varied and fascinating image of the time.

McCartney, Linda
  Linda's pictures: a collection of photographs / photographs and words by Linda McCartney; reviewed by Paul McCartney. – New York: Ballantine, 1977. – 148p.: chiefly ill., ports (some col.); 33cm. ISBN 0-345-27815-1
  Originally published: New York: Knopf, 1976.
Wife of Paul McCartney and keyboards player with Wings, Linda McCartney was a professional photographer for the American magazine *Town and Country*. This collection of her work includes photographs of many of the major popular music stars of the sixties and seventies. As part of the rock world's inner circle she has been able to obtain uniquely personal portraits which can be witty or tragic but always revealing and make this collection quite superb.

McCartney, Linda
  Photographs / Linda McCartney. – London: Pavilion Books, 1982. – 133p.: ill., ports; 36cm. ISBN 0-907516-15-1
A second collection of photographs which includes a wide range of subjects as well as some well-known artists. Many were taken over ten years before this publication and include Janis Joplin, Frank Zappa, the Who, the Rolling Stones and the Beatles during the late sixties. Beautifully produced, this is again an excellent collection.

Marks, J.
  Rock and other four letter words / J. Marks; photographs by Linda Eastman. – New York; London: Bantam Books, 1969. – 86p.: chiefly ill., facsims, ports; 18cm. ISBN 0-552-0433406 (pbk.)
This is mostly a collection of photographs taken by Linda McCartney, then Linda Eastman, during the years 1967 and 1968. The major stars of the period are all included. The format is unusual with page foldouts, drawings, some brief notes and song lyrics. Not informative, but a collage of the period.

Pictures and posters from 10 years of Circus: a rock & roll collectors anniversary edition / Gerald Rothberg, editor. – New York: Circus Enterprises, 1979. – 103p.: ill. (chiefly col.), facsims (chiefly col.), ports (chiefly col.); 28cm. (pbk.)
This is a beautifully produced selection of illustrations, covers and posters published by *Circus* magazine either in the magazine itself or as independent items. The colour printing is excellent and all the major artists and changing musical styles of the seventies are represented.

Rock'n'roll personality parade. – London: Weekly film news, 1957. – 33p.: chiefly ill., chiefly ports; 25cm. (pbk.)
This rare early collection of photographs of the first rock'n'roll stars includes the major American innovators as well as their British mimics. Valuable as an historical record, but the poses are frequently difficult to take seriously.

Rowlands, John
  *Spotlight heroes: two decades of rock and roll superstars as seen through the
  camera of John Rowlands.* – New York: McGraw-Hill, 1981. – 146p.: ill.,
  ports; 27cm. ISBN 0-0705-4159-0 (pbk.)
A fine collection of photographs from the sixties and seventies including the
Beatles, Rolling Stones, Bob Dylan, Rod Stewart and the Faces. It is interesting to see shots from early in their careers juxtaposed with the more recent
pictures.

Seeff, Norman
  Hot shots / photographs by Norman Seeff. – New York; London: Flash
  Books, 1974. – 90p.: chiefly ill., chiefly ports; 21cm. ISBN 0-8256-3903-4
  (pbk.)
A collection of photographs of mainly American artists by one of the most
widely acclaimed photographers of the American popular music press. Amusing and unusual, although posed, these portraits are sharp reflections of the
personalities and their world, carefully chosen to make a well-balanced and
original collection.

Yates, Paula
  Rock stars in their underpants / Paula Yates. – London: Virgin Books, 1980. –
  86p.: chiefly ill., ports; 28cm. ISBN 0-907-08005-7 (pbk.)
Paula Yates is the girlfriend of Bob Geldof of the Boomtown Rats group. She
has persuaded many of the lesser-known names in the rock world to remove
their trousers and has recorded this dubious event for posterity. The result is
pretentious, vulgar and not at all amusing. Peter Cook has written a biting
introduction which still fails to make this publication any more than a piece of
cheap commercialism.

3.8 PAINTINGS

Burns, Mal
  Visions of rock / compiled by Mal Burns. – London; New York: Proteus,
  1981. – 63p.: chiefly ill. (chiefly col.), chiefly ports (chiefly col.); 28cm.
  ISBN 0-906071-42-9 (pbk.)
Compiled by the former editor of *Record Mirror* and editor of *Flexipop*
magazine, this is a collection of caricatures of the major artists in rock music.
Divided into five sections, the first two spotlight foremost solo artists and bands
respectively, the third is devoted to rock legends, the fourth to modern cult
performers with vigorous but not wide followings, and the last section is a
collection of wildly exaggerated cartoons. Many of the performers included are
from the new wave. The intention to reflect the image of the artists' music and
stage presentation generally works, but the paintings are from a wide range of
artists, and thus the overall effect is patchy and very varied in style.

Ocean, Humphrey
  The Ocean view / Humphrey Ocean; preface by Paul McCartney. – London:
  Plexus, 1983. – 70p.: ill. (chiefly col.), ports (chiefly col.); 21cm.
  ISBN 0-85965-066-9
Paul McCartney commissioned portrait painter Humphrey Ocean to ac-
company Wings on their 1976 tour of America. The result is this excellent
collection of paintings depicting life on the road.

Peellaert, Guy
  Rock dreams / Guy Peellaert, Nik Cohn; introduction by Michael Herr. –
  London: Picador, 1982. – 154p.: chiefly col. ill., col. ports; 30cm.
  ISBN 0-330-26958-5 (pbk.)
  Originally published: London: Pan Books, 1974.
  Also published: New York: Popular Library, 1974.
This book uses the technique of photomontage, which ccombines retouched
photographic portraits superimposed on paintings that express the feel of the
artist's music and image. It is a remarkable collection of pictures which begins
with a youthful Frank Sinatra in the forties and covers the leading figures in
every area of popular music up to the early seventies, ending with an ageing
Sinatra. The images, which consistently strike the perfect mood, are annotated
with brief comments by the amusing Nik Cohn.

Sandison, David
  Oxtoby's rockers / David Sandison. – Oxford: Phaidon, 1978. – 80p.: ports
  (chiefly col.); 30cm. ISBN 0-7148-1854-2 (pbk.)
  Also published as *'The art of rock visions'*: New York: Dutton, 1978
David Oxtoby is a modern painter who has devoted his career over the past,
almost twenty years, to painting musicians from rock'n'roll stars to pop and
blues artists. He has the gift of frequently translating the essence of the
excitement of the music into a visual form, and this collection of paintings and
etchings contains good examples of such work. The reproductions are well
produced with interesting, informative notes.

3.9 RECORD SLEEVES

Album cover album / edited by Storm Thorgerson (Hipgnosis) and Roger
  Dean; introduced by Dominy Hamilton. – Limpsfield, Surrey: Dragon's
  World, 1977. – 160p.: chiefly col. ill., col facsims; 31cm. Includes index.
  ISBN 0-905895-00-2 (cased). ISBN 0-905893-01-0 (pbk.)
After an introduction including the biographies of the major designers and an
outline history of the development and increasing importance of album covers
as art and as a significant marketing factor, the reproduced album covers are
arranged first chronologically and then, for more recent designs, by style and
theme. There are brief notes on each theme and each reproduction has full

details of artist, designer and company of production. An appendix describes their creation from design stage to printing. The indexes provide easy access to a fascinating collection.

Album cover album: the second album / edited by Storm Thorgerson, Roger
    Dean & David Howells. – Limpsfield, Surrey: Dragon's World, 1982. –
    158p.: chiefly col. ill., col. facsims; 31cm. Includes index.
    ISBN 0-905895-72- X (cased). ISBN 0-905895-71-1 (pbk.)
A second volume including the significant examples of album-cover design which appeared since 1977. Arranged like the first volume, it is of the same high standard and an excellent complementary work.

Benedict, Brad
    Phonographics: contemporary album cover art & design / by Brad Benedict
    and Linda Barton. – New York: Collier Books, 1977. – 137p.: chiefly col. ill.,
    col. facsims; 31cm. Includes index. ISBN 0-02-000100-2 (pbk.)
With no attention to theme, artist or period, this collection claims to be the best work of the decade 1967 to 1977. It is a well-produced but very confusing jumble.

Dean, Roger
    Views / Roger Dean; text by Dominy Hamilton and Carla Capalbo in
    association with Roger Dean. – Ae Hendrik ido Anbacht, The Netherlands:
    Dragon's Dream; distributed by WHS Distributors, 1982. – 155p.: chiefly
    col. ill., col. facsims., col. ports; 31 cm. ISBN 90-6332-761-7 (cased).
    ISBN 90-6332-891-5 (pbk.)
    Originally published: Limpsfield, Surrey: Dragon's Dream, 1975.
Roger Dean was one of the most successful album-cover artists of the early seventies. His designs, which include the sleeves for Yes and Osibisa, present strange, timeless landscapes, curious creatures and surreal images. After a brief assessment of his work, his techniques are described in detail and his best-known designs reproduced. The text of this recent edition is in English although the new imprint is Dutch.

Errigo, Angie
    The illustrated history of the rock album cover / by Angie Errigo and Steve
    Leaning. – London: Octopus Books, 1979. – 160p.: ill. (chiefly col.), facsims
    (chiefly col.); 31cm. Includes indexes. ISBN 0-7064-0915-9 (pbk.)
A history of album covers since the late fifties grouped broadly by theme. There are many full-size reproductions as well as a chronologically arranged series of the most outstanding covers of the seventies. The indexes are to the cover designers, the record labels and recording artists.

Fame / compiled by Brad Benedict. – London: Elm Tree Press, 1981. – 119p.:
    ill. (some col.), ports (some col.); 25cm. ISBN 0-241-10537-4 (pbk.)
    Originally published: New York: Harmony Books, 1980.

Not exclusively devoted to music, and including some film stars, this collection of publicity materials, poster designs and record sleeves is well chosen and beautifully reproduced with no concept of categorizing themes or images.

Goldmann, Frank
  The gimmix book of records / edited by Frank Goldmann and Klaus ·
  Hiltscher. – London: Virgin Books, 1981. – 128p.: ill. (chiefly col.), facsims
  (chiefly col.); 30cm. Includes index. ISBN 0-90708-017-0 (pbk.)
The curiosities of the packaging and format of gramophone records are looked at with beautiful reproductions. The picture disc, which is a playable record imprinted with a picture, often but not always of the album-cover design, takes up a large portion of the book. Rare record sleeves, odd-coloured vinyls, curiously shaped records, promotional records and even records released in metal boxes are all here. Picture discs first appeared in the thirties and experienced a wide distribution in the late seventies. They have become, as have these other oddities, collector's items and this is the major single source of information on them.

Graphics: record covers / edited by Walter Herdeg. – New York: Hastings
  House, 1974. – 192p.: ill. (some col.), facsims (some col.); 26cm.
Including predominantly American record sleeves with a good collection of reproductions, this is a sound history up to the early seventies. There is more text than usual with a description of printing processes and the creative method.

Pollock, Bruce
  The face of rock & roll: images of a generation / text by Bruce Pollock; design
  by John Wagman; with a foreword by Pete Fornatale. – London: New
  English Library, 1978. – 184p.: chiefly col ill., facsims (chiefly col.); 28cm.
  Includes indexes. ISBN 0-450-04301-0 (pbk.)
  Originally published: New York: Holt, Rinehart and Winston, 1978.
Arranged by theme or the image that is portrayed. The development of the album-cover art is traced with beautifully produced reproductions and short well-written notes. Themes are taken, for example images of women, and a range of sleeve designs, juxtaposed, strike the changes in visual images over twenty years. Other themes are more musically based with the British invasion and the images of the West Coast style reflected in their covers. Included are albums ranging far wider than the rock-music field, jazz and blues being well considered. Indexes are to photographers, illustrators, designers and the recording artists.

Rock art: fifty-two record album covers / edited by Dennis Saleh. – Seaside,
  California: Comma Books, 1977. – 134p.: chiefly col. ill., facsims (chiefly
  col.); 28cm. Includes index. ISBN 0-930-75001-2 (pbk.)
A beautifully produced collection of the sleeve designs of albums released in America. Included are several albums of British artists. There is no grouping by themes or image: the editor's aim is to include aesthetically his favourite collection.

Thorgerson, Storm
An ABC of the work of Hipgnosis: 'Walk away Rene' / compiled by Hipgnosis and George Hardie; text by Storm Thorgerson; dedicated to Vanji. – 2nd ed. – Limpsfield, Surrey: Paper Tiger, 1979. – 159p.: ill. (chiefly col.), facsims (chiefly col.); 31cm. Includes index. ISBN 0-905895-09-6 (cased). ISBN 0-905895-08-8 (pbk.)
Previous edition: Limpsfield, Surrey: Dragon's World, 1978.
Storm Thorgerson, under the pseudonym Hipgnosis, is one of the most successful album-cover designers. He presents his work explaining techniques, inspirations and the creation of album covers from their inception to production. Loosely categorized by theme or by one of his various styles, the reproductions of his work are beautifully presented.

3.10 POSTERS

Farren, Mick
Get on down: a decade of rock and roll posters / edited by Mick Farren. – London: Big O Publishing Limited, 1977. – 95p.: ill. (chiefly col.), facsims (chiefly col.); 38cm. ISBN 0-905664-01-0 (pbk.)
A collection of reproductions of posters from the period 1966–75. A good introduction traces the development of this art form from its establishment as an important factor in the advertising and image-building process of the music business. As well as the psychedelic West Coast concert posters of 1966 the collection includes record advertisements and tour posters. Although some of the reproductions appear a little flat, they are faithful to the originals and make this a valuable and very good collection.

Mouse & Kelley. – Limpsfield, Surrey: Paper Tiger, 1979. – 127p.: chiefly col. ill., col. facsims: 28cm. ISBN 0-905895-30-4 (pbk.)
Stanley Miller, known as Mouse, and Alton Kelley have been leading designers of album covers and posters since the sixties. This collection of their work includes their well-known poster designs for the Grateful Dead and Steve Miller Band as well as their more recent efforts for Wings' American tours of the late seventies.

3.11 FASHION. IMAGE. TASTE

Cool Cats: twenty-five years of rock'n'roll style / edited and designed by Tony Stewart. – London: Eel Pie Publishing , 1981. – 160p.: ill., ports; 27cm. ISBN 0-906008-47-6 (pbk.)
This does not attempt any kind of sociological or artistic analyses but with over 300 photographs traces the development of the visual images and fashions presented by the stars since the mid fifties. There are five essays by three journalists and singers Ian Dury and Paul Weller of the Jam. As a collection of

portraits this is excellent but the concept requires more study than this superficial presentation. The recurrence of particular fashions is a point of particular emphasis, developing the theme of the evolution of style and the influence of the earlier on more recent stylists.

Raker, Muck
  Rock bottom: the book of pop atrocities / Muck Raker. – London; New York:
  Proteus, 1981. – 143p.: ill., facsims, ports; 28cm. ISBN 0-906071-79-8 (pbk.)
A collection of the kitsch of popular music. Examples of the most tasteless stage shows of groups such as Kiss and Alice Cooper, tasteless album sleeves, names of groups such as the 'Dead Kennedys', bad lyrics and awful compositions and the bottom-twenty albums and bottom-thirty singles charts. There are amusing examples of the least-memorable careers and failed comebacks. With the publication comes a flexidisc including some dreadful recordings. An amusing idea which almost works but is neither a serious study nor simply a humorous excursion.

CHAPTER FOUR

The popular-music business

Social expression, political commentary and artistic value are all subjects of this growing body of literature and a continuing source of debate. What is accepted, however, is that popular music has a solid, commercial motivation: it is a wealthy industry; a business. There are few artists who are not largely attracted by the potential wealth; if not as an end in itself, then certainly as a means of personal and hopefully artistic freedom: a too-frequently illusory ideal.

Originally the industry, known as Tin Pan Alley, was based on music publishing. During the first half of the twentieth century the greatest source of income came from sheet-music sales and rights. Songwriters and their publishers were the hallowed figures until the radio and the gramophone took over from the piano as the major producers of music in the home.

Record companies then took the place of publishers and songwriters and their position has grown to dominate the industry. New professions of recording engineers and record producers joined A & R men and session musicians as creative people, with a whole army of publicists, promoters, agents and pluggers engaged in selling the product: their artists, or more specifically their artists' recordings.

There is a wide variety of material on the business beginning with surveys of the complex industry, explaining how its many facets interrelate, to songwriting manuals and guides for would-be rock stars. There are histories of record companies, record-company discographies and works on activities such as festivals, concerts and touring which demonstrate the scale and complexities involved in such enterprises.

Sub-sections are, where necessary, arranged as follows: General works; Collected lives and works; Discographies.

Bygrave, Mike
  Rock / author Mike Bygrave; art director Linda Nash; special consultant
  Paul Murray. – London: Hamish Hamilton, 1977. – 61p.: ill. (some col.),
  ports (some col.); 30cm. ISBN 0-241-89643-6
  Also published: New York: Gloucester Press, 1978.
An informal glimpse of the world of rock and pop music for the school child. After a brief definition of current popular music with a section on how sound is transmitted, the author describes simply the theory of amplification and how electric guitars work. There follows a description of a successful career in the

music business, touring, recording and the disc jockey's role. After a history, which leads up to the present period and attempts to include the major styles, there is a section on jobs in the music industry other than that of performer. The illustrations are well selected and arranged, making this a good introduction. An index would have been helpful and is included in the American edition.

Cable, Michael
   The pop industry inside out / Michael Cable. – London: W. H. Allen, 1977. –
   128p.; 22cm. Includes index. ISBN 0-491-02381-2

Written by the former showbusiness correspondent of the *Daily Mail* who contributes to most national papers, this is a good survey of the development of the popular-music industry in Britain. There is a great deal of statistical information presented in an excellent section of tables and graphs. The share of the market actually taken by the various positions in the charts is a fascinating breakdown. Best-selling artists and records of all time are also listed. Every aspect of the business is covered with case studies and lengthy quotations. Two chapters of particular interest are one on pop stars who have faded from the limelight, including Brian Poole and Dave Clark, and another on the effects of stardom on the individual with the examples of Elton John and Gary Glitter. Thoroughly researched, the author's final speculation on the future of the music business is intelligent, conjecturing on the video boom which has arrived sooner than he imagined.

Chapple, Steve
   Rock'n'roll is here to pay: the history and politics of the music industry / Steve
   Chapple & Reebee Gorofalo. – Chicago: Nelson-Hall, 1977. – xv, 354p.;
   24cm. Includes bibliography and index. ISBN 0-88229-395-8 (cased).
   ISBN 0-88229-437-7 (pbk.)

This is an analysis of the growth and structure of the music industry. The first part deals with the history and economics and the second looks at the social and political nature. The constituent parts of the industry, the contributions of performers, executives, producers, advertisers and promoters are discussed in depth. Specific artists are cited as examples with profiles of their careers, statistics and economic breakdowns of their gross earnings, showing how the vast income is absorbed by the enormous multinational corporations of which even companies such as RCA are just tiny parts. The role of black people in music is discussed as is the growing power of women. The bibliography is excellent and the index thorough. This offers by far the best economic analysis of the music business available.

Dachs, David
   Anything goes: the world of popular music / David Dachs. – Indianapolis:
   Bobbs-Merrill, 1964. – 328p.: ill.; ports; 24cm. Includes index.
   Also published: Toronto: Thomas Allen, 1964.

A thorough survey of the music scene of the early sixties with some historical background but mainly an impressionistic view of changing fashions and the evolution of styles. The rock'n'roll era is well covered, as is the growth in importance of the technicians, producers, managers and promoters. There are extensive quotes from interviews with some of these behind-the-scenes figures which reflect their growing influence.

Dann, Allan
   How to succeed in the music business / Allan Dann and John Underwood. – London: Wise Publications, 1978. – 87p.: ill., facsims; 26cm.
   ISBN 0-86001-454-1 (pbk.)
A good outline of the music business for the prospective songwriter, singer and musician, by two authors who have worked in music publishing and artist management. Although very brief, this guide is well organized and extremely informative with lists of publishers, record companies and studios. There is an appendix of contracts, a guide to royalties and a glossary. The legal advice, particularly on the laws of copyright, is extremely well explained.

Dove, Ian
   Electric experience: rock and popular music / by Ian Dove. – Milwaukee: Raintree Publishers, 1976. – 128p.: ill., ports; 25cm. Includes index.
   ISBN 0-8172-0501-2 (cased). ISBN 0-8172-0500-4 (pbk.)
The world of popular music is presented here for pupils in the first years of American high schools. Informative, the lifestyle of stars is described as are the business aspects of publicity, promotion and management and a simple background to record production.

Dufour, Barry
   The world of pop and rock / written and devised by Barry Dufour; special consultant Dave Laing. – London: Macdonald Educational, 1977. – 61p.: ill., ports; 29cm. Includes bibliography, filmography and index.
   ISBN 0-356-05591-4 (cased). ISBN 0-356-05763-1 (pbk.)
Aimed as a general outline of the popular-music industry for use in schools; after a brief historical outline, there is a survey of the various facets of the business from writing and recording to management and promotion. There is a description of how the record charts work and details of the major record companies.

Farmer, Paul
   Pop / Paul Farmer. – London: Longman, 1979. – 24p.: ill., facsims, music, ports; 23cm. ISBN 0-582-21577-3 (pbk.)
A brief introduction for schools, this includes a survey of the business, an introduction to musical analysis and a section of questions and answers. Modern recording techniques and musical instruments are skilfully covered.

Hatch, Tony
   So you want to be in the music business / Tony Hatch. – London: Everest Books, 1976. – 240p., 4p of plates: ill., facsims, music, ports; 20cm.
   ISBN 0-903925-95-8 (cased). ISBN 0-903925-44-3 (pbk.)
Tony Hatch is a successful British songwriter and record producer. He has written dozens of hit songs and television themes. This guide to the music

business is practical, advising the reader on how to get started and describing techniques and pitfalls. There is a very good section on music publishing, managers and agents, explaining legal problems, and another on the rudiments of musical arrangement, scoring and harmony.

Making music: the guide to writing, performing & recording / edited by
George Martin. – London: Pan Books, 1983. – 352p.: ill., facsims, ports; 24cm. Includes bibliography and index. ISBN 0-330-25945-3 (pbk.)
An excellent, thorough guide to the music business with essays by leading artists, producers and writers. Jimmy Webb, Paul Simon and Sting write on songwriting, Paul McCartney on playing bass, Eric Clapton and John Williams on playing guitar. Everyone at the top seems to have contributed. With technical information, this is by far the best source.

Miller, William Robert
The world of pop music and jazz / William Robert Miller. – St. Louis,
Missouri; London: Concordia, 1965. – 112p.; 18cm. (pbk.)
A superficial look at the music business in the early sixties with a distinct moralizing tone. A great deal of useful information, however, can be found.

Monaco, Bob
*The platinum rainbow : how to succeed in the music business without selling
your soul* / Bob Monaco and James Riordan. – Sherman Oaks, California: Swordsman Press, 1980. – 239p.: 22cm. Includes index.
ISBN 0-940018-00-4 (pbk.)
A guide to survival in the music business for the aspiring performer and writer, it offers a straightforward survey of the industry with a tendency to oversimplify the more complex areas. An American bias is not evident.

Pike, Jeff
Rock world / Jeff Pike. – London; Marshall Cavendish Children's Books,
1979. – 61p.: col. ill., col. ports; 29cm. Includes index. ISBN 0-85685-675-4 (cased). ISBN 0-85685-738-6 (pbk.)
An outline of the music business for children and young teenagers. There is a brief analysis of the forms of popular music, hints on songwriting, forming a group, instruments, recording and aspects of the financial side. The vocabulary is carefully chosen for its aimed readership and the information is made interesting and easily available.

Plimmer, Martin
The rock factory / by Martin Plimmer. – London; New York: Proteus, 1982. –
160p.: ill., ports; 23cm. ISBN 0-86276-052-6 (cased). ISBN 0-86276-051-8 (pbk.)
This survey of the workings of the contemporary music business focusses on the world behind the stars. The roles of producers, managers, engineers and agents are well defined in a simple, readable way. The role of the music press, corruption, economics and exploitation are dealt with forthrightly but mildly.

Pollock, Bruce
It's only rock and roll / Bruce Pollock. – Boston, Massachusetts: Houghton
Mifflin, 1980. – 232p.: ill., ports; 24cm. Includes index. ISBN 0-395-29182-8
An introduction to the American contemporary music industry for the young
reader, in which all aspects are covered from production and music publishing
to performing. It is a good guide and well illustrated.

Powell, Peter
Peter Powell's book of pop / Peter Powell; illustrated by Dave Bowyer. –
London: Armada, 1980. – 123p., 16p. of plates: ill., ports; 18cm.
ISBN 0-00-691735-6 (pbk.)
An outline of the music business for the young teenager which includes
information on life on the road, record companies, the charts, inside the radio
studio and brief biographies of popular stars. There are puzzles, a simple
glossary and some good illustrations. An entertaining, accessible outline which
includes a great deal of information expressed in a simple way.

Rublowsky, John
Popular music / John Rublowsky. – New York; London: Basic Books, 1967.
– 164p., 14p. of plates: ill., ports; 24cm. Includes index.
Offering some historical background on the development of the music industry
in America, this book covers the whole spectrum of popular music. The careers
of particular artists are briefly discussed as examples. The structure of the
business, the functions of agents, managers, promoters, arrangers and so on
are all well described. It does, of course, reflect the state of the art in the mid
sixties and certain aspects (for example, recording, which is described in some
detail) have changed significantly.

Spitz, Robert Stephen
The making of superstars: artists and executives of the rock music business / by
Robert Stephen Spitz. – Garden City, New York: Anchor Press; Doubleday,
1978. – xx, 325p.; 22cm. Includes index. ISBN 0-385-12413-9
After an introduction which describes the many styles of music described by the
author as rock, this is a series of autobiographical accounts of the careers of a
selection of performers, managers, writers, producers, promoters, executives
and publicists. It is concerned with the American music business and the
subjects include major names such as John Hammond, Janis Ian, Barry
Manilow, Jon Landau, Dave Marsh, Neil Sedaka and many others. The only
British artist interviewed is Peter Frampton. The author has worked hard to
produce revealing accounts which tend to show the contrived, strategic effort
and hard work that is required for sustained success in music. Of particular
interest are the stories of these artists' early careers, the disappointments and
lucky breaks. The index is well produced, making this a useful outline of the
industry in America.

Watson, Pat
Inside the popscene / by Pat Watson. – Gloucester: Thornhill Press, 1977. –
45p : ill., ports; 22cm. Includes bibliography. ISBN 0-904110-57-5 (pbk.)

An outline of the pop scene for the teenager, this book includes a surprising amount of information. Many of the artists whose biographies are used to illustrate the road to success were at their peak two or three years earlier than the published date and it is therefore considerably out of date. Nevertheless, the information is here in a readable form with a brief guide to further reading.

4.1 Music publishing

Since the aim of the music industry changed from selling sheet music to selling gramophone records, the function of the music publisher has also evolved.

The publisher acts as an agent for the songwriter, finding recording artists, record companies, broadcasting outlets, selling rights and ensuring the income from the performing rights and royalties due. Sheet music has now taken a very low place in the publisher's order of priorities.

Goldberg, Isaac
> *Tin Pan Alley: a chronicle of American popular music* / Isaac Goldberg. With a supplement from sweet and swing to rock'n'roll / by Edward Jablowski. – New York: Frederick Ungar Publishing, 1961. – 371p. : ill., ports; 20cm.

A detailed history of the American music industry and particularly of music publishing and songwriting. The brief supplement updates the author's original text, which reaches the early fifties. The rambling style often detracts from this informative, background work.

Meyer, Hazel
> *The gold in Tin Pan Alley* / by Hazel Meyer. – Westport, Connecticut: Greenwood Press, 1977. – 258p.: 23cm. ISBN 0-8371-9694-9
> Originally published: Philadelphia, Pennsylvania: J. B. Lippincott, 1958.

A history of the music-publishing industry in America which includes the early days of rock'n'roll. The development of promotion techniques is a particular theme. Famous songs are cited as examples with their individual stories.

Rogers, Eddie
> *Tin Pan Alley* / by Eddie Rogers; as told to Mike Hennessy. – London: Robert Hale, 1964. – 196p.: ill., ports; 23cm.

Eddie Rogers was a leading song plugger in the fifties and early sixties. This is a collection of anecdotes concerning the way in which the music-publishing industry functioned at the time. The manipulation and 'hype' is seen here in its seminal period.

4.2 Songwriting

If one knows the secret of writing hit songs then it is surely a sorry waste of time to write a guide for others. Although there are hints on publishing, legal aspects and recording, in general songwriting guides are at best misleading and at worst nonsense.

Bolte, Carl E.
Successful songwriting / by Carl E. Bolte, Jr. – Kansas City, Montana: Holly
Productions, 1978. – 193p.: ill., music; 22cm.
A poor guide to songwriting technique with American-biased information.

Decker, Tom W.
So you wrote a song, now what?: a complete guide for songwriters / by Tom
W. Decker. – 2nd ed. – Tampa, Florida: Prepare the Way, 1978. – 128.: ill.,
music; 22cm. (pbk.)
A brief guide with hints on structures, themes and lyrics as well as the
background to the publishing business. Legal aspects are naturally American.

Glaser, Hy
How to write lyrics that make sense. . .and dollars / Hy Glaser. – Hicksville,
New York: Exposition Press, 1977. – 110p.: 21cm. ISBN 0-6824-8764-3
With examples of rhyming patterns, rhythmic structure and advice on writing
meaningful lyrics for various themes, this is a poorly produced, misleading
attempt.

Harris, Rolf
Write your own pop song with Rolf Harris. – London: Wolfe; Keith Prouse
Music Publishing, 1973. – 111p.: ill., facsims, music; 23cm.
ISBN 0-7234-0509-3
Rolf Harris is not only a television personality and artist but has written and
recorded a number of successful songs. This guide for the budding songwriter
has advice on composition, scoring simple melody lines, making demonstration
recordings and finding a music publisher. Accurate in information, obviously
oversimplified and overlooking the rather important facet of creativity, this is a
useful attempt.

Kasha, Al
If they ask you, you can write a song / Al Kasha and Joel Hirschhorn. – New
York: Simon and Schuster, 1979. – 352p.: ill., music; 24cm. Includes index.
ISBN 0-671-24149-4
A better-than-average attempt to impart songwriting technique to the hopeful
amateur. A strong American bias is, naturally, evident in areas of law and
business method but musical guidance is sound.

Lindsay, Martin
Teach yourself songwriting / by Martin Lindsay. – London: English
Universities Press, 1956. – x, 164p.: ill., music; 19cm.
A simple guide to composition, rhymes and the structure of popular songs,
there are many musical examples illustrating the text. Although recording
one's results is mentioned, there is little guidance to making professional
demonstration records which was almost unheard of at the time.

McNeel, Kent
How to be a successful songwriter / Kent McNeel and Mark Luther. – New
York: St. Martin's Press, 1978. – 222p.: ill., music; 28cm.

ISBN 0-3123-9586-8 (cased). ISBN 0-3123-9587-6 (pbk.)
A guide to songwriting for the American market with details on technique, musical examples, lyric methods and harmonic theory. The American music business and its contractual system is described.

Neal, Roy
Compose your own tunes : the Roy Neal tune-tutor / Roy Neal. –
Peterborough: Sceptre Publishers, 1981. – 32p.: ill., music; 31 cm. (pbk.)
A guide to the composition of pop songs with musical examples and brief notes. Simple but unlikely to be effective.

Pincus, Lee
The songwriter's success manual / by Lee Pincus. – 2nd ed. – New York:
Music Press, 1976. – 160p.: ill., music; 22cm.
Previous edition: New York: Music Press, 1974.
Techniques of lyric rhyming, simple composition and structuring songs are described, followed by methods of recording demonstration records, and then publishing and contractual problems.

Rachlin, Harvey
The songwriter's handbook / by Harvey Rachlin. – New York: Funk & Wagnalls, 1977. – xvi, 172p.: ill., facsims, music; 24cm. Includes index.
ISBN 0-308-10321-1
Written by an American songwriter, record producer and music publisher, this is a thorough, practical guide to songwriting. It covers scoring the song, making the demonstration records, copyright, publishing, arranging and contractual law in considerable detail. Although hints on the actual creation of songs are simplistic, it is the practical information that is valuable. There are appendices of record companies, music publishers, advertising agencies, a self-testing questionnaire and even musical exercises. Naturally the addresses of organizations, and much of the legal advice on copyright, are irrelevant for the British reader.

Revere, Don
How to put your song together : the rhythmograph method / by Don Revere. –
Cleveland, Tennessee: Educative Publications, 1978. – 113p.: ill.; 21cm.
A system of songwriting based on a series of rigid rhythmic structures and rhyming patterns : very odd indeed.

Warner, Jay
How to have your hit song published / by Jay Warner. – Murphys, California:
Music Bank Publications, 1978. – 197p.: ill., music; 22cm.
A general guide to songwriting, recording demonstration tapes, scoring and arranging songs. The legal and contractual advice is American, but this is a reasonable practical guide.

Wilbur, Perry
How to write songs that sell / L. Perry Wilbur. – Chicago: H. Regnery, 1977. –
x, 200p.: ill., music; 22cm. Includes index. ISBN 0-8092-7861-8 (cased).
ISBN 0-8092-7846-4 (pbk.)

A serious attempt to offer detailed advice on songwriting. Musical examples, legal aspects and an outline of the music-publishing business are all included for the American situation.

Songwriting: Collected lives and works

Staveacre, Tony
  The songwriters / Tony Staveacre. – London: British Broadcasting
  Corporation, 1980. – 191p.: ill., facsims, ports; 24cm. ISBN 0-563-17638-5
Covering the period from 1890 to 1979, this is a collection of short biographical essays of those considered to be the most influential popular songwriters. The more recent include Tim Rice and Andrew Lloyd Webber, Lionel Bart and John Lennon and Paul McCartney. The essays attempt to describe simply their method of working and inspirations and to analyse their music as well as to give outline biographies. Unhappily the analysis is superficial and the style turgid.

4.3 RECORD INDUSTRY

The image of the gargantuan record-company conglomerates, faceless and multinational in structure, cynically manipulating popular taste, resolved in the destruction of art in exchange for the dollar but always thwarted, just, by the tiny independent label, is shown in these surveys to be a very dramatic concept. Instead, the industry is shown to be as most others with the many aspects of intricate human institutions.

Davis, Clive
  Clive: inside the record business / by Clive Davis with James Willwerth. –
  New York: Ballantine, 1976. – 300p.: ill., ports; 24cm. ISBN 0-688-02872-1
  (pbk.)
  Originally published: New York: Morrow, 1975.
Written by a record-company executive in a style that is both informative and arrogant, here is a detailed description of how the record business worked in America from the mid sixties until 1972. During this period the independent record companies were absorbed by the conglomerates and the industry continued to boom in spite of the fact that a search for a new Beatles had failed. Although much of the narrative concerns the purely business aspects, it is readable and in places fascinating.

Denisoff, R. Serge
  Solid gold: the popular record industry / R. Serge Denisoff. – New
  Brunswick, New Jersey: Transaction Books, 1975. – 504p.: ill., ports; 22cm.
  Includes bibliography and index. ISBN 0-87855-586-2 (pbk.)
An excellent analysis of popular music and its industry which covers the problem of definition by a lengthy essay on just how extensive popular taste can be. There are chapters on the music press and the influence of disc jockeys as

well as a great deal of detail on the workings of the record business itself. There
is an enormous quantity of facts and statistics and a real insight into the
unscrupulous side of the business. This is a well researched, well-indexed work
with a superb bibliography and useful tabulated results of surveys on musical
taste related to age ranges within the population.

The music goes round and round: a cool look at the record industry / edited by
    Peter Gammond and Raymond Horricks. – London: Quartet Books, 1980. –
    183p., 16p. of plates: ill., facsims, ports; 23cm. ISBN 0-7043-2239-0 (pbk.)
This collection of essays is a glimpse of the record industry written by the
backroom workers: the producers, engineers, executives and promoters. Each
writer explains his personal contribution. The history of the industry is outlined
with a good collection of illustrations. Avoiding technicalities, the recording of
all types of music is discussed. The transcripts of interviews are also included
and offer a revealing slant to some of the subjects. There is an appendix of
biographical notes on the contributors.

Schicke, C. A.
    Revolution in sound: a biography of the recording industry / C. A. Schicke. –
    Boston, Massachusetts: Little, Brown, 1974. – 246p.: ill., ports; 24cm.
    Includes index. ISBN 0-316-77733-6
A thorough history from early in the century to the beginning of the seventies,
systematically describing developments. Technical innovations as well as the
politics of the industry, its influences and power, are analysed.

Stokes, Geoffrey
    Star-making machinery: inside the business of rock and roll / by Geoffrey
    Stokes. – New York: Vintage Books, 1977. – 234p.: ill., ports; 24cm.
    Includes index. ISBN 0-394-72432-1
    Originally published as '*Star-making machinery: the odyssey of an album*':
    Indianapolis: Bobbs-Merrill, 1976.
Regarded by many as the best study of the American recording industry and its
workings. The author spent a period of several months studying Commander
Cody and His Lost Planet Airmen, a country-rock band, as they recorded an
album and watched it fail to become successful. His conclusion is that the
musician is merely a worker for the giant media corporations and essentially
powerless to do anything to affect the sales of his work. His arguments are
convincing.

RECORD COMPANIES

Atlantic Records

Formed as a small independent company in 1947, Atlantic was to become one
of the most influential forces in black music for the next three decades. Early on

featuring jazz and rhythm & blues records, its small subsidiary Cat label released the song Sh'boom, regarded by many as the first authentic rock'n'roll record. Later dominated by soul music, Atlantic was eventually taken over by the Warner Corporation.

Gillett, Charlie
Making tracks: Atlantic records and the growth of a multi-billion-dollar industry / Charlie Gillett. – St. Albans: Panther, 1975. – 238p., 32p. of plates: ill., ports; 18cm. ISBN 0-586-04018-8 (pbk.)
Originally published: London: W. H. Allen, 1975.
The history of Atlantic Records is traced from its rise as a small, independent company which grew during the fifties from obscurity to prominence and absorption. The growth of the independent record labels had much to do with the growth of rock'n'roll and in the case of Atlantic the exposure of black musicians to a larger white audience. This is not simply a look at the business, however, but an insight into its relationship with the creators of the music itself, their exploitation and successes.

Ruppli, Michel
Atlantic Records: a discography / compiled by Michel Ruppli. – Westport, Connecticut: Greenwood Press, 1979. – 4v.: ill., ports; 24cm. Includes indexes. ISBN 0-313-21170-1
A unique four-volume work, this lists almost 40,000 recordings released by Atlantic Records between 1947 and 1978. Ranging from jazz to soul, white rock to disco, the main arrangement is by Atlantic's master-numbering system. Volume 1 covers the period up to 1966, volume 2 1966 to 1970, volume 3 1970 to 1974 and volume 4 1974 to 1978. Citations include title and recording date with details of the personnel involved and even material recorded at each session but not released. Indexes of artists' names offer an alternative approach but are not well prepared.

Brunswick

The Brunswick-Balke-Collender Company of Chicago began producing records after the First World War and its British company began in 1930. It evolved into the British outlet of American Decca and was maintained until 1968 when MCA, into which American Decca had been absorbed, became an independent label. Brunswick was responsible for the British release of the two enormously successful records White Christmas by Bing Crosby and Rock Around the Clock by Bill Haley.

British Brunswick singles history: 1952 to 1967. – Bromley, Kent: Record Information Services, 1978. – 41p.; 30cm. (unbound)
A straightforward chronological arrangement by record number. There is no artist index. The label history and editorial notes are excellent. There is a twelve-page supplement, published in June 1980, which gives amendments as well as additional matrix and US catalogue-number information.

Capitol

Songwriter Johnny Mercer, Paramount Pictures executive producer Buddy da Sylva and a Hollywood record-store magnate formed the Capitol company in 1941. Peggy Lee, Nat King Cole, Dean Martin, Les Paul and Mary Ford and Frank Sinatra made it an enormous success. In 1955 EMI gained a controlling interest in Capitol, giving the company an American outlet as well as a share of a thriving market. In the early sixties Capitol's artists included the Beach Boys and the Beatles and by the late sixties and seventies Helen Reddy, Neil Diamond, Paul McCartney and Diana Ross. Variety has been the key to success but the acquiring of such big names has been costly and has added to the company's current financial difficulties.

British Capitol singles & E.P.s, Part One: 1948–1955. – London: Record
Information Services, 1977. – 41p.; 30cm. Includes index. (unbound)
Arranged in chronological record-number order with an artist index, Capitol's 1955 releases include no rock'n'roll but crooners of the time such as Dean Martin and Frank Sinatra, as well as jazz.

Pelletier, Paul M.
British Capitol 45 r.p.m. singles catalogue: 1954–1981 / Paul M. Pelletier. –
Chessington, Surrey : Record Information Services, 1982. – 71p. : ill.,
facsims; 21cm. ISBN 0-907872-00-X (pbk.)
Showing a great improvement in quality of production, this is the first of a new series of discographies from Paul Pelletier's Record Information Services. Arranged by record number and including releases of December 1953, each record is meticulously listed. There are illustrations of the changing design of Capitol's record labels and some excellent editorial notes and history of the company.

London

The London label was established in New York in 1947 by the British Decca company and introduced in Britain in 1949. Originally London records were pressed in Britain and exported to the USA but this soon changed. Slim Whitman and Billy Daniels were early London successes and in November 1953 Bill Haley and the Comets had an early release. Jim Reeves, John Lee Hooker, Fats Domino, T-Bone Walker, as well as Little Richard and Pat Boone, show the variety and importance of artists on the label.

British London / London Jazz E. P. listing. – 2nd ed. – London: Record
Information Services, 1976. – 33p.; 30cm. (unbound)
Previous edition; London: Record Information Services, 1975.
Arranged chronologically, by record number, with an artist index, this covers releases from November 1954 to June 1956. The wide variety of music on the label is notable.

British London Jazz complete L. P. listing. – London: Record Information
Services, 1976. – 49p.; 30cm. (unbound)

Arranged chronologically by record number, with no index, this covers from November 1955 to June 1962. Mostly mainstream jazz; Ray Charles is included.

British London singles / Felsted popular singles & EPs listing: Part One. – 2nd ed. – London: Record Information Services, 1976. – 39p.; 30cm. (unbound) Previous edition: London: Record Information Services, 1975.

Arranged chronologically by record number, with no index, this covers London releases from October 1949 to September 1961. The Felsted label was created by Decca in 1954 to deal with continental jazz artists. In 1958 and 1959 it released twenty-nine records by popular singers, transferring activities to London.

Sue

The Sue label was established in Britain at the end of 1963 as a subsidiary of the Island label formed in 1961 by Chris Blackwell. Sue was actually an American label, owned and formed by Juggy Murray in 1957. Between 1963 and 1968 Sue concentrated on releasing American material, mainly of black artists with some early rhythm & blues and rock'n'roll releases. The final record was released in June 1968.

British Sue complete singles, E. P.s & L. P.s listing. – London: Record Information Services, 1976. – 25p.; 30cm. (unbound)

The complete listing of this rare label arranged chronologically, in record number sequence. There is a history of the label and an index by artist.

Sun Records

After working as an engineer at the WERC radio station in Memphis, Sam Phillips began his recording service, which was to become Sun Records, in 1950. For four dollars one could make one's own 78 r.p.m. record with the crudest of equipment. Famous black artists such as Howlin' Wolf, B. B. King and Bobby Bland recorded in the studio and their records became hits. The first Sun release was in March 1952 and it was in the autumn of 1953 that Elvis Presley walked into the studio to make a birthday recording for his mother, or so legend has it. In July 1954 Elvis made his first professional recording for Phillips, who saw in the young singer the fusion of black rhythm & blues and white country music; the rest is history. After Elvis, Jerry Lee Lewis, Johnny Cash, Roy Orbison and a host of others were to follow, all taking advantage of the famous Sun sound, which is regarded as authentic rockabilly.

Escott, Colin
Catalyst: the Sun Records story / Colin Escott and Martin Hawkins. – London: Aquarius Books, 1975. – 173p., 24p. of plates: ill., facsims, ports; 21cm. Includes bibliography, discography and index. ISBN 0-9046-1900-1 (pbk.)

Well organized and packed with information, this is a disappointing attempt at an important subject. Nevertheless, the major artists are here and there is an emphasis on the influence of Phillips on his young protégés, his recording techniques and artistic importance.

Escott, Colin
   Sun Records: the brief history of the legendary record label / Colin Escott and Martin Hawkins. – New York; London: Omnibus Press, 1980. – 184p.: ill.; facsims, ports; 23cm. Includes bibliography and discography.
   ISBN 0-86001-775-3 (pbk.)
A brief version of the authors' *Catalyst* which includes the essential information as well as an appendix of biographies of the best-known artists. The illustrations are well selected and there is a complete list of recordings and a good bibliography.

Top Rank / Stateside

Top Rank Records was formed in January 1959 by the Rank Organisation. The only consistently successful artist was Craig Douglas and in 1960 the company sold out to EMI. The new company continued with the label until April 1962 when it was discontinued. The British artists were transferred to other labels and the American artists transferred to Stateside. During the sixties this label took over from Decca's London label in the importing of American artists. In April 1974 the label was finally discontinued when EMI introduced the EMI label to include its British Columbia and Parlophone as well as American imports.

British Top Rank — Stateside Long-Play listing. – London: Record Information Services, 1975. – 43p.; 30cm. (unbound)
This title covers Stateside albums up to December 1970 beginning with Top Rank albums of 1959, including some 10″ discs. The later Stateside records precede the earlier Top Rank releases. There is full discographical information with track titles arranged chronologically by record number. The notes by Paul Pelletier are excellent.

British Top Rank — Stateside — Triumph — Palette singles / E. P. Listing. – London: Record Information Services, 1976. – 2nd ed. – 41p.; 30cm.
   Previous edition: London: Record Information Services, 1975. (unbound)
A complete listing of Top Rank and Stateside singles as well as those of the small Triumph and Palette subsidiary companies. Arranged chronologically by record number, it has no artist indexes but excellent notes and histories.

Tamla Motown

The Tamla Motown organization, which is the largest black-owned corporation in America, was formed by Berry Gordy Jr. in 1960. He was working on the production line of a Detroit car factory and writing songs in his spare time when in 1958 one of them became an enormous hit for Jackie Wilson. He followed this with another success in 1959 and decided he could do better with his own label. He named it Tamla and Motown, short for the 'motortown', or Detroit. He distributed records for his sister's company, the Anna label, and had his first success with the classic song Money in 1961. From then on he signed the Miracles, the Supremes, Diana Ross, Marvin Gaye, the Four Tops, the Temptations, Stevie Wonder and many more successful black acts. In addition, he had a powerful songwriting trio of Eddie and Brian Holland and Lamont Dozier, as well as a superb production team which evolved a distinctive 'Motown' sound. By the mid sixties Tamla Motown was the biggest independent record company in America with the two most commercially successful acts of the period in the Supremes and the Four Tops. A rock label, Rare Earth, was launched in 1971 and the company also moved to the West Coast. The music became more sophisticated and some of the major artists began to leave. Nevertheless Diana Ross, Marvin Gaye and Stevie Wonder continued to sell millions of records and in 1975 Tamla Motown offered the latter a record twelve-million-dollar contract. The company had become one of the top record-producing organizations in the world.

Benjaminson, Peter
The story of Motown / by Peter Benjaminson. New York: Grove Press, 1979. – 180p: ill., ports; 30cm. Includes discography and index.
ISBN 0-394-17554-9 (pbk.)
A well-illustrated history of the Tamla Motown record company which has a concise and informative text. There is a list of every single to reach the American top-twenty charts between 1961 and 1971 with full discographical details. This is a reasonable outline but not a definitive history.

British Tamla Motown complete listing: Part One (1959 to 1970 inclusive). – New Malden, Surrey: Record Information Services, 1980. – 41p.: ill., facsims; 21cm. (unbound)
Originally published : New Malden, Surrey : Record Information Services, 1976.
Arranged chronologically in record-number order, this listing includes Tamla Motown records released in Britain on Fontana, Stateside, Oriole and London labels. There are full discographical details and a brief history of the company.

British Tamla Motown complete listing: Part Two (1971 to August, 1975). – London: Record Information Services, 1977. – 41p.; 30cm. (unbound)
Arranged chronologically by record number, the first section includes singles followed by albums with full discographical information listing each track.

Morse, David
Motown and the arrival of black music / David Morse. – London: Studio Vista, 1971. – 111p.: ill., facsims, ports; 21cm. ISBN 0-289-70131-7 (cased). ISBN 0-289-70136-9 (pbk.)
Originally published: New York: Macmillan, 1971.
A good, brief outline of the rise of Motown. There are illustrations of all the major artists, biographical notes and some analysis of their styles. It unfortunately lacks a discography and an index would have been useful.

4.4 RECORD PRODUCTION

Record production, or the recording, balancing and mixing of instruments and voices to construct a cohesive work, has increasingly become recognized as a significant creative facet in successful records. There are many general works on tape-recording techniques but here are books which aim to describe the methods of production towards a specifically musical end.

Anderton, Craig
> *Home recording for musicians* / by Craig Anderton. – New York: Guitar Player Books, 1978. – 187p.: ill.; 28cm. Includes bibliography and index. ISBN 0-89122-019-4 (pbk.)

A guide which describes all aspects of recording from the placing of microphones and the dynamics of different instruments to the technical complexities of tape machines and multi-track recording. There are technical specifications, detailed illustrations and an audiodisc of examples of recording techniques.

Connelly, Will
> *The musician's guide to independent record production* / Will Connelly. – Chicago, Illinois: Contemporary Books, 1981. – 208p.: ill.; 22cm. ISBN 0-8092-5969-9 (cased). ISBN 0-8092-5968-0 (pbk.)

A guide to the setting up of a small recording studio as a commercial venture and method of producing one's own demonstration records. A sound manual from both a technical and business standpoint. The American bias detracts in no way from the usefulness of this very good guide.

Lambert, Dennis
> *Producing hit records* / by Dennis Lambert; with Ronald Zalkind; foreword by Al Coury. – New York: Schirmer Books; London: Collier Macmillan, 1980, 196p.: ill.; 24cm. ISBN 0-02-871950-6 (cased). ISBN 0-02-871960-3 (pbk.)

Written by an American producer with over fifteen years' experience, this covers every aspect of making records. The book gives technical advice on equipping the studio, organizing sessions, recording specific instruments and mixing tapes. The roles of producers, engineers, arrangers and A & R men are well defined, and there is advice on financial aspects from raising initial capital to contracts. It comes with an enclosed audiodisc of some examples of recording techniques which is, unfortunately, very poor.

Rapaport, Diane Sward
> *How to make and sell your own record: the complete guide to independent recording* / Diane Sward Rapaport. – New York: Quick Fox, 1979. – 167p.: ill., facsims, ports; 28cm. Includes index. ISBN 0-8256-9932-0 (pbk.)

Until the late seventies the concept of the small, independent record company had not been a reality in Britain whereas it had been commonplace in the USA for many years. This is a guide to setting up your own record company, from detailed guidance on recording and mixing techniques, to designing and producing record sleeves, promotion and the legal aspects of contracts and performing rights. Although this latter area relates to American law, the guidance offered in the practical and technical aspects is exceptionally useful, particularly in the areas of planning the total project which even covers details such as stock control and printing.

Talmy, Shel
  How to succeed in recording by really trying / Shel Talmy. – London: Mills
  Music, 1964. – 19p.: ill., ports; 19cm. (pbk.)
Born in Chicago, the author came to Britain in the early sixties and became one of the most creative record producers of the period. He worked with the Who, the Kinks, Manfred Mann and the Easybeats among others and produced many classic records including My Generation and Waterloo Sunset. He left the recording industry in the early seventies to become a book publisher, returning only to produce an album for Ralph McTell in 1976 which failed to be released. He offers an extremely brief look at the state of the art of recording in 1964. Talmy had produced a series of successful songs by this time but was yet to produce his masterpieces. From an historical point of view this is an interesting little work which gives an insight into the simple techniques and equipment of the period.

Record production: Collected lives and works

Tobler, John
  The record producers / John Tobler & Stuart Grundy. – London: British
  Broadcasting Corporation, 1982. – 248p.: ill., ports; 30cm. Includes
  discographies and index. ISBN 0-583-17958-9 (pbk.)
Published to complement the BBC radio series of the same title, this is an excellent collection of the career biographies of the best-known producers including Phil Spector, Tom Dowd, Bill Szymczyk, Todd Rundgren, Chris Thomas, Roy Thomas Baker, George Martin, Mickie Most, Tony Visconti, Chinn and Chapman and Richard Perry. Each chapter is followed by a separate discography of the work of the preceding producer. Filled with quotations and technical background, there is a great deal of information here which takes the mystique from the stars and demonstrates the significance of producers and engineers in the creation of musical sounds.

RECORDING STUDIOS

Southall, Brian
  Abbey Road: the story of the world's most famous recording studio / Brian
  Southall; foreword by Paul McCartney; preface by George Martin;
  additional research and original idea by Peter Vince and Allan Rouse. –
  Cambridge: Patrick Stephens, 1982. – 217p.: ill., ports; 24cm. Includes
  discography and index. ISBN 0-85059-601-7
The fifty-year history of Abbey Road, the studios of the EMI record company, is written with considerable detail by the company's chief press officer. Abbey

Road is associated heavily with the Beatles, who named an album after the studio, and a remarkable number of all-time famous recordings have been made there. The book includes lengthy reminiscences from producers, engineers and artists, a great deal of fascinating historical and technical background, and an excellent collection of illustrations. There is a glossary of technical terms and a discography of all number-one hits recorded at the studio. This is, therefore, a history of a studio and the development of recording technique.

4.5 RADIO DISC JOCKEYS

Radio has always been the natural medium for the spreading of recorded music and played a significant part in popularizing the jazz and dance music of the thirties and forties. In the USA, with its proliferation of local stations playing for specific tastes, the influence of radio has been very important. Many artists gained wide popularity either by being resident musicians on regular shows or working as disc jockeys: Elvis Presley certainly gained his feel for black music from the local Memphis rhythm & blues station. Before most people in the mid-West and southern states of America owned a gramophone, Nashville's weekly Grand 'Ole Opry radio show was building the following of country music, while without the work of disc jockey Alan Freed rock'n'roll might never have gained its hold on a mass audience.

In Britain for a long time the only commercial station available to most receivers was Radio Luxembourg and thus until the explosion of commercial private radio in the mid sixties, the influence of the disc jockey, not a general feature on the BBC, was limited. Luxembourg's Honey Hit Parade with Kent Walton was an exception and Jack Jackson's shows on the BBC Light Programme were always innovative and influential. In the mid sixties with Radios Caroline, London, North Sea International, Jackie and all the others, the pattern changed, leading to a revolution in BBC broadcasting, the legalizing of commercial stations and the evolution of local radio.

By the late sixties the disc jockey had become an important figure in the United Kingdom: if Tony Blackburn featured a single on his Breakfast Show it was assured a place in the charts and a play on John Peel's Top Gear gave an album track credibility with the 'underground'.

Works included here are specifically concerned with radio as a medium of popular music and with the disc jockey's role.

Alex, Peter
   Who's who in pop radio / by Peter Alex. – London: New English Library,
   1966. – 128p.: ill., ports; 19cm. (pbk.)
Brief biographies of the leading disc jockeys of the time. They had just come to real prominence in Britain with the growth of the pirate radio stations. There are portraits and photographs of contemporary equipment and conditions of work which are of particular interest.

Harris, Paul
  When pirates ruled the waves / by Paul Harris. – London: Impulse
  Publications, 1968. – x, 206p.: ill., ports; 23cm.
An excellent survey of the British pirate-radio phenomenon which was such an
important influence on current independent broadcasting. Operating from
ships anchored in the Channel, stations such as Caroline and Radio London not
only beat the restrictions on broadcasting for several years but also trained
most of the current leading disc jockeys. Most of the stations are included here
with insight into their organization and their leading personalities. Written
without the benefit of hindsight, there is no analysis of their true significance,
for without them and their pop-dominated shows the BBC would not have
been forced into forming Radio One from the old Light Programme.

Passman, Arnold
  The deejays / by Arnold Passman. – New York: Macmillan, 1971. – 320p.:
  ill., ports; 24cm. Includes index
Beginning with a general history of the growth of radio in the USA the main
theme is its change from a diverse medium into a disc-playing one. The style is
very turgid but the book gives a great deal of information, particularly on Alan
Freed, Dick Clark, Tom Donahue and others who promoted the development
of rock'n'roll.

Radio 1 on show. – Bristol: Radio 1 Offers, 1979. – 36p.: chiefly ill. (some col.),
  ports (some col.); 30cm. (pbk.)
A collection of portraits of the BBC Radio One disc jockeys and each of their
favourite recording artists. There are advertisements, a quiz and illustrations of
the disc jockeys involved in promotional activities, playing football and with
their fans.

Rosko, Emperor
  Emperor Rosko's DJ book / ideas by Rosko; translated into English and
  written by Johnny Berling. – London: Everest Books, 1976. – 224p., 24p. of
  plates: ill., facsims, ports; 20cm. Includes index. ISBN 0-903925-92-3
  (cased). ISBN 0-903925-91-5 (pbk.)
Written by the well-known BBC Radio One disc jockey and an executive
producer with the BBC. After outlining Rosko's career, the book develops into
a useful guide for the aspiring DJ. There is advice on auditioning, presentation
and programming as well as information on sources of records, record companies and the technical side of equipment. The index is good and there is a
useful collection of illustrations.

See, David
  How to be a disc jockey / David See. – London: Hamlyn, 1980. – 87p.: ill.
  (some col.), facsims, ports (some col.); 29cm. Includes index.
  ISBN 0-600-34642-0
Written by a leading club disc jockey and contributor to the magazine *Disco
International*, this is a genuine attempt to give a brief guide to the techniques of

working as a disc jockey. There is considerable technical detail, photographs of equipment, flow charts, hints on programming and even advice on legal aspects and insurance: in general a well-produced guide.

Williamson, Bill
  The dee jay book / research by Bill Williamson. – London: Parnell, 1969. – 156p.: ill., ports; 26cm.
A look behind the scenes at the work of the leading disc jockeys including those from pirate stations Radio Caroline and Radio London. Jimmy Savile and a youthful Tony Blackburn are featured.

4.6 ARTISTS, GROUPS, BANDS

How to become a pop or rock artist, what the job is actually like and advice on how to conduct one's career are the themes of the following works. Not an inspiring collection, but *How to run a beat group*, by the Hollies, is a very interesting early exception.

Barlow, David
  The Instant Sunshine book with hints for struggling supergroups / David Barlow; songs by Peter Christie; drawings by Heath. – London: Robson, 1980. – 96p.: ill.; 24cm. ISBN 0-86051-119-7
A vaguely humorous look at the lifestyle of rock musicians, written by Instant Sunshine, a comedy act who specialize in satirical, sometimes witty, songs. The songs included here are not witty.

Collier, James Lincoln
  Making music for money / by James Lincoln Collier; illustrations by Robert Censoni. – London: Franklin Watts, 1979. – 63p.: ill.; 24cm. Includes index. ISBN 0-85166-797-X
  Originally published: New York: Franklin Watts, 1976.
A simple guide to forming a group and playing for money. It is written and aimed at the early teenager and concentrates on the very basic aspects, including extremely sparse information on equipment, but such concepts as leadership and practical guidance on managing rehearsals are here. It neither glamorizes the popular music world nor does it make the process of success seem easily obtainable but it fails to be a really useful practical guide.

Gelly, David
  The facts about a pop group: featuring Wings / introduction by Paul McCartney; by David Gelly; photographed by Homer Sykes. – London: Whizzard with Deutsch, 1976. – 47p.: ill. (some col.), facsims, music, ports (some col.); 29cm. ISBN 0-233-96771-0
A look at a famous pop group with an emphasis on the organization supporting the performers. Aimed at the teenage reader, there is a serious attempt to offer information not available elsewhere. There is a complete list and diagram of

the staff and equipment required to set up a tour, down to the accommodation problems. The making of a record from the composition of the song, to the recording and production and then marketing, is dealt with concisely and accurately. Well illustrated and concisely written, this is a good attempt to offer a serious approach to a young reader.

Gorman, Clem
Backstage rock: behind the scenes with the bands / Clem Gorman;
    photographs by Jan Turvey. – London: Pan Books, 1978. – 205p., 8p. of
    plates: ill., ports; 18cm. Includes index. ISBN 0-330-25583-5 (pbk.)
Starting with a look at the complex organization of presenting live perform-ances for a rock band, the author portrays the rock world as one with a rigidly feudal structure. He sees the performers as the knights, the promoters and producers as the lords, the road crew as the peasants and so on. The book then develops into a more general look at all aspects of the popular-music business from types of venues and record companies to the politics and finances involved, the implications of contracts and groupies. Although using examples of some specific artists, this general survey ends with the author's personal view of how the industry will develop. This is a good look at the business, filled with useful facts and written by an inquisitive fan.

Hollies, The
How to run a beat group / as told to Anne Nightingale; pictures by Bruce
    Fleming. – London: *Daily Mirror*, 1964. – 100p.: ill., ports; 19cm. (pbk.)
Formed in Manchester in 1963 by Allan Clarke, Tony Hicks, Bobby Elliott, Eric Haydock and Graham Nash (who was later to form the internationally successful Crosby, Stills and Nash group), the Hollies were one of the most successful British groups of the Beat period and between 1963 and 1970 they had a sequence of twenty-one top-twenty hits. After Nash left in 1968 he was replaced by Terry Sylvester. The group continued to add to their success until 1971 when Clark left to pursue a solo career, but inexplicably a record made some time before suddenly reached the top of the American charts and he returned. The Hollies continued to have a successful cabaret career and in 1976 they released an album of their live show which reached the British charts, followed the next year by a greatest-hits album. The Hollies still command a position of respect in British popular music, having had more top-twenty single records than any other group including, surprisingly, the Beatles.

This title was a guide for aspiring young musicians at that time, with advice on choosing equipment, transport, engagements, stage dress and performance. The Hollies were regarded very widely as one of the groups with the most professional approach and this guide gives an excellent picture of life on the road in the sixties. That things have changed makes it more valuable historically.

How t'make it as a rockstar / editor Zip Lecky, assistant editor Tony Benyon. –
    London: IPC Magazines, 1977. – 36p.: chiefly ill. (some col.); 30cm. (pbk.)
Produced in magazine format, this is a superficial guide to entering the music business as a performer. It outlines the structure of the business, the vast army

of people who work behind the scenes in support, and the pitfalls of stardom. The illustrations are not very instructive and the text is of little informational value.

Lawrence, Sharon
So you want to be a rock & roll star / Sharon Lawrence. – London: Star
Books, 1978. – 175p., 8p of plates: ill., ports; 18cm. ISBN 0-352-30162-7
(pbk.)
This claims to tell you everything about the music business from the standpoint of the performer, from how to get your first bookings to how to deal with stardom. The information was gathered from a variety of sources including interviews with top stars, executives, technicians and writers. The glib, journalistic style, however, often detracts from any real information and practical guidance on, for example, legal aspects or economics is far too generally expressed. In conclusion, it succeeds only in increasing the mystique and exclusiveness and is frequently sensational in approach.

Paige, David
The day in the life of a rock musician / by David Paige; photography by Roger
Ruhlin. – Mahwah, New Jersey: Troll Associates, 1980. – 32p.: ill.; 24cm.
ISBN 0-8937-5225-8 (cased). ISBN 0-8937-5229-0 (pbk.)
Written for a reading age of about ten, it is in a series which aims to involve children with topics that encourage reading, extend vocabulary and introduce contemporary information. It is informative, depicting the technical and mundane side of a musician's life, the hard work as well as just a little of the glamour.

Professional rock and roll / Herbert H. Wise, editor. – London: Collier;
Collier-Macmillan, 1968. – 94p.: ill., music; 28cm. (pbk.)
Originally published: New York: Amsco Music, 1967.
Written by experts in their various fields as a basic introduction to the business, here is advice on forming and playing in a band. The book contains technical information, advice on the choice of instruments, musical hints and information on music publishing and management. Now in many ways out of date, in its time it was a useful guide but with a definite American bias.

Rappoport, Victor D.
Making it in music / Victor D. Rappoport. – Englewood Cliffs, New Jersey:
Prentice-Hall, 1979. viii, 311p.; 20cm. Includes index. ISBN 0-1354-7612-7
(cased). ISBN 0-1354-7604-6 (pbk.)
Aimed as a practical guide for the singer-songwriter, this offers advice on how to break into the music business. The early steps of recording demonstration records, hints on songwriting and auditioning are all here. The advice on the legal and contractual aspects is in an American context, which makes it less useful to the English reader.

4.7 CONCERTS

Farren, Mick
  Rock'n'roll circus: the illustrated rock concert / by Mick Farren and George
  Snow. – London: Pierrot Publishing Ltd., 1978. – 117p.: ill. (some col.),
  facsims, ports (some col.); 26cm. ISBN 0-905301010-1 (pbk.)
This is a collection of photographs of performing musicians, the preparation of
setting-up equipment, backstage shots of the tense anticipation and nervous
antics. Included are illustrations of artists across a wide spectrum of rock music.

Lewis, Laurie
  The concerts / Laurie Lewis; with a foreword by John Peel. – Limpsfield:
  Paper Tiger, 1979. – 119p.: col. ill., col. ports; 31cm. ISBN 0-95089-542-8
  (pbk.)
  Also published: New York: A & W Visual Library, 1979.
After a brief introduction, this is a visual history of the rock concert from the
late sixties to the late seventies. The beautifully produced colour photographs
include the Band, Jimi Hendrix and the Rolling Stones, as well as groups such
as the Sex Pistols and the Damned.

TOURING

Gold, Mick
  Rock on the road / edited and photographed by Mick Gold. – London:
  Futura Publications, 1976. – 160p.: ill., ports; 25cm. ISBN 0-8600-7323-8
  (pbk.)
A look at the life of touring musicians. The author toured with a series of the
most successful groups of the early seventies. Both the hectic lifestyle and the
complex organization are looked at, as well as the effect on the musicians.
There is a good collection of photographs.

4.8 FESTIVALS

When one thinks of the pop festival the image of Woodstock is always to the
fore. Music festivals have in fact been held since the early fifties in the USA.
The Newport Jazz Festival and, in England, the Cambridge Folk Festival were
always events of fraternal enjoyment and as early as 1958 there was a large jazz
festival in Richmond, Surrey, organized by Harold Pendleton. In 1963 the
Rolling Stones, Georgie Fame and Long John Baldry were featured, so that
this year saw the beginnings in Britain of true pop, rock festivals. The peak was
in the late sixties and early seventies. Festivals still continue on both sides of the
Atlantic but without the fervour of those early days. The violence of the
notorious Rolling Stones festival at Altamont in 1969 probably marks the end
of the idealism of such events.

Gahr, David
The festival song book / photographs by David Gahr; text by Paul Nelson and Tony Glover. – New York: Simon and Schuster, 1974. – 350p.: ill., ports; 24cm. ISBN 0-671-20983-3

A pictorial account of the development of the music festival from its beginnings in the folk revival of the fifties to the great rock festivals of the late sixties. Paul Nelson's essay examines the social aspects of the phenomenon. It is the photographic record which is unusual, however, offering a superb collection of candid shots of artists and audiences. There is an appendix of song lyrics.

Hopkins, Jerry
Festival!: the book of American music celebrations; San Jose rock festival, Newport folk festival, Woodstock music & arts fair, Monterey jazz festival, Ann Arbor blues festival, Memphis blues festival, Big Sur folk revival, Salinas country and western music festival, Galar, Va., fiddlers convention, North Carolina bluegrass and squaredance festival, Mt. Clemens pop festival, Berkeley folk festival, Amen! / text Jerry Hopkins; photographs Jim Marshall, Baron Wolman. – New York: Macmillan; London: Collier-Macmillan, 1970. – 191p.: ill., ports; 29cm. ISBN 0-02-580170-8 (cased). ISBN 0-02-061950-2 (pbk.)

Hopkins' excellent essays on some of the major American music festivals of the late sixties are combined with some superb atmospheric photographs. Some of the text originally appeared in *Rolling Stone* magazine and one article is in the author's book *The rock stars*.

Sandford, Jeremy
Tomorrow's people / Jeremy Sandford, Ron Reid. – London: Jerome Publishing Co., 1974. – 128p.: ill. (some col.), ports (some col.); 30cm. ISBN 0-904125-05-X (pbk.)

After a brief outline of the history of pop-music festivals, this is a detailed survey of festivals organized in Britain between 1967 and 1973. There is far more detail of the later festivals of this period, profusely illustrated with photographs of the hippie audiences and some of the musicians. Sandford, author of socially aware television plays such as Cathy Come Home and Edna the Inebriate Woman, always has an eye for the social reasons behind such gatherings, the social vacuum existing for young people, their need to create an alternative culture and so on. Far from satisfactory, this does offer an insight into being involved in such festivals, and nostalgia for those of us who have had the privilege.

Santelli, Robert
Aquarius rising: rock festival years / Robert Santelli. – New York: Dell Publishing, 1980. – 292p.: ill., ports; 24cm. Includes bibliography and index. ISBN 0-440-50956-4 (pbk.)

This definitive history of American music festivals covers the period between 1967 and 1978, giving detailed descriptions of all the major occasions. There is a list of each event listing performers, attendance, place, time and notes on additional notable features. There is much information on the economics of festivals with a fascinating list of Woodstock's expenses. The illustrations are well chosen and the bibliography limited but useful. Many of the events described will be unknown to the British reader and this offers a unique source of information on these.

Altamont

Aimed by the Rolling Stones as a sequel to Woodstock, at which they did not play, the Altamont concert was held in December 1969. Hell's Angels were to act as marshals but during the frenzy induced by building tension and by the excellent performance of the Jefferson Airplane, second on the bill to the Stones, the Angels brutally abused the audience as well as Marty Balin of the Airplane. The culmination was the savage stabbing to death of Meredith Hunter, a member of the audience. The action was well reproduced in the filmed documentary, Gimme Shelter, released in 1970. If Woodstock is regarded as the height of Hippie culture, Altamont is the end.

Eisen, Jonathan
  Altamont: death of innocence in the Woodstock generation / Jonathan Eisen.
  – New York: Avon, 1970. – 168p.; 18cm. (pbk.)
Eisen looks at the festival, analysing the reasons for its disastrous result. Blame is largely placed on the Stones themselves but he regards the disaster as inevitable in the context of time and a sad reflection on human nature.

Cambridge Folk Festival

After the success of the Newport Folk Festival, which first took place in 1959, similar annual gatherings began to spring up all over America. The festival first held in Cambridge, Massachusetts, in 1962 was a leading event which featured the major artists and acted as a showcase for new talent. A feature of Cambridge was its progressive view of folk music and inclusion of electric bands, folk rock and singer-songwriters.

Von Schmidt, Eric
  *Baby, let me follow you down: the illustrated story of the Cambridge folk
  years* / by Eric Von Schmidt & Jim Rooney. – Garden City, New York:
  Anchor Books, 1979. – 314p.: ill., ports; 28cm. ISBN 0-385-14456-3 (pbk.)
With a brief text, this fine collection of photographs clearly shows the importance of Cambridge as a venue for influential new talent as well as established artists. Bob Dylan, Muddy Waters, Joan Baez, Maria Muldaur, Tom Rush, Taj Mahal, Bonnie Raitt and Paul Butterfield are all included, demonstrating the range of music from protest to authentic blues and folk rock.

Woodstock

The Woodstock Music and Arts Fair took place on a dairy farm owned by Max Yasgar in White Lake, New York State, between August 21st and 24th 1969; 450,000 young people gathered to listen to a remarkable selection of rock music including such artists as the Grateful Dead, the Jefferson Airplane, Canned Heat, Joe Cocker, the Who, Country Joe, John Sebastian, Crosby, Stills, Nash and Young and many more. It is regarded with enormous nostalgia as the very pinnacle of the flower-power period of the late sixties with its totally peaceful atmosphere and overwhelming feeling of community. The recording of the festival's performances became a successful album and an even more successful film directed by Michael Wadleigh and released in 1970. Martin Scorcese worked on the film's editing and it includes a variety of excellent effects, notably the use of split screens.

Spitz, Robert Stephen
   Barefoot in Babylon: the creation of the Woodstock Music Festival 1969 /
   Robert Stephen Spitz. – New York: Viking Press, 1979. – xviii, 513p., 2
   leaves of plates: ill., maps, ports; 24cm. Includes index. ISBN 0-6703-1168-5
   (cased). ISBN 0-6701-4801-6 (pbk.)
A detailed story of the legendary festival exhaustively researched. The motives, personalities and economics of Woodstock are all here. Lengthy recollections of artists and spectators attempt to offer the atmosphere of the event but ten years have passed and the detail does not make up for the contemporary enthusiasm. The illustrations are unusual and the production exceptionally good.

Young, Jean
   Woodstock: festival remembered / by Jean Young and Michael Lang. – New
   York: Ballantine, 1979. – 127p.: ill. (some col.), ports (some col.); 31cm.
   ISBN 0-345-28003-2 (pbk.)
An account of the festival written by two of the organizers with the benefit of ten years' hindsight and much lost idealism. There is a fine selection of illustrations of the performances, the artists relaxing backstage and the audience's antics. Illustrations are included of performances which were not incorporated into the film. The problems and unforeseen mishaps of the organization are described as well as the behaviour and involvement of the audience.

4.9 EQUIPMENT

There are many works which deal with musical instruments as physical objects, discuss their history and development in general, or take a particular company, such as Fender guitars or Steinway pianos, and offer a detailed history. Such works are not within the purview of this book as an instrument may be used to produce any form of music and it is the musician and the technique which provide the creative style.

The following titles, therefore, include some introductions to the technical side of modern musical instruments and earn their own place by including information on artists, their equipment and styles of playing forms of popular music.

Denyer, Ralph
  The guitar handbook / Ralph Denyer; with Isaac Guillory and Alastair
  M. Crawford. – London: Dorling Kindersley, 1982. – 256p.: ill. (some col.),
  music, ports (some col.); 30cm. Includes index. ISBN 0-86318-004-3 (pbk.)
With an introduction by Andy Summers of the Police, the first section comprises brief essays on fifteen guitar innovators and includes Django Reinhardt, Chuck Berry, Bo Diddley, Duane Eddy, Eric Clapton, Pete Townshend, Frank Zappa, Stanley Clarke, Jimi Hendrix and other major names. This is followed by sections on how acoustic and electric guitars work with excellent diagrams and thorough, beautifully illustrated descriptions of every important model of instrument. A large section is devoted to playing the guitar with chord charts, notes on technique, comments by well-known guitarists and information on tuning, musical styles and some music theory. Finally, guitar maintenance and customizing, amplification and recording are covered in detail with consistently fine illustrations and well-written text. With a full chord dictionary as an appendix, this is a superb guide to the guitar, orientated towards popular music, beautifully produced and a mine of accessible information.

Jenkins, John
  Electric music: a practical manual for musicians / John Jenkins and Jon
  Smith. – Newton Abbot: David & Charles, 1975. – 168p.: ill.; 22cm. Includes
  index. ISBN 0-7153-6912-1
This comprehensive guide to the technical side of forming an electric group is a unique, excellent and well-written work. The physics of sound and its amplification and production by electric instruments is described in easy language and illustrated with fine diagrams. Hints on the recording of each individual instrument, of the best use of instruments and a guide to the choice of instruments for particular applications are all here. Both authors have long personal experience as musicians as well as technical training and this is evident. This practical manual is an asset to anyone playing in a band or working as a sound engineer.

Mackay, Andy
  Electronic music / Andy Mackay. – Oxford: Phaidon Press, 1981. – 124p.: ill.
  (some col.), ports; 27cm. ISBN 0-7148-2176-4
Andy Mackay has been the saxophone player with the avant-garde group, Roxy Music, since 1971. He is also a composer whose works include the music for the British television series Rock Follies. This is a survey of the growth in the use of electronics in music from recording and sound amplification to complex synthesizers and effects. Arranged chronologically with photographs and diagrams, the book has a section of biographical notes and portraits of the major innovators and musicians.

Rock hardware: the instruments, equipment and technology of rock / edited by
  Tony Bacon. – Poole, Dorset: Blandford Press, 1981. – 224p.: ill. (some
  col.), ports (some col.); 31cm. Includes discography and index.
  ISBN 0-7137-1190-6

After an introduction outlining the history of the development of the various instruments and sound equipment used by today's musicians, each instrument is taken separately in a full chapter. Acoustic guitar, electric guitar, bass, keyboards, drums, synthesizers, woodwind, brass and strings, effects and the PA system are described in detail. The influence of instruments on the music is examined with detailed cross-section diagrams, photographs of well-known musicians in action and excellent technical notes. Chapters on recording and playing live are followed by lists of the addresses of major manufacturers, a glossary, discography and well-constructed index. The illustrations throughout are beautifully presented and the facts are fascinating although there are a few minor errors. This is a superbly produced work for the musician as well as the enthusiast.

Hammond, Ray
   The musician and the micro / Ray Hammond. – Poole, Dorset: Blandford
   Press, 1982. – 192p.: ill.; 22cm. ISBN 0-7137-1298-8 (cased).
   ISBN 0-7137-1299-6 (pbk.)
Written by an experienced sound engineer and musical journalist. The author describes the development and massive advances in computer-aided music. There is a survey of the range available and a discussion of their applications.

Lawrenson, David
   The complete guitar guide / David Lawrenson. – London: Virgin Books,
   1982. – 199p.: ill., ports; 30cm. Includes index. ISBN 0-907080-39-1 (pbk.)
A good, well-illustrated guide to the guitar for musicians of all styles. It gives a guide to the selection of guitars and amplification, separate biographies of lead, acoustic and bass guitarists and an introduction to chords. Prices are included, which will make for fast obsolescence.

Wheeler, Tom
   The guitar book: a handbook for electric and acoustic guitarists / Tom
   Wheeler. – Rev. ed. – London: Macdonald Futura, 1981. – xvii, 343p.: ill.,
   ports; 29cm. Includes index. ISBN 0-354-04682-9 (cased).
   ISBN 0-354-04683-7 (pbk.)
After a foreword by B. B. King this gives a history of the guitar which includes references to a number of well-known guitarists with brief comments on their contribution to technique. Chapters follow on acoustic and electric guitars with hundreds of illustrations, including most well-known models. How to choose the right guitar, guitar strings, maintenance, an introduction to harmonics, amplifiers and effects are all well covered. Finally there are appendices including details on picks and capos followed by scanty chord charts. Unfortunately lacking coloured illustrations, this is an informative and thorough source.

CHAPTER FIVE

Forms of popular music

Modern popular music is an amalgam of black music, with its negro blues roots, and white country music, with its traditional folk roots, which has been refined by the commercial pressures of Tin Pan Alley, with its roots in vaudeville, the music hall and light music.

The arrangement here to some extent reflects these threads. General works on black music are followed by works on specific styles arranged chronologically in terms of their appearance. The white music tradition follows in a similar progression from folk to country to rock'n'roll and its subsequent manifestations and branches.

General, introductory works for subjects not within the direct purview of this book are briefly included. Where jazz meets popular music with jazz–rock fusion, works are included which cover the major artists. Similarly there is a folk section for contemporary folk, protest, skiffle and folk rock, and works on musicals are included which cover contemporary shows and rock operas.

Within each form, there is a brief introduction followed, with the exception of country music, by a simple classified arrangement where justified: General works; Bibliographies; Discographies. Because of the volume of material on country music there is a more specific arrangement (*see* section 5.4, Country music).

5.1 BLACK MUSIC

Black popular music was born in the iniquity of the cotton fields of the southern USA. The African rhythms and chants transported by the slave ships were to evolve and revolutionize the white man's culture with a vengeance.

The country blues of the fields would become the urban blues of the Chicago ghettos and the jazz of New Orleans. The spiritual of the Church would become popular gospel, and rhythm & blues would emerge and lead on to soul music and its more commercial companions in Tamla Motown, Phillie and disco, while in the West Indies Jamaica was to evolve its distinct sound of reggae.

All these are forms of black music with the essence of struggle and intensity that was a powerful ingredient in the formation of rock'n'roll and its descendants.

Black music / editor and designer Gavin Petrie. – London: Hamlyn, 1974. –
    128p.: ill. (some col.), ports (some col.); 28cm. ISBN 0-600-31343-3
This glossy, superficial look at the major stars of black music is arranged into
styles. The notes are brief and there are no discographies but some fine
illustrations. Contemporary stars are emphasized with only brief reference to
their important forerunners.

Garland, Phyl
    The sound of soul / Phyl Garland. – Chicago: Henry Regnery, 1969. – 246p.,
    24p. of plates: ill., ports; 21cm. Includes discography and index
By the music critic of *Ebony* magazine, this is a good introduction to black
music. The author gives an outline history of the various forms which have
evolved into popular current styles. She looks at country and urban blues,
gospel and jazz before describing the scene as it was in the late sixties. Her
definition of soul is a wide one including the Tamla Motown and Philadelphia
sound. The discography is American but a good guide to selection.

Giants of black music / edited by Pauline Rivelli and Robet Levin; new
    introduction by Nat Hentoff. – New York: Da Capo, 1981. – 128.: ill., ports;
    22cm. ISBN 0-306-80119-1 (pbk.)
    Previously published as '*The black giants*': New York: World Publishing,
    1970.
A collection of articles and interviews which first appeared in the American
magazine *Jazz and Pop*. Many of the major figures in black music of the sixties
are included: Smokey Robinson, Eddie Floyd, Diana Ross and the Supremes
and Stevie Wonder, to name a few.

Gill, Chris
    The illustrated encyclopedia of black music / Chris Gill and Jon Futtrell. –
    London: Salamander Books, 1982. – 224p.: ill. (chiefly col.), col. facsims,
    ports (chiefly col.); 30cm. Includes discographies and index.
    ISBN 0-86101-145-7 (pbk.)
Covering the whole spectrum of black music from rhythm & blues to disco
and reggae, this is arranged by decades from the forties to the eighties.
Introductory essays set the scene by describing the major developments and
influences in the music of the time. These are followed by alphabetically
arranged bibliographical sketches with a superb collection of portraits, reproductions of record sleeves and discographies. Well written and informative,
this is the best single reference source to date.

Jones, Hettie
    Big Star fallin' mama: five women in black music / Hettie Jones. – New York:
    Viking Press, 1974. – 150p.: ill., facsims, ports; 24cm. Includes bibliography,
    discography and index. ISBN 0-670-16408-9
The biographies of the blues singers Ma Rainey, Bessie Smith and Billie
Holiday, the gospel singer Mahalia Jackson and soul singer Aretha Franklin
present the development of women in black music. Only Aretha Franklin
really falls into the contemporary popular field but the historical background is

valuable. Other major black women singers are listed. There is a selective discography and a good bibliography. The illustrations are rare and include facsimiles of early posters.

Lydon, Michael
  Boogie lightnin' / Michael Lydon. – New York: Dial Press, 1974. – 229p.: ill., ports; 24cm. ISBN 0-8037-2061-0
Comprising entirely reprints of magazine articles. The author's theme is the contribution of black music in all its forms to American culture. There is a fascinating article on the development of the electric guitar and its playing, as well as profiles of John Lee Hooker, Bo Diddley, Aretha Franklin, Ray Charles, the Chiffons and many more.

Pascall, Jeremy
  The stars & superstars of black music / produced by Jeremy Pascall and Rob Burt. – London: Phoebus, 1977. – 128p.: ill. (some col.), col. facsims, ports (some col.); 31cm. ISBN 0-7026-0010-5
  Also published: Secaucus, New Jersey: Chartwell Books, 1977.
Originally published in the twenty-six part serial The History of Pop, this is basically a collection of biographical essays of the major artists from the mid fifties to the mid seventies. Mixed with these are introductory outlines describing the styles of the record companies, for example Motown, Philadelphia, Atlantic and Stax. The illustrations are good and although it has no cohesive approach, this is a good popular outline.

Roach, Hildred
  Black American music: past and present / by Hildred Roach. – Boston: Crescendo Publishing Company, 1973. – vii, 199p.: ill., ports; 24cm. ISBN 0-8759-7079-6
As a history of the development of black music in the USA this unfortunately has large gaps. The general themes, however, are all here such as the move of the blues from the country to its urban manifestation and its influence on white music. The author covers the whole field of jazz with extreme brevity but is strong on the development of small black record labels and the acceptance of black artists in the wider market. The illustrations of old performers are useful.

Roberts, John Storm
  Black music of two worlds / John Storm Roberts. – London: Allen Lane, 1973. – x, 286p.: music; 23cm. Includes bibliography, discography and index. ISBN 0-7139-0536-0
  Also published: New York: Morrow, 1974.
By far the best analysis of the evolution and influence of black music and probably one of the best books available on popular music. The music of the black nations in Africa and the Caribbean is analysed in social and musical terms. The movement of the music and its development in white countries, principally England and America, and its influence on their indigenous music is presented in a scholarly but thoroughly readable way.

Rublowsky, John
  Black music / John Rublowsky. – New York: Basic Books, 1971. – 150p.: ill.,
  ports; 22cm. Includes index. ISBN 0-4560-0697-3
A well-structured, informative survey of the rise of black music from folk
culture to the driving force behind modern commercial popular music. The
blues and jazz are covered and developed into rhythm & blues and soul styles
with some unusual illustrations and excellent analysis.

The soul book / edited by Ian Hoare. – London: Eyre Methuen, 1975. – ix,
  206p., 16p. of plates: ill., ports; 20cm. Includes discography and index.
  ISBN 0-413-32150-9 (pbk.)
  Also published: New York: Delta, 1975.
A collaboration of four well-known writers (Simon Frith, Tony Cummings,
Clive Anderson and Ian Hoare) has produced this well-written outline to black
music. The title is misleading as the book covers not just the narrow area of soul
music but also a brief history of the development of black music from its blues
roots and includes chapters on the popular areas of Tamla Motown and the
Philadelphia sound. Tony Cummings deals with the historical section describing the career of Sam Cooke, and the rise of James Brown and Clyde
McPhatter. Simon Frith continues with the story of Tamla Motown. Clive
Anderson's subject is soul music itself with its roots in Memphis, the Stax label
and the growth of funk, leaving Ian Hoare to analyse the relationship of black
music with its contemporary white counterpart. In all, an excellent collection of
essays.

Shaw, Arnold
  The world of soul: black America's contribution to the pop music scene / by
  Arnold Shaw. – New York: Cowles Book Company, 1970. – xiii, 306p., 16p.
  of plates: ill., ports; 22cm. Includes discography and index.
  ISBN 0-402-12291-7
This is a detailed history of the evolution of American black music from the
itinerant country bluesmen to the classic blues singers such as Bessie Smith
through the jazz era of Billie Holiday and Ella Fitzgerald to the recent pop and
rhythm & blues artists. Shaw's definition of soul is a wide one covering all
modern black music. His analyses of musical growth and the description of the
changes in styles are set against their sociological background. His approach in
relating the music to its roots in poverty and deprivation is always poignant.
The recent major artists are given considerable attention and the index makes
access to the information easy.

Southern, Eileen
  The music of black Americans: a history / Eileen Southern. – New York:
  W. W. Norton, 1971. 552p.: ill., ports; 22cm. Includes bibliography and
  index. ISBN 0-393-02156-4 (cased). ISBN 0-393-09899-0 (pbk.)
A scholarly collection of essays on a wide range of subjects centred on black
music and its social significance. Jazz is well covered as are folk sources, but the
development of gospel, rhythm & blues and soul music is covered to a lesser
extent although in a succinct and intelligent way.

Southern, Eileen
  Readings in black music / Eileen Southern. – New York: W. W. Norton,
  1972. – xii, 302p.; 22cm. Includes bibliography and index.
  ISBN 0-393-02165-3 (cased). ISBN 0-393-09892-3 (pbk.)
Covering jazz particularly well from its beginnings to the avant garde and jazz
fusion, this also provides superficial analysis of the development of popular
black music. Great areas such as the rhythm & blues vocal groups of the fifties
are not included but the evolution of soul music is well chronicled.

Walton, Ortiz M.
  *Music, black, white and blue: a sociological survey of the use and misuse of
  Afro-American music* / Ortiz M. Walton. – New York: Morrow, 1972. –
  180p.: ill.; 24cm.
Written by a black American who studies the development of black music from
folk art to its commercial forms in the context of the social conditions that
produced it and those which prevail. The exploitation of performers and
writers is a common theme explored, but less usual is the concept of the white
manipulation of black people through the financial control of their music and
thus, later, the rise of independent black record companies. Not an easily read
work, but packed with information and arguments from a particular standpoint.

Black music: Bibliographies

Skowronski, Jo Ann
  Black music in America: a bibliography / by Jo Ann Skowronski. –
  Metuchen, New Jersey; London: Scarecrow Press, 1981. – 733p.; 23cm.
  Includes index. ISBN 0-8109-1443-9
In listing over 14,000 articles and books, the aim is to cite writings which trace
the history of the impact of black culture on American music. Divided into two
sections, the first focusses on ninety-seven musicians from a wide range of
music including jazz, opera and popular music. This is followed by a general
section on historical aspects of black music and is concluded by a section on
reference materials listing bibliographies, encyclopedias and indexes. References are listed chronologically by date of publication within each subject
heading. There is an intricate network of cross references and an author index.
A good guide, this is very selective with the briefest of annotations.

Black music: Discographies

Gonzalez, Fernando L.
  *Disco – file: the discographical catalog of American rock & roll and rhythm
  and blues vocal harmony groups; race, rhythm & blues, rock & roll, soul:
  1902–1976* / Fernando L. Gonzalez. – 2nd ed. – Flushing, New York:
  Gonzalez, 1977. – 49p.; 28cm. Includes indexes. ISBN 0-960109-01-3
  Previous edition: Flushing, New York: Gonzalez, 1974.
This rare, privately published discography is the result of the compiler's real
labour of love and meticulous research over a number of years. It is the

discographical history of the development of black harmony-singing groups from blues and gospel through the fifties rock'n'roll and rhythm & blues phase to the rise of the Tamla Motown style, and its contemporaries of the sixties, up to the dominance of Philadelphia in the mid seventies. Chronologically arranged with artist and song indexes, only American releases are included, but it is a valuable guide for any serious record collector.

Osborne, Jerry
    Blues, rhythm & blues, soul / by Jerry Osborne and Bruce Hamilton. –
    Phoenix, Arizona: O'Sullivan Woodside, 1980. – 160p.: ill., facsims; 28cm.
    Includes index. ISBN 0-89019-071-2 (pbk.)
A guide for record collectors, arranged alphabetically by artist. There are full discographical details and an indication of current values in the USA.

Tudor, Dean
    Black music / Dean Tudor and Nancy Tudor. – Littleton, Colorado:
    Libraries Unlimited, 1979. – 262p.; 24cm. – (American popular music on
    Elpee) Includes bibliography. ISBN 0-87287-147-9
Part of a four-volume series (the others include *Jazz*, *Contemporary popular music* and *Grassroots music*). The excellent introduction is followed by sections on each musical form. The emphasis is on the blues but rhythm & blues, gospel, soul and reggae are well represented. Significant recordings are grouped, rather than artists, avoiding the problem of artists who record in various styles but creating some confusion. The 'best and most enduring' albums in each genre are included with an annotation of around three hundred words apiece. There is an excellent bibliography, making this a thoughtful and well-researched contribution.

GOSPEL

Descending from the spiritual, gospel music arose from the upsurge in fundamentalist church-going in black urban communities in the twenties. The call-and-response style is a distinctive feature. This form evolved into rhythm & blues and soul in their purest manifestations, where the gospel elements remain prominent. Sam Cooke, Aretha Franklin and many other leading soul singers were gospel stars before going on to sing more secular material.

Anderson, Robert
    Gospel music encylopedia / Robert Anderson & Gail North, introduction by
    Don Butter. – New York: Sterling Publishing; London; Sydney: Oak Tree
    Press, 1979. – 320p.: ill., music, ports; 26cm. Includes discography. ISBN
    0-8069-0174-8 (Sterling). ISBN 0-7061-2670-X (Oak Tree)
An informative reference source which covers the contemporary American gospel-music scene in detail. There is an alphabetical sequence of biographical notes, a guide to radio stations and a hall of fame which includes all the leading gospel singers of the past. This is the sole source of many of the portraits of the lesser-known artists.

Heilbut, Tony
The gospel sound: good news and bad times / Tony Heilbut. – New York:
Simon and Schuster, 1971. – 350p.: ill., ports; 24cm. Includes index.
ISBN 0-671-20983-3

A scholarly study of gospel music this century which aims to show, rightly, how
the black experience has been instrumental in giving birth to the major modern
musical forms. The author relates blues, jazz and rhythm & blues to the more
religiously based gospel and is often scathing about and very hostile to popular
music. Nevertheless this is a definitive study and provides a good background
to the overall understanding of black music.

JAZZ

The literature of jazz is exceptionally well covered in:

Kennington, Donald
The literature of jazz: a critical guide / by Donald Kennington and Danny
L. Read. – 2nd ed. – London: Library Association, 1980. – 236p.; 22cm.
Includes indexes. ISBN 0-85365-663-0 (pbk.)
Previous edition: London: Library Association, 1970.

It has been the intention throughout the present work to avoid duplication of
Kennington, but some has inevitably occurred in fringe areas.

Below are listed two general reference sources which provide excellent introductions to the subject of contemporary jazz and the jazz–rock fusion, plus the
sole in-depth book on the fusion itself.

Case, Brian
The illustrated encyclopedia of jazz / Brian Case and Stan Britt; photographs
Val Wilmer; editor Trisha Palmer. – London: Salamander Books, 1978. –
224p.: ill. (some col.), facsims (some col.), ports (some col.); 30cm. Includes
index. ISBN 0-86101-026-4 (pbk.)

A well-produced, well-written encyclopedia aimed at the popular market, this
gives a good introduction to its subject. Included here not just because there is
some overlap with entries on jazz-rock musicians such as Chick Corea and
Weather Report (although there is no personal entry for Larry Coryell) but
because it is an excellent quick-reference source to blues artists and related
rock-music influences.

Feather, Leonard
The encyclopedia of jazz in the seventies / by Leonard Feather and Ira Gitler;
introduction by Quincey Jones. – London: Quartet Books, 1978. – 393p.:
ill., ports; 26cm. Includes bibliography and discography.
ISBN 0-7043-2175-0

A detailed reference source, meticulously compiled with not only an alphabetical, detailed biographical dictionary, but appendices of information on jazz education, films, discography and books published. Included are many jazz-influenced rock musicians such as Frank Zappa, the Pointer Sisters, Charlie Musselwhite and Blood, Sweat and Tears. It is interesting to see who in the popular-music field the authors regard as respectable enough to include. An excellent reference source.

JAZZ–ROCK FUSION

Rock music had developed partly from rhythm & blues, which itself was partly inspired by jazz, but the division between rock'n'roll and jazz was firmly maintained on both sides until the mid sixties when artists such as Gary Burton and Miles Davis began to experiment with electric instrumentation in their bands. When in 1969 Miles Davis recorded his album In a Silent Way, the jazz–rock fusion was born. Incorporating the improvisation of jazz with rock rhythms, with multiple electric keyboards, electric guitars and their associated effects, the result is neither true jazz nor rock. Musicians associated with the form are Chick Corea, Weather Report, Herbie Hancock, John McLaughlin, Frank Zappa and sometimes Miles Davis himself.

Coryell, Julie
   Jazz–rock fusion: the people, the music / Julie Coryell & Laura Friedman;
   preface by Ramsey Lewis. – London: Marion Boyars, 1978. – xi, 300p.; ill.,
   ports (some col.); 28 × 22cm. Includes bibliography and discography.
   ISBN 0-7145-2667-3 (cased). ISBN 0-7145-2662-2 (pbk.)
   Originally published: New York: Delacorte Press, 1978
   Also published; New York: Dell, 1978
A collection of interviews and biographical essays on all of the major jazz-rock musicians arranged in sections by type of instrument played. Julie Coryell's husband Larry is an eminent guitarist, giving her excellent access to the jazz world. There is a comprehensive discography and a very good portrait of each artist. This is a particularly well-written work and the best single source of information on this musical form.

REGGAE

Reggae evolved in Jamaica from a mixture of American rhythm & blues and soul and the local bluebeat and ska forms. It is characterized by a syncopated beat with scratchy, staccato guitar and a curious, erratic bass line. Lyrically reggae is associated with the religious and social messages of the Rastafarian cult. The style has influenced the work of musicians in all areas of popular music. It is by far the major form of popular music in Jamaica with a wide following in Britain, but with only a minor cult following in the USA

(*See also* Chapter 2, Subcultures: Rastafarians.)

Clarke, Sebastian
Jah music / by Sebastian Clarke. – London: Heinemann Educational, 1980. – 224p.: ill., ports; 20cm. Includes discography and index.
ISBN 0-435-82140-7 (pbk.)
The author was born in Trinidad and has contributed articles on reggae music to the American music press for a number of years. This is a well-written, scholarly account of the evolution of reggae from its Jamaican roots. The cult of Rastafarianism is outlined and its sociological basis and link with reggae well described. The international expansion of the music is discussed as are the major artists. The discography is excellent.

Davis, Stephen
Reggae bloodlines: in search of the music and culture of Jamaica / text by Stephen Davis; photographs by Peter Simon. – London: Heineman Educational, 1979. - 216p.: ill., facsims, music, ports; 28cm. Includes discography. ISBN 0-4359-8190-0 (pbk.)
The deprivations of the slums of Kingston, Jamaica and the growth of the Rastafarian movement are inevitably linked here to illustrate the background to reggae's wide appeal. The author avoids becoming too sociological in his approach, however, and the emphasis is strongly on the music with musical illustrations explaining reggae's rhythms and style as well as portraits of the major performers. The discography is brief but well selected.

Davis, Stephen
Reggae international / Stephen Davis, Peter Simon. – London: Thames and Hudson, 1983. – 191p.: ill. (some col.), ports (some col.); 31cm.
ISBN 0-500-27279-4 (pbk.)
Beautifully illustrated with many full-page colour photographs, this gives a brief history of Jamaica, outlining African culture and its evolution into the West Indies' own culture. The evolution of reggae from ska is followed by a brief discussion of Rastafarianism. There are biographies and criticism of the major Jamaican artists as well as a look at white reggae and the two-tone movement. As well as the author's narrative other contributors include Chris May on reggae in England, Dick Hebdige on two-tone, Peter Simon on the group Steel Pulse, Timothy White on Bob Marley and the Wailers and historical notes by Gareth White and Randall Grass. In all a well-produced, very good introduction, well written and informative.

Farmer, Paul
Steelbands & reggae / Paul Farmer. – London: Longman, 1981. – 24p.: ill., map, music, ports; 23cm. (Longman music topics). ISBN 0-582-20097-0 (pbk.)
A brief introduction to West Indian music for schools with musical analysis, question-and-answer exercises and portraits of the leading artists.

Johnson, Howard
Reggae: deep roots music / Howard Johnson and Jim Pines; photographs by Howard Johnson. – London; New York: Proteus, 1982. – 128p.: ill. (some col.), ports (some col.); 29cm. ISBN 0-86276-119-0 (cased).

ISBN 0-86276-117-4 (pbk.)
Published as tie-in text for the six-part Channel 4 television series, this is a good
survey of the music. A history of the development of the contemporary
Jamaican style from ska, the influence of the disc jockeys, a section on Bunny
Lee, the spiritual side of the music and Rastafarianism, the business and the
music's impact in Britain are all topics briefly covered with some photographs.

Kallyndyr, Rolston
  Reggae: a people's music / Rolston Kallyndyr, Henderson Dalrymple. –
  Sudbury, Middlesex: Carib-Arawak Publications, 1977. – 38p.: ill., ports;
  21cm. (pbk.)
A brief outline of reggae which describes the evolution from bluebeat and ska
to its popularization in Britain. There is a short description of Rastafarianism
and lyrics reflecting the significant emotions of the cult are reproduced.

5.2 RHYTHM & BLUES

The black-American popular music from the late forties and early fifties,
rhythm & blues, or R & B, was a synthesis of swing rhythms and blues vocal
techniques with the intensity of gospel music. An urban style, it had regional
variations in New Orleans, Chicago, New York and so on. Although widely
followed, it was regarded as a somewhat inferior form compared with its jazz
contemporary, Be-bop. Much of rhythm & blues was transmitted to rock'n'roll
and many of the leading artists moved quite happily between the forms. Fats
Domino, Bo Diddley and Chuck Berry are good examples while Ray Charles
was both a rhythm & blues artist and an innovator of soul music.

Broven, John
  Walking to New Orleans: the story of New Orleans rhythm & blues / John
  Broven. – 2nd ed. – Bexhill-on-Sea, Sussex: Flyright, 1977. – 248p.: ill.,
  ports;
  23cm. Includes discography and index. (pbk.)
  Previous edition: Bexhill-on-Sea, Sussex: Flyright, 1974.
  Also published: Gretna, Louisiana: Pelican Publishing, 1978.
A scholarly work by an English contributor to the journal *Blues Unlimited*, this
covers the development of the music in New Orleans from 1946. There are lists
of successful singles and albums as well as detailed analysis of the development
of local record companies. The biographical notes and rare portraits are
superb.

Given, Dave
  *The Dave Given rock'n'roll stars handbook: rhythm and blues artists and
  groups.* – Smithtown, New York: Exposition Press, 1980. – 328p.: ill., ports;
  24cm. Includes discography and index. ISBN 0-682-49577-8
Well illustrated. The author covers not only the well known, but also many

obscure rhythm & blues performers from the fifties through to the seventies. There are brief, but informative notes on their careers and good analyses of their music.

Groia, Philip
They all sang on the corner: New York City's rhythm and blues vocal groups of the 1950s / by Philip Groia. – Setauket, New York: Edmond Publishing, 1947. – 147p.: ill., ports; 22cm. Includes discography. ISBN 0-9129-5408-6 (pbk.)
The forerunners of the Doo-wop, rock'n'roll, vocal groups, according to the myth these early rhythm & blues groups, known as 'street corner singers', practised in the street unaccompanied. This history is the main source of information on these obscure, important early innovators, few of whom gained any wide recognition. The discography is of rare American releases and the illustrations are rare indeed.

Kamin, Jonathan Liff
Rhythm & blues in white America: rock and roll as acculturation and perceptual learning / Jonathan Liff Kamin. - Ann Arbor, Michigan: University Microfilms, 1975. – 309p.; 24cm.
Prepared as a Ph. D. thesis at Princeton University, this detailed study analyses the evolution of white rock'n'roll from black rhythm & blues. The author is both sociological and musicological in approach, often using musical themes to illustrate wider cultural points. An in-depth study, this is yet to be published for wider circulation.

McCutcheon, Lynn Ellis
Rhythm and blues: an experience and adventure in its origin and development / Lynn Ellis McCutcheon. – Arlington, Virginia: Beatty, 1971. – ix, 305p.: ill., ports; 20cm. Includes bibliography, discography and index. ISBN 0-8794-8000-9
Written with the skill of an historian, this detailed history covers the early formation of the blues in both its country and later urban forms. The major artists are described, their music and influence analysed and rhythm & blues' influence on music in general discussed. There are detailed references, a collection of rare photographs, an extensive bibliography and selective discography, naturally of American releases.

Redd, Lawrence N.
Rock is rhythm and blues: the impact of mass media / by Lawrence N. Redd. – East Lansing, Michigan: Michigan State University Press, 1974. – xviii, 167p.; 24cm. ISBN 0-87013-180-X
This analysis sets out to examine the thesis that present-day rock music which has grown from the rock'n'roll of the fifties is a direct descendant of black rhythm & blues. Furthermore, early white singers such as Elvis were simply white carbon copies of black singers such as Bo Diddley. Writing in the context of the relatively recent assertion of black people that their culture has played such a major part in shaping the wider American culture, the author claims that

the terms rock'n'roll and pop music, as opposed to the black rhythm & blues or soul, are different simply in that white performers have constantly failed to do the music justice in their performances. Packed with quotations from lyrics, detailed historical background and detailed bibliographic citations, the final section of the book is a collection of the author's interviews with six major performers, B. B. King, Brownie McGhee, Dave Clark, Arthur 'Big Boy' Crudup, Jerry Butler and Jesse Whitaker. All in all, this is an excellent work that makes its point — one which few people could dispute.

Rowe, Mike
   Chicago breakdown / by Mike Rowe. – New York: Drake, 1975. – 226p.: ill., ports; 24cm. Includes discography and index. ISBN 0-87749-813-X
A well-researched, exhaustive chronicle of the growth of urban blues in Chicago. The author describes the establishment and development of each of the record companies in the city, whether large or small. There are interviews with well-known and obscure performers and a fine collection of rare illustrations. The discography is brief but offers a wide selection of, alas, unobtainable records reflecting the variety of styles of the Chicago style of rhythm & blues.

Shaw, Arnold
   Honkers and shouters: the golden years of rhythm and blues / by Arnold Shaw. – New York: Macmillan, 1978. – xxvii, 555p.: ill., ports; 24cm.
   Includes bibliography, discography and index. ISBN 0-026-10000-2
   Also published: New York: Collier Macmillan, 1978.
Shaw's experience in music publishing in the fifties gives an unusual view of the great performers and leading figures associated with rhythm & blues. He is often inaccurate in his analysis of rock'n'roll and its development but his biographies of blues, rhythm & blues and related performers, as well as producers and executives, make this an important contribution to the history of the music in this period, from its roots to its evolution into rock, soul and other popular forms. There are portraits of little-known artists not published elsewhere, an excellent discography and a good bibliography of background material. As in other histories of the early development of modern popular music, the part played by the independent record companies is regarded as a major contribution and the structure of Shaw's account is based around the various growing companies with all his inside knowledge.

Discographies

Ferlingere, Robert D.
   A discography of rhythm & blues and rock'n'roll vocal groups, 1945 to 1965 / compiled by Robert D. Ferlingere. – Pittsburg, California: Ferlingere, 1976. – 700p.; 29cm. Includes indexes
A rare, privately published discography which exhaustively lists the full details of every record released by mainly black vocal groups in the rock'n'roll and rhythm & blues style over the twenty-year period indicated by its title. The development of rhythm & blues into rock'n'roll is thus reflected by the records released. Notes on the artists are sparse but if this can be obtained, it is a useful, remarkable piece of research.

Leichter, Albert
A discography of rhythm & blues and rock & roll circa 1946 – 1964: a reference manual / compiled by Albert Leichter. – Staunton, Virginia: Leichter, 1975. – 189p.; 30cm.
A rare, privately published discography which describes the development of rhythm & blues in its more ethnic and later commercial, vocal group forms, its adoption by white singers and its development into rock'n'roll. The content is of American releases and the arrangement is chronological and then by artist. Certainly not comprehensive, it is an interesting personal selection.

SOUL

Sometimes used as a term to describe all black music, soul evolved out of rhythm & blues in the late fifties, adapting gospel intensity into a secular form. Many of the songs were simply rewritten gospel songs. Ray Charles was instrumental in taking a series of basically sacred songs and presenting them with erotic lyrics. He was followed by Ben E. King and Sam Cooke. Soul arrangements also brought sophistication to black music with a new, complex orchestration. The Drifters are a good example. The productions of Jerry Leiber and Mike Stoller introduced the group to a wider, white audience. Atlantic, Stax and Motown record companies developed the form throughout the sixties with major artists such as Otis Redding, Wilson Pickett, Aretha Franklin, Curtis Mayfield, James Brown and many more. Soul continues to flourish in its modified forms, a long way from its rhythm & blues roots.

Haralambos, Michael
Right on: from blues to soul in black America / Michael Haralambos. – London: Eddison Press, 1974. – 187p.: ill., ports; 23cm. Includes bibliography, discography, and index. ISBN 0-85649-016-4
Also published: New York: Drake Publishers, 1975; New York: Da Capo Press, 1979.
Written by an English authority on the blues, this is a history of the development of the black blues music into the modern soul style. The influences of each form of blues are discussed in terms of its region of origin and urban or country style. The evolution of soul itself from gospel is particularly well described with hundreds of song references and extracts from lyrics. There is an excellent selection of rare illustrations of many black soul singers not published elsewhere. The bibliography includes background material as well as references to blues and soul biographies. There is a selective discography of significant records which reflect the evolution of the music. This is a concise and well-presented outline.

Larkin, Rochelle
Soul music: the sound, the stars, the story / Rochelle Larkin. – New York: Lancer Books, 1970. – 189p.: ill., ports; 21cm. (pbk.)
A brief outline of the growth of black music in the USA, this covers the early days of country and urban blues and follows the development of the independ-

ent black record labels in the fifties. The biographies of the stars of the soul boom of the sixties are brief but informative. The illustrations are well chosen and unusual.

GIRL GROUPS

A long way from the aggressive lady rockers of the seventies and early eighties, 'girl groups' described the female vocal groups, mainly composed of black singers, of the sixties, who projected perfectly the image of adolescent fantasies of the period. The style of their music certainly evolved from the earlier rhythm & blues vocal groups from the gospel tradition with lyrics suited to the white teenage audience. The Shirelles took the lead in 1960 and were followed by the Crystals, the Dixie Cups, the Ronettes, the Chiffons and many more, not forgetting the Shangrilas, who were a white group but very much in the same style. Phil Spector was the greatest creator of girl-group hits, utilizing and developing his Wall of Sound system behind often gentle vocal harmonies. Groups such as the Supremes in the late sixties and Three Degrees in the seventies are direct descendants of this important form.

Betrock, Alan
 Girl groups: the story of a sound / by Alan Betrock. – New York: Delilah
 Books, 1982. – 175p.: ill., ports; 28cm. Includes discography.
 ISBN 0-933328-25-7 (pbk.)
A good history which includes the stories of all the major artists: Chiffons, Shirelles, Crystals, Angels, Toys, Dixie Cups, Ronettes, Shangrilas and so on, as well as some unsuspected ones such as Lesley Gore and Mary Welles. The discography is very selective including only 131 major hits, but the illustrations are well chosen and rare.

TAMLA MOTOWN

The music released on the Tamla Motown label is often seen as a genre of highly produced black pop music and the terms 'Motown' or 'Tamla' used to describe it. Essentially, however, the company has been involved in a wide spectrum of music although it is perhaps artists such as the Supremes, Marvin Gaye and Stevie Wonder who symbolize the company's image.

(*See* Chapter 4.3. Record companies: Tamla Motown.)

PHILADELPHIA (PHILLIE)

The Phillie sound has been in existence with local record labels since the late fifties. Chubby Checker became its first big star when he launched the Twist dance style in 1959. Throughout the sixties black and white artists recorded in

Philadelphia but not until the early seventies did it become the centre of the most successful sound of that period. Billy Paul, the O'Jays, Delfonics, Labelle and the Three Degrees are all part of the Phillie sound, which is a lush blend of modern orchestration and vocal harmony produced together with great precision.

Cummings, Tony
   The sound of Philadelphia / Tony Cummings. – London: Eyre Methuen, 1975. – 157p.: ill., facsims, ports; 27cm. Includes index.
   ISBN 0-413-34080-5 (pbk.)
A particularly well-researched history of the evolution of the Phillie sound by this English journalist, who covers the very early days of recording in Philadelphia including Mario Lanza's early career. Jazz is included along with disc jockey Dick Clark's launching of white teenage idols such as Bobby Rydell, Frankie Avalon and Fabian. The detail in which he covers the black groups of the sixties and seventies is considerable and there are illustrations of even the most obscure artists. Curiously, the book has not been published in the USA. This is a fine source of information with a well-constructed index.

DISCO

Disco is an abbreviation of the word discothèque, which described a dancing club in which disc jockeys played records through powerful sound systems. These clubs originated during the Twist dance craze of the early sixties. In the late seventies, however, the term came to describe a style of music aimed specifically at dancing and with the release of the film Saturday Night Fever a boom occurred with the emergence of more and more clubs and the production of thousands of records. The style is notable for its lack of emotion, the use of repetitive rhythms and, more recently, the use of synthesizers. It is often dismissed as the most manufactured of all pop music. Its leading artists include Donna Summer, the Bee Gees and Boney M, as well as many American and British groups who simply changed their soul styles to comply with the trend.

Blackford, Andy
   Disco dancing tonight / Andy Blackford. – London: Octopus Books, 1979. – 80p.: ill. (chiefly col.), ports (chiefly col.); 30cm. Includes index.
   ISBN 0-7064-1019-X (pbk.)
Although there is a brief attempt to trace the development of the disco movement from its beginnings in the seventies, the general theme here is to depict the glamour of discos with their exotic dancers. Illustrations are mainly of models in the most fashionable, colourful outfits. There are also stills from disco films and a sequence of frozen-frame dance movements. The author fails in his aim to give an exciting impression of disco and also does not offer any analysis or information.

Fox-Cumming, Ray
  Disco fever / Ray Fox-Cumming. – London: Mandabrook Books, 1978. –
  95p., 8p. of plates: ill., ports; 18cm. ISBN 0-427-00429-2 (pbk.)
Written for the fan, this superficial guide to the disco boom describes the
beginnings of the phenomenon with brief biographies of John Travolta, the
Bee Gees and Olivia Newton-John. The films Saturday Night Fever and
Grease are discussed and there is emphasis on the fashions created by these
films. The author attempts to set disco in the context of its evolution from
earlier forms of pop music but with no thoroughly-thought-out argument.

Goldman, Albert
  Disco / Albert Goldman. – New York: Hawthorn Books, 1979. – 174p.: col.
  ill.; 24cm. ISBN 0-8015-2128-9
Attempting a definitive historical survey of the growth of discothèques in the
sixties and the development of music aimed specifically at them, the author
writes at the peak of the disco boom. Disco is depicted as of more musical
importance than it deserves. The major stars are all discussed, as is the role of
the disc jockey, fashion, dances and the more famous elaborate clubs.

Lovisone, Carter
  The disco hustle / by Carter Lovisone. – London: Ward Lock, 1979. – 95p.:
  ill.; 28cm. Includes index. ISBN 0-7063-5865-1 (pbk.)
  Also published: New York: Sterling Publishing, 1979.
After a brief essay on the beginnings of disco, four dances are described in
detail with dozens of frozen-frame illustrations. This is a good manual of the
most popular disco dances.

Ryzin, Lani van
  Disco / by Lani Van Ryzin. – London: Franklin Watts, 1979. – 60p.: ill.;
  24cm. Includes index. ISBN 0-85166-793-7
A simple guide to disco, not for the prospective musician, but for the disc
jockey, promoter and dancer. There are dancing charts for the most popular
dances as well as photographs. There are brief biographies of the major artists.
In general this is a superficial guide which is of little practical value.

JAZZ FUNK

In no way a true jazz form, jazz funk is a black American dance music which
appeared during the disco craze of the late seventies. It is dominated by
complex rhythms and often sophisticated record production. British disc
jockeys, notably Chris Hill, fostered its following in Britain, attracting a multi-
racial audience of real enthusiasm calling themselves the Family.

Brown, Chris
  The Family album / compiled and written by Chris Brown. – Woking, Surrey:
  Hitman, 1980. – 96p.: ill. (some col.), ports (some col.); 28cm. Includes
  bibliography. (pbk.)

The brief text describes the growth of interest in the music in Britain and features the leading disc jockeys. The illustrations include no artist but fans and disc jockeys mainly in discothèque settings. The racial harmony of the Family is the main feature.

5.3   FOLK MUSIC

Folk music is music of the oral rather than written tradition. Since the eighteenth century considerable work has been done on the collection and study of folk songs by the likes of Cecil Sharpe in England and the Lomax brothers for the Library of Congress. More recently in the USA, the protest movement, born out of the politically motivated songs of Woody Guthrie and his followers such as Pete Seeger and later Bob Dylan, was itself a product of the folk scene. Such singer-songwriters were termed folk singers not because of their style or the political content of their songs, but because of their tradition. The later singer-songwriters brought an intellectual and literary approach to popular song which fostered a seriousness and respectability which had not appeared before. The works here are concerned with the contemporary folk movement and not traditional, revivalist song.

Baggelaar, Kristin
    The folk music encyclopedia / by Kristin Baggelaar and Donald Milton. –
    London: Omnibus Press, 1977. – 419p.: ill., ports; 25cm.
    ISBN 0-86001-309-X (pbk.)
    Also published: New York: Thomas Y. Crowell, 1979.
This is an encyclopedia of the American folk scene including some information on the styles of American folk music but concentrating mainly on biographical information on artists. The definition of 'folk' is extremely wide and included are all the major country-music stars, folk-rock artists, singer-songwriters and many rock performers. Bias is American and although often informative, the coverage is confusing and lacking in discographies.

De Turk, David A.
    The American folk scene: dimensions of the folk song revival / edited and with
    an introduction by David A. De Turk and A. Poulin Jr. – New York: Dell,
    1967. – 334p.; 18cm. (pbk.)
An outline of the folk revival in the USA in the fifties and sixties, this book comprises a series of articles which previously appeared in a wide range of American magazines.

Myrus, Donald
    Ballads, blues and the big beat / by Donald Myrus. – New York: Macmillan;
    London: Collier-Macmillan, 1966. – 136p.: ill., ports; 24cm. Includes
    discography and index
This surveys the work of folk singers and singer-songwriters in the mid sixties.

The background influences of country music, blues and bluegrass are discussed, as is the work of the earlier songwriters such as Leadbelly and Woody Guthrie. The acceptance of the rock'n'roll influence also creeps in with a detailed look at the work of Bob Dylan. The influence of folk on the Beatles is suggested. A wide spectrum is taken in by the author and the discography suggests a varied range of listening. This is an interesting view from the context of the mid sixties before the development and acceptance of folk rock.

Stambler, Irwin
> *Encyclopedia of folk, country and western music* / by Irwin Stambler and Grelun Landon. – London: St. James' Press; New York: St. Martin's, 1969. – ix, 396p.: ill., music, ports; 25cm. ISBN 0-9009-9724-9

A well-illustrated, informative and well-arranged source which includes biographical detail on folk performers, singer-songwriters and country artists. The American bias is such that few British artists are included at all, although as a source of information on obscure country and western stars it is unequalled. The term 'folk' refers to the contemporary American scene.

SKIFFLE

Skiffle emerged in the early fifties in Britain out of the jazz movement. Originally its goal was to revive the sound of the early black blues performers. Homemade basses and washboards were included in its lineup and with this simple rhythm section, or back line, augmented by banjo and guitars, the front-line instruments of the jazz band were replaced by vocals. The early groups emerged from established traditional jazz bands such as Ken Colyer and Chris Barber. Thousands of skiffle groups sprang up all over Britain with Lonnie Donegan, who had played banjo with Barber, as the undisputed leader. He drew his early songs from American sources, notably Leadbelly and Woody Guthrie. By the early sixties skiffle had been superseded by electric instrumental groups and later beat groups. The lasting influence of skiffle is that the vast majority of musicians to form beat groups had learnt their instruments and singing techniques in skiffle groups. John Lennon, for example, had led the Quarrymen while still at school.

Bird, Brian
> *Skiffle: the story of folk-song with a jazz beat* / by Brian Bird; with a foreword by Lonnie Donegan. – London: Robert Hale, 1958. – 125p., 13p. of plates; 20cm. Includes bibliography and index

Brian Bird sets skiffle firmly as a style emerging from the mainstream of jazz. He gives a concise history of the development of jazz and its growth in Britain. He defines the style of music, emphasizing its definite beat, and then gives potted biographies of the major skiffle groups. It is interesting to note that while many of the groups have now totally faded into obscurity, some became notable as folk groups or reverted to straight traditional jazz after the skiffle boom. There is a chapter on the future of skiffle which now appears very naive but this is a contemporary and serious examination of a style of popular music and as such a rare effort.

PROTEST

During the thirties Woody Guthrie began writing and singing songs condemning the ills of the Depression. His songs reflected the mood of the novels of Steinbeck, lyrically describing the struggles of the dirt farmers of the mid-West, their bankruptcies and evictions. The spirit of Guthrie was revived in the sixties in a movement evolving out of the folk revival of the fifties, notably by Joan Baez, Pete Seeger, Phil Ochs and Bob Dylan. Beginning in university campuses and the coffee houses of Greenwich Village, New York, the movement grew to world-wide proportions. Its decline came with the growth of folk rock and the psychedelia of 1967. Leading artists, such as Bob Dylan, left protest and explored wider musical expression and found commercial success.

(*See also* section 2.5, In politics.)

Denisoff, R. Serge
   Great day coming: folk music and the American left / R. Serge Denisoff. –
   Urbana; London: University of Illinois Press, 1971. – 220p.: ill., ports; 26cm.
   Includes bibliography, discography and index. ISBN 0–252–00179–6
A scholarly study of the political content, relevance and influence of the American protest movement. There is some historical background, much about Woody Guthrie, Pete Seeger and, of course, Bob Dylan and the protest singers of the sixties. Sometimes turgid, it is informative and well indexed with an excellent bibliography. The discography is of American releases which are often obscure.

Denisoff, R. Serge
   Sing a song of social significance / R. Serge Denisoff. – Bowling Green, Ohio:
   Bowling Green University Press, 1972. – 227p.: ill., ports; 24cm. Includes
   bibliography and index. ISBN 0–87972–036–6
A survey of the growth of the protest movement from the work of Guthrie to the likes of Paul Simon, Bob Dylan and the upsurge of the sixties. More involved in the political and social aspects of the movement than in its music.

Denisoff, R. Serge
   Songs of protest, war and peace: a bibliography and discography / R. Serge
   Denisoff. – Revised ed. – Santa Barbara, California; Oxford: ABC-Clio,
   1973. – xvi, 70p.; 23cm. ISBN 0-87436-121-4 (pbk.)
   Previous edition: Los Angeles: Center for Study of Armament and
   Disarmament, California State College, 1970.
An exhaustive bibliography of anti-war and other social themes in American folk song with a detailed discography of American releases.

Rodnitsky, Jerome L.
   Minstrels of the dawn: the folk-protest singer as cultural hero / Jerome
   L. Rodnitsky. – Chicago: Nelson-Hall, 1976. – xx, 192p., 4p. of plates: ill.,
   ports; 23cm. Includes bibliography, discography and index.

ISBN 0-8829-284-6

Written with a mood of nostalgia and lost idealism, the history of the protest movement is examined from Guthrie to its decline. The lives and careers of the major performers are well discussed with lengthy reference to songs and quotations by the artists and their friends. There is a final chapter analysing the decline and the move of the major artists into other forms of music. The bibliography is exhaustive, the discography a good guide and the index well constructed.

SINGER-SONGWRITERS

A singer-songwriter is an artist who both writes and performs his or her own material and who is usually able to perform solo playing (for example, acoustic guitar or piano). There was a particularly strong movement in this field in the early seventies with such artists as Joni Mitchell, Neil Young, James Taylor, Jackson Browne, Randy Newman, Cat Stevens, Janis Ian and David Ackles.

Sarlin, Bob
  Turn it up! (I can't hear the words) / Bob Sarlin. – London: Coronet, 1975. –
  239p., 4p. of plates: ill., ports; 18cm. ISBN 0-340-17848-5 (pbk.)
  Originally published: New York: Simon and Schuster, 1974.
An account of the birth of what the author calls songpoetry. The work of the major artists is analysed in the context of their lyrics. There is a strong American bias and some notable omissions but, in general, this is a good survey of the growth of an influential movement with good illustrations and interesting quotes.

FOLK ROCK

Folk rock was born in 1965 when Bob Dylan's album Bringing It All Back Home was released. This collection of songs, which would have previously been set to a simple acoustic backing, were now augmented with electric instrumentation and a rock'n'roll beat. Subsequently the Byrds beautifully recorded a series of Dylan songs with their intelligent, political themes, using folk-style harmonies and jangling, electric-guitar sound and, after a world-wide success, established this new style. In Britain during the sixties the Fairport Convention began experimenting with English traditional folk music and electric instruments and produced English folk rock which was to be popularized by Steeleye Span in the early seventies.

The electric muse: the story of folk into rock / Dave Laing, Karl Dallas, Robin
  Denselow & Robert Shelton. – London: Eyre Methuen, 1975. – 182p., 18p.
  of plates: ill., ports; 20cm. Includes discography and index.
  ISBN 0-413-31860-5 (pbk.)

An excellent work by four respected music journalists which describes the folk movement of the fifties and its origins and its development into the singer-songwriter boom of the sixties and seventies in the USA. Britain is not neglected, however, and the final quarter of the book is devoted to British folk rock and its development from the traditional folk revival. Written with great attention to detail and accuracy, with notes on all the major exponents of the form and a good discography, this is the best source of information on folk rock.

Vassal, Jacques
   Electric children: roots and branches of modern folk rock / Jacques Vassal; translated and adapted by Paul Barnett. – New York: Taplinger Publishing Company, 1976. – 270p., 18p. of plates: ill., ports; 23cm. Includes bibliography, discography and index. ISBN 0-8008-2382-6
   Originally published in French as *'Folksong: une histoire de la musique populaire aux Etats-Unis'*: Paris: Albin Michel, 1971.
   Also published: Ontario, Canada: Burns & MacEachern, 1976.
A well-researched study of the development of folk rock from its roots in the traditional folk music of both sides of the Atlantic. There is a significant American bias, but a chapter is included on the development of folk rock in Britain. Information on the singer-songwriters, who emerged out of the folk revival of the late fifties and sixties and became the leading writers and performers in the seventies, is included as well as notes on the more purist exponents.

5.4 COUNTRY MUSIC

Originally described as country and western, country music is based on the music of the rural southern and southwestern USA. With its roots firmly in the white folk music of the Appalachians, country music was founded in the twenties with the early recordings of Jimmie Rodgers and the Carter Family. Transmitted to wider audiences by radio, namely programmes such as the Grand 'Ole Opry, it has continuously evolved over the past sixty years and in the last twenty years has become established as a major branch of commercial pop music. It has both fused with rock music to form country rock in the sixties, and has more recently been influenced by rock's tougher side with the work of the likes of Waylon Jennings and Willie Nelson, known as outlaw music. Even in the soft rock or AOR fields, artists such as the Eagles show distinct commercial country influences in their style and the recording studios of country music's capital, Nashville, are used by a wide range of artists from Paul McCartney to Elvis Costello.

An interesting feature of country is its wide appeal and since the early seventies its popularity in Britain has grown until it is now the most widely enjoyed single style of pop music, particularly by the older followers of popular music.

The range and quantity of books on country clearly displays the obvious interest in the form. The literature ranges from serious histories and detailed discographies to collections of portraits with brief notes for the fan.

A detailed arrangement is required to organize the volume of material available: Encyclopedias; Histories; Surveys; Collected lives and works; Yearbooks; Almanacs; Discographies; Quizbooks.

Encyclopedias

Brown, Len
  The encyclopedia of country and western music / by Len Brown and Gary
  Friedrich. – New York: Tower Publications, 1971. – 191p.: ill., ports; 18cm.
  (pbk.)
A poorly produced, alphabetically arranged encyclopedia which contains biographical information about the major artists from the twenties to the late sixties. There are no discographies and a limited number of portraits.

Dellar, Fred
  The illustrated encyclopedia of country music / Fred Dellar, Roy Thompson,
  Douglas B. Green. – London: Salamander Books, 1977. – 256p.: ill. (some
  col.), facsims, ports (some col.); 31cm. Includes discographies and index.
  ISBN 0-86101-012-4 (pbk.)
  Originally published: New York: Harmony Books, 1977.
A well-written and well-illustrated brief encyclopedia arranged in an alphabetical sequence of artists, forms of music and instruments. It includes the historical figures of country music as well as modern performers, and attempts to include major artists from country rock and the cabaret fringe of country. For the British reader this is the best introductory reference work to this form of music with excellent discographies and index.

Gentry, Linnell
  A history and encyclopedia of country, western, and gospel music / by Linnell
  Gentry. – St. Clair Shores, Michigan: Scholarly Press, 1972. – vi, 380p.;
  23cm. ISBN 0-4030-1358-5 (pbk.)
  Originally published: Nashville, Tennessee: Clairmont Corp., 1961.
  Previous edition: Nashville, Tennessee, Clairmont Corp., 1969.
Divided into two sections: part 1 is a collection of reproductions of seventy-six articles which have appeared in journals, newspapers and pamphlets between 1908 and 1968; and part 2 is a collection of six hundred biographies of major artists. The articles vary from lengthy, detailed academic pieces to simple, single-page reports from magazines such as *Newsweek* and *Time*. Not an encyclopedia: the author says his aim is to provide biographical information as well as a range of historical sources. Access is difficult, badly needing an index.

Kash, Murray
  Murray Kash's book of country music / Murray Kash. – London: Star books,
  1981. – 509p.; 18cm. Includes discographies. ISBN 0-3523-0443-X (pbk.)
Written by the Canadian journalist who organizes the annual festival of country music at Wembley, this is an alphabetically arranged encyclopedia

mainly of biographical notes as well as a few definitions of styles of music, musical terms and notes on instruments. It is comprehensive, if often a little brief, and includes British artists. The discographies are particularly useful, highlighting artists' better albums. The lack of portraits, however, is a handicap to this otherwise useful reference source.

Shestack, Melvin
>*The country music encyclopedia* / by Melvin Shestack. – London: Omnibus
>Press, 1977. – 375p.: ill., ports; 25cm. Includes discography.
>ISBN 0-86001-308-1 (pbk.)
>Originally published: New York: Thomas Y. Crowell, 1974.

This comprehensive encyclopedia includes biographies of all the major and many less well known country-music artists. To the British reader many of the artists, all of whom are American, will be unknown. A few country-rock performers are included but only those leaning far more heavily towards country. The discography is good, including American details only. There are many portraits unavailable elsewhere.

Histories

Gaillard, Frye
>*Watermelon wine: the spirit of country music* / Frye Gaillard. – New York: St.
>Martin's Press, 1978. – xv, 236p.: ill., ports; 25cm. ISBN 0-3128-5697-0

A thorough, but not scholarly look at the evolution of country music up to the late seventies. The emphasis is on the themes of the music and the influences of the writers and the performers. The historical background is well analysed but the author does not sustain particular historical themes; he merely sets the contemporary scene in context. There are extensive examples of lyrics.

Green, Douglas B.
>*Country roots: the origins of country music* / Douglas B. Green; foreword by
>Merle Travis. – New York: Hawthorn Books, 1976. – 238p.: ill., ports; 28cm.
>Includes bibliography, discography and index. ISBN 0-8015-1781-8 (cased).
>ISBN 0-8015-1778-8 (pbk.)

A good, well-illustrated background to modern country music which includes chapters on the various styles that have developed into the popular country music of Nashville. There is also a chapter on rockabilly and a final one on Nashville. There are portraits of all the major stars. The discography includes only American releases but is extensive. There is also a chronology of significant events in the music between 1877 and 1975 which includes all top-five hit records between 1923 and 1975. The bibliography is selective and again American but offers a good guide for material on the history of the subject and is classified by style: for example, cajun, gospel, blues, singing cowboys and so on.

Hemphill, Paul
>*The Nashville sound: bright lights and country music* / by Paul Hemphill. –
>New York: Simon and Schuster, 1970. – 289p.; 22cm. Includes index.

ISBN 0-671-20493-9

Beginning with the pre-war days of the Grand 'Ole Opry, the career of Jimmie Rodgers and leading up to Johnny Cash and Merle Haggard, the author shows the development of fortunes in country music up to 1970. The work is informative, describing the recording studios and radio stations as well as the major artists throughout the thirty years of its coverage, and is thoughtful and journalistically researched. What the author saw as a peak in country music at the time of writing, was, in retrospect, only the beginning of its establishment as a form with a world-wide following.

The illustrated history of country music / by the editors of *Country Music* magazine; edited by Patrick Carr. – Garden City, New York: Dolphin Books, 1980. – 359p.: ill., ports; 27cm. Includes index. ISBN 0-385-15385-6 (pbk.)
Originally published: Garden City, New York: Doubleday, 1979.

This is a history which traces country music from its origins in the Old World to its development in the east of the USA and finally into its present popular form. There are chapters on the phases in its evolution with extensive information on Nashville and modern, popular country styles. Rockabilly is well covered with early illustrations of the major performers. There is a well-produced index for artists, songs, recording studios and styles.

Malone, Bill C.
Country music U.S.A.: a fifty year history / by Bill C. Malone. – Austin, Texas; London: University of Texas Press, 1968. – xii, 422p., 16p. of plates: ill., ports; 24cm. Includes bibliography, discography and index.
ISBN 0-292-78377-9

This well-documented, scholarly history was written by the Professor of History at Murray State University, Kentucky. His slant is that of the traditionalist. The folk roots of country music are analysed in depth touching on black and white traditions as well as the music hall. The early commercial period of the twenties and thirties is outlined with excellent biographical notes, especially on Jimmie Rodgers. This leads on to the background to modern country music and its folk and pop associations. There is a great deal of information here, an excellent bibliography and a well-constructed index.

Price, Steven D.
Take me home: the rise of country and western music / Steven D. Price. – New York: Praeger, 1974. – 184p.; 22cm. Includes bibliography, discography and indexes. ISBN 0-275-53610-2

This book traces the story of country music from its folk origins in Irish ballads and Scottish border ballads, through the early Nashville days, and then on to the later wave of songwriters such as Kris Kristofferson and Johnny Cash. The various influences from bluegrass, black music and rock'n'roll are all discussed along with country music's reciprocal influences. There are detailed notes, a section of fifty short biographies and a helpful general index and song indexes. Written for the intelligent reader, this is a very good introduction to the subject.

Shelton, Robert
The country music story: a picture history of country and western music /
Robert Shelton; photographs by Burt Goldblatt. – Indianapolis: Bobb-
Merrill, 1966. – 256p.: ill., ports; 26cm. Includes discography and index.
A well-illustrated history with a brief commentary outlining the development
of country music from the twenties to the sixties. The selective discography is of
American releases.

Stambler, Irwin
Golden guitars: the story of country music / Irwin Stambler and Grelun
Landon. – New York: Four Winds Press, 1971. – 186p.: ill., ports; 24cm.
Includes index.
A brief but well-written history with biographies of the leading performers
from the twenties to the sixties with portraits of many of them. The develop-
ment of bluegrass as well as commercial country music is covered, and the
influence of radio is an important theme.

Tosches, Nick
Country: the biggest music in America / Nick Tosches. – New York: Dell,
1979. – 258p.: ill., facsims, ports; 24cm. Includes discography and index.
ISBN 0-4451-440-1 (pbk.)
Originally published: New York: Stein & Day, 1977.
A good outline history, this is well illustrated and has discographical information on old recordings. The British reader may find the hilarious style and some
of the detail rather esoteric and mildly shocking in its frankness about the
lifestyle and the behind-the-scenes of Nashville society. Nevertheless, a great
deal of information has here been made accessible.

Walthall, Daddy Bob
The history of country music / Daddy Bob Walthall. – Houston, Texas:
Walthall Publishing, 1978. – 210p.: ill., ports; 22cm. Includes index.
ISBN 0-8601-5820-0
The first volume of a proposed lengthy history which includes some rare
illustrations and background to the modern styles of country music. Not
scholarly in approach but informative, with real appreciation of the music and
personal knowledge of many of the performers.

Wolfe, Charles K.
Tennessee strings: the story of country music in Tennessee / by Charles
K. Wolfe. – Knoxville, Tennessee: University of Tennessee Press, 1977. – x,
118p.: ill., ports; 23cm. Includes bibliography, discography and index.
ISBN 0-8704-9224-1
Tennessee has become the centre of commercial country music, with Nashville
its capital. This is a well-organized, well-researched history with a detailed
bibliography of sources and a good collection of illustrations.

Surveys

Bart, Teddy
Inside Music City, U.S.A. / by Teddy Bart. – Nashville, Tennessee: Aurora,
1970. – 164p.: ill., ports; 24cm.
A simple look at the activities which make Nashville the centre of country
music. Promoters, agents, studios and musicians are all covered in an uncritical
way.

Chalker, Bryan
Country music / written by Bryan Chalker; edited by Jeremy Pascall;
designed by Rob Burt. – London: Phoebus, 1976. – 95p.: ill. (some col.),
ports (some col.); 31cm. ISBN 0-7026-0015-6
A popular, simple introduction: there is a good essay outlining the range of
styles of country music, biographical notes on the major performers and a brief
look at Nashville and the Grand 'Ole Opry.

Corbin, Everett J.
Storm over Nashville: a case against modern country music / Everett
J. Corbin. – Nashville, Tennessee: Ashlar Press, 1980. – 202p.: ill., ports;
22cm. ISBN 0-932534-17-9
The author considers that the country-music industry is ruining the tradition of
the music by overt commercialism and thereby losing sight of its roots. It is a
good analysis of the contemporary scene but obsessive and biased.

Cornfield, Robert
Just country: country people, stories, music / Robert Cornfield; with Marshall
Fallwell, Jr. – New York: McGraw-Hill, 1976. – 176p.: ill., ports; 28cm.
Includes index. ISBN 0-0701-3184-8 (cased). ISBN 0-0701-3178-3 (pbk.)
Well illustrated, with some informative, chatty essays, this is a good survey of
country music with an excellent analysis of the developing styles. There are
biographical notes on leading artists which make real attempts at analysis.

Dellar, Fred
The best of country music / Fred Dellar and Richard Wootton; foreword by
Don Williams. – London: Octopus, 1980. – 96p.: ill. (chiefly col.), ports
(chiefly col.); 31cm. ISBN 0-7064-1204-4 (pbk.)
A beautifully illustrated but superficial look at contemporary country music,
with the briefest of notes on the major stars.

Grissim, John
Country music: white man's blues / by John Grissim. – New York: Paperback
Library, 1970. – 299p.: ill., ports; 18cm. (pbk.)
A good survey of the Nashville scene at the turn of the decade, this is
comprehensive with some well-selected illustrations. Country music's evolution in the seventies, however, does make it seriously dated, not simply
because of the new artists that have emerged but because of the general mood,
attitude, confidence and creativity of some of the recent country stars.

Hill, Thomas A.
Country music / by Thomas A. Hill. – New York: Franklin Watts, 1978. –
87p.: ill., ports; 24cm. Includes index. ISBN 0-5310-1405-3
Written as a first introduction to country music for children with a reading age
of around ten, this has a good, simple text with some fine photographs. The
major singers are all included: old and modern.

Hume, Martha
*Martha Hume's guide to the greatest in country music: you're so cold I'm
turning blue* / Martha Hume. – New York: Viking Press; Penguin Books,
1982. – xiii, 202p.: ill., facsims, ports; 24cm. ISBN 0-670-24417-1 (cased).
ISBN 0-14-006-348-X (pbk.)
The author's aim has been to produce a book which not only conveys a great
deal of information, but also her love of the music and the mood of the country-
music scene. The result is that the reader is bombarded with quizzes and lists of
seemingly arbitrary collections of facts. For example, the ten best songs of class
consciousness; best cowboy songs; useful addresses; artists' former day jobs;
ten best cheatin' songs; and so on. In addition, there are some unusual essays
and interesting illustrations. Amusing and potentially informative, but the lack
of an index is a pity.

Lazarus, Lois
Country is my music! / by Lois Lazarus. – New York: J. Messner, 1980. –
192p.: ill., ports; 22cm. Includes index. ISBN 0-6713-2953-7
A contemporary survey featuring the major stars with emphasis on the outlaw
movement and the rock-orientated new stars of Nashville. The portraits are
well chosen and there is considerable musical analysis, unusual for books on
country.

Sakol, Jeannie
The wonderful world of country music / by Jeannie Sakol. – New York:
Grosset & Dunlap, 1979. – 240p.: ill., ports; 28cm. Includes index.
ISBN 0-448-14392-5 (cased). ISBN 0-448-14393-3 (pbk.)
An alphabetically arranged collection of facts about country music from the
biographies of its major stars to lists of the winners of awards, booking
agencies, films, American radio stations and even a glossary of recording
terminology. Well illustrated, this is not a comprehensive encyclopedia and
lacks a well-organized discography but it is, nevertheless, a source of information available nowhere else in book form in the UK.

Worth, Fred L.
The country & western book / Fred L. Worth. – New York: Drake
Publishers, 1977. – 94p.: ill., ports; 23cm. ISBN 0-847-31575-4
An outline of the contemporary country-music scene, this collection of bio-
graphical notes and portraits offers a good introduction without analysing the
music or looking at the commercial background.

Collected lives and works

David, Andrew
  Country music stars: people at the top of the charts / Andrew David; edited by
  Ray Levin. – Chicago: Domus Books, 1980. – 96p.: ill., ports; 29cm.
  Includes index. ISBN 0-8919-6063-5
  Also published: New York: Galahad Books, 1980.
A collection of brief biographies with portraits of the major current country-
music stars, this is biographically informative but lacks detail of their work and
discographical information.

Davis, Paul
  New life in country music / by Paul Davis; with foreword by Cliff Richard and
  introduction by George Hamilton IV; illustrations by Richard Deverell. –
  Worthing: Henry Walker, 1976. – 111p.: ill., ports; 18cm.
  ISBN 0-85479-591-X (pbk.)
A collection of biographies of country singers, this is written from a Christian
standpoint with a central theme of their religious belief and how their enlight-
enment has enlivened their music. The artists include Pat Boone, Johnny Cash,
Skeeta Davis and George Hamilton IV.

Dew, Joan
  Singers & sweethearts: the women of country music / by Joan Dew. – Garden
  City, New York: Dolphin Books, 1977. – 148p., 1 leaf of plates: ill., ports;
  28cm. ISBN 0-385-12595-X
A well-illustrated collection of informative biographical sketches of the major
female stars in country music. Included are Loretta Lynn, Tammy Wynette,
June Carter, Dolly Parton and Tanya Tucker. There are no discographies but
their recordings are discussed in the text.

Gray, Andy
  Great country music stars / Andy Gray. – London: Hamlyn, 1975. – 176p.: ill.
  (some col.), facsim., ports (some col.); 31cm. ISBN 0-600-33979-3
A collection of brief biographies and portraits of the major artists of country
music. Although it is mostly of recent performers, some of the pioneers of the
style are included.

Hollaran, Carolyn
  Meet the stars of country music / Carolyn Rada Hollaran. – Nashville,
  Tennessee: Aurora Publishers, 1977. – 179p.: ill., ports; 28cm.
  ISBN 0-8769-5204-X (pbk.)
A survey of the contemporary country-music scene. Informative, with a very
good collection of portraits, the emphasis is on the story of Nashville rather
than the new-wave, Texas-based artists.

Hollaran, Carolyn
  Meet the stars of country music: volume 2 / Carolyn Rada Hollaran. –
  Nashville, Tennessee: Aurora Publishers, 1978. – 191p.: ill., ports; 28cm.

ISBN 0-8769-5212-0 (pbk.)
A second volume with the intention of becoming an annual survey. An excellent collection of portraits with an informative text.

Hollaran, Carolyn
   Your favourite country music stars / by Carolyn Hollaran. – New York:
   Popular Library, 1975. – 283p.: ill., ports; 18cm. ISBN 0-445-03076-3 (pbk.)
Brief biographies of the leading contemporary country stars, this is an informative book with portraits. A few surviving or influential stars of earlier eras are included.

Kosser, Michael
   Those bold and beautiful country girls / by Michael Kosser. – Leicester,
   Leicestershire: Windward, 1979.– 127p.: ill; 28cm. ISBN 0-7112-0022-X
   (pbk.)
A collection of biographical essays on the leading female stars of country music. Full of glamorous portraits and brief notes of little substance.

Krishef, Robert K.
   Western stars of country music / Robert K. Krishef and Bonnie Lake. –
   Minneapolis: Lerner Publications, 1978. – 71p: ill., ports; 21cm. Includes
   index. ISBN 0-8225-1407-9 (pbk.)
This controlled-vocabulary text is aimed at a reading age of about ten for American schools. It is a well-selected collection of brief biographies and portraits, mainly of the country-music artists described as the cowboy singers. Although some are more recent, most of these thrived in the forties and fifties.

Rubenstein, Raenne
   Honky tonk heroes: a photo album of country music / photographs by
   Raenne Rubenstein; text by Peter McCaber. – New York: Harper & Row,
   1975. – 154p.: ill. (chiefly col.), ports (chiefly col.); 30cm. ISBN 0-61-28924-5
   (cased). ISBN 0-61-28922-3 (pbk.)
A good collection of photographs of the major stars, contemporary and of the past, with very brief biographical notes.

Stars of country music: Uncle Dave Macon to Johnny Rodriguez / edited by Bill
   C. Malone and Judith McCulloch. – Urbana, Illinios: University of Illinois
   Press, 1975. – xii, 476p., 16p. of plates: ill., ports; 24cm. Includes index.
   ISBN 0-2520-0527-9
Uncle Dave Macon was born in 1870 and died in 1952. A superb banjo player, he was the mainstay of his style of country music until his death, which took place one year after Johnny Rodriguez, one of the youngest hopes of country, was born. In between the two, every major name is discussed in considerable detail. This is a serious work, describing the development of the music in its various styles. The emphasis is historical but recent important stars are treated with the same authority and interest.

Zanderbergen, George
Nashville music: Loretta Lynn, Mac Davis, Charlie Pride / by George
Zanderbergen. – Mankato, Minnesota: Crestwood House, 1976. – 47p.: ill.
(some col.), ports (some col.); 25cm. ISBN 0-9139-4050-X
Written for a reading age of around ten for American schools, this is a well-
produced collection of biographies, informative and well illustrated.

Yearbooks

British Country Music Association
Yearbook: British Country Music Assocation 1976 –. – Newton Abbot,
Devon: British Country Music Association, 1975 –. Annual. 1982. – 1981. –
80p.: ill., ports; 21cm. ISSN 0308-4698
The British Country Music Association was formed in 1975. Its yearbook is
both an annual survey of the country-music scene internationally as well as a
directory of the domestic scene. Advertisements for clubs and other local
country-music venues are of particular value. There are brief album reviews
and portraits of notable artists of the year.

Almanacs

Wootton, Richard
The illustrated country almanac: a day by day history of country music /
Richard Wootton. – London: Virgin Books, 1982. – 192p.: ill., ports; 28cm.
Includes index. ISBN 0-907080-53-7 (pbk.)
A daily list of important events in the country-music calendar which com-
memorates anniversaries, deaths, birthdays and a wide range of other signifi-
cant dates. Entertaining and informative, this is well designed with a good
selection of illustrations.

Discographies

Osborne, Jerry
55 years of recorded country & western music / by Jerry Osborne; edited by
Bruce Hamilton. – Phoenix, Arizona: C.O.L. Publishing, 1976. - xii, 164p.,
32p. of plates: ill., facsims; 28cm. Includes index. ISBN 0-89019-060-7
After an introductory history to country music and its recording, there is an
alphabetical arrangement by artist listing American releases. Details include
albums, singles with full label details and an indication of their value, graded by
condition. Old 78 r.p.m. records are included. A glossary, a list of gold records,
and an essay on rockabilly are interesting additional features, as is a lengthy
index to major record dealers arranged by state.

Tudor, Dean
Grassroots music / Dean Tudor and Nancy Tudor. – Littleton, Colorado:
Libraries Unlimited, 1979. – 367p.; 24cm. – (American Popular Music on
Elpee). Includes bibliography. ISBN 0-87287-133-9
Part of a four-volume series (the others include *Jazz, Black music* and

Contemporary popular music). After an excellent historical introduction the work is divided into sections covering folk music, old-time music, bluegrass, cowboy music, country music, sacred music and troubadour music. The authors' aim is to group significant recordings together and to include the best and most enduring. Each album has a three-hundred-word annotation and there is a fine bibliography. The series is one of real scholarship and offers a guide of unusual authority.

Quizbooks

Humphreys, Don
  The country music quizbook / Don and Barbara Humphreys. – Garden City,
  New York: Dolphin Books, 1978. – 167p.: ill., ports; 21cm.
  ISBN 0-385-12397-3 (pbk.)
For the country-music expert, this is a well-produced book of questions and answers with some very searching picture quizzes. As might be expected, no British country singers are included.

GRAND 'OLE OPRY

Since 1925 the Grand 'Ole Opry radio show has been broadcast weekly from Nashville and has had a significant effect on the promotion of country music. For many years it was a necessity to be played regularly on the Opry in order to become established in the country field. It was the brainchild of George D. Hay, who originally called his show the National Barn Dance. One night, however, the show was to follow a broadcast of a grand opera. Hay jokingly announced, 'Now we will present the Grand 'Ole Opry'. The phrase stuck. The younger 'outlaws' of country music reject the Opry as passé and the major stars no longer need to appear. Its days of supremacy have passed but it is affectionately thought of by most old country enthusiasts.

Hurst, Jack
  Nashville's Grand 'Ole Opry / text by Jack Hurst: introduction by Roy Acuff.
  – New York: Harry N. Abrams, 1975. – 404p.: ill. (chiefly col.), music, ports
  (chiefly col.); 36cm. Includes discography and index. ISBN 0-8109-0268-0
A history of the Opry to the mid seventies with brief, informative notes and lavish portraits of the major stars. The discography is very brief but it is for the illustrations that the work was produced.

Krishef, Robert K.
  The Grand 'Ole Opry / Robert K. Krishef. – Minneapolis: Lerner
  Publications, 1980. – 71p.: ill., ports; 21cm. Includes index.
  ISBN 0-8225-1405-2
Written for a reading age of around ten for American schools, this is a brief, controlled-vocabulary history of this radio institution. The approach suits the age range well. The illustrations are good and the text informative.

Wolfe, Charles K.
The Grand'Ole Opry: the early years, 1925–35 / Charles K. Wolfe. – London:
Old Time Music, 1975. – 128p.: ill., ports; 30cm.
A large format, well-illustrated look at the original stars of the show; a few
survived into the seventies but are seen here in the early stages of their careers.

BLUEGRASS

The term bluegrass was coined in the early fifties. It describes a vocal and
instrumental treatment of a certain type of traditional or composed folk song.
The vocal sound has a dominant, nasal tenor voice above which are a series of
high harmony voices. The instrumentation is traditional with no electric
instruments but banjos, guitars, violin and string bass. Basically a traditional
form, the style became established when Bill Monroe, Earl Scruggs, Lester
Flatt and Chubby Wise began releasing records in the late forties. It is featured
in country-music concerts, where it is appreciated for the virtuosity of the
musicians, and remains a popular form.

Artis, Bob
*Bluegrass: from the lonesome wail of the mountain lovesong to the
hammering of Scruggs-style banjo, the story of an American tradition* / Bob
Artis. – New York: Hawthorn Books, 1975. – xviii, 182p., 12 leaves of plates:
ill., ports; 25cm. Includes bibliography, discography and index.
ISBN 0-8015-0758-8
A detailed reference source on the bluegrass idiom with biographical notes on
its main artists, a lengthy discography, lists of magazines, radio stations and
portraits. Well indexed. The bibliography is very brief.

Price, Steven D.
Old as the hills: the story of bluegrass music / Steven D. Price. – New York:
Viking Press, 1975. – 110p.: ill., ports; 22cm. Includes discography and
index. ISBN 0-670-52204-X
This book traces the evolution of bluegrass from its purely folk roots. There are
brief biographies of the major artists, past and present, and an analysis of the
style and its origins. The discography is American and includes recordings of
most of the significant performers in the field.

OUTLAWS

Led by Waylon Jennings, Willie Nelson, Tompall Glaser and Jessi Colter, the
outlaws movement began in the early seventies as a revolt against the orchestral blandness which had grown up in Nashville. The new style was grittier and
more exciting rhythmically with more personalized, contemporary lyrics
tending in presentation towards rock'n'roll.

Bane, Michael
    The outlaws: revolution in country music / Michael Bane. – New York:
    Country Music Magazine Press; Doubleday, 1978. – 154p.: ill., ports; 28cm.
    ISBN 0-3851-2596-8
With an informative text and good illustrations, this looks at the growth of the
outlaw movement into a major force in country music. There are short
biographies of the major artists and brief analyses of their styles. In short, this is
a concise and perceptive analysis which is popular in presentation and of high
quality in content.

Claypool, Bob
    Saturday night at Gilley's / by Bob Claypool; principal photographer Tony
    Bullard. – New York: Delilah; Grove Press, 1980. – 176p.: ill., ports; 26cm.
    ISBN 0-394-17727-4 (pbk.)
Gilley's is the country-music night club in Houston, Texas which was the centre
of the John Travolta film Urban Cowboy. The film generated a trend in
country-music clubs throughout the USA in 1980. This book describes the club,
discusses the growth of the modern, outlaw style of country music and cowboy
dress in America.

Krishef, Robert K
    More new breed stars / Robert K. Krishef. – Minneapolis: Lerner
    Publications, 1980. – 71p.: ill., ports; 21cm. Includes index.
    ISBN 0-8225-1410-9
Written for a reading age of around ten for American schools, this is a
controlled-vocabulary text of short biographies of the most recent country-
music stars with some good illustrations.

Krishef, Robert K.
    The new breed / Robert K. Krishef. – Minneapolis: Lerner Publications,
    1978. – 71p.: ill, ports; 21cm. Includes index. ISBN 0-8225-1406-0
This collection of biographies and illustrations of the stars of the late seventies
country-music scene is written for a reading age of about ten for American
schools.

Reid, Jan
    The improbable rise of redneck rock / by Jan Reid; photographs by Melinda
    Wickman. – New York: Da Capo Press, 1977. – xviii, 342p.: ill., ports; 23cm.
    ISBN 0-306-80065-9 (pbk.)
    Originally published: Austin, Texas: Heidelberg Publishers, 1974
Written with almost missionary zeal, this is a thorough survey of the evolution
of country-rock as manifested in Texas. Early influences of people like Janis
Joplin are discussed, as is the fusion of styles making the music, from blues,
rock to gospel. There is an emphasis on the major performers, particularly
Willie Nelson, Kinky Friedman and the Texas Jewboys, Willis Alan Ramsey,
Guy Clark and Michael Murphy. There is an excellent collection of photographs of the major performers, unknown to all but ardent country fans. Sadly
lacking are an index and discography.

5.5 ROCK'N'ROLL

A much misused and abused term, rock'n'roll is frequently used to describe all modern popular music. It is, in fact, the seed from which current popular music has evolved. The fusion of white country music and black rhythm & blues, it has influenced all existing forms, from black music to country music, from folk music to jazz.

If Elvis Presley was the real catalyst, Bill Haley was the first to make a wide impact in 1954 and the Chords' record Sh'boom, even earlier in 1954, is often claimed to be the first rock'n'roll hit.

The debate will continue without conclusion; many of the artists who are regarded as the early rockers were country musicians or black rhythm & blues singers, and would have regarded themselves as strictly in one of those two categories.

To the purist, rock'n'roll died when Elvis Presley entered the army in 1958 and in a strict sense this event can be seen as the end of this first era.

In its original form rock'n'roll continues to be enjoyed by both its original fans as well as by their children and its pervasive influence continues to evolve throughout contemporary popular music.

Brown, Len
Encyclopedia of rock & roll / by Len Brown and Gary Friedrich. – New
York: Tower Publications, 1970. – 217p.: ill., ports; 18cm. (pbk.)
There is a strong American bias in this alphabetically arranged work which covers the biographies of most major artists from the fifties, including the details of their careers into the sixties – where they survived. Some black musicians are included, notably the rhythm & blues singing groups. There are no discographies and the production is poor with limited illustrations.

Busnar, Gene
It's rock'n'roll / Gene Busnar. – New York: Julian Messner, 1979. – 247p.:
ill., ports; 24cm. Includes bibliography, discographies and index.
ISBN 0-671-32977-4
Also published: New York: Wanderer Books, 1979.
Prompted by the rock'n'roll revival of the late seventies which was started by the films Grease and the Buddy Holly Story, this is a well-organized retrospective survey with an earnest attempt to describe the development of rock'n'roll accurately. After a brief outline, the biographies of the major artists are classified in their particular styles: for example, Northern band music, rockabilly, Chicago vocal-group music and so on. Each section and individual biography includes an excellent discography.

Colman, Stuart
They kept on rockin' / Stuart Colman. – Poole, Dorset: Blandford Press,
1982. – 160p.: ill., ports; 25cm. Includes index. ISBN 0-7137-1217-7 (pbk.)
Written by a BBC Radio London disc jockey whose programme features

authentic rock'n'roll and who has been the producer of Shakin' Stevens' hit records, this aims to be the story of the original stars of rock'n'roll who have survived and are still involved in music. Not all are still performing rock'n'roll and some, such as Elvis Presley and Bill Haley, have not survived but, nevertheless, this is an excellent collection of well-written, informative biographies including not only the American greats, such as Jerry Lee Lewis, Chuck Berry and Fats Domino but also British rockers, such as Cliff Richard, Wee Willie Harris, Marty Wilde and Johnny Kidd. Their important records are mentioned in the text and the illustrations are rare and well chosen.

Elson, Howard
   Early rockers / by Howard Elson. – London; New York: Proteus, 1982. – 128p.: ill., ports; 27cm. ISBN 0-86276-087-9 (cased). ISBN 0-86276-086-0 (pbk.)
A good survey of the influential figures of fifties rock'n'roll. Of particular interest is the coverage of lesser-known but important artists, such as Louis Jordan and Larry Williams, who are often overlooked. This is a good source of early illustrative material

Goodgold, Edwin
   Rock'n'roll trivia / Edwin Goodgold and Dan Carlinsky. – New York: Popular Library, 1970. – 138p: ill., ports; 28cm. (pbk.)
A mass of information about music of the fifties including white rock'n'roll as well as inffluential black rhythm & blues performers. Biggest-selling records, most-recorded songs, extracts from charts, details of musicians and a good collection of photographs make this an entertaining work, packed with facts which are unfortunately difficult to find.

McColm, Bruce
   Where have they gone?: rock'n'roll stars / by Bruce McColm & Doug Payne. – New York: Tempo Books, 1979. – 254p.: ill., ports; 18cm. ISBN 0-4481-7025-6 (pbk.)
A retrospective look at the early stars of American rock'n'roll, rockabilly and rhythm & blues. All the major stars are included: those whose careers continue as well as those now forgotten. Of particular interest are a whole range of artists completely unknown to the British audience.

Pollock, Bruce
   When rock was young: a nostalgic review of the top forty era / by Bruce Pollock. – New York: Holt, Rinehart & Winston, 1981. – 214p.: ill., ports; 22cm. Includes index. ISBN 0-03-049836-8 (cased). ISBN 0-03-049841-4 (pbk.)
Concerned with the fifties and early sixties, this is basically, as the subtitle states, a nostalgic look at the early days of rock'n'roll along with black artists and pop singers of the period. The major stars are all here but the British reader will probably not recognize some of the artists included and one will not find the likes of Cliff Richard, Johnny Kidd, Marty Wilde or even Tommy Steele.

Rogers, Dave
  Rock'n'roll / Dave Rogers. – London: Routledge & Kegan Paul, 1982. –
  148p.: ill., ports; 23cm. Includes bibliography, discography and index.
  ISBN 0-7100-0938-0
After setting rock'n'roll in the historical context of the fifties with its associated
subculture, the Teddy Boys, the author explains its evolution from rhythm &
blues and country music in some detail. The major artists, with particular note
of their significance in Britain, are all here. The author concludes with an
epilogue which notes the revival in the seventies but fails to develop the legacy
of rock'n'roll in the best music of the sixties through to punk rock and its effect
on all other music on the way. Nevertheless, suitable for use as a textbook and
with a very good index and glossary, this is a good introduction.

Shaw, Arnold
  The rockin' '50s: the decade that transformed the pop music scene / Arnold
  Shaw. – New York: Hawthorn Books, 1974. – xv, 296p.: ill., ports; 25cm.
Arnold Shaw's experience of the music business in the fifties as an executive in
music publishing makes this survey particularly important. Well illustrated
with unusual photographs of many of the significant personalities of the period,
the book's main theme is the way in which the advent of rock'n'roll transformed the existing, sterile popular-music scene. Shaw acknowledges the
overwhelming influence of black musicians and 'race music' on the growth of
rock'n'roll and develops this theme to show how, by the late fifties, black
musicians themselves were becoming accepted at last as a highly significant
element in the American music industry.

The stars of rock'n'roll. – London: Alan Keen, 1966. – 48p.: ill., ports; 29cm.
  (pbk.)
The stars of rock'n'roll: Book 2. – London: Alan Keen, 1970. – 16p.: ill., ports;
  28cm. (pbk.)
Two collections of portraits of rock'n'roll stars with very brief biographical
sketches. They appeared with an interval of four years, produced by an
enthusiast who presumably mistimed the music's revival.

Whitcomb, Ian
  Whole lotta' shakin': a rock'n'roll scrapbook / Ian Whitcomb. – London:
  Arrow Books, 1982. – 190p.: ill., facsims, ports; 30cm. ISBN 0-09-927170-2
  (pbk.)
Covering the period from 1955 to 1965, presented in the form of a fan's
scrapbook. The author has compiled an excellent collection of press extracts,
reproduced as facsimiles, and presents the most important artists of the period
as seen by the general and music papers. There is a brief introductory essay to
each year with some intelligent observations. There are charts, lifelines and
some rare illustrations. The *New Musical Express, Record Mirror* and *Daily
Mirror* are the most-used sources.

Wood, Graham
  An A–Z of rock and roll / Graham Wood. – London: Studio Vista, 1971. –

128p.: ill., facsims, ports; 21cm. Includes discography and filmography. ISBN 0-289-70006-X (cased). ISBN 0-289-70005-1 (pbk.)
After a brief foreword which firmly places rock'n'roll accurately as the seminal influence on modern popular music, this is a good biographical dictionary of those involved in the music between 1955 and 1961. The major groups and solo artists are included, as well as many little-known ones. There are portraits of the majority of artists, a list of million-selling records and a list of films featuring rock'n'roll performers.

Discographies

Ferlingere, Robert D
A discography of rhythm & blues and rock'n'roll vocal groups, 1945 to 1965 / compiled by Robert D. Ferlingere. – Pittsburg, California: Ferlingere, 1976. – 700p.; 29cm. Includes indexes
A rare, privately published discography, this reflects clearly the development of rhythm & blues into rock'n'roll through the releases of mainly black vocal groups. Notes are sparse but the research involved here was immense.

Leichter, Albert
A discography of rhythm & blues and rock & roll circa 1946–1964: a reference manual / compiled by Albert Leichter. – Staunton, Virginia: Leichter, 1975. – 189p.; 30cm.
Privately published, this rare discography traces the development of rhythm & blues in its more ethnic and later commercial forms, its adoption by white singers and the subsequent emergence of rock'n'roll. The contents are of American releases which are arranged chronologically and then alphabetically by artist. Certainly not comprehensive, it is an interesting personal selection.

ROCKABILLY

When Elvis Presley fused the southern country-music traditions and guitar sounds with the feel and rhythms of black music giving birth to rock'n'roll, the earliest form of his Sun label recordings is described as rockabilly. The essential ingredients of this first true form of rock'n'roll are an upright acoustic bass played in a style which gives a slapping, rhythmic backbeat, a light guitar rhythm and an essentially country-style, electric-guitar solo. Drums are an optional extra and not for the purist. The music of the Stray Cats offers a commercially successful modern form.

Garbutt, Bob
Rockabilly queens / Bob Garbutt. – Toronto, Ontario: Ducktail Press, 1979. – 80p.: ill., ports; 21cm. Includes bibliography and discography. (pbk.)
A collection of short biographies of the leading women singers loosely defined as rockabilly artists: they include Lucille Starr, Joan Campbell, Rose Maddox, Wanda Jackson, Janis Martin, Jackie de Shannon, Brenda Lee and Lillian

Briggs. Country-music followers would probably claim some of these ladies, but this is an informative work with much information not available elsewhere.

Guralnick, Peter
Lost highway: journeys & arrivals of American musicians / Peter Guralnick.
– Boston, Massachusetts: David R. Godine, 1979. – x, 362p.: ill., ports; 23cm. Includes bibliography, discography and index. ISBN 0-87923-293-5 (cased). ISBN 0-87923-294-3 (pbk.)
A well-written, scholarly work on the influences and evolution of rockabilly. The author examines the careers of selected artists: Sleepy Lebeef and Charlie Feathers, obscure white singers, are included as well as country-blues artists such as Rufus Thomas, Howlin' Wolf and Otis Span. With an excellent essay on the early Elvis Presley and an analysis of the work of country artists Merle Haggard and Waylon Jennings, this work clearly demonstrates the difficulty of categorizing popular music.

5.6 BEAT MUSIC

By 1962 the excitement of rock'n'roll had subsided and the British record charts were dominated by former British rockers singing ballads, instrumental groups with American artists, notably black groups, adding some innovation to an otherwise stagnant period. The Merseybeat movement in Liverpool was still a very local source of enthusiasm. On October 5th 1962 the Beatles' first single, Love Me Do, was released by EMI to a confused national audience and was followed by Please Please Me on January 12th 1963. The confusion immediately changed into an unprecedented excitement and beat music was born.

The Beatles were followed by Brian Epstein's stable of Liverpool acts: Gerry and the Pacemakers, Billy J. Kramer and the Dakotas, the Fourmost, and others such as the Searchers and the Swinging Blue Jeans. Soon other groups emerged from all parts of the country: the Animals from Newcastle; the Dave Clark Five from London; the Hollies from Manchester; the Rockin' Berries from Birmingham; Brian Poole and the Tremeloes from Dagenham, Essex and hundreds of others. By 1964 the Rolling Stones were also established with their brand of British rhythm & blues but they, along with the Kinks and Yardbirds, represented a continuation of the impetus begun by the Beatles.

For the first time British artists made a big impression on the American record charts and for a period in 1963 America was dominated by this British beat movement, termed the British Invasion.

Cross, Colin
Encyclopedia of British beat groups & solo artists of the sixties / compiled by Colin Cross with Paul Kendall & Mick Farren. – London: Omnibus Press, 1981. – 96p.: ill., ports; 27cm. Includes index. ISBN 0-86001-638-2 (pbk.)
This covers the whole period of the sixties including British artists who emerged after the beat boom of the mid sixties. The alphabetical arrangement

is complemented by an index from individual artist to the group of which he was a member. The biographical notes are, however, brief and discographical information is sparse. Illustrations are well chosen, including rare portraits of lesser-known artists. This is an interesting work but sometimes inaccurate and rather too selective.

Ellis, Royston
   The big beat scene / Royston Ellis. – London: Four Square Books, 1961. – 124p.: ill., ports; 18cm. (pbk.)
Aimed at being an outspoken exposé of the teenage world of rock'n'roll, in retrospect this gives an interesting insight into British attitudes to the music and its fans before the emergence of the Beatles. Amusingly naive in parts, this is the first serious attempt to look into the British pop scene and became quite an influential work, establishing the author as the leading British pop writer up until 1966.

Gardner, Graham
   Then and now / by Graham Gardner. – Shepperton, Middlesex: Graham Gardner, 1981. – 89p.: ill., ports; 21cm. (pbk.)
Twelve British recording artists of the late fifties and early sixties have been interviewed recently by the author. Included are Marty Wilde, Kenny Lynch, Ricky Vallance, Jerry Lordan, Michael Cox, Alvin Stardust, Jess Conrad, Joe Brown, John Leyton, Craig Douglas and Heinz. There are twenty-year-old and contemporary portraits, and a fascinating collection of reminiscences reflecting on lost opportunities, lost money and faded talent.

May, Chris
   British beat / Chris May & Tim Phillips. – London: Socion Books, 1974. – 104p.: ill., ports; 29cm. Includes discographies. ISBN 0-903985-01-2 (pbk.)
Covering the period from 1962 to 1967 and dividing the music geographically into Merseybeat, London R & B, the Provinces and so on, the authors give a brief biography with an illustration of all the British groups who had a hit record in that period. There are full discographies and appendices which list hundreds of unsuccessful groups who performed at the time, as well as lists of films and important events. It unfortunately lacks an index but is a valuable source of information on the early careers of the major artists of the late sixties and seventies and the only source for many of the minor groups who faded away.

Schaffner, Nicholas
   British invasion: from the first wave to the new wave / Nicholas Schaffner. – New York: McGraw-Hill, 1982. – 316p.: ill., ports; 24cm. Includes index. ISBN 0-07-055089-1 (pbk.)
Written by an American who is acknowledged as an expert on the Beatles, this is an excellent account of the impact of British popular music on the USA since the early sixties. The major breakthrough by the Beatles and the Rolling Stones is well described and the author goes beyond a simple factual account to add his own intuitive analyses. The book is strongest on the sixties; the

superstars of the early seventies and the new wave of the later part of that decade and early eighties are treated with a little less enthusiasm. An excellent book from this intelligent American standpoint.

Trow, Michael-Arthur
   The pulse of '64: the Mersey Beat / Michael-Arthur Trow. – New York:
   Vangate Press, 1979. – 36p.: ill., ports; 21cm. ISBN 0-533-03396-9 (pbk.)
This curious little book describing the invasion of America by the Liverpool groups in 1964 and its effect on American culture is well written with some rare illustrations. Too brief to cover the subject thoroughly, it does offer a personal American perspective, although as the author was seven years old at the time its authority can be questioned.

HEAVY METAL

Originally 'heavy metal' described sluggishly rhythmic heavy rock of the late sixties and early seventies. Such bands as Grand Funk Railroad, Black Sabbath and Deep Purple were classic examples. They all basically distorted the blues using very powerful amplification. Since the late seventies there has been a so-called heavy-metal revival in Britain with such bands as Whitesnake, Rainbow, Motorhead and Gillan. With a following of largely working-class young people termed 'headbangers' because of their dancing movements, this style of music flourishes.

Halfin, Ross
   The power age / by Ross Halfin, Pete Makowski. – London: Eel Pie, 1982. –
   128p.: chiefly ill.: ports; 27cm. ISBN 0-906008-58-1 (pbk.)
With very little text, this is a well-produced collection of photographs containing the stars of the heavy-metal revival both in action and off-stage. All the major artists from both sides of the Atlantic are included. As an attempt to evoke the atmosphere and attitudes of the music, it is a very poor effort.

Harrigan, Brian
   Encyclopedia metallica / Brian Harrigan and Malcolm Dome. – London:
   Bobcat Books, 1980. – 92p.: chiefly ill., ports; 28cm. ISBN 0-86001-805-9
   (pbk.)
Described as the story of heavy-metal music from Cream and Jimi Hendrix to Rush and other heavy-metal groups of the eighties, this is a poor effort, badly arranged with illustrations of the major musicians and very brief notes. Although, for a time, the sole work on the subject, it is of little informational value with poorly reproduced portraits in comically tough poses.

Harrigan, Brian
   The HM A–Z / by Brian Harrigan. – London: Bobcat Books, 1981. – 64p.:
   ill., ports; 27cm. Includes discographies. ISBN 0-86001-928-4 (pbk.)
Arranged alphabetically and listing prominently the personnel of each band,

this is an improvement on the author's earlier attempt. Existing and defunct groups are included with full histories of line-ups and brief discographical information of album releases. The illustrations are quite good although there are too many inaccuracies for it to be a good reference source. There is also a full-size pull-out electric guitar.

Jasper, Tony
   The international encyclopedia of hard rock & heavy metal / Tony Jasper and
   Derek Oliver. – London: Sidgwick & Jackson, 1984. – 256p.: ill., ports;
   22cm. ISBN 0-283-99000-7 (pbk.)
A very good, alphabetically arranged source of information on a wide range of rock bands. Focussing on what is currently defined as heavy metal, it covers American AOR bands such as REO Speedwagon, progressive European rock bands and many lesser-known British bands. Well illustrated, and the text is factual and to the point. This is the best source on the subject.

PROGRESSIVE

Progressive music was a term used in the late sixties and early seventies to describe rock music with pretensions towards being an art form. It includes groups such as the Pink Floyd, the Nice and, later, Emerson, Lake and Palmer, Caravan and even Hawkwind. Such groups would later be described as playing art rock, pomp rock, jazz rock or even heavy metal.

McAleer, Richard
   A progressive rock portfolio / by Richard McAleer. – Syacuse, New York:
   Central New Yorker, 1970. – 96p.: ill., ports; 18cm. (pbk.)
This short book on the music at the turn of the decade covers a wide range of musicians, analysing types of music in depth, but it is oddly wrong in its perception of the future of rock.

5.7 WEST COAST

A loose term covering a wide range of musical forms which have emerged in Los Angeles and San Francisco. Surf music, folk rock, acid rock, soft rock and many of the singer-songwriters have flourished in California.

West Coast story / edited by Rob Burt and Patsy North. – London: Hamlyn;
   Phoebus, 1977. – 96p.: ill. (some col.), ports (some col.); 31cm.
   ISBN 0-600-39393-3
This is a well-illustrated outline history of the evolution of the musical styles associated with California throughout the sixties and seventies. It includes surf music and folk rock as well as psychedelic, acid rock and singer-songwriters.

Although brief, the book provides a surprisingly comprehensive outline. The Grateful Dead, the Byrds, Joni Mitchell, the Jefferson Airplane, the Beach Boys, Creedence Clearwater, the Doors, Steve Miller and the other names are all well covered with excellent illustrations.

SURF MUSIC

Basically a southern Californian trend, surf music began in the late fifties. The original staccato guitar sound was actually programme music for surfers, designed to simulate the feel of riding the waves. It was Brian Wilson of the Beach Boys who made this local phenomenon into a national craze. Wilson used the vocal ideas of Jan and Dean, which were a tribute to the sun, surf and youth, depicting a lifestyle of cars, girls, the beach and irresponsibility. The trend died out in 1966 with the advent of psychedelia, which made these old concepts of fun seem frivolous. The total absence of rebellion often gives surf music the reputation of having made rock'n'roll safe for middle-class ears but, nevertheless, in so doing it offered a new, wider, acceptable appeal.

Blair, John
   The illustrated discography of surf music, 1959–1965 / compiled & edited by
   John Blair. – Riverside, California: J. Bee Productions, 1978. – vi, 52p.: ill.,
   facsims, ports; 28cm. ISBN 0-9601-8800-2 (pbk.)
A beautifully printed and illustrated book; the author has produced a superb discography. He has excluded hot-rod music and imitations of the Beach Boys' vocal style. There are reproductions of rare labels, original posters and rare photographs. John Blair believes that unlike other trends in rock music surf music was sufficiently localized in California to make a truly comprehensive discography a realistic goal.

SPACE ROCK

Space rock is rock music with either lyrical themes concerned with science fiction or a musical sound evoking the atmosphere of space, the cosmos and the unknown. David Bowie, Hawkwind, the Pink Floyd and, for a brief period, the Byrds may all be described as having performed this type of music at some time.

Downing, David
   Future rock / David Downing. – St. Albans: Panther, 1976. – 172p.; 18cm.
   Includes discography. ISBN 0-586-04308-X (pbk.)
An attempted analysis of the themes of certain rock writers and their songs to show their significant, optimistic visions of the future. It is interwoven with references from John Wyndham, Orwell, Tolkien, D. H. Lawrence and other major writers. The result is a pretentious, rambling text which fails to make any point at all and leaves the reader bemused as to what the original thesis was.

5.8 NEW WAVE

By the mid seventies rock music had become a well-established form with many of its stars having maintained their position for a decade. These élite were seen as living glamorous, jetset lifestyles, seldom playing concerts and then only in large, impersonal venues. The essence of early rock'n'roll, the contact between the performer and the audience, the merging of the two into one with common aspirations, had gone. In 1976 a reaction came with its roots in the New York new-wave movement, but distinctly and aggressively English. Beginning with the punk groups such as the Clash, Sex Pistols and the Damned, their lyrics nihilistically attacked the establishment. Their presentation was the antithesis of the long-haired glamorous musicians of the rock establishment. They wore short hair, safety pins in their ears and hideous clothes with the intention of being ugly. A range of musical styles followed which are defined as new wave and include the futuristic, synthesizer-based music of the likes of Gary Numan, the Human League and Ultravox; the pop music of the Tourists, Toyah, Blondie and the Pretenders; and the two-tone music of Selector, the Beat, Specials and Madness.

In the USA the definition is different and refers to more avant-garde musicians with artistic pretensions: the Talking Heads are a good example.

The only cohesion between these artists, therefore, is that they reject the stagnant status quo, make an effort to be contemporary and poignant and have emerged since 1976.

Baker, Glenn A.
  The new music / Glenn A. Baker & Stuart Coupe. – London: Ring
  Publications, 1980. – 128p.: ill. (some col.), ports (some col.); 30cm.
  Also published: New York: Harmony Books, 1981. ISBN 0-858-35493-4
  (pbk.)
A well-illustrated survey of the new-wave styles of music with superficial notes on the major groups. There is no systematic analysis of the various forms and no discography.

Coupe, Stuart
  The new rock'n'roll / Stuart Coupe and Glenn A. Baker. – London:
  Omnibus Press, 1983. – 192p.: ill. (some col.), facsims (some col.), ports
  (some col.); 30cm. ISBN 0-7119-0173-2 (pbk.)
Arranged alphabetically by artist, this is a very good encyclopedia of the new wave. It claims to cover comprehensively those artists who have emerged since 1977 and in general this is an accurate statement. There is information here on the more obscure artists which certainly is unavailable elsewhere. It does fall down, however, on its coverage of black music. There are some excellent illustrations and an intelligent text.

The new wave encyclopedia / edited by Miles. – London: Omnibus Press, 1981.
  – 128p.: ill., ports; 27cm. ISBN 0-86001-962-4 (pbk.)

The widest definition of new wave was applied in the compilation of this reference source. Early punk acts such as the New York Dolls and Lou Reed in the USA and David Bowie in Britain are included, as are the late-seventies performers including the Sex Pistols and Clash, up to the new romantics of the eighties such as Spandau Ballet and Ultravox. Notes are brief but informative and there are some excellent photographs.

Palmer, Myles
   New wave explosion: how punk became new wave became the 80's / by Myles
   Palmer. – London; New York: Proteus, 1981. – 128p.: ill. (some col.), ports
   (some col.); 27cm. ISBN 0-906071-49-6 (pbk.)
Well designed as a mixture of comment, quotes and illustrations. The author presents the growth of the new-wave movement since 1976, tracing the development of many of its stars into the new musical establishment. The scope is wide, covering the more commercial elements such as Blondie, two tone groups such as the Specials, the avant-garde such as the Talking Heads and the more political such as the Clash. Superficial, but this does offer a good overall impression of the scope of the movement.

Discographies

International new wave discography: Vol.II / edited by B. George and
   Martha Defoe; with Henry Beck, Nancy Breslaw & Jim Linderman;
   graphics by Pam Meyer. – London: Omnibus Press, 1982. – 736p.: ill.; 25cm.
   ISBN 0-7119-0050-7 (pbk.)
   Originally published as *'Volume: international discography of the new wave'*:
   London: One Ten Records, 1980.
   Previous edition: London: Omnibus Press, 1982.
Originally published in a small format with a poor production, the first Omnibus Press edition had just ninety-two pages. The latest, greatly expanded edition includes 7,500 artists and groups, listed in one alphabetical sequence. 16,000 records are cited with a secondary listing of 3,000 record labels. The bias was distinctly British in the early editions but coverage has now expanded considerably to include American and European artists. This is certainly the most comprehensive source of information on new-wave recordings, with hundreds of obscure artists and tiny labels appearing which are impossible to trace elsewhere.

Shaw, Greg
   New wave on record 1975–1978: volume one England and Europe / by Greg
   Shaw. – Burbank, California: Greg Shaw, 1979. – 48p.: ill., facsims; 26cm.
   (pbk.)
Arranged alphabetically by artist and with a second sequence by record company, all styles of music loosely associated with the term 'new wave' are covered, but far from exhaustively. There are reproductions of record labels, full discographical details and a few brief annotations. Although compiled in America, it is accurate and includes the European releases of British artists. A title index would make this a far more useful reference tool.

PUNK

The leading form of the new-wave movement, punk rock, emerged from London in 1976. It is the ultimate reaction to the rock-music establishment. Boasting no musicianship, it is characterized by a relentless guitar and drum rhythm over which politically inspired lyrics are shouted. Derived from American groups such as the New York Dolls, Stooges and M.C.5, the surviving early British punks, notably the Clash and Siouxsie and the Banshees, have since become decidedly refined in their approach, while in America the Ramones continue their hectic style.

The bible. – London: Big O Publications, 1978. – 80p.: ill., facsims, ports; 30cm. ISBN 0-86044-489-9 (pbk.)
In 1976 Mark P, or Perry, produced the first issue of *Sniffin' Glue* which was to become the most influential of the fanzines of the London punk movement of the period. This is a collection of reproductions of the first ten issues of the now defunct publication. The production is rather better than that of the fanzine itself, with clear print and well-produced photographs, but the typescript, felt-tip graphics and layout are all faithful to the original. Included are interviews, reviews of concerts, club performances and record releases of the leading acts of the time including the Clash, Jam, Damned and the Adverts, chronicling the rise of the movement.

Boston, Virginia
Shockwave / Virginia Boston; with introductions by Danny Baker & Ian Rakoff. – London: Plexus, 1978. – 128p.: ill., facsims, ports; 30cm. ISBN 0-85965-020-0 (pbk.)
Also published as '*Punk rock*': New York: Penguin Books, 1978.
A collection of illustrations of the major punk groups operating in London during 1977. There are portraits, lists of personnel, extracts from lyrics and brief comments by the members as well as introductory notes. Quite detailed on the complement of the groups, and with information on the major fanzines.

Burchill, Julie
The boy looked at Johnny: the obituary of rock and roll / Julie Burchill and Tony Parsons. – London: Pluto Press, 1978. 96p.: ill., ports; 20cm. ISBN 0-86104-030-9 (pbk.)
By two young journalists on the *New Musical Express*, this is a rambling outline of the rise of the punk-rock, new-wave movement from its birth in New York and its establishment in London in 1976 to what the authors see as its decline in 1978. Their thesis is that the leaders of the punk-rock movement as a revolt against the old rock-industry establishment obtained record contracts and simply replaced it with a new establishment. The major figures in rock music past and present are demolished because of their lack of political integrity. An interesting, totally cynical comment, this book gives a great deal of information on the growth of punk, offering some ideas behind its beginnings and its decline.

Coon, Caroline
> *1988: the new wave punk rock explosion* / Caroline Coon. – London: Orbach
> and Chambers, 1977. – 128p.: ill., ports; 28cm. Also published: New York:
> Hawthorn Books, 1977. ISBN 0-427-00416-0 (pbk.)

Caroline Coon was one of the first British journalists to investigate the new-
wave movement in London while writing for the *Melody Maker*. She attempts
here to give an impression of what the new wave was about, reproducing lyrics
of the more important groups, illustrations of outrageous behaviour, extracts
from newspaper headlines and descriptions of performances. The essays on the
individual groups are informative and the rejection of the status quo is well
depicted. Ironically, it all appears terribly out of date.

Davis, Julie
> *Punk* / edited by Julie Davis. – London: Millington, 1977. – 128p.: ill.,
> facsims; ports; 30cm. ISBN 0-86000-098-2 (pbk.)

A collection of short articles, interviews and reviews from fanzines. There are
pieces on most of the leading punk artists as well as on punk attitudes and the
new-wave movement generally. The illustrations of the fans and artists are well
produced. There is a list with addresses of the major fanzines which were
available in London in 1976 and 1977. The view of punk here is actually written
by the fans and lacks the filter of formal journalism.

Hennessy, Val
> *In the gutter* / by Val Hennessy. – London: Quartet Books, 1978. – 94p.: ill.
> (some col.), ports (some col.); 26cm. ISBN 0-7043-3230-2 (pbk.)

This is an odd attempt to juxtapose photographs of primitive people resplen-
dent in their ritual adornments with pictures of the eccentric appearance and
antics of British punk rockers. The illustrations are interspersed with passages
of quotes from press articles on the punk movement and its music, together
with comments by the author. The exotic early illustrations of artists such as
Siouxsie and the Damned show quite clearly their recent relative conservatism.
The idea of relating the basic ritualistic elements in primitive and civilized
societies is interesting, but the treatment here is superficial and fails.

> *Not another punk book!* / text by Anscombe. – London: Aurum Press, 1978. –
> 96p.: chiefly ill., facsims, ports; 30cm. ISBN 0-9060-5306-4 (pbk.)

Photographs of extraordinary punk fashions, extracts from newspapers and
reviews of leading bands of the genre. The brief text offers a short analysis of
punk's reaction against the music and fashion establishments of the mid
seventies. The format resembles a fanzine with typewriter script.

> *Punk* / text by Dike Blair. – New York: Urizen Books, 1978. – 56p.: chiefly ill.
> (some col.), ports (some col.); 24cm. ISBN 0-9163-5458-X (pbk.)

Brief notes on the punk movement in London are accompanied by photographs of some leading groups, but mainly of more bizarre examples of fashion.

Vermorel, Fred
> *The punk encyclopedia* / by Fred and Judy Vermorel. – London: Omnibus
> Press, 1981. – ill., ports; 27cm. ISBN 0-86001-927-6 (pbk.)

An alphabetically arranged source of information on the punk groups of the late seventies with some reference to their earlier influences. There are brief biographies and portraits of the major exponents and some attempt to analyse punk and place it as a significant cultural movement.

OI!

Appearing in 1981 as a later manifestation of British punk rock, Oi!˙is characterized by abrasive vocals and a driving, tuneless guitar sound. The groups display a skinhead image with cropped hair and an exaggerated working-class manner. The lyrical themes are nihilistic and often overtly racist. Such groups played at National Front meetings and to provocatively nationalistic audiences at venues in Southall during the riots of 1981. Groups include the 4 Skins, Rose Tattoo and J J All Stars. None of the bands within this category has attained commercial success, although some have record contracts with independent labels.

Johnson, Gary
   The story of Oi: a view from the dead-end of the street / Gary Johnson. –
   Manchester: Babylon Books, 1981. – 46p.: ill., ports; 28cm. (pbk.)
Including photographs and profiles of the leading groups associated with Oi!; there are also interviews with angry young skinheads. The author does attempt a superficial analysis of the sources of the nothingness and racism: born out of unemployment and lack of a defined moral code and so on. A depressing book, it does communicate the general attitude of the musicians and their fans but the analysis is simplistic.

TWO-TONE

Originally the name of a record label which included the major artists of the genre, this style of music appeared as part of the new wave in Britain in the late seventies and had established itself by 1980. Based on West Indian ska or reggae rhythms, the lyrics of the songs tend to be of working-class themes with general criticism of the establishment. The main groups include the Specials, Madness, UB40, Selector and Bad Manners. One of the notable points about the groups is that they tend to include both young black and white musicians, complementing the rhythmic and vocal style of the music.

Miles
   The 2-tone book / text by Miles; book design Perry Neville and Jimmy
   Egerton. – London: Omnibus Press, 1981. – 80p.: chiefly ill., ports; 27cm.
   ISBN 0-86001-901-2 (pbk.)
This is a collection of illustrations of groups playing this musical style. The text is brief and not very informative but the major protagonists of the music are all here in one volume.

NEW ROMANTICS

Evolving from the sparseness of the punk movements in 1980, the new romantics dress extravagantly. Influenced by David Bowie, they have extraordinary-coloured hair, extravagant make-up and period clothes of romantic fashions. The music has no cohesive style but tends to use synthesizers, has very obscure lyrics and exaggerated vocal presentation. The leading groups include Visage, Landscape, Ultravox and Spandau Ballet.

The book with no name / Text editor Ian Birch; designer Pearce Marchbank. –
London: Omnibus Press, 1981. – 72p.: ill. (chiefly col.), ports (chiefly col.); 24cm. ISBN 0-86001-928-X (pbk.)
Lavishly illustrated, this look at the new romantics offers no analysis of the motivations or the ideas behind the movement, but does show the main groups, as well as the leading fashion-conscious stylists.

5.9 MUSICALS

A mixture of theatre and music, the musical is the modern manifestation of light opera, operetta or musical comedy.

Certainly many songs from musicals have become popular standards but, in general, this is a fringe area, somewhere between an accepted form of light music and middle-of-the-road popular taste.

In recent years the so-called rock opera has appeared, notably with the work of Tim Rice and Andrew Lloyd Webber, but this is an often misused term which includes not only the relatively traditional work of these two but also such works as Pete Townshend's Tommy and Quadrophenia.

Included here are general works which give an introduction to musicals in general and include information on the more contemporary works, as well as the few works on individual shows.

Bordman, Gerald
American operetta: from H.M.S Pinafore to Sweeny Todd / Gerald
Bordman. – New York: Oxford University Press, 1981. – viii, 206p., 16p. of plates: ill., ports; 22cm. Includes index. ISBN 0-19-502869-4
An historical account of the development of operetta in America into the modern musical show. Only a small section describes recent musicals but the treatment is both scholarly and readable. The index is excellent and there is an appendix of principals and credits of important works.

Druxman, Michael B.
The musical: from Broadway to Hollywood / by Michael B. Druxman. –
South Brunswick, New York: A.S. Barnes; London: Yoseloff, 1980. – 202p.: ill.; 29cm. ISBN 0-498-02282-X

Taking twenty-five musicals which were subsequently adapted into films it, gives brief accounts of the original productions and subsequent changes. Adopting a popular approach, it is, nevertheless, informative and well produced with some very good illustrations.

Green, Stanley
Encyclopedia of the musical / Stanley Green. – London: Cassell, 1977. – vii, 488p.; 24cm. Includes bibliography and discography. ISBN 0-304-29930-8
Originally published as '*Encyclopedia of the musical theater*': New York: Dodd, Mead, 1976.
An alphabetically arranged encyclopedia of shows, singers, actors, composers, lyricists and songs, all in one straightforward sequence. Informative, it tends to be patchy for more recent works. For example, there is no entry under Tim Rice or Andrew Lloyd Webber, but Jesus Christ Superstar is included. The discography is lengthy but lacking detail. The bibliography includes the music and lyrics from shows.

Green, Stanley
The world of musical comedy: the story of the American musical stage as told through the careers of its foremost composers and lyricists / Stanley Green. – 4th edition. – San Diego, California; New York: A. S. Barnes; London: Tantivy Press, 1980. – xiv, 480p.: ill., ports; 29cm. Includes discography and index. ISBN 0-498-02344-3
Written by an American journalist, author and reviewer who has specialized in the musical and its history for many years, this is a detailed history which spans the development from 1866 to date. Arranged chronologically, each of the major composers and lyricists is discussed in depth and his works analysed. There are photographs of the stage presentations and portraits of the writers. An appendix lists every Broadway musical produced since 1894 with details of songs, performers, directors and full discographical information. The index is well constructed giving good access to the main sequence by shows and writers.

Jackson, Arthur
The book of musicals: from Show Boat to Evita / by Arthur Jackson; foreword by Clive Barnes. – London: Mitchell Beazley, 1979. – 208p.: ill. (some col.), facsims, ports (some col.); 29cm. Includes bibliography, discography, filmography and indexes. ISBN 0-85533-191-7 (pbk.)
Originally published: Exeter: Webb & Bower, 1979.
Previously published: Exeter: Webb & Bower, 1979.
After a sketchy outline history of the production of musicals from the turn of the century to 1976, the work has an excellent section of indexes giving access to a wide range of information. There is a biographical dictionary of composers, lyricists and writers, a chronology of major performances from 1866 to 1979, a song index and a brief list of shows with their plots. Hollywood musicals are included and the illustrations are superb. As a brief source of information on the subject and a general introduction, this is well produced and easy to access.

Discographies

Hodgins, Gordon W.
The Broadway musical: a complete LP discography / by Gordon W. Hodgins.
– Metuchen, New Jersey; London: Scarecrow Press, 1980. – 188p.; 23cm.
Includes indexes. ISBN 0-8108-1343-2

The main sequence of the work is a listing covering 331 Broadway musicals with a total of 424 recordings. Each performance is described in detail with full credits, discographical notes and brief criticism. In addition, there are composer, lyricist, author, song and performer indexes. Appendices include major composer and lyricist partnerships and their associated productions and releases by the major record companies, in number order. This is an excellent reference source for those interested in the field, but not for the casual reader.

Rust, Brian
London musical shows on record 1897–1976 / by Brian Rust; with Rex Bunnett. – Harrow: Gramophone Publications, 1977. – 672p.; 22cm.
ISBN 0-90247-007-8

A thoroughly researched work produced with a typewriter typeface. The first section is a chronological listing of every production since 1894, beginning with Shop Girl and ending with A Little Night Music, which first appeared in 1975. Information includes date of opening, length of run and the name of the theatre in which the show was initially launched. This is followed by an alphabetically arranged sequence listing each musical, with no synopses, but very full, meticulously researched details of productions, writers and recordings. There is full discographical information with label numbers and full credits.

Individual works

Cats

Cats is based on T. S. Eliot's *Old Possum's book of practical cats*, published in 1939. Andrew Lloyd Webber began to set the poems to music in late 1977. Working with Trevor Nunn, the main body of Eliot's work was scanned for feline themes to complete the structure of a stage production. Gillian Lynne choreographed the action and John Napier designed the atmospheric sets. It has been an extremely successful show with a wide range of performers, selected from modern disco and classical ballet, cast in the roles of the cats.

Cats: the book of the musical, music by Andrew Lloyd Webber; based on Old Possum's book of practical cats by T. S. Eliot / Photographs and drawings by John Napier; edited by John Bodley; designed by Roger Huggett. – London: Faber & Faber, 1981. – 110p.: ill. (chiefly col.), ports (chiefly col.); 28cm.
ISBN 0-571-11862-3 (cased). ISBN 0-571-11863-1 (pbk.)

Beautifully produced with coloured reproductions of costume designs and photographs from the stage production. Eliot's poems used as the libretto are included in full. Ostensibly produced as a souvenir from the show, this stands alone as an attractive work.

Hair

Billed as 'the American tribal love–rock musical', Hair opened at New York's Biltmore Theater, after a year off Broadway, in April 1968 and in September of that year at the Shaftesbury, London. It played for 1,705 performances in New York and 1,999 in London. With music by Galt MacDermot and lyrics by James Rado and Jerome Ragni, it captured the mood of the Hippie movement of the time and neatly packaged the idealism into a very commercial show which eventually played in twenty-two countries. A film version directed by Milo Forman appeared in 1979, far too late to become successful. Albums of the songs from Hair were as successful as the show itself but now seem part of a lost era. Sadly Hair is remembered by many only for the notoriety gained by certain nude scenes.

Davis, Lorrie
    Letting down my Hair / by Lorrie Davis; with Rachel Gallagher. – London:
    Paul Elek, 1974. – 279p., 8p. of plates; 23cm. ISBN 0-236-31072-0
    Originally published: New York: Arthur Fields, 1973.
The author was one of the stars of the Broadway production of the show. She describes with some bitterness and disillusionment the way in which the genuine early feeling of idealism, which the actors had at the beginning of the show's life, later disintegrated as it became successful. It is a jaundiced story of poor management, greed, drug taking, open violence and general hypocrisy.

Jesus Christ Superstar

Written by Andrew Lloyd Webber with lyrics by Tim Rice, Jesus Christ Superstar tells the story of the New Testament in contemporary terms. With its rival show Godspell it opened in London in 1971. After success at the Palace Theatre it was a hit on Broadway. It was made into a film in 1973 but although the soundtrack albums of both show and film were commercial triumphs, the film itself was only a moderate success.

Nassour, Ellis
    Rock opera: the creation of Jesus Christ Superstar from record album to
    Broadway show and motion picture / Ellis Nassour. – New York: Hawthorn
    Books, 1973. – 248p.: ill.; 24cm.
A thorough, well-researched study of the creation of the musical, with details of casts, directors and lengthy quotes from the writers as well as performers. A good insight into the production of a musical and the evolution of its form by different directors.

CHAPTER SIX

Lives and works

The cult of the star with its excesses and idolatry is perhaps a fundamental modern requirement. It had been exemplified by Rudolph Valentino and was firmly established by the Hollywood film industry for twenty years before Frank Sinatra became the first genuine pop star in the forties.

Radio, gramophone records and films created these glittering images and spread them to an ever-increasing audience. By the fifties television had added a new medium and to complement these, there were the popular press and magazines. The first example of a pop biography appeared in 1946 — *The voice*, by E. J. Kahn, on Frank Sinatra.

The vast majority of early publications on popular singers of the fifties either consisted largely of photographs in magazine formats, or, towards the end of the decade, were simple patronizing biographies or poorly ghosted autobiographies. The former were produced by publishers, notably Photoplay, who had previously concentrated on the cinema. The more substantial works varied greatly in quality: Adam Faith, Tommy Steele, Cliff Richard and, a little later, Helen Shapiro, have good examples. The wholesome, naive image with the concept that such fame can suddenly be sprung on any teenager is the persistent theme.

These two basic types of publication continued throughout the early sixties. The early books on the Beatles, Brian Epstein's ghosted autobiography and the first Rolling Stones autobiography were all bland, uncontentious efforts, augmented by smiling portraits.

In 1968 Hunter Davis produced the first serious pop biography, *The Beatles: the authorised biography*, which, although excessively reverent and uncritical set a more authoritative tone. This was followed by Anthony Scaduto's *Bob Dylan* and Jerry Hopkins' *Elvis*, which again were kind to their subjects but of high quality.

In 1974, Anthony Scaduto published his *Mick Jagger*, which was the first critical attack on a major star. From then on better-researched, more serious biographies began to appear from Mark Eliot's *Death of a rebel*, a biography of Phil Ochs, to Albert Goldman's character assassination of Elvis Presley, *Elvis*.

This does not mean that the poor efforts did not continue. They continue to thrive along with journalistic, contrived works which flow from the likes of George Tremlett, Miles, Howard Elson and Chris Welch.

Large-format works, mostly of portraits, have evolved considerably from the Photoplay type of production and various publishers, notably Omnibus

Press, Proteus, Eel Pie, Plexus, Quick Fox and Flash Books, have evolved presentations which provide a mixture of good texts and well-presented illustrations. Dave Marsh's *Bruce Springsteen: born to run,* Leonore Fleischer's *Joni Mitchell* and Roy Carr's *The Beatles: an illustrated record* and *The Rolling Stones: an illustrated record,* are good examples. The majority of works in this format, however, continue to have poor texts the function of which is to link a collection of coloured photographs.

A recent innovation has been the 'cut up' fanzine format which adopts the poor appearance of the cheaply produced 'fanzine' publications (*see* section 8.4). Here a collection of previously published articles and photographs are reproduced, linked with poorly written comments. This form, the most prolific publisher of which was Babylon Books, already seems to be fading and recent examples have adopted a more acceptable standard of production.

As interest and serious study of popular artists and their work has grown, a wide range of new, specialist publications has emerged. This explosion began in the mid seventies and Pierian Press, Scarecrow Press and on a more popular level, Omnibus Press, publish an increasing number of titles. In addition, university presses, fan organizations, and private individuals provide a growing volume of information.

The Beatles offer the most extraordinary variety. As well as the usual biographies and pictorial works, there are quotations, interviews, comprehensive discographies, bootleg discographies, a listing of public performances, a listing of songs broadcast on radio, quizbooks, works on memorabilia, collection of letters from fans, a detailed musicological and lyrical analysis, collections of lyrics, a concordance of lyrics, a day-by-day chronology of their career as well as books on their films.

The literature generated after Elvis Presley's death added to an already vast volume and is, at present, the single largest body. In addition to many of the forms above, there are several works of a spiritualist nature concerning posthumous contact with Elvis, works of a devotional nature, viewing him in a quasi-religious context, a collection of devotional portraits, a multitude of tributes, an analysis of his cultural impact, a bibliography and an outline of his film career.

Bob Dylan's bibliography includes several mystical works, writings, poems and a novel and, in general, he receives the most academic and literary attention of anyone.

For younger readers Christmas annuals have emerged on a recreational level with puzzles, quizzes and comic strips and the American publishers, EMC and Creative Education, have produced an excellent range of controlled-vocabulary texts. Some include a complementary audio cassette and are aimed both at musical education and the development of reading skills, using a subject close to the hearts of the age group.

In addition to works on individual artists and groups, included are the recollections and biographies of some managers, producers and songwriters.

By far the most extensive chapter, 'Lives and works' represents a diverse and fascinating body of literature remarkable not only for the variety of formats and approaches but also in the volume and quality.

ARRANGEMENT

Individuals and groups are arranged in one alphabetical sequence with linking references where appropriate. For example, information on many artists will appear in material on their associated groups as well as in works on them as an individual. In some cases a straightforward 'see' reference will be used:

WINGS, see McCARTNEY, PAUL AND WINGS

and in others a 'see also' reference:

THE ROLLING STONES; see also JAGGER, MICK
JAGGER, MICK; see also THE ROLLING STONES

Within each individual heading there is a brief biographical sketch followed by a simple classified arrangement: Artist (general works, biographies, autobiographies, pictorial works, quotations. . .); Songs (lyrics, analysis); Writings, poems, novels (where the artist writes other than songs); Bibliographies; Discographies; Quizbooks; Films; Periodicals (references to section 8.2, ARTIST).

ABBA

Four artists who had already become stars in their own right before forming into a group, Abba comprises Anni-Frid Lyngstad, born in 1945 in Norway but brought up in Tosholla, Sweden; Agnetha Faltskog, born in Jonkopping in 1950; Bjorn Ulvaeus, born in Gothenberg in 1945; and Benny Andersson, born in Stockholm in 1946. They came together in 1971 and spent two years writing songs and developing an act for a wider audience. They chose the 1974 Eurovision Song Contest to reach that audience and easily won the competition with the song Waterloo, cleverly sung in English; Europop had been created. Waterloo was a world-wide success which, after overcoming the stigma which usually befalls Eurovision winners, was followed by a string of topselling singles and albums. Abba have developed sophisticated record-production techniques with songs of exceptionally strong melody. Their lyrics, however, tend to be banal and simplistic, possibly because they are working in a foreign language. They continue to prosper, ever experimenting with new studio methods, seldom performing in concert but always successful. In 1980 they were listed as Sweden's most profitable export.

Abba
   Abba in their own words / compiled by Rosemary York. – London: W. H. Allen, 1982. – 128p.: ill., ports; 26cm. ISBN 0-491-02796-6
   Originally published: London: Omnibus Press, 1981.
Abba have never shunned interviews and since they became internationally successful a vast file of quotes has been amassed. Their views on the world make less than fascinating reading.

Abba annual 1976 –. – Knutsford, Cheshire: Stafford Pemberton, 1975. –
Annual. 1983. – 1982. – 45p.: ill. (some col.), ports (some col.; 26cm. ISBN
0-86030-380-2
A Christmas gift for the young fan with puzzles, quizzes, photographs and
messages from the group.

Borg, Christer
Abba by Abba / as told to Christer Borg. – Knutsford, Cheshire: Stafford
Pemberton, 1977. – 127p.: ill., ports; 20cm. ISBN 0-86030-069-2 (pbk.)
Despite the title, this is not an autobiography but a straightforward, uncritical
account of the group's history based on interviews with the artists. The cover
states this to be 'the only authorized biography' and therefore one would hardly
expect any real criticism, but included are some good illustrations and interesting facts about their solo careers.

Edgington, Harry
ABBA / Harry Edgington and Peter Himmelstrand. – Rev. ed. – London:
Magnum Books, 1978. – 181p., 16p. of plates: ill., ports; 18cm. ISBN 0-417-
03370-2 (pbk.)
Previous edition: London: Magnum Books, 1977.
Written by journalist Harry Edgington and Peter Himmelstrand, a close friend
of the group who has collaborated with them in songwriting, this is a lively,
informative biography which accepts their success without analysis and almost
ignores their music. The revision is slight, simply adding the briefest information concerning the marriage of Anni-Frid and Benny and Abba's 1978
successes.

Lindvall, Marianne
ABBA: the ultimate pop group / Marianne Lindvall. – London: Pop
Universal; Souvenir Press, 1977. – 95p.: ill. (some col.), ports (some col.);
28cm. Includes discography. ISBN 0-285-62312-5 (pbk.)
Also published: Edmonton, Alberta: Hurtig, 1977; New York: A & W
Visual Library, 1977.
Lavishly illustrated outline of Abba's career which includes the lyrics of some
of their hit songs and a short discography. The text is very brief and lacks even
the most rudimentary information on their backgrounds.

Tobler, John
ABBA for the record / John Tobler. – Knutsford, Cheshire: Stafford
Pemberton, 1980. – 96p.: ill. (chiefly col.), col. facsims, ports (chiefly col.);
30cm. ISBN 0-86030-272-5 (pbk.)
A beautifully illustrated work which focusses on the records of the group,
including their efforts as individuals, to plot their careers. Their album sleeves
are reproduced and portraits of the group and their earlier incarnations are
interspersed with brief journalistic accounts of their progress.

ABBA: SONGS

Ulvaeus, Bjorn
   ABBA: a lyrical collection 1972–1982 / all lyrics by Bjorn Ulvaeus and Benny
   Andersson. – Iver, Buckinghamshire: Century 21 Merchandising, 1982. –
   83p.: col. ill., col. ports; 22cm. Includes index. ISBN 0-907938-00-0 (pbk.)
Classified into rock, ballads, mid tempo, B sides and disco songs, there are
indexes to titles and first lines to this complete collection of recorded songs.
Few stand alone as interesting lyrical works, but the illustrations are well
printed and there are some very good portratis.

ABBA: PERIODICALS

(*See* section 8.2, Abba.)

AC/DC

Formed in the early seventies in Australia, AC/DC included brothers Angus
and Malcolm Young, and Cliff Williams, Philip Rudd and Bon Scott. The
Young's older brother, George, had been, with Harry Vanda, a leader of the
sixties group the Easybeats and now became a major influence in moulding this
newer project. After two successful albums in Australia, the group arrived in
Britain in 1976 and played in a small pub, the Red Cow, in Hammersmith,
London. Playing a frantic form of heavy-metal rock, they presented a curious
image with guitarist, Angus Young, dressed as a schoolboy with shorts, blazer
and satchel frantically cavorting around while playing earsplitting solos. By the
end of 1976 they had made an impression in Britain and this was followed by
American successes in 1979. Constantly touring and recording, they were early
leaders of the heavy-metal revival movement and have become the most
successful rock band to emerge from Australia. In 1980, singer Bon Scott died
and he was replaced by Brian Johnson from the defunct British band, Geordie.
Their popularity continues to grow.

Bunton, Richard
   AC/DC: hell ain't no bad place to be / by Richard Bunton. – London:
   Omnibus Press, 1982. – 80p.: ill., ports; 27cm. Includes discography
   ISBN 0-7119-0061-2 (pbk.)
A well-written brief history of the band's career which includes unusual
information on their road crew and sound equipment. The illustrations are not
exceptional but the discography includes official and bootleg releases with full
track and label details.

Dome, Malcolm
   AC/DC / Malcolm Dome. – London; New York: Proteus, 1982. – 96p.: ill.,
   ports; 27cm. Includes discography. ISBN 0-86276-011-9 (pbk.)

A straightforward, well-illustrated biography examining AC/DC's successes from the unlikely beginnings in the Australian rock scene to date. Each member of the group is given space and his contribution examined with a slight emphasis on Angus Young. Each album is well analysed and the discography is complete with full details.

ACUFF, ROY

Roy Acuff was born in 1903 in Maynardsville, Tennessee, and began playing the jaw harp and harmonica as a child. He suffered from several attacks of sunstroke in 1929 and 1930, and during convalescence learnt to play the fiddle. In 1932 he joined a travelling medicine show. By 1933 he had formed his own group, the Tennessee Crackerjacks, and soon was playing regularly on radio. He recorded his first tracks in 1936 and by 1938 he had begun playing in the Grand 'Ole Opry radio show. He became the most popular artist on the show by 1940 and in 1942 formed his own music-publishing company. He was even nominated to run as governor of Tennessee in 1944, 1946 and 1948, and although he failed, he gained enormous support. In 1962 he was the first living musician to be honoured as a member of the Country Music Hall of Fame and he gained the title 'King of Country Music.' He has sold thirty million records during his career and is the undisputed father of modern country music.

Dunkleberger, A.C
  King of country music: the life story of Roy Acuff / by A C. Dunkleberger. –
  Nashville: Williams, 1971. – 137p.: ill., ports; 23cm.
The place of Acuff as a force in country music is well described, his career traced and his music discussed, not analytically but in the context of its influence on other artists. His music-publishing influence and broadcasting career are well covered with some unusual illustrations. This book lacks a discography.

Schlappi, Elizabeth
  Roy Acuff: the Smoky Mountain boy / by Elizabeth Schlappi. – Gretna,
  Louisiana: Pelican Publishing, 1978. – viii, 289p., 8 leaves of plates: ill.,
  ports; 24cm. Includes index. ISBN 0-8828-9144-8
A detailed biography giving a straightforward account of Acuff's career and importance to country music. His position as a celebrity is assumed throughout, which appears odd to the British reader.

ADAM AND THE ANTS

Born Stuart Goddard in north London in 1954, after attending Hornsey Art School Adam became involved with early punk music in London as early as 1975. He was involved with Malcolm Maclaren, the Sex Pistols' creator, for a while but this involvement was shortlived. By the late seventies Adam and his group the Ants presented an image of leather, whips and menace. Described as 'hard core' punks, they flirted with sado-masochism in Adam's lyrics. In 1980, however, after their early records had been of only minor cult interest, they finally had a hit single, followed by a string of hits throughout 1981 and two topselling albums. The themes changed to songs of pirates, highwaymen and and the idealization of Red Indians. Tribal rhythms, two drummers and odd chord progressions made Adam and the Ants Britain's top pop group with a wide following of young teenagers.

Adam and the Ants annual. – Knutsford, Cheshire: Stafford Pemberton.
    Annual. 1983. – 1982. – 45p.: ill. (some col.), ports (some col.); 26cm.
    ISBN 0-86030-344-6
A Christmas gift for young Adam fans with puzzles, quizzes, portraits and a message from the star.

Adam and the Ants superstar. – Knutsford, Cheshire: Stafford Pemberton,
    1982. – 66p.: col. ill., col. ports; 28cm. ISBN 0-86030-374-8 (pbk.)
A brief, poorly written text is accompanied by a beautifully reproduced collection of coloured photographs, mainly of Adam in exquisite poses.

Maw, James
    The official Adam Ant story / James Maw. – London; Sydney: Futura
    Macdonald, 1981. – 160p., 24p. of plates: ill., ports; 18cm. Includes discogra-
    phy. ISBN 0-7088-2123-5 (pbk.)
An uninspired attempt: the facts of Adam's career are assembled in a dull and pedantic text. The discography is complete and includes his early releases.

Vermorel, Fred
    Adam and the Ants / Fred and Judy Vermorel. – London: Omnibus Press,
    1981. – 47p.: ill. (some col.), ports (some col.); 30cm. ISBN 0-86001-400-9
    (pbk.)
A brief biography by two friends of Malcolm Maclaren, who was Adam's early manager before he became the moulding influence of the Sex Pistols. The selection of illustrations is well presented with Adam in his various recent costumes and cosmetics. What is interesting about the Vermorels' effort, however, is their inside knowledge of his early career and they relate a series of interesting anecdotes which one can only hope come from their close source and are reliable.

Welch, Chris
    Adam & the Ants / Chris Welch. – London: Star Books, 1981. – 128p., 8p. of
    plates: ill., ports; 18cm. Includes discography. ISBN 0-352-30963-6 (pbk.)
A superficial biography which has all the symptoms of having been written and rushed into publication with the sudden establishment of Adam as a new, major attraction. Aimed at the young fan, it is trivial, with little mention of his musical innovations or even his obsession with visual presentation. The discography is complete up to publication but lacking in detail and including none of the early limited editions.

West, Mike
  Adam and the Ants / text by Mike West. – Manchester: Babylon Books,
  1981. – 36p.: ill. (some col.), facsims, ports (some col.); 29cm. Includes
  discography. ISBN 0-907188-08-4 (pbk.)
In fanzine style but with a production of a far higher quality than usual, this is a
good survey of Adam's career including a fascinating collection of extracts
from press coverage and some unusual illustrations. Although brief, the
author's commentary includes some perceptive musical analysis for a publication of this type.

ADAM AND THE ANTS: SONGS

Ant, Adam
  Adam and the Ants "Kings": the official Adam and the Ants song book /
  words and music by Adam Ant and Marco Pirroni; Text by Stephen Lavers.
  – London: Mirror Books, 1981. – 44p.: ill. (some col.), music, ports (some
  col.); 31cm. ISBN 0-85939-301-1 (pbk.)
A large-format collection of Adam's curious lyrics, with a few songs set to
music. There is a brief but informative biographical sketch and a collection of
posed photographs, mainly from his days of stardom.

THE ALLMAN BROTHERS BAND

Duane and Greg Allman were born in Nashville, Tennessee in 1946 and 1947
respectively. After playing in their band, the Allman Joys, and later in the Los
Angeles studio band, Hourglass, they formed the Allman Brothers Band in
1969. This included Richard Betts, like Duane a brilliantly innovative guitar
stylist. It was the twin guitar sound and boogie rhythm that was to become their
trademark. They embarked on a series of coast-to-coast American tours in
1970, always building on their reputation as excellent recording artists. In 1973
group member Berry Oakley and Duane were killed in motorcycle accidents,
making the band, already America's leading attraction, a legend. They became
more dominated by Betts at this time and their style moved towards soft rock
with country overtones.

By 1974, however, after having their biggest album successes and some
notice in Britain, internal conflicts between Greg and Betts were producing a
serious rift. The discord within the group culminated in Greg's testifying
against his long-serving road manager in a narcotics trial. After an uneasy
period the band finally dissolved. In late 1974 Greg Allman undertook a US
tour under his own name and has continued as a solo artist since then. Duane
Allman left a legacy of excellent work, and his slide guitar on other artists'
records (such as those of Eric Clapton, Wilson Pickett and Aretha Franklin)
did as much as the Allman Brothers Band's own music to give them success but,
nevertheless, their own albums are superb. They were predominantly an
American phenomenon who were only moderately successful in Britain.

Nolan, Tom
  The Allman Brothers Band; a biography in words and pictures / by Tom
  Nolan; edited by Greg Shaw. – New York: Sire Books; Chappell Music
  Company, 1976. – 55p.: ill., ports 30cm. – Includes discography. (pbk.)
A brief biography, but the only one available of the band, which traces the
early careers of the Allman brothers themselves and then the evolution of their
band. Their session work is not neglected and is included in the well-researched
discography. The tragedies of the band are not sentimentalized.

ARROWS

Formed in 1973, Arrows joined Mickie Most's RAK record company and were
launched to appeal to the teenybopper market which was so important at the
time. A three-piece group, Arrows consisted of Paul Varley, born in Preston in
1952, Alan Merrill, born in 1951 in New York, and Jake Hooker, born in 1952
also in New York. They were surprisingly competent musicians but after two
minor hit records they faded into obscurity.

Harry, Bill
  Arrows: the official story / Bill Harry. – London: Everest Books, 1976. –
  141p., 8p. of plates: ill., ports; 18cm. ISBN 0-9039-2561-3 (pbk.)
This is written for the young enthusiast, with personal interviews with the
group members, lists of their tastes and biographical details. It is the biography
of a group that did not actually achieve the stardom anticipated when it was
commissioned and because the subject is empty the formula style is even more
obvious.

AZNAVOUR, CHARLES

Born into a family of Armenian refugees in Paris after the First World War,
Charles Aznavour lived in poverty as a child and struggled for years as a night-
club entertainer and songwriter. Eventually he began selling his songs to
famous stars such as Maurice Chevalier and Edith Piaf and gradually became a
singer in his own right. He sings and writes in nine languages and his songs,
which are often lyrically very complex, are presented in a unique, narrative
style. He is one of the authentic international artists.

Aznavour, Charles
  Aznavour by Aznavour: an autobiography / Charles Aznavour; translated
  by Ghilaine Boulanger. – Chicago: Cowles Book Co., 1972. – 283p. : ill.,
  ports; 24cm.
A rambling biography covering his childhood reminiscences as well as his love
affairs and writing. There is much fascinating information about the lifestyles
of bohemian French society in the fifties.

Aznavour, Charles
    Yesterday when I was young / Charles Aznavour. – London: W. H. Allen,
    1979. – 202p., 16p. of plates: ill., ports; 23cm. Includes index.
    ISBN 0-491-02446-0
A candid, recent autobiography showing the honesty of a man relaxed in his
success. His anecdotes from his childhood and his struggling years are enthralling. He talks frankly about his affairs and marriages as well as his dramatic
relationship with Edith Piaf. There is real insight into his music and the
influences behind his lyrics.

BACHMAN–TURNER OVERDRIVE

Randy Bachman was originally a member of the top Canadian band the Guess
Who. In 1970 he left the group and after making a solo album he formed a band
with his brother Robbie, Chad Allen from the Guess Who and singer, bass
player Fred Turner. Allen left, a third brother Tim joined and Bachman–
Turner Overdrive was born. After two successful albums in Canada, a single
became a big hit in America and Britain in 1974, but since then they have failed
to achieve further success although for a period they were Canada's top
attraction in the rock field with their commercial but well-played style of
rock'n'roll.

Melhuish, Martin
    *Bachman–Turner Overdrive: rock is my life, this is my song: the authorized
    biography* / by Martin Melhuish. – Toronto: Methuen; New York: Two
    Continents, 1976. – 178p.: ill., ports; 23cm. Includes discographies.
    ISBN 0-8467-0104-9
A straightforward biography packed with quotations, particularly from Randy
Bachman. The importance of the band in Canada is difficult to appreciate for
the British reader but the author's enthusiasm comes through with some
impression of their impact in that country. The illustrations are well produced
and the discography complete.

JOAN BAEZ

Born in 1941 into a middle-class, academic family in New York City, Joan
Baez's remarkably pure voice gave her acclaim as a traditional folk singer. She
had her first success at the Newport Folk Festival in 1959 and in 1960 her first
album of traditional songs became a success on both sides of the Atlantic. She
began singing songs of protest (for example, We Shall Overcome) as early as
1961. Soon afterwards she began a relationship with Bob Dylan and was a great
help in starting his career. She became a symbol of anti-Vietnam war protest
and married a student protest leader who was imprisoned for draft evasion. She
began writing her own protest songs in the late sixties. In 1974 Joan Baez
released an album of later, simply good, commercially acceptable songs and

toured with Bob Dylan's Rolling Thunder review. This breakaway from her earlier idealism revived her career.

Baez, Joan
Daybreak / Joan Baez. – London: Panther, 1971. – 141p.; 18cm.
ISBN 0-586-03502-8 (pbk.)
Previously published: London: MacGibbon & Kee, 1970.
This is a collection of vignettes in which Baez outlines her upbringing, her parents, her Quaker background and her involvement and commitment to the non-violence movement. Her streams of consciousness are often revealing, if self-indulgent, with the narrative frequently breaking into prose poems.

BAEZ, JOAN: BIBLIOGRAPHIES: DISCOGRAPHIES

Swan, Peter
Joan Baez, a bio-disco-bibliography: being a selected guide to material in print, on record, on cassette and on film, with a biographical introduction / Peter Swan. – Brighton: Noyce, 1977. – 23p.: 30cm. (pbk.)
Poorly produced by Noyce, of Librarians for Social Change, this includes a full discography of Joan Baez but the other material is far from comprehensive. One is bound to compare this unfavourably with *Diamonds & rust*.

Swanekamp, Joan
Diamonds & rust: a bibliography & discography on Joan Baez / compiled and edited by Joan Swanekamp. – Ann Arbor, Michigan: Pierian Press, 1979. – 88p.; 25cm. ISBN 0-87650-113-7
A full discography of the recording career of Joan Baez as well as being a detailed, annotated bibliography of books and articles, arranged chronologically by title, covering the years from 1961 to 1977. The information is indexed by author, title, subject and periodical. Baez's work as politician and human-rights activist is covered in as much detail as her career as a musician. This is a thorough piece of scholarly research and an excellent reference source.

THE BAY CITY ROLLERS

Formed in Edinburgh in 1971, after a period of playing around Great Britain in small clubs and discothèques the 'Rollers' signed a contract with Bell Records and had a minor hit at the end of 1972. Their manager, Tam Paton, had created for them an image which appealed to the growing market of pre-teen and early teenagers known as 'teenyboppers'. Their hair was shorter than that of other groups of the early seventies and their stage dress was a variation on baseball kit with tartan trimmings and an androgynous, pure image. During 1973 and 1974 they became the major British teenybopper idols, competing with the Osmonds, with a string of topselling records. Their musical formula included very simple pop songs and simple Beach Boys-like harmonies with a very full production. They were criticized for being a manufactured group and were the object of a great deal of abuse from the music press. Their popularity had waned by the end of 1975 although they continued to record and perform, attempting to produce more sophisticated pop music for an older audience. They are yet to produce a revival although during 1981 they were playing in small clubs in America.

Allen, Ellis
> *The Bay City Rollers* / Ellis Allen. – St. Albans: Panther, 1975. – 157p., 16p.
> of plates: ill., ports; 18cm. ISBN 0-586-04325-X(pbk.)

Based on interviews and observations made while touring with the group, this is obviously for the young fan in the tradition of the early sixties. It is totally uncritical, avoiding discussion of their music and depicting them as fun-loving, clean-living boys, unaffected by fame and fortune.

> *Bay City Rollers Annual 1975* –. – Knutsford, Cheshire: Stafford Pemberton,
> 1974–. Annual. 1977. – 71p.: ill. (some col.), ports (some col.); 25cm.
> ISBN 0-86030-005-6

Appearing for the three years 1975, 1976 and 1977, this was aimed at the Christmas gift market. It contained portraits, a comic strip, interviews and puzzles, all suitable for the pre-teenager.

Golumb, David
> *The Bay City Rollers picture scrapbook* / by David Golumb; photographer by
> special appointment to the Bay City Rollers; all words by Tony Jasper. –
> London: Queen Anne Press, 1975. – 96p.: chiefly ill., chiefly ports; 19cm.
> ISBN 0-3620-0252-5 (pbk.)

An uninspired collection of pictures of the teenybop phenomenon with a few brief comments for the teenage reader.

Paton, Tam
> *The Bay City Rollers* / Tam Paton with Michael Wale. – London: Everest
> Books, 1975. – 154p., 16p. of plates: ill., ports; 18cm. ISBN 0-9039-2560-5
> (pbk.)

Written by their manager with Michael Wale, who is a journalist and well-known television presenter, the narrative describes the Bay City Rollers' formation and career in a simple, factual style. Obviously uncritical, it makes no mention of their music or analysis of their success. There are chapters devoted to interviews with each member of the group and a selection of illustrations covering the group's early line-ups. Written at a higher level than that appropriate to the group's following, this is too subjective to offer an insight into the manipulation of such a pop group, which would have made interesting reading.

> *Rollers in America: exclusive souvenir of the Rollers' trip to America* / photo-
> graphs by Alan Ballard; text by Bess Coleman. – London: Queen Anne
> Press; Phoebus, 1975. – 50p.: chiefly ill. (some col.), chiefly ports (chiefly
> col.); 30cm. (pbk.)

Produced as a publicity publication, this is an extravagant celebration of a non-event.

THE BEACH BOYS

The Wilson brothers Brian, Carl and Dennis with their cousin Mike Love and friend Al Jardine had sung together while still at high school, occasionally playing at local school dances. In 1961 they recorded a Brian Wilson composition, Surfin', which was released on the Candix label and became a local and then an international hit. Their style, featuring lyrics about surfing, complex harmonies and high falsetto vocals, was totally new and became known as the surfing sound. After touring America in 1962 they signed with Capitol Records and a series of successes followed. By 1965 Brian Wilson had decided to give up touring and was replaced by Bruce Johnston. Their records began to display new signs of sophisticated innovation. In 1966 they released the album Pet Sounds which achieved real critical acclaim and great success in Britain, although receiving only a mediocre response in America. This was followed by Good Vibrations, regarded by many as the most brilliantly conceived pop single of all time. Brian Wilson had by now become obsessed with a competitive battle with the Beatles and when the latter's Sergeant Pepper's Lonely Hearts Club Band album was released in the summer of 1967, he conceded defeat and withdrew into a totally reclusive lifestyle. There followed a string of poor albums and occasionally successful singles.

In 1971 the Beach Boys received enormous critical acclaim after performing at a festival in Monterey and a renewed following as they played at charity concerts on the fashionable 'ecology' bandwagon. This was followed by a very successful album, Surf's Up, which received brilliant reviews. The personnel of the group was enhanced at this time by South Africans Ricky Fataar and Blondie Chaplin, who have since departed. Although they continued to be a major concert attraction, since the early seventies few new records have been released by the Beach Boys though a number of compilation albums of their earlier singles sold in their millions and continue to do so. They remain one of the most innovative American groups with an important place in the history of modern popular music.

Barnes, Ken
   The Beach Boys / by Ken Barnes; edited by Greg Shaw. – New York: Sire Books; Chappell Music Company, 1976. – 55p.: ill., ports; 30cm. Includes discography. (pbk.)
A brief but very good source of information on the group with some rare illustrations. The discography is complete and there is an interesting listing of Brian Wilson songs that have been recorded by other artists, which however includes no cover versions of Beach Boys' songs or songs written in collaboration with people like Jan and Dean. Some of the content is surprising, showing an often overlooked versatility.

Golden, Bruce
   The Beach Boys: southern California pastoral / Bruce Golden. – San Bernadino, California: Borgo Press, 1976. – 186p.: ill., ports; 22cm. Includes discography. ISBN 0-8787-7202-2 (pbk.)

A rare biography of the group which celebrates their music as a reflection of the changing face of Californian youth culture. The evolution of their music is well chronicled with some poignant analysis by the author and excellent background to their inspirations and techniques not found elsewhere. The discography is full, with complete details of American releases including unofficial bootlegs.

Leaf, David
   The Beach Boys and the California myth / David Leaf. – New York: Grosset & Dunlap; Today Press, 1978. – 192p.: ill., facsims, ports; 28cm.
   ISBN 0-4481-4625-8 (cased). ISBN 0-4481-4626-6 (pbk.)
A highly critical history of the Beach Boys which focusses largely on Brian Wilson who is depicted as the brilliant Hollywood genius who is destroyed by his family, friends and drugs. The clean-living, wholesome Californian myth is nowhere to be found: only one of the Beach Boys, the author maintains, could surf. Instead here are dissolution, corruption and decadence. There are some excellent photographs, rare reproductions of posters for early live performances and some good journalistic writing. Sometimes the severity of the criticism does seem rather too harsh but this in itself is refreshing.

Preiss, Byron
   The Beach Boys: the authorised illustrated biography / by Byron Preiss. –
   New York: Ballantine Books, 1978. – 160p.: ill., ports; 29cm. Includes discography. ISBN 0-345-27950-6 (cased). ISBN 0-345-27398-2 (pbk.)
A beautifully illustrated but poorly written biography with some useful information on the Beach Boys' early lives and careers but no analysis of Brian Wilson's writing or their experimental studio techniques. The discography is also lacking in detail, including only American releases with the briefest of information.

Tobler, John
   The Beach Boys / John Tobler. – London: Hamlyn; Phoebus, 1977. – 96p.: ill. (chiefly col.), ports (chiefly col.); 31cm. Includes discography.
   ISBN 0-600-31434-0
A well-illustrated and particularly well-designed biography of the group which includes a brief but surprisingly informative and intelligent text. The author does not attack his subject in an overtly critical way but includes a good deal of gentle sarcasm. The discography includes only British releases and although it gives dates of release, there are no listings of album tracks or label numbers.

THE BEACH BOYS: DISCOGRAPHIES

Elliott, Brad
   Surf's up!: the Beach Boys on record, 1961–1981 / by Brad Elliott. – Ann Arbor, Michigan: Pierian Press, 1982. – 512p.: ill., ports; 23cm. Includes bibliography and indexes. ISBN 0-87650-118-8
A superbly designed and informative source, this is a complete guide to the

work of the group. The main section is a chronological discography of American releases with which members of the group have been associated in a variety of roles. This is followed by an alphabetical list of these record releases with full credits. There is a fascinating list of unreleased songs with remaining sections devoted to promotional records, records by relatives and friends, week-by-week chart activity from *Billboard*, a brief bibliography and a general index. In addition, there are over one hundred photographs of the group, many of which are unavailable elsewhere.

THE BEAT

The Beat were formed in 1979 as one of the original bands to join the Two-tone record label. Their line-up comprises Dave Wakeling, Saxa, Andy Cox, Ranking Roger, Everett Morton and David Steel, three black and three white musicians. They blend a style which is a fusion of reggae, ska and straight-forward British pop music. They have achieved real commercial success with several singles and by the end of 1981 had produced two topselling albums. They are yet, however, to match on record the excitement of their live shows.

Halasha, Malu
  The Beat: twist and crawl / by Malu Halasha. – London: Eel Pie, 1981. – 96p.:
  ill., ports; 25cm. Includes discography. ISBN 0-906008-24-7 (pbk.)
The best source of information on the group: there are over fifty black-and-white photographs and an interesting, informative text. Their early career, musical influences and recording techniques are briefly, but well, covered. Their European tour of 1981 concludes a well-written work.

THE BEATLES

All born in Liverpool in the early forties, John Lennon, Paul McCartney, George Harrison and Ringo Starr became one of the most significant influences in the history of popular music. Lennon had played in a school skiffle group called the Quarrymen when he met Paul McCartney and a very young George Harrison and they soon began playing together. Later, at Liverpool College of Art, Lennon met Stuart Sutcliffe, who joined their group. After a few local engagements they gained work with impresario Larry Parnes and toured Scotland as the Silver Beatles, with fifties rock'n'roll singer Johnny Gentle. They had no regular drummer, however, and after Allan Williams, their first manager, had secured them work in Hamburg, they recruited Pete Best. They undertook five hectic stints of playing to the sailors and prostitutes of the red-light district and served a tough apprenticeship, sometimes playing ten hours per night and living in squalid conditions. After their fifth visit to Hamburg, during which they made their first recordings, with British singer Tony Sheridan, Stuart Sutcliffe decided to stay in Germany and continue his artistic studies. In April 1962 he died of a brain haemorrhage.

On returning to Liverpool the group was spotted by Brian Epstein. From a comfortable middle-class family Epstein was drawn to the contrasting rawness of the Beatles and their brand of anglicized rhythm & blues. He took over as their manager and after a succession of failures finally persuaded George Martin of Parlophone Records to offer them a contract. Martin was to be their guiding figure for most of the next decade. After they had replaced Pete Best with new drummer Richard Starkey, or Ringo Starr, their first single was a minor success in December 1962 and their second became a topseller in early 1963. After two more hits and a topselling album in Britain, the Beatles were promoted by Capitol Records and by the time of their tour in April 1964 they held the top five places in the American singles charts. This was Beatlemania at its height with massive crowds at airports and unprecedented publicity, particularly in America. In late 1963 they appeared on the Royal Variety Show, an event which in retrospect may be seen as significant in the acceptance of rock'n'roll music by the establishment. John Lennon also showed literary talents in publishing two books of poems and the Beatles always displayed in their interviews a mocking intelligence and interest in the world that had not been openly manifested before in pop singers. In 1965 they appeared in the honours list as MBEs in recognition of the massive income they had generated by leading the British invasion of popular music to America.

After two successful films, immense wealth and critical success, the group turned its attention to the development of record production and to writing ever more sophisticated songs. In 1967 the Sgt. Pepper's Lonely Hearts Club Band album was released. This is regarded by many as a turning point in popular music and by some as the most brilliantly complete work pop music has created. Artistic credibility had at last been achieved and even the music establishment would in future begin consciously to take notice and be unconsciously deeply influenced.

In 1967 Brian Epstein died, leaving the Beatles deeply involved in Eastern mysticism and in financial trouble with their Apple Corps, the commercial organization. Their decline followed. Lennon and McCartney, who had written most of the Beatles songs, had worked separately since 1963 and had always displayed distinctive styles. McCartney's melodic sweetness contrasted with Lennon's increasingly experimental music and political lyrics. Allen Klein, an experienced American showbusiness manager, was brought in to save their dwindling finances but his presence only resulted in further rifts. After two more albums, made largely by McCartney with the others playing as session musicians, the Beatles finally disintegrated in late 1970 and their parting was officially announced early in 1971. A sad episode of litigation and bitterness followed.

The Beatles' significance to popular music is even now difficult to calculate. Their records are bought in vast quantities, they still have armies of devoted fans and until John Lennon's death in 1980 there was always the vain hope of a reconciliation. The Beatles' solo careers which followed the break-up have never achieved their joint artistic heights of the mid sixties. Their talent may be analysed in their perfectly pitched harmonies, the complex, intuitive key modulations of their songs or in the innovation of their recording techniques but the reality is that, as with all real art, they somehow seem to epitomize their period, the sixties, with a lasting excitement and a wealth of creative images.

(*See also* EPSTEIN, BRIAN; HARRISON, GEORGE; LENNON, JOHN; McCARTNEY, PAUL; MARTIN, GEORGE; TAYLOR, DEREK.)

Adler, Bill
   Love letters to the Beatles / selected by Bill Adler; illustrated by Osborn. – London: Blond, 1964. – 91p.: ill., facsims; 15cm. (pbk.)
Bill Adler was given access to 250,000 fan letters in a New York warehouse and chose this limited collection. They are amusing, sad, pathetic, but offer reflections of vulnerable, adolescent emotion.

Alico, Stella
   Elvis Presley – the Beatles / by Stella H. Alico; illustrated by E. R. Cruz and Ernie Guanlao. – West Haven, Connecticut: Pendulum Press, 1979. – 63p.: ill., ports; 24cm. ISBN 0-88301-364-9 (cased). ISBN 0-88301-352-5 (pbk.)
The story of the Beatles, and Elvis, is told for American schools. Composition and comprehension exercises are included with a straightforward quiz.

Bacon, David
   The Beatles' England / David Bacon and Norman Maslov. – London: Columbus Books, 1982. – 142p.: chiefly ill. (some col.), ports; 22cm. ISBN 0-86287-008-9 (pbk.)
This includes some interesting photographs of the group and the places associated with them and mentioned in their songs: The Cavern club, Abbey Road, Strawberry Fields and Penny Lane are all here.

Beatles, the
   Beatles in their own words / compiled by Miles; edited by Pearce Marchbank. – London: W. H. Allen, 1982. – 128p.: ill., ports; 26cm. ISBN 0-491-02936-5 Originally published: London: Omnibus Press, 1978.
A well-chosen collection of quotes from the Beatles taken from interviews, press conferences, their writings and songs. It is arranged by subject: for example, drugs, politics, films and songwriting. Not to be taken too seriously, they are witty, entertaining and sometimes very thoughtful.

The Beatles by royal command: their own story of the most fabulous night in their career. – London: Daily Mirror, 1963. – 29p.: chiefly col. ill., col. ports; 23cm. (pbk.)
Just one year after the release of their first record, the Beatles were asked to perform at the Royal Variety Performance at the Prince of Wales Theatre on November 4th 1963. They had been accepted by the establishment. In his introduction to the song Twist and Shout, John Lennon invited the audience in 'the dearer seats' to 'rattle your jewellery'. This has become a legendary example of Lennon's impudence. This collection of photographs depicts their day, from rehearsal and the performance to the royal presentation and there are amusing shots with the other stars including Marlene Dietrich.

The Beatles for the record. – Knutsford, Cheshire: Stafford Pemberton, 1981. –
  96p.: ill. (chiefly col.), col. facsims, ports (chiefly col.); 30cm.
  ISBN 0-86030-340-3 (pbk.)
Although this includes some beautifully presented photographs of the group,
the text is superficial and the result is a very well designed, but poor attempt to
give a popular outline of their career.

The Beatles in America: their own exclusive story, and pictures / photographs by
  the Beatles' special photographer Robert Freeman. – London: Daily Mirror,
  1964. – 32p.: ill., ports; 23cm. (pbk.)
Quotes and posed photographs from the first Beatles' tour of the USA: there
are many rare illustrations but no insight into the tour itself.

The Beatles: the fabulous story of John, Paul, George and Ringo / material
  compiled by Robert Burt and Jeremy Pascall. – London: Octupus Books,
  1975. – 82p.: chiefly col. ill., facsims, ports (chiefly col.) ; 31cm.
  ISBN 0-7064-0446-7
Originally this was published as part of the periodical, *The Story of Pop*, a tie-in
with the BBC radio series of the same title. With a brief, sketchy text this is a
collection of illustrations in vivid, even garish, colour. There is little information, but a good visual impression of their changing styles from 'mop tops' to
world-weary business tycoons.

Blake, John
  All you needed was love: the Beatles after the Beatles / John Blake. – Feltham:
  Hamlyn Paperbacks, 1981. – 227p., 8p. of plates: ill., ports; 18cm.
  ISBN 0-600-20466-9 (pbk.)
  Also published: New York: Putnam, 1981.
After a brief resumé of their rise to fame, John Blake focusses on the death of
Brian Epstein as the beginning of the end of the Beatles. He skilfully, though
briefly, examines the failure of their Apple Corps organization and describes
their break-up in detail. The second half of the book considers the lives of the
four musicians after their parting. The author's very real contribution to the
literature of the group is his talent for portraying the Beatles as individual, very
separate, personalities with their own distinctive lives, loves and talents. His
treatment is sympathetic, often moving and never sensational. He skilfully
avoids taking sides and makes no pretence of musical analysis but is content to
describe the events, adding occasionally some inspired comment. Published
after the extensive work, *Shout!*, by Philip Norman, this is complementary and
as good in every way.

Braun, Michael
  Love me do: the Beatles' progress / Michael Braun. – Harmondsworth:
  Penguin, 1977. – 143p.: ill., ports; 18cm. (pbk.)
  Originally published: Harmondsworth: Penguin, 1964.
By far the best of the early books on the group. The author travelled with the
Beatles on their first American tour, as well as joining them while they were
recording in London and touring Britain. It is unusually candid and revealing

for the period and was considered by John Lennon to give the truest impression of the early days of Beatlemania. There is an excellent collection of illustrations and, taking into account the time at which it was written, some intelligent analysis of the group's success. The transcripts of press interviews and general quotes are another interesting feature and give a good impression of their early, cheeky, public image.

Brown, Peter
    The love you make: an inside story of the Beatles / Peter Brown and Steven Gaines. – London: Macmillan, 1983. – xii, 401p., 16p. of plates: ill., ports; 24cm. Includes index. ISBN 0-333-36134-2
    Also published: New York: McGraw-Hill, 1983; London: Pan, 1984.
Peter Brown was the manager of NEMS Enterprises, the Beatles' business affairs, a director of Apple and best man at John Lennon's wedding. In a candid and remarkably matter-of-fact-style, he gives us a catalogue of excess and silliness which although not surprising in itself is at times shocking in its extent. Their alleged drug taking, orgies and paternity suits are frankly discussed in what frequently appears to be a very hostile way. It is, however, simply a frank, factual memoir by someone close to the Beatles as individuals and who understands that what he has described was all part of the whole that created their art and their lifestyle which in turn was part of the culture and mood of a past decade which they helped to fashion.

Bunt, Jan de
    The Beatles concert-ed effort / Jan de Bunt and friends. – Alphen aan de Rijn: Beatles Unlimited, 1978. – 108p.: ill., facsims, ports; 21cm.
    ISBN 9-06419-010-0 (pbk.)
This is a complete list of the live performances and the radio and television broadcasts made by the Beatles as a group, as solo performers and with other artists. It begins with their dates when they were the schoolboy group, the Quarrymen, and includes details of some 294 performances at the Cavern Club and, rather sketchily, their career in Hamburg. The concerts of Paul McCartney's Wings and a live appearance made by Ringo, in 1976, are the last to be noted. The information of songs performed, venues, times and dates, is remarkably full. It is unfortunate that their first British television broadcast, Granada's Tuesday Rendezvous in October 1962, is omitted, but this is a unique, well-indexed work with some rare, but badly reproduced, illustrations of performances.

Carr, Roy
    The Beatles: an illustrated record / by Roy Carr and Tony Tyler. – Rev. ed. – London: New English Library, 1982. – 136p.: ill. (some col.), col. facsims, ports (some col.); 30cm. Includes discography. ISBN 0-450-85228-1 (pbk.)
    Originally published: London: New English Library, 1975.
    Previous edition: London: New English Library, 1978.
    Also published: London: Tribune Books, 1978; New York: Harmony Books, 1978.
Chronologically arranged and beautifully illustrated, this is a history of the

Beatles' recording career with brief introductory notes on their beginnings and their solo activities. There is a reproduction of each of their record sleeves, some full size, with extensive details of the songs, the period at which the record was made and a detailed critical review. There are numerous additional illustrations of the group, posed and performing, with press cuttings and other reproduced memorabilia. The latest edition fully updates the work to include John Lennon and Yoko Ono's later records and his death. More than a discography, this is an excellent pictorial representation of their career, style and influence.

Catone, Marc A.
  An American generation remembers the Beatles / by Marc A. Catone. – Ann Arbor, Michigan: Pierian Press, 1982. – 256p.: ill., ports; 23cm.
  ISBN 0-87650-137-4
Published to coincide with the eighteenth anniversary of their first American tour, this is a collection of 160 letters and seventy drawings from Beatles fans, now all aged around thirty years of age. The memories of the heady days of Beatlemania are nostalgically and enthusiastically described. Not a major contribution to Beatle literature, but amusing

Davis, Hunter
  The Beatles: the authorised biography / Hunter Davies. – Rev. ed. – London: Mayflower, 1978. – 400p., 40p. of plates: ill., facsims, ports; 18cm. Includes discography. ISBN 0-583-11530-6 (pbk.)
  Previous edition: London: Heinemann, 1968.
  Also published: New York: McGraw-Hill, 1968; New York: Dell, 1968.
This title was originally published at the peak of the Beatles' career and now appears very out of date. The revised edition adds only a brief chapter to cover the break-up of the group and subsequent solo careers. An experienced journalist, the author was given access to the Beatles' inner circle and was able to interview them as well as their closest associates and friends. Their early backgrounds and early career are described as well as their successes. This well-written, well-illustrated biography does get behind the glamorous facade to give a picture of the very ordinary personalities that produced their extra-ordinary phenomenon, but it is altogether too reverent.

Davis, Edward E.
  The Beatles book / edited by Edward E. Davis. – New York: Cowles, 1968. – vii, 213p.; 24cm.
Written from the perspective of 1967, this is a collection of essays on the Beatles from fourteen contemporary pundits including Ned Rorem, William F. Buckley and Timothy Leary. The essays are intelligent, often adversely critical but always interesting.

DiLello, Richard
  The longest cocktail party / Richard DiLello. – London: Charisma Books, 1973. – x, 325p.: ill., ports; 23cm. Includes discography, ISBN 0-85947-006-7 (pbk.)

Originally published: London: Charisma Books, 1972.
Also published: New York: Playboy Books, 1973.
Written by an employee of the Apple Corporation, this is an entertaining, inside view of the Beatles' bizarre business organization. The internal wrangles associated with Allen Klein are well described. Lennon's drift away from the others and his involvement with Yoko Ono is discussed from this unusual standpoint. The little-known characters involved with Apple such as Derek Taylor, Peter Asher and Magic Alex are not neglected and there is some useful information about the recording artists like Badfinger and White Trash. There is a full discography of every record released on the Apple label and a superb collection of photographs from DiLello's camera.

Fenick, Barbara
Collecting the Beatles / by Barbara Fenick. – Ann Arbor, Michigan: Pierian Press, 1982. – 296p.: ill., ports; 23cm. ISBN 0-87650-147-1
A guide to collecting Beatles memorabilia, this has a general historical essay, hints on spotting counterfeit items, hints on shopping and a price guide. Records are included and there is an appendix listing the merchandising licences granted during the 1963–64 period in America when Brian Epstein was somewhat lacking in his control. A reference source for the real fanatic, this in itself an oddity.

Freeman, Robert
Beatles Ltd / designed and photographed by Robert Freeman. – London: Newnes, 1964. – 26p.: chiefly ill., ports; 31cm. (pbk.)
A collection of early photographs at the height of Beatlemania, the image cultivated by Epstein of four happy, innocent lads is well portrayed.

Friede, Goldie
The Beatles A to Z / by Goldie Friede, Robin Titone and Sue Weiner. – London: Eyre Methuen, 1981. – 248p., 1p. of plates: ill., facsims, ports; 28cm. ISBN 0-413-48380-0 (pbk.)
An alphabetically arranged encyclopedia of Beatles facts listing songs, places, associates and events in some way related to the group. The information is very detailed and as a source of discographical information, it is very good, including details of songs performed and written by the Beatles as solo artists. It has over one hundred unusual photographs and three thousand entries. There are lists of useful adddresses, television appearances, tours, special performances and reproductions of album sleeves.

Friedman, Rick
The Beatles: words without music / compiled by Rick Friedman; introduced by Joe O'Brien. – New York: Grosset and Dunlap, 1968. – 80p.: ill., ports; 21cm. (pbk.)
A collection of Beatles quotations taken from American press conferences and interviews. The portraits are unusual and much of the comment is not available in similar works published in Britain.

Fulpen, H. V.
The Beatles: an illustrated diary / H. V. Fulpen. – London: Plexus, 1983. –
176p.: ill., facsims, ports; 28cm. ISBN 0-85965-071-5 (cased).
ISBN 0-85965-070-7 (pbk.)
Put together by the president of the Dutch Beatles Fan Club, this is a
chronology of the group's career illustrated with photographs, record sleeves,
merchandising materials and a range of other fascinating items. Not as informative as some works, but entertaining and well produced.

Grove, Martin A.
Beatle madness / Martin A. Grove. – New York: Manor Books, 1978. –
128p.: ill., ports; 18cm. ISBN 0-532-19179-X (pbk.)
A retrospective view of the group's conquest of the USA in 1964: a simple
account with no attempt to analyse the extraordinary hysteria but including an
excellent collection of illustrations depicting the event. There are interesting
accounts of their concert appearances, the first to take place in the large-
stadium venues.

Hamblett, Charles
Here are the Beatles / Charles Hamblett. – London: Four Square, 1964. –
127p.: ill., ports; 19cm. (pbk.)
Full of rare early photographs, this is a journalistic account of the early days of
Beatlemania in Britain. It is filled with memories of the Cavern, brief,
expurgated references to their days in Hamburg and descriptions of what
carefree, unspoiled young men they were. Amusing from a distance of almost
twenty years, this is a typical reflection of the Beatles' public image at the time.

Harry, Bill
The Beatles who's who / Bill Harry. – London: Aurum Press, 1982. – 192p.:
ill., facsims, ports; 25cm. Includes index. ISBN 0-906053-38-2 (pbk.)
This is a collection of three hundred biographies and one hundred photographs
of well-known and obscure figures who had something to do with the lives and
career of the Beatles. The illustrations are a particularly interesting feature as
the vast majority are not available elsewhere.

Harry, Bill
Mersey Beat: the beginnings of the Beatles / edited and introduced by Bill
Harry. – London: Omnibus Press, 1977. – 96p.: ill., facsims, ports; 33cm.
ISBN 0-86001-415-0 (pbk.)
Mersey Beat was a fortnightly Liverpool music magazine set up by Bill Harry in
July 1961. Harry was a former student with John Lennon at Liverpool College
of Art and a close friend of the Beatles. Produced in a tabloid newspaper
format, the paper covered the local music scene at the crucial time in the
evolution of the Liverpool sound. The publication finally ceased in late 1964
when this had become internationally accepted. Harry has selected extracts
which feature the Beatles and some of their fellow artists with interesting
contemporary comment and photographs reflecting the remarkable local
enthusiasm.

Humphery-Smith, Cecil Raymond
Up the Beatles' family tree / by Cecil R. Humphery-Smith, Michael
G. Heenan and Jennifer Mount; illustrated by John Bainbridge. –
Northgate, Kent: Achievements Ltd., 1966. – 12p.: ill., geneal. tables, ports;
25cm. (unbound)
This contains family trees researched by a notable writer on genealogy, and
portraits of the Beatles and their relations. A curious, rare publication, it is
unique within the subject.

Hoffman, Dezo
With the Beatles: the historic photographs of Dezo Hoffman. – London:
Omnibus Press, 1982. – 96p.: ill., ports; 30cm. ISBN 0-7119-0111-2 (pbk.)
A collection of early photographs of the Beatles taken by their publicity
photographer: many of the examples are unique to this publication. Their
image during this 1963 and 1964 period is well shown with brief captions.

Howlett, Kevin
The Beatles at the Beeb 62–65: the story of their radio career / Kevin Howlett.
– London: British Broadcasting Corporation, 1982. – 128p.: ill., ports; 20cm.
Includes bibliography and discography. ISBN 0-563-20128-6 (pbk.)
The Beatles first made a radio broadcast in March 1962. The body of this book
lists every song broadcast live by the group between 1962 and 1965 with dates
and shows. There is the transcript of an early interview, a list of radio
programmes, a discography of record releases during this period and a good
selective bibliography.

Keenan, Debra
On stage, the Beatles / text by Debra Keenan; design concept Larry Soule. –
Mankato, Minnesota: Creative Education, 1975. – 47p.: ill., ports; 23cm.
ISBN 0-91191-487-5
Aimed at a reading age of around ten for American schools, this a well-
designed controlled-vocabulary text with some very well selected illustrations.

Larkin, Rochelle
The Beatles, yesterday, today and tomorrow / Rochelle Larkin. – New York:
Scholastic Book Services, 1977. – 180p.: ill., ports; 18cm. Includes
discography. ISBN 0-590-09866-7 (pbk.)
An uninspiring account of the Beatles as a group and as solo artists, this is
aimed at American high schools. The text is dull but the illustrations very good.

Leach, Sam
Beatles on Broadway / written and compiled by Sam Leach. – London:
World Distributors, 1964. – 32p.: ill., ports; 30cm.
A superficial account of their first American tour: the excellent, rare illustra-
tions and brief captions are full of Beatlemania and excitement.

McCabe, Peter
Apple to the core: the unmaking of the Beatles / Peter McCabe & Robert

D. Schonfield. – London: Martin Brian & O'Keeffe, 1977. – 209p.; 18cm.
ISBN 0-85616-090-3
Originally published: London: Martin Brian & O'Keeffe, 1972; New York:
Pocket Books, 1972.
Also published: London: Sphere, 1973; New York: Scholastic Books, 1977.
The author knew the Beatles in their early days before he moved to New York
to work as a journalist. This is a well-researched study which attempts to
unravel the financial intrigue that destroyed Apple Corps and ultimately the
Beatles. Their naivety and idealism is set against the sophisticated business
brain of Allen Klein. The prolonged litigation and financial detail is meticulously described, demonstrating the blacker side of the music business.

Maugham, Patrick
   The Beatles / story Patrick Maugham; pictures Dezo Hoffman. – London:
   Pyx Publications, 1964. – 30p.: ports; 25cm. (pbk.)
This early work presents the Beatles as happy 'mop tops'. There is very little
text but some unusually natural photographs for the period.

Nimmervoll, Ed
   1000 Beatle Facts: (and a little bit of hearsay) / by Ed Nimmervoll & Euan
   Thorburn. – Sydney, New South Wales: J. Albert, 1977. – 71p.: ill., ports;
   20cm. ISBN 0-8691-3044-7
Arranged into broad categories, a random collection of Beatles information
some of which is very spurious indeed but much of which is entertaining.

Noebel, David A.
   The Beatles: a study in drugs, sex and revolution / by David A. Noebel. –
   Tulsa, Oklahoma: Christian Crusade Publications, 1969. – 64p.; 20cm.
   Originally published as '*Communism, hypnotism, and the Beatles*': Tulsa,
   Oklahoma: Christian Crusade Publications, 1965. (pbk.)
In February 1965 John Lennon, always outspoken, made the unfortunate
remark that the Beatles were 'more popular than Jesus Christ'. This was more
than the American southern states could take and throughout the Bible belt
there were burnings of Beatle publications and records. In this curious book
the author accuses the Beatles of being a communist plot to indoctrinate
American youth. Originally published in 1965, the 1969 edition denounces
their drugtaking and involvement in Eastern religion as well as the blasphemies
described in the first edition.

Norman, Philip
   Shout!: the true story of the Beatles / Philip Norman. – London: Corgi, 1982. –
   426p., 16p. of plates: ill., ports; 20cm. ISBN 0-552-11961-X (pbk.)
   Originally published: London: Elm Tree Books, 1981.
Philip Norman is an English journalist who has written regularly for *The
Sunday Times* on rock and blues as well as writing novels and short stories. This
is an extensively researched biography. The author interviewed hundreds of
friends, associates and relations of the Beatles and Brian Epstein. Unfortunately, however, although he has interviewed the Beatles in the past in his

journalistic capacity, he was unable to meet them during the research period for this biography. Recent quotations are therefore secondhand. In many ways the author gives considerable emphasis to Brian Epstein and brings into the open his secret life and inept handling of the Beatles' merchandising affairs. Their childhood, musical influences and days in Hamburg are described sympathetically and in detail. This is intelligently written and well illustrated but not, however, without inaccuracies and would have been improved by an index.

Parkinson, Norman
  The Beatles book / by Norman Parkinson; with words by Maureen Cleave. – London: Hutchinson, 1964. – 32p.: ill., ports; 32cm.
A collection of illustrations from the Beatlemania days. The book is full of pictures of innocent poses from the early tours, television appearances and concerts, and there are sparse comments by a well-known pop writer of the period.

Pirmanten, Patricia
  The Beatles / text Patricia Pirmanten; illustrator Dick Brude. – Mankato, Minnesota; Creative Education, 1974. – 31p.: ill. (some col.), ports (some col.); 25cm. ISBN 0-8719-1396-8
Written for a reading age of about ten, this is a well-produced controlled-vocabulary biography for American schools.

Russell, Ethan A.
  The Beatles get back / photographs by Ethan A. Russell; text by Jonathan Cott and David Dalton. – London: Apple, 1969. – 133p.: chiefly col. ill., ports (chiefly col.); 29cm. (pbk.)
Originally packaged with early American editions of the Let It Be album but sold separately in Britain, this is a rare collection of 276 photographs from the Let It Be film set, not stills from the film. There is an amusing dialogue from the Beatles and commentary from the authors. Not a book of the film, the period of their break-up is beautifully captured in these excellent photographs.

Schaffner, Nicholas
  The Beatles forever / Nicholas Schaffner. – New York: McGraw-Hill, 1978. – 224p., 4p. of plates: ill., facsims, ports; 28cm. Includes bibliography, discography and index. ISBN 0-07-055087-5
  Originally published: Harrisburg: Stackpole, 1977.
An immense source of information about the Beatles arranged in the chronology of their record releases. It contains details of concerts, publicity materials, tickets, souvenirs and album sleeves as well as a narrative full of information about their career which extends beyond their break-up to 1977. The discography is international and the bibliography is annotated and detailed.

Schaffner, Nicholas
   The boys from Liverpool: John, Paul, George, Ringo / Nicholas Schaffner. –
   New York: Methuen, 1980. – 184p.: ill., ports; 25cm. Includes index.
   ISBN 0-4163-0661-6
This biography complements the author's work, *The Beatles forever*, in that it
takes the result of the author's years of research on the group and sets them in a
biographical narrative. It is unfortunate for the author that his biography was
published in the same year as Philip Norman's less enthusiastic but on the
whole better book.

Schaumberg, Ron
   Growing up with the Beatles: an illustrated tribute / by Ron Schaumberg. –
   New York: Harvest; Harcourt Brace Jovanovich, 1978. – 160p.: ill., facsims,
   ports; 28cm. ISBN 0-15-637387-4
   Originally published: New York: Pyramid Books, 1976.
This is a personal account of the story of the Beatles written by someone who
has never met them but who was simply another fan living in Kansas City. It is
in effect a chronological collection of memories of the period between 1964 and
1976 which relates the author's own development with the Beatles, reflecting
the way in which popular music impresses itself on us by representing and
reminding us of particular times in our lives.

Schultheiss, Tom
   The Beatles: a day in the life: the day by day diary 1960–1970 / compiled by
   Tom Schultheiss. – London: Omnibus Press, 1980. – xviii, 335p.: ill.,
   facsims, ports; 23cm. Includes index. ISBN 0-86001-809-1 (pbk.)
   Originally published: Ann Arbor, Michigan: Pierian Press, 1980.
Using all the available printed sources, the author has constructed a chronological, almost daily list of events relating to the Beatles, between 1960 and
1970 in meticulous detail. In addition, earlier events are listed, including the
dates of birth of the Beatles, their families and associates. The remarkable
detail is accessed superbly by an index of varied typefaces highlighting different
aspects. This is a unique work and very well produced.

Shepherd, Billy
   The true story of the Beatles / Billy Shepherd; illustrated by Bob Gibson. –
   London: Beat Publications, 1964. – 224p.: ill., ports; 19cm.
   Also published: New York: Bantam, 1964.
Published by the Beatles Monthly Book, this is a superficial and often fictitious
look at the Beatles' lifestyle, tastes and background. Symptomatic of the
Beatlemania period, it is aimed at the young fan and is amusing if not objective.
It is, however, an interesting reflection of their early success as viewed at the
time and includes many unusual illustrations.

Spence, Helen
   The Beatles forever / Helen Spence; designed by Philip Cucas. – New
   Malden, Surrey: Colour Library International, 1981. – 96p.: ill. (chiefly
   col.), ports (chiefly col.); 30cm. Includes discography. ISBN 0-9065-5980-5

Although containing only brief, superficial biographical notes, this is a superb collection of unusual pictures of the Beatles from throughout their careers up to the death of John Lennon.

Stokes, Geoffrey
  The Beatles / text by Geoffrey Stokes; introduction by Leonard Bernstein; art direction by Bea Feitler. – London: W. H. Allen; Omnibus Press, 1981. – chiefly ill., facsims, ports; 32cm. ISBN 0-491-02953-0 (W. H. Allen) (cased). ISBN 0-86001-821-0 (Omnibus) (pbk.)
  Originally published: New York: Times Books, 1980.
Andy Warhol's portraits of the Beatles are reproduced on the dust jacket and characterize this otherwise average biography. A brief book, it offers more of an impression of their rise to stardom than an informative account. The illustrations, however, are well chosen mainly from American sources and there are some fascinating facsimiles of newspaper reports of their tours.

Sutton, Margaret
  We love you, Beatles / written and illustrated by Margaret Sutton. – Garden City, New York: Doubleday, 1971. – 48p.: col. ill., ports; 21cm.
Published after the group's demise, this is a children's book of the Beatles' story. The illustrations are imaginative and the production very good. Obviously naive, it is an unusual book underlining the diverse types of material available on the group.

Swenson, John
  Yesterday seems so far away / John Swenson. – New York: Zebra Books, 1977. – 110p.: ill., ports; 18cm. ISBN 0-89083-146-6 (pbk.)
A brief recap of the Beatles' story told at a hectic pace: surprisingly informative but with no time for serious comment. The illustrations are a disappointing collection of often-reproduced clichés.

26 days that rocked the world. – Norfolk, Virginia: Tony Saks, 1980. – 64p.: ill., ports; 38cm. (pbk.)
Taken from over forty American newspapers, this collection of reproduced articles includes concert reports and interviews made during the Beatles' 1964 tour. There are 150 photographs. This rare, fascinating collection is arranged chronologically.

Williams, Allan
  The man who gave the Beatles away / Allan Williams and William Marshall. – Sevenoaks: Coronet, 1976. – 237p., 8p. of plates: ill., ports; 18cm. ISBN 0-340-21016-8 (pbk.)
Allan Williams became the Beatles' first manager and it was he who arranged their bookings in Hamburg. His recollections of their youthful days in Liverpool as a struggling, unknown group without a regular drummer are particularly absorbing. He revels in the unsavoury aspects of their education in Hamburg but the account is nostalgic and lacks bitterness. John Lennon regarded this account as reasonably accurate whereas Paul McCartney dismissed it as largely

fiction. Whatever the reality, it is an entertaining book and the author was used extensively by Philip Norman as a source for *Shout!*.

Woffinden, Bob
　The Beatles apart / Bob Woffinden. – London; New York: Proteus, 1981. –
　144p.: ill. (some col.), ports (some col.); 27cm. Includes bibliography.
　ISBN 0-906071-90-9 (cased). ISBN 0-906071-89-5 (pbk.)
Beginning in 1967 with the release of the Sergeant Pepper's Lonely Hearts Club Band album, the fall of the group is briefly charted. The author continues the story by tracing their solo careers, basing his information on personal interviews. The story of the break-up of the group is oversimplified but in general this is informative with some unusual illustrations.

Zanderbergen, George
　The Beatles / by George Zanderbergen. – Mankato, Minnesota: Crestwood
　House, 1976. – 47p.: ill. (some col.), ports (some col.); 25cm.
　ISBN 0-9139-4054-2
Written for a reading age of around ten for American schools, this is a well-produced biography suitable for the age group with some interesting illustration.

THE BEATLES: SONGS

Aldridge, Alan
　The Beatles illustrated lyrics: volume one / edited by Alan Aldridge. –
　London: Macdonald Futura, 1980. – 156p.: ill. (chiefly col.), ports; 28cm.
　Includes index. ISBN 0-354-04221-1 (pbk.)
　Originally published: London: Macdonald, 1969.
　Also published: New York: Delacorte Press; Dell, 1969.
Aldridge, Alan
　The Beatles illustrated lyrics: 2 / edited by Alan Aldridge. – London:
　Macdonald Futura, 1980. – 123p.: ill. (chiefly col.); 28cm. Includes index.
　ISBN 0-354-04221-1 (pbk.)
　Originally published: London: BPC Publishing, 1971.
　Also published: New York: Delacorte Press, 1971.
Alan Aldridge, an artist and contributor himself, commissioned forty-five other artists for the first volume and fifty-one for the second to interpret the images of the Beatles' songs. The result is a collection of illustrations which beautifully reflect the psychedelic, outrageously kitsch style of the late sixties. Both volumes are well designed with a brief introduction by Aldridge and an index of song titles with the identity of the artists. The second volume includes both the Abbey Road and Let It Be albums as well as early songs missed in volume one. The current edition is usually packaged in a two-volume set.

Beatles, the
　The Beatles lyrics / with an introduction by Jimmy Savile. – London: Futura
　Publications, 1979. – 219p.; 18cm. ISBN 0-8600-7478-1 (pbk.)

Previously published with 64p. of plates: London: Futura Publications, 1975. A complete collection of the 192 songs written by the Beatles up to 1970, including those recorded by other artists as well as by the writers. The 1975 edition included an excellent collection of photographs.

Beatles, the
The complete Beatles lyrics. – London: Omnibus Press, 1982. – 224p.: ill., ports; 25cm. Includes discography and index. ISBN 0-86001-754-0 (pbk.)
Every song written by the four Beatles as a group is included. There is a full chronological discography of official British releases with recording dates.

Beatles, the
Golden Beatles: book one the words of 50 Beatles hits / by John Lennon, Paul McCartney and George Harrison. – London: Northern Songs, 1966. – 53p.: ill., ports; 21cm.
Well produced, these lyrics of the earlier songs are presented as poems.

Beatles, the
Pocket Beatles complete / music edited by Clive A. Sansom; compilation by Pearce Marchbank and Jane Coke; designed by Pearce Marchbank. – 383p.: ill., music, ports; 20cm. Includes discography. ISBN 0-86001-667-6
A collection of 184 songs written by John Lennon, Paul McCartney, Ringo Starr and George Harrison, this includes not only the full lyrics but the musical tabulature of the melody lines and the guitar chords.

Campbell, Colin
Things we said today: the complete lyrics and a concordance to the Beatles' songs, 1962–1970 / by Colin Campbell and Allan Murphy. – Ann Arbor, Michigan: Pierian Press, 1980. – 430p.: ill., facsims; 25cm.
ISBN 0-8765-104-8
Unique to the field of popular music, this covers 182 songs written and recorded by the Beatles as a group. The concordance section lists every line in every song in which a particular word is used in chronological order of use over the years. The line number and song title follow the line itself. This is followed by an alphabetical-frequency listing of every word in the Beatles' song vocabulary with an indication of the number of times the word appears and a numerically descending frequency listing of each word. In all, although marred by its poor paper quality, this is a remarkable book.

Cowan, Philip
Behind the Beatles songs / by Philip Cowan; illustrated by Robert Rankin. – London: Polytantric Press, 1978. 63p.: ill., 26cm. Includes discography.
ISBN 0-905150-09-0 (pbk.)

In two parts, here is a collection of anecdotes with humorous cartoon illustrations about the inspiration behind individual songs of the Beatles followed by a section of facts and statistics about the Beatles' performances, broadcasts, contributions to the work of other artists and a full discography including unofficial bootleg recordings. A useful source of facts about the Beatles.

Doney, Malcolm
  Lennon and McCartney / Malcolm Doney. – London: Omnibus Press, 1982.
  – 136p.: ill., ports; 22cm. Includes discography. ISBN 0-7119-0051-1 (pbk.)
  Originally published: Tunbridge Wells, Kent: Midas Books; New York:
  Hippocrene Books, 1981.
This long, rambling essay is an unsatisfactory attempt at serious analysis. The
author's conclusions are totally unoriginal and little is added to the body of
literature on the subject.

Mellers, Wilfrid
  Twilight of the Gods: the Beatles in retrospect
  (*See* section 3.2, Musical criticism and analysis, p.82)

THE BEATLES: BIBLIOGRAPHIES

Harry, Bill
  Paperback writers: the history of the Beatles in print / Bill Harry. – London:
  Virgin Books, 1984. – 192p.: ill., facsims; 24cm. Includes index.
  ISBN 0-863690-21-1 (pbk.)
This first full bibliography of the Beatles includes not only books, magazines,
fanzines, music collections and European publications but also a few general
books which include interesting Beatle information. It is well written and on
the whole a very good piece of work, but it has some surprising omissions and
some bad errors in citations including errors in titles.

THE BEATLES: DISCOGRAPHIES

Castleman, Harry
  All together now: the first complete Beatles discography 1961–1975 / by Harry
  Castleman and Walter J. Podrazik. – New York: Ballantine, 1976. – xv,
  379p.: ill., facsims, ports; 24cm. Includes indexes. ISBN 0-87650-075-0
  Originally published: Ann Arbor, Michigan: Pierian Press, 1975.
The most exhaustive chronological list of all the Beatles' recorded songs with
detailed credits including the recordings of other artists. There is a full
international list of releases by the Beatles with the record number as well as
detailed annotations. In addition to the main chronological sequence there are
indexes by song and recording artist.

Castleman, Harry
  The Beatles again? / by Harry Castleman and Walter Podrazik. – Ann Arbor,
  Michigan: Pierian Press, 1977. – xxiii, 280p., 1 plate: ill., facsims, ports;
  24cm. Includes index. ISBN 0-87650-086-0
This is an excellent addendum and update to be used with *All together now*.
Again, it is well arranged and indexed.

Guzek, Arnot
Beatles discography / Arnot Guzek. – Alphen aan de Rijn: Beatles Unlimited, 1978. – 84p; 21cm. (pbk.)
A publication of the Dutch organization specializing in the Beatles, this is neither well produced nor comprehensive.

Janssen, Roos
Dig it: the Beatles bootleg book / by Roos Janssen and Erik M. Bakker. –
Alphen aan de Rijn: Beatles Unlimited, 1979. – 34p.; 21cm. (pbk.)
Although not well produced, this brings together information on unofficial releases from a wide range of sources. By definition it is impossible for there to be any control over bootlegs and there is no claim here of comprehensiveness.

Miles
The Beatles: an illustrated discography / by Miles. – London: Omnibus Press, 1981. – 96p.: ill., facsims, ports; 20cm. ISBN 0-86001-958-6 (pbk.)
A brief, well-designed discography, this covers Beatles' releases as the group and as solo artists, from their first German recordings to George Harrison's 1981 album. Some bootlegs are included. There is a section on their work as producers and as session musicians for other artists. This is not the most detailed of discographies but it is a good introduction to their work.

Reinhart, Charles
You can't do that: Beatles bootlegs and novelty records, 1963–1980 / by
Charles Reinhart. – Ann Arbor, Michigan: Pierian Press, 1981. – 350p.: ill., facsims, ports; 24cm. Includes indexes. ISBN 0-87650-128-5
This is by far the fullest collection of information on the Beatles' unofficial releases. It includes almost 900 bootlegs and counterfeits and also a curious collection of almost 400 novelty records about the group. There are detailed indexes to personal names, record labels and songs. The illustrations include a wide range of rare record sleeves and labels.

Russell, Jeff
The Beatles: album file and complete discography / Jeff Russell. – Poole,
Dorset: Blandford Press, 1982. – 256p.: ill., facsims; 23cm. Includes index.
ISBN 0-7137-1277-5 (cased). ISBN 0-7137-1294-5 (pbk.)
Each of the Beatles' albums is studied in detail from the early German recordings to the recent record-company compilations. Dates, the writer of each song, who played which instrument, how many versions exist and which was released, as well as full discographical information, are all meticulously chronicled. Unissued recordings, songs given to other artists, rehearsal tapes and a few bootlegs are noted with a full listing of American versions of albums. This is not the most comprehensive work on the subject, but it is well written and absorbing.

Stannard, Neville
The long and winding road: a history of the Beatles on record / by Neville
Stannard; edited by John Tobler. – London: Virgin Books, 1982. – 239p.:
ill., facsims; 24cm. Includes bibliography. ISBN 0-907080-46-4 (pbk.)

Well researched with very good annotations, the bulk of the book consists of two chronological sections devoted to British and American releases. Each record has a complete recording history, track length, discographical details and record sleeve, where appropriate. Appendices list songs recorded by other artists, chart data, unreleased songs and a chronology of recording sessions. This is one of the best discographies available on the Beatles, not because of its exhaustiveness (it is, for example, poor as a source for bootlegs and unreleased material) but because it is well written and carefully designed.

Stannard, Neville
   Working class heroes: the history of the Beatles' solo recordings/ Neville
   Stannard & John Tobler. – London: Virgin Books, 1983. – 239p.: ill.,
      facsims, ports; 24cm. Includes bibliography. ISBN 0-907080-92-8 (pbk.)
The second discography by Stannard, this time with the help of John Tobler, this book lists the record releases of the group after their demise. In addition to a straightforward description of the records, there are anecdotes about the period in their careers, the recording sessions, the ideas behind the writing and so on. Each album cover is reproduced with some promotional material. There is a chronological listing of the Beatles' British releases followed by their American releases and a list of Yoko Ono's solo efforts.

THE BEATLES: QUIZBOOKS

Goodgold, Edwin
   The compleat Beatles quiz book / compiled by Edwin Goodgold and Dan
   Carlinsky. – New York: Warner Books, 1975. – 206p.: ill., ports; 18cm.
   ISBN 0-446-76889-8 (pbk.)
Here are hundreds of questions and answers, puzzles, picture quizzes and a wide variety of games. The level of the inquisition ranges greatly from the very simple to the utterly obscure. Not the best in quizbook design or production, it is still very entertaining.

House, Jack
   The Beatles quiz book / compiled by Jack House. – London: Collins, 1964. –
   32p: ill., ports; 23cm. (pbk.)
A rare, early example of a pop quizbook, this was published at the height of Beatlemania and is packed with trivial information. There are some interesting early photographs, but some very misleading answers and certainly some very wrong ones.

Rosenbaum, Helen
   The Beatles trivia quizbook / by Helen Rosenbaum. – New York: Signet,
   1978. – 154p., 8p. of plates: ill., facsims. ports; 18cm. ISBN 0-451-08225-7
   (pbk.)
Arranged by broad categories ranging from commonly known to the most trivial pieces of spurious information, included are hundreds of entertaining questions and answers. There is a good picture-quiz section and some particularly searching sections on the group's songs.

THE BEATLES: FILMS

Harry, Bill
　　Beatlemania: an illustrated filmography / by Bill Harry. – London: Virgin
　　Books, 1984. – 224p.: ill., ports; 24cm. Includes index. ISBN 0-86369-041-9
　　(pbk.)
Covering film appearances of the four Beatles, not only as a group but also as
individuals, this is very detailed with synopses, stills and detailed credits.

A Hard Day's Night

Released in 1964 and directed by Richard Lester in black and white, A Hard
Day's Night was the Beatles' first film, made at the height of Beatlemania. It
attempted to depict the group's hectic lifestyle hampered by Paul's grand-
father, brilliantly played by Wilfrid Brambell. Lester's direction and innovative cutting of the film was to set a trend for dozens of films during the
swinging London period of the mid sixties. The overall effect of the film, which
won it an Academy Award nomination, remains today despite the lack of any
real storyline and is due to the natural wit of the group and an excellent
collection of songs.

The Beatles in Richard Lester's A Hard Day's Night: a complete pictorial record
　　of the movie / editor J. Philip di Franco; introduction Andrew Sarris. –
　　Harmondsworth: Penguin, 1978. – 297p.: ill., ports; 28cm.
　　ISBN 0-1400-4786-7 (pbk.)
　　Originally published: New York: Chelsea Publications, 1977.
Using stills and dialogue, this is a superbly designed presentation of the action.
It captures the mood of Lester's innovative direction particularly well. There is
a transcript of a lengthy interview with Richard Lester, the lyrics of the songs
heard on the film's soundtrack and an introductory essay analysing the style of
direction and its influence.

The Beatles: starring in 'A Hard Day's Night'. – London: World Distributors,
　　1964. – 34p: chiefly ill.; 30cm. (pbk.)
A large-format selection of stills with little text which capture the atmosphere
of the film admirably.

Burke, John
　　A Hard Day's Night / by John Burke. – London: Melita Music, 1977. – 126p.,
　　8p. of plates: ill.; 18cm. (pbk.)
　　Originally published: London: Pan Books, 1964.
An attempt to set down the action of the film into novel form. The storyline is
simply too thin to sustain a cohesive narrative.

Pop pics: the Beatles film. – London: Newnes, 1964. – 47p.: chiefly ill.; 30cm.
　　(pbk.)
A good selection of stills published to coincide with the release of the film.

Help!

The Beatles' second film, directed by Richard Lester and released in 1965, was shot in colour and was an altogether more sophisticated effort than their first. Eleanor Bron, Victor Spinetti, Roy Kinnear and Leo McKern joined the group in a frantic comedy in which a religious sect, followers of the goddess Kali, pursue the Beatles around the world in an attempt to retrieve their sacrificial ring from Ringo's finger. It was generally regarded as rather less successful than A Hard Day's Night, though the Beatles provided a superb collection of songs for the soundtrack and gave good acting performances.

Hine, Al
   The Beatles in 'Help!' / novelisation by Al Hine. – London: Mayflower, 1965.
   – 158p., 8p. of plates: ill.; 19cm. (pbk.)
   Also published: New York: Dell; New York: Random House, 1965.
Not a good attempt to represent the film's Goon-inspired plot, the story appears humourless and thin. The American editions included thirty pages of song lyrics and stills in an attempt to represent the action more closely.

Yellow Submarine

Made by George Dunning and released in 1968 as the Beatles' third film, Yellow Submarine was a beautifully coloured animation. The storyline concerned the fantastic journey of the little characters, the Lonely Hearts Club Band, who resemble and sound like the Beatles. Very much in the vein of sixties psychedelia, the soundtrack includes old Beatles songs and some of the characters come from Lennon's writings. George Martin supplied additional incidental music which appears on the soundtrack album.

*The Beatles in 'Yellow Submarine': starring Sgt. Pepper's Lonely Hearts Club
   Band* / produced by Al Brodax, written by Lee Minoff (and others) from an
   original story by Lee Minoff based upon the songs by John Lennon & Paul
   McCartney. – London: New English Library, 1968. – 128p.: chiefly col. ill.:
   18cm. ISBN 0-4500-0156-3 (pbk.)
Published to coincide with the release of the film, this collection of beautifully coloured stills perfectly reproduces the feel of the film. The dialogue is well chosen to correspond with the action.

THE BEATLES: PERIODICALS

(See section 8.2, The Beatles.)

THE BEE GEES

The brothers Barry (born 1946) and twins Maurice and Robin Gibb (born

1949) emigrated from their birthplace, Manchester, to Australia as children and by their late teens had established themselves as Australia's top pop group. They returned to Britain in 1966 and with two additional musicians began to produce a consistent chain of million-selling singles. Their strength was the astute management of Robert Stigwood, an ability to write songs with strong melodies and their own unusual, blended vocal harmonies.

Their success began to wane by 1970, however, and the group had drifted into the background until 1975 when they released the album Main Course, which included a series of songs produced in the black style later to be known as disco. The sound they produced was close to that of black soul groups, maintaining their strong melodies sung in high falsetto harmonies. After a sequel album in 1977 they provided most of the sound track for the disco film Saturday Night Fever and became the leading exponents of the enormously successful disco style of music which in the late seventies became a major force in pop music. Their success in album and singles sales of their own records and in the recordings of their songs sung by other artists made them the most successful British writers of the late seventies. The Saturday Night Fever soundtrack album was the bigest seller of all time until overtaken by Michael Jackson's Thriller in 1983.

Billboard salutes the Bee Gees. – Los Angeles: Billboard Publications, 1978. – 117p.: chiefly ill. (some col.), ports (some col.); 37cm. (pbk.)
A large-format American tribute to the Bee Gees, published at the height of their disco success in the USA, not informative but beautifully illustrated.

Gibb, Barry
    Bee Gees: the authorized biography / by Barry, Robin and Maurice Gibb; as told to David Leaf. – London: Octopus Books, 1979. – 160p.: ill. (some col.), col. facsims, ports (some col.); 28cm. ISBN 0-7064-7091-2
    Also published: New York: Dell, 1979; New York: Chappell, 1979.
A well-illustrated biography packed with personal as well as publicity photographs of the Gibbs and their album covers. A list of their songs and versions recorded by other artists is included as well as an impressive list of their awards, but unfortunately no discography. A good, if superficial, lighthearted outline of their changing fortunes from their point of view which occasionally offers an insight into their songwriting technique and musical influences.

Pryce, Larry
    The Bee Gees / Larry Pryce. – St. Albans: Panther, 1979. – 141p.: 16p. of plates; ill., ports; 18cm. ISBN 0-586-04854-5 (pbk.)
Produced in the wake of the Bee Gees' 1978 revival. The author covers their early career well. The style is straightforward with some good illustrations but the result, although informative, is dull.

Schumacher, Craig
    Bee Gees / by Craig Schumacher. – Mankato, Minnesota: Creative Education, 1980. – 31p: ill. (some col.), ports (some col.); 25cm.

ISBN 0-9719-1697-5 (cased). ISBN 0-686-70890-3 (pbk.)
Written for a reading age of around ten and aimed at American schools, this is a well-illustrated controlled-vocabulary biography. There is an emphasis on the Bee Gees' more recent disco successes but their early career is covered briefly.

Stevens, Kim
  The Bee Gees / Kim Stevens. – New York; London: Quick Fox, 1978. – 92p.; ill., ports; 26cm. Includes discography. ISBN 0-8256-3923-9 (pbk.)
With only a brief mention of their early career, this is a sketchy, but well illustrated, biography which covers mainly the period between their renewed success in 1975 and the making of their film, Sgt. Pepper's Lonely Hearts Club Band, in 1978.

Tatham, Dick
  The incredible Bee Gees / Dick Tatham. – London: Futura Publications, 1979. – 144p.; 18cm. Includes discography. ISBN 0-7088-1687-8 (pbk.)
An uninspiring, journalistic biography which does not attempt to analyse their songs or recording techniques. Their very early career in Australia and success during the sixties is well covered, and a full discography is included.

THE BEE GEES: FILMS

Sgt. Pepper's Lonely Hearts Club Band

Produced in 1978 by Robert Stigwood and directed by Michael Schultz, Sgt. Pepper's Lonely Hearts Club Band was a vehicle for the Bee Gees and Peter Frampton, with dozens of other stars in guest appearances. The soundtrack of Beatles songs produced by George Martin is very poor. The overall effect is a very bad film, with no plot, no cohesion and embarrassing acting performances.

Edwards, Henry
  Sgt. Pepper's Lonely Hearts Club Band / Henry Edwards. – London: Star Books, 1978. – 190p., 16p. of plates: ill.; 18cm. ISBN 0-352-30360-3 (pbk.)
  Originally published: New York: Pocket Books, 1978.
The storyline of the film is described with the Beatles' lyrics and a few stills. A very bad tie-in, underlining the weakness of the film itself.

Stigwood, Robert
  The official Sgt. Pepper's Lonely Hearts Club Band scrapbook / by Robert Stigwood and Dee Anthony. – New York: Wallaby Pocket Books, 1978.
  80p.: ill. (some col.), ports (some col.); 30cm. ISBN 0-671-79038-X (pbk.)
This lavishly produced book describes the action of the film using stills, and goes on to describe its making. A souvenir to recall a non-event.

BEEFHEART, CAPTAIN

Born Don Van Vleit in Glendale, California, in 1941, Captain Beefheart worked closely with Frank Zappa for many years. Impossible to categorize, his music, which is a blend of blues, rock and free-form jazz, with its futuristic production and strange lyrics, made his Magic Band an original phenomenon and a firm favourite of the sixties' underground movement. In recent years his work has become more conventional but always surprising in its inventiveness.

The lives and times of Capt. Beefheart. – Manchester: Babylon Books, 1979. –
　　60p.: ill., facsims, ports; 25cm. Includes discography. (pbk.)
A cut-up, fanzine-format biography arranged chronologically with a fascinating collection of press cuttings, writings, illustrations and lyrics. The discography is brief and information is difficult to access.

Muir, John
　　The lives and times of Captain Beefheart / edited by John Muir. – Manchester:
　　Babylon Books, 1980. – 72p.: ill., facsims, ports; 28cm. Includes discography. ISBN 0-907188-03-6 (pbk.)
A completely revised version of the Babylon book of the same title. There is no resemblance. This edition has a far superior production and includes a fuller discography. The cut-up format is still maintained, but with a much improved selection of writings, newscuttings, lyrics and illustrations. Access to the information is no easier than for the earlier version but this is the fullest source available on Captain Beefheart, with a lengthy essay by the editor.

BERRY, CHUCK

Born in St. Louis, Missouri, in 1931, Charles Edward Bury learned to play the guitar in his early teens. After spending three years in a reform school for attempted robbery, he worked for General Motors and then began training as a hairdresser. He began playing guitar semi-professionally and in 1955 moved to Chicago. He met the great bluesman Muddy Waters, who was impressed by his guitar style and recommended him to the head of Chess Records with whom he signed a contract. His first record, Maybelline, was an immediate success in 1956 which he followed with the classic song Roll Over Beethoven. His style was a blend of rhythm & blues and country music: the result was pure rock'n'roll into which he added witty, satirical lyrics which he enuciated with unusual clarity. He appeared in four films and continued to write and record hit records until he was imprisoned in 1959, after a trial lasting almost two years, for moral offences under the Mann Act, involving a fourteen-year-old hat-check girl in his club. He has always maintained his innocence but the fact that he was successful and black was against him.

　　He was finally released in 1964 and although the music scene had changed dramatically, it was to his advantage. The new leaders, the Beatles and the Rolling Stones, had been so influenced by his work that they had recorded many of his songs and achieved hits with them. The Rolling Stones have recorded twelve alone. He immediately began making more records although he was not to regain his earlier success in the singles charts, apart from one comic record in 1972. Chuck Berry has continued since then to be a massive magnet for concert audiences. He has played a season in Las Vegas and a multitude of rock festivals, as well as extensive tours. Chuck Berry remains one of the most influential figures in rock'n'roll. He arguably made the lyric a significant part of the music. He is one of the richest of all black artists.

Dewitt, Howard A.
   Chuck Berry: rock'n'roll music / by Howard A. Dewitt. – Fremont,
   California: Horizon Books, 1981. – 228p.: ill., ports 20cm. Includes
   bibliography and discography. ISBN 0-938840-01-0 (cased).
   ISBN 0-938840-00-2 (pbk.)
Poorly produced with a typescript typeface, this is by far the best source of information on Chuck Berry. Written in a direct, factual style with an excellent collection of photographs, the author analyses Berry's musical influences in some depth and begins to explain and describe his far-reaching influence. The discography includes full details of his recording sessions, musicians, songs, release dates and some bootlegs. There is a full listing of cover versions by other artists.

Reese, Krista
   Chuck Berry: Mr Rock and Roll / by Krista Reese. – London; New York:
   Proteus, 1982. – 128p.: ill. (some col.), ports (some col.); 28cm. Includes
   discography. ISBN 0-86276-018-6 (pbk.)
A well-produced, but superficial biography; it claims to uncover the enigmatic side of Berry's life but reveals no information that has not been available for years. There are excellent illustrations, including eight colour plates, which to some extent compensate for the poor text.

BLACK SABBATH

Originally formed in Birmingham as Earth, Tony Iommi, Ozzie Osbourne, Geezer Butler and Bill Ward changed their name to Black Sabbath and moved to London in late 1969. They were associated, as their name implies, with mystical beliefs and the occult, popular interests at the time, and their first album soon appeared in the charts followed by an internationally successful single. Their use of the guitar-riff-based songs and barrage of sound made them early exponents of British heavy metal. After a period during the mid seventies when their style was unfashionable, they re-emerged with the revival of interest in heavy metal in the eighties. Ronnie James Dio has now taken over from Osbourne on vocals and Vinnie Appice from Bill Ward, on drums. They continue to sell records and attract enormous followings to their concerts from both new fans and longterm devotees.

Welch, Chris
   Black Sabbath / by Chris Welch. – London; New York: Proteus, 1982. – 96p.:
   ill. (some col.), ports (some col.); 28cm. Includes discography.
   ISBN 0-86276-015-1 (pbk.)
A brief, well-illustrated biography which includes the bare facts, but there is no
analysis of their music, or heavy metal as a whole, or any attempt to explain
their prolonged success. It is the only substantial source of information on the
group, however, and is well designed and well produced.

BLONDIE

After a varied career around show business, Deborah Harry formed her group,
the Stilettoes, in 1973 and with the addition of Chris Stein this evolved into
Blondie. Based in New York, they were part of the early punk movement
which had a strong influence on the London new-wave movement of 1976,
Debbie Harry being called the 'punk princess'. Their music is a cross between
fifties and sixties pop with the earthy lyrics of the new wave. Blondie's greatest
asset has always been Debbie Harry, whose incredibly youthful looks and
sensual presentation, as well as distinctive voice and unusual songwriting
ability, have given Blondie a wide appeal across the popular-music audience.
Since 1976 they have had a series of successful singles and albums, although
their concerts are often disappointing.

Bangs, Lester
   Blondie / Lester Bangs. – London: Omnibus Press, 1980. – 94p.: ill. (some
   col.), ports (some col.); 28cm. ISBN 0-86001-711-7 (pbk.)
   Also published: New York: Simon and Schuster, 1980.
Written by a well-known American music journalist, this is very well illustrated
and includes information from a series of news interviews. Especially revealing
are those from former associates and musicians. This is not a chronological
outline but an episodic impression of the group with some serious analysis of
their music and criticism of their albums.

Blondie. – Manchester: Babylon Books, 1979. – 56p.: ill., facsims, ports;
   25cm. (pbk.)
In a cut-up, fanzine format, this is a collection of material on the group, poorly
reproduced with little new text and few original photographs. Nevertheless, it
is a guide to sources of articles and does include information available from no
other source and exposés of Debbie Harry's past.

Blondie. – London: Omnibus Press, 1980. – 96p.: ill. (some col.), ports (some
   col.); 28cm. ISBN 0-86001-711-7 (pbk.)
A well illustrated, brief biography which does not concentrate on Deborah
Harry as a pin-up but discusses the contributions of all the members of the
group and their musical evolution.

Harry, Debbie
   Making tracks: the rise of Blondie / Debbie Harry, Chris Stein and Victor
   Bockris. – London: Elm Tree Books, 1982. – 192p.: ill. (some col.), ports
   (some col.); 29cm. ISBN 0-241-10838-1 (pbk.)
Blondie's singer and lead guitarist give an autobiographical account of the
group's rise to fame. Well-designed, with some excellent illustrations, this
book gives an authoritative account of the birth of the American new-wave
movement from the inside. All major American, as well as many British, new-
wave artists are included in the illustrations and are cleverly woven into the text
as they cross Blondie's path. The music is not analysed in any depth but their
career, in a commercial context, is carefully traced.

Schruers, Fred
   Blondie / Fred Schruers. – London: Star Books, 1980. – 134p., 16p. of plates:
   ill., ports; 18cm. ISBN 0-352-30778-1 (pbk.)
An outline biography, this includes transcripts of lengthy interviews with the
group. Of particular interest is the account of their power structure, of how
they share their profits, how songs are chosen for recording and the details of
their recording techniques. If not a revealing biography in a sensational sense,
it does give an indication of the business-like approach required of such a
successful pop group.

BOLAN, MARC

Born in Hackney, London, in 1947, Marc Bolan began his musical career in the
mid sixties as a budding young mod male model with aspirations of becoming a
pop singer. In 1966, after an abortive solo attempt, he was persuaded by his
manager, Simon Napier-Bell, to join the group John's Children. With Bolan
adding his distinctive vocals and songwriting talent, the group had some minor
hits but it was not until he formed the duo, Tyrannosaurus Rex, in 1968 and
became the darling of the London hippies, that he gained wider attention. His
initial success faded after four albums of his naive, mystical little songs
presented with a sparse acoustic accompaniment.
   In late 1970 he reappeared and with the addition of a full electric band,
T. Rex, suddenly he reached a new, younger audience in their early teens.
Their hysterical following had not been seen in Britain since the days of the
Beatles in the early sixties. Bolan led this movement, termed glam rock, until it
subsided in 1974. At one period, it was claimed that T. Rex were actually
selling records at a greater rate than the Beatles at their peak; this is doubtful.
In 1977 Bolan was killed when his car crashed into a tree. He is regarded by
many of his fellow writers and musicians as one of the most creative artists
of the late sixties and early seventies. Certainly he had a unique style
and a determination to become a star in a world of changing moods and
fashions.

Marc Bolan: songs, photos, lyrics, interviews, memorabilia, letters, notes,
   snapshots, memories. . . . . a tribute / compiled and edited by Ted Dicks and

Paul Platz. – London: Essex House Publishing, 1981. – 127p.: ill., facsims, music, ports; 29cm. Includes discography. ISBN 0-86001-840-7 (pbk.)
Originally published: London: Essex House Publishing; Springwood Books, 1978.
A collection of reminiscences by Bolan's associates and friends; this is not a biography, but a celebration of his 'genius' and 'humanity'. Included are some of his most famous songs and a good collection of illustrations.

Sinclair, Paul
Marc Bolan: the Marc Bolan story / Paul Sinclair. – London: Omnibus Press, 1982. – 96p.: ill., ports; 26cm. Includes discography. ISBN 0-7119-0054-X (pbk.)
Written by the editor of *Cosmic Dancer*, the first Marc Bolan fanzine, this is a serious attempt to give an authoritative account of his life and work. Well illustrated, the text is too brief to offer an in-depth study, but is full of informed comment.

Tremlett, George
The Marc Bolan story / George Tremlett. – London: Futura Publications, 1975. – 126p., 16p. of plates: ill., ports; 18cm. ISBN 0-860-07068-9 (pbk.)
Written in the author's thorough, journalistic style with the usual detailed chronology, this has a good collection of illustrations and lengthy quotations from the author's personal interviews with the subject.

Welch, Chris
Marc Bolan: born to boogie / by Chris Welch and Simon Napier-Bell. – London: Eel Pie, 1982. – 128p.: ill., ports; 27cm. ISBN 0-906008-65-4 (pbk.)
Written by a well-known rock journalist and Bolan's first manager, this is a sketchy outline of his career, full of anecdotes but lacking analysis and serious criticism. The illustrations are well chosen and many appear in no other publication.

BOLAN, MARC: SONGS

Bolan, Marc
Marc Bolan lyric book. – London: Essex Music International, 1972. – 86p.; 20cm. (pbk.)
A complete collection of Bolan's song lyrics from his hippie days to the pop classics of the early seventies. Few stand up as even approaching poems but for pop songs they are often amusing and certainly different.

BOLAN, MARC: DISCOGRAPHIES

Bramley, John
Marc Bolan: the illustrated discography / by John and Shan Bramley. – London: Omnibus Press, 1982. – 96p.: ill., facsims, ports; 20cm.

ISBN 0-7119-0108-2 (pbk.)
A well-organized, chronological listing of all his British and American releases
including some bootlegs. The illustrations are good, including record sleeves,
and the notes are particularly well written and informative.

BONEY M

Boney M, a Jamaican vocal group of three women and one man, were the most
successful British-based perpetrators of the late seventies disco boom. They
had a series of very successful hit records between 1976 and 1980 which were
mostly remakes of old pop songs with the faintest hint of a reggae rhythm and
occasionally interesting harmonies. Their success was probably largely due to
their glamorous, exotic presentation and to the shrewd management of Frank
Farian. They were the first pop group to be invited to play in Moscow. Their
cosmopolitan image made them one of the best known of the exponents of
Europop. They continue to perform on the international cabaret circuit with
occasional record releases and television appearances.

Shearlaw, John
  Boney M / John Shearlaw and David Brown. – Feltham, Middlesex:
  Hamlyn, 1979. – 140p., 8p. of plates: ill., ports; 18cm. ISBN 0-600-20009-4
  (pbk.)
A superficial biography with lengthy quotes from their manager underlining his
skilful manipulation with a good deal of smugness and certainly no excuses.
Nevertheless, the Boney M fan would find much of interest here, particularly in
the way their stage fashions were designed and in the background information
on the relatively anonymous members of the group.

THE BOOMTOWN RATS

Formed in Dun Laoghaire, Ireland, in 1977, the Rats were a leading band of
the British new wave. Led by singer Bob Geldof, they had a powerful stage act
with some well written, exciting songs. With their first hit in 1977, there
followed a succession of hits into the eighties with their biggest success, I Don't
Like Mondays, a major hit in the summer of 1979. Geldof with his bright
comments on a range of subjects is frequently to be seen on television but the
band itself seems to have passed its peak.

Stone, Peter
  The Boomtown Rats: having their picture taken / Peter Stone. – London: Star
  Books, 1980. – 94p.: chiefly ill., ports; 28cm. ISBN 0-352-30768-4 (pbk.)
Mainly a collection of photographs of the Rats on tour, including in the USA,
with pictures of the band in concert as well as relaxing and travelling. Not a
good collection, it fails to capture the feel of the tour and does not get near to
transmitting the group's dynamic stage presentation.

BOONE, DEBBIE

Born in 1955, the third daughter of singer Pat Boone, Debbie began singing with her family's act in 1969. She appeared on numerous television shows and in 1977 made her first solo recordings. Her first release was an enormous success in America and one of the biggest sellers of all time for a female vocalist. She has so far made little impression in Britain.

Eldred, Patricia Mulrooney
   Debbie Boone / by Patricia Mulrooney Eldred; designed by Mark
   Landkamer. – Mankato, Minnesota: Creative Education, 1980. – 31p.: ill.
   (some col.), ports (some col.); 25cm. ISBN 0-87191-719-7 (cased).
   ISBN 0-89812-099-8 (pbk.)
Aimed at a reading age of around ten for American schools, this controlled-vocabulary text is well designed and well illustrated.

BOONE, PAT

Born Charles Eugene Boone in Jacksonville, Florida, in 1934, Pat Boone was one of the most successful popular singers of the mid fifties. By 1960, after appearing in a number of poor films, his popularity had waned but he continued to remain in the public eye because of his work on behalf of the Christian church. He appeared on a wide range of American television shows and by the mid seventies he had begun a new phase of his career, appearing with his wife and daughters as the 'Boone Family'. They continue as a cabaret and television act.

Boone, Pat
   A new song / Pat Boone. – London: Lakeland, 1972. – 192p.; 18cm.
   ISBN 0-551-00406-1 (pbk.)
   Originally published: New York: Creation House, 1970.
After recalling the successes of his career during the fifties, Pat Boone describes his decline in the early sixties and his turning to Christianity: an event which saved his family. The tone is self-indulgent in the extreme.

Boone, Pat
   Together: 25 years with the Boone Family / by Pat Boone; photos selected by
   Shirley and Laury Boone. – Nashville, Tennessee: T. Nelson, 1979. – 128p.:
   ill., ports, 29cm. ISBN 0-8407-5165-5
A homely biography covering the whole of Boone's life. He was a young family man and part of his appeal in the fifties was this wholesome family image and four young daughters. There is much emphasis here on his family life as a support to his career through its various phases as well as the influence of Christianity on his personal philosophy.

Bowie, David

Born David Jones in south London in 1947, Bowie began playing saxophone in local groups in 1963. His own group, David Jones and the Lower Third, made an obscure, unsuccessful album and disbanded a little later, after which he joined a dance troupe led by mime artist Lindsay Kemp. At about this time, he changed his name to Bowie to avoid confusion with David Jones of the Monkees. The experience with Kemp would later show itself in Bowie's development of theatrical presentation. In 1969 he released his first album and had a big success with a single. He left the limelight, however, to set up the Arts Lab in Beckenham, Kent, but found time to release an album in 1970 and another in 1971. Both of these received serious critical attention. It was in 1972 with his album Ziggy Stardust and the Spiders from Mars, and its supporting tour, that he established himself as a major talent. His theatrical staging of the album, make-up and innovative stage dress, as well as an excellent collection of songs, soon gave him his first million seller. Each subsequent album has experimented in new musical styles and themes and has been accompanied by a change in Bowie's presentation of his visual image. In 1976 he starred in Nicolas Roeg's film, The Man Who Fell to Earth, and in 1982 he played the title role in the BBC television production of Brecht's play, Baal.

Bowie stands as a leading figure in contemporary popular music, turning his hand to any form from disco to soul, from futuristic to pop, but always imaginatively and always with the finest degree of execution. His most important contribution to popular culture remains his development of the fusion of rock music with theatre which many others continue to emulate but none has approached.

Bowie, Angela

Free spirit / Angela Bowie. – London: Mushroom Publishing, 1981. – viii, 176p., 16p of plates: ill., ports; 18cm. ISBN 0-907-39403-5 (pbk.)

Angie Bowie, former wife of David, describes her life of fame by proxy. Her own attempts at modelling, acting and singing achieving little success, she concentrates on her and David's bi-sexual relationships, their style of open marriage and its final break-up. The development of Bowie's career is well chronicled from this unique standpoint but badly distorted by sensationalism. Included are some of the author's poems and a collection of photographs which is a mixture of interesting early family snapshots and posed studio portraits.

Bowie, David

Bowie in his own words / compiled by Miles; designed by Perry Neville. – London: W. H. Allen, 1982. – 128p.: ill., ports; 25cm. ISBN 0-491-02946-2
Originally published: London: Omnibus Press, 1980.

A collection of David Bowie's quotes and views on his work, attitudes and philosophies of life. Arranged by subject, this is well illustrated and brings together information available elsewhere only in magazines and newspapers.

Cann, Kevin
  David Bowie: a chronology / Kevin Cann. – London: Vermilion Books,
  1983. – 239p., 16p. of plates: ill., ports; 23cm. Includes bibliography,
  discography and filmography. ISBN 0-09-153831-9 (pbk.)
The life of Bowie is presented here as a day-by-day calendar. It is full of
information for the real fanatic. The illustrations are excellent, but the bibliography is very limited. Nevertheless this book is a good addition to the
literature of the artist.

Carr, Roy
  David Bowie: an illustrated record / by Roy Carr and Charles Shaar Murray.
  – London: Eel Pie, 1981. – 120p.: ill. (some col.), col. facsims, ports (some
  col.); 30cm. ISBN 0-906008-25-5 (pbk.)
Based on Bowie's recording career, this is a chronologically arranged biography which includes reproductions of his album sleeves and over two hundred
photographs, many of which are not available in other sources. There is full
discographical information and listings of the songs on each album. The text is
well written and informative with some interesting information on Bowie's
early career.

Charlesworth, Chris
  David Bowie: profile / by Chris Charlesworth. – London; New York:
  Proteus, 1981. – 96p.: ill. (some col.), ports (some col.); 27cm. Includes
  discography. ISBN 0-906071-82-8 (cased). ISBN 0-906071-87-4 (pbk.)
Although basically a chronologically arranged collection of photographs, many
not available elsewhere, there is also a brief but interesting text. The author
attempts not merely to describe Bowie's career but also to analyse the development of his music and stage presentation. The early illustrations are particularly unusual. The discography includes only bootlegs and is very limited in
its listing of these.

Claire, Vivian
  David Bowie / by Vivian Claire. – New York; London: Flash Books, 1977. –
  80p.: ill., ports; 26cm. Includes discography. ISBN 0-8256-3911-5 (pbk.)
A superficial, but well-presented biography with a good collection of typically
posed illustrations. The discography is detailed and there is considerable
analysis of Bowie's writing, performance and influences, as well as transcripts
of interviews.

Juby, Kerry
  David Bowie / by Kerry Juby. – London: Midas Books, 1982. – 156p., 8p. of
  plates: ill., ports; 22cm. Includes discography. ISBN 0-85936-233-7
A serious look at the evolution of Bowie's career; his alter egos are analysed in
depth. The author also gives probably the best analysis of Bowie's songwriting
technique to date.

Kelleher, Ed
  David Bowie: a biography in words and pictures / by Ed Kelleher. – New

York: Sire Books; Chappell Music Company, 1977. – 63p.: ill., ports; 30cm.
Includes discography. (pbk.)
For its size, this is an excellent biography. Well written and informative, there
is a well-selected, unusual collection of photographs. The discography is
detailed but includes only official American releases.

The lives and times of David Bowie / Manchester: Babylon Books, 1979. – 56p.:
ill., facsims, ports; 25cm. Includes discography. (pbk.)
Produced in the fanzine style, this is a chronological collection of reproduced
articles and photographs from the music press. The illustrations are very poorly
printed. The discography is good and includes some foreign labels and
bootlegs.

Miles
The David Bowie black book / text by Miles; designed by Pearce Marchbank.
– London: Omnibus Press, 1981. – 128p.: ill. (some col.), facsims (some
col.), ports (some col.); 29cm. Includes discography. ISBN 0-86001-808-3
(pbk.)
A detailed biography, this is particularly well illustrated with many rare
photographs from Bowie's early days as well as portraits in his various guises.
Each of his album sleeves is reproduced with full discographical information
and there are interesting reproductions of the labels of his early singles.

Tremlett, George
The David Bowie story / by George Tremlett. – London: Futura
Publications, 1974. – 159p., 16p. of plates: ill., ports; 18cm.
ISBN 0-8600-7051-4 (pbk.)
Also published: New York: Warner Paperback Library, 1975.
Based on original research including interviews with Kenneth Pitt, Bowie's
manager, Marc Bolan, the group Mott the Hoople and the subject, this covers
Bowie's career in depth up to 1974. There is a detailed chronology and the
author's usual formula provides a readable, informative biography with an
interesting collection of illustrations.

BOWIE, DAVID: DISCOGRAPHIES

Fletcher, David Jeffrey
David Robert Jones Bowie: the discography of a generalist, 1962–1979 / by
David Jeffrey Fetcher; edited by Rose Winters. – 3rd ed. – Chicago:
Ferguson, 1979. – 123p.: ill., facsims, ports; 28cm. (pbk.)
A chronologically arranged, well-annotated work, this attempts to be exhaustive including world-wide releases and hundreds of bootlegs. There are
recordings of Bowie's songs made by other artists and his work on other artists'
records as musician, singer and producer. There are obviously some gaps, but
this is still a very detailed work and a result of considerable research.

Hoggard, Stuart
David Bowie: an illustrated discography / compiled by Stuart Hoggard. –
London: Omnibus Press, 1980. – 93p.: ill., facsims, ports; 20cm.
ISBN 0-86001-772-9 (pbk.)

A detailed chronological listing of David Bowie's official American and British recordings with full discographical details, reproductions of album sleeves and portraits of Bowie in his various theatrical postures. There is a separate section of bootleg recordings and some good explanatory annotations which both describe the contents of each record and comment on its significance in the development of the artist's music and career.

BOYCE, MAX

Max Boyce was born in 1945 in Glyn Neath, South Wales. His father was killed in a coalmining accident. Although he studied as an electrical engineer, he began singing in folk clubs, writing songs with Welsh themes of pithead baths, mining disasters and rugby, and gaining for himself a large following. His act, which includes long anecdotes as well as his songs, is based on overt chauvinism and constant attacks on the English. His presentation of the Welsh as quaint, rugby-loving scoundrels, however, makes him not at all popular with the real nationalists. He is often criticized for his music-hall Welshness, but, nevertheless, his albums have sold millions and his popularity extends far beyond the Welsh borders.

BOYCE, MAX: SONGS

Boyce, Max
'*I was there*' / Max Boyce; with drawings by Gren. – London: Weidenfeld and
Nicolson, 1979. – 94p.: ill. (chiefly col.), facsims, ports (some col.); 29cm.
ISBN 0-2977-7609-6

A collection of song lyrics reproduced with portraits and witty little drawings, this includes some of Max Boyce's best-known songs with two of the lyrics in Welsh.

Boyce, Max
Max Boyce, his songs and poems / introduction by Barry John; cartoons by
Gren. – St. Albans: Panther, 1976. – 63p.: ill., facsims; 18cm.
ISBN 0-5860-4621-6 (pbk.)

A collection of lyrics, including two in Welsh. The introduction is supplied by Barry John, the famous Welsh rugby star.

BUSH, KATE

Kate Bush was born in 1958 in Bexley, Kent; her father worked as a general practitioner in Welling. When only sixteen she took her songs to EMI, where she was given an advance and told to return when she was eighteen. This she did after studying dance in the meantime. One of the original songs, Wuthering Heights, was her first release and became one of the most successful records ever produced by a British female singer. Her deceptively vague public manner belies her skill as a songwriter, singer and recording artist. She enhances her live performances with mime and theatre, providing spectacular stage shows. She has won dozens of awards and gold records for her songs, and has become one of Britain's major singers.

Bush, Kate
   Leaving my tracks / Kate Bush. – London: Sidgwick & Jackson, 1982. –
   144p., 8p. of plates: ill. (some col.), ports (some col.); 30cm.
   ISBN 0-283-98698-7 (cased). ISBN 0-283-98799-5 (pbk.)
In this beautifully illustrated book Kate Bush gives an account of her approach to her work, techniques, inspirations and lifestyle. An interesting, unselfconscious attempt at autobiography, it does not appear to be written with the aid of a ghost writer and is surprisingly fluent.

Kerton, Paul
   Kate Bush: an illustrated biography / Paul Kerton. – London; New York:
   Proteus, 1980. – 111p.: ill., ports; 30cm. Includes discography.
   ISBN 0-906071-22-4 (pbk.)
This biography is well illustrated and attempts to give an impression of the hectic nature of the lifestyle of a young star. It never gets behind the songs, however, and is basically aimed at the young fan.

Vermorel, Fred
   Kate Bush / Fred and Judy Vermorel. – Rev. ed. – London: Omnibus Press,
   1982. – 80p.: ill., ports; 30cm.
   Previous edition: London: Target Books, 1980.
   ISBN 0-7119-0152-X (pbk.)
A short, superficial biography which attempts to give an impression of Kate Bush's family background and inspirations. She is portrayed as a product of suburbia – this is an account not without sarcasm.

THE BYRDS

Formed in 1964 in Los Angeles and originally called the Beefeaters, the Byrds were publicized as the American answer to the Liverpool sound and as the American Beatles. The original line-up, which was to undergo a series of changes throughout the life of the group, included Jim McGuinn, David Crosby, Gene Clarke, Michael Clark and Chris Hillman. All the members had been involved in some way in the West Coast folk scene. In 1965 they recorded Bob Dylan's song Mr Tambourine Man, shortening the verses and using an electric twelve-string guitar which was to become their trademark. This was the beginning of folk rock music. The record was a massive success and was followed by a whole series of singles and albums which were world-wide hits. Gene Clarke left the group in 1966 and David Crosby joined the famous Crosby, Stills and Nash in 1968. He was replaced by country-music guitarist Gram Parsons and their next album, Sweetheart of the Rodeo, created the style of country rock. By the next year Hillman and Parsons had left to form the Flying Burrito Brothers, leaving McGuinn as the only original member. With a different line-up the Byrds continued through the seventies, McGuinn producing solo albums as well as with the group. They never regained their early success but were one of the most influential groups of the sixties, constantly experimenting and creating the new movements: folk rock, country rock, raga rock, space rock and even Jesus rock. They developed new recording techniques and were, ironically, a major influence on the Beatles. Their sound can still be heard in the style of more recent groups such as the Pretenders and Tom Petty and the Heartbreakers.

Rogan, Johnny
  Timeless flight / John Rogan. – London: Scorpion Publications; Dark Star, 1981. – 192p.: ill., facsims, ports; 22cm. Includes discography.
  ISBN 0-905906-30-6 (pbk.)
Considering their success and seminal influence it is surprising that this is the only substantial work on the Byrds and that it is written by an Englishman. It is thoroughly researched with an excellent appendix listing sources. The author interviewed all former members of the group, their producers, managers and Derek Taylor, their one-time publicist. Their music is analysed in depth, their influences discussed and the problems of their personalities, changes in line-up and gradual loss of popularity are carefully described. The discography is exhaustive and lists all the members of the band followed by full discographical details of the recordings on which they played, their solo efforts and even recordings with other groups. There is a section on bootleg tapes and information about unreleased recordings. This is a good biography with an excellent collection of rare illustrations.

Scoppa, Bud
  The biography of the Byrds / Bud Scoppa. – New York: Scholastic Book Services, 1972. – 96p.: ill., ports; 18cm. ISBN 0-590-09227-1 (pbk.)
A brief biography for American high schools with some good illustrations and a suitable, informative text.

Scoppa, Bud
  The Byrds / Bud Scoppa. – New York: Quick Fox, 1971. – 136p.: ill., ports; 24cm. Includes discography. ISBN 0-8256-2657-9 (pbk.)
With some good illustrations, this is a brief biography which covers the rapidly changing personnel of the group up to 1971, but never gets beyond the surface. Not a bad effort, but too brief to devote the time necessary to deal with such significant artists.

CAHN, SAMMY

Born in New York City in 1913, since the thirties Sammy Cahn has been one of the world's leading lyricists. He has written innumerable songs which have become classics, songs for musicals and songs written to order for the likes of Frank Sinatra. He appears frequently on British and American chat shows because of his humorous anecdotes and cutting, very Jewish wit.

Cahn, Sammy
   I should care: the Sammy Cahn story / by Sammy Cahn. – London: W. H.
   Allen, 1975. – 253p., 16p. of plates: ill., ports; 23cm. Includes index.
   ISBN 0-491-01973-4
An amusing autobiography; Cahn's use of language and real wit are proven in this collection of anecdotes from his career. He spares no one in his often caustic sarcasm, discussing artists such as Doris Day, Sinatra, Artie Shaw and Phil Silvers, as well as producers and directors. The index gives useful access. There is a list of his successful songs and the lyrics of thirty of his best-known songs are reproduced in full.

CAMPBELL, GLEN

Born in Delight, Arkansas, in 1938, Glen Campbell moved to Los Angeles in 1961 and worked as a session musician. After playing briefly with the Beach Boys he signed a contract with Capitol Records in the late sixties and was launched as a solo artist. He achieved almost immediate success with songs written by Jim Webb, and also worked in a duo with Bobbie Gentry. His middle-of-the-road country style and clear voice have won him eleven gold records, film parts and his own television series. He continues to be a family entertainer of considerable popularity.

Kramer, Freda
   The Glen Campbell story / by Freda Kramer. – New York: Pyramid
   Publications, 1970. – 125p., 8p. of plates: ill., ports; 18cm. (pbk.)
An uncontroversial biography which describes his humble beginnings as part of a family of eleven. His rise to fame and fortune is well described, emphasizing his thoroughly wholesome nature. There is no attempt to discuss his work or to reflect on his success.

CAPTAIN AND TENNILLE

Born in Montgomery, Alabama, in 1952, Toni Tennille moved with her family to Los Angeles in 1962 where she studied the piano and acted in the South Coast Repertory Theatre. She wrote a musical called Mother Earth for the theatre and while working in the show met Daryl Dragon, who played keyboards. Daryl and Toni toured together with the Beach Boys and Mike Love, singer of that group, gave Daryl the name Captain Keyboards. In 1977 Captain and Tennille finally made a breakthrough with the song Love Will Keep Us Together, written by Neil Sedaka. This was followed by more American hits and their own television series. Their middle-of-the-road style has a very wide appeal in America but they have had only minor success in the United Kingdom.

Spada, James
> *Captain and Tennille* / by James Spada; designed by Mark Landkamer. – Mankato, Minnesota: Creative Education, 1978. – 31p.: ill., ports; 25cm. ISBN 0-87191-393-0

Aimed at a reading age of around ten for American schools, this controlled-vocabulary biography is well produced and well illustrated.

The Carter Family

One of the most influential forces in country music, the original line-up was headed by Alvin Pleasant (A. P.) Delaney Carter. He married Sara Dougherty in 1915 and they were joined by Maybelle Carter, A. P.'s sister-in-law, in 1926. They made their first records in 1927 and over the next fifteen years recorded hundreds of classic songs. A. P. died in 1960 but the Carter family continued with an all-female line-up of Maybelle and her daughters June, Helen and Anita. Over the years the family has, in its various forms, continued to produce successful albums on the country record charts and Maybelle has become a mother figure for a new generation of country stars.

Atkins, John
> *The Carter Family* / by John Atkins. – London: Old Time Music, 1973. – 63p.: ill., facsims, ports; 30cm. ISBN 0-9043-9500-6 (pbk.)

A short but well-researched and presented history of the Carters with an emphasis on their early career and contribution to country music. Many of the illustrations are available only in this publication.

Krishef, Robert K.
> *The Carter Family* / by Robert K. Krishef and Stacy Harris. – Minneapolis: Lerner Publications, 1978. – 71p.: ill., ports; 21cm. Includes index. ISBN 0-8225-1403-6

Written for a reading age of around ten for American schools, this is a controlled-vocabulary history of the family with some good illustrations.

Cash, Johnny

Born in Dyess, Arkansas, in 1932, Johnny Cash joined Sun Records in 1955 and became one of the early rockabilly performers. He had a series of successful records but by the late fifties his personal problems had led to drug dependency. In the mid sixties he met June Carter, an established singer and writer of country music, and, after working together for some time, they were married. His career gained momentum at this point and he began to record dozens of hit records as well as turning his hand to acting. He is a prolific recording artist and writer. His style is to project his tough, masculine voice over a usually predictable, simple backing. His songs, however, deal with varied aspects of American life and rarely appear on his own albums. He is now generally regarded as a country-music performer and is currently one of the most successful artists in that field without strictly being a country singer at all.

Bowman, Kathleen
  On stage Johnny Cash / text Kathleen Bowman; design concept Larry Soule. –Mankato, Minnesota: Creative Education, 1976. –47p.: ill., ports; 23cm. ISBN 0-87191-486-7
A controlled-vocabulary biography aimed at a reading age of around ten for American schools, this has a lucid writing style with simple sentence structure. The account of Cash's life is straightforward and suitable for the age group.

Carpozi, George
  The Johnny Cash story / by George Carpozi. – New York: Pyramid Publications, 1970. – 128p.: ill., ports; 18cm. (pbk.)
A well-illustrated, but poorly written, superficial biography which fails to delve into a complex subject. The author avoids Cash's drug addiction and does not discuss his writing talent. The artist's turn to religion and help to convicts and ex-offenders, however, are described at great length.

Cash, Johhny
  Man in black / Johnny Cash. – London: Hodder and Stoughton, 1977. – 224p., 8p. of plates: ill., ports; 18cm. ISBN 0-340-22173-9 (pbk.)
  Previously published: London; Hodder and Stoughton, 1976.
  Originally published: Grand Rapids, Michigan: Zondervan, 1975.
A candid autobiography covering not only Cash's early career and later successes but much about his personal problems and drug addiction. There is no real insight into his songwriting or performing but a good deal about his personal 'salvation'. Johnny Cash turned to religion in the late sixties and the evangelical tone comes through in his writing. This book does, however, give a very personal look at the man himself.

Conn, Charles Paul
  The new Johnny Cash / Charles Paul Conn. – London: Hodder and Stoughton, 1973. – 93p., 8p. of plates: ill., ports; 18cm. ISBN 0-340-17962-7 (pbk.)
Cash is represented as a man driven to despair and drugs by the pressures of stardom, seeing the error of his ways, turning to Christianity and going on to greater heights. A blatant misrepresentation of the truth – certainly at the time of its writing this was a version which the singer did not strenuously deny.

Govoni, Albert
   A boy named Cash / Albert Govoni. – New York: Lancer Books, 1970. –
   190p.: ill., ports; 18cm. (pbk.)
A superficial biography, this avoids the more controversial elements of Cash's
life, concentrating on his public image and career. The illustrations are well
chosen.

Taylor, Paula
   Johnny Cash / text Paula Taylor; illustrator John Keely. – Mankato,
   Minnesota: Creative Education, 1974. – 31p.: ill. (some col.), ports (some
   col.); 25cm. ISBN 0-87191-391-7
This is a controlled-vocabulary biography written for a reading age of about ten
for American schools. Informative and well illustrated, the information has
been suitably selected for the age group.

Wren, Christopher S.
   Johnny Cash: winners get scars too / Christopher S. Wren. – London:
   Abacus, 1974. – 221p., 24p. of plates: ill., ports; 20cm. Includes discography.
   ISBN 0-3491-3740-4 (pbk.)
A biography supporting Cash's cultivated macho image, but this does attempt
to examine his music in some depth. His musical background and influences are
analysed and his recording techniques and work in Nashville with Bob Dylan
are described in detail. On the whole, this is well written, thoughtful and
informative.

CASH, JOHNNY: DISCOGRAPHIES

Smith, John L.
   Johnny Cash discography and recording history (1955–1968) / by John
   L. Smith. – Los Angeles: John Edwards Foundation, 1969. – 48p.: ill., ports;
   23cm.
A rare piece of research, this is exhaustive up to 1968 and includes not only
Cash's solo recordings but his work as a session musician and as a songwriter for
others.

CASH, JUNE CARTER

Born in Maces Springs, Virginia, in 1929, June Carter is a member of the most
famous family in country music. She began performing with her sisters, Helen
and Anita, as the Carter Sisters in the mid forties and in 1960 the girls joined
their mother, Maybelle, and began working as the new Carter Family. In 1961
they joined Johnny Cash's Road Show Company and in 1966 became regular
guests on his television programme. June became Cash's second wife and they
have one son. She has made solo albums, many others with the Carter Family,
and some with her husband.

Cash, June Carter
Among my klediments / June Carter Cash. – Grand Rapids, Michigan:
Zondervan, 1979. – 152p., 4p. of plates: ill., ports; 22cm.
ISBN 0-3103-8170-3 (cased). ISBN 0-3103-8171-1 (pbk.)
A straightforward autobiography by June Carter, the most interesting aspects
of which are her childhood memories of the early days of the Carter family. She
reveals little about her relationship with Johnny Cash and no more about her
musical influences and other interests.

CASSIDY, DAVID

David Cassidy was born in New York in 1950, son of actor Jack Cassidy and
singer Evelyn Ward. His parents had separated by the time he was ten and he
moved with his mother to Los Angeles in 1960. He learned to play guitar and
drums at high school and did some amateur acting in his mid teens. After
working on Broadway in the Allen Sherman show The Fig Leaves Are Falling,
he secured a leading part in the television series The Partridge Family. The
series, about a family pop group, was a big success throughout the world and
Cassidy, with his fresh-faced appearance, became for a while the leading idol of
the pre-teens age group. After a series of hit records with the Partridge Family,
he began working solo and this success was even bigger. He is unquestionably
talented with a clear, full voice suited to big ballads and an ability to write some
good songs. He had some trouble shaking off his teenage image but after he
posed naked in *Rolling Stone* magazine, many of his admirers were shocked.
By the late seventies Cassidy had faded from the scene but he is always likely to
return.

Cassidy, David
David in Europe: exclusive! David's own story in David's own words . . . /
David Cassidy. – London: Daily Mirror, 1973. – 47p., 1 folded leaf: chiefly
ill. (some col.), ports (some col.); 30cm. ISBN 0-8593-9014-4 (pbk.)
In magazine format David Cassidy's brief words on his European tour are
meticulously quoted but the real point of the publication is photographs of the
star looking beautiful.

David Cassidy annual 1974. – Manchester: World Distributors, 1973. – 78p.:
ill. (some col.), ports (some col.); 27cm. ISBN 0-7235-0210-2
Comic strip of his wonderful life, lots of pretty pictures and even a board game:
a Christmas present for the pre-teenager. It appeared just the once.

Gregory, James
The David Cassidy story / by James Gregory. – Manchester: World
Distributors, 1973. – 158p., 8p. of plates; ill., ports; 18cm.
ISBN 0-7235-5000-X (pbk.)
Much about Cassidy's childhood, his parents' break-up and the effect on his

subsequent early career, covering the time up to shortly after he left the Partridge Family and the release of his solo records. Included are lengthy quotations from interviews undertaken by the author.

CASSIDY, SHAUN

Shaun Cassidy was born in 1959, the son of Shirley Jones and Jack Cassidy and step-brother of David Cassidy. He was a child television actor and in 1977 he became a star of the television series The Hardy Boys. This was followed by a series of top-twenty hits in America and a massive campaign to package him in the way his once famous brother had been. His appeal to the young, pre-teenagers continues in America but never really happened in Britain.

Schumacher, Craig
    Shaun Cassidy / by Craig Schumacher. – Mankato, Minnesota: Creative Education, 1980. – 31p.: ill. (some col.), ports (some col.); 25cm.
    ISBN 0-87191-717-3 (cased). ISBN 0-89812-097-7 (pbk.)
Written for a reading age of around ten for American schools, this is a well-produced controlled-vocabulary biography with a subject very well suited to the age range.

CHARLES, RAY

Born in Albany, Georgia, in 1930, Ray Charles became blind at the age of six. He was orphaned at fifteen and formed his own band at seventeen, working on the West Coast and in Washington. He made recordings with independent record companies before his contract was bought by Atlantic Records. During the next few years he made a major contribution to the development of popular music by fusing gospel and blues into a unique style featuring his technique of call-and-response antiphonies. He recorded a series of classic singles through-out the late fifties and sixties. His stage act became extravagant and orchestral but his private life sank into drug addiction and imprisonment. He continues to perform and owns his own record company. He is regarded by many as a genius.

Charles, Ray
    Brother Ray: Ray Charles' own story / Ray Charles and David Ritz. –
    London: Futura Publications, 1980. – 340p., 8p. of plates: ill., ports 18cm.
    Includes discography. ISBN 0-7088-1734-3 (pbk.)
    Originally published: New York: Dial Press, 1978.
    Also published: London: Macdonald and Janes, 1979.
A fascinating, autobiographical account, journalistically cobbled together by Ritz. Ray Charles's struggle as a child and the development of his musical style, as well as his personal emotions about his drug addiction, women, religion, money and the acceptance of his blindness, are all described. Occasionally sensational. The discography is excellent with detailed notes.

Mathis, Sharon Bell
   Ray Charles / by Sharon Bell Mathis; illustrated by George Ford. – New
   York: Crowell, 1973. – 31p.: ill. (some col.), ports (some col.); 24cm.
   ISBN 0-6906-7065-6
For American schools: this introductory biography is well illustrated with a
brief but informative text.

CHER

Born Cherily Sakisian in El Centro, California, in 1946, Cher was originally
part of the Sonny and Cher duo. After her estrangement from Sonny she began
a solo career in modelling, had a series of successful singles and her own
American television programme. In 1975 she married Greg Allman of the
famous American band, the Allman Brothers. This also failed to last and her
latest romantic attachment is with the leader of the group Kiss. In the USA she
continues to be a leader of chic fashion circles.

(*See also* SONNY AND CHER.)

Carpozi, George
   Cher / by George Carpozi. – New York: Medallion Books, 1975. – 178p.: ill.,
   ports; 18cm. ISBN 0-425-02973-5 (pbk.)
A survey of Cher's career in which the author's journalistic devices tend to
detract from the otherwise interesting account. There are some well-chosen,
but poorly reproduced illustrations, and lengthy quotations from interviews
with the artist.

Jacobs, Linda
   Cher: simply Cher / by Linda Jacobs. – St. Paul, Minnesota: EMC, 1975. –
   34p.: ill., ports; 20cm. ISBN 0-88436-186-1 (cased). ISBN 0-88436-187-X
   (pbk.)
This controlled-vocabulary text for a reading age of about ten, aimed at
American schools, is well illustrated and covers Cher's career with Sonny and
Cher as well as her solo successes. Well designed and produced, the book is also
available with an audio cassette.

CHICAGO

Originally formed in 1968 and called the Big Thing, they changed their name to
the Chicago Transit Company and moved to Los Angeles to work with
producer James Guercio. Their originality is based on the fact that they
augmented a standard four-piece rhythm section with a brass trio playing jazz-
orientated harmonies with the occasional long solo. They were very successful
in the USA in the early seventies but their style has become increasingly

mechanical and lacking real depth or soul. They achieved a world-wide success in 1976 with the single If You Leave Me Now but failed to follow it up. They continue to produce sophisticated, if dull, albums.

O'Shea, Mary J.
  Chicago / by Mary J. O'Shea. – Mankato, Minnesota: Creative Education, 1977. – 31p.: ill. (some col.), ports (some col.); 25cm. ISBN 0-8719-1458-1 (cased). ISBN 0-89812-114-0 (pbk.)
This sole book on Chicago is a controlled-vocabulary text written for a reading age of around ten for American schools. It is well produced with some good illustrations.

CLAPTON, ERIC

Born in Ripley, Surrey, in 1945, Eric Clapton did not begin learning to play the guitar until he was seventeen years old. After playing in several unknown groups during the British rhythm & blues movement of the early sixties, he finally joined the Yardbirds. When they achieved commercial success, however, he left in the spring of 1965 to join the more authentic John Mayall's Bluesbreakers. After establishing himself as the top British guitar hero, he formed the first 'supergroup', Cream, in 1966, with Jack Bruce and Ginger Baker. They became enormously successful throughout the world with their lengthy improvisations and virtuoso playing from each member of the group. Cream split up in November 1968 and Clapton formed Blind Faith and later toured America with Delaney and Bonnie and Friends. With the demise of Blind Faith by 1970 Eric Clapton made several guest appearances with other artists but not until he released the album Layla later that year did he seem to be finding his own style. The song Layla was written for Patti Boyd (the former wife of George Harrison of the Beatles) who later married Clapton. Clapton struggled with drug addiction and severe depressions throughout the seventies but sustained a succession of album releases which have varied in success and have been erratic in terms of creativity. Nevertheless, he is still regarded as one of the greatest of all guitarists and is still capable of filling the largest auditoriums in the world.

Clapton, Eric
  Conversations with Eric Clapton / Steve Turner. – London: Abacus, 1976, – 116p., 24p. of plates: ill., ports; 20cm. Includes discography.
  ISBN 0-349-13402-2 (pbk.)
Interviewed by the journalist Steve Turner, Clapton talks of his early career, his struggle with coming to terms with unexpected commercial success with Cream, his drug addiction and his romantic relationships. There are some good illustrations and a detailed discography but in general this is an unsatisfactory, unrevealing series of interviews.

Pidgeon, John
  Eric Clapton: a biography / John Pidgeon. – St. Albans: Panther, 1976. –

144p., 8p. of plates: ill., ports; 18cm. Includes discography.
ISBN 0-586-04292-X (pbk.)
A well-written biography covering Clapton's childhood, his time with his various groups and his solo career. There is much personal information and intimate detail of his personal problems as well as an analysis of his songwriting and particularly his style of guitar playing. The discography is a complete list of all his recordings with each of his groups, his sessions and solo work.

CLARK, DICK

Born in New York in 1929, Dick Clark followed Alan Freed as America's leading disc jockey after the latter was discredited during the 'payola' bribery scandal. Clark began working as a disc jockey in local radio stations in 1952 and by 1956 was the presenter of ABC television's American Bandstand, which was made in Philadelphia and networked throughout the USA. By 1958 he was also presenting the Dick Clark Show from New York. He was responsible for introducing hundreds of young artists of the period from Chuck Berry to Johnny Mathis and Tom and Jerry, later to become Simon and Garfunkel. He was one of the most influential disc jockeys and television presenters in a period when their influence was at its height.

Clark, Dick
  Rock, roll & remember / Dick Clark and Richard Robinson. – New York:
  Popular Library, 1978. – 305p.: ill., ports; 18cm. Includes index.
  ISBN 0-445-04178-1 (pbk.)
  Originally published: New York: Crowell, 1976.
Clark's recollections map the changes in popular music during two decades and notably the growth of the influence of rock music and the ascendancy of black musicians. Sometimes sensational, there are hundreds of accounts here that may be fictional but are always entertaining.

CLARK, PETULA

Born in Ewell, Surrey, in 1932, during the Second World War Petula Clark was a child star on British radio and between the ages of eleven and eighteen made more than twenty films. In 1955 she signed with Pye Records, leaving Polygon with whom she had had some minor hits in the UK, and during the sixties she achieved a number of number one, million-selling singles. In 1964, with Downtown, she was the second British woman ever to top the American charts. (The first was Vera Lynn.) Married to Claud Wolff, publicity director for Vogue Records in France, she lives in France and since the early seventies has grown into a performer of international stature. Often compared with Julie Andrews, a comparison she hates, she prefers a stage image nearer to that of her heroine Edith Piaf. She is a fine singer who made the unusual transition from child star to adult artist without the frequent disastrous side-effects.

Kon, Andrea
    This is my song: biography of Petula Clark / Andrea Kon. – London: Comet,
    1984. – 256p., 16p. of plates: ill., ports; 24cm. Includes index.
    ISBN 0-8637-9030-5 (pbk.)
    Originally published: London: W. H. Allen, 1983.
A chatty biography, this is well-written and produced. Lacking excitement, it
is very personal in its approach with a few very forthright opinions and
criticisms of other performers put to the author during extensive interviews.
Petula is shown to be a thoroughly professional, sometimes tough individual.

THE CLASH

Formed in 1976, the Clash were second only to the Sex Pistols as leaders of the
new-wave movement in London. Their lyrics, energy and political commitment gave them a fanatical following. Joe Strummer and Mick Jones write of
unemployment and deprived neighbourhoods of London in a way that is often
primitive but always exciting. When they signed a record contract with CBS in
1977 they were accused of selling out and lost some of their early support, but
they have made some successful albums and now lead the remnants of the
politically motivated punks. Paul Simonon has played bass since the group's
beginning but drummers have included Terry Chimes and more recently Nicky
Headon. By late 1982 the position of drummer was vacant and session players
seemed to be commonly used.

Miles
    Clash / text by Miles; art direction Perry Neville; design Andy Morton. –
    London: Omnibus Press, 1981. – 32p.: chiefly ill., ports; 27cm.
    ISBN 0-86001-803-2 (pbk.)
This is largely a collection of photographs of the group with a brief text and a
few quotations and extracts from press articles. Of little informational value, it
does no justice to its subject.

Smith, Pennie
    The Clash: before & after / photographs by Pennie Smith; with passing
    comments by Joe Strummer, Mick Jones, Paul Simonon and Topper
    Headon. – London: Eel Pie, 1980. – 154p.: chiefly ill., ports; 29cm.
    ISBN 0-906008-23-9 (pbk.)
A large collection of photographs of the group taken on tour, mainly in
America. Stylishly produced, the occasional comments are quite amusing and
sometimes almost intelligent.

CLINE, PATSY

Born in Winchester, Virginia, in September 1932, Patsy Cline's real name was
Virginia Patterson Hensley. She began playing the piano at the age of eight. By

her teens she was playing in local clubs and in 1948 she won an audition to play in Nashville. It was after winning a talent contest in 1957 that she released her first record, however, with immediate chart success in both the country and national listings. In 1961 she released I Fall to Pieces, which became a massive hit and was followed by a series of big sellers. During this period she became a regular singer on the Grand 'Ole Opry and soon became ranked as country music's leading female artist. On March 5th 1963 she was killed in a plane crash at Camden, Tennessee. After her death, her records continued to sell throughout the sixties. In 1973, she was elected to the Country Music Hall of Fame. She remains an influential figure who was remarkably versatile with a natural talent for communicating a real sense of emotion.

Nassour, Ellis
    Patsy Cline / by Ellis Nassour; introduction by Dottie West. – New York: Tower Books, 1981. – 410p.: ill., ports; 20cm. Includes discography and index. ISBN 0-505-51679-9 (pbk.)
    Originally published: New York: Twayne Publications, 1981.
Based largely on the recollections of Patsy Cline's contemporaries in Nashville, this is an extensive and detailed biography. Her influence as a female country-music star in a male-dominated period is clearly shown.

THE COASTERS

Originally known as the Robins, the group changed their name to the Coasters in 1956 when they signed a recording contract with the Atlantic Records label. They immediately began working with the team of Jerry Leiber and Mike Stoller who were not only innovative songwriters, but also excellent record producers. Throughout the late fifties they had a series of big-selling hit singles which included a strong sense of satirical humour within a rhythm & blues vocal style. They were a big influence on the British beat groups of the early sixties and a major factor in the acceptance of black music by a mass white audience.

Millar, Bill
    The Coasters / by Bill Millar. – London: Star Books, 1975. – 206p., 8p. of plates: ill., ports; 18cm. Includes discography. ISBN 0-352-30020-5 (pbk.)
A meticulously researched biography reflecting an important period in the music industry for black artists. There is a superb discography and a full list of Leiber and Stoller compositions from 1951 until 1970. The ever-changing personnel of the Coasters is well documented in an appendix of brief, but informative, biographical notes.

COHEN, LEONARD

Born in Montreal in 1934, Cohen had written some widely published poems and two novels before he began to compose and set some of his verse to music.

Judy Collins recorded one of his songs in 1966 and from then his solo career began. He was introduced to Britain largely by disc jockey John Peel and his first album, released in 1967, gathered for him a cult following. Tony Palmer made the film Bird on the Wire, featuring Cohen's 1971 European tour. He has produced a series of six albums over the past fifteen years: a sparse but steady output of intense quality. If Cohen lacks the ability to compose memorable melodies he has introduced to popular music the literary tradition of classical poetry.

COHEN, LEONARD: POEMS

His collections of poetry include many of his song lyrics demonstrating quite clearly the way in which they stand alone as poems.

Cohen, Leonard
Death of a ladies' man / Leonard Cohen. – London: Deutsch, 1979. – 216p.; 23cm. Includes index. ISBN 0-233-97172-6
Originally published: Toronto: McClelland and Stewart, 1978.

Cohen, Leonard
Flowers for Hitler / Leonard Cohen. – London: Cape, 1973. – 154p.; 23cm. ISBN 0-224-00840-4 (cased). ISBN 0-224-00841-2 (pbk.)
Originally published: Toronto: McClelland and Stewart, 1964.

Cohen, Leonard
Poems 1956–1968 / by Leonard Cohen. – Abridged ed. – London: Cape, 1969. – 94p.; 22cm. Includes index. ISBN 0-224-61776-1 (pbk.)

Cohen, Leonard
Selected poems 1956–1968 / Leonard Cohen. – Harmondsworth: Penguin Books, 1978. – x, 246p.; 20cm. Includes index. ISBN 0-14-042266-8 (pbk.)
Originally published: New York: Viking Press, 1968.
Also published: London: Cape, 1969.

Cohen, Leonard
The spice-box of earth / Leonard Cohen. – London: Cape, 1973. – 93p.; 23cm. ISBN 0-224-00648-7 (cased). ISBN 0-224-00649-5 (pbk.)
Originally published: Toronto: McClelland and Stewart, 1961.

COHEN, LEONARD: NOVELS

Cohen, Leonard
Beautiful losers / Leonard Cohen. – St. Albans: Panther, 1972. – 239p.; 18cm. ISBN 0-568-03578-8 (pbk.)
Originally published: Toronto: McClelland and Stewart, 1966.
Also published: London: Cape, 1970.

Written in an experimental, stream-of-consciousness style which is often difficult to penetrate, the author's thoughts modulate between the present and the mystical figure of Catherine Tekakwitha, an Iroquois Indian who lived in the seventeenth century. A disjointed attack on sexual, racial and political exploitation; its reviews were very mixed.

Cohen, Leonard
    The favourite game / Leonard Cohen. – St. Albans: Panther, 1973. – 219p.;
    18cm. ISBN 0-586-03617-2 (pbk.)
    Originally published: New York: Viking Press, London: Secker and
    Warburg, 1963.
    Previously published: London: Cape, 1970.
A semi-autobiographical novel of a young Lawrence Breavman, starting life in the Montreal Jewish community. He absorbs himself in the writing of his poetry and after working as a manual labourer and a period of frantic womanizing in New York, he decides that his only valid future is in the well-springs of his past. The first of Cohen's novels to appear, it is relatively straightforward in style and often amusing.

COLLINS, JUDY

Judy Collins was born in 1939 in Denver, Colorado. Her father was a well-known figure in radio in Denver and on the West Coast. She studied classical piano from the age of six but by the time she was at the University of Colorado her interest in folk music had taken over. She began singing traditional music and moved to Chicago where she made her first album. By the third album she was singing contemporary protest songs. Throughout the sixties her music developed from singing the compositions of others to writing her own romantic songs. She has a fine voice and sense of musical interpretation, and has been instrumental in bringing to the public's attention the work of little-known writers. She continues to perform and record modestly successful albums. Her major contribution has been the recording of the songs of people such as Leonard Cohen and Joni Mitchell and bringing them to general notice.

Claire, Vivian
    Judy Collins / by Vivian Claire. – New York: Flash Books, 1977. – 78p.: ill.,
    ports; 26cm. Includes discography. ISBN 0-8256-3914-X (pbk.)
A brief biography tracing her career recording by recording, with detailed description and analysis. Her own writing is looked at without serious criticism but with warmth and insight. The discography is full.

COOKE, SAM

The son of a Baptist minister, Sam Cooke was born in Chicago in 1935. He began singing with the gospel group the Soul Stirrers in the early fifties. He started to record pop songs while still with the Soul Stirrers, releasing them under the pseudonym Dale Cooke. He was finally forced to leave the group and his first, self-composed, hit record followed and sold over one million copies. In 1960 he moved from the small Keen record label to RCA and over the next four years had a succession of hits. In December 1964, he was murdered in sordid circumstances in a Los Angeles motel. After his death artists such as Aretha Franklin and Otis Redding recorded his songs, as well as British rhythm & blues-influenced groups such as the Animals. His importance is that, along with Ray Charles, he created the soul-music style by merging a gospel tradition with secular, although often trivial, lyrics. His influence can be heard today in the music of Rod Stewart, Gladys Knight and the Pips, and hundreds of black vocal groups from the Motown, Stax and Philadelphia stables.

McEwen, Joe
    Sam Cooke: a biography in words & pictures / by Joe McEwen; edited by
    Greg Shaw. – New York: Sire Books; Chappell Music Company, 1977. –
    46p.: ill., facsims, ports; 30cm. Includes discography. ISBN 0-1445-7631-5
    (pbk.)
The only source of information on Sam Cooke of any length. He is represented, correctly, as an innovator of great importance and his career set in the evolving place of black people in American society. His era was that of the Watts riots, the Montgomery bus strikes and the growth of black power. He died before the Beatles were established but could see the effects of his work on the acceptance of black music by a mass white culture. Not long enough, but a good biography. There is an excellent discography.

COOPER, ALICE

Born Vincent Furnier in 1948, in Detroit, Alice Cooper was brought up in Phoenix, Arizona. He formed a band with schoolfriends Glen Buxton, Michael Bruce, Dennis Dunaway and Neal Smith and began playing Rolling Stones material under the names Earwigs, Spiders and later Nazz. They moved to Los Angeles and after a poor start signed a contract with Frank Zappa's Straight record label in 1969. After unspectacular results they moved to Detroit and in 1970 with the production of Bob Ezrin had their first major success. Widely regarded as poor musicians, they compensated with bizarre stage shows. Performing with a live python, chopping up dolls and using props such as gallows while wearing feminine clothes and make-up were the norm. They had a series of enormously commercially-successful singles and albums in a high-energy, heavy style, but by 1975 the appeal had gone. Alice Cooper's only saving feature is his honesty and uncompromising admittance of being simply commercial. He continues to record and retains a small following.

Demorest, Steve
    Alice Cooper / Steve Demorest. – New York: Popular Library, 1974. – 159p.:
    ill., ports; 18cm. Includes discography. (pbk.)

Written for *Circus* magazine and including a large collection of illustrations from its files, this is a biography of idolatry. Alice Cooper's limited success in the United Kingdom makes it difficult for the British reader to relate to the biographer, who blatantly exaggerates his importance, even in America. This is a poor biography with little analysis or insight into the music and no explanation of the success.

Gaines, Steven
  Me, Alice: the autobiography of Alice Cooper / with Steven Gaines. – New York: Putnam, 1976. – 254p., 16p. of plates: 22cm. Includes discography. ISBN 0-3991-1535-8
A detailed biography based on lengthy interviews with Alice and the group. Their music is discussed in depth, as is the development of the bizarre stage act and their backgrounds. The author takes Alice rather more seriously than he has ever done himself.

COSTELLO, ELVIS

Elvis Costello was born Declan Patrick MacManus in Twickenham, Middlesex, in 1954. His father, Ross, was the vocalist with the Joe Loss Orchestra. Ross MacManus still sings on the northern England cabaret circuit since leaving Loss in 1969. Declan left school at sixteen and moved to Liverpool. He could already play guitar and began learning to write songs, playing in local country-style groups. He moved back to London in 1970, working as a computer operator in Acton while his bluegrass-style group, Flip City, became regulars at London's Marquee Club. In 1976 he answered an advertisement looking for talent for the newly formed Stiff Records and was quickly signed by Jake Riviera. His sophisticated lyrics, catchy tunes and skill as a performer and record producer have made him an international success. His Buddy Holly appearance with large spectacles and unglamorous dress made him a darling of the new wave. He has had a string of successful singles and albums and produces other artists' records, the most famous being Squeeze.

Reese, Krista
  Elvis Costello: completely false biography based on rumour, innuendo and lies / Krista Reese. – London; New York: Proteus, 1981. – 127p.: ill. (some col.), ports (some col.); 27cm. Includes discography. ISBN 0-906071-62-3 (pbk.)
Written by an American journalist inspired by the success of Costello's 1981 tour, this attempts to intrude into Costello's private life and well-guarded views. It fails to succeed as the research is based on hearsay, spurious facts of acquaintances, the music press and the author's impressions. Her musical analysis is, however, very good, and the discography detailed with bootleg and full label information.

CREEDENCE CLEARWATER REVIVAL

Formed in the San Francisco Bay area and led by John Fogerty with Tom Fogerty, Stu Cook and Doug Difford, the Creedence Clearwater Revival made their first impact in 1968. From then until 1973 they became probably the most successful American group of all time in the context of the singles charts. Fogerty wrote songs with working-class themes, unusual for a Californian. The songs were often set deep in the Louisiana bayous and termed swamp rock because of their strangely atmospheric production and austere arrangements. The group disbanded in October 1972. John Fogerty has since released three solo albums and the other members have played in various groups and as session musicians. It is remarkable that the creator of swamp rock wrote his most important, authentic songs without ever having been to Bayou country.

Hallowell, John
    Inside Creedence / by John Hallowell. – New York: Bantam, 1971. – viii,
    88p., 64p. of plates: ill., ports; 18cm. Includes discography.
    ISBN 0-552-66901-6 (pbk.)
The sole biography of Creedence and a superficial one although it includes a good selection of illustrations and a full, early discography. There is no analysis of Fogerty's writing or of their record production.

CROCE, JIM

Born in Philadelphia in 1942, Jim Croce attended Villanova University and after graduating he had a series of manual jobs but played guitar and sang in coffee bars in his spare time. He signed a contract with Capitol and in 1971 recorded his first compositions. In the spring of 1972 an album was released which was soon successful. This was followed by two other albums and a single which was to top the American charts. His songs were witty and well observed, reflecting American blue-collar aspirations. He was tragically killed in a plane crash in September 1973.

Jacobs, Linda
    Jime Croce: the feeling lives on / by Linda Jacobs. – St. Paul, Minnesota:
    EMC, 1976. – 40p.: ill., ports; 23cm. ISBN 0-88436-215-9 (cased).
    ISBN 0-88436-216-7 (pbk.)
With a controlled-vocabulary text, written for a reading age of about ten for American schools, this is a well-produced biography. The illustrations are rare. Although it was written for children this is one of the few sources of information on Croce. It is also available with an audio cassette.

CROSBY, STILLS AND NASH

Graham Nash, formerly of the British pop group the Hollies, David Crosby, formerly of the Byrds, and Stephen Stills, formerly of the Buffalo Springfield, came together in 1968 and released their first album the following year. Characterized by beautiful, complex harmonies, a predominantly acoustic backing and some excellent, sophisticated songs, it was not only a massive commercial success, but also set a new standard of musicianship and subtlety for rock music. Later in 1969 they were joined by Neil Young, also formerly of the Buffalo Springfield, and in 1970 released their second album, Déjà Vu. At least as good as the first, this was followed by a live album of the same high quality. Since the early seventies there have been other, less satisfactory albums and some confusion over whether the group existed as a unit or not. Each of the musicians has pursued his own, independent projects with Neil Young becoming one of the most influential writers in the field of rock to have so far emerged.

(*See also* YOUNG, NEIL.)

Zimmer, Dave
  Crosby, Stills & Nash: the authorized biography / text by Dave Zimmer; photographs by Henry Diltz; foreword by Graham Nash. – London: Omnibus Press, 1984. – xviii, 268p.: ill., ports; 27cm. Includes discography. ISBN 0-7119-0534-7 (pbk.)
  Originally published: New York: St. Martin's Press, 1984.
Incredibly, the first book to appear on this important group of artists, it is well designed, packed with a fine collection of photographs and very well written. There are many quotations from the musicians and a real feeling that the author knows his subject. This discography is detailed, making this a long awaited, but fine example of a rock biography.

DANKWORTH, JOHN

Primarily a serious jazz performer, John Dankworth has now certainly gained a far wider appeal than any other British artist in the field. After emerging in the fifties as the leader of the Johnny Dankworth Seven, Dankworth has become a prolific writer and orchestrator for films and television, as well as working closely with his wife, Cleo Laine, who spans the categories of blues, jazz, opera and popular vocalist with ease. They have created at their home a remarkable workshop for musicians of all kinds and are patrons of many young performers.

Collier, Graham
  Cleo and John: a biography of the Dankworths / Graham Collier. – London: Quartet Books, 1976. – 187p., 34p. of plates: ill., ports; 22cm. Includes index. ISBN 0-7043-2113-0
Written by a jazz musician and journalist, this is a well-researched biography which includes interviews with the subjects and musical analysis. The illustrations are plentiful and the comments by their associates and friends are revealing, if uncritical.

DARIN, BOBBY

Born in New York, in 1939, at the start of his career Bobby Darin epitomized the manufactured, callow, teenage idol typical of the late fifties. By 1960 he had already won three gold recrods for bland, pop hits, but in 1960, he released Mack the Knife, from Brecht's Threepenny Opera, and this was to mark a distinct change in style and approach. He subsequently had hits with songs by Tim Hardin and Johnny Cash and began to build an older, more serious following. In 1963 he set up his own music-publishing company and recording firm, TM Music. In addition, he had already begun to act in films and had received some real critical acclaim for his dramatic, as well as his comedy roles. With frequent television appearances on NBC Television's The Flip Wilson Show, engagements at the Las Vegas hotels and seasons in the most prestigious night spots in New York and Los Angeles, by the seventies Darin was established as a versatile star with a wide appeal. He had always suffered from problems with his heart and in 1971 underwent open-heart surgery for the insertion of artificial valves. His health seemed to improve until in late 1973 he was taken into Cedars Lebanon Hospital in Hollywood for another operation and died on December 20th. It is difficult to assess his talent but his potential was certainly never realized.

DiOrio, Al
  Borrowed time: 37 years of Bobby Darin / Al DiOrio. – Philadelphia,
  Pennsylvania: Running Press, 1981. – 256p.: ill., ports; 24cm. Includes
  bibliography, discography and index. ISBN 0-89471-110-5 (cased).
  ISBN 0-89471-111-3 (pbk.)
A thorough, well-documented and authoritative biography, this is packed with quotations from interviews with friends and associates. Offering the view of a sympathetic, modest, but multi-talented individual, the author displays enthusiasm but avoids exaggeration and idolatry. In general this is a noteworthy work in the field.

DAVIS, SAMMY, JR.

Born in Harlem, New York, in 1925, Sammy Davis Jr. began performing as part of a family act at the age of two. Over the past fifty years his versatility has become the essence of his status as an entertainer. He has starred in dozens of films and musicals and has a regular annual spot in Las Vegas. A close friend of Frank Sinatra and Dean Martin, over the years he has provided a string of successful albums and successful television programmes. He is an exceptionally gifted dancer, notable jazz vocalist and multi-instrumentalist as well as being a comedian and gifted actor. He remains one of the top performers, often described as 'Mr Entertainment'.

Davis, Sammy, Jr.
  Hollywood in a suitcase / Sammy Davis, Jr. – London: Star Books, 1981. –
  255p., 8p. of plates: ill., ports; 18cm. ISBN 0-352-30965-2 (pbk.)

Originally published: St. Albans: Panther, 1980.
An entertaining memoir in which Sammy Davis reflects on his association with
Hollywood. Anecdotes from his own film career are combined with recollections of his friends and associates. Many of the great stars of the last thirty years
are included. His friendships with Elvis Presley and Marilyn Monroe are
described, as well as his closer association with Sinatra and his Rat Pack. Little
about his musical career but a lively biography.

Davis, Sammy, Jr.
  Yes I can: the story of Sammy Davis, Jr. / by Sammy Davis, Jr. and Jane and
  Burt Boyar. – New York: Pocket Books, 1966. – 626p., 16p. of plates; 18cm.
  (pbk.)
A fascinating biography which although naturally entertaining, is also tinged
with Davis's tragic side. Life in vaudeville and his problems as a black
performer in a less enlightened America are candidly described in an outspoken style.

DEEP PURPLE

Formed in early 1968, Deep Purple was to undergo many changes in its eight
years of existence and was to spawn the leading bands of the British heavy-
metal revival of the late seventies. The original line-up included Ritchie
Blackmore on guitar, Jon Lord on keyboards and Rod Evans as vocalist. Evans
was replaced by Ian Gillan in 1970 and this led to a change in style with a new,
ambitious approach, fusing heavy rock with the sound of the Royal Phil-
harmonic Orchestra. Their Concerto for Group and Orchestra was innovative
but not wholly successful. They were, however, established by late 1970 and
continued to be productive. In 1973 Gillan left and was replaced by David
Coverdale and in 1975 Blackmore left. This was the beginning of the end and by
the middle of 1976 the inevitable finally occurred. Ritchie Blackmore went on
to form Rainbow, David Coverdale to form Whitesnake and Ian Gillan to
form his band Gillan.

(*See also* RAINBOW; WHITESNAKE.)

Charlesworth, Chris
  Deep Purple: the illustrated biography / Chris Charlesworth. – London:
  Omnibus Press, 1983. – 96p.: ill. (some col.), ports (some col.); 29cm.
  Includes discography. ISBN 0-7119-0174-0 (pbk.)
Plotting the rise and demise of Deep Purple, the book treats each year of its
existence as a separate chapter with details of recording activity and concert
tours. There is a well-presented collection of photographs and a full discography.

DENE, TERRY

Born in 1938 in London, Terry Dene was one of the earliest British rock'n'roll stars. He suffered lost popularity, however, after serious mental health problems on joining the army for his National Service. After a spell in a psychiatric hospital, he recovered and later turned to Christianity as a member of the Salvation Army.

Wooding, Dan
    I thought Terry Dene was dead / by Dan Wooding. – London: Coverdale House, 1974. – 160p., 8p. of plates: ill., ports; 18cm. ISBN 0-902088-55-6 (pbk.)
This retrospective look at Dene's life gives a good picture of the pop-music scene in London in the fifties. The apeing of American rock'n'roll and the manipulation are well described. Often amusing in its naivety, this is nevertheless a sad little story.

DENVER, JOHN

Born in New Mexico in 1943, John Denver joined the Chad Mitchell folk trio in 1964 and toured with them until 1969. In that year Peter, Paul and Mary recorded his song Leaving on a Jet Plane, and John Denver began his solo career. Not until 1971, however, did he achieve his first real success with a million-selling single and album. From then on throughout the seventies he continued to build an ever-growing commercial success based on the wide appeal of his folk-based, sentimental, sing-along lyrics and clear, soaring voice. In 1975 he sold more records than any other artist in the world, completely against trends.

Dachs, David
    John Denver / David Dachs. – New York: Pyramid Books, 1976. – 93p., 16p. of plates: ill., ports; 18cm. Includes discography. ISBN 0-5150-4172-6 (pbk.)
An uncritical biography which does attempt to analyse the inspiration behind his songwriting. His early career is mentioned briefly but the main theme is his spectacular success in the seventies and his wide appeal.

Fleischer, Leonore
    John Denver / by Leonore Fleischer. – New York; London: Flash Books, 1976. – 80p.: ill., ports; 26cm. Includes discography. ISBN 0-8256-3909-3 (pbk.)
This is a well-illustrated, but superficial biography of the performer the author describes as 'the embodiment of the American dream', with his image of 'good guy', 'filthy rich but Mr Clean'. There is nothing here to contradict this.

Jacobs, Linda
    John Denver: a natural high / by Linda Jacobs. – St. Paul, Minnesota: EMC, 1976. – 40p.: ill., ports; 23cm. ISBN 0-88436-211-6 (cased). ISBN 0-88436-212-4 (pbk.)

This controlled-vocabulary text is aimed at a reading age of about ten and written for American schools. The illustrations and production are very good. It is also available with an audio tape.

McGreane, Meagan
 On stage John Denver / text Meagan McGreane; design concept Larry Soule. – Mankato. Minnesota: Creative Education, 1976. – 47p.: ill., ports; 23cm. ISBN 0-87191-483-2
A controlled-vocabulary text aimed at a reading age of around ten for American junior high schools. The simple sentence structure and informative content suit the age range.

Martin, James
 John Denver: Rocky Mountain wonderboy / James Martin. – London: Everest Books, 1977. – 148p., 16p. of plates: ill., ports; 18cm. ISBN 0-9050-1856-7 (pbk.)
A superficial, homely biography which outlines his childhood and describes his career. His songs are discussed without analysis and his remarkably wide audience is accepted without comment.

Morse, Charles
 John Denver / text Charles and Ann Morse; illustrator John Keely; design concept by Mark Landkamer. – Mankato, Minnesota: Creative Education, 1974. – 31p.: ill. (some col.), ports (some col.); 25cm. ISBN 0-8719-1392-5
This controlled-vocabulary biography is written for a reading age of about ten for American schools. This is an informative biography with some well-chosen illustrations.

DIAMOND, NEIL

Born in Brooklyn, New York, in January 1941, Neil Diamond began his career by hawking his songs around New York record companies and was at last taken on as a staff writer with Sunbeam Music. This was in 1963 and he had to wait until 1966 for his first successful song, I'm a Believer, which was recorded by the Monkees and became a world-wide success. Then he had a minor hit of his own and after changing record companies to Uni, he began to make a long list of hits which have continued from the late sixties to date. In 1970 he began writing more lyrical, grander compositions including The African Trilogy, which attempted to illustrate the three stages of man's development – birth, maturity and death – using musical devices such as tribal rhythms and gospel choirs. This was followed by the film score for the film Jonathan Livingstone Seagull. All very pretentious; he was making an attempt to change his image as the smooth writer of catchy songs to something more substantial. In 1980 he starred in the remake of the film The Jazz Singer for which he wrote the songs, proving that he still does write catchy, quality songs and sings them in a limited but effective style. He signed a record five-million-dollar contract with the CBS company in 1973 and in 1975 held the record for being the highest-paid performer for a single performance.

O'Regan, Suzanne K.
  Neil Diamond / text Suzanne K. O'Regan; illustrator John Keely; design
  concept Mark Landkamer. – Mankato, Minnesota: Creative Education,
  1975. – 29p.: ill. (some col.), ports (some col.); 25cm. ISBN 0-87191-446-6
  (cased). ISBN 0-89812-115-9 (pbk.)
The only book available on Diamond, this is a controlled-vocabulary text
written for a reading age of around ten for American schools. It is well
illustrated and well produced, but uncritical.

DIRE STRAITS

Dire Straits was formed in 1977 with Mark Knopfler on lead guitar, David
Knopfler on rhythm guitar, John Illsley, bass, and Pick Withers, drums. To
begin with the group lived and worked in Deptford, south London. After
financing their own demo tapes, they toured with the Talking Heads in January
1978 and began to be noticed. In May their first record was released and
received critical attention and later that year their first album began to sell well
in America, Canada, Germany, Holland and France, but not until the following year in the United Kingdom. Since then they have become a major band
with five hit albums. Alan Clark joined them on keyboards in 1981 and David
Knopfler left to be replaced by Hal Lindes. It is unquestionably Mark Knopfler
who fronts the band, writing the songs, singing, and playing lead guitar. It is in
fact his unique style of playing which gives them their peculiar sound. He is one
of the finest guitarists playing today and an unusual phenomenon as a guitar
hero to emerge from the late seventies.

Oldfield, Mike
  Dire Straits / Mike Oldfield. – London: Sidgwick & Jackson, 1983. – 152p.:
  ill., ports; 28cm. Includes discography and index. ISBN 0-283-98990-4
  (cased). ISBN 0-283-98995-5 (pbk.)
A very good biography of the band's career, packed with quotations and giving
some real insight into Knopfler's songwriting and playing style. An unusually
straightforward and factual narrative with a fine collection of well-selected
photographs.

DOONICAN, VAL

Born in Waterford, Ireland, in 1927 into very humble circumstances, Val
Doonican first became a professional entertainer in 1947. He moved to
England, working in holiday camps, music halls and clubs. His style is a mixture
of homely Irish humour and standard country and western songs, sung with a
deep, rich accent. After seventeen years of obscurity, in 1964 he appeared at
the London Palladium on the Sunday night television show and immediately
became a popular success. He has achieved nine successful singles and won a
variety of awards as well as having his own longstanding television series.

Doonican, Val
  The special years: an autobiography / Val Doonican. – London: Sphere
  Books, 1981. – 181p., 8p. of plates: ill., ports; 18cm. ISBN 0-7221-3603-1
  (pbk.)
  Originally published: London: Elm Tree Books, 1980.
An autobiography which modestly describes Doonican's success story. The
poverty of his childhood is described with humour, with numerous witty
anecdotes of his family and particularly of his father. In all a homely story of a
nice man.

THE DOORS

See MORRISON, JIM AND THE DOORS

THE DRIFTERS

The Drifters was the name of Atlantic Records' most successful vocal group of
the fifties and sixties. The personnel changed continuously between 1955 and
1968, maintaining the name and outputting a series of classic hit singles which
were a mixture of rhythm & blues and pop, often with Latin American
rhythms. They reached a white teenage audience in a period when other black
groups aimed their music at black audiences. A Drifters line-up still performs
on the American cabaret circuit.

Millar, Bill
  The Drifters: the rise and fall of the black vocal group / Bill Millar. – London:
  Studio Vista, 1971. – 102p.: ill., ports; 21cm. Includes bibliography and
  discography. ISBN 0-2897-0133-3
  Originally published: New York: Macmillan, 1971.
A well-researched, meticulously described account of the Drifters reflecting
their complicated history and the situation of black musicians in the fifties,
together with their relationship with the record companies.

THE DUBLINERS

All born in Dublin between 1936 and 1944, the Dubliners, Ciaran Bourke,
Ronnie Drew, Luke Kelly, Bob Lynch, Barney Mackenna, John Sheahan and
Jim McCann, were all deeply interested in the folk music of Ireland at an early
age. Like many young Irish musicians they began playing in pubs in the late
fifties and by 1963 they had joined together as a group. They signed their first
record contract with Transatlantic Records after appearing at the Edinburgh
Folk Festival in 1963 and soon gathered a considerable Irish folk following. In
1967 they changed record companies and signed with Major Minor, appearing
at the Albert Hall in February 1968. Their new record company promoted their

music on the popular pirate radio station, Radio Caroline. In March 1968 they had a single in the British charts with some sexual innuendo called Seven Drunken Nights – it was banned in Ireland. They had two more successful singles in 1967 and since then have become an established group with a wide following, extending interest in Irish music.

Hardy, Mary
   The Dubliners scrapbook / by Mary Hardy. – London: Wise Publications, 1978. – 96p.: ill., facsims, ports; 25cm. ISBN 0-86001-530-0 (pbk.)
Based on hundreds of press cuttings of the group, the author links them chronologically with the development of their career, adding biographical facts and criticism of their records.

DYLAN, BOB

Born Robert Zimmerman in May 1941, in Duluth, Minnesota, he changed his name to Dylan after his hero Dylan Thomas. He left the University of Minnesota after a year and moved to Greenwich Village, New York, where he began performing in the folk clubs, becoming part of the growing folk circle. He was spotted by John Hammond of Columbia Records and made his first album in 1961. Released in March 1962 the material was mainly traditional songs with a sparse backing of Dylan's acoustic guitar and harmonica behind his grating voice. His next album, however, included only Dylan's own compositions which commented on contemporary social and political events and firmly put him at the head of the protest singing movement. By 1965 his songs had become more surreal and introspective and when he appeared that year at the Newport Folk Festival, backed by the Paul Butterfield Blues Band, an all-electric group, he left his folk roots and folk rock was born. After three innovative albums which completely changed the concepts of the content of popular songs with strange streams of consciousness and complex imagery, Dylan produced nothing for two years. The official press release was that he was almost killed in a motorcycle accident.

He re-emerged in 1968 with simpler songs and a smoother vocal style, which he has maintained. Throughout the seventies he produced a series of creative albums which are all totally different in concept and approach but never fail to be experimental or successful.

Bob Dylan's influence on the development of popular music in the last twenty years is only rivalled by the Beatles. Like them he gave it a respectability and acceptable social position which has been influential on the awareness and cultural attitudes of a whole generation. He broke down the barriers between the highbrow attitudes of the folk world of the fifties and the earthiness of rock'n'roll, making rock at last acceptable to the aspiring intellectual. He has appeared in several films: Don't Look Back in 1965; Pat Garratt and Billy the Kid with Kris Kristofferson, directed by Sam Peckinpah, in 1973; his own effort of direction, Renaldo and Clara, in 1977 and Martin Scorsese's The Last Waltz, in 1978. Film exists of Dylan's Rolling Thunder Review tour of the northeast of America, in 1975, but it has appeared only in short television extracts. During the late seventies his philosophy took a turn towards religion and he announced his position as a reborn Christian. His albums, Slow Train and Saved, were emphatically carrying an evangelical message. During 1981 he toured Britain with a black gospel vocal group and new band playing modern, heavy rock but the audiences still called for his classic songs of the sixties. Rumour has it that he has more recently left the flock.

Beal, Kathleen
 Bob Dylan / text Kathleen Beal; illustrator John Keely. – Mankato,
 Minnesota: Creative Education, 1974. – 31p.: ill., (some col.), ports (some
 col.); 25cm. ISBN 0-8719-1399-2
A controlled-vocabulary biography for a reading age of about ten written for American schools, this is a good introduction to Bob Dylan reflecting his early evolutions in style. There is a good collection of illustrations and some intelligent comment on his music. It is with considerable skill and sensitivity that the author conveys to such an age group the significance of Dylan's themes. She attempts, with some success, to interpret simpler symbolism and the concept of protest songs. Even his drug-orientated phase of writing is touched upon and explained away as simply a phase of the lifestyle of the sixties.

Bob Dylan: a retrospective / edited by Craig McGregor. – Rev. ed. – London:
 Angus and Robertson, 1980. – 237p.: ill., ports; 22cm. ISBN 0-207-14352-8
 (pbk.)
 Previous edition: London: Angus and Robertson, 1973.
 Also published: abridged edition: London: Pan Books, 1975
Edited by an Australian journalist, this is an excellent selection of writings on Bob Dylan and transcripts of interviews brought up to date by the revised edition. The pieces cover the whole of Dylan's career and included are some unusual photographs. The articles are by such noted writers as Jon Landau, Studs Terkel, Lillian Roxon, Wilfrid Mellers, Jann Wenner, Nik Cohn and Richard Goldstein.

Dylan: a commemoration / editor Stephen Pickering: asst. editor Scott
 Sullivan. – 2nd ed. – Berkeley, California: No. Limit, 1971. – 64p.: ill.,
 facsims, ports; 37cm. (pbk.)
A rare, poorly produced publication which is a collection of writings on Dylan, reviews of books on him, reviews of his records and numerous portraits. A section written by the author entitled 'Bob Dylan approximately', which is an extended essay full of statements of idolatry with the general theme of Dylan as the Jewish mystic, is a well-known piece often referred to. This is a good example of how pretentious writing on a popular artist can become.

Dylan, Bob
 Bob Dylan in his own words / compiled by Miles; edited by Pearce
 Marchbank; designed by Perry Neville. – London: Omnibus Press, 1978. –
 128p.: ill., ports; 26cm. ISBN 0-86001-542-4 (pbk.)
 Also published: New York: Quick Fox, 1978.

A collection of Bob Dylan's remarks on his work, life and rock lifestyle. An entertaining collection which has been well edited – a necessary factor to make Dylan's quotations comprehensible.

Gross, Michael
   Bob Dylan: an illustrated history / produced by Michael Gross; with a text by Robert Alexander. – London: Elm Tree Books, 1978. – 149p.: ill., facsims, ports; 29cm. Includes bibliography. ISBN 0-241-10038-0 (pbk.)
   Originally published: New York: Grosset & Dunlap, 1978.
An outline biography up to 1976 which, with the help of a chronology of events, sets Dylan's career in perspective. Particularly strong on the transitional period from folk singer to rock artist, the illustrations are well chosen with album sleeves, posters, magazine covers and concert-ticket reproductions.

Heylin, Clinton
   Rain unravelled tales (the Nightingale's code examined): a rumourography / by Clinton Heylin et al. – 2nd ed. – 4, Rue Morgue Avenue, Juarez: Ashes and Sand Publications, 1982. – 135p.: ill., facsims, ports; 30cm. (spiral)
   Previous edition: 1981.
Privately published by the author, not at the address above but in Sale, Cheshire (the imprint place comes from a Dylan song). The criterion for including facts here is that not only are they spurious, but they are unsubstantiated. Rumours, obscure recordings and legendary performances make fascinating reading for the real fanatic.

Knockin' on Dylan's door. – London: Michael Dempsey; Cassell, 1975. – 137p., 4p. of plates: ill., ports; 20cm. ISBN 0-86018-104-9
   Originally published: New York: Pocket Books, 1974.
In 1974 Bob Dylan made his first tour of the USA since 1966. The editors of *Rolling Stone* magazine reported the concerts in this series of essays. A good and varied collection, it includes an interview and a list of songs performed on the tour. Strictly to be read in the context of the early seventies; Dylan's later changes in direction are not anticipated.

Kramer, Daniel
   Bob Dylan / by Daniel Kramer. – New York: Pocket Books, 1968. – 214p.: ill., ports; 18cm. (pbk.)
   Originally published: Secaucus, New Jersey: Castle Books, 1967.
Between 1964 and 1966 Kramer took thousands of photographs of Dylan. He describes the context of the sessions and Dylan's changing personality at this crucial time in his development.

Miles
   Bob Dylan / by Miles. – London: Big O Publishing, 1978. – 64p.: ill., facsims, ports; 30cm. ISBN 0-905-66409-4
A series of brief essays on Dylan's career up to 1978; although episodic, this is intelligent and factual with some material from early interviews. His recent work is also covered well with information of his association with new-wave artists.

Pickering, Stephen
  Bob Dylan approximately: a portrait of the Jewish poet in search of God; a
  Midrash / Stephen Pickering; photographs by George Gruel, Peter Vogl and
  others; designed by Jon Goodchild. – New York: David Mackay, 1975. –
  204p.: ill. (some col.), ports (some col.); 26cm. ISBN 0-679-50493-1 (cased).
  ISBN 0-679-50529-6 (pbk.)
A collection of writings focussing on his 1974 tour. Dylan is seen as a Jewish
mystic. With a section of religious chants, this is dull and very pretentious.

Ribakove, Sy
  Folk-rock: the Bob Dylan story / by Sy and Barbara Ribakove. – New York:
  Dell, 1966. – 143p.: ill., ports; 18cm. Includes discography. (pbk.)
The earliest book on Dylan, it is surprisingly informative and well written.
With the development of his music into rock, there is some excellent analysis of
his transitional albums. The illustrations are also particularly interesting.

Rinzler, Alan
  Bob Dylan: the illustrated record / by Alan Rinzler; designed by Jon
  Goodchild. – New York: Harmony Books, 1978. – 120p.: ill. (some col.),
  facsims, ports (some col.); 30cm. Includes bibliography. ISBN 0-517-53354-5
  (cased). ISBN 0-517-53355-3 (pbk.)
Designed as an elaborate discography, Dylan's career is chronologically traced
in the context of his album releases. Each album cover appears as a full-page,
full-size illustration, with details of its contents, analysis of the songs and the
style, followed by illustrations of Dylan at that period, quotations, extracts
from reviews and biographical detail. It is a beautifully presented, well
designed and edited biography covering the period up to 1978, which gives a
good impression of his changes in style, approach and influences. The bibliography is very selective.

Scaduto, Anthony
  Bob Dylan / by Anthony Scaduto. – London: Abacus, 1972. – 280p., 8p. of
  plates: ill., ports 20cm. Includes discography and index. ISBN 0-491-00662-4
  (pbk.)
  Originally published: New York: Grosset and Dunlap, 1971.
  Also published: London: W. H. Allen, 1972.
  Revised American edition: New York: New American Library, 1979.
Scaduto, without any doubt, treats Dylan as only a devotee can, with considerable deference. On reading the manuscript Dylan gave reserved approval to
the author. He corrected some factual errors and added some personal views
on important issues in his life. It is easily the best biographical work on Dylan,
whose notoriously secretive and elusive approach to journalists is so effective.
The information about his early life and influences is very detailed and shows
evidence of a great deal of research in which the author interviewed dozens of
the associates who have worked with Dylan at different stages of his career. Of
particular interest is the analysis of Dylan's change from folk singer to rock
singer. The index gives good access. The discography is very brief. The updated
American edition has added a short afterword by Steven Gaines which gives
very little extra information.

Shepard, Sam
Rolling Thunder logbook / by Sam Shepard. – Harmondsworth: Penguin,
1978. – 184p.: ill., ports; 26cm. ISBN 0-14-00-4750-6 (pbk.)
Originally published: New York: Viking, 1977
In 1975 Sam Shepard was engaged to travel with Bob Dylan's tour of the
northeastern USA, to write a screenplay and script for a proposed, but later
abandoned, film. Dylan took with him an entourage, named the Rolling
Thunder Review, of musicians and friends such as Joni Mitchell, Allen
Ginsberg and Joan Baez. This impressionistic diary comprises poems, extracts
from the aborted script and short prose pieces which add up to an unusual
picture of life on the road with a good collection of photographs.

Sloman, Larry
On the road with Bob Dylan: rolling with the thunder / by Larry Sloman. –
New York: Bantam Books, 1978. – 147p., 8p. of plates: ill., ports; 18cm.
ISBN 0-553-11641-X (pbk.)
A dedicated fan of Dylan, Larry Sloman travelled with the Rolling Thunder
Review. He describes the characters, the musicians, the performances and
atmosphere of the tour. The style is amusing, if full of idolatry, but the author's
knowledge and understanding of Dylan's writing is undeniable.

Thompson, Toby
Positively Main Street: an unorthodox view of Bob Dylan / Toby Thompson.
– London: New English Library, 1972. – 157p.: 18cm. ISBN 0-450-01012-0
(pbk.)
Originally published: New York: Cowan-McCann, 1971.
The author ruthlessly researched Bob Dylan's past, back to Hibbing,
Minnesota, in an attempt to gain a deeper understanding of his hero. Initially
appearing to be a typical piece of investigatory 'new' journalism, the result is an
almost reverent approach. This is not a conventional biography and describes
the investigation as well as the results, but it is full of details of Dylan's early
days not available elsewhere.

Thomson, Elizabeth M.
Conclusions on the wall: new essays on Bob Dylan. – edited by Elizabeth
M. Thomson. – Prestwich, Manchester: Thin Man, 1980. – 108p.: ill., ports;
21cm. Includes bibliography. ISBN 0-9507220-0-6 (pbk.)
Published to commemorate the second Bob Dylan convention, Dylan
Revisited '80, this is a collection of essays by some distinguished writers on
popular music. Michael Gray, Robert Shelton, Christopher Ricks and Wilfrid
Mellers look at various aspects of Dylan's creative personality. Mellers offers
his familiar musicological analyses while Elizabeth Thomson's essay on Dylan
as a composer gives a fascinating insight into his technique. Another particularly useful essay is Gabrielle Goodchild's critical interpretation of the novel
Tarantula. The pieces have all been written recently and there is much
discussion of his 'born again Christian' stance. This is not a comprehensive or a
cohesive view of Dylan, and is often contradictory, but it is intelligently written
and worth serious note. The illustrations are unusual but the bibliography poor.

Williams, Paul
Dylan: what happened? / Paul Williams. – South Bend, South Michigan: Ans
Books; Glen Ellen, California: Entwhistle Books, 1980. – 126p.: 16p. of
plates: ill., ports; 21cm. ISBN 0-89708-021-1 (pbk.)
In 1979 the themes of Bob Dylan's songs suddenly became religious as he was
reborn to the American non-conformist church. Paul Williams reviews some of
his recent songs and concert performances, attempting to find an explanation
for his change in philosophy. Not totally adverse in his criticism, Paul Williams
still finds some of Dylan's recent work full of inspiration and musically
satisfying.

DYLAN, BOB: SONGS

Dowley, Tim
Bob Dylan: from a hard rain to a slow train / by Tim Dowley and Barry
Dunnage. – London: Omnibus Press, 1982. – 177p.: ill., ports; 22cm.
Includes bibliography, discography and filmography. ISBN 0-7119-0060-4
(pbk.)
Originally published: New York: Hippocrene Books, 1981.
Also published: Tunbridge Wells, Kent: Midas Books, 1981.
Covering Dylan's changing preoccupations from the mid seventies to 1981, the
authors do not simply describe the changes, but study the subtle concept of the
pattern of his development. They suggest recurring themes and fixations which
manifest themselves in various forms. Interesting, but the informed reader will
find many of the arguments tenuous and some inaccuracies.

Gray, Michael
Song & dance man: the art of Bob Dylan / Michael Gray. – Rev. ed. –
London: Hamlyn, 1981. – 236p.: ill. (some col.), ports (some col.); 25cm.
Includes discography and index. ISBN 0-600-34170-4 (cased).
ISBN 0-600-34224-7 (pbk.)
Originally published: London: Hart-Davis MacGibbon, 1972.
Previous edition: London: Abacus, 1973.
This revised edition updates the artistic appreciation of Dylan's work to include
his 'born again Christian' work. The central theme is the significance of Dylan
as a major poet whose writing must be studied as a developing, coherent body
of work. He attributes Dylan with the changing of the public's awareness,
enabling art to be possible in popular music. The extensive quotations from
songs followed by textual analysis is sometimes tedious but as a disciplined
literary appreciation of popular lyrics it is unique and fascinating. The reader
not conversant with the songs in detail may find the notes pretentious and over-
analytical and the constant association with the works of poets, notably
Browning, Blake and Eliot, is often dubious. The illustrations are excellent in
the new edition and a great improvement on the previous editions.

Herdman, John
Voice without restraint: a study of Bob Dylan's lyrics and their background /

John Herdman. – Edinburgh: Paul Harris, 1982. – 164p.: ill., ports; 22cm.
Includes bibliography and index. ISBN 0-86228-019-2 (cased).
ISBN 0-86228-037-0 (pbk.)

Not an analysis of each Dylan song but a survey of his themes since 1966 with particular emphasis on his work in the seventies. The approach is basically literary but the author attempts to use information about Dylan's life and personality as a basis for some of his interpretation. Quite often his readings of Dylan's symbolism are simply affected. In short, Dylan certainly has a great talent and often uses language in a most unusual and creative way approaching poetry, but the author looks for the complex when the simple is more likely. An interesting work for the fanatic.

DYLAN, BOB: WRITINGS

Dylan, Bob
Writings and drawings / Bob Dylan. – St. Albans: Panther, 1974. – 478p.: ill.; 20cm. Includes index. ISBN 0-586-04088-9 (pbk.)
Originally published: London: Cape, 1973.

This is a complete collection of Dylan's lyrics and poems as well as miscellaneous drawings from the time of his first album in 1961, until 1972. The arrangement is chronological, displaying his change in style. The index is to the title, first line and key lines of the song or poem.

Dylan, Bob
Tarantula / Bob Dylan. – St. Albans: Panther, 1971. – 123p.: 18cm.
ISBN 0-586-03753-5 (pbk.)
Originally published: London: MacGibbon and Kee, 1971.

A rambling, surreal work combining prose and blank verse and which lacks any cohesive theme, it is generally incomprehensible. It is claimed to be an unfinished novel but whether this is true or not is difficult to detect.

DYLAN, BOB: DISCOGRAPHIES

Cable, Paul
Bob Dylan: his unreleased works / Paul Cable. – London: Scorpion Publications; with Dark Star, 1978. – 192p.: ill.; 22cm. ISBN 0-905906-17-9 (cased).
ISBN 0-905906-16-0 (pbk.)

A book for the Dylan enthusiast. This is the most complete list of the recordings of songs which appear on the unofficially recorded bootleg tapes and of those officially recorded songs which were not included on released albums. No other such list exists for any other artist or band which is so systematic or so comprehensive.

Hoggard, Stuart
Bob Dylan: an illustrated discography / Stuart Hoggard & Jim Shields. – 2nd ed. – Dumbarton: Transmedia Express, 1978. – 138p.: ill., facsims, ports:

20cm. Includes index and bibliography. ISBN 0-906344-00-X (pbk.)
Previous edition: Oxford: Transmedia Express, 1978.

Arranged chronologically, this is a meticulously annotated discography which includes bootleg albums, tapes of interviews, videos and films. The author divides Dylan's career into three separate periods, 1961–65, 1966–70, 1970–77, which conveniently and accurately demonstrates his changes in style. The illustrations are few but there are many reproductions of album-cover designs. The bibliography is sparse but as a source of basic information on Dylan's work this is excellent.

DYLAN, BOB: FILMS

Don't Look Back

Directed by D. A. Pennebaker in 1965, Don't Look Back is a *cinéma vérité* documentary of Bob Dylan's 1965 English tour. It is a fascinating look at the young Dylan preparing himself for a concert, destroying an unfortunate interviewer, at a party with Joan Baez and Donovan and performing. Dylan ordered the film's withdrawal in the mid seventies.

Pennebaker, D. A.
    Don't look back / by D. A. Pennebaker. – New York: Ballantine, 1968. –
    112p.: ill.; 18cm. (pbk.)
With an interesting collection of stills the director fails to translate his work to the printed page but includes some of the best dialogue.

THE EAGLES

The Eagles were formed in 1972 by Randy Meisner, formerly of Poco, Bernie Leadon, formerly of the Flying Burrito Brothers, Don Henley and Glenn Frey, who had played with Linda Ronstadt. Their first album of the year became an instant success in the USA. From then on their success grew and by 1976 they were the leading American band in terms of both singles and albums sales. Their original style can be loosely defined as country rock with complex harmonies in the tradition of such West Coast groups as the Byrds, Crosby, Stills and Nash and Poco. By 1976, however, their sound had become so smooth and lavishly produced that it became heavily criticized and described as middle-of-the-road or adult-orientated rock. Their line-up has changed by the addition of Joe Walsh, Don Felder and Timothy Schmidt and the departure of Leadon and Meisner. Their success has been considerable in Britain, but as nothing compared to their achievements in the USA.

Swenson, John
    The Eagles / by John Swenson. – New York: Ace Books, 1981. – 192p.: ill.,
    ports; 18cm. ISBN 0-448-17174-0 (pbk.)

Surprisingly the only book available on the group, this is an informative little work written in a straightforward, simple style. All the basic information is here, including details of the members' previous careers, but there is no real criticism or analysis of their music.

ECHO AND THE BUNNYMEN

After leaving the original version of the group which would become the Teardrop Explodes, Ian McCulloch formed Echo and the Bunnymen in 1978. Based in Liverpool, during their first year the group (which included Will Sergeant, guitar, Les Patterson, bass, Pete De Freitas, drums, and McCulloch on guitar and lead vocals) released a single on the independent Zoo label. After gaining considerable experience of performing live, they signed for Korova Records in late 1979 and by the end of 1980 their first album, Crocodiles, had entered the lower region of the charts. Extensive touring followed and their growing reputation began to make them into a cult band. Their second single was a minor hit and their stage look of camouflage clothes became a widely copied fashion. In January 1981 they made a film, They Shine So Hard, which received high critical acclaim. Their second album, which appeared in May 1981, again was hailed by the music press but was not a real hit. At the end of 1982, they remain an enigma, highly regarded but still to establish themselves commercially.

Cooper, Mark
   Liverpool explodes: The Teardrop Explodes, Echo and the Bunnymen /
   Mark Cooper. – London: Sidgwick & Jackson, 1982. – 96p.: ill., ports; 26cm.
   Includes discography and index. ISBN 0-283-98865-5 (pbk.)
Shared with the Teardrop Explodes, this is an informative account of a group about which there is very little available information. There is a good selection of photographs and a detailed discography with some intelligent and informed discussion of their music

THE ELECTRIC LIGHT ORCHESTRA

ELO was formed by Roy Wood and Bev Bevan, with the addition of Jeff Lynne, from the remnants of the sixties group, the Move. Although Wood left in 1971, the band (which was planned to provide live the kind of orchestral rock with which the Beatles had experimented in the studio) continued to become ever more successful. Their music includes a conventional rock-group line-up of electric guitars, keyboards and drums, augmented with cellos and violins. A fusion of classically trained, former London Symphony Orchestra members and rock'n'roll primitives, the group works together to provide a unique sound with an extremely wide appeal which has made ELO successful throughout the world and particularly in the USA. Jeff Lynne writes all the band's material as well as being the lead guitar player and vocalist.

Bevan, Bev
  The Electric Light Orchestra story / by Bev Bevan; edited by Garth Pearce. –
  London: Mushroom Books, 1980. – 174p.: ill., ports; 28cm. Includes
  discography. ISBN 0-907-394-00-0 (cased). ISBN 0-907-394-01-9 (pbk.)
After playing drums with the successful sixties group, the Move, Bev Bevan
was a founder member of ELO. This history of the group includes the evolution
of the band from the Move and is an edited compilation of Bevan's diaries
which he has maintained since first becoming involved in music in 1962. A well-
illustrated, surprisingly unsensational, personal account by someone who
enjoys being at the top of the rock industry but has avoided the excesses. There
is no real analysis of ELO's music or discussion of recordings or concert
performances.

EPSTEIN, BRIAN

Brian Epstein was born in Liverpool in 1934. After public school and RADA,
he joined his father's furniture business. Because of his love of music, he
opened a small record department in one of the shops. In November 1961 he
became aware of an early German recording of the Beatles because of the high
demand for the rare disc. Intrigued, he visited the Cavern Club and was so
impressed by the Beatles' raw talent that he became their manager, smoothing
out their image and finally arranging their record contract with EMI. He
subsequently signed other Liverpool acts such as Cilla Black, Gerry and the
Pacemakers, Billy J. Kramer and the Fourmost, all of whom gained considerable success. When the Beatles had become established as the most successful
group in the world his role became redundant. He bought and managed the
Savile theatre and dabbled in a variety of artistic ventures. He died of a drug
overdose on August 27th 1967 in London while the Beatles were away in
Bangor, Wales, with the Maharishi Yogi. After his death the Beatles began
their protracted decline.

(*See also* THE BEATLES.)

Epstein, Brian
  A cellarful of noise / Brian Epstein. – London: New English Library, 1981. –
  127p.; 18cm. ISBN 0-450-05388-1 (pbk.)
  Originally published: London: Souvenir Press, 1964; New York:
  Doubleday; Pyramid, 1964.
  Previous edition: London: New English Library, 1965.
Ghost-written by his personal assistant, Derek Taylor, this is an autobiography
in which Brian Epstein affectionately describes his upbringing and education.
His meeting with the Beatles and their early career is told factually, but a lot is
glossed over. Their lifestyle, which during the early tours they have admitted
was extremely wild, is all avoided as are Epstein's own personal problems and
depressions which led to his death. Nevertheless this is well written and his
artistic flair and analysis is well communicated.

Essex, David

Born in Hackney, London, in 1947, David Essex took the lead role in the London production of the musical Godspell in 1971. He followed this with film roles in That'll Be the Day and Stardust. His songwriting and singing then suddenly became remarkably successful and he achieved singles successes on both sides of the Atlantic. His style alternates between quite serious rock and light pop with an appeal to the younger end of the market.

Tremlett, George
   The David Essex story / George Tremlett. – London: Futura Publications,
   1974. – 140p., 16p. of plates: ill., ports; 18cm. ISBN 0-8600-7092-1 (pbk.)
   Also published: London: White Lion, 1976.
Based on personal interviews and his manager's personal file, this is another journalistically produced, informative biography by Tremlett. There is a chronology of events in David Essex's career and an appendix which includes synopses from That'll Be the Day and Stardust with biographical notes on the other actors. There is even an appendix of Essex's quotations on the set of Stardust, offering even more padding than usual.

The Faces

(*See* STEWART, ROD.)

Fairport Convention

Formed in Muswell Hill, London, in 1967 as the British answer to the Jefferson Airplane, the original line-up included Judy Dyble and Ian Matthews as vocalists, Richard Thomson, Simon Nicol, Ashley Hutchings and Martin Lamble. In 1968 Sandy Denny replaced Judy Dyble. Their early records consisted of some original songs mixed with American songwriters' contemporary material. On their third album, Unhalfbricking, they began experimenting by including an English traditional song and a violin played by Dave Swarbrick, an established folk artist. Ian Matthews had left by this time and Swarbrick joined along with a new drummer, Dave Mattacks. The resulting album, in 1969, Liege Lief, consisted of traditional songs and is considered to be the most important step in the formation of English folk rock.

Personnel changes continued throughout the seventies. Sandy Denny established a successful solo career until her death in 1978, Richard Thomson joined his wife, Linda, in a successful duo, Ian Matthews formed Southern Comfort and Plain Song, and Ashley Hutchings formed the Albion Dance Band and Steeleye Span. The group continued until 1979, led very much by Swarbrick, but finally disbanded, mainly because of his failing hearing. They join together each August for a commemorative festival. In its various forms, Fairport Convention was certainly one of the most interesting and innovative ensembles to emerge from the late-sixties folk-rock period and is responsible for helping to foster an interest in English folk song in a wider audience.

Humphries, Patrick
  Meet on the ledge: a history of Fairport Convention / Patrick Humphries. – London: Eel Pie, 1982. – 112p.: ill., ports; 25cm. Includes discography.
  ISBN 0-906008-46-8 (pbk.)
An excellent outline of the complex history of the group with a well-selected collection of illustrations and a family tree by Pete Frame. There are transcripts of interviews and a discography which lists the records of the group, as well as those made by members of the group as solo artists or as part of other units.

FAITH, ADAM

Born Terence Nelhams in Acton, London, in 1940, Adam Faith was second only to Cliff Richard as Britain's top pop idol for a short time in the early sixties. After singing with skiffle groups, he made his first record in late 1959. He would never claim to be a great singer, but with a soft, almost spoken style, slightly emulating Buddy Holly, he had a string of sixteen hit singles. He was always shrewd and after early appearances in films, he spent two years with a repertory theatre. He was the first pop singer to admit that his taste in music included Sibelius and that he actually read novels. He had the leading role in the television series Budgie, and in 1974 was a star of the film Stardust. He now owns a recording company and manages singer Leo Sayer, whose career he has shrewdly guided.

Faith, Adam
  Adam, his fabulous year / Adam Faith. – London: Picture Story Publications, 1960. – 67p.: ill., ports; 25cm. (pbk.)
Published after his initial, and most successful, year at the top, this is in an almost comic-strip format for the teenage fan of the period. The inane text is patronizing and disjointed and the author credit is dubious. A good example of the literature of the period.

Faith, Adam
  Poor me / by Adam Faith. – London: Four Square; Souvenir Press, 1961. – 95p., 16p. of plates: ill., ports; 18cm. (pbk.)
An early example of a pop singer's autobiography with no hint of the text being ghost-written; Faith simply outlines his background and describes life as a star of the early sixties. It is uncritical, ingenuous with little humour, but here is a singer attempting to be different from the general image of the time. The ironic title is taken from one of his song titles, which typically had a lame-dog theme.

Ferry, Bryan

Born in 1945 in County Durham, the son of a miner, Ferry graduated in fine arts from Newcastle University and moved to London to teach. He had sung in local groups since the mid sixties and after meeting bass guitarist Graham Simpson, Andy Mackay, Brian Eno and drummer Dexter Lloyd, he formed Roxy Music between November 1970 and early 1971. Their immediate success established them, and particularly Ferry, among the leading stylists of the early seventies. They were looked on as the visionaries of the period with their high-camp style and music influenced by the likes of John Cage. After Brian Eno left the group Ferry made Roxy a vehicle for his own provocative, humourless style with its urbane, very English image. His first solo album in 1973 was a success but subsequently he has been less so. In the summer of 1976 Roxy Music stopped performing together; they had lost their early innovation. In 1980 they reappeared and in 1981 had their first number-one hit with Jealous Guy, a tribute to John Lennon. Ferry remains a remarkable, distant figure, often criticized for his blandness, but one of the undoubted innovators in contemporary popular music.

(*See also* ROXY MUSIC.)

Balfour, Rex
> *The Bryan Ferry story* / as told by Rex Balfour. – London: Michael Dempsey, 1976. – 128p.: ill., ports; 20cm. Includes discography. ISBN 0-86044-015-X (pbk.)

Written before the decision to suspend Roxy Music's activities in 1976, this is a good survey of Ferry's career, lavishly illustrated. There is some attempt to analyse his musical influences, without any revelations. The value of the book is the information about Ferry's boyhood, education and the art-school, stylist approach in the formation of Roxy Music. This is the best source of information on an elusive star.

Fisher, Eddie

Born in Philadelphia in 1928, Eddie Fisher began singing on local radio in his teens. He moved to New York and began singing as a band vocalist at the Copacabana night club. In 1949 he was spotted by Eddie Cantor, the star of the thirties and forties, who signed him for a nationwide tour. He achieved his first successful record in the USA in 1951 and between 1953 and 1956 he had nine hit records in Britain, but then his crooning style became out of date. He was at one time married to Elizabeth Taylor. In the early seventies he suffered from acute drug addiction, but has since recovered.

Fisher, Eddie
> *My life, my loves* / Eddie Fisher. – London: W. H. Allen, 1982. – 320p.: ill., ports; 24cm. ISBN 0-491-02269-X

Originally published: New York: Harper & Row, 1981.
An autobiography containing recollections of Eddie Fisher's relationships with
not only the women in his life such as Ann Margret, Debbie Reynolds,
Elizabeth Taylor, Marlene Dietrich and Connie Stevens, but figures such as
John F. Kennedy, Lyndon Johnson, Frank Sinatra and Mike Todd. He makes
no excuses for his failures and indeed, at least for the sake of this memoir,
seems to relish them. The showbusiness world of the fifties and early sixties, its
gossip and leading characters, are all here. The book is sensational in its style
but an interesting insight.

Greene, Myrna
The Eddie Fisher story / by Myrna Greene. – Middlebury, Vermont: P. S.
Eriksson, 1978. – 210p.: ill., ports; 24cm. Includes discography and index.
ISBN 0-8397-8682-4
A detailed biography: Fisher's success in the fifties is described exhaustively.
His later career, planned comeback and problematical personal life are
discussed. The discography is complete and the index well constructed.

FLACK, ROBERTA

Born in Ashville, North Carolina, in 1939, Roberta Flack began playing the
piano at an early age and studied music at Harvard University. While teaching
in Washington in the mid sixties she played in clubs and accompanied opera
singers. In 1967 she left teaching and in 1969 signed a contract with Atlantic
Records. Her expressive, clear voice and jazz-influenced, slow, piano style
soon gave her comfnercial successes with singles as well as albums. She has
collaborated with jazz musician Donny Hathaway of late and although she is
regarded as a soul singer, her real achievement is that she has brought an
awareness of classical forms to popular music.

Jacobs, Linda
Roberta Flack: sound of velvet melting / by Linda Jacobs. – St. Paul,
Minnesota: EMC, 1975. – 37p.: ill., ports; 20cm. ISBN 0-88436-188-8
(cased). ISBN 0-88436-189-6 (pbk.)
Illustrated with excellent photographs, this is a brief, controlled-vocabulary
biography for a reading age of about ten, part of a series for American schools.
Well designed and produced, it is also available with an audio cassette.

Morse, Charles
Roberta Flack / text Charles and Ann Morse; illustrator Dick Brude. –
Mankato, Minnesota: Creative Education, 1974. – 31p.: ill. (some col.),
ports (some col.); 25cm. ISBN 0-8719-1396-8
Written for a reading age of about ten, this is a controlled-vocabulary biography in the series produced for American schools. It is a sensitive portrait,
suitable for the age range.

FLEETWOOD MAC

Formed in 1967 by Peter Green, John McVie and Mick Fleetwood (who had played together with John Mayall's Bluesbreakers), and later joined by Jeremy Spencer, Fleetwood Mac led the British blues movement of the late sixties. Their style has since then, however, continually changed as have the personnel of the band. In the late sixties they had a series of hit singles and albums mainly of Peter Green songs and even instrumentals. In 1971 Green finally left the group and John McVie's wife joined to play keyboards. After a series of different lead guitarists, in 1975 husband-and-wife team Lindsay Buckingham and Stevie Nicks joined to add their songwriting abilities as well as their voices. From then on Fleetwood Mac have had hugely successful record sales both of singles and albums, particularly in the USA, where they are the leading band in the AOR (adult-orientated rock) or soft rock style.

Carr, Roy
   Fleetwood Mac: rumours 'n' fax / by Roy Carr and Steve Clarke. – New
   York: Harmony Books, 1978. – 120p.: ill., ports; 22 x 28cm. Includes
   discography. ISBN 0-517-53364-2 (cased). ISBN 0-517-53365-0 (pbk.)
A well-arranged outline of the band's career in the context of their records, which are meticulously reviewed and interspersed with illustrations, press cuttings, anecdotes and biographical notes. There is a full discography of the recording work of every individual musician who has played with the band over its first ten years.

Graham, Samuel
   Fleetwood Mac: the authorized history / Samuel Graham. – New York:
   Warner Bros. Publications; Sire Books, 1978. – 104p.: ill., ports; 31cm.
   Includes discography. ISBN 0-89724-000-6 (pbk.)
Graham, Samuel
   Fleetwood Mac: the authorized history / Samuel Graham. – New York:
   Warner Books; distributed in the United Kingdom by New English Library,
   1978. – 175p.: ill., ports; 18cm. Includes discography. ISBN 0-446-89984-4
   (pbk.)
Although including identical illustrations and text, the first-listed edition is lavishly produced whereas the quality of the illustrations in the second is poor. This is a fair outline biography which discusses the records of the band and provides a full discography of the individual musicians who have constituted Fleetwood Mac, as well as the band itself.

FRAMPTON, PETER

Born in Beckenham, Kent, in 1950, Peter Frampton first reached prominence in 1967 as the singer and guitarist of the London pop group, the Herd. After being described as the 'face of '67' and a series of over-produced hits with the Herd, he emigrated to America and played first with Humble Pie and then

Peter Frampton's Camel. After moderate success in 1976 he released a live album which was the most successful record of that year in the USA and a world-wide top-selling hit. Since then he has achieved minor, but consistent, record sales.

Adler, Irene

Peter Frampton / by Irene Adler. – New York: Quick Fox, 1979. – 96p.: ill., ports; 26cm. ISBN 0-8256-3933-6 (pbk.)

Quite a good popular biography, well illustrated and informative, which describes Frampton's later career admirably but rather overlooks his ability as a songwriter.

Daly, Marsha

Peter Frampton / by Marsha Daly; edited by Barbara Williams Prabhu. – New York: Grosset & Dunlap, 1979. – 92p., 8p. of plates: ill., ports; 21cm. ISBN 0-44817-026-4 (pbk.)

Originally published: New York: Grosset & Dunlap, 1978.

A brief biography, slightly abridged from the earlier edition, this concentrates on Frampton's later career in the USA. There are lengthy quotations from interviews and some discussion of his musical influences and style.

Katz, Susan

Frampton!: an unauthorized biography / by Susan Katz; designed by Paul Gamarello. – New York: Jove Publications, 1978. – 190p.: ill., ports; 18cm. ISBN 0-5150-4603-5 (pbk.)

Covering Peter Frampton's earlier careers with the Herd and Humble Pie, as well as his solo successes in the late seventies, this is a sketchy biography with a good selection of photographs but little interesting comment.

FRAMPTON, PETER: FILMS

Sgt. Pepper's Lonely Hearts Club Band

Produced in 1978 by Robert Stigwood and directed by Michael Schultz, Sgt. Pepper's Lonely Hearts Club Band was a vehicle for the Bee Gees and Peter Frampton, with dozens of other stars in guest appearances. The soundtrack of Beatles' songs produced by George Martin is very poor. The overall effect is a very bad film, with no plot, no cohesion and embarrassing acting performances.

Edwards, Henry

Sgt. Pepper's Lonely Hearts Club Band / Henry Edwards. – London: Star Books, 1978. – 190p., 16p. of plates: ill.; 18cm. ISBN 0-352-30360-3 (pbk.)

Originally published: New York: Pocket Books, 1978.

The storyline of the film is described with the Beatles' lyrics and a few stills. A very bad tie-in, underlining the weakness of the film itself.

Stigwood, Robert
  The official Sgt. Pepper's Lonely Hearts Club Band scrapbook / by Robert
  Stigwood and Dee Anthony. – New York: Wallaby Pocket Books, 1978. –
  80p.: ill. (some col.), ports (some col.); 30cm. ISBN 0-671-79038-X (pbk.)
This lavishly produced book describes the action of the film using stills and goes
on to describe its making: a souvenir to recall a non-event.

FRANKLIN, ARETHA

Born in Detroit in 1942 into a family deeply involved in gospel music, Aretha
Franklin began singing in a Baptist choir as a child. At eighteen she began
singing blues and moved east to sign a contract with Columbia Records. After a
difficult period with Columbia, she moved to the more blues-and-soul-
orientated Atlantic Records, and immediately gained success. She became
known as 'Lady Soul' and later 'the Queen of Soul'. Her success has continued
because of her powerful voice and exceptional interpretation, although her
more recent records have tended to lack the dynamism and earthiness of her
early work.

Olsen, James T.
  Aretha Franklin / James T. Olsen; illustrator John Keely. – Mankato,
  Minnesota: Creative Education, 1974. – 31p.: ill. (some col.), ports (some
  col.); 25cm. ISBN 0-8719-1402-9
Written for a reading age of about ten for American schools this is a controlled-
vocabulary biography which is well illustrated and informative.

GARCIA, JERRY

Born in San Francisco in 1940, after a mixed early career heavily influenced by
bluegrass music Jerry Garcia formed the Grateful Dead in 1965. He was the
main writing force and a spectacular guitarist. His virtuosity is very much
underrated, probably because of his unpretentious presentation. He was a
leading figure of the acid-rock, psychedelic style of West Coast music and an
outspoken leader of the hippie movement.

(*See also* THE GRATEFUL DEAD.)

Garcia, Jerry
  Garcia: the Rolling Stone interview / by Charles Reich and Jann Wenner; plus
  a stoned Sunday rap with Jerry Charles and Mountain Girl. – San Francisco:
  Straight Arrow Books, 1972. – 252p.: ill., ports; 22cm. ISBN 0-87933-031-1
  (cased). ISBN 0-87933-030-3 (pbk.)
With a brief foreword by Jann Wenner and an introduction by Charles Reich,
these revealing interviews with Garcia offer an insight into both the music of

the Grateful Dead and the lifestyle and motivation of hippies. Often amusing, much of the idealism now seems sadly naive. Nevertheless, this is a rare look at a major figure.

GARFUNKEL, ART

(*See* SIMON AND GARFUNKEL.)

GARLAND, JUDY

Born in Grand Rapids, Michigan, in 1922, Judy Garland was the daughter of Frank and Ethel Gumm, both vaudeville performers. At the age of three she began singing with her parents and at twelve made her first film. In 1939 she made The Wizard of Oz and was established as a star. She is often credited with taking popular music into the concert hall, and the album of her performance at Carnegie Hall in 1961 sold well over one million copies. After poor health, unhappy marriages and problems with drugs and alcohol, she died in London in 1969. She was the mother of Liza Minnelli.

Deans, Mickey
  Weep no more, my lady: an intimate biography of Judy Garland / by Mickey Deans, her last husband, and Ann Pichot. – London: W. H. Allen, 1972. – 238p., 16p. of plates: ill., facsims, ports; 23cm. ISBN 0-491-00941-0
The pressures of stardom on one so young and the loss of a normal childhood are isolated as the reasons for her breakdowns and heavy drinking. That the end of her life was blissful is the expected conclusion from this particular author.

DiOrio, Al
  Little girl lost: the life and hard times of Judy Garland / by Al DiOrio. – London: Robson Books, 1975. – 298p.: ill., ports; 24cm. Includes discography, filmography and index. ISBN 0-903895-33-1
  Originally published: New York: Arlington House, 1973.
  Also published: New York: Woodhill, 1975.
A distinctly sensational account of her life. Judy Garland is portrayed as the victim of her ego and insecurity. There is little of her talent and much of her over-indulgence.

Edwards, Anne
  Judy Garland: a biography / Anne Edwards. – London: Constable, 1975. – 350p., 32p. of plates: ill., facsim., ports; 23cm. Includes discography, filmography and index. ISBN 0-09-461006-2
  Originally published: New York: Simon and Schuster, 1975.
The most sympathetic biography on this artist. The author conducted a great

number of interviews with her friends and associates, as well as studying existing printed sources. There is a collection of Judy Garland's poems and an excellent collection of photographs.

Finch, Christopher
    Rainbow: the stormy life of Judy Garland / by Christopher Finch; designed by Will Hopkins. – London: Michael Joseph, 1975. – 255p.: ill., ports; 27cm. Includes index. ISBN 0-7181-1439-6 (cased). ISBN 0-7181-1467-1 (pbk.)
    Also published: New York: Grosset and Dunlap, 1975.
A well-illustrated, journalistic biography, the facts of Judy Garland's career are all here with no analysis of her work. The author does not avoid the lurid aspects of her life but is relatively gentle in his approach.

Frank, Gerold
    Judy / Gerold Frank. – London: W. H. Allen, 1975. – xviii, 654p., 32p. of plates: ill., ports; 24cm. Includes index. ISBN 0-491-01735-9
    Also published: New York: Harper and Row, 1975.
By far the most extensive work on the artist. The author treats his subject with respect and provides a meticulously researched study. The standpoint is objective, occasionally even a little cold. but the result is a balanced portrait which avoids both sensation and sentimentality.

Morella, Joe
    Judy: the films and career of Judy Garland / by Joe Morella and Edward Z. Epstein. – London: Leslie Frewin, 1969. – 218p.: ill., facsims, ports; 29cm. Includes index. ISBN 0-09-100960-X
    Also published: New York: Citadel Press, 1970.
With a large collection of illustrations, including many stills from films, the author traces Judy Garland's career with care. There is an emphasis on her Hollywood days, but her later concert performances are well described. There is a refreshing lack of interest in her more decadent pursuits.

GENESIS

Genesis was formed at Charterhouse public school by Peter Gabriel, Tony Banks, Michael Rutherford and Anthony Philips. Early attempts to find an outlet for their songs were a failure. In 1969 they came to the attention of Jonathan King, who produced their first record for Decca, without success. They left Decca to join Charisma Records in 1970, and released their second album with little more interest being shown in them. During 1971 they began to develop a new, characteristic style with strong melodies and intriguing lyrics and a theatrical, often spectacular, stage presentation. The group also recruited drummer Phil Collins and guitarist Steve Hackett and went from strength to strength during 1973 and 1974 with large album sales and hugely successful concert tours. In 1976 Peter Gabriel, who for many symbolized Genesis, left and was replaced as vocalist by Phil Collins. Their success continued. In addition, both Gabriel and Collins have developed highly successful solo careers, both having had album and single successes. The group is now reduced to a line-up of three, but maintains a strong following and excellent stage show.

Gallo, Armando
  Genesis: I know what I like / story and photographs by Armando Gallo. – Los Angeles, California: D.I.Y., 1980. – 174p.: ill. (some col.), facsims, ports (some col.); 30cm. Includes discography an index. ISBN 0-283-98703-0 (pbk.)
  Originally published as '*Genesis: the evolution of a rockband*': London: Sidgwick & Jackson, 1978.
Well designed and beautifully produced, Genesis' history from their days at Charterhouse to 1979 is chronicled with an informative text and over three hundred photographs. Each member of the band's changing line-up has a section devoted to him with quotations from interviews and biographical details. The emphasis is on the development of the group's career and the changes in their presentation and personnel, rather than an analysis of the evolution of their music. The discography is complete and fully detailed with reproductions of the album-cover designs. The American version fully updates the earlier, British edition.

GENESIS: SONGS

Genesis
  Genesis lyrics / illustrated by Kim Poor; introduction by Jo Durden-Smith and Chris Welch. – London: Sidgwick & Jackson, 1979. – 100p.: ill. (chiefly col.), ports; 31cm. ISBN 0-283-98526-7 (cased). ISBN 0-283-98527-5 (pbk.)
Genesis' lyrics, always interesting and often complex, are interpreted here by beautiful paintings in vivid colour. Occasionally pretentious, more often the spirit of the song is perfectly captured.

GENESIS: DISCOGRAPHIES

Parkyn, Geoff
  Genesis: turn it on again / Geoff Parkyn. – London: Omnibus Press, 1984. – 125p.: ill., facsims, ports; 20cm. ISBN 0-7119-0442-1 (pbk.)
  Previously published: London: Omnibus Press, 1983.
A very detailed discography including all the manifestations of the band, as well as their solo efforts.

GERRY AND THE PACEMAKERS

Following the Beatles, Gerry and the Pacemakers were the second of Brian Epstein's groups to achieve national success. Gerry Marsden was born in

Liverpool in 1942. After learning to play the guitar while still at primary school, he began playing in a local skiffle group. After the demise of the skiffle craze, he formed a group with his brother, Freddy, on drums and bass player Les Chadwick. They were joined by Les Maguire, on piano, and began playing the Liverpool clubs. They had established themselves as local favourites before the Beatles were considered of any consequence, but it was not until the Beatles had established a national foothold that they were signed by Epstein. Their first single, written by Mitch Murray and rejected by the Beatles, was an immediate number-one hit. Between 1963 and 1966 they had a series of successful records but failed to adjust to the changing mood of the late sixties.

GERRY AND THE PACEMAKERS: PERIODICALS

(See section 8.2, GERRY AND THE PACEMAKERS.)

GLITTER, GARY

Gary Glitter was born Paul Gadd in Banbury, Oxfordshire; his age is a closely guarded secret. His early career was as Paul Raven, an unsuccessful solo singer during the fifties and sixties. In 1971 he changed his name to Gary Glitter and led the glitter-rock trend. He appeared wearing make-up, silver lurex costumes and boots with enormous platform soles. His outrageous attire and gyrating movements appealed both to the teenage fans on one level and to a different, amused audience attracted to his blatant parody. After a string of successful singles he retired in 1976 but was forced to make a comeback in 1980 because of financial troubles. He appears both in cabaret and as a cult figure in rock concerts.

Tremlett, George
   The Gary Glitter story / George Tremlett. – London: Futura Publications,
      1974. – 144p., 16p. of plates: ill., ports; 18cm. ISBN 0-8600-7094-8 (pbk.)
Written at the height of Gary Glitter's success and based on interviews with him and his associates, there is a brief outline of his earlier career. His opulent lifestyle and amusing approach to his music are well portrayed. There is a chronology of his musical career and a good selection of illustrations.

GODBOLT, JIM

Born in Battersea in 1922, after serving in the Royal Navy during the Second World War Jim Godbolt became manager of one of Britain's early traditional jazz bands, George Webb's Dixielanders. Later he became a successful band agent and promoter of jazz clubs and concerts. Eventually in the mid sixties he became involved with popular music and was agent for the Swinging Blue Jeans, a successful Liverpool group of the period.

Godbolt, Jim
  All this and 10% / Jim Godbolt. – London: Robert Hale, 1976. – 208p., 12p.
  of plates: ill., ports; 22cm. Includes index. ISBN 0-7091-5841-6
Although mainly concerned with the author's interest in jazz and his involvement in the British jazz movement of the fifties, this is a humorous look at the British music scene. It features people like George Melly and Mick Mulligan as well as the author's acquaintance with pop singers and entrepreneurs. Of particular interest is his personal involvement with the Swinging Blue Jeans' success. Written in his retirement with a sardonic, detached air, it is nevertheless an informative history of the growth of the influence of the popular-music business in Britain.

THE GRATEFUL DEAD

The Grateful Dead was formed by Jerry Garcia (born in San Francisco in 1942), who met Robert Hunter, the band's songwriter, at San Mateo College in 1959. Garcia began playing in clubs in the Bay area of San Francisco and it was here that he meet Bob Weir and Ron McKernan and became acquainted with Bill Kreutzmann. Garcia at this time was playing ethnic blues while the others were interested in rock. The direct antecedent of the Grateful Dead was Garcia's bluegrass band, Mother McCree's Uptown Jug Champions. Through a lack of following they gave up this style of country music and began playing electric blues, calling themselves the Warlocks, the original group being joined by Phil Lesh and Bill Sommers. They became heavily involved with Ken Kesey during the period documented in Tom Wolfe's *Electric Kool-Aid Acid Test*, in 1965, taking LSD and developing the style known as acid rock. They signed a contract with Warner Brothers in 1967 and began their successful recording career. Still regarded by many as the premier West Coast band, mainly for their live performances, their concerts were like rock festivals, putting forward a total idea of the Hippie lifestyle. After various changes in line-up the band reformed in 1977 and signed a new contract with Arista Records. Massively successful in the USA the Grateful Dead still have a cult following in Britain but have never achieved the same degree of commercial success. Their early, atmospheric acid rock has drifted into country rock and jazz-influenced styles but the musicianship, particularly of Garcia's guitar playing, is always superb.

(*See also* GARCIA, JERRY.)

Harrison, Hank
  The Dead / Hank Harrison. – Millbrae, California: Celestial Arts, 1976. –
  322p.: ill., ports; 20cm. Includes astrological charts. ISBN 0-89087-300-3
A detailed biography including considerable musical analysis. The preoccupation with astrology gives the book a curious slant and there is an appendix of full astrological charts of each of the Grateful Dead's musicians. The personal contribution of each member to the identity of the group and its musical styles is examined in depth.

Harrison, Hank
  The Grateful Dead / Hank Harrison. – London: Star Books, 1975. – 175p.,
  8p. of plates: ill., ports; 18cm. Includes discography. ISBN 0-352-30093-0
  (pbk.)
  Originally published as '*The Dead Book: a social history of the Grateful
  Dead*': New York: Links, 1973.
  Also published: New York; London: Flash Books, 1975.
An excellent, shorter biography of the Grateful Dead with details of the
individual members' early careers, their meeting and formation of the early
bands which would finally evolve into the Dead. There is a sensitive insight into
the Hippie movement and the LSD drug cult of the mid sixties. Their music is
not neglected, however, and its changes and developing styles are analysed
particularly well.

GUTHRIE, WOODY

Woody Guthrie was born Woodrow Wilson Guthrie in Okema, Oklahoma,
in 1912. After spending some time as a merchant seaman, he lived through
the Depression as a drifter and odd-jobman. He travelled with the hobos of
the period, singing and writing songs about the rural poor and the injustice
of the mid-Western landowners. He had a genius for presenting complex
political issues in simple terms, understandable to the people who were the
victims. His style embodied traditional folk, country tunes with harmonica
and simple guitar method. He was the idol and influence of such artists as
Bob Dylan, Phil Ochs, Tom Paxton, Pete Seeger, Donovan, Ry Cooder and
even Bruce Springsteen. His string of classic songs such as This Land is
Your Land, Pastures of Plenty and The Grand Coulee Dam, have become
anthems in the USA. He once said that he wrote his song Tom Joad after
he had read Steinbeck's novel, *The grapes of wrath*, for those who could not
afford to buy the book. He became the undisputed father of the protest
movement but achieved fame while dying of the hereditary disease, Hunting-
ton's chorea. He first entered hospital in 1954 and died in 1967. His son is singer
Arlo Guthrie.

Guthrie, Woody
  Bound for glory / Woody Guthrie; illustrated with sketches by the author. –
  London: Picador, 1974. – 320p.: ill.; 20cm. ISBN 0-330-24166-4 (pbk.)
  Originally published: New York: Dutton, 1943.
  First British edition: London: Dent, 1969.
A straightforward recollection, in which the author describes his childhood and
life in the Depression. Vivid and sometimes harrowing in its detail, his political
message is direct. In 1976 a film of the autobiography was released starring
David Carradine as Guthrie. His peformance was excellent and he was
nominated for an academy award. The film is an honest and touching tribute to
the book, the music and most important, the man himself.

Klein, Joe
　　Woody Guthrie: a life / Joe Klein. – London; Boston: Faber, 1981. – 476p.,
　　32p. of plates: ill., ports; 25cm. Includes index. ISBN 0-571-11736-8
Written from secondary sources by a regular contributor to *Rolling Stone* and
Esquire, this lengthy biography avoids idolatry and appears factual. Guthrie is
presented as a plain man with faults, often arrogant and prone to take
advantage of his friends, but still the father of the protest song. There is an
excellent collection of illustrations.

Yurchenco, Henrietta
　　A mighty hard road: the Woody Guthrie story / by Henrietta Yurchenco;
　　assisted by Marjorie Guthrie; introduction by Arlo Guthrie. – New York:
　　McGraw-Hill, 1970. – 159p.: ill., ports; 25cm.
A short personal biography written in close co-operation with Guthrie's widow
and with an introduction by his son. Not an in-depth study, but an interesting,
sensitive work.

GUTHRIE, WOODY: WRITINGS

Guthrie, Woody
　　Born to win / Woody Guthrie; edited by Robert Shelton. – New York:
　　Collier Books, 1967. – 250p.: ill.; 20cm. (pbk.)
　　Originally published: New York: Macmillan, 1965.
A collection of essays, prose poems, verse, journal notes, maxims, song lyrics,
letters and drawings, which shows a far more complex and intellectual charac-
ter than is displayed in his songs. Often intense, some pieces are harrowing and
others obscure.

Guthrie, Woody
　　Seeds of man: an experience lived and dreamed / Woody Guthrie. – New
　　York: Dutton, 1976. – 401p.; 24cm. ISBN 0-5251-9936-5
This is an autobiographical novel published some thirty years after it was
written, to coincide with the release of the film Bound for Glory. It tells of the
thirties, the dustbowls of mid-Western America, the dispossessed farmers and
their migrations. Atmospheric and rather long, it embodies the spirit of the
songs without the directness and immediacy.

HAIRCUT ONE HUNDRED

Haircut One Hundred was formed in summer 1980 in Beckenham, Kent, by
Nick Heyward, Graham Jones and Les Nemes. By late 1981 they were
established as the new idols of the early teenagers. Fresh boyish looks, profuse
smiles and innocuous but sometimes witty pop songs still seem to have their
place and a ready audience.

Haircut 100: not a trace of Brylcreem. – London: Mendura, 1982. – 36p.: ill. (some col.), ports (some col.); 28cm. ISBN 0-95080-770-2 (pbk.)

A poorly written account of the group's rise to fame with some unimpressive illustrations; an example of a publication contrived to meet a sudden demand.

Payne, Sally
    The Haircut One Hundred catalogue / by Sally Payne. – London: Omnibus Press, 1982. – 32p.: ill. (some col.), ports (some col.); 26cm.
    ISBN 0-7119-0112-0 (pbk.)

Brief notes from interviews by the press officer of Stiff Records, filled with smiling portraits, strictly for the screaming fan.

HALEY, BILL

Born in Detroit, Michigan, in 1925, Bill Haley began playing country and western music in his teens in the yodelling, cowboy style of the late forties. His group, the Four Aces of Swing, changed to Bill Haley and the Saddlemen and began to introduce rhythm & blues numbers into their act. Noting the favourable response, Haley evolved a style of music which combined elements of western swing with a constant, steady, up-tempo beat. The group's name changed again to the Comets and in 1951 he had his first record success and a second in 1953. He then joined the Decca label and gained more hits. In 1955, when his song Rock around the Clock was featured in the film Blackboard Jungle, he was established as the first star of rock'n'roll. He was always more popular in Britain than in America but his main problem was his stout physique and middle-aged appearance with a curious 'kiss curl' dangling on his forehead. He was soon deposed by Elvis Presley but refused to change his style and continued to have revivals throughout the sixties and seventies. Disillusionment led to heavy drinking and mental illness and in September, 1981, he died in Harlingen, Texas, mentally disorientated and alone. If he was not the greatest rock'n'roller, most people remember him as the first.

Swenson, John
    Bill Haley / John Swenson. – London: Star Books, 1983. – 174p., 8p. of plates: ill., facsims, ports; 18cm. ISBN 0-352-31303-X (pbk.)
    Originally published: London: W. H. Allen, 1982.

Amazingly the only biography on the artist. Swenson interviewed Haley's family, friends and colleagues; in addition, there is the transcript of an unpublished interview with Haley by Ken Terry and access was gained to his early diaries. The result is a sad story of a man confused by his position in popular music, lonely and destructive. The discography covers the period from 1948 to 1979 with full track listings and discographical detail. There is a collection of rare photographs, making this a useful, if not exceptional, work.

HALL, TOM T.

Born in Olive Hill, Kentucky, in 1936, Tom T. Hall learned to play the guitar at six and after leaving school at fourteen began playing on local radio when only sixteen. He worked as a disc jockey and then spent a period in the army, after which he returned to his radio station in 1961. In 1963 one of his early compositions became a major hit for country singer Jimmy Newman. This was followed by a series of successes for other artists until, in 1967, he achieved his first personal hit record. This was followed by an enormously successful, world-wide hit, Harper Valley PTA, sung by Jeannie C. Riley, which established him as a major country-music writer. He has failed to gain even the smallest personal success in Britain, possibly because his narrative tales are too American in theme, character and style. This is, perhaps, odd as it has not stopped other, lesser writers in the country-music genre.

Hall, Tom T.
   How I write the songs, why you can / Tom T. Hall. – New York: Chappell
   Music, 1976. – xi, 158p.: ill., facsims, ports; 24cm.
For those who know the songs of the author this songwriters' guide is also an interesting insight into his methods and inspirations. One of the most genuine pictures of the way in which a successful songwriter works.

Hall, Tom T.
   The storyteller's Nashville / Tom T. Hall. – Garden City, New York:
   Doubleday, 1979. – 221p., 10 leaves of plates: ill., ports; 22cm.
   ISBN 0-385-14690-6
Hall is often described as the Mark Twain of country music because of his narrative style: his band is named the Storytellers. An interesting autobiography of the artist giving the customary background to Nashville, its studios, promoters and radio shows, with some insight into Hall's songwriting.

HAMMOND, JOHN

Born of a wealthy family in New York in 1910, after classical music training at the Juillard, John Hammond joined Columbia Records. He began his successful association with Columbia supervising jazz recordings in the thirties and forties. He was involved with Benny Goodman and Duke Ellington and was responsible for bringing Billie Holiday to Columbia. In the early sixties he signed Pete Seeger and Aretha Franklin, and in 1961 he discovered Bob Dylan and produced his first album, although executives within the company described Dylan as 'Hammond's folly'. His incredible belief in his intuition continued into the seventies when he found and signed Bruce Springsteen. His unusual ability to spot talent and to produce it effectively has spanned four decades and still continues.

Hammond, John
   John Hammond on record: an autobiography / with Irving Townsend. –

Harmondsworth: Penguin Books, 1981. – 432p.: ill., ports; 20cm. Includes discography and index. ISBN 0-14-00-5705-6 (pbk.)
Originally published: New York: Ridge Press, 1977.

The bulk of this autobiography is concerned with Hammond's involvement in jazz in its golden age, but his later career and particularly his involvement with Bob Dylan and Bruce Springsteen is described in detail. He analyses the music of his artists, the development of recording technique and the changes in the music business. The discography of records he has produced is comprehensive and gives full discographical details. Overall this is a fascinating biography of one of the most significant figures in American popular music of the last fifty years.

HANSON, JOHN

Born John Stanley Watts in Oshawa, Ontario, Canada in 1922, he moved with his family to Scotland in 1928. He became interested in music and particularly light opera at an early age. He began studying singing seriously while working in the aircraft industry in Coventry in 1939 and began entertaining servicemen during the early forties. By the late forties he had graduated to performing professionally in musical shows with leading entertainers of the time. It was in the fifties that he began performing in light operas such as The Student Prince and The Desert Song. He was to become the leading singer in Britain in this field and even achieved a gold record in 1977. His most famous role, the Red Shadow in the The Desert Song, remains with him. He regularly appears on television and undertakes concert tours, singing a wide range of material.

Hanson, John
Me and my Red Shadow: the autobiography of John Hanson. – London: W. H. Allen, 1980. – 218p., 12p. of plates: ill., ports; 24cm. Includes index. ISBN 0-491-02359-6

A self-effacing autobiography giving an insight into British showbusiness of the last forty years. Many of the major entertainers are included with dozens of humorous anecdotes.

HARRISON, GEORGE

The youngest member of the Beatles and their lead guitar player, George Harrison was born in Liverpool in 1943. He influenced their style dramatically in the mid sixties as his growing interest in Indian philosophy and music began to show itself. He was not the first rock musician to use the sitar in a popular song but his influence made it widespread. He had written several songs for later Beatles' albums, but it was with their break-up in 1970, and the release of his own triple album, All Things Must Pass, that he showed himself to be a really creative writer in his own right. He has experimented with electronic music, started his own record company and made frequent guest appearances on other artists' albums as well as organizing the famous benefit concert for Bangladesh in 1971. Since the early seventies, however, he has failed to have the impact of his early solo efforts. He has continued to achieve fair commercial successes in the USA with his later albums but not in Britain.

(*See also* THE BEATLES.)

Michaels, Ross
> *George Harrison: yesterday and today* / by Ross Michaels. – London: Omnibus Press, 1982. – 80p. ill., ports; 25cm. Includes discography.
> ISBN 0-7119-0156-2 (pbk.)
> Originally published: London; New York: Flashbooks, 1977.

A superficial attempt to find Harrison's hidden secrets, this covers his Beatles and his solo career, but never attains any depth. There are many rare illustrations of the Beatles and quotations from interviews with Harrison. The breakup of the Beatles, his own legal affairs, his marriages and his ability as a guitarist are discussed superficially. The discography includes his work with the Beatles and includes detail of all his singles.

HARRISON, GEORGE: WRITINGS

Harrison, George
> *I Me Mine* / by George Harrison: with notes by Derek Taylor. – Guildford, Surrey: Genesis Publications, 1980. – 450p., 49p. of plates: ill. (some col.), facsims (some col.), ports (some col.); 24cm. Includes index.
> ISBN 0-904351-07-6

Published in a limited, signed edition of two thousand, this beautiful leatherbound work was priced at £164.00. The first section of the book consists of a preface describing how the book came about, with additional notes by Derek Taylor, the Beatles' press agent, who describes his involvement with Harrison in the mid sixties when they collaborated on a series of newspaper articles. There follows a brief biography of Harrison's sixties period followed by his thoughts on the influence of India upon him and his writing. After a collection of unique photographs, the second part of the book consists of the lyrics of eighty-three songs in both print and the original facsimile of his manuscript with doodles and notes on the meanings and stories behind the songs. This is an extraordinary example of fine book production which has already become a collector's item, not least because the limited edition of two thousand were signed.

Harrison, George
> *I Me Mine* / by George Harrison. – London: W. H. Allen, 1982. – 399p.: ill., facsims, ports; 24cm. Includes index. ISBN 0-491-02886-3

An unremarkable edition of Harrison's opus for the mass market, interesting but somehow even more pointless than the extravagant version.

HENDRIX, JIMI

Born in Seattle in 1942, Hendrix is regarded as a genuine virtuoso of the electric guitar. After being medically discharged from the US Paratroopers in 1963, he began working as a musician backing other black singers and it was in a club in Greenwich Village, New York, while backing Curtis Knight, that Hendrix was spotted by his manager-to-be, Chas Chandler. He brought Hendrix to London and formed a backing rhythm section, the Experience. In early 1967 he had his first hit single, immediately became a cult figure and was accepted by other guitarists, including Eric Clapton, to be a leading exponent. After making an appearance at the filmed Monterey Pop Festival he returned to the USA in triumph. His style, which began as a fusion of blues and psychedelic rock over which he drawled Dylan-like lyrics, evolved into something nearer avant-garde jazz. His record sales were enormous and continued throughout the seventies after his untimely death from a drink-and-drug overdose in September 1970. He changed the approach of electric-guitar players to their music by creating the sound produced not as an amplified acoustic guitar but something new and exciting. He was an early experimenter with electronic effects for use with the guitar and in his short four years at the top expanded the boundaries of rock music more than any other instrumentalist.

Henderson, David
    'Scuze me while I kiss the sky: the life of Jimi Hendrix / David Henderson. –
    New York: Bantam, 1981. – 416p.: ill., ports; 22cm. Includes discography
    and index. ISBN 0-553-01334-3 (pbk.)
    Originally published as *'Jimi Hendrix: voodoo child of the Aquarian age'*:
    New York: Doubleday, 1976.
A slightly abridged and retitled edition of the author's 1976 work, which is by far the most thorough biography of Hendrix. His well-known excesses are not avoided but are rightly treated as an aside with emphasis solidly on his songs, guitar technique and performance. His childhood, period in the army and his long apprenticeship with Curtis Knight, the Isley Brothers and lesser-known artists are all well covered with quotations from friends and colleagues. Perhaps including its share of idolatry, but in general one of the better biographies of a rock star; the title comes from one of his most successful songs, Purple Haze.

Hopkins, Jerry
    The Jimi Hendrix story / Jerry Hopkins. – London: Sphere Books 1983. –
    244p.: ill., ports; 25cm. ISBN 0-7221-4801-1 (pbk.)
    Originally published as *'Hit and run: the Jimi Hendrix story'*: New York:
    Putnam. 1983.
Not one of the author's better works or a particularly good attempt to look at this artist, Hopkins' approach is uncharacteristically superficial. There are some unusual illustrations and perhaps an almost redeeming feature is the information about Hendrix's childhood and his relationship with his father. But in short, this is a very disappointing biography.

Knight, Curtis
  Jimi: an intimate biography of Jimi Hendrix / Curtis Knight. – London: Star
  Books, 1975. – 223p., 8p. of plates: ill., ports; 18cm. Includes discography
  and index. ISBN 0-352-30047-7 (pbk.)
  Originally published: New York: Praeger, 1974.
  Also published: London: W. H. Allen, 1974.
Written by a musician with whom Hendrix played during his formative years
and with whom he sustained a friendship. The style is dull but the author writes
with authority on Hendrix's music, analysing each album in detail. There are a
few sensational anecdotes, but in general this is a good biography with a
detailed discography.

Nolan, Tom
  Jimi Hendrix: a biography in words & pictures / by Tom Nolan; edited by
  Greg Shaw. – New York: Sire Books; Chappell Music Company, 1977. –
  55p.: ill., ports; 30cm. Includes discography. (pbk.)
A superficial account of Hendrix's life, which is very sketchy about his early
career and time in the army. The discography includes most of the posthumous
albums. The illustrations are good, but this is an unworthy attempt.

Tarshis, Steve
  Original Hendrix / Steve Tarshis. – London: Wise Publications, 1982. – 64p.:
  ill., music, ports; 31cm. Includes discography. ISBN 0-7119-0015-9 (pbk.)
After an introductory appreciation of Hendrix's career, the author looks
specifically at his guitar style. There are profuse musical examples which
analyse his chord structures, solo styles and frequently used riffs. It is unlikely
that the artist would have understood a word of this analysis, but it is intriguing,
well written and impossible to copy.

Welch, Chris
  Hendrix: a biography / by Chris Welch; designed by Pearce Marchbank. –
  London: Omnibus Press, 1982. – 104p.: ill., ports; 26cm. Includes
  discography. ISBN 0-7119-0144-9 (pbk.)
  Originally published: London: Ocean Books, 1972.
  Also published: New York: Flash Books, 1975.
A well-illustrated, brief biography, this is surprisingly informative with tran-
scripts of interviews with a number of his musicians, friends and girlfriends.
The discography is complete but lacking in detail.

HOLLY, BUDDY

Born in Lubbock, Texas, in 1936, Buddy Holly's early influence was country
and western music. After playing at high-school dances, he made a series of
demonstration records between 1954 and early 1956. In mid 1956 he went to the
studio of Norman Petty, in Clovis, New Mexico, and with his group, the
Crickets, recorded a series of million-selling records. Petty was an early
innovator of multi-track recording and this, coupled with Holly's advanced

guitar style, made his sound distinctive. Many of Holly's own songs, lighter than the rock'n'roll of Elvis Presley, are now classics. On February 2nd 1959 he was killed in a plane crash after a concert at Clear Lake. His popularity grew after his death with vast record sales throughout the sixties. His influence can be heard in much of modern pop music. Paul McCartney now owns the rights to his songs and in 1977 a compilation album of his hits sold over a million copies in the United Kingdom alone.

Goldrosen, John J.
   Buddy Holly: his life and music / John J. Goldrosen. – St. Albans: Panther
   1979. – 258p., 16p. of plates; ill., ports; 18cm. Includes bibliography,
   discography and index. ISBN 0-586-04947-9 (pbk.)
   Originally published: Bowling Green, Ohio: Popular Press, 1975.
   Also published: London: Charisma Books, 1975.
On publication this was described by *Rolling Stone* as the best rock biography ever written. That may not be so, but it is an excellent study. Information about his recording sessions and guitar technique is fascinating. The discography is very detailed and the list of sources a fine guide to further reading.

Laing, Dave
   Buddy Holly / by Dave Laing. – London: Studio Vista, 1971. – 144p.: ill.,
   ports; 20cm. Includes discography. ISBN 0-289-70129-5 (cased).
   ISBN 0-289-70128-7 (pbk.)
   Also published: New York: Macmillan, 1972.
Laing's emphasis is artistic rather than biographical, offering an impressive analysis of Holly's work. His early work and influences are discussed in detail and his own legacy is intelligently placed in perspective.

Tobler, John
   The Buddy Holly Story / John Tobler. – London: Plexus, 1979. – 96p.: ill.,
   facsims, ports; 30cm. Includes discography. ISBN 0-85965-035-9 (pbk.)
Written to tie in closely with the film, The Buddy Holly Story, released in 1979, this is a superficial outline of Holly's career with no analysis of his work, but a section on his influence and legacy. Illustrations include original photographs as well as stills from the exceptionally good film.

HULL, ALAN

Alan Hull is the leader and main songwriter of the Newcastle group Lindisfarne. Formed in 1967, they became very successful in 1970 with the biggest-selling album in Britain for that year. In 1973 they split up and Alan Hull wrote and recorded two solo albums which greatly enhanced his status as a songwriter. He is yet to achieve real solo success but has a cult following. In 1978 the group reformed and released a successful album and single. They continue to work very much for a family audience.

HULL, ALAN: POEMS

Hull, Alan
   The mocking horse / Alan Hull. – London: Spice Box Books, 1973. – 64p.:
   ill.; 20cm. ISBN 0-85947-004-0 (pbk.)
A collection of poems without the expected Geordie themes or dialect words –
they are sensitive, intelligent and witty.

THE HUMAN LEAGUE

Formed in Sheffield, Yorkshire, in 1977, the Human League was an early
exponent of electronic-based pop music. After some early success, the original
line-up disbanded in 1979 leaving only Phil Oakey and Phil Wright to rebuild
their promising career. They added Ian Burden and Jo Callis on synthesizers
and Joanne Catherall and Suzanne Sulley on vocals. Martin Rushent, an
innovator in the use of programmed synthesizers, was brought in to produce
their records and during 1980 and 1981 they had a series of hits. They are now
established as an international attraction with their appeal based on strong,
melodic pop songs and a glamorous image. They were one of the groups to be
followed by the new romantics but their fans are now from a wide spectrum.

Nash, Peter
   The Human League / Peter Nash. – London: Star Books, 1982. – 143p., 4p.
   of plates: ill., ports; 18cm. Includes discography. ISBN 0-352-31151-7 (pbk.)
With some well-written analysis of the group's use of synthesizers and impec-
cable recording technique, this is an intelligent, readable account of their
career to date. The discography is complete with brief annotations.

Ross, Alaska
   The story of a band called the Human League / by Alaska Ross; photographs
   by Jill Furmanovsky. – London; New York: Proteus, 1982. – 32p.: ill. (some
   col.), ports (some col.); 27cm. Includes discography. ISBN 0-86276-103-4
   (pbk.)
A well-illustrated, but poor source of information on the group: the brief notes
avoid mention of their music and the discography lacks detail.

HUMPERDINCK, ENGELBERT

Englebert Humperdinck was born Arnold George Dorsey, in Madras, India, in
1936. In 1945 his family returned to Leicester. He began singing in local clubs at
the age of seventeen during his engineering apprenticeship and continued
during his national service. On leaving the army he had little success as a singer
until he was spotted by Gordon Mills, the manager of Tom Jones. Mills
changed his name from Gerry Dorsey to Engelbert Humperdinck and in 1967
his third record became a world-wide best seller. Thirteen hits followed until
late 1973. He followed Tom Jones to Las Vegas in 1968 and at one stage

seriously rivalled Jones as the top attraction with the over-thirties, female audience in America. He is a tall dark man whose powerful voice was far more suited to ballads than to up-tempo numbers and his main failing was his lack of versatility. He faded into wealthy obscurity in the late seventies but in 1981 attempted a comeback, this time called simply Engelbert. He continues to draw vast audiences on the international cabaret circuit and has also returned to an affectionate welcome in the clubs of northern England.

Short, Don
   Engelbert Humperdinck: the authorised biography / by Don Short. –
   London: New English Library, 1972. – 96p., 12p. of plates: ill., ports; 18cm.
   Includes discography. ISBN 0-450-01453-3 (pbk.)
The words 'a revealing portrait of one of the greatest singers of our time' which appear on the cover will give some idea of the kind of biography this is. Full of idolatry, sincere quotations and with an appendix of poems written by fans to Engelbert and a poem by him to them, this is a very poor example of a biography in any area of popular music. The illustrations are as bad as the text with poses that are unintentionally hilarious. The discography includes British releases with record numbers and lists the songs included on albums. There is even an appendix of the addresses of his forty-nine fan clubs throughout the world.

HUNTER, IAN

Born in Shrewsbury, allegedly in 1946 but probably much earlier, Ian Hunter was a founder member and vocalist of the group Mott the Hoople. Formed in 1969, the group had a slow start, finally achieving success in 1972 after recording a David Bowie song, All the Young Dudes. After becoming a major attraction in the USA in 1973, Hunter left the group in 1974. His brand of straightforward rock'n'roll with its simple lyrics and exciting arrangements was complemented by a flat vocal style not unlike Bob Dylan's. He has made three solo albums since leaving Mott the Hoople which have had little impact.

Hunter, Ian
   Diary of a rock'n'roll star / Ian Hunter. – St. Albans: Panther, 1974. – 159p.,
   8p. of plates: ill., ports; 18cm. ISBN 0-586-04041-2 (pbk.)
   Also published as *'Reflections of a rock'n'roll star'*: New York: Flash Books,
   1976.
In November and December 1972 after their first successful hit record, Mott the Hoople embarked on a five-week tour of the USA. This is a daily diary of the tour written at the time in hotel rooms, on buses and at airline terminals. It is not an account of high living or lurid tales of countless orgies but a down-to-earth description of travelling, meeting other musicians, the author's reaction to the group's performances and his day-to-day, seemingly ingenuous comments. It is the ordinariness of the lifestyle of the musicians that is the most remarkable aspect of the book but a second theme is the author's acceptance of his sudden success, always with the awareness of its frailty and imminent obscurity. An unusual, repetitive but revealing autobiography.

JACKSON FIVE (THE JACKSONS)

Originally called the Jackson Five, the Jacksons are five brothers born in Gary, Indiana, between 1951 and 1958. Joe Jackson, their father, was a guitarist in the Chicago group, the Falcons, and he encouraged his sons' musical interests. They turned professional in 1967 and in 1969 signed a recording contract with the Tamla Motown company. They were immediately successful and soon became Motown's top group. They left Motown in 1975 and signed with Epic Records and for contractual reasons changed their name. There was some suspicion in the early seventies that the Jacksons were simply a fabricated, black version of the Osmonds. This was totally false, however, as although young, the family were good musicians with an excellent stage sound. Michael Jackson's recent enormous success has made the group a leading contemporary act as his support.

(*See also* JACKSON, MICHAEL.)

The Jackson Five. – Hitchin: B. C. Enterprises; New English Library, 1972. –
    24p.: ill. (some col.), ports (some col.); 30cm. ISBN 0-9038-3500-2 (pbk.)
Well produced with some vividly coloured portraits, this is a quality publication for the pre-teenage fan of the Jacksons.

Manning, Steve
    The Jacksons / by Steve Manning; photographs by Kwarne Brathwaite. –
    Indianapolis: Bobbs-Merrill, 1977. – 64p.: ill., ports; 20cm.
    ISBN 0-672-52148-2 (pbk.)
    Originally published as '*The Jackson Five*': Indianapolis: Bobbs-Merrill, 1976.
Well illustrated with some exceptional photography, this brief look at the Jacksons is at the time of their establishment as adult artists. The text is brief but informative.

Morse, Charles
    Jackson Five / text Charles and Ann Morse; illustrator John Keely. –
    Mankato, Minnesota: Creative Education, 1974. – 31p.: ill. (some col.),
    ports (some col.); 25cm. ISBN 0-8719-1389-5
A controlled-vocabulary text written for a reading age of around ten for American schools, this is well illustrated with an informative text focussing on the Jackson Five's Tamla Motown period, before they emerged as a mature funk band in the late seventies.

Pitts, Leonard
    Papa Joe's boys: the Jacksons' story / Leonard Pitts, Jr. – Cresskill, New
    Jersey: Sharon Publications, 1983. – 96p.: ill., ports; 29cm. Includes
    discography. ISBN 0-89531-037-6 (pbk.)
A surprisingly full history of the Jackson family, packed with interesting photographs and hard information. The discography is complete with notes and full details.

JACKSON, MICHAEL

Born in August 1958, as early as 1972 Michael had begun to have solo hits on both sides of the Atlantic. In 1977 he starred in the film, The Wiz, an updated version of the classic, The Wizard of Oz, and during the following year he had a hit album, Off the Wall. It was with the album Thriller, released at the end of 1982, that he was suddenly established as the most exciting new phenomenon around. The album not only spawned some excellent singles, but the song, Thriller, was also the basis for a remarkably innovative and sophisticated video film. An accomplished singer and an excellent dancer, Michael Jackson is a painfully shy, curiously childlike, private person who has paid a great deal for his success. Thriller is reputed to be the fastest selling, most commercially successful album to date and it is obvious that Michael's potential is a long way from being fully realized.

Bego, Mark
   Michael!: the Michael Jackson story / Mark Bego. – London: Zomba Books,
   1984. – 128p.: ill., ports; 18cm. ISBN 0-946391-39-4 (pbk.).
   Originally published: New York: Pinnacle Books, 1984.
Written by the editor of the American magazine, *Modern Screen*, this is based on interviews with a number of well-known friends of the subject including Quincy Jones and Diana Ross. Quite informative, with some good photographs, but in general this is not an exciting attempt.

Brown, Geoff
   Michael Jackson: body and soul: an illustrated biography / Geoff Brown. –
   London: Virgin Books, 1984. – 128p.: ill. (some col.), ports (some col.);
   28cm. ISBN 0-86369-027-0 (pbk.)
With a fine collection of illustrations, this is a well-written, straightforward account of Michael's career from his singing with his brothers at the age of eleven. Brief, but the best effort to date.

George, Nelson
   The Michael Jackson story / George Nelson. – Sevenoaks, Kent: New
   English Library, 1984. – 128p., 16p. of plates: ill., ports; 18cm. Includes
   discography and filmography. ISBN 0-456-05751-8 (pbk.)
   Originally published: New York: Dell, 1984.
Poorly produced, this is a rambling, episodic account of the artist's career with no evident understanding of his real talent and no attempt at analysis. The discography is complete including all the work of the Jacksons and the filmography includes videos.

Magee, Doug
   Michael Jackson / by Doug Magee. – London; New York: Proteus, 1984. –
   64p.: ill. (some col.), ports (some col.); 27cm. Includes discography.
   ISBN 0-86276-238-3 (cased). ISBN 0-86276-237-5 (pbk.)
Quite well written and beautifully illustrated, this is a straightforward and factual brief biography. The discography is complete and detailed.

The magic of Michael Jackson. – London: Omnibus Press, 1984. – 66p.: ill.
  (chiefly col.), ports (chiefly col.); 28cm. ISBN 0-7119-0482-0 (pbk.)
With the transcript of some brief interviews and a random collection of facts
this is basically a collection of smiling portraits.

Michael in concert / text written by Phyl Garland. – London: Pan Books, 1984.
  – 62p.: chiefly col. ill., music, col. ports; 34cm. ISBN 0-330-28651-X (pbk.)
A very large-format collection of action photographs in beautifully printed
colour. It includes the words and music of a few songs and a very brief text
about Jackson concerts.

Michael Jackson. – London: Omnibus Press, 1984. – 36p.: chiefly col. ill., col.
  ports; 30cm. Includes discography. ISBN 0-7119-0479-0 (pbk.)
Tracing Michael Jackson's career in the form of photographs back to the days
of the Jackson Five, there is a useful chronology and a fold-out poster.

Michael Jackson fact file and official lyric book. – London: Omnibus Press,
  1984. – 36p.: ill. (chiefly col.), ports (chiefly col.); 30cm. ISBN 0-7119-0513-4
  (pbk.)
Some more smiling portraits, a pot-pourri of information and the lyrics of some
of Michael's best-known songs are well presented.

Regan, Stewart
  Michael Jackson / by Stewart Regan. – Guildford, Surrey: Colour Library,
  1984. – 64p.: chiefly col. ill., ports (chiefly col.); 30cm. ISBN 0-86283-189-X
A beautifully produced collection of mainly coloured portraits of Michael with
some good action shots.

JAGGER, MICK

Mick Jagger was born in Dartford, Kent, in 1943. His father was a physical
education lecturer at Avery Hill College in Eltham, Kent. After studying
briefly at the London School of Economics, Mick Jagger left to become a
founder member of the Rolling Stones. Always the front man, he is the co-
writer of all of the group's songs, with Keith Richards. His importance to rock
music is his development of an exciting, arrogant stage act and larger-than-life
persona which has kept him in the public eye for almost twenty years. His chic
lifestyle, numerous relationships with the world's most desirable women and
his marriage and divorce from his former wife, Bianca, have all contributed to
the image. He remains one of the most important figures in popular music and
an underrated songwriter.

(*See also* JONES, BRIAN; RICHARDS, KEITH; THE ROLLING STONES.)

Dowley, Tim
  Mick Jagger and the Stones / by Tim Dowley. – Tunbridge Wells, Kent:
  Midas Books, 1982. – 152p.: ill., ports; 22cm. ISBN 0-85936-234-5

Focussing on Jagger as the charismatic leader, innovator and creative force behind the Stones, this is a good attempt to survey his career in a serious, analytical way. His love of money is gently referred to, but this is a pro-Jagger biography with an avoidance of Jagger's usual 'Lucifer' image.

Jagger, Mick
   Mick Jagger in his own words / compiled by Miles; designed by Pearce
   Marchbank and Sue Trilton. – London: Omnibus Press, 1982. – 128p.: ill.,
   ports; 26cm. ISBN 0-86001-930-6 (pbk.)
A collection of quotations from throughout Jagger's career: they evolve from the rebellious, to the outrageous and finally to his more recent, world-weary, dilettante-Englishman stance. They are arranged broadly by subject.

Marks, J.
   Mick Jagger: the singer, not the song / J. Marks. – London: Abacus, 1974. –
   156p., 32p. of plates: ill., ports, 20cm. ISBN 0-349-12288-1 (pbk.)
   Originally published: New York: Curtis Books, 1973.
A well-illustrated, personal account of Jagger's life, performances, lifestyle and backstage activities. Not a good biography, being too subjective and probably including a good deal of imaginative material, it does, however, give a strong impression of his powerful charisma.

Scaduto, Anthony
   Mick Jagger / Anthony Scaduto. – St. Albans: Mayflower, 1975. – 290p.,
   24p. of plates: ill., ports; 18cm. ISBN 0-583-12302-3 (pbk.)
   Originally published as '*Mick Jagger: everybody's Lucifer*': New York:
   David McKay, 1974.
   Also published: London: W. H. Allen, 1974.
Scaduto had already written his enthusiastic work on Bob Dylan when he turned his attention to Jagger. His attitude to his new subject was certainly not that of an admirer. From the outset, it is Jagger's egocentricity, which results in his poor relationships with associates and friends, that is the theme. In particular, his treatment of Brian Jones, founder member of the Stones and regarded by many as by far their most talented musician, is pursued at length. The author did not interview his subject in the preparation for the book and relied heavily on information gleaned from the press and interviews with an assortment of former girlfriends, acquaintances and colleagues. Scaduto admits that some of the detail is fictional, as is the case with much popular biography, but one must observe that he seems at all times prepared to accept the very worst view of situations and interpretation of facts. At the time of publication this was the most outspoken, critical biography of a popular singer. In this respect it has been surpassed, but it remains an entertaining study, if totally biased.

Schofield, Carey
   Jagger / Carey Schofield. – London: Methuen, 1983. – 248p., 20p. of plates:
   ill., ports; 24cm. Includes bibliography and index. ISBN 0-413-51580-X
Avoiding a sensational approach, a difficult job when dealing with this subject,

the author depicts Jagger as one who has been able to live the life of an adolescent into manhood. Brian Jones is seen as an arrogant character and not the victim of Jagger's ego, which is the usual attitude. The background to the British blues scene of the late fifties and early sixties has been very well researched. A good, factual biography; those viewing it with prurient expectation will be disappointed.

JAGGER, MICK: FILMS

Ned Kelly

In 1970 Mick Jagger acted in the starring role of Tony Richardson's film, which was the story of a notorious, armour-wearing Australian bandit. It was neither a critical, nor a box-office success. Jagger's Irish accent was hilarious.

Mick Jagger is Ned Kelly / photographs by Robert Whitaker. – London: Corgi
   Books, 1970. – 32p. of ill.; 28cm. ISBN 0-552-98490-6 (pbk.)
A collection of stills from the film augmented by a few other photographs taken on the set; this is a rare but uninspiring book.

THE JAM

The Jam emerged from Woking, Surrey, in 1976, as one of the many London-based new-wave groups. With Paul Weller, guitar, Bruce Foxton, bass, and Rick Buckler, drums, they produced a sound reminiscent of the early Who. This similarity extended beyond their music and their stage image developed into the 'mod' look of the mid sixties. Weller's lyrics were abrasive and politically inspired, as with many of the punk groups of the period, but they do not fall into the punk category as the Jam's music, and particularly the quality of the songs, always possessed a strong element of sophistication. They signed a contract with Polydor in February 1977 and released their first, excellent album the following May. From then on they became the most successful of the British new-wave groups with a series of top-selling albums and singles. After a farewell tour of Britain at the end of 1982, the group decided to divide with a single at the top of the charts. In 1983 Paul Weller reappeared with Style Council.

Honeyford, Paul
   The Jam: the modern world by number / Paul Honeyford. – London: Eel Pie,
   1980. – 111p.: ill., ports; 26cm. Includes discography. ISBN 0-906008-22-0
   (pbk.)
A large-format account of the group's career with a substantial, intelligent text, this makes a serious effort to set the Jam's music and Weller's songs in the context of their being a natural development of the English rock tradition.

Honeyford, Paul
The Jam: the modern world by number / Paul Honeyford. – London: Star
Books, 1982. – 125p., 4p. of plates: ill., ports; 18cm. Includes discography.
ISBN 0-352-31135-X (pbk.)
With much the same text as the earlier, large-format work, this is updated to
include their successes of 1981. The excellent illustrations have been cut to a
minimum.

Miles
Jam / text by Miles; art direction Perry Neville; design Andy Morton. –
London: Omnibus Press, 1981. – 32p.: chiefly ill., ports; 27cm.
ISBN 0-86001-800-8 (pbk.)
The brief text, selected quotations and extracts from press articles offer very
little real information. The illustrations are, however, well chosen and will
delight the fan.

Nicholls, Mike
About the young idea: the story of the Jam 1972–1982 / Mike Nicholls. –
London; New York: Proteus, 1984. – 126p.: ill. (some col.), ports (some
col.); 28cm. Includes discography. ISBN 0-86276-177-8 (cased).
ISBN 0-86276-176-X (pbk.)
A brief history of the Jam from inception to demise. Weller's writing is
discussed in a limited way. The illustrations are good and the discography
complete and detailed.

JAPAN

Japan was formed in southeast London in 1974. David Sylvian, Mick Karn,
Richard Bardieri and Steve Jansen began playing at the end of the British glam-
rock period, modelling themseles very much on the New York Dolls. Even
before making their first record in 1977, however, they had transformed into a
synthesizer-based band more inspired by early Roxy Music. They were joined
by guitarist Rob Dean for their first album which, with its two immediate
successors, failed to find success in Britain but gained some acclaim in Europe.
In 1981 they moved from the Ariola record label to Virgin and, at last, achieved
the kind of success they had long promised. Their overtly glamorous image,
particularly that of David Sylvian, their innovation in composition and their
accomplishment as musicians have given them a wide appeal. After a period of
uncertainty followed by almost assured massive success, by the end of 1982
they had decided to complete a major tour and part company.

Pitt, Arthur A.
A tourist's guide to Japan / Arthur A. Pitt. – London; New York: Proteus,
1981. – 32p.: ill. (some col.), ports (some col.); 30cm. Includes discography.
ISBN 0-86276-172-7 (pbk.)

This book has a brief, but informative, text which includes many quotations from the group concerning the evolution of their musical style, and the illustrations are well produced and beautifully posed. Unusually for such a small publication there is much emphasis on the group's writing.

JEFFERSON AIRPLANE

The Jefferson Airplane was formed in 1965 in San Francisco by Marty Balin, Paul Kantner and Signe Anderson, who were joined originally by Skip Spence and Jack Casady. They were not musically very adept at the beginning, but their enthusiasm and empathy with the Hippie community of Haight Ashbury soon earned them a local following. They were one of the first San Francisco groups to sign a major recording contract. In 1966 singer Signe Anderson was replaced by Grace Slick and jazz drummer Spencer Dryden took over from Skip Spence, who left to form Moby Grape. Grace Slick brought to the Airplane an unusual, powerful voice and a real songwriting talent. In 1967 their album, Surrealistic Pillow, established them as the leading acid-rock band on the West Coast. Their style, which was originally described as folk rock, began to emerge as a fusion of jazz, folk, blues and rock, with unusual guitar parts and complex harmonies and lyrics laced with drug references.

A succession of successful albums followed, growing ever more political, reflecting the radical politics of the period, but by 1969 the Hippie culture of San Francisco and its mood had faded. Balin left the group in 1970 and Slick and Kantner recorded their own album. Casady and guitarist Jorma Kaukonen formed Hot Tuna. Airplane albums became more and more self-indulgent and by 1974 the group no longer existed. In that year Slick and Kantner formed Jefferson Starship which, after a successful tour reproducing old Airplane songs and solo efforts, has produced a series of successful albums of new material. Jefferson Airplane never really achieved the popularity in Britain they have in America, but are critically regarded as one of the outstandingly creative bands of the sixties and, to a lesser extent, the seventies.

(*See also* SLICK, GRACE.)

Gleason, Ralph J.
   The Jefferson Airplane and the San Francisco sound / Ralph J. Gleason. –
   New York: Ballantine Books, 1969. – 340p.: ill., ports; 19cm. (pbk.)
Gleason was a jazz critic for the *San Francisco Chronicle* before becoming interested in rock music in the sixties. He believes that rock is the expression of the 'youth revolution' and he sees the Jefferson Airplane as the prime example of the movement. The main substance of the book is a series of rambling interviews with members of the band concerning such issues as drugs, Vietnam and 'straight society'. He is in passionate sympathy with their radical political stance. The book is regarded by many as an important impression of one side of American society in the late sixties, though much is lost in the poorly edited text. It is, nevertheless, a frequently cited and well-regarded work.

JENNINGS, WAYLON

Born in Littlefield, Texas, in 1937, Waylon Jennings began playing the guitar in his early teens and played bass for Buddy Holly until Holly's death in 1959. After playing around Phoenix, Arizona, he signed a contract with RCA in 1965. Concerned with the rigid control imposed by RCA's hierarchy on their country artists and particularly with the formula sound of the Nashville session musicians and studios, he negotiated his own arrangements, allowing him to use his band and influence his production. His choice of songs talked not of the comfortable world associated with Nashville but were harder, disillusioned and couched in 'outlaw' imagery far more slanted towards rock. Indeed with Willie Nelson, Jessi Colter and Tampall Glaser, he has become a leader of the outlaw movement within contemporary country music.

Allen, Bob
  Waylon and Willie / Bob Allen, – New York: Flash Books, 1979. – 128p.: ill., ports; 26cm. Includes discographies. ISBN 0-8256-3941-7 (pbk.)
Brief biographies of the two leading outlaws. This is not a big enough book to do justice to such important artists, but is still quite useful.

JOEL, BILLY

Born in the Bronx, New York, in 1949, Billy Joel began studying the piano at the age of seven. In 1964 he began playing in rock groups and occasionally working as a session musician, without much success. In 1970 he decided to work as a solo performer, writing his own material and playing in small clubs. After four marginally successful albums, in 1977 he finally had a big hit with his album The Stranger. There followed several successful singles and another hit album and by the end of 1978 he was established as one of America's leading singer-songwriters. It is his wide appeal both to middle-of-the-road and rock audiences that ensures his continued success. His songs have been recorded by numerous other artists and he views himself primarily as a songwriter.

Gambaccini, Peter
  Billy Joel: a personal file / by Peter Gambaccini. – New York: Quick Fox, 1979. – 128p.: ill., ports; 26cm. Includes discography.
  ISBN 0-8256-3940-9 (pbk.)
A well-illustrated, matter-of-fact biography. There is no idolatry, no sensationalism, simply a straightforward description of Joel's life and work with a central theme of his being an example of hard work and talent eventually paying off.

JOHN, ELTON

Born in Pinner, Middlesex in 1947, as Reg Dwight, Elton John played in a soul group, Bluesology, on leaving school at sixteen. The group was spotted by the blues singer Long John Baldry and became his regular backing group unitl 1968. After the break-up from Baldry, Elton answered an advertisement in the *New Musical Express* and was given a collection of the lyrics of Bernie Taupin, another hopeful who had answered the ad. After composing songs from the lyrics, Elton and Taupin began working for Dick James Music, attempting to write pop songs for other artists. In 1969, however, Elton recorded one of their songs himself and in 1970 he finally had record successes in England with a single and albums. In late 1970 Elton broke through in the USA and his success then continued throughout the seventies. His distinctive voice, melodic piano playing augmented by good arrangements of tuneful, lyrically interesting songs have made him one of the richest pop stars ever. His style varies from gentle ballads to raucous rock'n'roll and although his original success was in the mode of a singer-songwriter, he is impossible to categorize. In 1977 he split with Bernie Taupin only for them to reunite in 1981 and although he continues to record, he spends a great deal of his energy on being chairman of Watford Football Club.

Gambaccini, Paul
  A conversation with Elton John and Bernie Taupin / by Paul Gambaccini. – London; New York: Flashbooks, 1975. – 112p.: ill., ports; 26cm. Includes discography. ISBN 0-8256-3063-0 (pbk.)
Gambaccini, Paul
  Elton John and Bernie Taupin / editor Paul Gambaccini. – London; Star Books, 1975. – 117p., 16p. of plates: ill., ports; 18cm. Includes discography. ISBN 0-352-30058-2 (pbk.)
Although the Flashbooks edition contains far more illustrations, these two formats are the same transcripts of interviews with Elton John and his lyricist. Amusing and open, the interviews are not deeply revealing, but do give some insight into the extravagant artist and his more retiring writer.

Jacobs, Linda
  Elton John: Reginald Dwight & Co. / by Linda Jacobs. – St. Paul, Minnesota: EMC, 1976. – 38p.: ill., ports; 20cm. ISBN 0-88436-188-8 (cased).
  ISBN 0-88436-189-6 (pbk.)
Well illustrated with some unusual photographs, this is a controlled-vocabulary biography written for a reading age of about ten for American schools. Very well designed and well produced, it is also available with an audio cassette.

John, Elton
  The Elton John tapes: Elton John in conversation with Andy Peebles. – London: BBC Publications, 1981. – 55p.: ill., ports; 20cm.
  ISBN 0-563-17981-3 (pbk.)
An interview made by BBC disc jockey Andy Pebbles for a radio broadcast is here reproduced in its entirety. Not particularly searching, with Elton as witty, yet cautious as ever, it is entertaining but not a good piece of journalism.

Newman, Gerald
  Elton John / by Gerald Newman with Joe Bivona; introduction by Henry
  Edwards. – London: New English Library, 1976. – 159p.: 18cm. Includes
  discography. ISBN 0-450-03235-3 (pbk.)
  Also published: Bergenfield, New Jersey: Signet Books, 1976.
Although based very much on previously published articles in the music press
and not on new sources, this is a thorough survey of Elton John's career,
containing a good deal of information about its business side. Each of his
albums is separately criticized and the contents described.

Shaw, Greg
  Elton John: a biography in words & pictures / by Greg Shaw. – New York:
  Sire Books; Chappell Music Company, 1976. – 56p.: ill., ports; 30cm.
  Includes discography. (pbk.)
A brief but well-illustrated and informative biography with some good analysis
of Elton John's songwriting. The discography is detailed but American.

Stein, Cathi
  Elton John / Cathi Stein. – London: Futura Publications, 1975. – 144p., 16p.
  of plates; ill., ports; 18cm. Includes discography. ISBN 0-86007-201-0
  (pbk.)
  Originally published: New York: Popular Library, 1975.
Covering Elton John's career up to 1973 and the establishment of his Rocket
Record Label, this is an idolatrous biography written originally for *Circus*
magazine and including good coverage of his early days. The author includes
quotes from numerous interviews and describes some of his American concert
performances in detail. The period covered does not include the recording of
the album Goodbye, Yellow Brick Road, probably Elton John's greatest
achievement, but it is thorough with, at times, some good analysis. The brief
discography includes American releases.

Tatham, Dick
  Elton John / Dick Tatham and Tony Jasper. – London: Octopus Books;
  Phoebus, 1976. – 92p.: chiefly ill. (chiefly col.), ports (chiefly col.); 31cm.
  Includes discography. ISBN 0-7064-0548-X (pbk.)
A collection of photographs of Elton, many displaying his more exaggerated
forms of stage dress, strung together with a readable, informative text. There is
a chronology summarizing his career, and a brief but complete discography.

Taupin, Bernie
  Elton: it's a little bit funny / text by Bernie Taupin, pictures by David Nutter;
  dedication by Elton John. – Harmondsworth: Penguin, 1977. – 144p.: ill.
  (some col.), ports (some col.); 28cm. ISBN 0-14-00-4680-1 (pbk.)
  Originally published: New York: Viking Press, 1977.
An account of his 1976, year-long tour which covered most of the world. The
text by his lyricist is intimate and amusing and the illustrations give an idea of
the size and complexity of such a tour.

Taylor, Paula
> *Elton John* / text Paula Taylor; illustrator John Keely; design concept Mark
> Landkamer. – Mankato, Minnesota: Creative Education, 1975. – 31p.: ill.
> (some col.), ports (some col.); 25cm. ISBN 0-8719-1457-3

Written with a controlled vocabulary for a reading age of about ten for
American schools, this is a brief, informative and well-illustrated biography.

JOHN, ELTON: SONGS

Taupin, Bernie
> *Bernie Taupin, the one who writes the words for Elton John: complete lyrics
> from 1968 through to Goodbye, Yellow Brick Road* / with an introduction by
> Elton John; illustrated by various hands; edited by Alan Aldridge and Mike
> Dempsey. – London: Cape, 1976. – 144p.: ill. (chiefly col.), facsims (chiefly
> col.), music, ports (some col.); 28cm. ISBN 0-224-01236-3 (pbk.)
> Originally published: New York: A. A. Knopf, 1976.

Bernie Taupin is unique as a non-performing lyricist in that he has always been
given a great deal of credit for Elton John's success and has become a celebrity
in his own right. This collection of lyrics includes his best work with amusing
illustrations. The range of his imagination and observation is a notable feature.
Few of the lyrics may aspire to poetry but they are, nevertheless, of the best in
their field.

JOHN, ELTON: DISCOGRAPHIES

Finch, Alan
> *Elton John: an illustrated discography* / by Alan Finch. – London: Omnibus
> Press, 1981. – 96p. – ill., facsims, ports; 20cm. ISBN 0-86001-926-8 (pbk.)

Including full details of British and American releases and some of the many
bootlegs, this is a thorough discography including information of track timings
and the musicians involved in each recording. There are some good illustrations and reproductions of album sleeves. The author briefly but intelligently
describes the mood and contents of each record and shows real understanding
of Elton's work.

JONES, BRIAN

Born in Cheltenham in 1942, Brian Jones left school at fifteen and began
playing the clarinet with local jazz musicians. By the age of sixteen his
notorious local reputation was greatly enhanced by his fathering two illegit-
imate children. He met Alexis Korner, father of the British rhythm & blues
movement, at a performance of Korner's Blues Incorporated band in
Cheltenham and subsequently moved to London and began playing at the
Ealing Blues Club where Blues Incorporated were the resident band. It was
here that he met Keith Richards, Mick Jagger and Charlie Watts. After playing

with them as part of various improvised bands, in June 1962 (billed as 'Brian Jones and Mick Jagger & the Rolling Stones') they supported Blues Incorporated on a radio broadcast and their own following began to grow. A fine guitarist, Brian Jones had a very real feel for the blues and was also to become an excellent blues harmonica player. He was probably the most musically creative member of the Rolling Stones, turning his hand to a range of other instruments.

None of his songs, however, was recorded by the Stones and tensions grew between him and Jagger. Unreliable, unpleasant and heavily dependent on a wide range of drugs, by 1969 he no longer wanted to perform in live concerts and on June 9th 1969 he left the group. On July 3rd he was found dead in the swimming pool of his house in Hartfield, formerly the residence of A. A. Milne. Mick Jagger quoted from Shelley in memorial of Jones before the group's famous free concert in Hyde Park. He was buried on July 10th with a coroner's verdict of misadventure. He was very much the archetypal rock star of the sixties and Rolling Stones fans will always debate his qualities and some will blame Jagger for his demise.

(*See also* JAGGER, MICK; RICHARDS, KEITH; THE ROLLING STONES.)

Aftel, Mandy
  Death of a Rolling Stone: the Brian Jones story / by Mandy Aftel. – London: Sidgwick & Jackson, 1983. – 205p.: ill., ports; 23cm. ISBN 0-283-98952-1 (cased). ISBN 0-283-98955-9 (pbk.)
  Originally published: New York: Delilah Communications, 1982.
The author is an American psychotherapist who was able to interview Keith Richards in the course of her research. She supports Jones against the victimization of Jagger, she overemphasizes his importance to the Stones and exaggerates his musical skills, considerable though they were. Her intimation that he might have been murdered finally makes this in general interesting, if one-sided, biography lose credibility.

JONES, GRACE

Born in Jamaica, the daughter of a clergyman, Grace Jones moved to Syracuse, New York, in her early teens. After high school, she began a career in modelling and moved to Europe for much of her work. She became involved in dance and later singing and brought to her music an unusual approach, with a strong emphasis on the visual image and startling presentation. Her imposing physical stature, curiously-cropped, masculine hairstyle and aggressive attitude give her a unique style. Her music is strictly aimed at the disco audience with a fusion of basically West Indian rhythms, black disco themes and sophisticated lyrical pretensions. She has released a series of albums and singles on the Island label, finally achieving a wider audience in 1981 with a hit album, Nightclubbing. In that year she played a season at London's Drury

Lane Theatre billed as a 'one-man show'. Criticized as superficial, the result of hype and unable to give a convincing live performance, she is an enigmatic figure of uncertain potential.

Goude, Jean-Paul

Jungle fever / Jean-Paul Goude. – London: Quartet, 1982. – 114p.: ill. (some col.), ports (some col.); 29cm. ISBN 0-7043-2339-7 (pbk.)

Photographer Jean-Paul Goude is art director of *Esquire* magazine. This collection of his photographs, mainly of Grace Jones, shows very clearly his obsession with his subject. The text explains this preoccupation with her as well as briefly outlining her career. The book is exciting but lacking in information.

JONES, TOM

Tom Jones's powerful voice, developed in the local choir, made this coal-miner's son a popular entertainer in South Wales clubs. In 1964, he was spotted by Gordon Mills, who became his manager, took him to London and secured a recording contract. By 1965 he had a number-one hit single with an up-tempo pop song, It's Not Unusual. From then on his aggressive, macho stage act, sensual poses and open-chested shirts, as well as his fine voice, gave him a series of hit singles in the late sixties and made him the toast of the Las Vegas cabaret throughout the seventies. He remains one of the truly international stars.

Jones, Peter

Tom Jones: biography of a great star / by Peter Jones. – London: Barker, 1970. – 161p., 24p. of plates: ill., ports; 23cm.
Also published: Chicago: Regnery, 1970.
ISBN 0-213-00247-7

A 'rags-to-riches' biography in the classic style, there are a few interesting recollections of his early years and many poorly posed photographs. The quotations seem contrived throughout and Jones is presented in a thoroughly artificial way with a mid-Atlantic accent and worldly-wise banalities.

JOPLIN, JANIS

Born in 1943, in Port Arthur, Texas, at an early age Janis Joplin became interested in Bessie Smith and Leadbelly and she began singing country and blues music in 1960. In 1961 she worked in Austin, Texas and in 1962 she moved to San Francisco. After a short spell at the University of Texas, she returned to San Franciso in 1966 and became the lead singer with Big Brother and the Holding Company. The group gained a large following but when they appeared at the Monterey Pop Festival in August 1967 Janis immediately became a star. Her powerful, hoarse voice and frantic stage performance covered her deep personal loneliness and insecurity. As her standing grew she signed a management contract with Albert Grossman and by the end of 1968 she had left the group. Her commercial success continued in the USA but never occurred in Britain. In October 1970 she was found dead in her Hollywood hotel room, the result of a heroin overdose. Her outrageous lifestyle, heavy drinking and erratic behaviour made her performances either brilliant experiences or tragic spectacles – they were rarely mediocre. She remains a female legend in the long list of rock music's victims.

Caserta, Peggy
    Going down with Janis / Peggy Caserta; as told to Dan Knapp. – London:
    Futura Publications, 1976. – 276p.; 18cm. ISBN 0-8600-7231-2 (pbk.)
    Originally published: Secaucus, New Jersey: Lyle Stuart, 1975.
    Also published: London: Talmy Franklin, 1975.
This is the autobiographical account of the period when Peggy Caserta was the lover of Janis Joplin. This corresponds with her rise to stardom and eventual tragic overdose. It describes a sordid, outrageous lifestyle which often stretches one's credence but is, nevertheless, often captivating and very entertaining.

Dalton, David
    Janis / written and edited by David Dalton. – London: Calder and Boyars;
    New English Library, 1972. – 154p.: ill., facsims, ports; 28cm.
    ISBN 0-7145-0943-4 (pbk.)
    Originally published: New York: Simon and Schuster, 1972.
This is a collection of the author's own thoughts and writings as well as a well-edited selection of pieces by other journalists, of interviews, accounts of concerts and reviews of recording. It is sensitive, sympathetic and sad, with a superb collection of photographs which clearly show the extremes of Janis Joplin's personality.

Friedman, Myra
    Buried alive: a biography of Janis Joplin / Myra Friedman. – London: Star
    Books, 1975. – 284p., 8p. of plates: ill., ports; 18cm. ISBN 0-3523-0077-9
    (pbk.)
    Originally published: New York: Morrow, 1973.
    Also published: London: W. H. Allen, 1974.
Myra Friedman was a close friend and associate of Janis and worked in the office of Albert Grossman, her manager. This book contrasts with Peggy Caserta's account in being altogether less sensational and giving a more detailed background to her musical activities. It is well written, with some well-chosen photographs; Janis's warmth shines through the tough public image and is described with a gentle understanding of her complex, confused personality.

Landau, Deborah
    Janis Joplin: her life and times / Deborah Landau. – New York: Paperback
    Library, 1971. – 159p.: ill., ports; 18cm. Includes discography. (pbk.)
A well-written biography with a good selection of photographs; the author

avoids the more sensational aspects of Janis's life. She expresses both an enthusiasm for her subject as a performer and a sympathetic view of her life without really attempting to understand her self-destructive excesses.

KENNY

Signed by Mickie Most's record company, RAK, in 1973, Kenny appeared in the wake of the Bay City Rollers. They had one hit record in late 1974, three in 1975 and subsequently faded into obscurity. Their style was simple, catchy pop for the pre-teenager, an example of the teenybop trend.

Kenny annual 1977. – Manchester: World Distributors, 1976. – 77p.: ill. (some col.), ports (some col.); 25cm. ISBN 0-7235-0406-7

Appearing only once, reflecting the group's short life, this was aimed at the Christmas gift market. It is a collection of portraits, games and brief interviews for the pre-teenager.

KING, B. B.

Born Riley King in 1925 in Itta Bena, Mississippi, B. B. King had an impoverished childhood as the foster son of a sharecropper. He moved to Memphis and worked as a disc jockey and was nicknamed Blues Boy, B. B. He played guitar in his spare time with jazz and blues artists. He made his first record in 1951 and had a succession of blues hits throughout the fifties with his very clean, almost jazz style of guitar playing. In 1969 he made an album produced by Bill Szymczyk, the producer of the Eagles. One side was a live recording and the other a studio session with top session men. Finally, after being a major influence on the electric-guitar playing of top artists, B. B. suddenly became a major attraction himself. He continues to be the world's leading blues guitarist. He is superb showman but he cannot play rhythm guitar, only solos, and cannot sing while playing.

Sawyer, Charles
  B. B. King: the authorised biography / Charles Sawyer. – London: Quartet, 1982. – 288p., 16p. of plates: ill., ports; 21cm. Includes discography and index. ISBN 0-7043-3415-1 (pbk.)
  Originally published as '*The arrival of B. B. King*': Garden City, New York: Doubleday, 1980.
  Also published: New York: Da Capo, 1981; Poole, Dorset: Blandford Press, 1981.
Charles Sawyer, a freelance journalist and photographer, lived and toured with his subject over a period of twelve years. The result of his observations is an excellent biography which goes far beyond a simple description of B. B. King's career. There is an analysis of his background, the sociology of the American

southern states, the establishment of the blues as an influential art form and the influence of B. B. on other guitarists. The musical analysis is extensive and the cited sources of background materials impressive. The full discography includes unreleased tracks and covers 1949 to 1980. The photographs are extensive, giving a glimpse of life in the black southern states as well as portraits of the artist. There are unusual musical examples in explanation of his style.

KING, CAROLE

Carole King was born Carole Klein in Brooklyn, New York, in 1942. After a teenage interest in pop music she went to Queens College and met Gerry Goffin, who was later to become her husband. With him she wrote a string of successful songs during the early and mid sixties. They were to become the most successful American songwriting team and second only to Lennon–McCartney in the world. Carole made a hit record of her own in 1962 and another under the name of the Cookies. She was divorced from Goffin in 1965. She began playing with an obscure New York band, the City, and then moved to Los Angeles, appearing on the albums of other artists such as James Taylor. She was continuing writing at this time and in 1970 she released a solo album, Writer. She toured with James Taylor in 1971 and released a second album, Tapestry, which was immediately an enormous success and has become the fourth-biggest-selling album ever. She has continued to be a leader of the singer-songwriter movement, but is yet to repeat the quality of Tapestry. She remains, however, one of the most prolific writers in popular music.

Cohen, Mitchell S.
  Carole King: a biography in words & pictures / by Mitchell S. Cohen: edited by Greg Shaw. – New York: Sire Books; Chappell Music Company, 1976. – 55p.: ill., ports; 30cm. Includes discography. (pbk.)
A well-illustrated but brief survey of Carole King's career which does cover her early writing career with Gerry Goffin but concentrates on the singer-songwriter period of the seventies. Included is a list of her songs and the artists who recorded them, as well as a detailed discography.

Taylor, Paula
  Carole King / text by Paula Taylor; illustrator John Keely; design concept Mark Landkamer. – Mankato, Minnesota: Creative Education, 1976. – 31p.: ill. (some col.), ports (some col.); 25cm. ISBN 0-8719-1465-4
Written with a controlled vocabulary for a reading age of about ten aimed at American schools, this is a brief but informative and well-illustrated biography.

KING, CAROLE: SONGS

King, Carole
  You've got a friend: poetic selections from the songs of Carole King / edited by

Susan Polis Schutz; with illustrations by Stephen Schutz. – Boulder,
Colorado: Blue Mountain Press, 1978. – 61p., ill., ports; 22cm.
ISBN 0-88396-030-3 (pbk.)
A collection of Carole King's most beautiful lyrics are interpreted by a
collection of illustrations which add very little.

THE KINKS

Formed in London in 1964 by Ray Davies, Dave Davies, Mick Avory and Pete
Quaife, the Kinks began playing rhythm & blues. Ray was still at Hornsey Art
School when they signed their contract with Pye, but it was not until their third
release, You Really Got Me, produced by Shel Talmy, that they made an
impact. This became a top seller in Britain, reached the American charts and
has become a classic, often cited as the first heavy-metal record. After a
succession of similar-sounding records, in late 1965 their style changed to a very
English sound, with satirical lyrics and its roots deeply in the music hall. By
1967, Ray Davies was writing collections of songs which formed concept
albums. These initially were difficult for the British audience to accept but by
the early seventies the group's popularity had consolidated in America with
works discussing such subjects as the power structure in the music industry and
the manipulation of the mass media. Davies saw their future as being in the
USA and with growing record successes and even more successful concert
tours, by 1980 the Kinks were more popular than ever.

Their current musical style is far harsher, almost reverting to the sound of the
mid sixties; it is nevertheless well played with much character and the same
biting wit. The group is still very much fronted by Ray Davies with Dave Davies
on lead guitar, original drummer Mick Avory, Jim Rodford on bass and Ian
Gibbons on Keyboards.

Rogan, Johnny
 The Kinks: a mental institution / Johnny Rogan. – London; New York:
 Proteus, 1982. – 128p.: ill. (some col.), ports (some col.); 27cm. Includes
 discography. ISBN 0-86276-065-8 (cased). ISBN 0-86276-064-X (pbk.)
Surprisingly the first work to appear on such an important group; the author
knows his subject but the format fails to do it justice. A good collection of
illustrations is complemented by a straightforward, informative text which
lacks any real interpretation or depth. The discography is complete but lacking
in detail.

Rogan, Johnny
 The Kinks: the sound and the fury / Johnny Rogan. – London: Elm Tree
 Books, 1984. – 242p.: ill., ports; 24cm. Includes index. ISBN 0-241-11307-5
 (cased). ISBN 0-241-11308-3 (pbk.)
This is the first substantial biography of the group to appear. Rogan's rock
biographies improve with each publication. Well researched with extensive
interviews with musicians who have played with the group over the years,

managers, friends and associates, this is a very direct history of the Kinks' career. The competitive nature of the relationship between Dave and Ray Davies is discussed at some length and the author makes a real attempt to delve into Ray's extraordinarily diverse songwriting. The discography is excellent with full track details and includes some bootlegs.

Savage, Jon
> *The Kinks: the official biography* / Jon Savage. – London: Faber, 1984. – 176p.: ill., ports; 27cm. Includes discography. ISBN 0-571-13379-7 (cased). ISBN 0-571-13407-6 (pbk.)

Although based on extensive interviews with members of the group, this is not a brilliantly written biography but it is revealing and does have a very personal feel about it. The illustrations, of which there are about one hundred, have been well selected and many are unique to this work.

Schruers, Fred
> *The Kinks: the story of a legend* / Fred Schruers. – London: Vermilion, 1984. – 192p., 8p. of plates: ill., ports; 24cm. Includes discography. ISBN 0-09-158561-9 (pbk.)

Concentrating heavily on Ray Davies and the development of his songwriting, this is a well-written biography which unfortunately fails to get close to the group as individual personalities. The photographs are very good.

KISS

One of the more bizarre exponents of heavy-metal rock, Kiss were formed in New York in 1973 with Ace Frehley, guitar, Paul Stanley, guitar, Gene Simmons, bass and vocals, and Eric Carr, drums. They combine a very loud sound with a theatrical performance in which they are dressed in monster costumes, eat fire and drink simulated blood in the midst of explosions and a smoke-shrouded stage. Never successful in Britain, they were the most successful heavy rock band in the USA in the late seventies. They have never been photographed without their disguises.

Duncan, Robert
> *Kiss* / Robert Duncan. – Manchester: Savoy Books; in association with New English Library, 1980. – 176p., 16p. of plates: ill., ports; 20cm. Includes index. ISBN 0-86130-141-8 (pbk.)

Celebrating their outrageous antics, this is extremely difficult for the British reader to appreciate. It gives, however, an impression of the excesses into which popular music can degenerate.

Swenson, John
> *Kiss* / John Swenson. – Feltham: Hamlyn, 1979. – ill., ports; 18cm. Includes discography. ISBN 0-600-20109-0 (pbk.)

Accepting the visual 'monster movie' presentation of Kiss as a valid approach to rock music, the author analyses the group's recording in a serious, critical way. The British reader will be surprised at the importance which the author gives this, thankfully, American phenomenon.

Tomarkin, Peggy
   Kiss: the real story authorised / by Peggy Tomarkin. – New York: Delilah
   Communications, 1980. – 111p.: ill., ports; 28cm. ISBN 0-440-04834-6
   (pbk.)
This book is full of a large collection of bizarre illustrations but the group's music is briefly discussed. The author regards them as a major new expression of rock music and applauds their creative approach. The very idea of the group being taken seriously for their music is a novel one. Included are quotations from interviews and comments to the press.

KITT, EARTHA

Born in the USA in 1928, Eartha Kitt appeared to British audiences first in the early fifties as a sultry night-club singer. She became a favourite on British television in the fifties, singing in a coquettish, comic style, often performing lying on a fur rug. She had one hit single in Britain in 1955 but her career has always focussed on cabaret and musicals rather than recording successes. She experienced a renaissance in Britain in the late sixties and early seventies in the clubs of the North of England and had a series of very successful seasons at the, then prestigious, Batley Variety Club. She continues to work in cabaret with a faithful, if limited, following.

Kitt, Eartha
   Alone with me: a new biography / by Eartha Kitt. – Chicago, Illinois:
   H. Regenery, 1976. – xii, 276p., 3 leaves of plates: ill., ports; 24cm.
   ISBN 0-8092-8351-4
In an autobiographical updating of Eartha Kitt's career into the sixties and seventies, the musicals and television series are discussed at length with revealing comments on the behind-the-scenes relationships and indeed the men in her life. The cabaret tours of the English clubs are also affectionately recalled. The style of her writing is intelligent, witty and self-effacing.

Kitt, Eartha
   Thursday's child / Eartha Kitt. – London: Cassell, 1957. – 248p., 17p. of
   plates: ill., ports; 20cm. Includes index
An early autobiography written for the then growing number of British fans, much of the book is concerned with the poverty of her early years and, although not in any way political, the problems of the American black performer are well described. She writes of her hardships, unsuccessful marriage and final success with a great sense of humour.

KOOPER, AL

Born in New York in 1944, Al Kooper had his first success in 1958, at the age of thirteen, with the Royal Teens. He made his name, however, as a gifted session musician, playing keyboards for Bob Dylan and later in forming the early jazz-influenced rock band, Blood Sweat and Tears. After leaving the band, he continued to work as a session player as well as making solo albums. One of his most important projects was the album Super Session, made in 1968. It featured Mike Bloomfield, Steve Stills and himself improvising brilliantly. More recently he has continued to record but has become more involved as a producer.

Kooper, Al
  Backstage passes: rock'n'roll life in the sixties / by Al Kooper; with Ben
  Edmonds. – New York: Stein and Day, 1976. – 254p.: ill., ports; 24cm.
  ISBN 0-8128-1840-7
This-ghosted autobiography is particularly well written and gives a fascinating view of the world of rock from a central, informed standpoint. The cynicism, mismanagement, drugs and pure extortion are described along with the success stories. Al Kooper worked with most of the important figures of the period and talks about them very candidly.

KRISTOFFERSON, KRIS

Kris Kristofferson was born in Brownsville, Texas, in 1936. After obtaining a doctorate at Pomona College, he studied at Oxford on a Rhodes scholarship. Preferring to join the army rather than become an academic, he began writing songs and singing while serving in Germany. In 1965, after leaving the army, he moved to Nashville and, after a period of failure, well-known artists such as Roger Miller, Johnny Cash and Janis Joplin began to record his songs. He then began to build a following as a performer and with his low, underplayed, country style, he had a number of successful albums. He has also established himself as something of an actor with roles in such films as A Star is Born, Pat Garrett and Billy the Kid, Convoy and Alice Doesn't Live Here Anymore. He is married to singer Rita Coolidge, with whom he records and tours.

Kalet, Beth
  Kris Kristofferson / by Beth Kalet. – New York: Quick Fox, 1979. – 96p.: ill.,
  ports; 26cm. Includes discography. ISBN 0-8256-3932-9 (pbk.)
A superficial biography, this fails to give an adequate picture of an unusual and complex artist. Kristofferson's mixture of academic background and country-music influence is noted but not examined in the context of his work. The discography is full and his films are noted in the text but not listed.

LAINE, CLEO

(*See* DANKWORTH, JOHN.)

LAST, JAMES

James Last was born in Germany in the early thirties and began his career playing and writing arrangements for ensembles of various sizes before finally forming his own orchestra in the early sixties. In the mid sixties he set about finding an instrumental sound that would fill the vacuum which had emerged in the area of light instrumental music. He eventually developed a distinctive style which takes popular melodies and augments them with a lush brass arrangement, adding sing-along vocals. Clinically produced, his records sell in their millions. Often described as 'Muzak', Last's offerings represent one of the blandest forms of contemporary popular music.

Elson, Howard
    James Last / Howard Elson. – London; New York: Proteus, 1982. – 64p.: ill.
    (some col.), facsims, ports (some col.); 28cm. Includes discography.
    ISBN 0-86276-174-3 (cased). ISBN 0-86276-120-4 (pbk.)
A superficial account of James Last's career with no musical analysis. There is a large collection of illustrations of Last conducting his orchestra from various angles. Whether James Last fans would appreciate this kind of publication is a mystery. The discography is complete with label details.

Willox, Bob
    James Last / Bob Willox. – London: Everest Books, 1976. – 207p., 16p. of
    plates: ill., ports; 23cm. Includes discography. ISBN 0-905018-12-5
This is a well-written biography by an English journalist who went on tour with Last, attended his recording sessions and interviewed him at length. His background and the evolution of his musical style are described in depth. His success, however, is described but not explained.

LED ZEPPELIN

Formed in 1968 as the New Yardbirds, from the remnants of that legendary British rhythm & blues group, Led Zeppelin are credited with creating heavy-metal music but their work is actually diverse in its forms and often acoustic and subtle. Guitarist Jimmy Page had been a prolific session musician, playing on countless hit records of other artists throughout the sixties, as had bass and keyboards player John Paul Jones. Drummer John 'Bonzo' Bonham and singer Robert Plant, although not as well known, had also acquired a good deal of experience before being recruited by Page. Their manager, Peter Grant, had managed to secure a contract with Atlantic Records, a company which was beginning to take an interest in white heavy-rock groups, and, after a brief tour of Scandinavia, their debut album was quickly made and released in late 1968. Although musically derivative, it was applauded as a masterpiece with Page's excellent guitar technique and Plant's soaring, intense vocals. There followed a tour of America with the band supporting the likes of the Vanilla Fudge and particularly the Jeff Beck Group. The latter were at the point of their self-destruction and Zeppelin were eagerly ready to fill the vacuum.

The management of Peter Grant has had a great influence on the band's career; he has been described as ruthless and over-protective and often compared to Presley's Colonel Tom Parker. They have always concentrated on and been more successful in the USA than in Britain but with their world-wide following they are still one of the three most successful bands ever in terms of record sales and concert returns. Their reputation as exciting performers is only equalled by their reputation for outrageous living, wrecking hotel rooms and an amazing appetite for the more decadent pursuits of rock stars. In 1980 John Bonham died after a drinking spell and since then no new work has come from the group.

(*See also* PAGE, JIMMY; PLANT, ROBERT.)

Bunton, Richard
    Led Zeppelin: in the light 1968–1980 / Richard Bunton & Howard Mylett. – London; New York: Proteus, 1981. – 96p.: ill. (some col.), ports (some col); 27cm. Includes discography. ISBN 0-906071-65-8 (pbk.)
This chronologically arranged, pictorial look at the twelve-year history of Led Zeppelin has a fine collection of photographs as well as a brief but informative text. The discography covers only official British releases. There is no attempt to discuss their music in any depth but some descriptions of their stage performances.

Burston, Jeremy
    Led Zeppelin: the book / by Jeremy Burston. – London; New York: Proteus, 1982. – 160p.: ill., ports; 27cm. Includes discography. ISBN 0-86276-144-X (cased). ISBN 0-86276-113-1 (pbk.)
A well-written, concise and surprisingly thorough account of their career. Much of the author's research is from first-hand sources including lengthy personal interviews with the musicians and their manager. It is Peter Grant's comments which are the most revealing here and he makes it quite clear how important he sees the role of manager. The discography is brief, including only official British releases.

Kendall, Paul
    Led Zeppelin: a visual documentary / by Paul Kendall. – London: Omnibus Press, 1982. – 96p.: ill. (some col.), ports (some col.); 27cm. ISBN 0-7119-0094-9 (pbk.)
A chronologically arranged collection of photographs of the band with brief explanatory notes, there is also a section giving sketchy biographies of the musicians. The career of the band is briefly chronicled here but although well designed, this is not primarily an information source.

Led Zeppelin
  Led Zeppelin in their own words / compiled by Paul Kendall. – London:
  Omnibus Press, 1981. – 128p.: ill., ports; 26cm. ISBN 0-86001-932-2 (pbk.)
An interesting collection of quotes giving some insight into the band's motivations and musical development as well as some amusing refutations concerning
their off-stage reputation. John Paul Jones is revealed as being particularly
intelligent.

Mylett, Howard
  Led Zeppelin / Howard Mylett. – Rev. ed. – St. Albans: Panther, 1981. –
  209p., 16p. of plates: ill., ports; 18cm. ISBN 0-586-04390-X (pbk.)
  Previous editions: St. Albans: Panther, 1976; St. Albans: Panther, 1978.
Written by a real Led Zeppelin fan, this not only describes their career in
considerable depth but analyses in detail each of their officially recorded songs
although it includes no discography. The revised edition includes details of the
making of their film, The Song Remains the Same. There are also biographical
notes for each of the group plus their manager Peter Grant, focussing on their
earlier careers and including details of interviews. This is a well-written,
informative biography giving a close, serious look at a major group without
being too sensational about their lifestyle.

Yorke, Ritchie
  The Led Zeppelin biography / Ritchie Yorke. – New York: Two Continents,
  1976. – 192p.: ill., ports; 23cm. Includes discography. ISBN 0-8467-0103-0
  (pbk.)
  Also published: Toronto: Methuen, 1976.
A well-illustrated but superficial biography which tends to be sensational and
fails to get behind the public image of the group. There is no analysis of their
work, merely some descriptions of their performances and comments on their
tours.

LEIBER, JERRY AND STOLLER, MIKE

Jerry Leiber and Mike Stoller are generally accepted as the most influential
songwriting and production team of the fifties and early sixties. Writing
basically in a rhythm & blues style, Stoller wrote memorable tunes with Leiber
adding unusually well-observed lyrics for the time. They were contracted to
Atlantic Records and worked with the Coasters and the Drifters as well as
writing for Elvis Presley. Their list of successes is enormous and they had a
revival after a break of ten years or so, with a series of successes during the early
seventies. These included songs for Stealer's Wheel, Procol Harum and Elkie
Brooks.

Palmer, Robert
  Baby, that was rock & roll: the legendary Leiber & Stoller / by Robert Palmer;
  introduction by John Lahr. – New York: Harcourt Brace Jovanovich, 1978. –
  131p.: ill., ports; 31cm. Includes discography. ISBN 0-1561-0155-6 (pbk.)

With a brief text, this traces the Leiber–Stoller successes with an excellent collection of photographs of themselves and their recording artists. A well-produced publication but with no insight into their writing method or discussion of their changes in style. The discography includes all their major hits, but is far from comprehensive. An interesting introduction to their work; a fuller, more analytical study is required to do justice to their position as major writers.

LENNON, JOHN

Born in October 1940, in Liverpool, after attending Quarry Bank High School and Liverpool School of Art, John Lennon became the rhythm guitarist and co-writer of the Beatles. It was Lennon who brought the toughness and acid wit to Paul McCartney's sense of melody. He was the first of the Beatles to branch out on his own projects with two works of verse and drawings, *John Lennon: in his own write*, in 1964, and *A Spaniard in the works*, in 1965, and in an acting role in the film How I Won the War, in 1967. It was Lennon who was outspoken on political matters, who stated that the Beatles were more popular than Christ and, as the Plastic Ono Band, released his solo records before the Beatles' final demise. His marriage to Yoko Ono alienated him from many of his early fans and by the seventies he was an established leader of the anti-establishment. Lennon's work during the seventies ranged from the superb, with albums like Imagine, to the boring. It culminated in a collection of rock'n'roll classics which were badly over-produced by Phil Spector. He spent a year estranged from Yoko, mostly spent on the West Coast drinking with Harry Nilsson, but on their reunion he retired from music to live in the Dakota apartment building in New York and bring up his second son, Sean. His househusband stance was a manifestation of the political radicalism which was to permeate his later work.

Finally, at the end of 1980, an album appeared, poignantly shared with Yoko. The album had already received excellent reviews when, on December 8th 1980, he was murdered outside his home – a tragic end to one of the most important figures in popular culture. He was killed by a maniacal fan, the ultimate victim of his own fame. His final album and a series of singles immediately achieved unprecedented sales. The shock of his death remains as one of the final steps in a phase of the development of popular music, for the hope that the Beatles would reunite to bring a renaissance to the eighties died with him.

(*See also* THE BEATLES; ONO, YOKO.)

The ballad of John and Yoko / the editors of *Rolling Stone*; edited by Jonathan Cotton and Christine Doudna; art direction Bea Feitler. – London: Michael Joseph, 1982. – xxiii, 317p., 16p. of plates: ill. (some col.), facsims, ports (some col.); 24cm. Includes index. ISBN 0-7181-2186-4 (cased). ISBN 0-7181-2208-9 (pbk.)
Also published: New York: Doubleday, 1982.
The beginning of John and Yoko's life together coincided with the birth of

Rolling Stone magazine. Lennon was on the cover of the first edition and over the years received a great deal of attention from its writers. This is a selection of articles, interviews and reviews covering the period from 1967 to 1980 with some excellent new tributes and critical essays. Oral appreciations by a variety of people from Frank Sinatra to Ray Charles and Norman Mailer complement an excellent collection of photographs by Annie Leibovitz. In all a beautifully edited, worthy tribute.

Carpozi, George
    John Lennon: death of a dream / George Carpozi Jr. – New York: Manor
    Books, 1980. – 254p.: ill., ports; 18cm. Includes discography.
    ISBN 0-532-23466-9 (pbk.)
Hurriedly produced within two weeks of Lennon's death, this is a very poor account of Lennon's career and murder. Included is a chapter on the Beatles' films and a discography of the Beatles' recording as a group and as individuals. In fact, the author has used every device to pad out and produce quickly this very extreme example of cynicism.

Connolly, Ray
    John Lennon 1940–1980 / Ray Connolly. – London: Fontana Paperbacks,
    1981. – 191p., 32p. of plates: ill., facsim., ports; 20cm. Includes discography
    and index. ISBN 0-00-636405-5 (pbk.)
Written by the popular-music critic of the *Standard* and *The Sunday Times*, this is an intelligent, sensitive biography. Published after Lennon's death, this is in no way a hurried, clumsy work but is well written with an excellent collection of photographs. The chapters on his early life and the early days of the Beatles are particularly revealing but the years of success are also described in a balanced way. Certainly there is an air of reverence but it is not so overt as to detract from what is one of the best biographies on Lennon to date.

Doncaster, Patrick
    Tribute to John Lennon: his life, his loves, his work and his death / written by
    Patrick Doncaster. – London: Mirror Books, 1981. – 32p.: ill., facsims,
    ports; 36cm. ISBN 0-85939-266-X (unbound)
Published in a tabloid, newspaper format soon after Lennon's death, this is surprisingly well written with good illustrations.

Fawcett, Anthony
    John Lennon: one day at a time: a personal biography of the seventies / by
    Anthony Fawcett. – London: New English Library, 1977. – 192p.: ill.,
    facsims, ports; 26cm. Includes bibliography and discography.
    ISBN 0-456-03073-3 (pbk.)
    Originally published: New York: Grove Press, 1976.
This biography, which includes an account of the break-up of the Beatles, the collapse of their Apple business organization and the subsequent career of John Lennon, is full of excellent illustrations. There is a detailed chronology of Lennon's life during this period. Interesting, but neither a revealing insight nor critically objective.

Garbarini, Vic
  Strawberry Fields forever: John Lennon remembered / by Vic Garbarini and
  Brian Cullman; with Barbara Graustark; special introduction by Dave
  Marsh. – New York: Delilah Books; Bantam Books, 1980. – 177p., 16p. of
  plates: ill., ports; 18cm. ISBN 0-553-20121-2 (pbk.)
Published within three weeks of Lennon's death, this is a poorly produced work
comprising a biographical essay, interviews and a chronology of his life.
Although there are some interesting comments on his writing, both with the
Beatles and after, this includes nothing not available in earlier biographies
apart from an account of his last days, the murder and illustrations of the
aftermath.

Harry, Bill
  The book of Lennon / Bill Harry. – London: Aurum Press, 1984. – 223p.: ill.,
  facsims, ports; 24cm. ISBN 0-906053-74-9 (pbk.)
By a longtime friend of Lennon, this is an encyclopedia. It is divided by topic:
people, places, records and so on, each of the six hundred entries being
arranged alphabetically within its section. There is much useful information
here with some interesting illustrations.

John Lennon / edited by George Darby and David Robson; designed by
  Michael Rand and John Tennant; pictures by Vincent Page. – London:
  Times Newspapers, 1980. – 60p.: ill. (some col.), facsims, ports (some col.);
  29cm. Includes discography. (unbound)
Published within days of his death in the format of *The Sunday Times Colour
Supplement*, this is a well-designed tribute with some unusual photographs and
intelligent text.

John Lennon: a Melody Maker tribute. – London: IPC Magazines, 1981. – 54p.:
  ill. (some col.), ports (some col.); 28cm. (unbound)
Some quite well written notes and illustrations but still a hastily-put-together
collection of idolatry.

John Lennon: a tribute in words pictures and lyrics. – Hastings: Disco 45; Chart
  songwords publications, 1981. – poster; 28cm. (unbound)
This consists of a fold-out poster, with illustrations, lyrics and notes on the
reverse.

John Lennon: Beatles memory book. – New York: Harris Publications 1981. –
  66p.: ill. (some col.), ports (some col); 28cm. (unbound)
Although it includes many rare illustrations, this was hurriedly brought
together after Lennon's death and adds nothing.

John Lennon: give peace a chance. – Nottingham: Croft Publishers, 1981. –
  50p.: ill. ports; 28cm. Includes discography. (unbound)
A reasonable tribute with some rare illustrations and a discography.

John Lennon: summer of 1980 / Yoko Ono with eight photographers. –
London: Chatto & Windus, 1984. – 110p.: chiefly ill., chiefly ports; 23cm.
ISBN 0-7011-3931-5 (pbk.)
Originally published: New York: Perigree Books, 1983.
A beautiful collection of photographs of Yoko and John taken during the
summer of 1980 by eight well-known photographers including Bob Gruen,
Allen Tannenbaum, Jack Mitchell and Annie Leibovitz. All of them give their
recollections of the sessions and there is an introduction by Yoko. This is a
moving little volume.

Lennon, Cynthia
A twist of Lennon / Cynthia Lennon. – London: Star Books, 1978. – 173p.,
8p. of plates: ill., ports; 18cm. ISBN 0-352-30196-1 (pbk.)
This is an autobiographical account, in no way sensational, by John Lennon's
former wife of the rise and fall of the Beatles up to the time of his leaving her for
his second wife, Yoko Ono. Cynthia Lennon briefly outlines her childhood and
early days with Lennon and then describes the effect of sudden, enormous
success on the Beatles and particularly her husband. Filled with fascinating
anecdotes not available elsewhere, this is not the account of an embittered ex-
wife but a sympathetic, retrospective record of part of the author's life which
was to her enthralling and exciting.

Lennon, John
John Lennon: in his own words / compiled by Miles; designed by Pearce
Marchbank. – London: W. H. Allen, 1981. – 126p.: ill., ports; 26cm.
ISBN 0-491-02975-X (pbk.)
Also published: London: Omnibus Press, 1980.
Hastily produced just weeks after John Lennon's death, this is a collection of
quotations from interviews and poignant remarks for which he was famous.
Although well selected, apart from a few of the illustrations there is nothing
here that is not available elsewhere.

Lennon, John
Lennon remembers: the Rolling Stone interviews / by Jann Wenner. –
Harmondsworth: Penguin Books, 1973. – 190p.: ill., ports; 23cm.
ISBN 0-1400-3581-8 (pbk.)
Originally published: New York: Straight Arrow Books, 1971.
Also published: London: Talmy, 1972.
Widely regarded as a classic piece of journalism, this series of interviews was
undertaken soon after the Beatles' demise. It is witty, revealing, often vitriolic
but always outspoken, mainly intelligent and interesting. Lennon is openly
critical of Paul McCartney and patronizing about George Harrison's early solo
efforts. There is a fine collection of photographs and as a background to the end
of the Beatles it is biased but fascinating.

Lennon, John
*The Lennon tapes: Andy Peebles in conversation with John Lennon and
Yoko Ono 6th December 1980.* – London: BBC Publications, 1981. – 84p.;
20cm. ISBN 0-563-17944-9 (pbk.)

The BBC disc jockey, Andy Peebles, recorded a lengthy interview with the Lennons just two days before the murder. This is a full transcript of those tapes, in which Lennon reveals the secrets of his newly found settled lifestyle and restored creativity. It is a warm interview by a sympathetic inquisitor, made the more remarkable by its tragic timing.

Lennon, John
   The Playboy interviews with John Lennon and Yoko Ono / conducted by
   David Sheff; edited by G. Barry Golson. – Sevenoaks, Kent: New English
   Library, 1982. – 193p., 8p. of plates: ill.. ports; 21cm. ISBN 0-450-05489-6
   (pbk.)
   Originally published: New York: Playboy Press, 1981.
This book is composed of the transcripts of taped interviews. A brief version was to have appeared in *Playboy* magazine in December, 1980, but was withdrawn because of Lennon's death. Concerned largely with his recent liberated attitudes towards sexual roles, his recent lifestyle and his marriage, much of this information appears in other works.

Lennon, John
   *Search for liberation: featuring a conversation between John Lennon and
   Swami Bhaktiredanta; Lennon '69.* – Los Angeles; London: Bhaktiredanta
   Book Trust, 1981. – viii, 66p.: ill., facsims, ports; 18cm. ISBN 0-89213-109-8
   (pbk.)
An interview undertaken in 1969 with Lennon by a leading member of the international Society of Krishna Consciousness. This curious publication reflects his philosophies at the time, offering an unusual perspective.

Lennon: up close / editor Timothy Coreen Beckley. – New York: Sunshine
   Publications, 1980. – 160p.: ill., ports; 18cm. ISBN 0-89596-296-9 (pbk.)
Another addition to the material rushed into publication on Lennon's death; this is an attempt at his biography. In places inaccurate, it is poorly produced, poorly written and childish in approach.

Lennon: what happened! / editor Timothy Green. – New York: Sunshine
   Publications, 1980. – 160p.: ill., ports; 18cm. ISBN 0-89596-297-7 (pbk.)
Appearing within weeks of the murder, this is another very poor effort, looking at Lennon's recent years living in New York. It leads up to a ghoulish account of the killing.

Nelson, Paul
   John Lennon: a biography in words & pictures / by Paul Nelson; edited by
   Greg Shaw. – New York: Sire Books; Chappell Music Company, 1976. –
   56p.: ill., ports; 30cm. Includes discography. (pbk.)
Written at a time when Lennon's career was at a low ebb, this is a reasonable, brief biography with some intelligent discussion of his writing.

Pang, May
> *Loving John* / May Pang and Henry Edwards. – London: Corgi Books, 1983.
> – 352p.: ill., ports; 24cm. ISBN 0-552-99079-5 (pbk.)
> Originally published as '*Loving John: the untold story*': New York: Warner
> Books, 1983.

May Pang was Lennon's personal assistant and later, during his estrangement
from Yoko Ono, his companion and lover. A sympathetic account of this
difficult period in Lennon's life, it is not without its criticisms of Yoko and errs,
on occasion, towards the sensational. The accounts of Lennon's escapades with
Harry Nilsson are very amusing indeed.

Ryan, David Stuart
> *John Lennon's secret* / by David Stuart Ryan. – London; Washington D.C.:
> Kozmik Press Centre, 1982. – 256p.: ill., facsims, geneal. table, ports; 23cm.
> Includes bibliography and index. ISBN 0-905116-07-0 (cased).
> ISBN 0-905116-08-9 (pbk.)

With the aim of unfolding the mysteries of Lennon's genius and offering an
insight into his writing, this is a poor attempt which focusses on the sensational
aspects of his life and adds very little new information. An appendix includes
the lyrics of a few of his best-known songs with brief analyses and a full list of his
songs, including collaborations. There are a few interesting illustrations, but
this an insensitive, unworthy work written from a distant, American, standpoint.

Shotton, Pete
> *John Lennon: in my life* / by Pete Shotton and Nicholas Schaffner. – London:
> Coronet Books, 1984. – 208p.: ill., ports; 28cm. ISBN 0-304-34699-X (pbk.)
> Originally published: New York: Stein & Day, 1983.

This is a collaboration between Pete Shotton, a lifelong friend of Lennon, and
Nicholas Schaffner, the Beatles expert and prolific author. It is a sympathetic,
well-written biography with good musical analysis and a fine collection of
photographs. The anecdotes from the fifties and sixties are particularly
interesting and well drawn.

Tremlett, George
> *The John Lennon story* / George Tremlett. – London: Futura Publications,
> 1976. – 160p., 16p. of plates: ill., ports; 18cm. ISBN 0-8600-7294-0 (pbk.)

A journalistic portrait which combines personal interviews with much material
from secondary sources. There is a useful chronology.

A tribute to John Lennon. – London; New York: Proteus, 1982. – 96p.: ill.,
> facsims, ports; 22cm. ISBN 0-906071-80-1

A selection of posthumous tributes in a cased edition; the effect is mawkish.

Tyler, Tony
> *John Lennon: working class hero; the life and death of a legend 1940–1980* /
> mainly written by Tony Tyler. – London: IPC Magazines, 1980. – 37p.: ill.
> (some col.), ports (some col.); 30cm. (unbound)

A particularly poor tribute, hastily produced with a chronology full of errors.

Young, Paul
The Lennon factor / by Paul Young. – New York: Stein & Day, 1972. – 42p.;
26cm. ISBN 0-8128-1465-7 (pbk.)
An unusual, whimsical, free-verse retelling of how Lennon and his followers
have changed the world. The humour is unfortunately not sustained throughout.

LENNON, JOHN: WRITINGS

Lennon, John
John Lennon in his own write / by John Lennon. – Harmondsworth: Penguin
Books, 1980. – 78p.: ill., facsims; 18cm. ISBN 0-14-00-5928-8 (pbk.)
Originally published: London: Cape, 1964.
When originally published, it was the first time that a pop singer's work had
appeared as 'literature'. The verses are reminiscent of Lear, Carroll and
Milligan.

Lennon, John
John Lennon in his own write and a Spaniard in the works. – London: Cape,
1981. – 154p.: ill. (some col.), facsims (some col.); 21cm. ISBN 0-224-02921-5
Also published: New York: Simon and Schuster, 1981.
This cased edition of both works was published as a posthumous tribute.

Lennon, John
The Penguin John Lennon. – Harmondsworth: Penguin Books, 1966. –
157p.: ill. (some col.), facsims (some col.); 20cm. ISBN 0-14-00-2540-5
(pbk.)
The first edition of both works in one volume, it has remained in print.

Lennon, John
A Spaniard in the works / by John Lennon. – Harmondsworth: Penguin
Books, 1980. – 94p.: ill. (some col.), facsims (some col.); 20cm.
ISBN 0-14-00-5929-6 (pbk.)
Originally published: London: Cape, 1965.
Lennon's collection of verse, perhaps even more eccentric than the first, was
published as a single volume in paperback following his death.

LEWIS, JERRY LEE

Born in Ferriday, Louisiana, in 1935, Jerry Lee Lewis was taught to play piano
by his father, Elmo, as a child. After studying to be a minister of religion at the
Assembly of God Institute, Wazahachie, Texas, he went to Sun Records to
audition in 1956. His first record was a hit in America and his second was also
successful in Britain and earned him his first gold disc. His next release, Great
Balls of Fire, was even bigger, becoming top of the British charts. He was firmly
established by now as rock'n'roll's wildest white performer, often demolishing

his piano in his frantic assault. In 1958 he married his thirteen-year-old cousin, Myra, and caused a massive public outcry on both sides of the Atlantic which resulted in the ruin of his career. During the sixties and seventies he gradually rebuilt the remnants of his following, working in the country-music field and he is now the surviving father figure of rock'n'roll. Calling himself 'the Killer', he has a reputation for hard drinking and blatant arrogance which has made him somewhat unpopular with his fellow artists. In 1980 he almost died but recovered to continue to thrill his loyal followers.

Cain, Robert
  Whole lotta shakin' goin' on: Jerry Lee Lewis, the rock years, the country years, the triumphs and the tragedies / Robert Cain. – New York: Dial Press, 1981. – 143p.: ill., ports; 26cm. ISBN 0-686-85874-3 (pbk.)
With a fine collection of photographs, this is an episodic, impressionistic attempt to recreate the mood of his career. There are interesting interviews with many of his associates, including Jerry Kennedy, his early producer.

Lewis, Myra
  Great balls of fire: the true story of Jerry Lee Lewis / Myra Lewis with Murray Silver. – London: Virgin Books, 1982. – 319p.: ill., ports; 23cm. Includes index. ISBN 0-907080-75-8 (pbk.)
  Originally published: New York: Morrow, 1982.
From the recollections of his third wife, this commemorates their twenty-five years of marriage and estrangement with a catalogue of sensational tales. Entertaining and probably factual, the story is told with considerable relish.

Palmer, Robert
  Jerry Lee Lewis / By Robert Palmer. – London: Omnibus Press, 1981. – 128p.: ill., ports; 30cm. ISBN 0-86001-956-X (pbk.)
Well written, with some excellent illustrations, the brief but informative text carefully concentrates on his musical contribution, avoiding the lurid.

Tosches, Nick
  Hellfire: the Jerry Lee Lewis story / Nick Tosches. – London: Plexus, 1982. – 228p., 16p. of plates: ill., ports; 24cm. ISBN 0-85965-053-7 (cased). ISBN 0-85965-052-9 (pbk.)
  Originally published: New York: Delacorte, 1982.
Jerry Lee Lewis is represented here as an American anti-hero, torn between evangelism and dissipation. The author has a genuine understanding of Lewis's music and a sympathetic, intelligent view of the man.

LIGHTFOOT, GORDON

Born in Orillia, Ontario, Canada, in 1939, Gordon Lightfoot moved to Los Angeles in 1958 to study orchestration at Westlake College. After working as an arranger, session musician and producer of advertising jingles, he became interested in folk music. His early compositions had strong country-music overtones but his style changed after he heard Bob Dylan, becoming far more folk-based and remaining that way. His songs have been recorded by major artists in the country, pop and rock music fields and, although he has never been regarded as a major or a fashionable artist, he has consistently sold albums and is a prolific songwriter.

Gabiou, Alfrieda
    Gordon Lightfoot / Alfrieda Gabiou. – New York; London: Quick Fox, 1979. – 128p.: ill., ports; 26cm. Includes discography. ISBN 0-8256-3148-3 (pbk.)
    Also published: Toronto: Gage, 1979.
Although surprisingly scant in detail about his songwriting and songs, this is a good outline biography with a full discography of Gordon Lightfoot's recordings. The list of his songs recorded by other artists, however, is far from complete. Much of the information is based on interviews with the author, who toured with her subject. This is by far the major source on the artist.

LORD, BOBBY

Born in Sandford, Florida, in 1934, during the fifties Bobby Lord was a member of Red Foley's Jubilee USA Show as well as later becoming a regular on the Grand 'Ole Opry. A conventional singer and guitarist in the commercial, country-music mode, he had a series of hits in the late sixties and early seventies but has never made any impression in Great Britain.

Lord, Bobby
    Hit the glory road! / Bobby Lord. – Nashville, Tennessee: Broadman Press, 1969. – vii, 143p.: ill., ports; 21cm.
This is the autobiography of a little-known singer with some interesting background to Nashville in the fifties and sixties.

LYNN, LORETTA

Daughter of a mineworker in Kentucky, born in 1935, after a harsh childhood of real poverty Loretta Lynn formed a band with her brother and achieved her first successful record in 1960. She then moved to Nashville and became the most successful maker of hit records in country music throughout the sixties. In 1972 she became the first woman to be voted Country Music Association Entertainer of the Year. In 1981 a film of her autobiography was released.

Krishef, Robert K.
    The story of Loretta Lynn / by Robert K. Krishef. – Minneapolis: Lerner Publications, 1978. – 184p.: ill., ports; 21cm. Includes index.
    ISBN 0-8225-1401-X (pbk.)

A controlled-vocabulary biography aimed at American schools, this follows closely her autobiography, *Coal Miner's Daughter*. Her humble beginnings are not overemphasized. There is a good deal of detail of life in Nashville, some simple analysis of her work and good illustrations. A good biography for the age group.

Lynn, Loretta
 Coal miner's daughter / Loretta Lynn; with George Vecsey. – St. Albans:
 Panther, 1979. – 256p., 16p. of plates: ill., ports; 18cm. ISBN 0-586-04832-4
 (pbk.)
 Originally published: Chicago: Regnery, 1976.
This was a bestselling autobiography when first published 1976. It is an honest, personal account of the rise to fame of the 'Queen' of country music. It does give an insight into life in Nashville, but not into her approach to singing nor to country music.

LYNN, LORETTA: DISCOGRAPHIES

Zwisohn, Laurence J.
 Loretta Lynn's world of music: including an annotated discography and
 complete list of songs she composed / Laurence J. Zwisohn. – Los Angeles:
 Palm Tree Library; John Edwards Memorial Foundation, 1980. – 115p.: ill.,
 facsims, ports; 25cm. ISBN 0-933266-01-4 (pbk.)
A detailed list of her recording career with descriptions of her recording sessions and critical annotations of her resulting disc releases.

LYNOTT, PHIL

Born in 1944 in Dublin, son of an Irish mother and Brazilian father, Phil Lynott is the writer and founder member of the group Thin Lizzy. He is a charismatic figure, a black Irishman, with a distinctive voice and unusual, positive bass guitar style. His writing covers a wide range of topics and is arguably the secret of the group's success.

(*See also*: THIN LIZZY.)

LYNOTT, PHIL: WRITINGS

Lynott, Philip
 A collected works of Philip Lynott. – London: Chappell, 1979. – 104p.: ill.;
 22cm. (pbk.)
A collection of Lynott's poems and song lyrics displaying his themes which range from wild-western folklore to Celtic myth and include tender love songs. There are drawings illustrating song titles.

McCartney, Mike

Born in Liverpool in 1944, Peter Michael McCartney is the younger brother of Paul McCartney of the Beatles and Wings. After school at the Liverpool Institute, he became involved with the Merseyside Arts Festival and the group of young writers known as the 'Liverpool poets' which included Roger McGough. John Gorman, another organizer of the festival, McGough and Mike McCartney formed a satirical group calling themselves the Scaffold which, in the style of the period, read poems and performed sketches. So as not to use his brother's name he became known as Mike McGear. The Scaffold became a successful recording and performing group in Britain with hit records and one, Lily the Pink, reached the top of the singles charts in 1968. In the early seventies he released a solo album with the help of his brother. The Scaffold continue to make occasional concert appearances.

McCartney, Mike
    Thank U very much: Mike McCartney's family album. – London: Arthur
    Barker, 1981. – 192p: ill., facsims, ports; 29cm. ISBN 0-213-16816-2
Mike McCartney briefly and wittily outlines his family history and goes on to describe in some detail his childhood, and the early days of the Beatles and his own career. Comments on stars he has met include an interesting view of Jimi Hendrix. The photographs, the author's own, include some of the earliest and most unusual available of the Beatles.

McCartney, Paul and Wings

Born in Liverpool in 1941, Paul McCartney was the bass player and co-writer of the Beatles songs who gave them their very strong sense of melody. By the late sixties he had become the driving force of the group. He foresaw and attempted to avoid the demise and contributed the majority of effort to their last three albums. At the time of the break-up he released his own, very simple, solo album and then followed it by forming his group, Wings, which included his wife Linda on keyboards and former Moody Blues singer Denny Laine. Wings became one of the most successful attractions of the seventies. Paul McCartney is undisputedly the wealthiest musician Britain has produced, with a keen business sense and keener feel for popular taste. His record of Mull of Kintyre, a traditional Scottish tune, is the biggest-selling British record of all time. He is also the possessor of most gold discs and the biggest income, and has a series of entries in the *Guinness book of records*.

(*See also* THE BEATLES.)

Gambaccini, Paul
    Paul McCartney in his own words / written and edited by Paul Gambaccini;
    designed by Pearce Marchbank. – London: Omnibus Press, 1976. – 112p.:
    facsims, ports; 26cm. Includes discography. ISBN 0-8600-1239-5 (pbk.)

Mostly taken from a series of taped conversations in 1973 with a short piece added during Wings' tour of America, here is Paul McCartney's side of the Beatles' success and break-up. He discusses his songwriting, his relationship with John Lennon and the formation of Wings. The author's questions are searching and the transcript informative and entertaining but not controversial.

Gelly, David
  The facts about a pop group: featuring Wings / introduction by Paul
  McCartney; by David Gelly; photographed by Homer Sykes. – London:
  Whizzard with Deutsch, 1976. – 47p.: ill. (some col.), facsims, music, ports
  (some col.); 29cm. ISBN 0-233-96771-0 (cased)
  Also published: New York: Harmony Books, 1977.
A look at a famous pop group with emphasis on the organization supporting the performers. Aimed at the teenage reader, it makes a serious attempt to offer information not available elsewhere. There is a complete list and diagram of the staff and equipment required to set up a tour, down to the accommodation problems. The making of a record, from the composition of the song, the recording and production to the marketing, are dealt with succinctly and accurately. Well illustrated and concisely written, this is a good attempt to offer a serious approach for the young reader.

Grove, Martin A.
  Paul McCartney: Beatle with Wings / Martin A. Grove. – New York: Manor
  Books, 1978. – 142.: ill., ports; 18cm. ISBN 0-532-17191-8 (pbk.)
Paul McCartney's career with the Beatles is briefly outlined but the author's emphasis is on the formation of Wings, the various line-ups and recording successes. Each of the successful albums up to 1977 is discussed in detail and the American tour of 1976 is well covered. Not an in-depth study but a fairly good, superficial peep.

Hands across the water: Wings tour USA / design Hipgnosis; all photographs by
  Aubrey Powell; graphics and illustration by George Hardie; edited by Storm
  Thorgerson & Peter Christopherson.– London: Paper Tiger; Los Angeles:
  Reed Books, 1978. – 150p.; chiefly ill.: 29cm. ISBN 0-89169-500-1 (pbk.)
A photographic record of Wings' 1976 tour of the USA which concentrates on backstage shots, attempting to catch the mood, the operation and the atmosphere of the places where they played.

Jasper, Tony
  Paul McCartney and Wings / Tony Jasper. – London: Octopus Books, 1977.
  – 93p.: ill. (some col.), ports (chiefly col.); 30cm. ISBN 0-7064-0663-X
A well-illustrated look at the group with a brief section on McCartney's days with the Beatles. There are descriptions of Wings' tours and details of their entourage of road crews, engineers and equipment.

Mendelsohn, John
Paul McCartney: a biography in words & pictures / by John Mendelsohn;
edited by Greg Shaw. – New York: Sire Books; Chappell Music Company,
1977. – 55p.: ill., ports; 30cm. Includes discography. ISBN 0-1445-8431-5
(pbk.)
A brief biography of Paul McCartney from his childhood and early days with
the Beatles to the height of his second success with Wings. There is some
emphasis on his marriage and family life. The discography is complete and
there is an additional list of his songs recorded by other artists.

Ocean, Humphrey
The Ocean view / Humphrey Ocean; preface by Paul McCartney. – London:
Plexus, 1983. – 70p.: ill. (chiefly col.), ports (chiefly col.); 21cm.
ISBN 0-85965-066-9
Paul McCartney commissioned portrait painter Humphrey Ocean to ac-
company Wings on their 1976 tour of America. The result is this excellent
collection of paintings depicting life on the road.

Pascall, Jeremy
Paul McCartney & Wings / Jeremy Pascall. – London: Hamlyn; Phoebus,
1977. – 96p.: ill. (some col.), ports (some col.); 31cm. ISBN 0-600-39394-1
Also published: Secaucus, New Jersey: Chartwell Books; London: Phoebus,
1977.
After a brief outline of McCartney's career with the Beatles and of the break-
up of the group, this is an informative account of the forming of Wings and its
various line-ups to 1976. There is a good deal of discussion of McCartney's
music and songwriting and the transcript of an interview.

Tremlett, George
The Paul McCartney story / George Tremlett. – London: Futura Publications, 1975. – 192p., 16p. of plates: ill., ports; 18cm. ISBN 0-8600-7200-2
(pbk.)
Also published: London: White Lion, 1976
Written to the author's usual formula with a detailed chronology as an
appendix, this covers Paul McCartney's life from childhood, through the
Beatles to the formation of Wings up to 1974. The author based much of his
information on interviews with the subject and on his journalistic sources. A
good biography.

MCCARTNEY, PAUL: SONGS

McCartney, Paul
Paul McCartney: composer/artist. – London: Pavilion Books; Michael
Joseph, 1981. – 272p.: ill., music, ports; 31cm. ISBN 0-907516-01-7 (cased).
ISBN 0-907516-00-9 (pbk.)
A well-produced collection of McCartney's forty-eight most famous songs,
including some credited to Lennon–McCartney as well as to McCartney

alone. Each song is juxtaposed with a simple line drawing, supposedly an image associated with the song. The lyrics are reproduced as poems as well as part of the scored song with guitar chord shapes. McCartney writes in an introduction that he was trained neither as an artist nor a songwriter, and his drawings certainly demonstrate his lack of an art-school education. This is a good collection but one cannot help feeling that the author is trying to follow George Harrison's *I, me, mine* on a more commercial scale.

McKuen, Rod

Born in Oakland, California, in 1933, McKuen had established himself as a popular poet before becoming a noted lyricist and performer of his own songs. Frank Sinatra recorded a McKuen song, I Will Drink the Wine, which became a hit single in 1971. In 1974 McKuen achieved his greatest success with the song Seasons in the Sun written in collaboration with composer Jacques Brel, which was a world-wide success for Terry Jacks. During the seventies McKuen made regular appearances on British television although his own recordings have never been commercial successes in the United Kingdom.

McKuen, Rod
  Finding my father: one man's search for identity / Rod McKuen. – London:
  Elm Tree Books, 1977. – 155p.: ill., facsim., ports; 23cm. Includes bibliography and index. ISBN 0-241-89625-8
  Originally published: Los Angeles: Coward McCann and Geoghegan, 1976
McKuen's sole work of prose, an autobiographical account of his search for his origins. Pretentious, lacking cohesion, this is of little informational value.

McKUEN, ROD: POEMS

His collections of poetry include many of his song lyrics.

McKuen, Rod
  Alone / by Rod McKuen. – London: Star Books, 1976. – 256p.: ill., ports;
  18cm. ISBN 0-352-39845-0 (pbk.)
  Originally published: New York: Pocket Books, 1975.

Mckuen, Rod
  Beyond the boardwalk / Rod McKuen. – London: Elm Tree Books, 1980. –
  111p.: ill.; 22cm. ISBN 0-241-10432-7
  Originally published: Los Angeles: Cheval Books, 1975.

McKuen Rod
  Caught in the quiet / Rod McKuen; drawings by Anthony Goldschmidt. –
  London: W. H. Allen, 1973. – 96p.: ill.; 23cm. ISBN 0-491-01051-6
  Originally published: Los Angeles: Stanyan Books, 1970.

McKuen, Rod
Come to me in silence / Rod McKuen. – London: W. H. Allen, 1974. – 120p.;
23cm. ISBN 0-491-01611-5
Originally published: New York: Simon and Schuster, 1973.

McKuen, Rod
Coming close to earth / Rod McKuen. – London: Elm Tree Books, 1977. –
160p.: ill.; 22cm. ISBN 0-241-89717-3. ISBN 0-241-89762-9 (limited edition)

McKuen, Rod
Fields of wonder / Rod McKuen. – London: W. H. Allen, 1972. – 106p.;
22cm. ISBN 0-491-00743-4
Originally published: New York: Cheval Books, 1970.

McKuen, Rod
In someone's shadow / Rod McKuen. – London: Michael Joseph, 1971. –
107p.; 22cm. ISBN 0-7181-0864-7
Originally published: New York: Cheval Books, 1969.

McKuen, Rod
Listen to the warm / by Rod Mckuen. – London: Michael Joseph, 1968. – viii,
113p.; 22cm.
Originally published: New York: Random House, 1967.

McKuen, Rod
Lonesome cities / Rod McKuen. – London: Michael Joseph, 1971. – 111p.;
22cm. ISBN 0-7181-0863-9
Originally published: New York: Random House, 1968.

McKuen, Rod
Moment to moment / Rod McKuen. – London: W. H. Alien, 1973. – xii, 91p.;
23cm. ISBN 0-491-01041-9
Originally published: Hollywood: Cheval Books, 1972.

McKuen, Rod
The sea around me — the hills above / Rod McKuen. – London: Elm Tree
Books, 1976. – 152p.: ill.; 23cm ISBN 0-241-89505-7. ISBN 0-241-89539-3
· (limited edition)

McKuen, Rod
Seasons in the sun / Rod McKuen. – London: Star Books, 1974. – 237p.: ill.,
ports; 19cm. Includes index. ISBN 0-352-30026-4 (pbk.)

McKuen, Rod
Stanyan Street and other sorrows / by Rod McKuen. – London: Michael
Joseph, 1968. – 82p.; 22cm.
Originally published: Hollywood: Stanyan Music, 1966.

McKuen, Rod
  Twelve years of Christmas / Rod McKuen. – London: W. H. Allen 1972. –
  52p.; 22cm. ISBN 0-491-00803-1
  Originally published: New York: Cheval Books, 1969.

McKuen, Rod
  We touch the sky / Rod McKuen. – London: Elm Tree Books, 1979. – 160p.;
  22cm. ISBN 0-241-89956-7

MANILOW, BARRY

Born in Brooklyn, New York, in 1941, Barry Manilow studied at the City
College of New York before moving to the New York College of Music and
finally to the Juillard Academy. He worked as a postroom boy at CBS, as well
as a piano player in various bars, and by chance a director asked him to write
some arrangements for a television show. After taking this step, he next
became Bette Midler's musical director, arranger and pianist and produced her
first album. In 1975, he had his first personal success with the Scott English
song, Mandy, and from then on he has grown into the world's leading middle-
of-the-road singer. He is much satirized as the epitome of the bland, insincere
side of showbusiness, but his extravagant stage productions, well-chosen
repertoire, including some of his own songs, clear voice and professionalism
give him an exceptionally wide appeal and a popularity throughout the world
with concert tours, television specials and as a recording artist.

Barry Manilow. – London: Grandreams, 1982. – 64p.: ill. (some col.), ports
  (some col.); 27cm. ISBN 0-86227-070-7
In the format of a Christmas annual, this is a brief resumé of his career. There is
a good collection of portraits, his vital statistics and a quiz.

Bego, Mark
  Barry Manilow: an authorised biography / by Mark Bego; edited by Barbara
  Williams Prabhu. – Rev. ed. – New York: Grosset & Dunlap, 1979. – 88p. :
  ill., ports; 21cm. ISBN 0-448-17035-3 (pbk.)
  Previous edition: New York: Grosset & Dunlap, 1977.
The revised edition describes Manilow's more recent successes, although the
text has been considerably abridged. It is superficial and uncritical, with no
analysis of his songwriting and a very poorly written biographical narrative.

Clarke, Alan
  The magic of Barry Manilow / Alan Clarke. – London: Prize Books, 1981. –
  48p.: ill., ports; 28cm. Includes discography. ISBN 0-86276-009-7 (pbk.)
A very brief biography, this combines a collection of portraits, mainly posed,
with a superficial text. Simple idolatry. Manilow's songwritting is not mentioned.

Elson, Howard
Barry Manilow / Howard Elson. – London; New York: Proteus, 1981. –
48p.: ill. (some col.), ports (some col.); 27cm. ISBN 0-86276-009-7 (pbk.)
A well-designed, superficial biography, the illustrations represent well the
extravagant showmanship of Manilow's stage act.

Jasper, Tony
Barry Manilow / Tony Jasper. – London: W. H. Allen, 1982. – 159p., 8p. of
plates: ill., facsims., ports; 22cm. Includes discography. ISBN 0-491-02877-6
Originally published: London: Star Books, 1981.
A poor biography with a section of quotations from inane press interviews, a
full discography and incomplete listings of songs performed.

Morse, Ann
Barry Manilow / by Ann Morse; designed by Mark Landkamer. – Mankato,
Minnesota: Creative Education, 1978. – 31p.: ill., ports; 25cm.
ISBN 0-8719-1617-7
A controlled-vocabulary text for a reading age of about ten for American
schools, this is lively and informative with some well-chosen illustrations.

Peters, Richard
The Barry Manilow scrapbook: his magical world in works and pictures / by
Richard Peters. – London: Pop Universal; Souvenir Press, 1982. – 96p.: ill.
(some col.), ports (some col.); 27cm. Includes discography.
ISBN 0-285-62548-9 (pbk.)
A superficial, glossy portrait, this is a very poor effort with no redeeming
feature.

Weir, Simon
Barry Manilow for the record / written by Simon Weir; art editor Alan
Murray. – Knutsford, Cheshire: Stafford Pemberton, 1982. – 96p.: ill.
(chiefly col.), col. facsims, ports (chiefly col.); 30cm. ISBN 0-86030-5 (pbk.)
Beautifully produced, this has a poor text but some very good illustrations.

MANILOW, BARRY: PERIODICALS

(*See* section 8.2, MANILOW, BARRY.)

MARLEY, BOB AND THE WAILERS

Born in 1945 in Jamaica, the son of an English army captain and a Jamaican
woman, Bob Marley made his first recording in 1962. He formed the Wailers in
1964, writing most of their material, and became associated with Johnny Nash
and recorded with him. In 1971 Nash had a successful record in Britain with a
Marley song. After a series of Jamaican hits throughout the sixties the Wailers
finally signed a contract with the Island record company in 1973 and achieved

their first international success, which has been consistently followed. His songs have always had social themes, telling of the ghettos of Kingston and the plight of black people. Since the early seventies Marley and his group have been associated with the revolutionary doctrine of Rastafarianism. They have been seen as leading preachers of the faith, which believes that Haile Selassie of Ethiopia was the reincarnation of Christ and that it is the birthright of all black people to return to Ethiopia. The use of marijuana is an intrinsic part of the religion as is the wearing of the believers' hair in plaited dreadlocks. The reggae style of music played by Marley with its odd rhythm patterns, its stops and starts and staccato guitar, has developed from Jamaican ska and bluebeat styles. Reggae is the natural popular music of Jamaica as well as being widely popular in Britain. In the USA, however, it has only a minority following. The Wailers' line-up has varied over the years with such members as Peter Tosh and Bunny Wailer becoming stars in their own right. After fighting cancer for four years, Bob Marley died in a Miami hospital on May 11th 1981 at the age of thirty-six. He was one of the most influential figures to emerge from popular music; not only as a creative artist, but also as a potent political and religious activist.

Dalrymple, Henderson
  Bob Marley: music, myth & the Rastas / Henderson Dalrymple. – Sudbury,
  Middlesex: Carib-Arawak Publishers, 1976. – 78p.: ill., ports; 21cm.
  ISBN 0-95056-880-5 (pbk.)
This includes a brief history of Rastafarianism and of the development of reggae. The biographical notes on Marley are informative. The general theme is the lack of understanding of his music by white critics and the spread of the originally localized form. There is little musical analysis.

Davis, Stephen
  Bob Marley: the biography / Stephen Davis. – London: Arthur Barker, 1983.
  – 248p., 16p. of plates: ill., ports; 24cm. Includes bibliography and index.
  ISBN 0-213-16855-3 (cased). ISBN 0-213-16859-6 (pbk.)
Author of *Reggae bloodlines* and *Reggae international*, Stephen Davis has written widely on reggae for some years and has interviewed his subject on several occasions. After setting the scene with a brief history of Jamaica and black self-realization back to the black hero Marcus Garvey, the author describes Marley's childhood, his early associations with music and the influence of his friends and neighbours. The greater part of the book deals directly with his career, displaying a real understanding of his lyrics but dealing rather less well with the musical concepts behind the words. Nevertheless, this is not only the best work on Marley but one of the better biographies of any figure in popular music. It is sympathetic, unpretentious and communicates perfectly Marley's uniqueness as not only a wonderfully innovative artist but also a religious enigma and powerful political force.

Goldman, Vivien
  Bob Marley: soul rebel — natural mystic / Vivien Goldman, Adrian Boot. –

London: Eel Pie; Hutchinson, 1981. – 62p.: chiefly ill., ports; 28cm. Includes discography. ISBN 0-09-146481-1 (pbk.)

Published after his death, this is mainly a collection of portraits of Marley and the Wailers. The brief text offers little biographical information. The discography is comprehensive, covering his entire career and citing British discographical details.

McKnight, Cathy

Bob Marley: and the roots of reggae / Cathy McKnight and John Tobler. – London: Star Books, 1977. – 160p., 8p. of plates: ill., ports; 18cm. Includes discography and index. ISBN 0-352-39622-9 (pbk.)

A particularly well researched biography of the artist with a good general introduction to the Rastafarian cult and its association with the deprivations of Jamaican society. There is a detailed discography of official recordings as well as more obscure recordings of Marley and his band. There is an emphasis on his writing and considerable analysis of the music.

White, Timothy

Catch a fire: the life of Bob Marley / Timothy White. – London: Elm Tree Books, 1983. – xvii, 380p.; 23cm. Includes bibliography, discography and index. ISBN 0-241-10956-6 (cased). ISBN 0-241-10957-4 (pbk.)

The author has written extensively on Marley, reggae and Caribbean culture for *Rolling Stone, The New York Times, Crawdaddy* and many other prestigious American publications and his acknowledgements include interviews with everyone, it seems of importance in Marley's life, including the man himself. The result is, however, very unsatisfactory. In an effort to convey the mystical Jamaican atmosphere in which the artist's unique creativity was spawned, White spends half the book in a rambling narrative which attempts to create events in Marley's life with full dialogue in curiously-spelled-out patois. When dealing with historical events, social conditions and particularly Rastafarianism, the author is superficial and often patronizing. The treatment of Marley's career is thus left to the second half of the work and, although factual, it provides no analysis of the lyrics or music of his songs. The illustrations are very good, however, and the discography, which is some forty-seven pages in length, includes all Jamaican releases and is excellent. These features sadly do not save a disappointing attempt which tried too hard to capture the artist's sense of magic but failed completely.

Whitney, Malika Lee

Bob Marley: reggae king of the world / Malika Lee Whitney, Dermott Hussey; with foreword by Rita Marley. – London: Plexus, 1984. – 204p.: ill. (some col.), facsims (some col.), ports (some col.); 30cm. Includes discography. ISBN 0-85965-061-3 (cased). ISBN 0-85965-068-5 (pbk.)

With a superb collection of illustrations, a fascinating selection of press cuttings and a detailed chronology of his tours, this is a beautifully designed work. If the text is superficial compared with White's and Davis's, the power of Marley's art is certainly expressed by many profound and well-presented visual images.

Martin, George

Born in London in 1926 and classically trained, in 1950 George Martin joined EMI and became an arranger and record producer with Parlophone Records. he recorded classical ensembles, the Goons, jazz musicians and later even the Beyond the Fringe Revue. In 1962, however, after the Beatles had had numerous rejections from other record companies, he decided to record them. Throughout their career he encouraged and influenced their music and was responsible for their recording innovations as well as many beautiful arrangements and added instrumentation.

Martin, George
All you need is ears / George Martin; with Jeremy Hornsby. – London:
Macmillan, 1979. – 285p., 16p. of plates; ill., ports; 24cm. Includes index.
ISBN 0-333-23859-1
A fascinating biography which traces the development of record production over thirty years through Martin's career. The major focus of interest, however, is on his association with the Beatles and his first-hand accounts of the creation of their recordings, their temperaments and aberrations. The technical and musical detail is never omitted but clearly explained.

Mathis, Johnny

Born in 1935, in San Francisco, Johnny Mathis was taught by his father to sing when he was only ten years old. Although at high school he was a promising athlete, and even had the potential to join the US Olympic squad as a high-jumper, he opted for showbusiness. After brief experience in clubs, he had his first hit record in 1956 and has since then been not only one of the most successful singers in his middle-of-the-road style, but also one of the most prolific recording artists around. His strength is a high, clear voice with a distinct vibrato and indefinable stage presence. In the late seventies he recorded with Deniece Williams and continues to sell millions of records and to undertake extensive world tours.

Jasper, Tony
Johnny: the authorised biography of Johnny Mathis / Tony Jasper. – London:
Comet, 1984. – 268p., 16p. of plates: ill., ports; 24cm. Includes filmography
and discography. ISBN 0-8637-9011-9 (pbk.)
Originally published: London: W. H. Allen, 1983.
A thorough, uninspired biography of a major star, with a good collection of photographs and a great deal of personal information. Appendices include very extensive listings of songs Mathis has recorded, his records, chart information, UK, US and European LPs and EPs and a list of film and television appearances.

Meatloaf

Born in Dallas, Texas, in 1948, Marvin Lee Aday played in a succession of local bands before moving to California and singing with the heavy-metal band of Ted Nugent, Free-for-all. In 1976 he met writer Jim Steinman and after a year working together they added singer Karla Da Vito to their band and signed with Epic Records. Calling themselves Meatloaf, because of Aday's bulk of nineteen stones, their powerful stage act and first album, produced by Todd Rundgren, soon made them a success. They continue to be a major American band in the mainstream rock field and have an increasing British following which by the beginning of 1982 had given them a single in the top ten of the British charts.

Robertson, Sandy
  Meatloaf / by Sandy Robertson. – London: Omnibus Press, 1981. – 48p.: ill., ports; 27cm. ISBN 0-86001-965-9 (pbk.)
Giving brief biographical information about the musicians and an outline of their career, this is mainly a collection of action photographs of Meatloaf's sweaty stage performance. A poor attempt, even for the fan market.

Midler, Bette

Born in New Jersey in 1945, Bette Midler grew up in Hawaii and moved to New York in 1965. After working in the Broadway production of the show, Fiddler on the Roof, she began working in cabaret in New York, coming to prominence in 1970 in the unlikely setting of a Turkish baths catering for homosexuals. Her repertoire is wildly eccentric, including songs from shows, blues and rock'n'-roll, as well as standards which she presents in an overtly showy style. Her performance and stage dress reach the extremes of kitsch but her clear, powerful voice has given her a series of successful albums in the USA since 1973. By the end of the seventies she was a major American singer and in 1980 starred in the film The Rose, based loosely on the lifestyle of Janis Joplin.

Baker, Robb
  Bette Midler / by Robb Baker. – London: Angus and Robertson, 1980. – 160p., 4p. of plates: ill., ports (some col.); 25cm. ISBN 0-207-95906-4
  Originally published: New York: Fawcett Books, 1975.
Baker, Robb
  Bette Midler / Robb Baker. – London: Coronet, 1980. – 256p.: ill., ports; 18cm. ISBN 0-340-25327-4 (pbk.)
An episodic biography originally published in 1975 in the USA, full of quotes from interviews with Bette Midler. The new British editions are considerably updated and cover the making of the film The Rose. There is considerable detail of her performances, her songs and her recent career, but little of her early life. The hardback edition is very well designed and illustrated, contrasting with the paperback's basic, poor production and illustrations.

Midler, Bette
  A view from a broad / Bette Midler; photography by Sean Russel. – London:
  Sphere Books, 1980. – 160p.: ill. (chiefly col.), col. ports; 25cm.
  ISBN 0-7221-6048-8 (pbk.)
  Originally published: New York: Sphere Books, 1980.
A humorous autobiography which does not attempt to be comprehensive but
gives an impressionistic view of her world tour. The illustrations are good and
an unusual feature is a series of witty questionnaires. Bette Midler's approach
to her work is well portrayed.

MIDLER, BETTE: FILMS

The Rose

Produced in 1979 and directed by Mark Rydell, The Rose was a vehicle for
Bette Midler and co-starred Alan Bates, who was badly miscast as her
manager. It told the story of Rose, a rock singer played by Midler, based
loosely on the character of Janis Joplin. Her insecurity has led to drug abuse
and heavy drinking, which result finally in her death while performing on stage.
The music and performance of Bette Midler won her the Grammy Award for
the best female singer in 1980 and an Academy Award nomination.

Watson, Diane Masters
  The Rose: an illustrated book / Diane Masters Watson and Mimi Maxwell;
  edited by Bonnie Schiffer. – New York: Twenty First Century Communications, 1979. – 98p.: chiefly ill. (some col.); 31cm. ISBN 0-930-36874-6 (pbk.)
The story of the film is presented by using stills with brief descriptive notes on
the action taking place. The notes, however, are not well written and the effect
is a narrative with no cohesion. The lyrics of the main songs from the soundtrack are reproduced.

MINNELLI, LIZA

Born in Hollywood, California, in 1946, the daughter of Judy Garland and
film director Vincente Minnelli, Liza became a fashionable figure of the early
seventies. Her first major acting role, in 1967, was a non-singing part but with
the film Cabaret, in 1972, she became established as a major star of musicals.
Stage successes and albums followed. She continues her success in musical films
and concert appearances.

Parish, James Robert
  Liza: her Cinderella nightmare / James Robert Parish; with Jack Ano. –
  London: W. H. Allen, 1975. – vi, 186p., 16p. of plates: ill., ports; 23cm.
  Includes discography and filmography. ISBN 0-491-01574-7
  Originally published: New York: Pocket Books, 1974.

Although her childhood was hardly deprived, Liza certainly did not enjoy a stable family upbringing. Her early years are described at length. Not a rags-to-riches story, but a struggle against the overpowering reputation of her mother and the final achievement of recognition in her own right. The author paints a sympathetic portrait without sentimentality.

MITCHELL, JONI

Born in McLeod, Alberta, in 1943, Joni Mitchell attended art college at Calgary and trained as a commercial artist. She became interested in traditional folk music and in 1964 moved to Toronto where she spent time singing in coffee bars and writing songs. She married Chuck Mitchell in 1965 and moved to Detroit. The marriage soon ended but she stayed in Detroit, gaining a wider following and working in New York. She eventually became known to more people after Judy Collins recorded some of her songs in 1967. Her first album, produced by David Crosby, appeared in 1968. Since then she has progressed and experimented with each successive record. Originally writing and performing in a folk style, she has developed her music into a mixture of jazz, rock and folk, always with complex, extremely personal lyrics reflecting her numerous romantic attachments. She is one of the most important contemporary songwriters, in the same league as Bob Dylan and Neil Young, and certainly by far the most important of the woman singer-songwriters.

Fleischer, Leonore
  Joni Mitchell / by Leonore Fleischer. – New York; London: Flash Books,
  1976. – 79p.: ill., facsims, ports; 25cm. ISBN 0-8256-3907-7 (pbk.)
A superficial biography with a cover subtitle, 'her life, her loves, her music', which concentrates on the influences of the various men in Joni Mitchell's life. Her songs are dealt with in passing, however, as are her albums up to 1975, and there are some unusual photographs. It is the sole biography and major source of information on a major artist, but unfortunately it fails to give the space, time and sensitivity required to do justice to the subject.

THE MONKEES

In 1966 Mickey Dolenz, Peter Tork, Mike Nesmith and Davy Jones were auditioned and selected to provide an American-made television series in the style of the Beatles' films. The music for the series was written by accomplished pop-song writers, such as Neil Diamond, and was commercially very successful. After a little over two years, and ten gold records, they disbanded. Mike Nesmith became involved with the First and Second National Bands and received his sought-after critical acclaim. The Monkees were the first 'manufactured' pop group and also the first to appeal to a new, predominantly preteenage audience. In retrospect, however, they provided some good pop music and did not lack talent.

Adler, Bill
    Love letters to the Monkees / edited by Bill Adler; illustrated by Jack Davis. –
    New York: Popular Library, 1967. – 127p.: ill., facsims, ports; 18cm. (pbk.)
Another of Adler's collections of fan letters, easily dismissed by adults, but the
feelings of these young people are often touching, if misplaced.

Meet the Monkees. – London: Daily Mirror Newspapers, 1967. – 80p.: ill.,
    ports; 28cm. (pbk.)
A poorly produced publication filled with stills from the early television shows.

The Monkees: a 'Mirabelle' colour photo souvenir. – London: Newnes, 1967. –
    16p.: ill. (some col.), ports (some col.); 28cm. (pbk.)
In magazine format, this collection of photographs of the group with a brief text
was published by *Mirabelle*, a weekly magazine for teenage girls, at the height
of the Monkees' initial success.

MONROE, BILL

Born in Rosine, Kentucky, in 1911, William Smith Monroe is the undisputed
founder of bluegrass music. He was the youngest of eight children. As his
eyesight was poor he learnt to rely on a fine ear for harmony and to play the
mandolin. In 1929 he joined his older brothers Birch and Charlie playing at
dances and local parties. In 1934 the Monroe Brothers turned professional and
in 1936 made their first records. Bill parted from his brothers in 1938 and began
to evolve his Bluegrass Boys line-up including Earl Scruggs and Lester Flatt. It
was Scruggs' syncopated banjo sound and the wide harmony of the vocals that
was to become bluegrass. His records and those of his musicians have remained
successful to date, influencing following generations. He was a major performer during the folk revival of the sixties.

MONROE, BILL: DISCOGRAPHIES

Rosenberg, Neil V.
    Bill Monroe and his Blue Grass Boys / compiled with an introduction and
    commentaries by Neil V. Rosenberg. – Nashville, Tennessee: Country
    Music Foundation Press, 1974. – v., 122p.: ill., facsims, ports; 21cm.
    Includes index.
Detailed and well presented, full discographical information, the musicians
involved in sessions and the solo albums of the musicians are included. There
are reproductions of album sleeves and portraits of various line-ups.

MOON, KEITH

Born in 1946, Keith was the youngest member and drummer of the Who. A
brilliant musician with a unique, driving style he became more famous for his

outrageous lifestyle and wild antics. The legends grew, with stories of his demolition of hotel rooms, wrecking of motor cars and overindulgence. He died of a drug overdose in September 1978.

(*See also* THE WHO.)

Butler, Dougal
Moon the loon: the rock and roll life of Keith Moon — the most spectacular drummer the world has ever seen / Dougal Butler, Chris Trengove and Peter Lawrence. – London: Star Books, 1981. – 231p., 8p. of plates: ill., ports; 18cm. Includes glossary. ISBN 0-352-30805-2 (pbk.)

Dougal Butler was born in West London in 1946. After being a fan of the Who as a teenager, he became one of their road managers in 1967. This is a sensational recollection of Moon's career and lifestyle. Often amusing, it is told with affection but little sensitivity. The glossary of Moon's west London terminology is an unusual idea. The author left the band over a year before Moon's death.

Waterman, Ivan
Keith Moon: the life and death of a rock legend / by Ivan Waterman. – London: Arrow Books, 1979. – 142p., 16p. of plates: ill., ports; 18cm. ISBN 0-09-920930-6 (pbk.)

In a sensational biography of the worst kind, the author indulges himself in Moon's drinking and violent antics. There is some discussion of his contribution to the Who but much more about his romantic escapades and liquid consumption.

MORRISON, JIM AND THE DOORS

James Douglas Morrison was born in Melbourne, Florida, in 1943, the eldest son of a rear admiral. In 1964 he left Florida State University and enrolled in the film school of University College Los Angeles, where he met Phil Manzarek. Eight years older than Morrison, Manzarek had been playing rhythm & blues for years and was a classically trained pianist. They decided to form a band after Morrison had read some of his poems to Manzarek, who saw their potential as innovative song lyrics. Robby Krieger and John Densmore were soon recruited and the Doors were formed. After playing in the small London Fog club in Los Angeles for a few months, they secured a contract with the small Elektra record company and when their first album was released in 1967 they were immediately established. Their style was blues-based but fused the contemporary sounds of acid rock with Morrison's literary lyrics, setting the group apart. Their following spanned a wide spectrum from the start and a number-one hit single was taken from the first album, making Morrison a teenage pin-up even though the band was acceptable to the underground intelligentsia. There followed a string of albums and singles, all of which sold in huge quantities. Morrison was always experimenting with the dramatic presentation of their stage act, dressed in leather and overtly sexual. In December 1967 he was arrested for using obscene language and in March 1969 for alleged indecent exposure on stage in Miami. After various other conflicts with the authorities he became disillusioned with his life as a rock star, concentrating on his poetry and changing his physical appearance by growing a beard and shedding the leather apparel. In 1971 his final album was completed, displaying even more urgent, critical lyrics and harsh images.

Morrison left America to work in Paris early in 1971. His health was by now in a bad state. He had always overindulged in drugs of all kinds and particularly in alcohol, which transformed him from an erudite, charming companion into a raging drunk likely to create a riot. He was found dead in the bath of his Paris flat on July 3rd 1971, with the cause of death diagnosed as a heart attack. His poems *The lords and the new creatures* were published in 1971. The Doors worked together for a few years and also made solo albums but with little real success. Far more successful in America and France than in Britain, Jim Morrison remains one of the martyrs of rock music. Not the literary genius he is sometimes called, he is an important figure whose major contribution is that he introduced to a wide audience poetic imagery and drama not experienced before in a heavy-rock context.

Hopkins, Jerry

No one here gets out alive / by Jerry Hopkins and Daniel Sugerman. – London: Plexus, 1980. – ix, 387p.: ill., ports; 23cm. Originally published: New York: Warner Books, 1980. Includes discography and filmography. ISBN 0-85965-039-1 (cased). ISBN 0-85965-038-3 (pbk.)

Jerry Hopkins decided to write Morrison's biography before the latter's death but waited for several years and then took four years to complete it. He then passed the manuscript to Sugerman, an associate manager of the Doors, who added to and edited it. The result is a mixture of Hopkins' well-written objective prose and idolatry, with no analysis of the Doors' music or techniques and an emphasis on sensationalism. There is an attempt to sow the seed of a possibility that Morrison did not die but escaped the pressures of stardom by faking his death. No evidence is put forward. With all its faults this book was a bestseller in the USA at the end of 1980 and is a captivating read for all those who enjoy the mythology of stardom.

Jahn, Mike

Jim Morrison and the Doors: an unauthorised book / Mike Jahn. – New York: Grosset & Dunlap, 1969. – 95p.: ill., ports; 21cm. (pbk.)

In the USA the Doors were by far the major American band of the late sixties and Mike Jahn reflects that fact with an enthusiastic text which captures very well the literary aspirations of the group members themselves and particularly those of Morrison. Written at the time of the Doors' height of popularity and prestige, the author speculates on their lasting importance and musical significance. It is easy from this side of the Atlantic, with hindsight and over a decade later to dimiss his enthusiasm, but suffice it to say the tone is over-zealous. Nevertheless, this is a well-written, intelligent work with an excellent collection of illustrations.

Lisciandro, Frank
  Jim Morrison: an hour of magic / photographs, text and design by Frank
  Lisciandro. – London: Eel Pie, 1982. – 160p.: chiefly ill. (some col.), ports
  (some col.); 30cm. ISBN 0-906008-60-3 (pbk.)
  Originally published: New York: Putnam, 1982.
With brief, recent quotations and anecdotes from surviving members of the
Doors and their associates, and a short biographical essay on Morrison's life,
the bulk of the book is an excellent collection of photographs. Many appear
here for the first time and few are available in other publications.

Sugerman, Danny
  The Doors: the illustrated history / Danny Sugerman. – London: Vermilion,
  1983. – 256p., 16p. of plates: ill. (some col.), ports (some col.); 31cm.
  Includes discography. ISBN 0-09-153821-1 (pbk.)
  Originally published: New York: Morrow; Quill, 1983.
Written by one of the band's associate managers, this is a factual, uninspiring
account of the Doors' career. What is interesting, however, is a good collection
of press cuttings and an excellent selection of photographs.

Tobler, John
  The Doors / by John Tobler and Andrew Doe. – London; New York:
  Proteus, 1982. – 128p.: ill. (some col.), ports (some col.); 27cm. Includes
  bibliography, discography and filmography. ISBN 0-86276-070-4 (cased).
  ISBN 0-86276-069-0 (pbk.)
Well illustrated with over fifty carefully selected photographs, this brief
attempt at a serious study of the band falls sadly short of the Hopkins
biography. The result is an unsatisfactory mixture of quotes from the Doors,
superficial facts, pretentious comment and interesting photographs in a well-
designed format.

MORRISON, JIM: SONGS

Morrison, Jim
  Jim Morrison: the story of the Doors in words and pictures. – London:
  Omnibus Press, 1982. – 96p.: ill., ports; 25cm. Includes discography.
  ISBN 0-7119-0150-3 (pbk.)
The lyrics to the Doors' songs transcribed from the recorded versions are
interspersed with an excellent collection of illustrations. Although the other
Doors certainly contributed to the writing of the songs, it is Jim Morrison who
is generally given credit for the lyrics.

MORRISON, JIM: POEMS

Morrison, Jim
  The lords & the new creatures / Jim Morrison. – New York: Simon and
  Schuster, 1971. – 141p.; 22cm. ISBN 0-671-20539-0 (cased).

ISBN 0-671-21044-0 (pbk.)

Previous edition: New York: Simon and Schuster, 1970.

Originally these two collections of poetry were published privately in limited editions of one hundred copies, but were later published by Simon and Schuster with a cover featuring the poet in his glamorous, unbearded pose. He was deeply anxious to be taken seriously as a poet and considered the cover offensive. When the paperback edition appeared the cover picture was changed to a larger, bearded image. His work has gained some critical acclaim since his death and possesses an eerie, hypnotic quality. After the success of the Hopkins biography, Simon and Schuster reprinted the collection.

MORRISON, VAN

Born in Belfast in 1945, from an early age Van Morrison was immersed in the blues. He first gained national success in 1965 with the rhythm & blues band, Them. After two big hits, he became disillusioned with the British music industry and moved to the USA. After success with a single, he recorded the album, Astral Weeks, in 1968. Although not representative of his later work, this collection of haunting songs is critically regarded as one of the most important albums in the field of rock music. His subsequent work has ranged in musical styles more diversely than that of any other major artist. He continues to write with remarkable intensity and introspection and is painfully critical of his own work to the extent of scrapping completed albums. He is a distant, mysterious figure who seldom ventures from his reclusive lifestyle.

Rogan, Johnny
    Van Morrison: the great deception / Johnny Rogan. – London; New York:
    Proteus, 1982. – 169p.: ill., ports; 23cm. Includes discography.
    ISBN 0-86276-045-3 (cased). ISBN 0-86276-040-2 (pbk.)
A reasonable attempt to understand Van Morrison's enigmatic personality, this is based exclusively on secondary sources. Nevertheless, the author has a real appreciation of his subject's work and has selected some good illustrations.

Yorke, Ritchie
    Van Morrison: into the music / Ritchie Yorke. – London: Charisma, 1977. –
    188p., 12p. of plates: ill., ports; 18cm. Includes discography.
    ISBN 0-85947-013-X (pbk.)
The author is the only journalist in whom Van Morrison has regularly confided and there are detailed transcripts of lengthy interviews. Each album is discussed in detail with copious reference to his lyrics and an excellent commentary.

MOTORHEAD

Motorhead were formed in London in 1975. After bass player and vocalist Lemmy Kilminster had left Hawkwind during their 1975 American tour, he included guitarist Larry Wallis and drummer Lucas Fox in his first line-up. They made one album, which was not released by their record company, United Artists, until 1980, who obviously lacked faith in the group at the time. Lemmy decided to find a new line-up and recruited Fast Eddie Clarke and Phil 'Philthy Animal' Taylor. They signed with the Chiswick record label and, in 1978, yet another contract with Bronze Records. At last they began to gather a following and from then on their brand of 'overkill' heavy-metal music has become louder, brasher and ever more popular. The image they have contrived is that of the ugliest, nastiest, most revolting band in the country. Their success has been achieved through hard work and an astute management.

Dadomo, Giovanni
  Motorhead / by Giovanni Dadomo. – London: Omnibus Press, 1981. – 48p.:
  ill., ports; 27cm. ISBN 0-86001-935-7 (pbk.)
A poorly designed, brief view of the group, lacking even the most fundamental biographical information and offering only an impression of their nasty image.

Motorhead: born to lose live to win. – Manchester: Babylon Books, 1981. –
  48p.: ill., ports; 25cm. Includes discography. (pbk.)
Produced in the fanzine format, this is even more disorganized than is usual in such publications. There is, however, a great deal of information here and some unusual, amusing, but poorly reproduced, illustrations.

NAPIER-BELL, SIMON

Born in London in 1939, after various jobs Simon Napier-Bell became involved in producing documentaries and television commercials in the mid sixties. At this time he met Vicki Wickham, who was partly responsible for the television show Ready Steady Go, the most important musical showcase of the time. After confessing an interest in the music business, she encouraged him to try to write song lyrics for Dusty Springfield. The song, which is also the title of his recollections, was a big hit. He later became the manager of the Yardbirds, one of the most prestigious groups of the mid sixties. Later he was to become involved with the group, John's Children, and to manage the career of Marc Bolan. In addition, he had a sucessful period as a record producer and was friend and confidant to many of the leading figures in the management of artists, such as Brian Epstein and Kit Lambert, manager of the Who.

Napier-Bell, Simon
  You don't have to say you love me / Simon Napier-Bell. – Sevenoaks, Kent:
  New English Library, 1982. – 178p., 8p. of plates: ill., facsims, ports; 18cm.
  ISBN 0-450-05504-3 (pbk.)
With the cover subtitle of *60's British rock backstage with its trousers down*, one is not surprised to find an attempt at an outrageous exposé. The result is a

catalogue of recollections in which the author admits his own involvement in the general manipulation and blatant hype of the music business. He presumably expects the reader to believe that this current little venture is a reformed, sincere approach. He implies, for example, that Brian Epstein's suicide was a result of his, Napier-Bell's, refusal to spend the weekend at Epstein's country house. Even if it were true, this is in extraordinarily bad taste, but much of the narrative is simply extravagant rubbish.

NELSON, WILLIE

Born in Abbott, Texas, in 1933, after serving in the Air Force, Willie Nelson settled in Waco, Texas, and obtained a job on a local radio station. From there he began playing around Fort Worth, working on radio and in bars and writing some very good songs. After working in Los Angeles, Nashville and Fort Worth, and making a series of albums, he became disillusioned with RCA of Nashville and signed a new record contract with Atlantic, determined to become a singer-songwriter on his own terms. He left Atlantic for Columbia Records in the mid seventies and his successes increased. Regarded by many critics as the leader of the Outlaw movement, he is an important figure and a very real stylist.

Allen, Bob
    Waylon and Willie / Bob Allen. – New York: Flash Books, 1979. – 128p.: ill., ports; 26cm. Includes discographies. ISBN 0-8256-3941-7 (pbk.)
Brief biographies of the two leading outlaws. This is not a big enough book to devote enough space to such important and complex artists, but is quite useful.

THE NEW YORK DOLLS

Formed in late 1973 in New York, the New York Dolls had a style very similar to that of the early Rolling Stones with singer, David Johannson, resembling Mick Jagger and guitarist, Johnny Thunder, looking not unlike Keith Richards. After their first drummer died of a heroin overdose, the other musicians included Sylvain Sylvain, Jerry Nolan and Arthur Kane. Their stage image relied on a transvestite theme, the decadence of which made them early leaders of the New York new-wave movement. In 1973 they recorded a promising album but the group had faded by 1975 when Malcolm Maclaren, later manager of the Sex Pistols, planned an abortive revival. In 1977 Thunder and drummer Jerry Nolan formed the Heartbreakers. They are recognized as a formative influence in the new-wave movement but little of this is in evidence in their recordings.

Morrissey, Steven
New York Dolls / Steven Morrissey. – Manchester: Babylon Books, 1980. –
52p.: ill., ports; 25cm. ISBN 0-907188-06-0 (pbk.)
This major source of information on the group is poorly produced in 'cut-up'
fanzine format. It is mostly composed of reproductions of articles and badly-
reproduced photographs from music papers.

NEWTON-JOHN, OLIVIA

Born in Cambridge, England, in 1948, the daughter of a Nobel Prize-winning
physicist, Olivia Newton-John spent her childhood in Australia. After singing
with a female vocal group in her teens, she moved back to England and in 1971
made her first album. There followed a series of successful singles in a country-
music style and by the mid seventies she was consistently successful in the
USA as well as the United Kingdom. In 1978 she starred, with John Travolta,
in the film Grease and suddenly her image and singing style were completely
transformed; and in the late seventies she became one of the most popular
female performers in the world, appealing to a younger, disco-orientated
audience.

Jacobs, Linda
Olivia Newton-John: sunshine supergirl / by Linda Jacobs. – St. Paul,
Minnesota: EMC, 1975. – 38p.: ill., ports; 20cm. ISBN 0-88436-184-5
(cased). ISBN 0-88436-185-3 (pbk.)
Written before her film success in Grease and her subsequent enormous world-
wide fame, this controlled-vocabulary biography is aimed at a reading age of
about ten for American schools. Well designed and beautifully illustrated, it is
also available with an audio cassette.

Morse, Ann
Olivia Newton-John / text Ann Morse; illustrator John Keely; design concept
Mark Landkamer. – Mankato, Minnesota: Creative Education, 1976. –
31p.: col. ill., col. ports; 25cm. ISBN 0-8719-1475-1
A controlled-vocabulary biography written for a reading age of about ten for
American schools. An informative, easy-to-read biography with some well-
chosen illustrations which covers Olivia Newton-John's career before her
success in Grease when she had already established herself as a popular country
singer in America.

Ruff, Peter
Olivia Newton-John / by Peter Ruff. – New York: Quick Fox, 1979. – 96p.:
ill., ports; 28cm. ISBN 0-8256-3934-4 (pbk.)
This is a homely biography, with a full, detailed discography; informative and
unsensational.

NEWTON-JOHN, OLIVIA: FILMS

(See TRAVOLTA, JOHN: GREASE.)

NIGHTINGALE, ANNE

Since the mid sixties Anne Nightingale has been one of Britain's most successful and consistent disc jockeys. Beginning on television, she moved to radio and in the late seventies became the host of the Old Grey Whistle Test television series. This programme deals with the more serious, album-orientated end of rock music and includes interviews with artists and considerable musical criticism. She moved into this job very easily and is exceptional as a successful disc jockey not only because she is a woman but also because she has an intelligent and critical approach.

Nightingale, Anne
    Chase the fade: music memories & memorabilia / Anne Nightingale. – Poole,
    Dorset: Blandford Press, 1981. – 125p.: ill., facsims, ports; 25cm. Includes
    index. ISBN 0-7137-1167-1
An episodic collection of reminiscences about such events as the break-up of the Beatles, the lifestyle of Keith Moon, her tour of the Far East with the Police and the British rock festivals of the early seventies. It gives some insight into personalities, and the relationships between the musicians, disc jockeys and the press, as well as a personal view of the unseen changes in the popular-music world over recent years. In general, however, this is a disappointing attempt at a new approach to biography in the field.

THE NOLANS

Tommy Nolan and his wife Maureen, both from Dublin, had been involved in Irish showbands for many years before moving to Blackpool in 1962. Bringing with them their growing family, they settled to play the many working-men's clubs of the Blackpool area. From an early age the two sons and six daughters of the family began to perform and in the early seventies the Nolan Sisters act was born, initially comprising Denise, Linda, Maureen, Anne and Bernadette. After singing on the club circuit of northern England, they moved to London in 1974 and signed a contract with Target Records. There followed television appearances and massive record sales of albums comprising popular music standards aimed at a wide, family audience. In 1979 Denise married and left the group. They changed their name to the Nolans, signed with Epic Records, and, in the same year, achieved their first hit single. The youngest sister, Coleen, joined the group and Anne left but rejoined in 1982, making the present number of five. Their career continues to flourish and they stand as one of the most successful British middle-of-the-road acts, able to appeal to a very wide audience from light disco and pop to cabaret.

Treasurer, Kim
>   *The Nolans: 'in the mood for stardom'* / Kim Treasurer. – Tunbridge Wells,
>   Kent: Midas Books, 1982. – 128p.: ill.,facsims, ports; 26cm. Includes
>   discography. ISBN 0-85936-104-7 (cased). ISBN 0-85936-122-5 (pbk.)
>   Also published: New York: Hippocrene Books, 1982.

With much background on the girls' childhood and parents, this is a well-written, well-designed, informative account which makes a very good attempt to make their narrow lives appear interesting. The discography is complete and the illustrations, which include family snapshots from over the years, are sometimes amusing but rather uninspired.

NUGENT, TED

Born in Detroit, Michigan, in 1949, Ted Nugent became a member of the Amboy Dukes in 1965. Most similar American groups of the time, often described as garage bands, soon disappeared, but the Amboy Dukes survived owing to their flair for the unusual and a simple pragmatism. They evolved through the excesses of the late sixties psychedelia into heavy metal with Nugent as a driving force. Working constantly, their stage act developed into extravagant shows with increasingly earsplitting guitar playing. Nugent claimed to be the greatest guitarist in the world, and if this is a typical piece of exaggeration, he is often accepted as the loudest. He also began to develop a wild stage image complete with loin cloth and bow and arrow. In 1975 he signed a solo contract with Epic Records and finally achieved a wider audience in the USA and some hit albums. He has never been very popular in Britain but has acquired a minor following since the heavy-metal revival.

Holland, Robert
>   *The legendary Ted Nugent* / by Robert Holland. – London: Omnibus Press,
>   1982. – 96p.: ill., ports; 26cm. Includes discography. ISBN 0-7119-0061-2
>   (pbk.)
>   Also published: New York: Savoy Editions, 1982.

Including a lengthy interview, but rather too much idolatry, this is well illustrated and by far the best source of information on the artist.

NUMAN, GARY

Born Gary Anthony James Webb in Chiswick, London, in 1958, Gary Numan spent his childhood in Stanwell, Middlesex. His schooldays were an unhappy and unsuccessful time but he learned to play the guitar in his early teens and was determined to become a musician. After playing in local groups, he made a demonstration record in 1977 with his friend and bass player, Paul Gardiner, and was signed by Beggars Banquet. His early idols had been Marc Bolan and David Bowie, as was soon to become evident. He shrewdly anticipated the trend of synthesizer-based music and cultivated a futuristic image with white face make-up and mechanistic stage movements. Numan's song lyrics were concerned with contemporary technology and isolation. In early 1979 he achieved his first hit with his group Tubeway Army. This was followed by a series of hit singles and albums which sold over ten million records in under three years. His approach, though inventive, is much criticized as being contrived, but he continues to be successful, always experimenting and recently becoming a little more human.

Coleman, Ray
    Gary Numan: an authorised biography / Ray Coleman. – London: Sidgwick
    & Jackson, 1982. – 128p.: ill., ports; 25cm. Includes discography and index.
    ISBN 0-283-98876-2 (pbk.)
The biggest source of information on Numan, this is filled with song lyrics and quotations, and gives a good biographical outline and some real analysis of his work. There is a good collection of illustrations and a complete, but not detailed, discography.

Vermorel, Fred
    Numan by computer / Fred and Judy Vermorel. – London: Omnibus Press,
    1981. – 64p.: ill. (some col.), ports (some col.); 27cm. ISBN 0-86001-813-X
    (pbk.)
Maintaining his futuristic image, some of Numan's ideas and quotations are displayed in a computer print-out style of typeface.

OCHS, PHIL

Phil Ochs was born in El Paso in 1940. After leaving military academy and studying journalism, he moved to Greenwich Village in the early sixties and soon became, with Bob Dylan, one of the leaders of the folk scene. His songs were even more political and abrasive than Dylan's and he was banned from both radio and television at a crucial time in his career. He did, however, sign a contract with Elektra Records and his first three albums all reached the American charts — a remarkable feat considering the lack of promotion. By 1966 he was one of the heroes of the American underground. He moved to Los Angeles in 1970, but his new material was receiving little response. He lived outside the USA for the next few years but his increasing bouts of acute depression finally led to his suicide on April 8th 1976. He remains a distant, enigmatic figure who stood alone in his refusal to compromise or to be consumed by the music industry establishment.

Eliot, Marc
    Death of a rebel / Marc Eliot. – Garden City, New York: Anchor Press;
    Doubleday, 1979. – 316p., 40p. of plates: ill., ports; 20cm. Includes
    discography and index. ISBN 0-385-13610-2 (pbk.)
A well-researched biography of exceptional detail which goes a long way to

explain the unusual, unbalanced character of Ochs. The discography is full and there are quotations from interviews with many of his musical associates and friends. The author rightly pays a great deal of attention to analysing his work and in emphasizing his considerable influence on the protest and singer-songwriter movements.

O'CONNOR, HAZEL

Born in Coventry in 1955, after a varied career as a model, cabaret singer and would-be songwriter, Hazel O'Connor first came to the attention of the general public in 1980 when she was cast in the leading role of the film Breaking Glass. This depicted the career of a young new-wave singer, hardly reflecting her own background. Nevertheless, after this image had been established, she sustained it in the real musical world and achieved success with a series of hit records and successful concert tours. By the end of 1981 she had become one of the three most popular British female singers with her distinct style, shouting her futuristic lyrics in a strange, distorted accent.

O'Connor, Hazel
  Hazel O'Connor: uncovered plus / by Hazel O'Connor. – London; New
  York: Proteus, 1981. – 128p.: ill. (some col.), facsims, ports (some col.);
  26cm. Includes discography. ISBN 0-906071-81-X (pbk.)
In this wittily written book, Hazel O'Connor describes her varied career, romantic attachments and final breakthrough to success. The photographs underline clearly her changing styles of dress and presentation of herself in the development of her current image.

ONO, YOKO

Born in Tokyo in 1934, Yoko Ono emigrated to America in the late forties with her parents and lived in the respectable New York suburb of Scarsdale. She attended Sarah Lawrence College and studied art and musical composition. In 1952 she married a Japanese musician and moved to Greenwich Village. She became part of Andy Warhol's art circle in the early sixties and gained a reputation as an avant-garde visual artist specializing in 'happenings'. In 1966 she moved to London and in that year met John Lennon of the Beatles. She had an immediate effect on Lennon's work even at this stage in their relationship. In March 1969 she and Lennon married in Gibraltar and then spent a honeymoon in bed in Amsterdam's Hilton Hotel where they invited the world's press to discuss their message of peace. Regarded by many as a primary cause in Lennon's radical change in musical direction and in his attitude to the Beatles as a group, she was probably more symptomatic of his desire to be taken seriously as an artist. After estrangement during the early seventies, she and Lennon became inseparable.They cooperated on several early musical projects and films but it was not until their joint effort, Double Fantasy, was released in 1980 that she appeared as a true musical partner. The album, a statement on their relationship, was completed only weeks before Lennon's death and is a lasting memorial to one of the most prominent and radical relationships in recent years.

(*See also* LENNON, JOHN.)

ONO, YOKO: WRITINGS

Ono, Yoko
  Grapefruit: a book of instructions / by Yoko Ono; introduction by John
  Lennon. – London: Peter Owen, 1970. 279p.: ill., facsims; 14cm.
  ISBN 0-7206-0121-5
This curious little book was originally produced as a set of cards. It features instructions and single words in surrealistic juxtapositions.

ORCHESTRAL MANOEUVRES IN THE DARK

Andy McCluskey and Paul Humphreys originally met at their primary school in West Kirby, Merseyside, in the early sixties. By 1975 they were involved in local groups and in 1977 began recording their own compositions. Working as a duo they developed performance techniques using a four-track tape recorder for their backing, playing only synthesizer and bass as live instruments to augment their voices. After minor successes, including a tour with Gary Numan, they had a big hit at the end of 1980 with the single Enola Gay, a song about the aircraft which dropped the first atomic bomb. This was followed, in 1981, by four further hit singles and a top-selling album. They continue to be successful with their interesting lyrical ideas and very melodic compositions. More recently they have enhanced their concert performances with additional musicians.

West, Mike
  Orchestral Manoeuvres in the Dark / by Mike West. – London: Omnibus
  Press, 1982. – 48p.: ill., ports; 27cm. Includes discography.
  ISBN 0-7119-0149-X (pbk.)
A straightforward, brief biography which does devote some time to OMD's use of electronics but fails to look into their musical influences or songwriting. There is a list of concert, radio and television performances and some dull illustrations.

ORLANDO, TONY

Born in New York in 1944, Tony Orlando's first success as a singer was in 1961 when he had three successful singles as a solo artist. He left singing for a while and was the general manager of the Columbia Records publishing division when, in 1970, he was asked to record a song with two black girl singers, Telma Hopkins and Joyce Vincent. This he did, and the group, calling themselves Dawn, had a series of hits throughout 1971, 1972 and 1973. Their material was always well-selected, simple pop songs, never aspiring above catchy commercialism, but totally professional in presentation and technique.

Morse, Ann
    Tony Orlando / text Ann Morse. – Mankato: Minnesota: Creative
    Education, 1978. – 32p.:. (some col.), ports (some col.); 25cm.
    ISBN 0-8719-1616-9
Written for a reading age of around ten for American schools, this is a controlled-vocabulary text with some good illustrations.

THE OSMONDS

The Osmond family, Mormons from Salt Lake City, Utah, began their careers as a child singing and dancing act in the early sixties. By the seventies they had developed their wholesome family image into the most successful world-wide pop attraction and had become the darlings of the teenyboppers. Their professional approach, the ingenious management of their father and careful publicity had produced a wide family appeal with large record sales, television spectaculars and concert tours. In addition, Donny, Jimmy and Marie Osmond have had solo successes and Donny and Marie, as a duet, had their own series on television.

Delaney, Monica
    The Osmonds / text Monica Delaney, Shannon Laney; illustrator John
    Keely; design concept Mark Landkamer. – Mankato, Minnesota: Creative
    Education, 1976. – 31p.: col. ill., col. ports; 25cm. ISBN 0-8719-1461-1
A controlled-vocabulary text written for a reading age of around ten for American schools, this is well illustrated, informative and a good choice of subject.

Dunn, Paul H.
    The Osmonds: the official story of the Osmond family / Paul H. Dunn. –
    London: Star Books, 1977. – 189p., 8p. of plates: ill., ports; 18cm.
    ISBN 0-352-39854-X (pbk.)
    Originally published: Salt Lake City, Utah: Bookcraft, 1975.
    Also published: London: W. H. Allen, 1975.
Well written for the young fan, hardly exciting but full of information about the development of the family's career and what a wonderful, happy crowd they are.

Eldred, Patricia Mulrooney
    Donny and Marie / by Patricia Mulrooney Eldred; designed by Mark
    Landkamer. – Mankato, Minnesota: Creative Education, 1978. – 31p.: ill.,
    ports; 25cm. ISBN 0-8719-1618-5

A controlled-vocabulary text for a reading age of around ten, it is well illustrated, informative and an ideal subject for the age range.

The fantastic Osmonds!. – London: Daily Mirror Books, 1972. – 48p.: chiefly
ill. (some col.), ports (some col.); 30cm. ISBN 0-6003-2890-2 (pbk.)
Published at the height of the group's popularity and to coincide with a European tour, here is a collection of smiling photographs with a few brief comments. A good example of well-produced ephemera.

Gregory, James
At last... Donny! / by James Gregory. – Manchester: World Distributors,
1973. – 125p., 16p. of plates; 18cm. ISBN 0-7235-5813-2 (pbk.)
The Osmonds' lifestyle, as told by Donny, in which their success story is covered in a fragmented style. Unashamedly sanctimonious, it is embarrassing and badly written.

Gregory, James
Donny and the Osmonds backstage / by James Gregory. – Manchester:
World Distributors, 1973. – 128p., 16p. of plates: ill., ports; 18cm.
ISBN 0-7235-5817-9 (pbk.)
The group's wholesome lifestyle, Christianity and the way pop music can be good, clean fun are the main themes. There are interviews with each member of the family and their parents, and a reasonable collection of portraits and photographs of the group in concert.

McMillan, Constance Van Brunt
Donny and Marie Osmond: breaking all the rules / by Constance Van Brunt
McMillan. – St. Paul, Minnesota: EMC, 1977. – 38p.: ill., ports; 23cm.
ISBN 0-88436-408-9 (cased). ISBN 0-88436-409-7 (pbk.)
A well-illustrated controlled-vocabulary text for American junior high schools, this series is particularly well designed.

Osmonds' world: the official year book of the Osmonds 1974–78. – London:
IPC Magazines, 1973–77. Annual. 1978. – 1977. – 70p.: ill. (some col.), ports
(some col.); 27cm. ISBN 0-8503-7378-6
This is the annual of *Osmonds' World,* their monthly magazine. Current photographs of the family, interviews, puzzles and games and brief news items were packaged for the Christmas gift market.

Roeder, Lynn
On tour with Donny & Marie and the Osmonds / by Lynn and Lisa Roeder. –
New York: Tempo Books, 1977. – 221p.: ill., ports; 18cm.
ISBN 0-448-13536-1 (cased). ISBN 0-448-14146-9 (pbk.)
The sixteen-year-old author and her younger sister, Lisa, toured with the Osmonds during their summer vacation. Filled with wonder, the book does contain some detailed description of the preparation, rehearsal and sophisticated equipment which was involved in their touring shows. The photographs are very poorly reproduced.

Tremlett, George
> *The Osmond story* / George Tremlett. – London: Futura Publications, 1974.
> – 168p., 16p. of plates: ill., ports; 18cm. ISBN 0-8600-7027-1 (pbk.)
> Also published: New York: Warner Paperback Library, 1975.

The author's usual formula of journalistic narrative, mainly acquired from other published sources, offers the only informative account of the group's career. As always there is an interesting chronology and some well-chosen illustrations.

THE OSMONDS: PERIODICALS

(*See* section 8.2, THE OSMONDS.)

PAGE, JIMMY

James Patrick Page, born in January 1944 in Heston, Middlesex, was already by the mid-sixties a leading session guitar player. It was his guitar on the Who's My Generation, Donovan's Hurdy Gurdy Man and the Kinks' You Really Got Me. He joined the Yardbirds in 1966 as the bass player and later switched to guitar. In 1968, with the final break-up of the original Yardbirds line-up, Page rounded up the musicians for the New Yardbirds. By the end of that year the name had changed to Led Zeppelin. Since then Jimmy Page has grown into the ultimate guitar hero with a superstar lifestyle, wild reputation, fascination with witchcraft and great wealth.

(*See also* LED ZEPPELIN.)

Mylett, Howard
> *Jimmy Page: tangents within a framework* / Howard Mylett. – London:
> Omnibus Press, 1983. – 96p.: ill. (some col.), ports (some col.); 26cm.
> ISBN 0-7119-0265-8 (pbk.)

Written by a longtime fan and writer on Led Zeppelin. The author knows his subject and writes with excitement and authority. The illustrations are very well chosen and there are many quotations from interviews with Page.

PARTON, DOLLY

Dolly Parton was born the fourth child of twelve in Locust Ridge, Sevier County, Tennessee, in 1946. After high school she moved to Nashville and in 1967 signed her first recording contract. She worked with country-music star Porter Wagoner until deciding to work as a solo act in 1974. Her music, although deeply rooted in commercial country, is light and avoids the usual clichés of that style. Her appearance, with enormous wigs and a spectacular figure, belies her real talent and it is her songwriting that is most impressive, with ambitious lyrics which transcend the limiting themes of standard country music and which have been widely recorded by other artists. Her appeal has become increasingly wider and her instrumentation and arrangements make her acceptable to some rock audiences. Her record successes, which have been consistent in the USA, have been fewer in Britain where she is nevertheless regarded as the top female country singer. In 1981 she gave an impressive acting performance in the film Nine to Five.

Berman, Connie
The official Dolly Parton scrapbook / by Connie Berman; foreword by Dolly Parton. – New York: Grosset & Dunlap, 1978. – 96p.: ill., ports; 28cm. Includes discography. ISBN 0-4481-6176-1 (cased). ISBN 0-4481-6183-4 (pbk.)
A large collection of photographs is augmented by an informative biographical essay and transcripts of interviews with the subject. A chapter is devoted to her songwriting, but unfortunately it is disappointing, failing to penetrate her inspirations and techniques. The discography is selective.

James, Otis
Dolly Parton / Otis James. – New York; London: Quick Fox, 1978. – 95p.: ill., ports; 26cm. Includes discography. ISBN 0-8256-3922-0 (pbk.)
Not an informative biography, this is well illustrated and has interesting comments about Dolly Parton's songwriting, but little else. The discography is complete but lacks detail.

Keely, John
Dolly Parton / by John Keely. – Mankato, Minnesota: Creative Education, 1980. – 31p.: ill. (some col.), ports (some col.); 25cm. ISBN 0-8719-1695-9 (cased). ISBN 0-89812-095-0 (pbk.)
This controlled-vocabulary biography is written for a reading age of about ten for American schools. It is well produced and well illustrated, presenting an attractive profile of the country singer.

Krishef, Robert K.
Dolly Parton / Robert K. Krishef. – Minneapolis: Lerner Publications, 1980. – 71p.: ill., ports; 21cm. Includes index. ISBN 0-8225-1411-7
Written for a reading age of about ten for American schools, this is a controlled-vocabulary biography with some good illustrations.

Nash, Alanna
Dolly / Alanna Nash. – St. Albans: Panther, 1979. – 397p., 8p. of plates: ill., ports; 18cm. Includes discography. ISBN 0-586-05051-5 (pbk.)
Originally published: Danbury, New Hampshire: Addison House, 1979.
A lengthy, personal biography, based on the author's interviews with her subject as well as with her friends and fellow musicians. In addition, she accompanied Dolly on tour and was with her on several recording sessions.

There is a great deal of information about her childhood and early career and a complete discography, although analysis of her songs is neglected. It does, however, give a real insight into her lifestyle and attitudes.

PERKINS, CARL

Carl Perkins was born in 1932 in Lake City, Tennessee. After performing at country dances he signed a contract with Sun Records in 1954, where Elvis Presley was already recording. He wrote and recorded Blue Suede Shoes, which became an enormous hit early in 1956, but while driving to a television engagement he was severely injured in a car crash; his brother was killed. On leaving hospital after almost a year he had been left behind by Elvis and, although he continued to record, his style of rockabilly had passed its height of popularity. He has continued to be a name in the country-music field and works frequently with Johhny Cash.

Perkins, Carl
  Disciple in blue suede shoes / Carl Perkins; with Ron Rendleman. – Grand
  Rapids, Michigan: Zondervan, 1978. – 145p., 4p. of plates ill., ports; 22cm.
  ISBN 0-3103-6730-1
This is not an embittered hard-luck story of what might have been but a well-balanced, ghosted autobiography with much interesting information about the early days of Sun Records.

PIAF, EDITH

Edith Piaf was born in Belleville, a poor district of Paris, in 1915. Her father was a circus performer and her mother a café singer. At the age of two months her mother left and she was brought up by her grandparents in Bernay, Normandy. She travelled with her father on his circus tours and began to sing in the circus and later in market places and cafés. At fifteen she left for Paris and after numerous unsuccessful auditions she ended up singing in the street for centimes. At last she was spotted by Louis Leplée, who booked her for his fashionable night club, giving her ten new songs and changing her name to Piaf, slang for sparrow. She began to gain recognition and by 1935 she had successfully appeared at large Parisian theatres and had extended her repertoire with haunting blues-type ballads. Jean Cocteau wrote a play for her in 1940 and after the war she began to appear in films. Her dramatic stage performance, simple black dress and powerful, husky voice, which seemed incongruous from such a tiny frame, created for her a cult following in France and world-wide fame. In addition, her traumatic romantic life and abuse of drink and drugs make her pre-date later stars in her excesses. She died in October 1963, in the middle of a series of concert engagements. Her own song, No Regrets, has become an anthem to her memory.

Berteaut, Simone
  Piaf / Simone Berteaut; translated from the French by Ghislaine Boulanger.
  – Harmondsworth: Penguin, 1973. – 434p., 8p. of plates: ill., ports; 19cm.
  Includes index. ISBN 0-14-003669-5 (pbk.)
  Originally published as '*Piaf*': Paris: Laffont, 1969.
  Previous English edition: W. H. Allen, 1970.
The author was Piaf's half-sister. Jean-Baptiste Berteaut gave her his name but
her father was Louis Gassion, Piaf's father. Born in 1917, Simone Berteaut
began working in a factory at the age of eleven and at thirteen started singing in
the streets with her older sister Edith. She tells Edith's story with warmth and
humour and does not spare the reader the degradations and hardships.
Without sensationalism, she tells of Piaf's drug abuse, alcoholism and lovers,
and of how she gave birth to a child at fifteen. The tragic death of her two-year-
old infant was to leave a bitter, but little-known, scar. With great knowledge
of Piaf's work, she discusses it without real analysis but presents a lengthy,
personal biography which is a pleasure to read.

Lange, Monique
  Piaf / Monique Lange. – London: W. H. Allen, 1982. – 256p.: ill., facsims,
  ports; 26cm. ISBN 0-491-02826-1
  Originally published as '*Piaf*': Paris: Editions Ramsay, 1979.
  Previous English editions: New York: Seaver Books; London: Plexus. 1981.
A well-illustrated biography written from secondary sources, the author,
nevertheless, deals with her subject with sensitivity and an appreciation of her
art. The choice of illustrations is of particular note, but the reproduction does
not always match the quality of the selection or the depth of the writing.

Piaf, Edith
  The wheel of fortune: the autobiography of Edith Piaf / translated from the
  French by Peter Trewartha and Andre Masoin de Virton. – London:
  Mayflower, 1968. – 140p.; 18cm. ISBN 0-5831-1245-5 (pbk.)
  Originally published as '*Au bal de la chance*': Paris: Jeheber, 1958.
  Previous English edition: London: Owen, 1965.
Although this book on occasion is rather earthy, one cannot help thinking that
Piaf's early life was probably even worse than she remembers it. Her tragic, and
not so tragic, love affairs are chronicled as well as her more platonic friendships
with the great names of the French arts. This is no way sensational but an
emotional, nostalgic recollection.

PINK FLOYD

Formed originally in Cambridge, Pink Floyd achieved their first regular
booking in early 1966 at the Marquee Club with a show called the Spontaneous
Underground. They later became a regular feature at London's UFO and
Middle Earth clubs. By 1967 they were the leading British psychedelic rock
group, producing a sound that was a mixture of loud feedback guitar mixed
with electric organ. They created strange moods with surreal fairytale lyrics

and complex lighting effects, employing liquid slide projectors like those used by the San Francisco acid-rock bands. In March 1968 Syd Barret, the main songwriter of the group, left to pursue a solo career. The group's music then changed direction and throughout the seventies their records and concerts continued to become more spectacular, their futuristic, space-travel images oddly mixed with straightforward social statements. The Floyd continues to change its style and is always innovative. Their record sales are consistently high throughout the world and two of their albums, Dark Side of the Moon and The Wall, are among the all-time biggest sellers.

Miles
   Pink Floyd / by Miles. – London: Omnibus Press, 1981. – Rev. ed. – 140p.:
   ill. (some col.), facsims, ports (some col.); 29cm. ISBN 0-86001-641-2 (pbk.)
A beautifully illustrated chronology of the group's career from 1965 to 1980: there are brief biographical notes, and then their concerts, recording sessions, changes in personnel and record releases are all meticulously and accurately tabulated.

Sanders, Rick
   The Pink Floyd / Rick Sanders. – London: Futura Publications, 1976. –
   143p., 16p. of plates: ill., ports; 18cm. Includes discography.
   ISBN 0-8600-7264-9 (pbk.)
A good, brief history of Pink Floyd's career. There is a good analysis of the evolution of their music and stage presentation. There are listings of their concerts and a detailed discography including bootlegs and the work of Syd Barrett.

PINK FLOYD: SONGS

Waters, Roger
   Pink Floyd lyric book / lyrics by Roger Waters. – Poole, Dorset: Blandford
   Press, 1982. – 80p.: ill., ports; 29cm. ISBN 0-71371-280-5 (pbk.)
This book contains two interviews with the writer (in 1975 and 1982) and the lyrics of many of the best-known recent songs, including the songs from The Wall.

PINK FLOYD: DISCOGRAPHIES

Miles
   Pink Floyd: another brick / by Miles. – London: Omnibus Press, 1984. – 64p.:
   ill., facsims, ports; 20cm. ISBN 0-86001-783-4 (pbk.)
   Previously published: London: Omnibus Press, 1981.
A chronological discography with full details with some bootlegs, and reproductions of album sleeves. The author's notes and illustrations are very good.

PINK FLOYD: FILMS

The Wall

Directed by Alan Parker and released in 1982, The Wall is the dramatization, written by Roger Waters of the Floyd, of the Pink Floyd's successful album. The theme concerns the barriers which people progressively build around themselves to insulate themselves from the rest of society. Animated parts of the films are by Gerald Scarfe, the soundtrack is a revised version of the album and the leading role is played by Bob Geldof of the Boomtown Rats.

Pink Floyd The Wall / Lyrics by Roger Waters; photographs by David
  Appleby; book design by Carroll and Dempsey. – Godalming, Surrey: LSP
  Books, 1982. – 144p.: col. ill.; 29cm. ISBN 0-380-81521-X (pbk.)
Stills from the film are linked by the lyrics with extracts from the animations. The book is beautifully produced. There is also a brief biography of the Pink Floyd.

PLANT, ROBERT

Born in Bromwich, Staffordshire, in 1948 Robert Plant played in local groups and recorded with a little-known Midlands group, the Band of Joy. He was spotted by Jimmy Page and, although it was his second choice, was finally asked to join the New Yardbirds, later to be renamed Led Zeppelin. Throughout the seventies Zeppelin were probably the most popular band in the world with Plant as their lead singer. His high vocal range, tall physique and masses of blonde hair, along with his reputation as a hellraiser and remarkable womanizer, have made him the classic rock idol.

(*See also* LED ZEPPELIN.)

Gross, Michael
  Robert Plant / Michael Gross. – New York: Popular Library, 1975. – 159p.:
  ill., ports; 18cm. (pbk.)
Written for *Circus* magazine and illustrated with unusual photographs from its files, this is a unique biography of Robert Plant. It briefly covers his career before joining Led Zeppelin and relates something of his personal life, but it is not as sensational as might be expected. In brief, there is much information here not available elsewhere.

THE POLICE

Formed in 1977 when Stewart Copeland, a longtime professional drummer who had worked with Curved Air, met Gordon Sumner, known as Sting, who was teaching by day and playing bass in a Newcastle jazz band by night. The line-up was completed by Henri Padovani on guitar. By September 1977, managed by Miles Copeland, Stewart's brother, they had released their first record and added Andy Summers, who had played with Zoot Money in 1964 and later with Kevin Ayers. In October 1978 the Police had their first, minor record success in Britain and suddenly appeared in the American charts. This was followed by a series of singles and albums which established them as the most successful British group by 1980. They have always unashamedly sought success, contriving an acceptable, new-wave image early on by dyeing their hair blond. Their music comprises simple lyrics, strong melodies with complex chord changes and catchy reggae rhythms. Sting has become a leading pin-up and appeared in a number of films and in television drama.

Goldsmith, Lynn
　　The Police / photographs by Lynn Goldsmith. – London: Vermilion, 1983. –
　　110p.: chiefly ill., chiefly ports; 30 cm. ISBN 0-09-152401-6 (pbk.)
A good collection of photographs of the group including many taken in concert.

Miles
　　Police / text by Miles; art direction Perry Neville; design Andy Morton. –
　　London: Omnibus Press, 1981. – 32p.: chiefly col. ill., facsims (chiefly col.),
　　ports (chiefly col.); 27cm. Includes discography. ISBN 0-86001-801-6 (pbk.)
With only brief biographical notes, a few selected quotations, extracts from press articles and brief comments, this is largely a collection of portraits of the group making a chronological record of their career to date. Dates of events, concerts, recording sessions and record releases are tabulated on each page.

Police annual 1982 – . – Knutsford, Cheshire: Stafford Pemberton, 1981 – .
　　Annual. 1983. – 1982. – 45p.: ill. (some col.), ports (some col.); 25cm.
　　ISBN 0-86030-390-X
A Christmas gift for the young fan, there are brief biographies, a message from the group, illustrations, puzzles, quizzes and a short story.

The Police released. – London; New York: Proteus, 1980. – 96p.: chiefly ill.
　　(some col.), ports (some col.); 25cm. Includes discography.
　　ISBN 0-906071-27-2 (pbk.)
　　Originally published: London: Big O Publications, 1980.
A collection of photographs with a few comments by members of the group to inform the reader that the reason for their success is that beneath it all they are exceptionally intelligent.

Sutcliffe, Phil
　　The Police: l'historia bandido / by Phil Sutcliffe and Hugh Fielder. – London;
　　New York: Proteus, 1981. – 96p.: ill. (some col.), ports (some col.); 27cm.
　　ISBN 0-906071-77-1 (cased). ISBN 0-906071-66-6 (pbk.)
The authors joined the Police during their 1980 American tour. They describe

the tour, the performances and quote from extensive interviews which offer insights into the musicians' views, musical influences and backgrounds. The authors fill in the spaces with brief comments. The illustrations are amusing and well selected. In addition, the comments of their manager, Miles Copeland, are interesting, underlining their commercial attitudes and professional approach.

THE POLICE: SONGS

Woolf, Rossetta
  Message in a bottle / by Sting; illustrations by Rossetta Woolf and Sharon
  Burn. – London: Virgin Books, 1981. – 48p.: chiefly col. ill.; 28cm.
  ISBN 0-907080-14-6
Printed on board, spirally bound and in the shape of a bottle, this is a children's picture book for adults. The Police's song, Message in a Bottle, is taken line by line and each is illustrated as a painting in a simple, childlike style. This is a unique little work.

THE POLICE: PERIODICALS

(*See* section 8.2, THE POLICE.)

POP, IGGY

Born in Ann Arbor, Michigan, in 1947, Iggy Pop formed the Stooges after playing with the Prime Movers and Iguanas in Detroit. This was the beginning of early American punk. In 1969 they signed a contract with Elektra Records and built a following by being utterly tasteless and performing a variety of obscene acts on stage. After the Stooges split up in 1971, Iggy drifted into the background, only to be revived in 1973 by David Bowie, with subsequent record efforts during the rest of the seventies. His act is by far the most demented of all rock acts, and Iggy has frequently spent time in various mental institutions.

West, Mike
  The lives and crimes of Iggy Pop / by Mike West. – Manchester: Babylon
  Books, 1983. – 48p.: ill., facsims, ports; 28cm. ISBN 0-907188-15-X (pbk.)
The only source of information on Pop; there are many photographs of his ludicrous performances but a limited text.

PRESLEY, ELVIS

Born in East Tupelo, Mississippi in 1935, Elvis Aaron Presley was brought up by his mother Gladys and father Vernon in a poor, religious, family atmosphere. His twin brother Jesse died at birth, leaving Elvis a lonely child whose interest was almost exclusively singing. In 1948 the family moved to Memphis, Tennessee, and after leaving high school Elvis eventually drove a van for the Crown Electric Company. Many legends surround the young Presley's interest, knowledge and skill at reproducing the sound of black rhythm & blues singers but it is unlikely that he frequented the clubs and bars of the black ghetto of Memphis; more likely he was an avid radio listener.

In 1953 he made a demonstration recording at the studio of Sam Phillips, the owner of the famous Sun Records company. Almost a year later his vivid black style was remembered by the staff of the studio and he was called in by Phillips to work with studio musicians Scotty Moore and Bill Black. After experimenting with some country songs, the trio played a blues number by Arthur Crudup with a fast, country backing and the rich, black-sounding vocals of Elvis. This was rockabilly in its purest form. After plays on local radio stations, Elvis appeared on a number of country-music shows, gaining a considerable local following. In 1955, after appearing on television's Louisiana Hayride, he came under the management of Colonel Tom Parker. Parker, who had already gained a reputation as a showman, manipulator and entrepreneur, soon signed Elvis with RCA, buying his contract from Sun for $35,000. In January 1956 the song Heartbreak Hotel was released. It reached the top position in the American charts and the second in Britain. Within a year he had achieved six gold discs and made his first film.

It is difficult now to understand the effect Elvis had on the teenage audience and the musical establishment. No one had heard music like it before and rock'n'roll was established as a powerful force which was to reverberate throughout our culture. In 1958 he made two more films before entering the US Army late in that year. His mother, Gladys, died while he was in the service and this, along with an anxiety that he would never recover his previous success, meant that he had mellowed considerably on his discharge in 1960. His sideburns had disappeared, as had his pelvic gyrations, once regarded as too erotic for television. He moved to Hollywood and made a succession of bad films between 1960 and 1968. After a television special in 1968 Parker changed the direction of Elvis's career again and he began touring once more, regularly playing Las Vegas for two months each year. His charisma, remarkably, had survived and he was back at the top. His records continued to sell and films of his tours were highly successful.

In 1973 Presley's marriage to Priscilla Beaulieu was dissolved. This seems to have been a turning point in his life. He had always, it has since been revealed, been heavily reliant on drugs of different kinds in enormous quantities. In addition, he had lived a curious nocturnal lifestyle hidden away in his mansion, Graceland, with a group of doting bodyguards known as the Memphis Mafia. His vast excesses in drugs, women and, curiously, food increased. His weight grew to an obese seventeen stones, he collapsed on stage several times and more often produced degrading performances. On August 16th 1977 he died in Graceland at the age of forty-two. He was described as the 'King' of rock'n'roll, and this is not just another example of idolatry in a world prone to such an attitude. He was the first great rock'n'roll star and he sold more records than any other solo artist. His success and following continues as widely now as at any time since the fifties.

Adler, Bill
  Bill Adler's love letters to Elvis / Bill Adler. – New York: Grosset & Dunlap,
  1978. – 96p.: ill., facsims, ports; 23cm. ISBN 0-448-14717-3 (cased).
  ISBN 0-448-14733-5 (pbk.)
A collection of fan letters selected by Bill Adler showing the range of emotions
of Elvis's adolescent fans. They are amusing, sad and sometimes pathetic, all
displaying remarkable dedication. The portraits of Elvis are selected from
throughout his career.

Alico, Stelia H
  Elvis Presley – the Beatles / by Stella Alico; illustrated by E. R. Cruz and
  Ernie Guanlao. – West Haven, Connecticut: Pendulum Press, 1979. – 63p.:
  ill., ports; 25cm. ISBN 0-88301-364-9 (cased). ISBN 0-88301-352-5 (pbk.).
  ISBN 0-88301-376-2 (workbook)
The story of Elvis and the Beatles for American schools. The book is well
illustrated and informative. Comprehension questions and composition exer-
cises are included, as well as a straightforward quiz.

Bowman, Kathleen
  On stage, Elvis Presley / text Kathleen Bowman; design concept Larry Soule.
  – Mankato, Minnesota: Creative Education, 1976. – 41p.: ill. (some col.),
  ports (some col.); 23cm. ISBN 0-8719-1488-3
A controlled-vocabulary biography aimed at a reading age of around ten for
American schools, the style is lucid with simple sentence structures. A factual
account of his career, mercifully written before the later exposés.

Bowser, James W.
  Starring Elvis / James W. Bowser. – New York: Dell, 1977. – 184p.: ill.,
  ports; 24cm. ISBN 0-440-18241-7 (pbk.)
A brief outline of his career with good illustrations from concert appearances
and stills from films. There is no attempt to discuss his personal life.

Buckle, Philip
  All Elvis: an unofficial biography of the 'King of discs' / Philip Buckle. –
  London: Daily Mirror, 1962. – 64p.: ill., ports; 24cm. (pbk.)
Elvis was always a remote figure for the British fan and it was certainly Colonel
Parker's strategy to maintain the mystique. This publication, which appeared
after he had left the army, presents Elvis in just such an untouchable way. It
talks of a visit to Britain, an event which never occurred. The illustrations are
well known and poorly produced.

Canada, Lena
  To Elvis with love / Lena Canada. – New York: Scholastic Book Service,
  1979. – 126p.: ill., ports; 22cm. ISBN 0-590-05770-0 (pbk.)
  Originally published: New York: Everest House, 1978.
An uncritical account of his career written in a simple style, there is no hint of
the reasons behind his decline. The illustrations are very good.

Carr, Roy
Elvis Presley: the complete illustrated record / by Roy Carr & Mick Farren. –
London: Eel Pie, 1982. – 192p.: ill. (some col.), facsims (some col.), ports
(some col.); 31cm. Includes discography. ISBN 0-90600-54-9 (pbk.)

A chronological history of his recording career, this is well written and profusely illustrated. Not the best source of information on Elvis, but an
attractive biography which is as accurate as it is straightforward and
unsensational.

Cocke, Marian J.
I called him Babe: Elvis Presley's nurse remembers / Marian J. Cocke.–
Memphis, Tennessee: Memphis University Press, 1979. – 160p.: ill., ports;
24cm. ISBN 0-87870-053-6. ISBN 0-87870-056-0 (De Luxe edition)

Marian Cocke was Elvis's nurse during the period in which he suffered from
glaucoma. She later followed him on tour as well as living amid the Graceland
community. She recalls his strange lifestyle, the deterioration of his health and
his drug abuse. Neither sensational nor sentimental, the picture is a grotesque
one.

The complete Elvis / edited by Martin Torgoff; art direction Ed Caraeff. –
London: Sidgwick & Jackson, 1982. – 256p.: ill. (some col.), ports (some
col.); 28cm. Includes bibliography. ISBN 0-283-98853-X
Originally published: New York: Delilah Publications, 1981.
Also published: London: Virgin Books, 1982.

This is a collection of essays followed by a short encyclopedia. There is an
excellent essay on his literary legacy outlining the output of material since his
death, Lester Bangs writes on the Gracelands pilgrimage and Stanley Booth on
Presley's drug abuse. The encyclopedia includes entries on songs, films,
musicians, associates and places. Not the best source, but with its well-chosen
collection of illustrations and bibliography, which is not exhaustive and sometimes inaccurate but includes all the major publications, this is a well-produced
and useful work.

Covey, Maureen
Elvis for the record / written by Maureen Covey; compiled by Todd
Slaughter; designed by Michael Wells. – Knutsford, Cheshire: Stafford
Pemberton, 1982. – 96p.: ill. (chiefly col.), col. facsims, ports (chiefly col.);
30cm. ISBN 0-86030-376-4 (pbk.)

An outline of his career, this is beautifully illustrated but with a poor, uncritical
text. The basic information is here but the result is an uninspired effort.

Crumbaker, Marge
Up and down with Elvis Presley / Marge Crumbaker and Gabe Tucker. –
London: New English Library, 1982. – 209p., 16p. of plates: ill., ports; 18cm.
ISBN 0-450-05492-6 (pbk.)
Originally published: New York: Putnam, 1981.

Marge Crumbaker is a columnist for the *Houston Post* and Gabe Tucker an old
friend of Colonel Parker. Parker is seen as the real hero. He is the creator of

Elvis, maintaining his image and protecting him from his own stupidity. But, nevertheless, the callousness of the Colonel still appears through the white-wash, particularly in the anecdote which concerns his behaviour on hearing of Elvis's death. He decided to 'leave the grief to others' and immediately telephoned Vernon Presley, Elvis's father, to warn him against the exploitation of outsiders and to plan the development of his posthumous image. Only Goldman discusses Parker more, but from the opposite view. This work, with all its justifications, still leaves the reader unconvinced that the Colonel possesses any good points.

Elvis: a tribute to the King of rock'n'roll, remembering you. – London: IPC
  Magazines, 1977. – 62p.: ill. (some col.), ports (some col.); 30cm. (unbound)
A sentimentalized, posthumous tribute, this is published in a glossy magazine format with some well-selected photographs.

Elvis: images and fancies / edited by Jac L. Tharpe. – Jackson, Mississippi:
  University Press of Mississippi, 1980. – 179p.: ill.; 24cm. ISBN 0-87805-113-9
  (cased). ISBN 0-87805-114-7 (pbk.)
A collection of fourteen essays by a variety of writers including Richard Middleton, Jac L. Tharpe and Charles Wolfe on aspects of Elvis's career, his image and impact. Topics include an appreciation of the quality of his voice, his film roles, the influence of the gospel tradition on him, the relationship between his style and country music and his cultural significance. There is an interesting collection of illustrations, not of the star, but of such subjects as Graceland, the Memphis Mafia and his mourning fans. The general theme is his social effect, but there are three essays concerned with musical analysis.

Elvis: the man and his music. – Manchester: World International Publications,
  1981. – 92p.: ill., ports; 26cm. ISBN 0-7235-0969-7
Primarily for children, this is a surprisingly well-written biography with a good selection of illustrations, particularly of his early years.

Elvis lives!. – London: Galaxy Publications, 1978. – 49p.: ill. (some col.),
  facsims, ports (some col.); 30cm. (unbound)
Mainly comprising portraits with a brief text, this is a very poor, belated tribute.

The Elvis pocket handbook / edited by Albert Hand. – Heanor, Derbyshire:
  Albert Hand, 1961. – 64p., 31p. of plates: ill., ports; 19cm. (pbk.)
All that British fans could have wanted to know about their idol in 1961! This is confusingly designed with no cohesive structure to aid in retrieving the facts.

*Elvis Presley: his complete life story in words and illustrated with more than 100
  pictures.* – London: Photoplay; Illustrated Publications, 1956. – 64p.: ill.
  (some col.), ports (some col.); 29cm. (pbk.)
One of the earliest British publications on Elvis, this is of little informational value but contains some very rare early illustrations of the pre-military service period. A good example of a fan magazine of the period, this follows identically the style of film magazines of the fifties published by the same company.

Elvis Presley: Photoplay tribute. – New York: Cadrant Enterprises, 1977. –
128p.: ill. (some col.), ports (some col.); 28cm. (pbk.)
A sentimental posthumous tribute, the illustrations include many stills from his
films as well as some unusual early portraits.

The Elvis Presley encyclopedia / compiled by Roy Barlow, David T. Cardwell
and Albert Hand. – 2nd ed. – Heanor, Derbyshire: Albert Hand, 1964. –
57p.; 23cm.
Previous edition: Heanor, Derbyshire: Albert Hand, 1964.
A brief, alphabetically arranged collection of facts which is poorly produced
and lacking in depth.

Elvis Presley 1935–1977: a tribute to the King. – Wednesbury, Staffordshire:
Bavie Publications.
Cover title: Goodbye
1. – 1977. – 30 leaves: ill., ports; 30cm. (pbk.)
2. – 1977. – 33 leaves: ill., ports; 30cm. (pbk.)
3. – 1977. – 33 leaves: ill., ports; 30cm. (pbk.)
4. – 1977. – 34 leaves: ill., ports; 30cm. (pbk.)
5. – 1977. – 32 leaves: ill., ports; 30cm. (pbk.)
A series of collections of portraits and poetic tributes, cynically published soon
after his death – this series is in very bad taste.

Elvis Presley picture parade album. – London: New Musical Express, 1958. –
25p.: chiefly ill., ports; 27cm. (pbk.)
This is a unique collection of early photographs of Elvis at work and play. It
includes 120 excellent examples.

Elvis Presley poster book. – New York: Crown, 1977. – 68p.: ill. (chiefly col.),
facsims (chiefly col.); 32cm. ISBN 0-517-53296-4 (cased).
ISBN 0-517-53297-2 (pbk.)
A good selection of reproductions of film, concert and record posters, which
are chronologically arranged, underlining the changes in Presley's visual
image.

Elvis Special 1962–. – Manchester: World International Publications, 1961–.
Annual. 1983 / edited for the *Elvis Monthly* by Todd Slaughter. – 1982. –
62p.: ill. (some col.), ports (some col.); 26cm. ISBN 0-7235-6633-X
Since its inception, this popular annual has changed its imprint from Albert
Hand to World Distributors and recently to its current publisher, with its editor
always being closely involved. The mood of the work has changed since
Presley's death to that of an annual tribute: formerly it aimed at being a news
medium. It includes quizzes, crossword puzzles and a few brief articles.

Elvis the other side: world spirit message from Edie (spirit guide). – Houston,
Texas: Golden Rainbow Press, 1980. – 96p.; 18cm. ISBN 0-686-24725-6
(pbk.)
A spirit medium passes on to us Elvis's comforting messages.

The Elvis they dig. – Heanor, Derbyshire: Albert Hand, 1959. – 35p.: ill.,
   ports; 22cm. (pbk.)
The basic facts about Elvis's early career and background are presented here
for the English fan. The photographs are rare and well presented.

Elvis we love you tender / Dee Presley, Billy, Rick and David Stanley; as told to
   Martin Torgoff. – London: New English Library, 1980. – 426p., 32p. of
   plates: ill., ports; 22cm. Includes index. ISBN 0-450-04815-2 (cased).
   ISBN 0-450-05135-8 (pbk.)
   Originally published: New York: Delacourte, 1980.
A biographical account told by Presley's father's second wife and her three
sons. It is a sympathetic and gentle view which does not avoid the questionable
areas of Elvis's behaviour, but is unsensational. Dee Presley met Elvis and his
father during Elvis's military service in Germany and there is much interesting
information here about this elusive period. Well indexed, there is a fine
collection of illustrations.

Friedman, Favius
   Meet Elvis Presley / Favius Friedman. – New York: Scholastic Book Service,
   1971. – 52p.: ill., ports; 24cm. (pbk.)
In a series for American high schools which introduced important world figures
to children, this is well written and informative but lacks the design and
production of later controlled-vocabulary series.

Gehman, Richard
   Elvis Presley: hero or heel? / Richard Gehman; Mary Callahan editor; Steve
   Horrath, art editor. – London: L. Miller, 1957. – 66p., 1p. of plates: ill.,
   ports; 28cm. (pbk.)
A rare, early English publication about Elvis which reflects the naivety
expected of rock'n'roll fans of the period. This issue of whether an artist is a
virtuous person or not, which really is the theme of this publication, makes for
some amusing reading but also reflects the contemporary attitudes towards the
latent evils of rock'n'roll.

Goldman, Albert
   Elvis / by Albert Goldman. – Harmondsworth: Penguin, 1982. – 727p., 16p.
   of plates: ill., ports; 18cm. Includes index. ISBN 0-14-00-5965-2 (pbk.)
   Originally published: New York: McGraw-Hill, 1981.
   Also published: London: Allen Lane, 1981.
The most exhaustive biography of a singer yet to be published, it received
devastating criticism from all the major critics including Greil Marcus in an
extensive essay in *Time Out* magazine. It is generally condemned for simply
concentrating on the seamy, sensational aspects of Presley's life and ignoring
his talent and significance as an artist. Goldman is without question dismissive,
treating his subject with real contempt. His opening gambit explains the
singer's position as idol in the context of the American people's craving for a
monarchy – naturally ignoring the adulation bestowed on him from the rest of
the world. Few would not accept that the author's facts are based on truth –

indeed he reveals little not already covered in Jerry Hopkins' books – but it is his attitude that causes offence. Colonel Parker's exploitation is, as one might expect, revelled in, perhaps with some justification.

Greenfield, Marie
   Elvis: legend of love / Marie Greenfield. – Mountain View, California:
   Morgan-Pacific, 1981. – 154p.: ill., ports; 22cm. ISBN 0-686-71746-5
The work of a doting fan, this is not only uncritical but very frequently fictional. Nevertheless, the view of Elvis as a messiah who provided a focus for the affection of millions of people is adequately expressed.

Gregory, James
   The Elvis Presley story / edited by James Gregory. – London: Hillman,
   Thorpe & Porter, 1960. – 160p. of plates: ill., ports; 17cm. (pbk.)
For its time this is a reasonable attempt at the biography of a teenage idol. It retains to a degree the usual patronizing attitude but is generally factual. The early illustrations are a particularly interesting feature.

Gregory, Neal
   When Elvis died / by Neal Gregory and Janice Gregory. – Washington, D.C.:
   Communications Press, 1980. – 292p., 16p. of plates: ill., ports; 21cm.
   Includes bibliography and index. ISBN 0-89461-032-5
The authors conducted a scholarly piece of research analysing the way in which the media responded to the death of Elvis. A brief biography, with an emphasis on the influence of the media on his career, is followed by their unique study. The hysteria and genuine national mourning are balanced by the sordid sensationalism and exposés. There is a bibliography of ephemera, little of which has appeared on this side of the Atlantic.

Gripe, Maria
   Elvis and his friends / Maria Gripe; translated from Swedish by Sheila La
   Farge. – New York: Delacourte, 1976. – 224p.: ill., ports; 22cm.
   ISBN 0-440-02272-X (cased). ISBN 0-440-02273-8 (pbk.)
A curious, naive story of Presley's career. Written before the sordid exposures and published before his death, there are some interesting photographs.

Gripe, Maria
   Elvis and his secret / Maria Gripe; translated from Swedish by Sheila La
   Farge. – New York: Delacourte, 1976. – 208p.: ill., ports; 22cm.
   ISBN 0-440-02282-7 (cased). ISBN 0-440-02283-5 (pbk.)
Elvis's secret is deeply spiritual involvement, love of his home, family and his generosity. Actually not that well hidden behind his public image, these aspects of his personality were significant. His darker traits are nowhere to be found.

Grove, Martin A.
   Elvis: the legend lives / Martin A. Grove. – New York: Manor Books, 1978. –
   138p.: ill., ports; 18cm. ISBN 0-532-19197-8 (pbk.)

A brief recap of Elvis's successes, particularly featuring his later years of Las Vegas and the nationwide tours. His death is not discussed but the nationwide mourning and posthumous hysteria are dealt with at length.

Grove, Martin A.
  The King is dead: Elvis Presley / Martin A. Grove. – New York: Manor Books, 1977. – 252p., 4p. of plates: col. ill., col. ports; 18cm. Includes discography and filmography. ISBN 0-532-19162-5 (pbk.)
A tribute to Elvis, briefly outlining his career, this makes no real attempt at serious analysis of his importance as an artist. There are four beautifully reproduced colour plates of the slender, young Elvis.

Hand, Albert
  A century of Elvis / Albert Hand. – Heanor, Derbyshire: Albert Hand, 1959. – 34p.: ill., ports; 22cm. (pbk.)
An optimistic title for this early publication. There are interesting, early photographs, but the text is poor.

Hanna, David
  Elvis: lonely star at the top / David Hanna. – New York: Leisure Books, 1977. – 224p., 16p. of plates: ill., ports; 18cm. ISBN 0-8439-0532-9 (pbk.)
A poorly written, superficial biography rushed out soon after Presley's death. The author does not attempt to discuss his music but aims at the sensational aspects of his demise.

Harbinson, W. A.
  The life and death of Elvis Presley / by W. A. Harbinson. – Rev. ed. – London: Michael Joseph, 1977. – 160p.: ill., ports; 28cm. ISBN 0-7181-1680-1
  Previous edition entitled '*Elvis Presley: an illustrated biography*': London: Michael Joseph, 1975; New York: Grosset & Dunlap, 1976.
Written and compiled by the former editor of *Men Only, Club International* and *Club USA*. The slight revision and change of title after Presley's death represent little change to the original edition. An impressive collection of illustrations is accompanied by a brief text which makes some uncompromising observations on Presley's career and the way in which it was managed.

Harms, Valerie
  Trying to get to you: the story of Elvis Presley / by Valerie Harms. – New York: Atheneum, 1979. – 175p.: ill., ports; 22cm. ISBN 0-689-30726-8
An affectionate biography which avoids the less pleasant side of Elvis's life. Lacking in real biographical information but offering a sensitive knowledge of his work and appreciation of his talent.

Harper, Betty
  Elvis: newly discovered drawings of Elvis Presley / by Betty Harper. – New York: Bantam Books, 1979. – 91p.: chiefly ill., ports; 28cm. ISBN 0-553-01241-X (pbk.)

Betty Harper, who lives in Hendersonville, Tennessee, has drawn over 10,000 portraits of Elvis Presley. This collection of reproductions of her pencil drawings shows a remarkable range of expressions and detail from throughout his career. This book demonstrates a truly obsessive hero worship.

Hatcher, Holly
Elvis is that you? / Holly Hatcher; edited by Terry Sherf. – Beverly Hills, California: Great American Books, 1979. – 240p.: ill., ports; 20cm. ISBN 0-936790-00-8 (pbk.)
Holly Hatcher is privileged to have made contact with Elvis's spirit. She describes those fantastic occurrences and relays the wonderful messages.

Hill, Wanda June
We remember Elvis / Wanda June Hill. – Mountain View, California: Morgan-Pacific, 1978. – 86p.: ill., ports; 24cm. ISBN 0-89430-028-8 (pbk.)
A posthumous tribute in the uncritical mode with portraits, recollections and a few quotations – the book is short on information and poorly presented.

Holmes, Robert
The three loves of Elvis Presley: the true story of the Presley legend / Robert Holmes. – London: Hulton Press, 1959. – 63p.: ill., ports; 25cm. (pbk.)
A downhome, early biography of Elvis depicted as the clean-cut country boy, this book includes some early portraits. His love for the Church, mother and country is all based on truth but his other loves are discreetly ignored.

Holzer, Hans
Elvis Presley speaks / Hans Holzer. – London: New English Library, 1980. – 255p.; 18cm. ISBN 0-450-04773-3
Originally published: New York: Manor Books, 1978.
The author, a student of the paranormal, was convinced that Presley's spirit must still be alive in the world and embarked upon a programme of interviewing people who had experienced psychic phenomena relating to Elvis. Elvis's thoughts from the grave are meticulously recorded in a long, rambling text which would be dull but for its bizarre subject.

Hopkins, Jerry
Elvis / Jerry Hopkins. – London: Abacus, 1974. – 364p., 16p.: ill., ports; 20cm. Includes discography and filmography. ISBN 0-349-11717-9 (pbk.)
Originally published: New York: Simon and Schuster, 1971.
Also published: London: Macmillan, 1972.
Regarded by most as the definitive biography of Elvis Presley's rise to stardom, this is well written by someone who was both a Presley fan and a good writer. The research and meticulous attention to detail makes it one of the very best biographies in the popular-music field. There is no sense of the decay of the singer which emanates from the later works written since his death, which is refreshing. The discography is detailed but the filmography very brief.

Hopkins, Jerry
  Elvis: the final years / Jerry Hopkins. – London: Star Books, 1981. – 258p.,
  12p. of plates: ill., ports; 18cm. ISBN 0-352-30859-1 (pbk.)
  Originally published: New York: St. Martin's Press, 1980.
  Also published in larger format: London: W. H. Allen, 1980;
A sequel to the author's biography of Presley's career up until 1970, this covers
the years of his decline as well as offering a brief recap of his early career.
Written soon after his death, it avoids both the sentimental and sensational
attitudes of other authors. Sections of his later career are taken chronologically, showing the development of his Las Vegas period and national tours after
rejecting Hollywood, his drift towards right-wing politics, bizarre lifestyle and
confused attitudes on moral issues. The illustrations are well selected. This is a
revealing biography with the authority of the writer's experience as well as
considerable research.

James, Antony
  Presley: entertainer of the century / Antony James. – New York: Tower
  Books, 1976. – 246p.: ill., port; 18cm. ISBN 0-505-51239-4 (pbk.)
A poor biography by a California-based journalist with no insight into Presley's
lifestyle, little appreciation of his music and no first-hand research. The only
saving feature is an unusual collection of illustrations.

Jones, Peter
  Elvis / Peter Jones. – London: Octopus Books, 1976. – 88p.: ill. (chiefly col.),
  col. facsims, ports (chiefly col.); 31cm. ISBN 0-7064-0550-1
A beautifully illustrated brief biography for the fan. The theme is simply to
idolize the Elvis image and to emphasize the importance of the influence of his
music. His film career is widely covered with a good collection of stills.

Lacker, Marty
  Elvis: portrait of a friend / by Marty Lacker, Patsy Lacker and Leslie
  S. Smith. – New York: Bantam Books, 1979. – 369p., 16p. of plates: ill.,
  ports; 18cm. ISBN 0-553-13824-3 (pbk.)
  Originally published: Memphis, Tennessee: Wimmer Books, 1979.
Divided into three sections, one by each co-author, this is an outspoken
biography. Marty Lacker was Elvis's personal bookkeeper and best man at his
wedding. Although Lacker was eventually discarded by Elvis and treated
rather badly, his account is in no way vindictive and is often flattering. His wife,
Patsy, however gives a quite different picture of life in Graceland. She talks of
the drugs, nocturnal lifestyle and openly attacks most of the entourage. In the
final section Smith concentrates on Elvis's drug problem and the doctors who
provided the prescriptions. Interspersed with all three accounts are classic
Elvis stories of his patriotism and generosity told in an incongruously sentimental way.

Levy, Alan
  Operation Elvis / Alan Levy; illustrated by Dedini. – London: World
  Distributors, 1962. – 151p.: ill.; 18cm. (pbk.)
  Originally published: London: André Deutsch, 1960.

Elvis's conscription was used by the US Army as a vast public relations exercise. His time in Germany gave the army more news media coverage than it had received since the Korean War. This humorous, often sarcastic, description of this period with its cartoon sketches, offers a lighthearted, sobering view of the whole farcical affair.

Lichter, Paul
    The boy who dared to rock: the definitive Elvis / Paul Lichter. – London: Sphere Books, 1980. – 304p., 8p. of plates: ill. (some col.), facsims (some col.), ports (some col.); 28cm. Includes discography and filmography. ISBN 0-7221-5547-6 (pbk.)
    Also published: New York: Doubleday, 1978; New York: Dolphin Books, 1978.
Paul Lichter is the editor of the *Memphis Flash*, a bi-monthly magazine about Presley. He claims to be the world's authority on this subject. As a source of information and for its collection of illustrations this is excellent. The initial biographical notes, which are skilfully written, are followed by lists of every performance he ever made, each recording session and an extensive discography which includes discs released outside the USA, bootlegs and curiosities. There are reproductions of all of his album sleeves, although some of the foreign releases are selective. There is a transcript of a rare early interview. The filmography is a simple list of films without credits.

Lloyd, Harold
    The Graceland gates / Harold Lloyd and George Baugh. – Memphis: Modern Age Enterprises, 1978. – 184p.: ill., ports; 23cm. (pbk.)
Life with Elvis: quotations from his bodyguards and others in his organization. This is not as sensational as some accounts but is often bitter and sometimes spurious.

Long, Marvin R.
    God's work through Elvis / Marvin R. Long. – Hicksville, New York: Exposition Press, 1979. – 32p.; 18cm. ISBN 0-682-49294-9 (pbk.)
Until late in Elvis's life Colonel Parker was somehow able to surround him with a clean-living, God-fearing image. Indeed Elvis publicly professed a strict, naive Christian lifestyle, but in reality varied his allegiance from religion to religion. Here the author maintains this religious image with a theme of Elvis's life as an example to others, unspoilt by success.

Mann, May
    Elvis and the Colonel / May Mann. – New York: Drake Publishers, 1975. – 273p., 6p. of plates: ill., ports; 24cm. ISBN 0-8473-1004-3
A well-researched biography by the author who interviewed Presley, his former wife Priscilla, his manager Colonel Parker and other associates and family over a period of twenty years. Not without its share of idolatry, it does offer a personal view without the almost requisite exposures of the posthumous biographies. The relationship between Elvis and the Colonel, and particularly the latter's influence, is a central theme.

Marsh, Dave
Elvis / Dave Marsh; art direction by Bea Feitler. – London: Elm Tree Press,
  1982. – 245p.: ill. (some col.), ports (some col.); 30cm. Includes
  bibliography, discography and filmography. ISBN 0-241-10902-7
  Originally published: New York: Times Books, 1982.
Beautifully produced and illustrated with over 250 photographs, some
curiously colour tinted, the text is a brief, but sympathetic and intelligent
assessment of Elvis's life and career. The author defends Elvis's efforts of the
sixties as misunderstood and states that his work in the seventies was good but
not captured to effect on record. A refreshing summary from a good writer and
Elvis fan who has no interest in any prurient aspects of his life.

Matthew-Walker, Robert
Elvis Presley: a study in music / Robert Matthew-Walker. – London:
  Omnibus Press, 1982. – 160p.: ill., ports; 23cm. Includes discography,
  filmography and index. ISBN 0-7119-0086-8 (pbk.)
  Originally published: Tunbridge Wells, Kent: Midas Books, 1979.
Written by a classically trained musician who works as an executive in the
recording industry, this is a detailed analysis of Presley's recording career.
There is a brief biography setting his style into context followed by a chronological description of every recording session he had with details of the songs
performed, musicians and location, followed by a detailed analysis. The
filmography is complete, including casts and credits but not synopses. This is a
well-written, serious study which is not at all pretentious, nor over-technical,
and often addresses adverse criticism as well as praise.

The official FBI file on Elvis A. Presley. – Chicago: MEM Publishing, 1978. –
  96p.: ill., ports; 28cm.
Purporting to be a reproduction of a file kept by the Federal Bureau of
Investigation, Elvis's vital statistics and movements are all here. There are
numerous illustrations of the singer, his associates and family, as well as of his
house, cars and details of his considerable armoury.

Panta, Ilona
Elvis Presley: king of kings / Ilona Panta. – Hicksville, New York: Exposition
  Press, 1979. – 247p.; 21cm. ISBN 0-682-49266-3
Written by a Hungarian who lives in Ontario, Canada, this book is an account
of the author's extrasensory perception. She heard voices which told her that
Presley was the greatest prophet who has ever lived. She sensed his imminent
death, wrote to him and visited his mansion, Graceland. She was unable to save
him. 'What was his real mission on Earth?' Impossible to read seriously, this
was produced after Presley's death.

Parish, James Robert
The Elvis Presley scrapbook / James Robert Parish. – Rev. ed. – New York:
  Ballantine Books, 1977. – 218p.: chiefly ill. (some col.), facsims (some col.),
  ports (some col.); 30cm. Includes discography and filmography.
  ISBN 0-345-27594-2 (pbk.)
  Previous edition: New York: Ballantine Books, 1975.

An excellent collection of portraits, film posters, souvenirs, publicity items and other illustrative materials recalling the life of Elvis. The revised edition was issued soon after his death. There is a full discography with reproductions of album sleeves and a full filmography with posters and stills. In addition, there is a complete listing of all of his concert appearances as well as television and radio performances.

Parker, Edmund K.
  Inside Elvis / Ed Parker; sketches by George Bartell. – Orange, California: Rampart House, 1978. – x, 197p., 18p. of plates: ill., ports; 23cm.
  ISBN 0-8977-3000-3
Ed Parker was Elvis's karate instructor and the owner of a karate school in Memphis. During Elvis's final years he was a regular companion, travelling throughout the USA with the tours and living for long periods at Graceland. Published in a limited edition a year after Presley's death, this is a personal, uncritical but not sentimentalized biography. It gives an idealized picture, avoiding the more sensational issues of Elvis's later life.

Presley, Elvis
  Elvis in his own words / compiled by Mick Farren; edited by Pearce Marchbank. – London: W. H. Allen, 1981. – 128p.: ill., ports; 26cm.
  ISBN 0-491-02776-1
Originally published: London: Omnibus Press; New York: Quick Fox, 1977. Elvis Presley emerged before rock'n'roll singers were treated with any degree of seriousness by the media and during the sixties he was a very distant figure. Up until his death he disclosed few opinions or gave insights into his real personality. Here are brought together the early press interviews, radio comments and his last statement to the press. Well edited and illustrated and arranged by themes, this at least offers some indication of his attitudes and motives.

Presley, Vester
  A Presley speaks / by Vester Presley; as told to Deda Bonura. – Memphis: Wimmer Brothers, 1978. – vi, 150p.: ill., ports; 24cm. ISBN 0-9185-4411-4
This book is the result of interviews with Elvis Presley's uncle, who claims to have taught him the guitar. It offers an interesting account, obviously much romanticized, of Elvis's early years and his musical influences; the effect of stardom is described by someone who was close to him all his life.

Private Elvis / editor Diego Cortez; with photographs of Rudolph Paulini. – Stuttgart: Fey Verglas, 1978. – 199p.: chiefly ill., facsims, ports; 27cm.
  ISBN 3-88361-101-8 (pbk.)
Diego Cortez, a contributor to American arts magazines, lecturer and television director, discovered this large collection of photographs in a photographic studio in Munich. They were taken by Rudolph Paulini during Elvis's military service spent in Germany in 1958 and 1959. They are intimate photos of Elvis with dancers, barmaids and a stripper and a few of him in army uniform. The general mood is sleazy. There is an index to the photographs and several

pretentious essays in both English and German which fail to have any relevance. The press cuttings are, however, interesting but in all this is a curious compilation which simply shows photographs of the star, devoid of his usual glamour.

Reggero, John
    Elvis in concert / text and photographs by John Reggero; with an
    introduction by David Stanley. – New York: Dell, 1979. – 120p.: chiefly ill.
    (some col.), ports (some col.); 26cm. ISBN 0-440-02219-3 (pbk.)
With a brief text, this is a collection of photographs of Elvis performing in the mid seventies. He is by this time very overweight and wearing the most extravagant of stage costumes. The notes describe his performances as being energetic and charismatic but this is difficult to believe from his appearance.

Shaver, Sean
    The life of Elvis Presley / by Sean Shaver and Hal Noland; with intimate
    memories of Charlie Hodge, Dick Grab, Billy Smith; featuring the
    photography of Sean Shaver. – Memphis, Tennessee: Timur Publications,
    1979. – 299p.: ill. (some col.), ports (some col.); 24cm. ISBN 0-96028-260-2
Illustrated with unusual photographs of Elvis at home as well as in concert, this is not a factual biography but a collection of episodic accounts. The most interesting aspects are the memoirs of Charlie Hodge and Billy Smith, both members of the Memphis Mafia.

Slaughter, Todd
    Elvis Presley / Todd Slaughter. – London: Mandabrook, 1977. – 128p.;
    18cm. Includes discography. ISBN 0-427-00417-9 (pbk.)
Compiled by the secretary of Elvis Presley's British fan club, this brief biography is informative and well written. Published before his death, it covers the facts of his life without the sensational aspects. There is a series of appendices which include statistics of his record sales, a discography and information about the British fan club.

Staten, Vince
    The real Elvis: a good old boy / by Vince Staten. – Dayton, Ohio: Media
    Ventures, 1978. – 150p., 8 leaves of plates: ill., ports; 24cm.
    ISBN 0-89645-008-2
A posthumous defence of Elvis by a writer who is obviously a fan and far from objective. The author emphasizes the quality of his character, seeing this as more significant than the influence of his music.

Stearn, Jess
    The truth about Elvis / Jess Stearn; with Larry Geller. – New York: Jove
    Books, 1980. – 236p.: ill., ports; 20cm. ISBN 0-515-05154-3 (pbk.)
Centred around the spiritual side of Elvis, this book is based on the recollections of Larry Geller who was his beautician and self-confessed spiritual adviser. It is full of stories of Elvis's generosity and sympathy, which were a

genuine part of his character, but it is also frequently pretentious. The exchanges between Geller and Elvis as they discuss aspects of Eastern philosophy are particularly embarrassing.

Tatham, Dick
   Elvis: tribute to the king of rock / London: Phoebus, 1977. – 64p.: ill., ports; 30cm. (pbk.)
Rushed out after Presley's death, this is a superficial, brief tribute with unusual illustrations.

Taylor, Paula
   Elvis Presley / text Paula Taylor; illustrator Dick Brude. – Mankato, Minnesota: Creative Education, 1974. – 31p.: ill. (some col.), ports (some col.); 25cm. ISBN 0-8719-1394-1
A controlled-vocabulary biography written for a reading age of about ten for American schools. Written at the height of Elvis's Las Vegas period when his public image was still flawless, it expresses his importance as a seminal figure of rock'n'roll with some good illustrations.

Thornton, Mary Ann
   Even Elvis / Mary Ann Thornton. – Harrison, Arkansas: New Leaf Press, 1979. – 188p.: ill., ports; 24cm. ISBN 0-89221-063-X (pbk.)
A simple biography by a devoted follower who avoids any shadow falling on her hero's memory.

Wallraf, Rainer
   Elvis Presley: an illustrated biography / by Rainer Wallraf and Heinz Plehn; translation Judith Waldman; design Roland Siegrist. – London: Omnibus Press, 1979. – 199p.: ill. (some col.), facsims, ports (some col.); 30cm. Includes discography and filmography. ISBN 0-86001-613-7 (pbk.)
   Originally published in German: Dreieich: Abi Melzer, 1978.
A well-illustrated but superficial biography with a chronology and a full filmography which includes detailed synopses. The discography includes unofficial bootlegs, tributes by other artists and a fascinating list of collector's items. There are reproductions of album sleeves, posters and press cuttings. The text itself offers little information but the various listings are useful.

Ward, Fred L.
   All about Elvis / Fred L. Ward and Steve D. Tamerius. – New York: Bantam Books, 1981. – 414p.; 18cm. Includes bibliography. ISBN 0-553-14129-5 (pbk.)
A lengthy information source on Presley which is arranged in a strict alphabetical sequence. The information includes song titles, films, musicians, places, incidents, venues and girlfriends. The overall effect is overwhelming and some areas are difficult to access because of the choice of heading. Nevertheless it contains a wealth of information.

Wertheimer, Alfred
  Elvis '56: in the beginning / photographs by Alfred Wertheimer; text by
  Alfred Wertheimer and Gregory Martinelli. – London: Cassell, 1979. –
  160p.: chiefly ill., ports; 28cm. ISBN 0-304-30416-6 (pbk.)
  Originally published: New York: Macmillan, 1979.
Just after Elvis Presley signed his contract for RCA Victor from Sun Records,
the author was contracted by RCA to photograph their new artist. He took a
series of photographs throughout 1956 on tour, in concert and relaxing. The
notes are interesting and the portraits of the twenty-one-year-old singer during
the year which took him from obscurity to fame are fascinating.

West, Joan Buchanan
  Elvis: his life and times in poetry and lines / Joan Buchanan West. –
  Hicksville, New York: Exposition Press, 1979. – 48p.; 24cm.
  ISBN 0-682-49305-8
A tribute in verse which is more than occasionally unfortunately amusing.

West, Red
  Elvis: what happened? / Red West, Sonny West, Dave Hebler; as told to
  Steve Dunleary. – New York: Ballantine Books, 1977. – 332p., 16p. of
  plates: ill., ports; 18cm. ISBN 0-345-27433-4 (pbk.)
The inside story of Elvis's later years as told by three of his bodyguards whom
he had dismissed. The reliability of the account may be questioned as the tone
tends to be sour. They talk of their loyalty to the 'King' and their later, unjust
dismissal. Nevertheless, they do reveal aspects of Presley's life, such as his drug
addiction, womanizing and megalomania, which others avoided discussing
during his lifetime. Published just days before his death, Elvis did read it. Not
well written, not to be trusted, sensational but fascinating.

Wootton, Richard
  Elvis Presley: king of rock'n'roll / Richard Wootton. – London: Hodder and
  Stoughton, 1982. – 128p.: ill., ports; 24cm. Includes bibliography and index.
  ISBN 0-340-26954-5
Written by an Englishman who has contributed to the *Melody Maker, Rock
year book* and produced his own work, *Honky Tonkin': a travel guide to
American music*, this is an excellent biography for a reading age of around
twelve. Well designed with an excellent collection of illustrations, the text is
concise and informative. The author describes Elvis's strange lifestyle, decline
and death with exceptional skill without evading any of the questionable issues.

Yancey, Becky
  My life with Elvis / Becky Yancey with Cliff Linedecker. – London:
  Mayflower, 1978. – 254p., 16p. of plates: ill., ports; 18cm.
  ISBN 0-583-12923-4 (pbk.)
  Originally published: New York: St. Martin's Press, 1978.
  Also published: London: W. H. Allen, 1977.
Becky Yancey was Elvis Presley's secretary from 1962 to 1975. She lived at
Graceland and her observations of his women, drug abuse, odd tastes in

entertainment and food are all here. There is nothing really sensational, and she presents her exposures in a gentle way. His death and the effect on his closest friends is covered sympathetically.

PRESLEY, ELVIS: BIBLIOGRAPHIES: DISCOGRAPHIES

Whisler, John A.
  Elvis Presley: a reference guide and discography / by John A. Whisler. –
  Metuchen, New Jersey; London: Scarecrow Press, 1981. – 265p.; 23cm.
  Includes indexes. ISBN 0-8108-1434-X
The discographical section includes full details of over five hundred official recordings, listing songs and musicians. To support this listing there is also a separate song-title index. It is the reference source section which is of the most interest, however, with citations of hundreds of magazine articles and news-paper stories as well as books. There are in fact over one hundred abstracts from books and encyclopedias but several curious omissions of important books devoted to Elvis. In any event, this is an extremely useful reference tool.

PRESLEY, ELVIS: DISCOGRAPHIES

Aros, Andrew A.
  Elvis: his films & recordings / by Andrew A. Aros. – Diamond Bar,
  California: Applause Publications, 1980. – 64p.; 24cm. ISBN 0-932352-01-4
  (pbk.)
This is a comprehensive discography arranged chronologically with full details of songs, composers and place of recording. The information is entirely of American releases. The brief synopses and credit details of Presley's film career are very much a minor feature. The author's notes on each record release are particularly well written, demonstrating a genuine understanding of the work.

Barry, Ron
  The Elvis Presley American discography / by Ron Barry. – Phillipsbury,
  New Jersey: Spectator Services; Maxigraphics, 1976. – 221p.: ill. (chiefly
  col.), facsims (chiefly col.), ports (chiefly col.); 28cm.
Well produced with album sleeves reproduced and full details of songs and musicians, this is the complete discography of Presley's official releases in America. No bootlegs are included at all. Published before his death, the listing obviously predates the explosion in re-releases of his material subsequent to 1977.

Escott, Colin
  Elvis Presley: an illustrated discography / by Colin Escott and Martin
  Hawkins. – London: Omnibus Press, 1981. – 136p.: ill., facsims, ports;
  20cm. ISBN 0-86001-746-X (pbk.)
Written by the authors of the authoritative works on the seminal Sun Records

Company, this is a full and detailed discography. Included are biographical notes and details of the musicians on particular recording session as well as full discographical information. There is a schedule of bootlegs, which is far from complete, and a detailed index to every song title Presley recorded. The illustrations are also interesting with some good shots from his earliest tours.

Osborne, Jerry
  Presleyana: the complete Elvis guide / by Jerry Osborne and Bruce Hamilton. – Phoenix, Arizona: O'Sullivan Woodside, 1980. – 304p.: ill., facsims; 22cm. Includes index. ISBN 0-89019-073-9
This is an exhaustive discography by the compilers of a range of collector's guides. It is arranged chronologically with full discographical details of albums and singles, and each disc is given an estimated current American value. There is an index by song title and an essay on Elvis's recording career.

PRESLEY, ELVIS: FILMS

Lichter, Paul
  Elvis in Hollywood / Paul Lichter. – London: Hale, 1977. – 188p.: ill., col. facsims, ports; 28cm. ISBN 0-6712-2153-4 (cased) ISBN 0-6712-2154-X (pbk.)
A complete guide to Elvis Presley's film career with synopses of plots, stills and posters. There are details of each film's credits as well as the songs and musicians. This is the fullest source of information on his film career, well written and comprehensive.

Zmijewsky, Steve
  Elvis: the films and career of Elvis Presley / by Steven Zmijewsky and Boris Zmijewsky. – Secaucus, New Jersey: Citadel Press, 1976. – 223p.: ill., ports; 29cm. ISBN 0-8065-0511-7
A beautifully illustrated guide to Presley's Hollywood career which concentrates purely on his acting and the films and ignores his music almost entirely. Stills are included from all his films with synopses, credits, casts and details of the shooting, and relationships between Elvis and his co-stars, particularly his leading ladies. This is a good source of information on this particular side of his work.

PRESLEY, ELVIS: QUIZBOOKS

Nash, Bruce M.
  The Elvis Presley quizbook / Bruce M. Nash. – New York: Warner Books; London: distributed by New English Library, 1978. – 205p., 8p. of plates; ill., ports; 18cm. ISBN 0-446-89823-6 (pbk.)
Questions and answers on every detail of Elvis's life: arranged chronologically, it is not as demanding as many quizbooks and not for the real Presley expert.

Rosenbaum, Helen
   The Elvis Presley trivia quiz book / by Helen Rosenbaum. – New York:
   Signet, 1978. – 154p., 8p. of plates: ill., facsims, ports; 18cm.
   ISBN 0-451-08178-1 (pbk.)
A good collection of questions and answers which range from the very simple to
the very obscure. There is an interesting picture-quiz section which will test
even the most fanatical devotee.

PRESLEY, ELVIS: PERIODICALS

(*See* section 8.2, PRESLEY, ELVIS.)

THE PRETENDERS

The Pretenders emerged from the London new-wave scene in 1979 with a
moderate hit record which was a revived version of an old Kinks song, Stop
Your Sobbin'. This was followed by a number-one, chart-topping single, and
an album which was very successful both here and in the USA. The vocalist and
leader of the group, Chrissie Hynde, was born in Cleveland, Ohio, in 1952, and
after art college moved to London where she began working as a journalist. She
began learning to play guitar and was one of the first women to front a rock
group during the recent growth in the numbers of women musicians. She is the
main writer in the group and certainly the dominant personality. Their style is
heavily derived from the British beat sound of the sixties and characterized by
Chrissie Hynde's low vocals. They are not regarded as particularly creative or
skilful musicians, and their initial, big impact has to some extent waned.
Recent records have been minor hits and their concerts attract large audiences,
but their music does not appear to be developing.

Miles
   Pretenders / text by Miles; art direction Perry Neville; design Andy Morton.
   – London: Omnibus Press, 1981. – 32p.: chiefly ill., ports; 27cm.
   ISBN 0-86001-802-4 (pbk.)
There is a fine collection of illustrations of the group, particularly featuring
Chrissie Hynde, and brief biographical notes on each group member, the
group's formation and career to date. These notes are supplemented with press
extracts and quotations, but this is not a good information source.

Salewicz, Chris
   The Pretenders / by Chris Salewicz. – London; New York: Proteus, 1982. –
   ill. (some col.), ports (some col.); 27cm. ISBN 0-86276-023-2 (pbk.)
Well-designed and illustrated, the brief text is both informative and well
written. Details of early changes in the group's personnel will be found
nowhere else.

PREVIN, DORY

Born Dorothy Langan to rigidly Catholic Irish parents in Los Angeles, Dory Previn began her musical career as a chorus girl. She later became a model, folk singer and occasional actress and married conductor André Previn. After the marriage was dissolved, she began writing and recording her songs, which are always deeply personal and explicit. Her lyrics are often harrowing in their intensity, sung over plaintive arrangements. She has received three Academy Award nominations for films scores but although critically highly regarded, she has never achieved commercial success in Britain. In 1978, she turned her attention to the pursuit of a literary career.

Previn, Dory
  Bog-trotter: an autobiography with lyrics / by Dory Previn; drawings by Joby Baker. – London: Weidenfeld and Nicolson, 1980. – 383p.: ill.; 23cm.
  ISBN 0-2977-7773-4
A large selection of Previn's lyrics, including most of her best-known songs, is the basis of this autobiographical account of her songwriting career. She offers a detailed insight into her techniques and inspirations. Avoiding overt self-indulgence, this is a sensitive and unusual work.

Previn, Dory
  Midnight baby: an autobiography / Dory Previn. – London: Corgi, 1978. – 140p.; 18cm. ISBN 0-552-10643-7 (pbk.)
  Previously published: London: Elm Tree Books, 1977.
A beautifully written recollection of childhood which is a sensitively drawn and often pathetic account. Her formative years were spent in a household in which she was resented by her father and there was general discord and a great deal of drunkenness. Writing originally for therapeutic reasons while undergoing pysychiatric treatment, she exorcizes old ghosts and reveals to the reader unusually personal emotions.

PRIDE, CHARLEY

Born in Sledge, Mississippi, in 1938, Charley Pride is by far the most successful black singer in the white-dominated field of country music. He became a baseball player in 1954 for Memphis Red Sox but, after the army, never quite made the top. He had always sung on a semi-professional basis and in 1963, after appearing on a local radio show, he was asked to sign a contract with RCA. Since that time his popularity has continued to grow and he has become the most commercially successful singer on RCA since Elvis Presley. He has a warm baritone voice and sings love songs in a pure country style which originally presented a confusing image but one which the public has long since accepted. He has been only slightly successful in Britain.

Barclay, Pamela
   Charley Pride / text Pamela Barclay; illustrator Dick Brude; design concept
   Mark Landkamer. – 31p.: ill. (some col.), ports (some col.); 25cm.
   ISBN 0-8719-1397-6
A controlled-vocabulary text written for a reading age of around ten and aimed
at American schools, this is well produced and informative.

QUATRO, SUZI

Born in Detroit in 1950, Suzi Quatro began playing in a group called the
Pleasure Seekers with her three sisters at the age of fourteen. They changed
their name to Cradle and toured American bases in Vietnam as well as playing
the seamier clubs in America. The British pop entrepreneur Mickie Most
spotted the group whilst visiting Detroit, and offered to manage her. She
moved to Britain and in 1972 released her first record, which failed to make any
impact. Subsequently Mickie Most engaged Nicky Chinn and Mike Chapman,
the most successful English pop writers of the period, and from then on she had
a string of hits. Her image was that of a rebellious tomboy dressed in leather,
aggressively playing bass and singing in front of her own all-male band. She
continued to play and record and in the late seventies had another string of hits.
She was the first of the female musicians to front a group, pre-dating her new-
wave successors by half a decade.

Mander, Margaret
   Suzi Quatro / Margaret Mander. – London: Futura Publications, 1976. –
   142p., 8p. of plates: ill., ports; 18cm. ISBN 0-8600-7270-3 (pbk.)
This biography places Suzi Quatro as the 'world's only female punk rocker',
and gives her a somewhat higher status in the world of popular music than she
justifies. Nevertheless, the essential facts of her life are here and Most's
manipulation and promotional techniques are well described.

QUEEN

Queen were formed in 1972 when guitarist Brian May and drummer Roger
Taylor joined with Freddy Mercury, who had an antique stall in Kensington
Market. After auditioning a great number of bass players, they finally recruited
John Deacon and began rehearsing their blend of heavy metal, not unlike Led
Zeppelin's style, with the extravagant vocals of Mercury. This was presented
with the band dressed in the androgynous glam-rock style of the period. Their
first album, which appeared in 1973, featured rich harmonies over some superb
guitar playing. They began to achieve commercial success in Britain and
became the first heavy-metal band to do this. Brian May, who was still
completing his doctorate at Imperial College, London, was evolving a unique
guitar style using a complex variey of electronic effects in concert and producing a wide range of sounds on record, often sounding like an orchestra. In 1975

their single, Bohemian Rhapsody, a disjointed, operatic-sounding song, was top of the British singles charts for nine weeks: the longest stay of any record since 1957. Often criticized as pretentious and contrived, by the eighties Queen had become enormously popular and some of the richest musicians ever with each album achieving massive world-wide sales. Queen manage their own financial affairs as a limited, four-share company and in 1981 were the highest-paid directors in British industry.

Davis, Judith
   Queen / by Judith Davis. – London; New York: Proteus, 1981. – 96p., 8p. of plates: ill. (some col.), ports (some col.); 27cm. Includes discography. ISBN 0-906071-91-7 (pbk.)
Well illustrated with an informative text, the theme of this book is the band's changing style and wide appeal. There is some good musical analysis, quotes from interviews and descriptions of their spectacular stage performances, as well as detailed technical information about their equipment. The discography is of albums only, giving full details of tracks.

Lowe, Jacque
   Queen's greatest pix / compiled, edited & designed by Jacque Lowe. – London: Quartet, 1981. – 95p.: chiefly col. ill., ports (chiefly col.); 27cm. Includes discography. ISBN 0-7043-3389-9 (pbk.)
With very brief notes by Ray Coleman, Ray Connolly and Paul Gambaccini, this collection of beautifully printed, mainly coloured photographs of the band portrays well their career from the beginning. The discography is complete but lacking in detail.

Pryce, Larry
   Queen / Larry Pryce. – London: Star Books, 1976. – 124p., 8p. of plates: ill., ports; 18cm. Includes discography. ISBN 0-352-39746-2 (pbk.)
A view of the group in 1976 (after their establishment as a top attraction), this is full of extracts from interviews with much information about their song-writing and recording techniques. It is not a chronological history, although there are reminiscences by the musicians. There is an appendix of personal biographies. The illustrations are uninspiring and the discography brief.

Tremlett, George
   The Queen story / George Tremlett. – London: Futura Publications, 1978. – 142p., 16p. of plates: ill., ports; 18cm. ISBN 0-8600-7412-9 (pbk.)
Another of the author's journalistic biographies, this is based on interviews with the group's associates and families as well as a range of secondary sources. Informative, but unexciting, there is a chronology of their career, tabulated biographical details of the musicians and some well-selected photographs of the musicians, mostly in extravagant poses.

West, Mike
> *Queen: the first ten years* / Mike West. – London: Omnibus Press, 1981. –
> 112p.: ill. (some col.), facsims, ports (some col.); 29cm. Includes
> discography. ISBN 0-86001-940-3 (pbk.)
> Originally published: Manchester: Babylon Books, 1981.

An outline history of the group, this is well illustrated with brief individual biographies of the four musicians and a comprehensive discography. An interesting feature is a description of Queen's stage show with a look at their complex equipment and special effects.

RACE, STEVE

Steve Race was born in Lincoln in 1920. After studying at the Royal Academy of Music and serving in the RAF during the Second World War, he began a career with the BBC. For more than thiry years he has hosted music programmes and helped to form the BBC's musical entertainment on both radio and television.

Race, Steve
> *Musician at large* / Steve Race. – London: Eyre Methuen, 1979. – 224p., leaf
> of plate, 8p. of plates: ill., ports; 23cm. Includes index. ISBN 0-413-39740-8

An entertaining, well-written autobiography which includes recollections of Steve Race's association with hundreds of top musicians from all types of music. His accounts range from working with Duke Ellington to Sir John Barbirolli and the Beatles.

RAINBOW

Rainbow was formed in May 1975 by Ritchie Blackmore, who had left Deep Purple that same month. The original line-up lasted for one album and six months. Blackmore's exacting requirements have seen none of the original members survive but a consolidated success grew. Veteran session drummer Cozy Powell joined in late 1975 and is the second mainstay of the band. It has, with Whitesnake and Gillan (both spawned by Deep Purple) led the heavy-metal revival in Britain and it continues to flourish. Rainbow is the most successful of these British bands in terms of sales of albums and singles.

Makowski, Peter
> *Rainbow* / by Peter Makowski. – London: Omnibus Press, 1981. – 48p.: ill.,
> ports; 27cm. Includes discography. ISBN 0-86001-963-2 (pbk.)

The author, in his capacity as a journalist, has travelled with Rainbow on their world tours and has personal information about the group's relationships and balance. He gives some technical detail about their equipment and includes a full section devoted to the early career of Ritchie Blackmore, which is the best source of detailed information on this important guitarist.

THE RAMONES

The Ramones made their first public appearance in March 1974 in New York and soon became second only to Patti Smith as innovators of the new wave in America. They visited Britain in July 1976 and had a great influence on the new-wave, punk revolution happening in London. They are described as the fastest band in the world and attack their audience with a barrage of non-stop, high-speed, guitar-dominated noise. Their formula has not evolved since their beginning and their importance has to a great extent waned.

Miles
  Ramones / text by Miles; art direction Perry Neville; design Andy Morton. – London: Omnibus Press, 1981. – 32p.: chiefly ill., ports; 27cm.
  ISBN 0-86001-804-0 (pbk.)
Basically this is a collection of illustrations of the band with a brief text, some extracts from press articles and a few quotations. It is sadly of little value as a source of information.

RAY, JOHNNIE

Born in Dallas, Texas, in 1927, Johnnie Ray left home at seventeen and went to Hollywood to seek fame and fortune as an actor. He ended up singing and playing piano in clubs around Los Angeles, wrote many of the songs in his act and soon acquired Bernie Larg as his personal manager. He was spotted playing in a nightclub by a disc jockey named Robin Seymour who persuaded Columbia Records to sign him. He became the most successful singing phenomenon of the early fifties and the biggest success since Frank Sinatra. Between 1952 and 1960 he had seventeen successful records in America as well as in Britain. A feature of his performance was the point at which he broke down in tears. His success waned with the growth of rock'n'roll and bad publicity over alleged homosexual activities.

Sonin, Ray
  The Johnnie Ray story / by Ray Sonin. – London: Horace Marshall, 1955. – 83p.: ill., ports; 19cm. (pbk.)
This is one of the earliest biographies of a pop star, poorly written and produced. The basic facts of the singer's life are here with some description of his concert performances but no discussion of his songwriting. The illustrations are sometimes posed and sometimes of the more emotional moments of his concert performances.

REDDING, OTIS

Born in Dawson, Georgia, in 1941, Otis Redding followed the tradition of many black singers by starting singing in his church choir. His local hero was

Little Richard and in 1962 he began working as road manager and occasional singer with a local rhythm & blues group, Johnny Jenkins and the Pine-toppers. When the group went to the studios of the Stax Record company Otis persuaded Jim Stewart, the controller of the company, to record some of his compositions. Stewart signed him and his first record was a minor American success. His success continued and by 1966 he had also made an impact in Britain. Excelling at up-tempo numbers, he could also sing powerful ballads with a style of soul music which was accessible to white audiences. It is this that makes him an important figure in that he was instrumental in achieving an important musical breakthrough, particularly in his soul interpretations of white rock songs. He was killed in a plane crash in 1967 and has become one of the legendary figures of popular music. His major British success, his composition Sitting on the Dock of the Bay, was posthumous.

Schiesel, Jane
   The Otis Redding story / Jane Schiesel. – Garden City, New York:
   Doubleday, 1973. – 143p., 1 plate: port; 22cm. Includes discography.
   ISBN 0-38502-335-9
Disappointing as the major source of information on the singer, this lacks serious analysis. His influence on white artists and audiences is briefly discussed.

REED, LOU

Born in New York, in 1943, Lou Reed was the leader of the Velvet Under-ground, an innovative group of the late sixties, based in New York and supported by Andy Warhol. Their music was inspired by a mood of the decadent Berlin of the thirties and always avant-garde. They survived until the early seventies without gaining real success. Reed then made a solo album in London which was followed by Transformer, an influential work produced by David Bowie. After finally achieving the success which had eluded him, he has since made a series of poor, derivative albums that are almost a self-parody. He maintains a cult following and is a father figure of the new-wave movement.

(*See also* THE VELVET UNDERGROUND.)

Clapton, Diana
   Lou Reed / Diana Clapton. – London; New York: Proteus, 1982. – 128p.: ill.
   (some col.), ports (some col.); 27cm. Includes discography.
   ISBN 0-86276-056-9 (cased) ISBN 0-86276-055-0 (pbk.)
A well-selected collection of illustrations is linked by a poor text which includes the basic information but fails to delve into a complex subject.

Lou Reed: rock and roll animal. – Manchester: Babylon Books, 1979. – 52p.:
   ill., facsims. ports; 25cm. Includes discography. (pbk.)
Produced in fanzine format, this collection of cartoon strips, cuttings, writings and illustrations, is presented in a confusing, impenetrable arrangement.

Trevena, Nigel
  Lou Reed & the Velvets / written, designed and produced by Nigel Trevena. –
  Falmouth, Cornwall: Bantam, 1973. – 36p.: ill., ports; 24cm. Includes
  discography. (pbk.)
This is not a cohesive biography but a collection of pictures, quotations,
reviews, comic strips, lyrics and a short, episodic chronology. The reviews,
which are of the Velvet Underground's albums as well as Reed's solo efforts,
are thorough and intelligent. The discography includes albums as well as
singles and unreleased recordings. The production is poor.

REEVES, JIM

Born in Panola County, Texas, in 1923, Jim Reeves made his first radio
broadcast at nine years old. By high school he was regularly playing guitar and
singing at local dances but it was as a basketball player that he excelled at the
University of Texas in Austin. After leaving college he became a radio
announcer and disc jockey. One night Hank Williams, the country-music star,
failed to arrive for a performance and Reeves was asked to stand in; from there
he signed with Abbott Records. In 1953 he gained his first big hit and in 1955 he
signed with the bigger company, RCA. His successes continued and by late
1957 he had gained a wider audience as a ballad singer and was achieving
success on an international scale which was to continue. On July 31st 1964 he
was killed in an air crash just outside Nashville. His records continue to sell in
vast numbers and during the sixties he was continually having posthumous
successes in the British record charts.

Cook, Pansy
  The saga of Jim Reeves: country and western singer and musician / by Pansy
  Cook. – Los Angeles: Crescent Publications, 1977. – iv., 27p.: ill., ports;
  22cm. ISBN 0-8914-4029-1 (pbk.)
A superficial tribute to Reeves' career packed with illustrations but short on
information.

RICH, CHARLIE

Born in Colt, Arkansas, in 1934, Charlie Rich studied music at the University
of Arkansas and was heavily influenced by jazz and blues. After leaving the US
Air Force, he became involved with Sam Phillips' famous Sun Records. In 1959
he made a successful record in the rockabilly style after being told that he must
relearn his proficient piano playing and learn to play badly! He has continued to
be moderately successful since the late fifties, developing his style into country
music and becoming an important performer who also has a following from the
middle-of-the-road record buyers. His stage performance still includes songs
from the various stages of his career.

Eron, Judy
  Charlie Rich / text Judy Eron, Geoffrey Morgan; illustrator Johnny Keely;
  design concept Mark Landkamer. – Mankato, Minnesota: Creative
  Education, 1975. – 31p.: ill. (some col.), ports (some col.); 25cm.
  ISBN 0-8719-1463-8
Written for a reading age of about ten for American schools, this is a well-produced controlled-vocabulary text which is a useful source of information. The content concerns mostly his later career but his rockabilly period is covered briefly.

RICHARD, CLIFF

Born Harry Webb in Lucknow, India, in 1940, Cliff Richard formed a group, the Drifters, in his home town of Cheshunt, Hertfordshire. After local performances he began playing at the 2 I's coffee bar in Soho. Here he met Jet Harris and Hank Marvin and reformed his group into the line-up which would later be renamed the Shadows. He released his first single in 1958, which became a hit and Cliff was established as Britain's answer to Elvis Presley. He made a series of successful records and films between 1958 and 1968 but his public image by the late sixties had been transformed from a sultry rocker into a family entertainer. He had become associated with the Church and his style had become outdated but he stayed in the public eye with a successful television series and playing in pantomime. In 1976 his album I'm Nearly Famous suddenly restored his success. Subsequent albums have given him a new credibility with superb productions inspired by Bruce Welch, one of the Shadows. He is re-established as Britain's leading male vocalist and is certainly one of the longest-surviving of all pop singers with his unbelievably youthful appearance and in spite of his clean-living image.

(*See also* THE SHADOWS.)

Doncaster, Patrick
  Cliff / Patrick Doncaster & Tony Jasper; written in co-operation with Cliff
  Richard. – London: Sidgwick & Jackson; in association with New English
  Library, 1982. – 253p., 16p. of plates: ill., ports; 18cm. Includes
  bibliography, discography, filmography and index. ISBN 0-283-98918-1 (pbk.)
  Originally published: London: Sidgwick & Jackson, 1981.
This includes little detail of Cliff's renaissance in the late seventies but there is a great deal of information about his earlier career and particularly his Christian activities. Tony Jasper, himself an active Christian and writer on pop music and Christian subjects, has for many years been involved with Cliff's career, hence the coverage and emphasis. The appendices are packed with information and the discography includes full details of British releases, track by track, as well as foreign releases with record numbers. The filmography includes full credits, radio and television appearances, addresses of fan clubs and details of tours. These latter are, however, somewhat incomplete. Overall, this is the most informative source of information on the singer.

Ferrier, Bob
Cliff around the clock / Bob Ferrier. – London: Daily Mirror Newspapers, 1964. – 24p.: ill., ports; 31cm. (pbk.)
Published in a newspaper format and presented in a reporting style, this is a day in the life of the singer in the early sixties. For the consumption of fans, the text is patronizing and naive and the photographs poorly posed. Nevertheless, it gives a candid glimpse of the period.

Ferrier, Bob
The wonderful world of Cliff Richard / Bob Ferrier. – London: P. Davies, 1964. – 247p.: ill., ports; 21cm.
A lengthy, early biography of Cliff after he had established himself not only as a singer but also as a film actor. There are lengthy quotations, numerous stills from his films, portraits and shots of him singing. The text is poorly written but informative.

Harris, Jet
Driftin' with Cliff Richard: the inside story of what really happens on tour / by Jet Harris and Royston Ellis. – London: Charles Buchan's Publications, 1959. – 63p.: ill., ports; 25cm. (pbk.)
Jet Harris was the original bass player of the Shadows. This ghosted account of early rock'n'roll tours in Britain is glossy and in no way reflects the reality of lack of organization and often squalid conditions. It is a superficial account for the fan. Published in magazine format, it does have some interesting illustrations.

Jasper, Tony
Silver Cliff: a 25 year journal 1958–1983 / Tony Jasper. – London: Sidgwick & Jackson, 1983. – 136p.: ill. (some col.), ports (some col.); 29cm. Includes discography. ISBN 0-283-98928-9 (cased). ISBN 0-283-98927-0 (pbk.)
This is a year-by-year celebration of Cliff's career with some good illustrations but a dull text. The discography is of British releases and includes EPs and singles as well as albums.

Richard, Cliff
Cliff in his own words / compiled by Kelvin St. John. – London: W. H. Allen, 1981. – 128p.: ill., ports; 26cm. ISBN 0-491-02786-4
Originally published: London: Omnibus Press, 1981.
An extensive collection of quotes which span Cliff's twenty-three years in showbusiness: the obvious topics of Christianity, his childhood in India and survival for so long are covered, and there are some well-selected illustrations from his early career and a few more recent ones.

Richard, Cliff
It's great to be young / Cliff Richard. – London: World Distributors, 1961. – 128p., 24p. of plates: ill., ports; 17cm. Includes discography
Originally published: London: Souvenir Press, 1960.

This is a wholesome autobiography in the mode of the period, originally subtitled *My teenage story and life in show business*, which includes interesting details of his early, unsuccessful tour of the USA. Well illustrated for the time, this is a good example of an early pop autobiography.

Richard, Cliff
  Me and my Shadows / Cliff Richard. – London: Daily Mirror Newspapers, 1961. – 64p.: ill., ports; 24cm. (pbk.)

A superficial autobiography with brief text but a good collection of early illustrations. The Shadows are featured with a description of their formation, their early incarnation as the Drifters and the change of personnel. The line-up here includes Jet Harris and Tony Meehan, who were later to leave and pursue a career as a duo.

Richard, Cliff
  Top pops / by Cliff Richard; presented by Patrick Doncaster the 'Daily Mirror's' D. J. – London: Daily Mirror Newspapers, 1963. – 63p.: ill., ports; 24cm. (pbk.)

Poorly produced, even by the standards of the time, here is a survey of the music of the period, nominally by Cliff Richard. There are some rare, interesting illustrations of lesser-known performers.

Richard, Cliff
  Which one's Cliff?: the autobiography / by Cliff Richard. – London: Coronet, 1981. – 219p., 12p. of plates: ill., ports; 18cm. Includes discography.
  ISBN 0-340-27159-0 (pbk.)
  Originally published: London: Hodder and Stoughton, 1977.
  Previous edition: London: Hodder and Stoughton, 1978.

This is a well-written autobiography, whose coverage includes Cliff's remarkable renaissance in the late seventies. His honesty and ability not to take himself too seriously is refreshing. The discography is full and very detailed. It is interesting to compare this with the 1961 autobiography to observe not only the obvious maturity of the author but also the improved quality in writing, illustration and production and the changed attitude towards the reader. The 1978 edition was specially published to commemorate his twenty-one years in showbusiness and has a more elaborate production in a large format.

Sutter, Jack
  Cliff, the baron of beat / Jack Sutter. – London: Valex, 1960. – 20p.: ill., ports; 25cm. (pbk.)

A brief, early look at the lifestyle of Cliff Richard at the period when he was both the English answer to Elvis Presley and still, deep down, the clean-cut 'boy-next-door'. Aimed at the fan, it is another interesting example of the patronizing attitude to pop artists in the early sixties. The illustrations are self-conscious and amusing.

Tremlett, George
  The Cliff Richard story / George Tremlett. – London: Futura Publications, 1975. – 156p., 16p. of plates: ill., ports; 18cm. ISBN 0-8600-7232-0 (pbk.)

Written just before Cliff Richard's renewed popularity in 1977, this is an informative, if uncritical, journalistic biography. There is the usual chronology but the unfortunate timing of the book's publication makes it largely irrelevant as the view is mostly retrospective.

Winter, David
   New singer, new song: the Cliff Richard story / by David Winter. – London:
   Hodder and Stoughton, 1968. – 192p., 8p. of plates: ill., ports; 18cm.
   Includes discography and filmography. ISBN 0-340-10994-7 (pbk.)
   Originally published: London: Hodder and Stoughton, 1967.
Written by the editor of the Christian periodical *Crusade*, and author of several titles on religious subjects, this is a personal biography by someone who knows his subject very well. The accounts of Cliff's early career, his rock'n'roll years and his success in films are factual and well written. The author is particularly interested in his conversion to Christianity, his support of Billy Graham on his British Crusade and this exceptional stand for a personality in pop music. Occasionally this theme is laboured but the approach is honest. The chronological discography does not include record numbers but is complete up to April 1967.

RICHARD, CLIFF: WRITINGS

Richard, Cliff
   Happy Christmas from Cliff / Cliff Richard. – London: Hodder and
   Stoughton, 1980. – 96p.: ill. (some col.), ports (some col.); 28cm.
   ISBN 0-340-25836-5 (cased). ISBN 0-340-25835-7 (pbk.)
Cliff presents the Christmas message to children in a modern way.

Richard, Cliff
   Questions: Cliff answering reader and fan queries / Cliff Richard. – London:
   Hodder and Stoughton, 1970. – 96p., 8p. of plates: ill., ports; 18cm.
   ISBN 0-340-10545-3 (pbk.)
Concerned with simple, fundamental questions about Christianity, the answers are well written with an uncomplicated, direct message.

Richard, Cliff
   The way I see it / by Cliff Richard. – London: Hodder and Stoughton, 1970. –
   187p.; 12cm. ISBN 0-340-04433-0 (pbk.)
   Originally published: London: Hodder and Stoughton, 1968.
This is a straightforward book preaching the gospel with Cliff Richard's uncomplicated, often simplistic message.

Richard, Cliff
   The way I see it now / by Cliff Richard. – London: Hodder and Stoughton,
   1973. – 92p.: ill., ports; 18cm. ISBN 0-340-16581-2 (pbk.)
A revised version of the above in a larger format.

RICHARDS, KEITH

Born in Dartford, Kent, in 1943, Keith Richards first met Mick Jagger at primary school. They renewed their acquaintance in 1960 through their mutual interest in rhythm & blues music and began playing together. With Jagger and Jones he formed the Rolling Stones in 1962. He and Jagger are the songwriters of the band and it is Keith Richards' driving guitar that leads the Stones' hard-rocking style. Although a man of few words, he has consistently reached the headlines with his notorious lifestyle and succession of drugs charges and court appearances.

(*See also* THE ROLLING STONES)

Charone, Barbara
   Keith Richards / Barbara Charone. – London: Futura Publications, 1979. – 192p.: ill., facsim., ports; 25cm. Includes discography. ISBN 0-7088-1658-4 (pbk.)
This is written by an American freelance journalist who has contributed to the best of the American music papers. She became closely involved with Richards and his girlfriend, Anita Pallenberg, in 1977 at the time of his arrest for drug offences in Toronto. She portrays Richards as the real driving force behind the Stones' image and music. It is a candid portrait, well illustrated, but suffering from even more than the usual amount of idolatry.

RILEY, JEANNIE C.

Born in Anson, Texas, in 1945, Jeannie C. Riley moved to Nashville in 1965 and worked as a secretary. She made a few demonstration recordings with little success until Shelby Singleton signed her to his new Plantation record label. She recorded a song written by Tom T. Hall, Harper Valley PTA, which dealt with small town hypocrisy. Amazingly it sold four million records in America alone and also became a big hit in Britain in 1968: unusual for a country-style record. Subsequently she had a series of minor successes but never reached her earlier heights. Recently she has had little success with her records but continues to be a popular concert performer.

Riley, Jeannie C.
   From Harper Valley to the mountain top / Jeannie C. Riley with Jamie Buckingham. – Eastbourne: Kingsway, 1981. – 211p.; 18cm. ISBN 0-86065-155-X (pbk.)
   Originally published: Lincoln, Virginia: Chosen Books, 1981.
A straightforward autobiography of overnight success in Nashville. Riley's opinions on other country artists and writers and the working of the country-music industry are forthright and informative.

ROGERS, KENNY

Born in Houston, Texas, in 1941, or so he claims, Kenny Rogers studied music at the University of Houston. He played with various country and folk groups, including the New Christy Minstrels, until in 1967 he formed the First Edition and between 1968 and 1971 had a string of successful singles. In 1979 he left the group and began his even more successful solo career, selling singles and albums in vast quantities as well as being a successful cabaret and concert performer. His success is due to a wide appeal, spanning folk, country and middle-of-the-road pop audiences. His popularity continues to grow.

Hume, Martha
> *Gambler, dreamer, lover: the Kenny Rogers story* / by Martha Hume;
> photographs by John Reggero. – London: Delilah Tower, 1981. – 160p.: ill.
> (some col.), ports (some col.); 28cm. Includes discography.
> ISBN 0-452-25254-7 (pbk.)

With an emphasis on the quality of Rogers' character and his exceptional personal happiness, this is a poorly written biography lacking in musical analysis but containing the basic information on his career.

THE ROLLING STONES

Mick Jagger, Keith Richards, Charlie Watts, Bill Wyman and Brian Jones had been playing individually in various blues-based bands around London including occasionally with Alexis Korner, the so-called father of British blues. By 1963, after various changes of line-up, the Rolling Stones as listed above met Andrew Oldham, who was quick to begin to mould their image as one to provide an alternative to the already famous, clean-cut 'mop top' image of the Beatles. Their style of rhythm & blues, which accurately imitated the sound of black musicans, their unkempt appearance and rebellious antics soon gained them a wide following. After two minor-hit records they achieved a major success in June 1964 and after an American tour they were second in popularity only to the Beatles. By 1966 Mick Jagger and Keith Richards were writing the majority of their songs and Brian Jones, the early leader of the Stones, was suffering increasingly from drug problems. He left the group in June 1969 and was found dead in his swimming pool on July 3rd 1969 aged twenty-five. His position as guitarist was taken by Mick Taylor, who was later replaced by Ron Wood.

The Stones continued their career into the seventies with occasional prosecutions on drugs charges and with Mick Jagger's jet-set lifestyle reaching the headlines at regular intervals. They undertook a series of now-legendary concert tours and had a string of hugely successful albums and singles, billing themselves, with some justification, as the 'Greatest rock'n'roll band in the world'. If they are not as musically creative as the Beatles, the Stones' position as one of the major forces in popular music is due to the excitement of their live performance. Although they have recorded some of the classic rock singles, they have admitted that their strength has always been in concert, with Mick Jagger standing out as one of the major influences in the presentation of popular song in recent years. Their 1982 tour of America and Europe was, as usual, a sell-out success.

(*See also* JAGGER, MICK; JONES, BRIAN; RICHARDS, KEITH.)

Carr, Roy
   The Rolling Stones: an illustrated record / by Roy Carr. – London: New
   English Library, 1976. – 120p.: ill. (some col.), col. facsims, ports (some
   col.); 30cm. ISBN 0-450-03172-1 (pbk.)
   Also published: New York: Harmony Books, 1976.
This is a chronologically arranged biography of the Stones, based around their record releases. Each album cover appears as a full-size reproduction along with full discographical information and notes. There is a full American discography, a list of bootlegs, songs recorded by other artists and appearances on other artists' albums. There is a full American filmography and a detailed listing of each of the band's tours, with the posters. The illustrations are very well chosen and arranged and the biographical notes are well organized.

Elman, Richard M.
   Uptight with the Stones: a novelist's report / by Richard Elman. – New York:
   Charles Scribner's Sons, 1973. – 119p.: ill., port; 23cm. ISBN 0-684-13299-0
The author, an American novelist, travelled with the Stones on their 1972 American tour. The style of writing, with its lengthy descriptive passages, is novelistic but essentially factual, describing the progress of the tour. The weakness, however, is the author's remoteness from the Stones themselves: he observes them meticulously from afar but never penetrates the public image.

Greenfield, Robert
   A journey through America with the Rolling Stones / Robert Greenfield. – St.
   Albans, Hertfordshire: Panther, 1975. – 287p., 16p. of plates: ill., ports;
   18cm. ISBN 0-586-04195-8 (pbk.)
   Originally published: New York: Saturday Review Press; E. P. Dutton,
   1974.
   Also published: London: Michael Joseph, 1974.
A rambling account of the group's 1972 American tour which attempts to give an impression of the pressures involved. The narrative meanders through quotations, events and flashbacks of the group's career and produces far more than an account of the tour – it is more of an impressionistic collage of life as a rock star.

Jasper, Tony
   The Rolling Stones / Tony Jasper. – London: Octopus Books, 1976. – 92p.:
   ill. (some col.), ports (some col.); 30cm. Includes discography.
   ISBN 0-706-40549-8
With some rare, early photographs, this is an intelligent, well-illustrated account of the group's career with some interesting analysis of their survival.

Kamin, Philip
  The Rolling Stones live in America / photographs by Philip Kamin; text by
  Peter Goddard. – London: Sidgwick & Jackson, 1982. – 128p.: ill. (some
  col.), ports (some col.); 28cm. ISBN 0-283-98940-8 (pbk.)
Well illustrated, this covers the Stones' 1981–2 tour of the USA. The text
briefly describes, often critically, each performance, but the overall effect is a
close view of some ageing rock'n'rollers.

Luce, Philip Carmelo
  The Stones / by Philip C. Luce. – London: Allen Wingate-Baker, 1970. –
  117p., 16p. of plates: ill., ports; 26cm. Includes discography.
  ISBN 0-09305-190-5 (pbk.)
Written with the death of Brian Jones in recent memory, the group's formation
and early career are covered as well as their early American tours and legal
problems of the late sixties. The discography is full with details of American
album releases, and the illustrations include several unique to this work.

Martin, Linda
  The Rolling Stones in concert / text by Linda Martin; produced by Ted Smart
  and David Gibbon. – New Malden, Surrey: Colour Library International,
  1982. – 98p.: ill. (chiefly col.), ports (chiefly col.); 30cm. Includes
  discography. ISBN 0-86283-007-9
Published to coincide with their 1982 British tour, this is not a detailed source of
the Stones' concert career, but a collection of beautifully reproduced photographs of the group, mainly performing, with a brief text outlining their career.
There is a list of their tours from 1963 to 1981 but no details of venues. The
discography includes all British and American releases.

Norman, Philip
  The Stones / Philip Norman. – London: Elm Tree Books, 1984. – x, 373p.,
  8p. of plates: ill., ports; 24cm. Includes index. ISBN 0-241-11065-3
  Also published: New York: Simon & Schuster; Fireside Books, 1984.
After Philip Norman's Beatles biography, *Shout!*, this publication was awaited
with anticipation and high expectations. It is unfortunately a disappointing
effort, lacking the understanding and warmth of the earlier work. Whether it is
the author's lack of real affection for the people concerned or the fact that
playing rhythm & blues in Richmond, Surrey, lacks the romance of sweaty
cellars in Liverpool and Hamburg, is difficult to be sure about but the result is a
straightforward, unexciting history. Research on the early days is rather
sketchy and although Norman conducted many recent interviews, he was
unable to talk to Mick Jagger. This is probably because Jagger did not wish to
divert interest from his imminent autobiography. Keith Richards comes over
particularly well, Brian Jones is a definite hero and Anita Pallenberg is a
bewitching, but sympathetic character. There is thankfully no resort to
sensationalism and even the legendary 'Mars bar incident' is dismissed as
absurd media exploitation. An anti-climax; one ends a lengthy read feeling no
nearer any of the subjects.

Pascall, Jeremy
  The Rolling Stones / written and edited by Jeremy Pascall. – London:
  Hamlyn, 1977. – 96p.: ill. (some col.), ports (some col.); 31cm. Includes
  discography and filmography. ISBN 0-600-37596-X
A brief but very informative and well-illustrated biography which traces well
their changes in style and image. The early period of their career with Brian
Jones is particularly well represented. There is a film section that gives
synopses and casts of the films in which the Stones have appeared as performers
and in which Mick Jagger acts. The discography and a list of hit singles is
complete to 1976.

Rolling Stones, the
  Our own story / by the Rolling Stones, as we told it to Pete Goodman;
  illustrations by Bob Gibson. – Rev. ed. – New York: Bantam Books, 1970. –
  188p.: ill., ports; 18cm. (pbk.)
  Previous edition: London: Transworld, 1964.
This is an interesting, early collection of interviews with the group at the time of
their first success. It displays their rebellious pose, with their middle-class
backgrounds clearly showing through. Usually articulate, they do discuss the
rhythm & blues music which was the basis of their style. The revision adds
nothing to the original text, merely a brief summary of the events in their career
between 1965 and 1970.

Rolling Stones, the
  Rolling Stones in their own words / compiled by David Dalton and Mick
  Farren. – London: Omnibus Press, 1980. – 125p.: ill., ports; 25cm.
  ISBN 0-86001-541-6 (pbk.)
Quotations by the Stones since their early days until 1980 are classified into
subjects to bring together comments on, for example, drugs, sex, money and
songwriting. Sometimes amusing, it is a mediocre collection.

  The Rolling Stones / edited by David Dalton. – Rev. ed. – London: Star Books,
  1975. – 186p., 12p. of plates: ill., ports; 18cm.
  Originally published: New York: Amsco Music Publishing, 1972. Includes
  discography. ISBN 0-352-30092-2 (pbk.)
This is a collection of biographical essays on the group, highlighting periods in
their development and rise to the top with pieces on such topics as Altamont,
the loss of Brian Jones and their brushes with the law. It is well written but lacks
cohesion. The early Amsco Music edition was a beautifully produced publication with coloured illustrations, lyrics and scores of some songs.

  The Rolling Stones / edited by David Dalton. – New York: Quick Fox, 1979. –
  126p.: ill., ports; 26cm. Includes discography. ISBN 0-8256-3929-8 (pbk.)
This collection of essays on the career of the group is a mixture of pieces taken
from the earlier work edited by the author and more recent magazine articles.
There is a good section of interviews and a full discography.

  The Rolling Stones. – New York: Straight Arrow Books, 1975. – 96p.: ill. (some
  col.). ports (some col.); 30cm. (pbk.)

Focussing on the Stones' legendary American tours of the seventies, this is a collection of articles which had appeared in *Rolling Stone* magazine. There are some very good illustrations and the quality of the writing is very high.

The Rolling Stones: the first twenty years / compiled by David Dalton. –
 London: Thames and Hudson, 1981. – 198p.: ill. (some col.), facsims (some col.), ports (some col.); 27 × 30cm. Includes discography.
 ISBN 0-500-27261-1 (pbk.)
Published to celebrate the Stones' twenty years of existence, this is a chronologically arranged selection of reproductions of newspaper and magazine articles. Dalton introduces each period of their career with a short essay. There are over five hundred well-chosen photographs and reproductions of their album sleeves. The discography, entitled a sessionography, gives full details of every recording session on which the group has ever worked with full information on the resulting record releases.

The Rolling Stones on tour / introduced by Mick Jagger; photographs by Annie Leibovitz, Christopher Sykes; text by Terry Southern. – Cheltenham: Phin Publishing, 1978. – 143p.: chiefly ill. (some col.), ports (some col.); 30cm.
 ISBN 0-90619-607-8 (pbk.)
A photographic record of the Stones' American tour which they undertook in 1975. The complexity of the operation, the organization of the personnel, transport, the technical problems of the sophisticated sound system and stage presentation as well as security are all portrayed. In addition, the extravagant stage shows are well photographed in colour. The notes are very brief.

Sanchez, Tony
 Up and down with the Rolling Stones / by Tony Sanchez. – New York: William Morrow, 1979. – 309p., 9p. of plates: ill., ports; 24cm.
 ISBN 0-688-03515-9 (cased). ISBN 0-688-08515-6 (pbk.)
Tony Sanchez was an employee of Keith Richards for eight years. He recalls the Stones' lifestyle at its most outrageous. It is a sensational account of drugs, women and excess, but with a fine collection of rare photographs. The interest lies in the personal nature of the anecdotes with recollections of particular parties as well as mundane incidents. The relationship of the Stones with other rock stars is particularly revealing. Brian Jones is portrayed as the real innovator and the member of the group the others followed in the early period.

Tremlett, George
 The Rolling Stones story / George Tremlett. – London: Futura Publications, 1974. – 190p., 16p. of plates: ill., ports; 18cm. ISBN 0-8600-7128-6 (pbk.)
 Also published: London: White Lion, 1976.
A well-researched biography up to 1973 based on the author's files kept since 1963 and including his own interviews with the group, their road manager Ian Stewart, families and friends. There is a detailed chronology and some interesting photographs.

THE ROLLING STONES: BIBLIOGRAPHIES

Dimmick, Mary Laverne
The Rolling Stones: an annotated bibliography / Mary Laverne Dimmick. –
Rev. ed. – Pittsburgh: University of Pittsburgh Press, 1979. – xiii, 159p.;
21cm. Includes indexes ISBN 0-8229-3384-5
Previous editions: Pittsburgh: University of Pittsburgh Press, 1972; 1975.
A scholarly, annotated bibliography produced by a librarian at the University
of Pittsburgh which includes descriptions and critical annotations of 455
writings on the Rolling Stones. The vast majority of citations are periodical
articles but also included are the monographs on the group. Divided into
eleven sections, each section is preceded by an essay of the period in the Stones'
development. There is a detailed chronology, an author index and periodical
index. In all this is a well-produced, unique example of a serious bibliographic
approach.

THE ROLLING STONES: DISCOGRAPHIES

Miles
The Rolling Stones: an illustrated discography / compiled by Miles. –
London: Omnibus Press, 1980. – 95p.: ill., facsims, ports; 20cm.
ISBN 0-86001-762-1 (pbk.)
A complete, well-organized, chronological listing of the Rolling Stones'
officially released records in the USA and Britain combined with their solo
efforts, their session appearances, and over two hundred bootleg recordings.
There are reproductions of most of the official album sleeves, as well as many of
the bootlegs, and an appendix which lists British and American albums
separately.

THE ROLLING STONES: QUIZBOOKS

Rosenbaum, Helen
The Rolling Stones trivia quiz book / by Helen Rosenbaum. – New York:
Signet, 1979. – 145p., 8p. of plates: ill., facsims, ports; 18cm.
ISBN 0-451-08669-4 (pbk.)
A collection of hundreds of questions on the Stones with a picture-quiz section.
They vary from the very easy to the utterly obscure.

THE ROLLING STONES: PERIODICALS

(*See* section 8.2, THE ROLLING STONES.)

RONSTADT, LINDA

Born in Tucson, Arizona, in 1946, Linda Ronstadt moved to Los Angeles in
1964 and achieved moderate success with the group, Stone Poneys. She began a

solo career in 1969 with a country-music style and material which by 1971 had evolved into country rock. In 1971 she formed her own backing group of the musicians who were to become the very successful Eagles, and it was their style and approach which helped her growth in popularity. After a series of successful albums, by 1976 she had become America's leading female rock star and her air of lost innocence had made her something of a sex symbol. Her pure voice, varied choice of songs (including some of her own) and her excellent choice of backing musicians give her continued success in America but she has a lesser following in Britain.

Berman, Connie
  Linda Ronstadt: an illustrated biography / by Connie Berman. – London:
  Proteus, 1979. – 117p.: ill. (some col.), ports (some col.); 27cm.
  ISBN 0-906071-08-9 (pbk.)
A richly illustrated, brief biography which ignores Ronstadt's early days, touches briefly on the start of her career and deals little with her personal life. The effect of her manager, Peter Asher, is discussed in some detail and her records are briefly described.

Claire, Vivian
  Linda Ronstadt / Vivian Claire. – New York; London: Flash Books, 1978. –
  72p.: ill., ports; 26cm. Includes discography. ISBN 0-8256-3918-2 (pbk.)
A short but good biography which attempts to deal with her music and analyses each of her albums. Although the book is brief, the author does reveal something of Linda Ronstadt's personality, attitudes and musical influences.

Kanakaris, Richard
  Linda Ronstadt: a portrait / by Richard Kanakaris. – Los Angeles: L. A. Pop
  Publications, 1977. – 79p., 3 leaves of plates: col. ill., col. ports; 29cm.
  ISBN 0-686-22854-5 (cased). ISBN 0-686-22855-3 (pbk.)
A popular biography for the teenage fan with beautiful portraits but a poorly written text.

Moore, Mary Ellen
  The Linda Ronstadt scrapbook / by Mary Ellen Moore. – New York:
  Sunridge Press, 1978. – 121p.: ill., ports; 28cm. ISBN 0-441-48410-7 (pbk.)
Moore, Mary Ellen
  The Linda Ronstadt scrapbook / by Mary Ellen Moore. – New York: Tempo
  Books, 1978. – 154p.: ill., ports; 18cm. ISBN 0-441-48411-5 (pbk.)
Packed with illustrations, the author's theme is that of the struggle of becoming a star in an area of music dominated by men. There is no real discussion of Linda Ronstadt's music, a lot of comment on her as a sex symbol but no attempt to analyse her success or to look at her personal life. Both editions have identical text and illustrations but the first, large-format version has far better reproduced illustrations.

Ross, Diana

Born in Detroit in 1944, Diana Ross met Florence Ballard and Mary Wilson at high school. They began singing together and after changing their name from the Primettes to the Supremes they signed a contract with the Tamla Motown label in 1961. After an initial failure they had a series of successful singles between 1964 and 1967. In 1967 Florence Ballard left the group to be replaced by Cindy Birdsong. The group now changed its name to Diana Ross and the Supremes, highlighting Ross's talents more strongly. There followed more hits and in December 1969 she finally left the Supremes to form an even more successful solo career. Diana Ross has made three successful films, taking the starring roles in Lady Sings the Blues, The Wiz and Mahogany. Her international stardom continues: she is the toast of Las Vegas and still has worldwide hit records.

Berman, Connie
Diana Ross: Supreme lady / Connie Berman. – New York: Popular Library, 1978. – 158p.: ill., ports; 18cm. Includes discography. ISBN 0-445-04283-4 (pbk.)
An uncritical little biography covering her career with the Supremes, her solo success and move into films. The illustrations are good but the discography lacks detail.

Brown, Geoff
Diana Ross / Geoff Brown. – London: Sidgwick & Jackson, 1981. – 144p.: ill. (some col.), ports (some col.); 28cm. Includes discography and index. ISBN 0-283-98772-3 (cased). ISBN 0-283-98773-1 (pbk.)
Filled with excellent illustrations and with an informative if uncritical text, this is the best available biography of Diana Ross. It covers her early days with the Supremes and there is some detail about her later acting career with stills from Lady Sings the Blues, the Wiz and Mahogany. The discography includes all her recordings with the Supremes, as well as other artists, and gives full discographical details.

Eldred, Patricia Mulrooney
Diana Ross / text Patricia Mulrooney Eldred; illustrator John Keely; design concept Mark Landkamer. – Mankato, Minnesota: Creative Education, 1975. – 31p.: ill. (some col.), ports (some col.); 25cm. ISBN 0-8719-1462-X
A controlled-vocabulary biography aimed at a reading age of about ten for American schools, this is well written with some good illustrations.

Haskins, James
I'm gonna make you love me: the story of Diana Ross / by James Haskins. – New York: Dell, 1982. – 192p.: ill., ports; 20cm. ISBN 0-440-94172-5 (pbk.)
Originally published: New York: Dial Press, 1980.
Aimed at the early-teenage reader, this is a sensitive, sympathetic and informative biography with very good illustrations.

Itzkowitz, Leonore K.
  Diana Ross / Leonore K. Itzkowitz. – New York: Random House, 1974. –
  186p.: ill., ports; 22cm. ISBN 0-3941-2310-7 (pbk.)
An outline of Diana Ross's career up to her film debut: this is a poor,
uninformative effort.

ROSS, DIANA: FILMS

Lady Sings the Blues

Made in 1972 and directed by Sidney J. Furie, Lady Sings the Blues is roughly
based on the tragic life story of blues singer Billie Holiday. Born in Baltimore in
1915, she became the leader in her field during the thirties, recording with the
best jazz musicians of the period. Her success continued throughout the forties
but heroin addiction and alcohol were badly taking their toll. She was imprisoned for narcotics offences in 1948 and charged again in 1959, but died
under detention in the Metropolitan Hospital, New York. The film, starring
Diana Ross (who was nominated for an Academy Award), is regarded by jazz
enthusiasts as a travesty in terms of biographical accuracy and the quality of the
singing.

Holiday, Billie
  Lady sings the blues / Billie Holiday with William Dufty. – London: Abacus,
  1975. – 220p., 16p. of plates: ill., ports; 20cm. Includes discography.
  ISBN 0-349-11705-5 (pbk.)
  Originally published: Garden City, New York: Doubleday, 1956.
  Also published: London: Barrie and Jenkins, 1958.
  Previous editions: London: Barrie and Jenkins, 1973; London: Sphere
  Books, 1973.
This original autobiography is included here because it was revived to coincide
with the release of the film. It includes both original photographs of Billie
Holiday and stills of Diana Ross resembling her not at all.

ROXY MUSIC

Bryan Ferry formed Roxy Music in London in late 1970; Andy Mackay and
Brian Eno joined him in early 1971 and Phil Manzanera a little later that year.
They received early critical approval from live shows featuring an extravagant,
glam-rock image. In 1972 their first album was a big success. They were all
involved in avant-garde music, and their style ranged from rock'n'roll pastiche
to a stylized Englishness not far away from Noel Coward with, for the time, an
extensive use of synthesizers, Eno's innovation leading in this new field.
  In 1973 their second album displayed more experimental trends influenced
by John Cage and Terry Riley but personality problems between Ferry and
Eno, based on a conflict over the future direction of the group, soon led to

Eno's departure. Ferry's urbane, English style now dominated the group but Mackay and Manzanera began to contribute their lyrics to the group's repertoire. In 1973 and 1974 Ferry, Manzanera and Mackay made solo albums by which Ferry established himself as a solo artist of real importance. Although interest had been shown by the American audience it was not until 1975, with the success of their fifth album, that the group began to play at the enormous venues in the USA. In 1976 the group separated but reappeared in 1980. In 1981 with their tribute to John Lennon, Lennon's song Jealous Guy, they had their first number-one single. They remain one of the most creative, talented and literate bands Britain has produced.

(*See also* FERRY, BRYAN.)

Rees, Dafydd
   Bryan Ferry and Roxy Music / by Dafydd Rees and Barry Lazell. – London; New York, Proteus, 1982. – 96p.: ill. (some col.), ports (some col.); 28cm. Includes discography. ISBN 0-862760-033-X (cased). ISBN 0-862760-034-8 (pbk.)
A concise history which does not attempt to analyse their music or success in any depth but is informative and well illustrated. The solo efforts of the individual members of the group are briefly covered and although the emphasis is on Bryan Ferry, Mackay, Eno and Manzanera are all well treated.

Rogan, Johnny
   Roxy Music: style with substance – Roxy's first ten years / Johnny Rogan. – London: Star Books, 1982. – 219p., 12p. of plates; 18cm. Includes discography. ISBN 0-352-31076-6 (pbk.)
A very good study of the group's career not forgetting the solo efforts of all the members. There are lengthy quotes from the music press with an unusual section of notes of sources. The illustrations are interesting and the discography complete with full discographical details. The author's knowledge of Roxy Music's development in terms of artistic presentation as well as musical style is evident, making this stand above the usual group history.

RUSH

Formed in Toronto, Canada, in 1970 by Geddy Lee (keyboards, bass and vocals), Alex Lifeson (guitar and vocals) and John Rutsey (drums), Rush released their first album in 1973. In 1974 Rutsey left and was replaced by Neil Peart, who became their lyricist as well as their drummer. Heavily influenced by science-fiction writer Ayn Rand, Peart translated many of her ideas into music. The effect was that their second album, released in 1975, was an immediate success. Their success has grown world-wide since breaking through in America with their third album in 1976. They play a variety of heavy-metal music, more sophisticated than most, sometimes termed pomp rock or science-fiction rock. They have a small following in Britain.

Harrigan, Brian
  Rush / by Brian Harrigan. – London: Omnibus Press, 1981. – 80p.: ill., ports;
  27cm. Includes discography. ISBN 0-86001-934-9 (pbk.)
The sole substantial source of information about the band; by the news editor
of *Melody Maker*, who betrays himself as an enthusiast. Well illustrated, it
gives an educated analysis of their albums and descriptions of their concert
performances.

Savile, Jimmy

Born in Leeds, in 1926, Jimmy Savile began working as a miner but suffered a
bad accident at the Waterloo Colliery, near Leeds, and was forced to retire.
Having been told that he would never walk again, he resolved not only to do so
but also to change his life completely. He did both. He began working as a disc
jockey and joined the Mecca organization in the early fifties, working in the
then-popular dance halls. He began working with Radio Luxembourg and by
the sixties was a leading disc jockey and supporter of rock'n'roll and particularly of Elvis Presley. He was an early presenter of BBC Television's Top of
the Pops and by the late seventies his own television show, Jim'll Fix It, was a
leading entertainment. A remarkable philanthropist, he genuinely and self-
lessly works for hundreds of charities. Too good to be true, he is a unique
character who has diversified, but owes his start to playing pop records on the
radio.

Savile, Jimmy
  God'll fix it / by Jimmy Savile. – London: Mowbrays, 1979. – xvi, 64p., 8p. of
  plates: ill., ports; 18cm. ISBN 0-264-66457-4 (pbk.)
A light, devotional work, Savile's personal philosophy and gratefulness for his
success seem totally honest.

Savile, Jimmy
  Love is an uphill thing / Jimmy Savile. – London: Coronet, 1976. – 184p.;
  18cm. ISBN 0-340-19925-3 (pbk.)
  Originally published as '*As it happens*': London: Barrie and Jenkins 1974.
Sincere and certainly not sanctimonious, this includes Savile's recollections of
working as a disc jockey in the fifties and his meeting with Elvis Presley.

Seeger, Pete

Born in 1919 in New York, Pete Seeger was educated at Harvard and served
with the armed forces during the Second World War. He spent some time with
Alan Lomax, the folk-music historian, working in the archives of the Library of
Congress. He later travelled throughout the mid-West, singing and studying
folk song. He formed the Weavers folk group in 1949 and worked with Woody
Guthrie. He became involved in left-wing politics and wrote the anthem We

Shall Overcome, as well as many other protest songs. His songs have been widely recorded by the younger generation of protest singers and singer-songwriters, on whom he has been a major influence.

Dunaway, David King
  How can I keep from singing?: Pete Seeger / David King Dunaway. – New York: McGraw-Hill, 1981. – 386p.: ill., ports; 24cm. Includes bibliography, discography and index. ISBN 0-07-018150-0 (cased). ISBN 0-07-018151-9 (pbk.)
A lengthy, authoritative biography, this not only looks at Seeger's writing and performing career, but also at his social and political activites in considerable detail. There are lengthy quotations, some interesting illustrations and intelligent comment.

Seeger, Pete
  The incompleat folksinger / by Pete Seeger; edited by Jo Metcalf Schwartz. – New York: Simon and Schuster, 1976. – viii, 596p.: ill., ports; 25cm.
  Includes index. ISBN 0-6712-0954-X
Autobiographical notes and essays, lyrics and some excellent illustrations are gathered into this excellent representation of Seeger's work. His notes on both his own songs and traditional songs are particularly interesting.

The Sex Pistols

Johnny Rotten, Glen Matlock, Steve Jones and Paul Cook, the notorious Sex Pistols, were formed in 1975 by Malcolm Maclaren, who had managed the New York Dolls for a few months. They became the archetypal London punk band with spiky hair, safety pins and frantic, totally inept musicianship over raw vocals. They were signed by EMI Records, who terminated their exclusive contract within three months after considerable embarrassment. Their national tour was disrupted after ninety percent of towns in Britain refused to accept them because of their obscene behaviour on a Thames Television news programme. They signed with A and M Records and were sacked within a week, finally establishing a contract with Virgin Records. They achieved an album success and several single hits, including God Save the Queen, which was banned on radio and television but still became a number-one hit at the time of the Silver Jubilee in 1977. John Lydon, or Johnny Rotten, their writer and singer, left the band in 1978. The band continued, but when in February 1979 the replacement bass player, Sid Vicious, was found dead from a drug overdose, after recently having been indicted for murder, the Pistols had finally reached their end. The leaders of punk, they avoided the pitfalls of show-business stardom by their self-destruction.

(*See also* VICIOUS, SID.)

Stevenson, Ray
Sex Pistols file / edited by Ray Stevenson. – Rev. ed. – London: Omnibus
Press, 1980. – 72p.: ill., ports; 30cm. ISBN 0-86001-464-9 (pbk.)
Previous edition: London: Omnibus Press, 1978.
Updated to include the death of Sid Vicious, this is published in the cut-up,
fanzine style. It consists mainly of photographs and press cuttings, but inter-
spersed are comments by the Pistols on various topics. Arranged in a generally
chronological sequence, it offers a vague impression of their saga.

Vermorel, Fred
The Sex Pistols: the inside story / compiled and edited by Fred and Judy
Vermorel. – London: Star Books, 1978. – 224p., 8p. of plates: ill., facsims,
ports; 18cm. ISBN 0-426-18585-4 (pbk.)
Written by friends of Malcolm Maclaren, this inside story of the group's
lifestyle, motives and attitudes has some credibility. There are lengthy transcripts of interviews as well as the author's descriptions of the individual
musicians and their associations with record companies, the press and the
police. There are some fascinating interviews with the mothers of the group
members and with people who worked with them. Generally the chaos is well
communicated along with the pretentiousness and Maclaren's manipulation.
The music is largely ignored. There is an appendix of short biographies of all
the protagonists in the story.

THE SEX PISTOLS: FILMS

The Great Rock'n'Roll Swindle

Released in 1980 and directed by Julian Temple, The Great Rock'n'Roll
Swindle was the film of the Sex Pistols playing their unique brand of high-
energy, low-melody noise with interviews and animations cut together in a very
disjointed way. The Pistols' meeting with Ronald Biggs, the great train robber,
is a memorably bizarre sequence in an otherwise undistinguished film.

Moorcock, Michael
The great rock'n'roll swindle: a novel / by Michael Moorcock. – London:
Virgin Books, 1980. – 24p.: ill., ports; 58cm. ISBN 0-907080-07-3 (unbound)
Published to coincide with the release of the film and produced in an unusual
format resembling a large-style, folded newspaper with a collection of stills
from the film, this is not a description of the action or a novel but a series of
short, obscure, prose poems or short streams of consciousness purporting to be
'inspired by the film'. Certainly unreadable, its odd format is its only significant
feature.

Moorcock, Michael
The great rock'n'roll swindle / Michael Moorcock. – London: Virgin Books,
1980. – 128p.; 20cm. ISBN 0-907080-13-8 (pbk.)

Published as a conventional paperback but lacking illustrations, this has the same odd text as the other edition. Both are simply pretentious nonsense.

THE SHADOWS

In 1958, after his first successful record, Cliff Richard set about forming a backing group to tour Britain. This group, the Drifters, included Hank B. Marvin, Bruce Welch plus bass player Ian Samwell and drummer Terry Stuart. After the tour the latter musicians left and Jet Harris and Tony Meehan were introduced. During 1959 they changed their name to the Shadows to avoid confusion with the American group, who had objected. In July 1960 they achieved their first top-selling single, Apache, and over the next five years there followed a series of over twenty instrumental hits. Jet Harris left in 1962 and was replaced by Brian Locking who was himself replaced by John Rostill in 1963. Meehan left also in 1962 and was replaced by Brian Bennett. Jet Harris and Tony Meehan had five successful records in 1963 as a duo but then faded. The Shadows appeared in three Cliff Richard films and continued as a group until 1968 when they split up. They reformed in 1975 and since then they have rebuilt their career, going from strength to strength. There is no doubt that Hank Marvin was the most influential British guitarist of the early sixties, inspiring a generation of young, hopeful musicians.

(*See also* RICHARD, CLIFF.)

Geddes, George Thomson
    The Shadows: a history and discography / by George Geddes. – Glasgow:
    G. and M. Geddes, 1981. – 178p.; 30cm. Includes bibliography. (spiral)
A much-expanded version of the author's purely discographical publication, this includes a very good biographical essay.

Shadows, the
    The Shadows by themselves. – London: Consul Books, 1961. – 126p.: ill.,
    ports; 18cm. (pbk.)
An unusually good, early autobiography: the Shadows describe their back-grounds, musical influences and the influence of skiffle on their early music. Their interest in the electric guitar, amplification and its potential, is prophetic.

Shadows, the
    The story of the Shadows: an autobiography / with Mike Read. – London Elm
    Tree Books, 1983. – x, 246p., 8p. of plates: ill. (some col.), facsims, geneal.,
    ports (some col.); 24cm. Includes discography. ISBN 0-241-10861-6 (cased).
    ISBN 0-241-10887-X (pbk.)
The fullest source of information on the group, this is largely the transcripts of interviews held with Hank Marvin, Bruce Welch, Jet Harris, Tony Meehan and Brian Bennett, with notes on Licorice Locking and John Rostill. There is an

excellent, full discography and a fine collection of photographs. Mike Read, the disc jockey and presenter of the BBC television programme Saturday Superstore, skilfully strings together the pieces by each group member, adding contemporary facts to set the scene and context and making useful observations. One would not expect a lurid exposé of the Shadows and one finds a good, straightforward biography.

THE SHADOWS: DISCOGRAPHIES

Geddes, George Thomson
  Foot tapping: the Shadows 1958–1978 / George T. Geddes. – Glasgow:
  George Thomson Geddes, 1978. – 54p.; 30cm. (pbk.)
Privately published, this is an exhaustive listing of British and European releases. There are full discographical details, dates and excellent annotations.

SHAPIRO, HELEN

Born in Hackney, London, in 1947, Helen Shapiro made her first record at the age of fourteen under the guidance of Norrie Paramor, the chief A & R man of EMI's Columbia label. This became a hit in March 1961 and by the end of the year she was Britain's top female vocalist. She held this position until 1963 with a string of successful singles and several film appearances. She was a victim of the Mersey sound boom of 1963, superseded by Cilla Black. Since then she has had a less prominent, but persistent career in clubs and cabaret.

Janson, John S.
  Helen Shapiro: pop princess / by John S. Janson. – London: Four Square,
  1963. – 126p., 16p. of plates: ill., ports; 18cm. (pbk.)
  Originally published: London: New English Library, 1963.
An early British pop biography, this is patronizing to the subject as well as to the reader. In this way it reflects clearly the attitude of writers and journalists to the pop audience of the early sixties. Nevertheless, it also gives a view of the music business at the time and the concept that any schoolgirl could become a star overnight.

SIMON AND GARFUNKEL

Paul Simon, born in Newark, New Jersey, in 1941, spent his childhood in the comfortable, middle-class suburb of Queens, New York and met Art Garfunkel, born in New York in 1941, while at school. In 1957 they formed a singing duo called Tom and Jerry and had a minor hit record in America, but after a definite lack of further success they went back to college. Simon went to law school but left in 1964 and came to England where he played in folk clubs. On returning to New York he and Garfunkel began playing in clubs in

Greenwich Village and soon secured a record contract with Columbia Records. Their first album included some Simon songs, greatly inspired by Dylan's protest lyrics, and some traditional folk songs. However, one song, The Sound of Silence, was released as a single with an overdubbed electric accompaniment engineered in the absence of and without the knowledge of Simon. It became a top-selling single in 1965. This was followed by a further album and successful single releases. In 1967 Simon wrote the soundtrack for the film The Graduate, performed by Simon and Garfunkel, and they followed this with one of the biggest-selling albums of all time, Bridge over Troubled Water. Criticized for their unashamed sweetness, they have nevertheless been exceptionally popular.

In 1971 the duo split up. Garfunkel appeared successfully in a number of films and also recorded solo albums. Simon, performing alone, has continued to write better and better songs. Possibly without the immediate catchiness of his earlier work, his tasteful, sparse arrangements, sophisticated chord structures and curious lyrics gave him continued success. In 1981 Simon and Garfunkel performed together in Central Park, New York, an event which became a successful live album. They now plan to work together again. Musically a strange mixture of rock'n'roll, sophistication, folk-protest and sentimentality, they remain two of the major stars of popular music who will continue to fill venues throughout the world.

Cohen, Mitchell S.
Simon & Garfunkel: a biography in words & pictures / by Mitchell S. Cohen; edited by Greg Shaw. – New York: Sire Books; Chappell Music Company, 1977. – 55p.: ill., ports; 30cm. Includes discography. ISBN 0-1475-4631-5 (pbk.)

A good study of Simon and Garfunkel's work, mainly concerned with their period together but also including information about their later solo careers. The illustrations are well selected and Paul Simon's lyrics are discussed in some detail.

Humphries, Patrick
Bookends: the Simon and Garfunkel story / Patrick Humphries. – London; New York: Proteus, 1982. – 128p.: ill. (some col.), ports (some col.); 27cm. Includes discography. ISBN 0-86276-063-1 (cased). ISBN 0-86276-062-3 (pbk.)

A well-illustrated biography inspired by Simon and Garfunkel's reunion Central Park concert in 1981. Their careers together and as solo artists are briefly described with full joint and solo discographical details.

Leigh, Spencer
Paul Simon: now and then / by Spencer Leigh. – Liverpool: Raven Books, 1973. – 110p.: ill., ports; 21cm. Includes discography. ISBN 0-85977-008-7 (pbk.)

Written by a radio presenter with Radio Merseyside who has interviewed Paul Simon in depth on several occasions, this biography covers in some detail his career with Art Garfunkel as well as the early stages of his solo career. Informative and demonstrating considerable knowledge of Simon's work, it has a detailed analysis of the solo album There Goes Rhymin' Simon and a detailed discography of his records up to 1972 which includes the rare, earlier efforts as Tom and Jerry. This is a sensitive little study by an author who understands not only the songs but also to some extent the complexities of the artist himself.

Marsh, Dave
   Paul Simon / Dave Marsh. – New York: Quick Fox, 1978. – 128p.: ill., ports; 26cm. Includes discography. ISBN 0-8256-3916-6 (pbk.)
Paul Simon's varied career from teenage pop singer to folk artist and singer-songwriter is well chronicled. The author knows Simon's work well enough but his attempts at lyrical and musical analysis are trite and simplistic. The illustrations are well chosen with some early photographs not available elsewhere, but the discography is incomplete and lacks detail.

Matthew-Walker, Robert
   Simon and Garfunkel / by Robert Matthew-Walker. – Tunbridge Wells, Kent: Midas Books, 1982. – 168p.: ill., ports; 22cm. Includes discography. ISBN 0-85936-244-2
A good study of their careers together and as solo artists, Simon's writing is the essential focus but Garfunkel's voice and flair for arrangements is recognized. Garfunkel's successful solo recording career is also given considerable space with Simon's solo work. Their reunion and the concert in Central Park is the culminating action. This is probably the most authoritative work on the duo, which displays the author's musical knowledge and excellent writing style.

SIMON, CARLY

Born in 1945, in New York, into a wealthy publishing family, Carly Simon attended the exclusive Sarah Lawrence College. She began singing with her sister, Lucy, while at college, performing in folk clubs around New York, but the duo split up on her sister's marriage. A year later, in 1966, she met Albert Grossman, Bob Dylan's manager, who arranged some recording sessions with producer Bob Johnston. No album resulted and not until 1969 did she finally sign a contract with Elektra. Her first album appeared in 1971 and immediately demonstrated her style, smoother and more sophisticated than the other singer-songwriters of the period. Although this album was successful in the USA, it was her third album, No Secrets, which established her in Britain. The single You're So Vain, taken from this album, was an enormous success, featuring Mick Jagger as a backing vocalist. Whether the subject was Warren Beatty or Jagger himself stimulated even more interest. In 1973 she married singer-songwriter James Taylor and has produced only a few records since then. She occasionally recorded and appeared in concert with her husband and has achieved some success in her native country but has made little impact in Britain. In 1980 she appeared in the film No Nukes, giving an enthusiastic performance.

Albert Grossman originally saw her as a kind of female version of Bob Dylan and although she certainly has never justified such exaggerated comment, she has never received the serious critical attention that many believe she deserves.

Morse, Charles
Carly Simon / text Charles and Ann Morse; illustrator Dick Brude. –
Mankato, Minnesota: Creative Education, 1975. – 31p.: ill. (some col.),
ports (some col.); 25cm. ISBN 0-8719-1393-3
A controlled-vocabulary biography written for a reading age of about ten for American schools, this is informative with some well-chosen illustrations.

SINATRA, FRANK

Born in Hoboken, New Jersey, in 1915, Francis Albert Sinatra was the first pop star. After singing on a local radio-station talent contest in 1935 he spent four years touring and singing in small clubs before being spotted by bandleader Harry James in 1939. At the time the road to success for a vocalist was to be the band singer with an established orchestra. Sinatra quickly made an impression with James and in 1940 was offered a job with the Tommy Dorsey orchestra, one of the top bands in America. By 1943 he had been offered the major spot on a radio programme called Hit Parade and was established as a major new talent. In 1943 he was also offered his first acting role in the film Higher and Higher, as well as winning a gold disc. He was the first singing star to get the fan mail and screams which are now associated with such 'phenomena' and during the mid forties was known as 'the Voice'. During the early fifties his career and personal life began to suffer until in 1953 he not only helped finance but won an Oscar for his performance in the film From Here to Eternity. More good acting roles followed as well as successful records. During the sixties his name was rarely absent from the bestseller lists until 1971 when he announced his retirement. By mid 1973 he was planning a comeback which he achieved in spectacular style with an enormously successful album.

Sinatra's success is due not only to his distinctive voice with unusual phrasing and superb enunciation, nor simply to his very real acting talent but also to his ability to choose excellent songs from a wide range of sources and somehow to move with the times although always with his own, unique style.

Douglas-Home, Robin
Sinatra / Robin Douglas-Home. – London: Transworld, 1963. – 110p.: ill.,
ports; 19cm. (pbk.)
Originally published: London: Michael Joseph, 1962.
A well-illustrated, brief biography, this gives the basic facts of Sinatra's career up to 1960. There are stills from his films, photographs of his various wives and hints about his notorious lifestyle. It is unusual in that it is a British book about an American artist, rare for the time.

Frank, Alan
 Sinatra / Alan Frank. – London: Hamlyn, 1978. – 176p.: ill. (some col.),
 facsims, ports (some col.); 30cm. Includes discography, filmography and
 index. ISBN 0-600-38317-2
Written by an author whose other works are on cinema and who writes a
weekly, film-review column, this is an informative, uncritical biography.
Sinatra's early career is well covered and there is considerable discussion of his
musical style. His film career is given rather more emphasis than his music, as
might be expected, and the filmography includes credits, stills but no synopses.
The index is good and the discography selective, including British releases.

Gehman, Richard
 Sinatra and his rat pack: a biography / Richard Gehman. – London:
 Mayflower, 1961. – 223p.; 18cm. (pbk.)
The Rat Pack was a very select group of entertainers who originally centred
around Humphrey Bogart in the late forties and early fifties. After Bogey's
death the group, which had changed its membership, included Dean Martin,
Peter Lawford and Sammy Davis Jr. An unashamedly élitist clique, the group
generally enjoyed their notoriety with as much of it myth as reality. This
biography describes Sinatra's rise to the leadership of the pack, the members
and their friends, and Sinatra's career, which is a secondary feature of the
book. The book aims to be mildly outrageous and is very entertaining.

Howlett, John
 Frank Sinatra / John Howlett. – London: Plexus, 1980. – 176p.: ill., facsims,
 ports; 31cm. Includes discography and filmography. ISBN 0-85965-022-7
 (cased). ISBN 0-85965-021-9 (pbk.)
A brief biography which uncritically outlines Sinatra's career: there are good
illustrations, a full discography and an informative filmography with stills.

Kahn, E. J.
 The voice: the story of an American phenomenon / by E. J. Kahn, Jr. –
 London: Musician's Press, 1946. – 125p., 16p. of plates: ill., ports; 18cm.
 (pbk.)
The earliest biography of Sinatra, and included here because it is the earliest
example of a biography of any modern popular singer. It was written at the
height of his first phase of popularity when he was the idol of the 'bobby soxers'.
In appearance and style this predates the late-fifties examples of biographies
prepared for a wide, fan-orientated market by over a decade.

Lake, Harriet
 On stage, Frank Sinatra / text Harriet Lake; design concept Larry Soule. –
 Mankato, Minnesota: Creative Education, 1976. – 47p.: ill., ports; 23cm.
 ISBN 0-8719-1482-4
A controlled-vocabulary biography for a reading age of about ten and aimed at
American schools, this is well produced with some good illustrations. Although
Frank Sinatra is far from a cult figure with this younger age group, this offers
information in a well-presented and interesting format.

Peters, Richard
The Frank Sinatra scrapbook: his life and times in words and pictures / by
Richard Peters. Incorporating the Sinatra sessions: a complete list of all his
recording sessions, 1939–1982 / by Ed O'Brien and Scott P. Sayers, Jnr. –
London: Pop Universal; Souvenir Press, 1982. 160p.: ill., ports; 27cm.
Includes discography and filmography. ISBN 0-285-62529-2 (cased).
ISBN 0-285-62539-X (pbk.)
With a fine collection of about 150 photographs, including stills from several of
his films, the biographical section of the work is superficial. The chronological
listing of his recording sessions is, however, well laid out and detailed including
full information of songs recorded, musicians and resulting releases. Overall
this is an unsatisfactory attempt which is neither popular nor a good reference
source.

Scaduto, Anthony
Frank Sinatra / Tony Scaduto. – London: Sphere Books, 1977. – 159p., 8p. of
plates: ill., ports; 18cm.ISBN 0-7221-7656-2 (pbk.)
Originally published: London: Michael Joseph, 1976.
Although reading at times like a series of episodes rather than a cohesive
biography, this is nevertheless a sympathetic, entertaining account. The author
avoids sensationalism, even in the way he examines in detail Sinatra's alleged
Mafia connection. He refutes this completely. In general this is the least
successful biography by the author who has also written works on Bob Dylan
and Mick Jagger.

Shaw, Arnold
Sinatra: retreat of the romantic / Arnold Shaw. – London: Hodder
Paperbacks, 1970. – 381p.; 18cm. Includes discography and filmography.
ISBN 0-340-12644-2 (pbk.)
Originally published: London: W. H. Allen, 1968.
This is a straightforward, lengthy biography which tends to romanticize Sinatra
and depicts him as the vulnerable, tough character fighting his way up – his
preferred image. Nevertheless, it is informative, unsensational and full of
interesting anecdotes from all stages of his career. There is a section on his films
up to 1967, a brief discography and an amusing Sinatra glossary. There is also a
chronology of events.

Sinatra, Frank
Sinatra in his own words / compiled Guy Yarwood. – London: Omnibus
Press, 1981. – 128p.: ill., ports; 26cm. ISBN 0-86001-946-2 (pbk.)
Sinatra's interviews have been very rare over the years and in recent times he
has become even more remote. Here is a collection of comments made to the
press and quotes from the few occasions he has allowed his guard to drop.
Interesting, but not particularly revealing.

Taylor, Paula
Frank Sinatra / text Paula Taylor; illustrator John Keely; design concept
Mark Landkamer. – Mankato, Minnesota: Creative Education, 1976. –
30p.: ill., col. ports; 25cm. ISBN 0-8719-1460-3

A controlled-vocabulary biography written for a reading age of about ten for American schools. A brief outline of the public side of Sinatra's singing and film career with good illustrations.

Wilson, Earl
   Sinatra: an unauthorised biography / Earl Wilson. – London: Star Books, 1978. – xv, 377p., 8p. of plates: ill., ports; 18cm. ISBN 0-352-30194-5 (pbk.) Previously published: New York: Macmillan, 1976; London: W. H. Allen, 1976.
Throughout his work as a freelance journalist the author covered in detail the career of Sinatra. The result of his personal experience and lengthy research is this detailed, objective biography, which is sympathetic and unsensational. In an anecdotal style, Wilson's biography is thorough as well as entertaining, with some good illustrations.

SINATRA, FRANK: BIBLIOGRAPHIES: DISCOGRAPHIES: FILMOGRAPHIES

Lonstein, Albert I.
   The revised compleat Sinatra: discography, filmography, television appearances, motion picture appearances, radio appearances, concert appearances, stage appearances / by Albert I. Lonstein, Vito R. Manno. – Ellenville, New York: Sondra M. Lonstein, 1979. – xiv, 702p.: ill., facsims, ports; 26cm. Includes bibliography, discography and filmography.
   Previous edition: Ellenville, New York: Cameron Publications, 1970.
A meticulously compiled and beautifully produced source of information on Sinatra's work. The discographical listings include his early work with dance bands as well as his solo career in complete detail. There are lists of every performance he has ever made on television, radio, stage and on film. There are song indexes to the discography as well as to the performance listings. The filmography includes stills, synopses and credits. The illustrations are unusual and well selected. Included is a bibliography which includes some of the best articles in American magazines. This is the fullest single volume of information on the artist.

Ridgway, John
   The Sinatra file: part one / by John Ridgway. – Birmingham: John Ridgway Books, 1977. – x, 310p.: ill., facsims, ports; 25cm. ISBN 0-905808-00-2 (cased). ISBN 0-905808-01-0 (pbk.)
Published in a limited edition of 1,000, this part 1 includes comprehensive information about Sinatra's radio performances, television performances, concerts, a bibliography, detailed chronology and even details of his marriages. There are detailed song indexes to each section of performances and some rare illustrations.

Ridgway, John
  The Sinatra file: part two / by John Ridgway. – Birmingham: John Ridgway
  Books, 1978. – 309p: ill., facsims, ports; 25cm. ISBN 0-905808-02-9 (cased).
  ISBN 0-905808-03-7 (pbk.)

Again published in a limited edition of 1,000, part 2 is a remarkably detailed discography and filmography of Sinatra's career. The author obtained access to the original, recording-session worksheets and the detail described includes the musicians, number of takes, length of tracks and technical information on each and every record Sinatra has made. There are reproductions of sleeves and a song index. In addition there is considerable detail of his films with stills, credits, synopses and songs included.

These two volumes offer the most detailed information source on Sinatra in a well-presented and accessible form.

SINATRA, FRANK: DISCOGRAPHIES

Hainsworth, Brian
  Songs by Sinatra, 1939–1970 / compiled by Brian Hainsworth. – Bramhope,
  Leeds: Hainsworth, 1973. – 92p.; 21cm. Includes index. ISBN 0-950286-10-9
  (pbk.)

A privately published labour of love, this extensive listing of Sinatra's work includes information on each recording session, the musicians, the songs recorded and the release of the records with full details. The arrangement is chronological with a song index.

SINATRA, FRANK: FILMS

Ringold, Gene
  The films of Frank Sinatra / Gene Ringold and Clifford McCarty. – New
  York: Citadel Press, 1971. – 249p.: ill., ports; 29cm. Includes index.
  ISBN 0-8065-0262-2

The fullest, beautifully illustrated outline of Sinatra's film career; the authors include a remarkable amount of detail. Synopses, extracts from scripts, stills and credits are well presented. Anecdotes of the shooting of his films, the on-set problems and humorous incidents are all here.

SLADE

Formed in the mid sixties in the Midlands as the 'N Betweens, they changed their name to Ambrose Slade and began playing farther afield than their native Birmingham area. They were spotted playing in a London club by Chas Chandler, the former bass player with the Animals and the manager of Jimi Hendrix, who became their manager and changed their name to Slade. He took their working-class image and gave them a skinhead appearance to make them appear leaders of that particular adolescent subculture with cropped hair, braces and boots. Although that particular fad was shortlived, the power of Noddy Holder's vocals, their natural exuberance and the songwriting of Holder and Jimmy Lea, their bass player and pianist, soon made them extremely successful. Between May 1971 and 1974 they had a string of top-selling singles. They attempted to diversify their talents by making the film Flame, but although critically well received it failed to capture a wide audience. They also attempted to become accepted by the American public but failed on a number of occasions. By 1976 they had faded into obscurity, playing only occasional club performances. They are difficult to classify with their hard-, rocking style and their image, which evolved into the glitter-rock style. In late 1980 they achieved a revival of their success and the instrumental ability of drummer Don Powell, lead guitar player Dave Hill as well as Holder and Lea brought together in their powerful stage act continues to make them an outstanding group.

Slade. – Hitchin: B. C. Enterprises: New English Library, 1972. – 26p.: ill. (some col.), ports (some col.); 39cm. ISBN 0-9038-3501-0 (pbk.)
A good example of a quality publication for the young fan. In a very large format this includes information on the group, quotes from an interview and some large, almost poster-size illustrations.

Tremlett, George
   The Slade story / George Tremlett. – London: Futura Publications, 1975. – 128p., 16p. of plates: ill., ports; 18cm. ISBN 0-8600-7193-6 (pbk.)
Based on interviews with the group by Tremlett and his wife Jane, this is the usual well-constructed, uncritical biography with a detailed chronology.

SLADE: FILMS

(*See* Chapter 7, *Flame*, by John Pidgeon.)

SLICK, GRACE

Born in Chicago in 1943, Grace Slick moved to San Francisco and joined Paul Kantner, Marty Balin, Jorma Kaukonen, Jack Casady and Spencer Dryden in the band Jefferson Airplane in 1966. She brought to the Airplane a series of drug-orientated songs from her previous band the Great Society. After the album Surrealistic Pillow was recorded in 1967, the band produced a long list of creative and totally original records. She made her first solo album in 1973 and in 1974 the original line-up parted and she and Kantner formed the Jefferson Starship and continued to produce albums. Although regarded as one of the most significant bands of the late sixties and seventies, the Airplane and Starship have never achieved the success in Britain that they have in the USA. Grace Slick remains one of the most significant female singers and writers in rock music.

(*See also* JEFFERSON AIRPLANE.)

Rowers, Barbara
    Grace Slick: the biography / Barbara Rowers. – Garden City, New York:
    Doubleday, 1980. – 215p., 8 leaves of plates: ill., ports; 22cm. Includes
    discography. ISBN 0-3851-3390-1
This is a well-researched biography which treats Grace Slick's career with the
seriousness and gives it the significance that it deserves. The illustrations are
well chosen. The personal information about her life, attitudes and political
motivations are all examined with an unusual depth and sensitivity, revealing a
great deal about this remote artist.

SLIK

Originally named Salvation and formed in Glasgow in 1972, their name was
changed to Slik in 1974. They released their first record in January 1975 after
their management had become involved with the record producers of the Bay
City Rollers, Bill Martin and Phil Coulter. They had a number-one hit single in
January 1976, followed by one slightly less successful in May the same year,
then faded from sight. Regarded as simply being in the wake of the Bay City
Rollers, wearing their American baseball shirts and short hair, in reality Slik
were far more competent musicians who were manipulated towards the pre-
teenage market. After splitting up in 1978, guitarist Midge Ure joined Rich
Kids and then the successful band Ultravox.

Tremlett, George
    Slik / George Tremlett. – London: Futura Publications, 1976. – 144p., 16p.
    of plates: ill., facsims, ports; 18cm. ISBN 0-8600-7197-9 (pbk.)
George Tremlett's journalistic biographies are usually concerned with established stars. With Slik, however, he seems to have badly overestimated their
longevity and influence. As ever, well-researched and based on interviews with
the group and its management, the book has a chronology of their career and
personal details of the musicians.

SMITH, PATTI

Born in Chicago in 1946 but brought up in New Jersey, Patti Smith is one of the
most influential and literate writers of the new-wave movement. She made her
debut album in 1975 and this was considered the most powerful rock statement
for many years, if rather undisciplined. Her public persona is often outrageous
and tiresome, but she has a cult following and draws her inspiration from a wide
range of literary and musical sources from Rimbaud and Dylan to William
Burroughs. She is regarded by some as a more important poet than rock artist
and her published poetry has received critical acclaim.

Patti Smith: high on rebellion / Text by the Muir. – Manchester: Babylon
   Books, 1980. – 56p.: ill., facsims, ports; 29cm. Includes discography.
   ISBN 0-907188-00-1 (pbk.)
A collection in fanzine format of writings on Patti Smith and transcripts of
interviews interspersed with press photographs, album covers, posters and
drawings. The illustrations are poor but the discography, which includes
bootleg records, is complete.

Roach, Dusty
   Patti Smith: rock & roll madonna / Dusty Roach. – South Bend, Indiana:
   And Books, 1979. – 95p.: ill., ports; 25cm. Includes bibliography and
   discography. ISBN 0-87908-066-8 (pbk.)
This is a sympathetic analysis of Patti Smith's work and influence. It does not
aim to give a full outline of her career, but the glimpses are revealing. The
discography and bibliography are complete.

SMITH, PATTI: WRITINGS

Smith, Patti
   Babel / by Patti Smith. – London: Virago, 1978. – 202p.: ill.; 21cm.
   ISBN 0-86068-091-6 (pbk.)
   Originally published: New York: Putnam, 1978.
   Also published: New York: Berkley Publishing Corporation, 1979.
A revealing collection of poems, prose poems and pieces of prose on aspects of
rock culture, drugs and Patti Smith's fantasies – often strange and curious but
also original and thought-provoking.

Smith, Patti
   Witt / by Patti Smith. – New York: Gotham Book Mart, 1973. – 43p.; 21cm.
   ISBN 0-91066-434-X (cased). ISBN 0-91066-433-1 (pbk.)
A collection of Smith's early poems: more inhibited than *Babel* but imaginative
and inspired by a wide range of subjects.

Sonny and Cher

Sonny Bono, born in Detroit in 1935, and Cherilyn Sakisian, born in El Centro,
California, in 1946, married in 1964. Bono, already a successful songwriter,
and Cher, a session singer, began singing together. They presented an image of
early hippies and with the rise of folk rock, they had a classic hit in 1965 with the
song I Got You Babe. Their successful marriage, well-produced records and
eccentric appearance made them a major success. Cher had hits as a solo artist
in the late sixties and by the seventies they had their own television series and
cabaret act. They were divorced in 1974. Cher continues to be an important
attraction in the USA and has since married and separated from Greg Allman.

(*See also* CHER.)

Braun, Thomas
    Sonny and Cher / by Thomas Braun; designed by Mark Landkamer. –
    Mankato, Minnesota: Creative Education, 1978. – 31p.: ill., ports; 25cm.
    ISBN 0-8719-1620-7
A controlled-vocabulary biography aimed at a reading age of around ten for
American schools. By the time it was published interest in the duo had long
passed. It is, however, informative and well illustrated.

THE SPECIALS

The members of the Specials played in various other groups around the
Coventry area before coming together in 1979. Led by Terry Dammers,
Horace Pinter and Lynval Golding, they were involved in the formation of the
Two-tone record label and became that label's first successful act. Their style
was a fusion of bluebeat, rock steady or ska rhythms with interesting vocal
arrangements and socially conscious, working-class lyrics. They split up in 1981
and three of the group, Terry Hall, Neville Staples and Lynval Golding,
became the trio Fun Boy Three.

Specials illustrated / illustrated by Nick Davis; designed and produced by Ian
    Hayward and Nick Davis. – London: Plangent Visions Music, 1981. – 62p.:
    chiefly ill., ports; 30cm. (pbk.)
A collection of photographs of the group mixed with the lyrics of some of their
songs; the effect is amusing, if lacking in information.

SPECTOR, PHIL

Born in the Bronx district of New York in 1940, Philip Harvey Spector is one of
the most important innovators to appear in popular music in recent years. He
moved with his widowed mother to Los Angeles when he was twelve and
became influenced by the work of Leiber and Stoller. He formed a vocal trio,
the Teddy Bears, in 1958 and had a massive hit record. After failing to follow
up this success he turned to record production and after working briefly on the
West Coast moved to New York and formed his own record company, Philles,
following a short spell with Atlantic Records. He signed the girl groups the
Crystals and the Ronettes and had more success, followed by productions of
Ike and Tina Turner and the Righteous Brothers. His contribution to record-
production technique was his Wall of Sound which gave extended dimensions
to the thin sound then generally offered by gramophone records. During the
late sixties he was little heard of but he emerged again in the early seventies to
mix the tapes of the Beatles' final album, Let It Be, and to work with John
Lennon and George Harrison on a series of successful albums. He remains an
important figure in that not only did he write a number of well-known songs of
the sixties, but he was certainly the first record producer or engineer to be
regarded as an important contributor to a record's final sound and indeed to
have created his own 'Spector sound'.

Williams, Richard
  Out of his head: the sound of Phil Spector / Richard Williams. – London:
  Abacus, 1974. – 156p., 12p. of plates: ill., ports; 20cm. ISBN 0-349-13723-4
  (pbk.) Includes discography.
  Originally published: New York: Dutton, 1972.
  Also published: New York: Outerbridge & Lazard, 1972.
Detailed, comprehensive and well written by the former assistant editor of
Melody Maker and BBC jazz critic, this is both sympathetic to Spector's music
and revealing of his alienated character. Always the outsider, his image as 'the
first tycoon of teen', as Tom Wolfe called him, is seen as his protective shell.
His music is well analysed with lengthy quotations and excellent appendices
listing his songs, produced records and short notes on artists. The illustrations
are good and John Lennon provides an introduction.

SPRINGSTEEN, BRUCE

Born in Freehold, New Jersey, in 1949, Springsteen was launched with his first
album in 1973 as yet another new Dylan, and with his second album as the
'future of rock'n'roll'. He survived these labels, however, and has become the
most influential rock songwriter and performer of the seventies and early
eighties. His record sales, although considerable, have to date not reflected his
prestige and this may be due to his total refusal to compromise himself for all-
out commercial success. He writes of the street life of down-town America, of
the seldom-seen American working-class life of factories, of cars, of humble
aspirations and desperate love. His band, The East Street Band, is one of the
finest and most musically exciting units in the world, adding depth and colour to
one of the simplest and yet most dramatic stage acts that has ever been created
by a rock performer. His more recent work has involved a new simpler
approach in an attempt to find his musical roots, though to little artistic benefit.

Gambaccini, Peter
  Bruce Springsteen / Peter Gambaccini. – New York: Quick Fox, 1979. –
  127p.: ill., ports; 25cm. Includes discography. ISBN 0-8256-3935-2 (pbk.)
  Also published: New York: Jove Books, 1979.
Although this at first appears to have a serious, analytical approach with a great
deal of emphasis on his songwriting, it has largely been compiled from
secondary sources with little original comment. The result is a superficial, poor
attempt.

Marsh, Dave
  Springsteen born to run: the Bruce Springsteen story / by Dave Marsh. – Rev.
  ed. – London: Omnibus Press, 1981. – 192p.: ill., ports; 28cm.
  ISBN 0-8 001-807-5 (pbk.)
  Previous edition published as '*Born to run: the Bruce Springsteen story*':
  Garden City, New York: Doubleday, 1979.
  Also published: New York: Dell, 1981.

The author has demonstrated a love of Springsteen's music in articles in the music press for some years and has gained much knowledge on his subject. He not only appreciates Springsteen's influences but understands his work. The result is a well-written biography full of information as well as discussion and analysis of Springsteen's songs. A good deal of new research has gone into this work with unusual features such as a complete list of his songs and those songs performed by him, whether recorded or not, and a list of his shows from November 1972 until January 1979, but there is not a conventional disc-ography. The author has interviewed a long list of Springsteen's friends and colleagues as well as the musician himself who commented on the text. The result is a well-written biography full of interesting photographs and intelligent commentary. The Omnibus edition adds a chapter on his album, the River, and its associated tours but strangely does not update the song list or concert appearances.

STARDUST, ALVIN

Born Bernard William Jewry in 1942, he made his first public appearance in 1959 as a moody English replica of an American rock'n'roll singer. In 1961 as Shane Fenton, with his group the Fentones, he had his first record success. After several hits, most of them minor ones, he disappeared from view, another victim of the Liverpool groups and the British rhythm & blues movement. He toured the clubs in the north of England for much of the late sixties and suddenly reappeared in 1973 renamed Alvin Stardust, dressed in black leather, wearing enormous rings on all of his fingers and with his dyed blond hair now dyed black. He posed as a menacing, humorously sinister figure with jokingly suggestive gestures. His songs were average but he had four number-one records and was one of the leading figures in the glitter-rock trend with a following of predominantly young teenagers. He still occasionally has hit records and makes regular club appearances.

Tremlett, George
   The Alvin Stardust story / George Tremlett. – London: Futura Publications,
   1976. – 144p., 16p. of plates: ill., ports; 18cm. ISBN 0-8600-7301-7 (pbk.)
Based largely on interviews with Stardust, his family, associates and his songwriter and producer Peter Shelley, this book is in the author's usual straightforward, journalistic style. It includes a chronology and also covers Alvin Stardust's earlier incarnation as Shane Fenton.

STATUS QUO

Formed in London in 1962 by Francis Rossi, Alan Coughlan and Alan Lancaster, who were joined by Rick Parfitt from Woking, Surrey in 1966. They had two hit singles in 1968 with light attempts to emulate the psychedelic trend of the time. Success was short-lived and they decided to rebuild their following in a new musical direction. They reappeared in 1970 with a style of unadventurous, twelve-bar boogie rock'n'roll. Always unfashionable and critically condemned, they have gained a fanatical following and throughout the seventies moved from strength to strength. In 1980 Alan Bown joined them to play keyboards and in 1981, surprisingly, drummer Coughlan left and was replaced by Pete Kirchner from the Original Mirrors. In 1982 their twentieth anniversary concert in Birmingham was honoured by no less a presence than H. R. H. Prince Charles.

Hibbert, Tom
    Status Quo / by Tom Hibbert. – London: Omnibus Press, 1981. – 80p.: ill., ports; 26cm. Includes discography. ISBN 0-86001-975-8 (pbk.)
An outline, illustrated history of Status Quo since 1968 with some good photographs and a short discography but poor text.

Shearlaw, John
    Status Quo: the authorized biography / John Shearlaw. – Rev. ed. – London: Sidgwick & Jackson, 1982. – 168p.: ill. (some col.), ports (some col.); 29cm. Includes discography. ISBN 0-283-98897-5 (pbk.)
    Previous edition: London: Sidgwick & Jackson, 1979.
With a cover note that this is the twentieth-anniversary edition, the author, who was the editor of the *Record Mirror*, gives an attractive well-written account of Status Quo's career. He was given access to the group's organization and has produced a revealing look at life at the top. Of particular interest are not only the interviews with the musicians, but also with their roadcrew and management. The size of the operation is captured with particular clarity. The new edition updates the story with the change of drummer. The discography is complete up to 1980.

STEELE, TOMMY

Born Tommy Hicks in Bermondsey, London, in 1938, Tommy Steele left school at the age of fourteen and joined the Merchant Navy. In his travels he became exposed to American rock'n'roll early on for an Englishman and in 1956 he began singing in the 2 I's coffee bar in Soho. A young New Zealander, John Kennedy, spotted him and became his manager with a view to making him England's answer to Elvis Presley. By 1957 he had become the biggest teenage attraction in Britain and had a growing following in Europe. In retrospect his records were very poor imitations of their American originals but by the end of the fifties he was already looking to become an all-round entertainer, appearing in Shakespeare at the Old Vic and in the early sixties in the musical comedy, Half a Sixpence. The show moved to Broadway and was made into an internationally successful film. He continues to be a thoroughly professional entertainer, living quietly in Richmond, touring, performing and filming at will.

Kennedy, John
  Tommy Steele / John Kennedy. – London: Transworld, 1959. – 189p., 8p. of
  plates; 17cm. (pbk.)
With no author credit, this edited version of the author's Souvenir Press
biography is in the early Corgi Books format.

Kennedy, John
  *Tommy Steele: the facts about a teenage idol and an "inside" picture of show
  business* / by John Kennedy. – London: Souvenir Press, 1958. – 166p, 16p. of
  plates: ill., ports; 22cm.
Written by Steele's manager, who is quite frank about the hype involved in
launching a career in the music business, this is a fascinating early look at the
state of the business in the mid-fifties. Not without the usual presentation of the
period of the artist as a happy, mindless boy-next-door, this goes some way
towards presenting the tougher side of management and promotion.

Tatham, Dick
  The wonderful Tommy Steele: picture-story album / Dick Tatham. – London:
  Record Mirror, 1957. – 28p.: chiefly ill., chiefly ports; 28cm. (pbk.)
A collection of illustrations with brief notes on Tommy Steele's career: all
smiles and the cheeky cockney image, this is the usual fan-orientated publication.

STEVENS, SHAKIN'

Born in South Wales in 1948, the youngest of eleven children, Shakin' Stevens
began singing in semi-professional groups after leaving school at the age of
fifteen. He became an upholstery apprentice, playing clubs at night and turning
professional in 1970. He spent the next seven years touring Britain, playing his
style of fifties rock'n'roll at clubs and colleges. In 1977 he was cast as one of the
portrayers of Elvis Presley in the musical Elvis. He had perfected a convincing
Elvis imitation and after leaving the show continued the act on television
rock'n'roll shows, finally achieving success with a record release in February
1980 and following this with a series of singles. By the end of 1981 he had
become a leading attraction in Britain, with an audience of an extraordinarily
wide age range from the pre-teenagers to their parents, attracted by the
nostalgia of his Presley impressions.

Barrett, Paul
  Shakin' Stevens / Paul Barrett with Hilary Haywood. – London: Star Books,
  1983. – 160p., 8p. of plates: ill., ports; 18cm. Includes discography.
  ISBN 0-352-31274-2 (pbk.)
Paul Barrett was the manager of Shakin' Stevens and the Sunsets and a close
friend of Stevens for many years. He tells the story of the artist from the early
days in Cardiff to his success, in a simple, factual way. Not very inspiring, the
book unfortunately appeared rather too late to catch Stevens' period of big
success.

Leese, Martyn
  Shakin' Stevens / Martyn Leese. – London: Prize Books, 1981. – 48p.: ill.
  (some col.), ports (some col.); 27cm. Includes discography.
  ISBN 0-86276-010-0 (pbk.)
Published for the Shakin' Stevens fan, this is short on biographical information,
totally uncritical and including only recent photographs.

STEVENS, SHAKIN': PERIODICALS

(*See* Chapter 8.2, Stevens, Shakin'.)

STEWART, ROD

Born in north London in 1945, Rod Stewart made his first record in 1964. He
joined Long John Baldry's Hoochie Coochie Men in 1965 and when that
disbanded, he joined the Steampacket, a legendary, London-based rhythm &
blues band. He had by now built a considerable reputation as a blues singer
with his gravelly voice and trendy dress and become known as Rod the Mod.
When Steampacket failed he joined the guitarist Jeff Beck's group. After
recording two albums with Beck he was sacked and along with Ron Wood
joined the Faces. This group, formerly called the Small Faces, had lost their
singer Steve Marriott to Humble Pie. While singing with the Faces, Stewart
made two early solo albums which made some impact in the USA but not in
Britain. In the summer of 1971, however, he released Every Picture Tells a
Story and suddenly became a star throughout the world.
  Stewart's writing ability is often overlooked but his use of language in his
lyrics is particularly unusual. He is best known, however, for his stage performance, which is often outrageous and made more so by his reputation as a
hard drinker and womanizer.
  In 1975 Rod Stewart finally left the Faces and since then has had a series of
successful albums and singles. When not singing one of his own compositions,
he has an uncanny ability to choose perfect material for his voice and to be
backed by the best musicians available. He now lives and records in America.
In 1976 he began living with Britt Ekland, the Swedish film star, which changed
his rough, football-playing image to one of sophistication, but this relationship
lasted only until 1979.

Burton, Peter
  Rod Stewart: a life on the town / by Peter Burton. – London: New English
  Library, 1977. – 120p.: ill. (some col.), col. facsims, ports (some col.); 27cm.
  Includes discography. ISBN 0-450-03429-1 (pbk.)
A well-written, well-illustrated biography which gives a good impression of
Stewart's lifestyle, but although it reproduces the lyrics of his best songs, it
makes no attempt at analysis. When the biography was written Rod Stewart
was still with Britt Ekland.

Cromelin, Richard
> *Rod Stewart: a biography in words & pictures* / by Richard Cromelin; edited by Greg Shaw. – New York: Sire Books; Chappell Music Company, 1976. – 56p.: ill., ports; 30cm. Includes discography. (pbk.)

A brief biography with some good illustrations, this covers Rod Stewart's early career with the little-known groups as well as his years of success. The intelligent text considers his music in a serious, analytical way.

Jasper, Tony
> *Rod Stewart* / Tony Jasper. – London: Octopus Books, 1977. – 94p.: chiefly ill. (some col.), ports (chiefly col.); 31cm. Includes discography. ISBN 0-706-40666-4

A well-illustrated survey with a readable, informative text mostly concerned with Stewart's successful solo career. There are also photographs of his period with the Faces and some rare, early portraits. There is a chronology summarizing his career and a useful discography.

Nelson, Paul
> *Rod Stewart* / Paul Nelson & Lester Bangs. – London: Sidgwick & Jackson, 1982. – 160p.: ill. (some col.), ports (some col.); 28cm. ISBN 0-283-98836-3 (pbk.)
> Originally published: New York : Delilah Communications, 1981.

In his preface Lester Bangs says that he has always believed that rock'n'roll comes down to myth and that rock news is hype. Because of this belief he concludes that Rod Stewart, like other leading artists (being aware that they are in the business of building images and 'reinventing' themselves), has always misled interviewers and offered contradictory fabrications. Bangs concedes that much of this work is based on such sources but some has been exhaustively researched from new sources. It is, indeed, without the usual idolatry, often extremely critical and always entertaining. Gathered together are an excellent collection of photographs including many rare portraits of the Jeff Beck group, Steampacket and the Faces with a youthful Rod Stewart looking far from a superstar. There is a section of record reviews by Paul Nelson and a dialogue between the authors on Stewart's career to date. An epilogue describes Rod Stewart's dismissive attitude to the British new wave, suggesting that its basis is in insecurity.

Pidgeon, John
> *Rod Stewart and the changing Faces* / John Pidgeon. – St. Albans: Panther, 1976. – 144p., 8p. of plates: ill., ports; 18cm. Includes discography. ISBN 0-586-04650-X (pbk.)

A well-researched, detailed biography the rise of Rod Stewart and of the musicians with whom he and the Faces have been associated over a period of twelve years. There is a genealogical table explaining their various groups and a full, very detailed discography. This gives an unusual view of the way in which musicians and groups evolve and influence each other's styles.

Tremlett, George
The Rod Stewart story / George Tremlett. – London: Futura Publications,
1976. – 143p., 16p. of plates: ill., ports; 18cm. ISBN 0-8600-7351-3 (pbk.)
Based on interviews with Rod Stewart, the members of the Faces and early
colleagues and friends, there is the usual chronology of events in his life,
recording sessions, performances and so on, as well as an appendix including
the official press releases of his record company.

STREISAND, BARBRA

Born in New York in 1942, by the late sixties Barbra Streisand was already a
star of Broadway with her performances in musicals such as Funny Girl. When
this was made into a film her career took on new proportions and she soon
made a series of films with non-singing roles which were usually comedies,
using her New York, Bronx style of Jewish humour. Although she had
achieved record successes with songs from shows, she had experimented in the
rock field and with the production of A Star is Born in 1976, in which she plays
a rock singer, she took on yet a new dimension to her career. Since then she has
had a series of successful albums and hit singles. Her clear, exceptionally strong
voice added to a distinctive delivery makes her appeal very wide from disco
audiences to cabaret.

Brady, Frank
Barbra Streisand: an illustrated biography / by Frank Brady. – New York:
Grosset & Dunlap, 1979. – 151p.: ill., ports; 28cm. ISBN 0-4481-6534-1
(pbk.)
A well-illustrated, superficial biography full of stills from films as well as posed
portraits.

Eldred, Patricia Mulrooney
Barbra Streisand / text Patricia Mulrooney Eldred; illustrator John Keely;
design concept Mark Landkamer. – Mankato, Minnesota; Creative
Education, 1975. – 31p.: ill., ports; 25cm. ISBN 0-8719-1418-X
A controlled-vocabulary biography aimed at a reading age of about ten for
American schools, this is an informative, straightforward account of her stage,
film and recording career. There are some very good illustrations.

Jordan, Rene
Streisand: unauthorised biography / Rene Jordan. – London: W. H. Allen,
1976. – 253p.; 23cm. ISBN 0-491-01775-8
Also published: London: Star Books, 1976.
A popular biography of her career before her change of musical direction and
the film A Star is Born. There is some detail of her childhood and her private
life as well as her stage and film appearances. It fails to give any real insight into
her offstage personality or to discuss her qualities as a performer.

Keenan, Debra
   On stage Barbra Streisand / text Debra Keenan; design concept Larry Soule.
   – Mankato, Minnesota: Creative Education, 1976. – 47p.: ill., ports; 23cm.
   ISBN 0-87191-485-9
A controlled-vocabulary biography aimed at a reading age of around ten for
American schools. The simple sentence structure, informative text and excel-
lent design makes the subject well suited for the age group.

Spada, James
   Streisand: the woman and the legend / James Spada. – London: Comet
   Books, 1983. – 246p.: ill., ports; 28cm. ISBN 0-863-79010-0 (pbk.)
   Originally published: New York: Doubleday, 1981.
   Previously published: London: W. H. Allen, 1982.
Particularly well designed with over one hundred photographs integrated into
the text, the author's emphasis is on the private life of the star. Her relationships with Ryan O'Neal, Omar Sharif and Pierre Trudeau, as well as her
marriage to Elliot Gould, are dealt with in a sensational style. Spada interviewed Robert Redford, Garson Kanin and Vincente Minelli, all of whom have
worked closely with the subject. The result is, nevertheless, a visually impressive but poor biography of an important artist.

Teti, Frank
   Streisand through the lens / photo-edited by Frank Teti; written by Karen
   Moline. – London: Sidgwick & Jackson, 1982. – 144p.: ill. (some col.), ports
   (some col); 28cm. ISBN 0-283-98957-2 (cased). ISBN 0-283-98958-0 (pbk.)
   Originally published: New York: Delilah Communications, 1982.
This is a collection of photographs of Barbra Streisand, very well selected with
interviews with the photographers. It reflects well her distinct persona.

Zec, Donald
   Barbra: a biography of Barbra Streisand / Donald Zec and Anthony Fowles.
   – Sevenoaks, Kent: New English Library, 1982. – 384p., 32p. of plates: ill.,
   ports; 18cm. Includes discography, filmography and index.
   ISBN 0-450-05398-9 (pbk.)
A well-researched biography, with some emphasis on Streisand's acting career.
There is an excellent collection of stills and some intelligent analysis of her
success.

STREISAND, BARBRA: FILMS

Castell, David
   The films of Barbra Streisand / by David Castell. – 3rd ed. – Bembridge, Isle
   of Wight: BCW Publishing, 1977. – 47p.: ill., ports; 21cm.
   ISBN 0-90415-934-5 (pbk.)
   Previous edition: Bembridge, Isle of Wight: BCW Publishing, 1975.
Based on a well-selected collection of stills, this is a brief outline of Barbra
Streisand's film career.

SUMMER, DONNA

Donna was born in Boston, Massachusetts, in 1949. Her early career included modelling and working in the production of the musical Hair, in Munich. In 1975, however, the disco boom was imminent and she was launched as the 'Queen of Disco' with a series of over-produced singles featuring a good deal of heavy breathing and not a little innuendo. After world-wide success, she now seems to have passed her peak but she is a creative writer and skilful recording artist and always likely to produce more hit records.

Haskins, James
Donna Summer: an unauthorized biography / by Jim Haskins and Jim Stifle. – Boston; Toronto: Little, Brown, 1983. – 136p., 6p. of plates: ill., ports; 22cm. Includes discography and index. ISBN 0-316-35003-6
This is not only a good, straightforward biography of a leading American artist of the late seventies, but also a very direct account of the careful contrivance of a new style of music. It is very detailed with an uninspired collection of illustrations.

THE TALKING HEADS

Formed in late 1974 by students at Rhode Island School of Design, Providence, they made their first public appearance as a supporting group to the Ramones at New York's CBGB's club in June 1975. A part of the New York new wave, their style is described as avant-garde. They certainly never cease to initiate new ideas in both their music and lyrics and are often criticized as being over-intellectual in their approach. They have achieved far more popularity in the UK than in America.

Miles
Talking Heads / text by Miles; art direction Perry Neville; design Andy Morton. – London: Omnibus Press, 1981. – 32p.: chiefly ill., ports; 27cm. ISBN 0-86001-799-0 (pbk.)
Of little information value, this is largely a collection of illustrations with a brief text, extracts from the press and a few quotations.

Reese, Krista
The name of this book is Talking Heads / Krista Reese. – London; New York: Proteus, 1982. – 128p.: ill. (some col.), ports (some col.); 27cm. ISBN 0-86276-057-7 (pbk.)
A reasonable attempt to cover the Talking Heads' career to date which gives the British reader a good insight into the American new-wave movement of the mid seventies with some well-produced photographs.

TAYLOR, DEREK

Born in Liverpool in 1932, Derek Taylor worked as a journalist on a number of northern newspapers as well as on the *Sunday Express* before being appointed as Brian Epstein's personal assistant in 1964. He subsequently became the Beatles' press officer and travelled with them on their early tours of America and Europe. He left them in early 1965 and was involved in the promotion of other groups including the Byrds and the Beach Boys. He lived in California until 1968 when he moved back to London and became involved with the Beatles' Apple organization. He continues to write and in recent years has worked on the management side of several major record companies.

Taylor, Derek
  As time goes by / Derek Taylor. – London: Abacus, 1974. – 182p., 12p. of plates: ill., ports; 20cm. ISBN 0-349-13381-6 (pbk.)
  Originally published: London: Davis-Poynter, 1973.
  Also published: San Francisco: Straight Arrow Books, 1973.
Derek Taylor was commissioned by Prentice-Hall in 1968 to write a memoir of his experiences of the sixties music scene and particularly about the Beatles. He was unable to complete the task but what he did produce was a collection of essays which recollect particular episodes including the Beatles as well as a list of other significant characters of the period. He is always forthright in his summary of people, such as Allan Klein, but in general this is a fond memoir, amusingly written and giving real insight into an extraordinary period.

Taylor, Derek
  Fifty years adrift (in an open-necked shirt) / by Derek Taylor; introduction by George Harrison. – Guildford, Surrey: Genesis Publications, 1983. – 450p.: ill. (some col.), facsims (some col.), ports (some col.); 24cm.
  ISBN 0-904351-22-X
Following George Harrison's book, *I me mine*, this is a matching work, a superb example of book production. Taylor's autobiography is well written, covering his fifty years in a witty, perceptive style. The Beatles are naturally an important feature but he also comments at length on his associations with such people as Sinatra, Harry Nilsson, Fleetwood Mac and the Byrds, as well as hundreds of other musicians, writers and artists of all kinds. There is a fine collection of photographs, facsimiles of memorabilia, drawings and even a painting by Captain Beefheart. Edited and introduced by George Harrison, with an epilogue by Harry Nilsson, each of the 2,000 limited edition was signed with a pre-publication price of £148.00.

THE TEARDROP EXPLODES

Originally formed in Liverpool in 1977 by Julian Cope, the original line-up included Ian McCulloch, who later formed Echo and the Bunnymen, and Pete Wiley, who later formed Wah!. Playing a latterday version of psychedelic rock, they had established themselves as a leading group on Merseyside by 1980 when they signed a recording contract with Phonogram. After several changes of personnel, Cope, as vocalist, Gary Dwyer, drums, Troy Tate, guitar, David

Balfe, keyboards, and Ron Francois, bass, made up a touring band. With a series of singles and two successful albums, the group became a leader of the new wave, innovative and distinctive in both musical style and stage presentation. Julian Cope's interest in the music of sixties star Scott Walker is a point of note. In 1981 he contrived the release of a remixed compilation of Walker's recordings in an attempt to encourage a renaissance. The enterprise failed, but it did underline Cope's unusual and intriguing approach to music. In December 1982 Cope announced that the group was to split, each member to pursue solo projects.

Cooper, Mark
  Liverpool explodes: the Teardrop Explodes, Echo and the Bunnymen / Mark
  Cooper. – London: Sidgwick & Jackson, 1982. – 96p.: ill., ports; 26cm.
  Includes discography and index. ISBN 0-283-98865-5 (pbk.)
Shared with Echo and the Bunnymen, this is an informative account of the evolution of the group with a good selection of photographs and a detailed discography. Musical style, presentation and the inspiration behind Cope's unusual writing are all topics on which the author focusses his interest. The result is a brief, but intelligent and well-written account of a group of great unrealized potential.

10CC

Eric Stewart, Graham Gouldman, Lol Creme and Kevin Godley played in various groups in the Manchester area in the early sixties. Gouldman became a successful songwriter in the mid sixties, writing hits for the Yardbirds, the Hollies and Herman's Hermits. Eric Stewart also had a successful career with the Mindbenders while Godley and Creme went to art schools. In 1968 Stewart established Strawberry Studios in Stockport and invited his friends Godley and Creme to help him. Calling themselves Hotlegs, they had a hit single in 1970. After a British tour, Gouldman returned from the USA and the four returned to Stockport to work. The result was the composition Donna, which was a parody of the American vocal groups of the late fifties. There followed a string of more and more sophisticated hit singles and albums. Sometimes criticized as being cold and calculated in its approach, their music is literate, well performed and superbly produced. Creme and Godley left the group in late 1976 to concentrate on their own experimental instrument, the Gizmo, and video production. With added new musicians, Stewart and Gouldman continued to be a major attraction but have yet to repeat their earlier record successes.

Tremlett, George
  The 10cc story / George Tremlett. – London: Futura Publications, 1976. –
  142p., 16p. of plates: ill., ports; 18cm. ISBN 0-8600-7378-5 (pbk.)
Drawn from extensive interviews with the members of 10cc and their managers as well as from secondary sources, this is another informative, popular biography by the author. There is a good collection of illustrations and a chronology of events in their career.

THIN LIZZY

Formed in Dublin in 1970, Thin Lizzy moved to London in 1971. Led by Phil Lynott, their front man and writer, they have changed their line-up from three piece to four with two lead guitars. Their style is basically heavy metal, centred on Lynott's unusual bass playing. They have had a series of successful singles and albums and continued to maintain their success throughout the late seventies and early eighties.

(*See also* LYNOTT, PHIL.)

Pryce, Larry
  Thin Lizzy / Larry Pryce. – London: Star Books, 1977. – 121p., 16p. of
  plates: ill., ports; 18cm. Includes discography. ISBN 0-352-39600-8 (pbk.)
A journalistic account of the career of Thin Lizzy centred around Phil Lynott and including quotations from interviews. Superficial, it fails to give Lynott's writing or music the space it deserves.

TINY TIM

Tiny Tim appeared in the late sixties as a bizarre, ukelele-playing, flower-wearing performer of old popular songs. His enormous physical appearance contrasted with his falsetto voice, which only added to his eccentric presentation. Although generally regarded as a vaguely entertaining curiosity, he was taken quite seriously in America for a brief period.

Stein, Harry
  Tiny Tim / by Harry Stein. – Chicago: Playboy Press, 1976. – 243p., 4p. of
  plates: ill., ports; 22cm. ISBN 0-8722-3455-X
A biography including poems, writings and descriptions of Tiny Tim's twee lifestyle: a well-produced account of a strange phenomenon.

TOYAH

Born in the comfortable Birmingham suburb of Kings Heath in May 1958, Toyah Wilcox attended the Birmingham Old Rep Drama School. While still studying she appeared in various television plays during 1976 but did not come to the attention of the public as a singer until 1978. A tiny four feet ten inches tall, she compensates for her little stature with brightly coloured hair (usually orange) and elaborate make-up. Originally in the punk style, she has now developed a quite unique style all of her own. Toyah writes her own songs, which contain naive lyrics but catchy melodies, and performs them in a theatrical style. She received the BBC award for best British female singer for 1981. Although she had achieved minor successes before, 1981 saw both albums and singles constantly in the British charts. She continues to develop both her singing and acting careers.

Evans, Gayna
  Toyah / by Gayna Evans. – London; New York: Proteus, 1982. – 32p.: col.
  ill., col. ports; 27cm. ISBN 0-86276-102-6 (pbk.)
Beautifully illustrated in colour, demonstrating Toyah's gift for colourful
costumes and make-up, this brief biography is concise with little attempt to
look at her songwriting seriously.

West, Mike
  Toyah / Mike West. – London: Omnibus Press, 1982. – 80p.: ill. (some col.),
  ports (some col.); 26cm. Includes discography. ISBN 0-7119-0062-0 (pbk.)
With a brief but informative text, Toyah's career is competently outlined.
There is a good collection of illustrations of her in various guises, a discography
and a full list of television, film and theatrical appearances.

Travolta, John

Born in Englewood, New Jersey, in 1954, Travolta first became well known in
the USA as a television actor. He played the part of Vinnie Barbarino, a New
York high-school kid, in the series 'Welcome back Kotter', which has never
appeared in Britain. His television parts continued until his major, world-wide
breakthrough came in 1977 with the leading role of disco dancer Tony Manero
in the film Saturday Night Fever. He did not sing in this film but did in his next
one, Grease, which was followed by Urban Cowboy. He achieved a series of hit
singles both alone and with Olivia Newton-John, his co-star in Grease. He
continues to be a major pre-teenage idol on both sides of the Atlantic.

Munshower, Suzanne
  The John Travolta scrapbook: an illustrated biography / Suzanne
  Munshower. – London: Pop Universal; Souvenir Press, 1978. – 121p.: ill.,
  ports; 28cm. ISBN 0-285-62382-6 (pbk.)
  Originally published as *'Meet John Travolta'*: New York: Sunridge Press,
  1976.
A poorly written biography which covers in some depth his early acting career
on American television. His film appearances are naturally featured with many
stills as well as on-set photographs. The text covers Saturday Night Fever and
Grease but although there are illustrations from the Urban Cowboy set it is not
mentioned.

Reeves, Michael
  Travolta!: a photo bio / by Michael Reeves. – New York: Jove / HBJ, 1978. –
  272p.: ill., ports; 18cm. ISBN 0-515-04850-X (pbk.)
Although this lengthy, well-produced biography is certainly informative, it also
represents the worst kind of journalistic idolatry. The major themes are: how
the tough screen image belies the real, sensitive artist; how beautiful he is; how

talented he is; what a genuine person he is. Uncritical, it also takes only a superficial look at his work and concentrates on his 'platonic' friendships with a wide selection of well-known, beautiful women. The production and illustrations, however, are excellent.

Schumacher, Craig
   John Travolta / by Craig Schumacher. – Mankato, Minnesota: Creative
   Education, 1980. – 31p.: ill. (some col.), ports (some col.); 25cm.
   ISBN 0-8719-1698-3 (cased). ISBN 0-8981-2094-2 (pbk.)
Well produced, this is a controlled-vocabulary biography aimed at a reading age of around ten for American schools. Reasonably informative; the subject suits the age range very well.

TRAVOLTA, JOHN: FILMS

Grease

The musical Grease, written by Jim Jacobs and Warren Casey, was first produced on Broadway in 1972. Recalling nostalgically the fifties with rock'n'-roll, hot-rod cars and high-school romance, it had a weak plot but was full of atmosphere. In 1978 it was made into a film, directed by Randal Kleiser, as a vehicle for John Travolta to follow his success in Saturday Night Fever and to launch Olivia Newton-John into films. It was an enormous success, generating a successful soundtrack album and a series of singles.

De Christoforo, Ron
   Grease / by Ron de Christoforo; based on the screenplay by Bronte
   Woodard; adaptation by Allan Carr; based on the original musical by Jim
   Jacobs and Warren Casey. – London: Magnum Books, 1978. – 220p., 16p. of
   plates: ill.; 18cm. ISBN 0-417-03760-0 (pbk.)
   Originally published: New York: Pocket Books, 1978.
This lengthy novel faithfully adheres to the plot of the film and is unusually fluid in its style. The stills from the film are in monochrome.

Grease: a fotonovel publications fotonovel / based on the screenplay by Bronte
   Woodard; adaptation by Allan Carr; based on the original musical by Jim
   Jacobs and Warren Casey; original fotonarration by Michael Newman;
   cover and interior design by Michael Parish; graphic devices by Thames
   Warkentin. – Los Angeles: Fotonovel Publications, 1978. – 182p.: chiefly
   col. ill.; 18cm. ISBN 0-89752-000-9 (pbk.)
Using stills from the film with speech bubbles for the dialogue, the story of the film is presented as a comic strip. The lyrics of all the songs are reproduced.

The Grease album / edited by Armand Eisen; written by Michael Sollars. –
   Kansas City, Missouri: Ariel Books; Cheltenham: Phin, 1978. – 80p.: ill.
   (chiefly col.), ports (chiefly col.); 31cm. ISBN 0-78067-078-0 (pbk.)

After a brief history of the musical, this describes the making of the film with coloured stills and monochrome photographs of the behind-the-scenes action. There are brief biographies of the production team and the careers of the actors. The overall effect is a very good example of book design.

Saturday Night Fever

Based originally on a short story by Nik Cohn about Shepherd's Bush mods of the sixties, Saturday Night Fever is transposed into New York of the seventies. Directed by John Badham in 1977, John Travolta, in his first main film role plays Tony Romero, a member of a Brooklyn street gang who lives only for Saturday night at the discothèque where he is 'king'. A relationship with a sophisticated woman finally gives Tony a more mature view of his narrow existence. With a soundtrack based on the Bee Gees' songs including some disco classics, this film started the disco craze of the late seventies and certainly established Travolta as an idol. It is, in fact, an earthy film about urban teenage life with some scenes which, because of their dialogue and sexual content, were cut out of an expurgated version later released to cash in on Travolta's pre-teenage appeal.

Gilmour, H. B.
  Saturday Night Fever: a novelisation / by H. B. Gilmour; based on a screen-play by Norman Wexler; from a story by Nik Cohn. – New York: Bantam Books, 1977. – 182p., 1 folded leaf of plates: col. ill.; 18cm.
    ISBN 0-553-11565-0 (pbk.)
Faithfully following the film, the author makes a good attempt at constructing both the atmosphere of excitement in the discothèque and the aimless, seedy side of Brooklyn. For a novelization of a screenplay, this is good.

Urban Cowboy

Set in the atmosphere of the Texas country-music boom of the late seventies and directed by James Bridges, this film, released in 1980, was a vehicle for John Travolta to continue his dancing in a different context. As a country boy he arrives in Houston and marries. Marital problems soon follow, mainly arising from the couple's efforts to beat the mechanical bull at Gilley's Honky Tonk Ballroom, the famous country-music club. The film is overlong and lacking in plot. The soundtrack includes a wide range of modern country-rock performers.

Latham, Aaron
  Urban cowboy: a novel / by Aaron Latham; based on a screenplay by James Bridges and Aaron Latham. – London: Corgi Books, 1980. – 295p.; 18cm.
    ISBN 0-552-11517-7 (pbk.)
Published to coincide with the release of the film in Britain, this elaborates by embellishing the atmosphere of Gilley's but is no stronger in plot or character-ization.

THE VELVET UNDERGROUND

Formed in 1966, in New York City, with Lou Reed on guitar and vocals, John Cale bass and viola, Maureen Tucker drums and Sterling Morrison on guitar, they were later that year joined by German singer Nico. Spotted by pop artist Andy Warhol, they aimed to create the decadent atmosphere of the big city, indeed naming themselves after the book by Michael Leigh which was subtitled *The sexual corruption of our age*. Their songs were about hard drugs and sado-masochism, evoking images of pre-war Berlin and deliberately setting them-selves against the peace and love of flower power at its height on the West Coast. After an initial, successful album they failed to achieve commercial success with subsequent efforts and finally split up in 1971. Nico, John Cale and Lou Reed pursued successful solo careers, with Reed coming to real prom-inence in 1972. The Velvet Underground was an uncompromising, innovative band, the importance of which was firmly established when the punk-rock movement so clearly mimicked their style and sound.

(*See also* REED, LOU.)

Bockris, Victor
   Up-tight: the Velvet Underground story / by Victor Bockris, Gerard Malanga.
   – London: Omnibus Press, 1983. – 128p.: ill., ports; 27cm. Includes
   discography. ISBN 0-7119-0168-6 (pbk.)
With some excellent illustrations, this is a very good account of the Velvet Underground's career. There is much new information here and the author both knows and understands their work. The discography is a complete listing.

VICIOUS, SID

Born in Lewisham, south London, in 1957, Sid Vicious was the bass player with the Sex Pistols. His provocatively violent attitude, drug addiction and indict-ment for the murder of his girlfriend make him one of the most notorious figures of the of the London punk scene. He died in 1979 of a drug overdose in New York, while on bail.

(*See also* THE SEX PISTOLS.)

The Sid Vicious family album / all captions by Anne Beverley; designed by
   Pearce Marchbank. – London: Virgin Books, 1980. – 32p. of ill., facsims,
   ports; 33cm. ISBN 0-907080-02-2 (pbk.)
A collection of photographs of Sid Vicious from his childhood to his death, with notes by his mother: a tribute with a true sense of bad taste.

VINTON, BOBBY

Born in Cannonsbury, Pennsylvania in April, 1941, Bobby Vinton first achieved success in 1962. During the sixties he had a string of hit singles in the

USA of which he wrote a large proportion. He sustained his success into the seventies with his sentimental ballads, which somehow seemed to have become adapted perfectly to the middle-of-the-road taste. He achieved only two minor hits in Britain, in 1962 and 1963.

Vinton, Bobby

The Polish prince / by Bobby Vinton; with Robert E. Burger. – New York: M. Evans, 1978. – 189p., 16p, of plates: ill., ports; 22cm.
ISBN 0-8713-1270-0
A straightforward, ghosted autobiography which outlines Vinton's adaptable talents. His songwriting is an area that is given considerable emphasis and even though he is little known in Britain, many of his songs are familiar.

WAKEMAN, RICK

Born in London, in 1949, and a graduate of the Royal College of Music, Rick Wakeman worked with the bands the Strawbs and Yes before writing and producing his own solo albums. His virtuosity as a keyboard player and his use of electronic synthesizers and effects have enabled him to create a unique form of classically influenced rock music which is both spectacular in performance and widely appealing on record. He was one of the most successful performers to emerge from the United Kingdom in the seventies, an exponent of pomp rock.

Wooding, Dan

Rick Wakeman: the caped crusader / Dan Wooding. – St. Albans: Panther, 1979. – 192p.: ill., ports; 18cm. Includes discography and index.
ISBN 0-586-04853-7 (pbk.)
Originally published: London: Robert Hale, 1978.
A well-written biography which is certainly an appreciation of Wakeman but portrays him as a straightforward, hard-working musician with few pretensions.

WHITESNAKE

After Ritchie Blackmore left the successful late-sixties group Deep Purple, they struggled on for almost a year before finally splitting up in late 1977. Their third lead singer, David Coverdale, formed Whitesnake in January 1978. One of the leading bands of the heavy-metal revival, it was an immediate success and continues to produce hit records and sell-out concert performances.

Hibbert, Tom

Whitesnake / by Tom Hibbert. – London: Omnibus Press, 1981. – 48p.: ill., ports; 27cm. Includes discography. ISBN 0-86001-964-0 (pbk.)

Including the bare facts about the band's formation and its musicians, this is a poor effort with undistinguished illustrations and a badly designed layout.

THE WHO

Originally known as the Detours and the High Numbers, the Who gained the following of the London Mods movement in 1964 and with the help of Kit Lambert and Chris Stamp as their management, they achieved national success in early 1965. Pete Townshend wrote a series of simple, but lyrically biting songs which, with the aid of a stage act that included the destruction of their equipment, made them unique. After a number of successful singles during the mid and late sixties, Townshend wrote the ninety-minute rock opera, Tommy, and they sealed their position as a major live act in America by performing at the Woodstock festival in 1969. Tommy has had a great influence on the development of rock music with a film and numerous stage presentations as well as spawning the rock opera as an accepted form. Quadrophenia, Townshend's second 'opera', was also made into a film in 1979 and the Who continued to be one of the world's major live shows. John Entwhistle, the bass player, Roger Daltrey, the singer, Keith Moon, the original drummer and Townshend himself, have all made solo records and Daltrey has acted in several successful films. In 1978 Moon died and was replaced by Kenny Jones, formerly of the Faces. In 1982 Townshend announced the band's retirement but how permanent this is likely to be is questionable.

(*See also* MOON, KEITH.)

Ashley, Brian
    Whose Who?: a Who retrospective / Brian Ashley and Steve Monnery. –
    London: New English Library; Times Mirror, 1978. – 128p., 8p. of plates:
    ill., ports; 18cm. Includes discography. ISBN 0-4500-4417-3 (pbk.)
Written after the death of Moon; the authors, both journalists, worked together using separately acquired sources. There is some serious attempt to study the Who's work and they place the group in the context of fathers of the new wave.

Barnes, Richard
    The Who maximum r&b: an illustrated biography / by Richard Barnes. –
    London: Eel Pie, 1982. – 168p.: ill. (some col.), ports (some col.); 28cm.
    Includes discography. ISBN 0-906008-57-3 (pbk.)
Written by a long-time friend of Pete Townshend, this is a beautifully-illustrated history of the Who with press cuttings, promotional material, record sleeves and American and British discographies. There is a flexidisc included of unreleased versions of two of the Who's best-known songs.

Charlesworth, Chris
The Who: the illustrated biography / Chris Charlesworth. – London:
Omnibus Press, 1982. – 90p.: ill. (some col.), facsims, ports (some col.);
28cm. Includes discography. ISBN 0-7119-0053-1 (pbk.)
The group's career is plotted with a prominent year-date heading to each
section. The discography is complete and includes full details. The illustrations
are the most important feature of this book with very brief notes. Of particular
interest is the collection of unique photographs from their early days as the
Detours and High Numbers.

*A decade of the Who: an authorised history in music, paintings, words and
photographs* / text by Steve Turner; paintings and drawings by John Davis. –
London: Elm Tree Books; Fabulous Music, 1977. – 239p.: ill. (some col.),
music, ports (some col.); 28cm. Includes discography ISBN 0-2418-9809-9
(pbk.)
Beautifully produced, this is a collection of photographs, paintings, writings,
the best-known songs of Pete Townshend and brief biographical notes. The
paintings are, however, in the dated psychedelic style.

Goddard, Peter
The Who: the farewell tour / text by Peter Goddard; photographs by Philip
Kamin. – London: Sidgwick and Jackson, 1983. – 128p.: ill. (some col.),
ports (some col.); 27cm. ISBN 0-283-98979-3 (pbk.)
A documentary record of the Who's farewell tour, good to look at with eighty
coloured photographs, but this is not a significant contribution to literature on
the band.

Herman, Gary
The Who / Gary Herman. – London: Studio Vista, 1971. – 112p.: ill.,
facsims, ports; 21cm. Includes discography. ISBN 0-289-70134-1
Also published: New York: Macmillan, 1972.
Well illustrated and packed with quotations, mostly from Townshend, this has
a particularly good design and production. Emphasis is on their revival with
Tommy.

McKnight, Connor
The Who . . . through the eyes of Pete Townshend / by Connor McKnight &
Caroline Silver. – New York: Scholastic Book Services, 1974. – 110p., 6p. of
plates: ill., ports; 18cm. (pbk.)
A poorly produced, badly illustrated account of the group during the early
seventies with emphasis on their American success. There are interviews with
each member of the group, especially Townshend.

Marsh, Dave
Before I get old: the story of the Who / Dave Marsh. – London: Plexus, 1983. –
xiv, 546p., 48p. of plates: ill., ports; 24cm. Includes bibliography and index.
ISBN 0-85965-085-5 (cased). ISBN 0-85965-083-9 (pbk.)
Originally published: New York: St. Martin's Press, 1983.

Exceptionally detailed and particularly well written, with the full co-operation of the band, this is certainly the best book on the Who and one of the finest works so far on life in the rock-music business. Dave Marsh spent a long period with Pete Townshend during the book's preparation, and his close understanding of the man has enabled him to present an in-depth study of this complex figure. The illustrations are well chosen and many appear here for the first time in print.

Stein, Jeff
> *The Who* / by Jeff Stein and Chris Johnston. – 2nd ed. – New York: Stein and Day, 1979. – 90p.: chiefly ill., ports; 18cm. ISBN 0-8128-2612-4 (cased). ISBN 0-8128-6028-4 (pbk.)
> Previous edition: New York: Stein and Day, 1973.

A collection of photographs taken during the Who's three tours of the USA in 1970 and 1971. The photographs include exciting shots of the group performing as well as backstage pictures of them relaxing and rehearsing.

Swenson, John
> *The Who* / John Swenson. – London: Star Books, 1981. – 176p., 8p. of plates; 18cm. Includes discography. ISBN 0-352-30943-1 (pbk.)
> Originally published: New York: Tempo Books, 1979.

An American view of the Who's career, it contains great detail of their American tours and their rise to fame in the USA. There is some fascinating background to their famous performance at the Woodstock festival and a selection of good illustrations. The death of drummer Keith Moon is included together with his replacement Kenny Jones. The discography, although listing the titles of their albums and singles, has no discographical details.

Tremlett, George
> *The Who* / George Tremlett. – London: Futura Publications, 1975. – 125p., 16p. of plates: ill., ports; 18cm. ISBN 0-8600-7069-7 (pbk.)

Based almost entirely on the author's personal interviews with the Who over ten years, this is another well-constructed, popular biography by Tremlett, with a detailed chronology and some good portraits.

Who, the
> *The Who in their own words* / compiled by Steve Clarke. – London: Omnibus Press, 1980. – 128p.: ill., ports; 26cm. ISBN 0-86001-647-1 (pbk.)

A random selection of quotes from the members of the Who, including the late Keith Moon. Arranged by subject, the comments are often amusing but also revealing, giving an insight into the particular dynamics of the group.

THE WHO: DISCOGRAPHIES

Hanel, Ed
> *The Who: an illustrated discography* / by Ed Hanel. – London: Omnibus Press, 1981. – 144p.: ill., facsims, ports; 20cm. Includes bibliography. ISBN 0-86001-810-5 (pbk.)

An exhaustive discography which covers British, American and European releases. The author gives full discographical details and even variations between pressings. There are full biographical notes, some good illustrations, reproductions of album sleeves and details of some bootleg and unreleased tapes.

THE WHO: FILMS

Quadrophenia

Released in 1979 and directed by Franc Roddam, Quadrophenia is nostalgically set in 1964. Jimmy is a London 'mod' who looks forward to riding his motor scooter to Brighton to fight with 'rockers' during the notorious bank-holiday riots of the period. With little plot, the mood of the period is set with some contemporary songs and some cult detail but does not succeed very well. Quadrophenia, Pete Townshend's second rock opera, fails to possess the wide appeal of Tommy. Sting, singer with the Police, plays a leading mod in the film. The Who's songs, which complement the contemporary music, are good but are unable to redeem the film's general lack of impact.

Fletcher, Alan
    Quadrophenia / Alan Fletcher. – London: Corgi, 1979. – 190p.: 18cm.
    ISBN 0-552-11183-X (pbk.)
The novel of the film is reasonably well written, including lyrics and a great deal of period slang, not all of which is authentic. The overall effect is no more impressive than the film.

Tommy

Although not regarded as the first rock opera, Tommy has become the most widely known and most successful. Written by Pete Townshend, the leader of the Who, and initially simply recorded as an album for the band, the work has since been recorded with the London Symphony Orchestra. It became a Ken Russell film in 1975 as well as being performed countless times all over the world in various forms. It is the story of Tommy, a deaf, dumb and blind boy who becomes a pinball champion through his sense of smell, regains his faculties and leads a youth crusade from which he finally escapes because of the unleashed fanaticism. Townshend admits that the libretto leaves much to be desired as its over-simplicity, appropriate in 1968, could have been greatly enriched in the more sophisticated seventies. The allegory remains obvious, however, and the music is always good.

Barnes, Richard
    The story of Tommy / Richard Barnes & Pete Townshend. – Twickenham:
    Eel Pie Publishing, 1977. – 129p.: ill. (chiefly col.), facsims (some col.), ports
    (chiefly col); 31cm. ISBN 0-906008-02-6 (cased). ISBN 0-906008-01-8 (pbk.)

Pete Townshend describes the writing of Tommy from its early inspiration to production. The description of the making of the film is combined with coloured stills, facsimiles of the script and synopses. There are notes on the collaborators on the film and a full reproduction of the lyrics of the songs with appropriate illustrations.

WILLIAMS, ANDY AND DAVID

Young nephews of the famous singer, Andy Williams, Andy and David appeared on their uncle's television show while still at high school. Appealing to the young teenage audience, they had a big success in America in late 1972 which was a very minor hit in Britain early in 1973. They then disappeared without a trace.

Andy and David on the beach. – London: Daily Mirror Books, 1973. – 48p.:
   chiefly ill. (some col.), ports (some col.); 30cm. ISBN 0-8593-9015-2
   (unbound)
A collection of illustrations published to coincide with a brief British tour which was launched at the time of their solitary success: lacking information and poorly produced, this is an interesting example of faded ephemera.

WILLS, BOB ·

Born near Kosse, Texas, in 1905, James Robert Wills began playing the violin at dances when still in his early teens. He moved to Fort Worth in 1929 and formed a duo, the Wills Fiddle Band. The band later added a vocalist, and began broadcasting on local radio as the Crust Doughboys. By 1935 he had signed a contract with Brunswick and had formed a thirteen-piece band, which included not only country-music instruments but brass and woodwind, playing swing music with country overtones. The band was known as Bob Wills and His Texas Playboys. They recorded one of Wills's songs, San Antonio Rose, in 1940, and this sold a million copies and was followed by many more hits. The band split up during the war years and after Wills's own discharge from the army he formed a smaller band, playing his jazz-orientated style. He suffered a heart attack in 1962 and was forced to retire from his band-leading days in 1964. He continued to appear as a solo artist and attended his last recording session in 1973. He died in May 1975 and remains the creator of western swing music whose influence is acknowledged by many contemporary artists in the country-music field.

Townsend, Charles R.
   '*San Antonio Rose*': *the life and music of Bob Wills* / Charles R. Townsend;
   with a discography and filmography by Bob Pinson. – Urbana, Illinois;

London: University of Illinois Press, 1976. – xvii, 395p., 90p. of plates: ill.,
facsims, maps, ports; 26cm. Includes bibliography, discography,
filmography and index. ISBN 0-252-00470-1
A thoroughly researched, scholarly biography of Wills with an exhaustive
discography, a detailed list of sources and excellent illustrations.

WINGS

(*See* McCARTNEY, PAUL AND WINGS.)

WONDER, STEVIE

Blind at birth, Stephen Judkins was born in Michigan in May 1950. When only
twelve he signed a contract with the Tamla Motown record company and was
portrayed as a child genius and called 'Little' Stevie Wonder. He consistently
made successful singles throughout the sixties but on reaching twenty-one and
receiving the earnings from his teenage successes, he changed his musical
direction and began writing, producing and recording albums as complete
entities. This was a total change for Tamla Motown, but enormously successful. He toured the USA with the Rolling Stones in 1972 and gained an even
wider following. He is probably the most gifted and creative black musician
working in popular black music today, whose versatility as an instrumentalist
cannot be equalled. He plays all the instruments on his records and then
produces the final result himself. His range of theme and styles of music are
completely varied and unpredictable but always distinguishable by his excellent voice and the quality of musicianship. He has won numerous Grammy and
other awards and signed the biggest-ever recording contract of twelve million
dollars.

Dragonwagon, Crescent
   Stevie Wonder / by C. Dragonwagon. – New York: Flash Books, 1977. – 94p:
   ill., ports; 26cm. Includes discography. ISBN 0-8256-3908-5 (pbk.)
A brief, superficial biography which includes some interesting illustrations and
an analysis of his music with a full discography.

Edwards, Audrey
   The picture life of Stevie Wonder / by Audrey Edwards and Gary Wohl. –
   New York: Watts, 1977. – 48p. of ill. (some col.), ports (some col.); 23cm.
   ISBN 0-5310-1271-9 (pbk.)
A good collection of photographs of the artist from his childhood to 1977.

Elsner, Constanze
   Stevie Wonder / Constanze Elsner. – London: Everest Books, 1977. – 360p.,
   8p. of plates: ill., ports; 23cm. Includes discography and index.
   ISBN 0-905018-51-6

A well-researched, lengthy biography by a German journalist who is an avid fan. She conducted long interviews with her subject and although his early years are dealt with sketchily, she analyses many of his songs in depth and searches out his influences. The discography is very full, including American and British releases with details of their successes and of Wonder's numerous awards.

Fox-Cumming, Ray
> *Stevie Wonder* / Ray Fox-Cumming. – London: Mandabrook Books, 1977. –
> 123p.: 18cm. Includes discography. ISBN 0-427-00418-7 (pbk.)

A short biography which includes his early career and childhood and covers the period up to his Songs in the Key of Life album in 1976. This is not analytical of his work, but his relationship with other musicians and with Tamla Motown is well described. There is a chronology of the highlights in his career.

Hasegawa, Sam
> *Stevie Wonder* / text Sam Hasegawa; illustrator Dick Brude. – Mankato,
> Minnesota: Creative Education, 1975. – 31p.: ill. (some col.), ports (some
> col.); 25cm. ISBN 0-8719-1395-X

A controlled-vocabulary biography written for a reading age of about ten for American schools. It is informative and well illustrated, covering his early career as well as his successes of the early seventies.

Haskins, James
> *The Stevie Wonder scrapbook* / by Jim Haskins with Kathleen Benson. –
> London: Cassell, 1978. – 159p.: ill., ports; 28cm. Includes bibliography.
> ISBN 0-304-30461-1 (pbk.)
> Originally published: New York: Grosset & Dunlap, 1978.

A large collection of illustrations of Stevie Wonder which are interspersed with brief biographical notes up to 1977. The bibliography, which includes periodical articles and book extracts, is an unusual guide to sources and interviews.

Haskins, James
> *The story of Stevie Wonder* / James Haskins. – St. Albans: Panther, 1978. –
> 93p., 16p. of plates: ill., ports; 18cm. Includes discography and index. ISBN
> 0-586-04541-4 (pbk.)
> Originally published: New York: Lothrop, Lee & Shepard, 1976.

Written by a black American college teacher and writer on black culture, this attempts to place Stevie Wonder in his role as a black leader and to give an impression of the struggle of black musicians in the USA. There is no analysis of his work but a very full discography and some interesting illustrations.

Wilson, Beth P.
> *Stevie Wonder* / by Beth P. Wilson; illustrated by James Calvin. – New York:
> Putnam, 1979. – 61p.: ill., ports; 23cm. ISBN 0-399-61106-1

A brief biography for young readers, this is well illustrated with a well-written, informative text.

WYNETTE, TAMMY

Often referred to as the Queen of Country Music, she was born in Redbay, Alabama, in 1942. She went to Nashville in 1965 and met Billy Sherrill, who was combining string arrangements with the rawness of country music with a great deal of success. Tammy Wynette's image was that of a platinum-blonde, middle-American housewife singing of standing by her man no matter how she was treated and and perhaps dreaming of a more glamorous life in the big city. Her songwriting reflects these unfashionable sentiments but her success has become international and she is one of the two most successful female singers with the British country-music audience.

Wynette, Tammy
  Stand by your man / Tammy Wynette. – London: Arrow Books, 1981. –
  349p., 16p. of plates: ill., ports; 18cm. Includes index. ISBN 0-0992-4870-0
  (pbk.)
  Originally published: London: Hutchinson, 1980.
A personal biography with no evidence of having been ghosted, it is well written and gives an honest impression of her life. She discusses her five marriages without cynicism, recounts her early struggles and gives a good idea of the country-music world and of Nashville.

THE YARDBIRDS

Keith Relf, vocals, Chris Dreja, guitar, Paul Samwell-Smith, bass, and Jim McCarty, drums, were joined by Eric Clapton in October 1963 to form the Most Blueswailing Yardbirds. After gaining a following around London playing Chicago blues in a fairly authentic style, they took over from the Rolling Stones as resident band at Richmond's Crawdaddy Club. This period was followed by a tour of Europe with blues hero Sonny Boy Williamson and, in 1965, a British and American hit single. Clapton decided, however, that this path strayed too far from their blues roots and left to join John Mayall's Bluesbreakers. He was replaced by Jeff Beck and there followed further hit records. In 1966 Paul Samwell-Smith left, Dreja began playing bass and Jimmy Page joined on second guitar. This did not last, however, as Beck soon left to form his own group and after a general decline the band split up in July 1968. Jimmy Page was soon to form Led Zeppelin and Keith Relf the folk group, Renaissance. Although during their existence the Yardbirds achieved relatively modest successes, their influence on the growth of psychedelic rock and subsequently heavy metal is unquestioned as no one band has ever been such a training ground for guitar heroes. Keith Relf was killed by an electric shock in his house in May 1976.

Platt, John
  Yardbirds / John Platt, Chris Dreja, Jim McCarty. – London: Sidgwick &
  Jackson, 1983. – 160p.: ill., ports; 26cm. Includes discography and index.
  ISBN 0-283-98982-3 (pbk.)

John Platt is the editor and publisher of the fanzine *Comstock Lode*, which specializes in sixties music. Here he collaborated with two former members of the band to produce a disappointing memoir. The illustrations are good, the discography complete, but the text gives the reader no sense of the mood of the sixties and no feel for the characters of the band members. Jeff Beck, for example, a particularly enigmatic figure, lacks any kind of depth. The music itself is also severely neglected and one is left with no insight into why the Yardbirds were so special.

YES

A group with a constantly changing line-up, Yes was originally formed by Chris Squire and Jon Anderson in 1968. After two unsuccessful albums the original guitarist was replaced by the technically brilliant Steve Howe, who had considerable experience on the London underground scene of the late sixties with the group Tomorrow. In 1971 their third album was a great improvement and later that year they were joined by Rick Wakeman, the classically trained keyboards player who had already gained considerable status in playing with the Strawbs and in session work. Their style was now described as techno-flash with remarkable quasi-orchestral passages often regarded as pretentious and soulless but nonetheless impressive. There followed a series of enormously successful albums for the group. By 1975 each member of the group had produced his own albums, with Rick Wakeman's solo efforts becoming more successful than the group's efforts. Several changes in line-up followed and the final incarnation included Steve Howe, Alan White, Chris Squire, Geoff Downes and Trevor Horn, the last two being recent additions from the pop group Buggles. Yes finally split up in 1982 with Downes and Howe joining together with John Wetton and Carl Palmer to form Asia.

Hedges, Dan
    Yes: the authorised biography / Dan Hedges. – London: Sidgwick & Jackson, 1981. – 145p.: ill. (some col.), ports (some col.); 28cm. Includes disc-ography. ISBN 0-283-98751-0 (cased). ISBN 0-283-98761-8 (pbk.)
None of the eleven musicians who have been part of Yes in the last thirteen years has been ignored in this well-researched biography. Each has been interviewed at length. There are photographs of the band at each of its stages with good musical analysis and quotations from the group. The discography is complete and includes work by the musicians apart from with Yes. The production is of an exceptionally high standard.

YOUNG, JIMMY

Born in Cinderford, Gloucester, around 1925, Jimmy Young became one of the most popular British recording artists of the late fifties. He had a series of twelve hit singles between 1953 and 1964 and then embarked on a broadcasting career, becoming one of BBC Radio Two's most successful disc jockeys. His homely good humour, cooking hints and curious patter continue to make him a great favourite with the housewife audience.

Young, Jimmy
J.Y.: the autobiography of Jimmy Young. – London: Sphere Books, 1975. – 176p., 8p. of plates: ill., ports; 18cm. ISBN 0-352-30014-0 (pbk.)
Originally published: London: W. H. Allen, 1973.
Covering Young's singing career as well as his establishment as a broadcaster, this is an amusing, self-effacing account.

Young, Jimmy
Jimmy Young. – London: Michael Joseph; Rainbird, 1982. – 176., 32p. of plates: ill., ports; 23cm. Includes index. ISBN 0-7181-2142-2
An autobiographical account of Young's radio career during the seventies, this is written with humour and a degree of self-satisfaction.

YOUNG, NEIL

Born in Toronto in 1945, in 1966 Neil Young moved to Los Angeles and became part of the Buffalo Springfield. In early 1969 he released his first solo album and later that year joined Crosby, Stills and Nash to add his name to that important group. His next album, After the Goldrush, established him as a major figure and critically the most influential artist of the early seventies. He has continued to produce always innovative, melodic albums, which had by the late seventies become increasingly heavier in their texture with more electric instrumentation from his band Crazy Horse. Apart from his unusual guitar style, it is his ability to surprise his audience with his enigmatic lyrics and wailing voice over simple but beautiful melodies that have made him one of the most influential figures in rock music.

(*See also* CROSBY, STILLS AND NASH.)

Dufrechou, Carole
Neil Young / Carole Dufrechou. – London: Omnibus Press, 1981. – Rev. ed. – 128p.: ill., ports; 26cm. Includes discography. ISBN 0-7119-0092-2 (pbk.)
Previous edition: New York; London: Quick Fox, 1978.
A short biography for such an important artist, this does cover the various stages of his career but does not attempt to delve into the creation of his songs. There is a full discography of his solo albums as well as his work with his various bands. Written in a seemingly authoritative style but unfortunately a poor effort, the 1982 edition has brief additional information by Chris Charlesworth concerning Neil Young's recent albums and concert tours.

Rogan, Johnny
Neil Young: the definitive story of his musical career / Johnny Rogan. – London; New York: Proteus, 1982. – 170p., 16p. of plates: ill., ports; 23cm.

Includes discography. ISBN 0-86276-027-5 (cased). ISBN 0-86276-012-7 (pbk.)
With a keen knowledge of his work and using hundreds of examples of lyrics to illustrate the analysis, the author has made a good attempt at a serious study. Neil Young's whole career is covered in detail with a great deal of information on his more obscure Buffalo Springfield period. The discography includes bootlegs, appearances on the records of other artists, unreleased recordings and cover versions. The illustrations are not particularly well chosen and are limited.

ZAPPA, FRANK

Born in Baltimore in 1940, Frank Zappa moved to the West Coast of America with his parents in 1950. After writing film scores and pieces for other performers he joined a group called the Soul Giants who were soon renamed the Mothers of Invention. After early problems, in 1966 they recorded the first-ever double rock album called Freak Out, which was a satirical picture of Hippie underground culture in Los Angeles. It was an enormous success and was followed by a series of like albums. In late 1969 Zappa's style changed and he recorded Hot Rats, an album with French jazz violinist Jean-Luc Ponty, which demonstrated Zappa's ability as a composer of lengthy, sophisticated jazz-rock pieces and as a superb guitarist. Throughout the seventies he followed this path with a stream of less successful but creative and sophisticated albums.

The lives & times of Zappa and the Mothers. – Manchester: Babylon Books, 1979. – 64p.: ill., facsims, ports; 25cm. Includes discography. (pbk.)
A cut-up fanzine offering disorganized but rare information and illustrations of Zappa and his band. Arranged chronologically, this collection of press cuttings gives a revealing picture of just how outrageous and innovative they were. The discography is detailed.

Walley, David
No commercial potential: the saga of Frank Zappa then & now / by David Walley. – New York: Dutton, 1980. – 192p.: ill., facsims, ports; 25cm. Includes discography. ISBN 0-525-93153-8 (pbk.)
Previous edition entitled 'No commercial potential: the saga of Frank Zappa & the Mothers of Invention': New York: Outerbridge and Lazard, 1972.
This is the fullest biography of Frank Zappa as a solo artist as well as the leader of the Mothers of Invention. It is full of amusing quotations, analysis of his music, some excellent illustrations and a full discography. The later edition adds little to the original, reflecting Zappa's relative quietness during the late seventies.

ZAPPA, FRANK: DISCOGRAPHIES

Obermanns, Nobbi
  Get Zapped: Zappalog the first step to Zappology / edited by Nobbi;
  photographs by Petra and Nobbi. – Bremen: Dwarf Nebula Publications,
  1981. – 91p.: ill., facsims, ports; 24cm. (pbk.)
Published in Germany but written in English, this is an exhaustive, illustrated
discography which includes all official releases of Zappa and the Mothers of
Invention in their various versions throughout the world. In addition, the
author has tracked down a remarkable number of bootlegs. Apart from
reproductions of album sleeves and record labels, there are also some rare
photographs and details of every musician who has ever played with Zappa at
every one of his recording sessions.

CHAPTER SEVEN

Fiction

For a subject which so obviously captures the popular imagination, there exists a very poor body of creative literature concerned with modern popular music.

Thom Keyes' *All night stand* appeared in 1966 as the first attempt and was regarded, even then, as a poor, tame exposé. In 1967 Nik Cohn's *I am still the greatest says Johnny Angelo* approached genuine satire and the possibility of a good novel seemed imminent.

What has followed, however, has been a surprisingly small output of material of, with little exception, very poor quality. The subject attracts a sensational approach, often by authors who should have known and could have done better.

Mark Shipper's *Paperback writer*, 1978, is an exception. It is a genuinely funny book mixing satire with the confusion created by the hype of the media.

The controlled-vocabulary readers by Edmund Hildick and Richard Ward are well meaning and appropriate to the reading age, but uninspired.

The other source of fictional material is the cinema, and film tie-ins or novelizations that have appeared to coincide with many film releases. Ray Connolly's *That'll be the day* and *Stardust*, Leonore Fleischer's *Fame* and John Pidgeon's *Flame* are worth considering as works in their own right and make a real contribution to the literature.

Allen, Richard
   Glam / Richard Allen. – London: New English Library, 1973. – 125p.; 18cm. ISBN 0-450-01741-9 (pbk.)
The sequel to the author's *Teenybopper idol*, Johnny Holland continues his musical career under the guidance of manipulator Steve Morash. Narcissus, glam-rock star, and Holland are natural enemies. After a succession of trivial events, the novel climaxes with an open-air concert which degenerates into a mass riot incited by Narcissus and his cronies who are arrested. Holland and Morash look forward to further stardom. Even poorer than its predecessor.

Allen, Richard
   Teenybopper idol / Richard Allen. – London: New English Library, 1973. – 126p.; 18cm. ISBN 0-450-01721-4 (pbk.)
Bobby Sharp, American teenybopper idol, arrives in England a week before his first London concert appearance. His manager Steve Morash and promotion team manipulate the media to ensure that the preteenage fans are aroused

to fever pitch in anticipation of his live appearance on the television spectacular. Johnny Holland, an aspiring young singer, takes advantage of the hysterical situation by storming onto the stage with the other members of his band and stealing the show. The press acclaim Holland at the expense of the star. No characterization, no real plot, no moral and poorly written, this is the lowest level of pulp fiction, attempting to sell copies by offering an exposé of the teenybopper craze and the manipulation of the fans. No such issues are in fact approached.

Breeze, Paul
  Back street runner / Paul Breeze. – London: Michael Joseph, 1980. – 282p.;
  21cm. ISBN 0-7181-1892-8
In this sequel to *While my guitar gently weeps*, Billy has begun drumming in an unknown semi-professional band as a means of still being involved in music. While performing he is recognized by the witness to his third murder, who informs the police. He is once again on the run and is finally caught. His girlfriend is killed by a car and the novel ends with him in prison in silent anguish. Sad, a little melodramatic, there is interesting insight into playing in a band and a good deal of suspense.

Breeze, Paul
  While my guitar gently weeps / Paul Breeze. – London: Macdonald; Futura:
  1980. – 222p.; 18cm. ISBN 0-7088-1840-4 (pbk.)
  Originally published: London: Michael Joseph, 1979.
The title is taken from a song by George Harrison and is the first novel by this author. Billy Dancey is the lead guitarist of a group, Black Dog, about to break into the big time. After their first really important concert three attackers break his left hand so badly that two fingers are amputated. He ruthlessly tracks down the attackers and murders them in retaliation for ending his career. The novel ends with his being spotted while committing the third murder. With some accurate, atmospheric facts about life as a musician, it is a well written and compelling thriller. There is a proposal to make it into a film featuring Sting of the Police.

Burke, John
  Privilege / John Burke. – London: Pan Books, 1967. – 156p.; 18cm. (pbk.)
The film Privilege was released in 1967 and directed by Peter Watkins from a story by Johnny Speight. Paul Jones, formerly of the group Manfred Mann, and model Jean Shrimpton starred in this bizarre story set in a futuristic idea of the eighties. Jones plays a pop singer who is forced by the government to lead an evangelical crusade, an honest but very poor attempt to comment on political manipulation. Jones' acting and singing were very good throughout. This novel is a faithful description of the action of the film, told in a flat style which is readable but fails to capture the hysteria of the film.

Calvert, Robert
  Hype / Robert Calvert. – London: New English Library, 1981. – 221p.;
  18cm. ISBN 0-450-05244-3 (pbk.)

The author once worked as a lyricist with rock group Hawkwind. His novel concerns APR, a record company experiencing a slump in business. The executives decide to market excessively or 'hype' one of their artists, Tom Mahler, who has failed to achieve success. They change his image, his record producer and make his songs more commercial. In spite of the million-pound budget allocated to his marketing, Mahler still fails to recoup the investment made in him. At a concert he is shot dead while performing and immediately becomes a posthumous superstar. There is considerable background to the dubious side of the music business, such as the influencing and bribing of disc jockeys and the buying of records into the charts, but in general this novel lacks a good plot or any real characterization and offers only a superficial, sensational glimpse at the lifestyle of the rock business.

Carlile, Richard
  Drummer / Richard Carlile. – London: Tandem, 1971. – 123p.; 18cm.
  ISBN 0-4260-6015-6 (pbk.)
Ariston is a drummer in the top rock band, Satiety Incorporated. While performing at a concert before over 200,000 fans, there is a riot in which all the other members of the band are killed. Ariston is saved by the intervention of a helicopter sent by an initially anonymous benefactor who wants to obtain the secret aphrodisiac behind Ariston's sexual prowess, which he in fact obtains from the rubbish dump where he once lived. The benefactor is later killed by the disembodied hand of a writer he had swindled. Ariston runs away and is captured by a woman who tortures and mutilates him. He escapes in a boat and drifts out to sea. A bizarre fantasy which has little to do with music but at times works as a curious thriller.

Cohn, Nik
  I am still the greatest says Johnny Angelo / Nik Cohn. – London: Secker & Warburg, 1967. – 191p.; 20cm.
Written by the journalist and author on popular music, this is a satirical novel about a rock star. It is the bizarre story of Angelo who, after achieving success, finally commits murder and is shot by the police. His destructive influence on all who meet him is an important theme, as is the devastating portrait of his sycophantic associates. Not a realistic picture of the pitfalls of stardom but entertaining and original.

Connolly, Ray
  Stardust / Ray Connolly. – London: Fontana, 1974. – 159p.; 18cm.
  ISBN 0-00-613663-X (pbk.)
The novel of the film, Stardust, which was directed by Michael Apted and released in 1974. It was the sequel to That'll Be the Day, starring David Essex as Jim Maclaine, a product of the sixties whose sole aim is to become a pop star. He graduates from an early-sixties beat group into psychedelia and finally dies, a recluse, from a drug overdose. A simplistic look at the pressures of fame, the film included an excellent perfomance by Adam Faith as Maclaine's manager. The screenplay was written by Ray Connolly, who provides a very readable, well-written novel with a sense of real pathos.

Connolly, Ray
That'll be the day / Ray Connolly. – London: Fontana, 1973. – 127p.; 18cm.
ISBN 0-00-613271-5 (pbk.)
The novel of the film, That'll Be the Day, which was directed by Claude
Whatham and released in 1973. Set in the fifties, it starred David Essex and
Ringo Starr. The background is that of the fairgrounds and holiday camps so
typical of the period with rock'n'roll competitions and groups emulating their
American idols. Jim Maclaine, played by David Essex, drops out of school and
takes casual jobs in this atmosphere. He marries young, becomes suffocated by
the concept of a respectable life and the film ends with his buying a guitar and
joining a group. Ray Connolly wrote the screenplay and his novel provides a
beautiful picture of the period, well written and, in places, very amusing.

Edwards, Alexander
A star is born: a new novel / by Alexander Edwards from the screenplay by
John Gregory Dunne & Joan Didion and Frank Pierson; based on a story by
William Wellman and Robert Carson. – London: Star Books. 1977. – 236p.;
18cm. ISBN 0-352-39688-1 (pbk.)
The novel of the film, A Star is Born, released in 1976 and directed by Frank
Pierson. It was the third version of a well-known story: the previous ones were
in 1937 and 1954. Barbra Streisand starred as Esther Hoffman, an up-and-
coming rock singer, with Kris Kristofferson as John Norman, a fading rock
star. They inevitably form a romantic attachment which initially helps
Norman's drink and drugs problem and launches Esther to stardom, but ends
in Norman's final despair and death. This novel is a poor rendering of the
storyline of the film which was in itself mediocre, sentimental and often
embarrassing.

Fabian, Jenny
Groupie / Jenny Fabian & Johnny Byrne. – St. Albans: Mayflower, 1970. –
295p.; 18cm. ISBN 0-583-11793-7 (pbk.)
Originally published: London: New English Library, 1969.
Set in the swinging London era of the sixties, Katie is a girl whose aim is to sleep
with as many musicians as possible. Usually under the influence of some drug
or other, she spends her time at clubs and indulging in sex. Much publicized at
the time of publication, *Groupie* lacks plot and characterization and is a
superficial, inaccurate picture of the period and the culture.

Fleischer, Leonore
Fame: a novel / by Leonore Fleischer: based on the Alan Parker film;
screenplay by Christopher Gore. – London: Sphere Books, 1980. – 255p.;
18cm. ISBN 0-7221-3547-3 (pbk.)
The film, Fame, was directed by Alan Parker and released in 1980. It is the
story of a group of teenagers attending Manhattan's High School for the
Performing Arts. The very mixed group have the single ambition to make it in
showbusiness. The result was a very good film without pretensions of delving
into the deeper motivations of performers but offering an interesting, refresh-

ing view of New York. In 1982 the idea became a very popular television series, The Kids from Fame. Leonore Fleischer, always a good writer, very skilfully adapted the screenplay to recreate the mood of the film perfectly.

Fleischer, Leonore
   The Rose: a novel / Leonore Fleischer; based on the original screenplay by
   Bo Goldman, Michael Cimino and William Kirby. – London: Futura
   Publications, 1979. – 247p.; 18cm. ISBN 0-7088-1663-0 (pbk.)
The novel of the film, The Rose, which was produced in 1979 and directed by Mark Rydell. It was a vehicle for Bette Midler and co-starred Alan Bates, who was badly miscast as her manager. It told the story of Rose, a rock singer played by Midler, based loosely on the character of Janis Joplin. Her insecurity has led to drug abuse and heavy drinking which result finally in her death while performing on stage. The music and performance of Bette Midler won her the Grammy Award for best female singer in 1980 and an Academy Award nomination. Even Leonore Fleischer is unable to produce a reasonable novel from this trite material.

Glanville, Brian
   Never look back / Brian Glanville. – London: Michael Joseph, 1980. – 240p.;
   22cm. ISBN 0-7181-1953-3
Successful young rock star Russ Hope becomes disillusioned with fame and soured with his life although he owns a mansion in the British countryside and a beachhouse in California. He experiences drug addiction and despair. Even women and his homosexual relationship with his lyricist do not help. Finally, a comeback concert, the suicide of his girlfriend and his own violent death at the hands of a group of punks end this little fantasy. Trite images of the rock world are created here by an author and journalist who really should do better. It could all be an attempt at satire but is simply too weak.

Hildick, Edmund Wallace
   Birdy and the group / E. W. Hildick; illustrated by Richard Rose. – London:
   Pan Books; Macmillan, 1968. – 160p.: ill.; 18cm. – (Topliners).
   ISBN 0-330-02045-4 (pbk.)
   Originally published: London: Macmillan, 1968.
Hildick, Edmund Wallace
   Birdy in Amsterdam / E. W. Hildick; illustrated by Richard Rose. – London:
   Macmillan, 1970. – 127p.: ill.; 18cm. – (Topliners). ISBN 0-333-05987-5
   (pbk.)
Hildick, Edmund Wallace
   Birdy Jones / E. W. Hildick; illustrated by Richard Rose. – London: Pan
   Books; Macmillan, 1968. – 141p.: ill.; 18cm. – (Topliners).
   ISBN 0-333-09954-0 (pbk.)
   Originally published: London: Faber, 1963.
Hildick, Edmund Wallace
   Birdy swings north / E. W. Hildick; illustrated by Richard Rose. – London:
   Pan Books; Macmillan, 1969. – 128p.: ill.; 18cm. – (Topliners).
   ISBN 0-333-03673-3 (pbk.)

A series of stories written in a simple, controlled vocabulary for teenagers with reading problems. Birdy Jones leaves school determined to create a new pop sound as a whistler. His adventures in the music business are amusing and provide a suitable theme for the age group.

Hill, Susan
   Breaking glass / Susan Hill. – London: Star Books, 1980. – 160p.; 18cm.
   ISBN 0-352-30724-2 (pbk.)
The novel of the film, Breaking Glass, which was directed by Brian Gibson and released in 1980, launching Hazel O'Connor on her successful career. She plays a new-wave singer who finds the pressure at the top too much for her. Clichés abound. The setting is simply updated in the context of the late seventies with confrontations between the National Front (an extreme right-wing British political party) and the Anti-Nazi League. The stage performances are realistic, as is much of the dialogue between the musicians and the technical aspects of recording and performing. Jonathan Price, Jon Finch and Phil Daniels give good performances with Gary Holton and Zoot Money appearing in minor roles. The songs, written by Hazel O'Connor, are an acquired taste. As a novel, although well written and including much of the dialogue, the story is not strong enough.

Holden, Stephen
   Triple platinum / Stephen Holden. – London: New English Library; Times
   Mirror, 1980. – 317p.; 18cm. ISBN 0-450-04691-8 (pbk.)
Nick Young is an ambitious young former journalist who is the protégé of Craig Morrison, president of IMC Records, a New York-based company. A peculiar sexual arrangement between Nick and Craig's wife, Beverley, profuse drug taking and general corruption are the backcloth to Craig's poor business deals and the signing of a seven-million dollar contract with ageing rock star, Lance Macon. The story culminates with the murder of Macon, Craig's loss of his wife and the presidency of the company. Beginning promisingly with considerable detail of the American music press and the business processes in record companies, the book sadly degenerates into ludicrous characterization and a stereotyped storyline.

Hughes, Megan
   Yesterday's music / Megan Hughes. – New York: Leisure Books, 1980. –
   285p.; 18cm. ISBN 0-8439-0736-3 (pbk.)
Reta Friedland, a record-company executive, is given the job of organizing a joint country and rock music album with two major artists: rock singer Keats and country singer Buck Walker. She embarks on the task of persuading Keats to become involved in the venture and becomes emotionally involved with the drug-addicted star. After a series of traumatic events, Keats leaves for South America to find obscurity. The story of a feminist in the male-dominated rock world, which fails to happen.

Keyes, Thom

All night stand / Thom Keyes. – London: W.H. Allen, 1966. – 216p.; 20cm.

Launched in 1966 as a novel from a writer 'within the long haired generation', it is the story of a four-piece pop group from Manchester who achieve international success and finally degenerate into dissipation. Written to be a sensational fantasy with all the sex and drugs clichés of the pop world, mild then, it is simply amusing now. The style is in the first person, written in sections from the point of view of each member of the group in turn. It is not a well-written novel, however, and it is interesting only in that it reflects the way in which the 'swinging sixties' movement saw itself.

Lea, Timothy

Confessions from the pop scene / Timothy Lea. – London: Futura Publications, 1974. – 156p.; 18cm. ISBN 0-8600-7047-6 (pbk.)

In a series of fictional confessions featuring sexual exploits in a wide range of occupations, there is no story, no characterization and no real humour. This could be the worst work of fiction ever written; it is certainly the poorest to be included here.

Lewis, Stephen

The Regulars / Stephen Lewis. – New York: Leisure Books, 1980. – 476p.; 18cm. ISBN 0-8439-0735-5 (pbk.)

Set during the rock'n'roll revival of the late seventies, American television network TBS decide to revive a famous music show of the fifties, Dancetime USA!, which had been dramatically taken off the air during the 'payola' bribery scandals of the late fifties. The Regulars were a group of teenagers who appeared each week on the show and the survivors are tracked down and invited to reappear. The narrative concerns their lives during the intervening twenty years and their thoughts and feelings on the reunion. The book is full of detail about real figures such as Dick Clark, artists of the period, shows and old fan magazines and with a refreshing lack of sex and drugs. With its odd nostalgic slant, this is an acceptable light novel by any standards.

Mazer, Barry

Superstar / Barry Mazer. – New York: Tower Publications, 1977. – 216p.; 18cm. (pbk.)

Rick Lathen is a rock superstar heavily involved in the drugs and sex associated with such a position. His teenage friend John Stark receives a mysterious telegram in Portugal telling him to meet Rick in New York at his next concert. After a brief meeting the performance begins but Rick leaves the stage and disappears. Stark searches New York, meeting his old friend's girlfriend, friends, drug pusher and stepfather and finally uncovers the facts: Rick is the subject of a ten-year-old biographical film which will culminate in his staged suicide induced by drugs. The plot, created by his record company, manager and drug pusher, does end in Rick's death but also in their own ends. Really an average mystery novel superimposed on the world of drugs and rock, it is entertaining but the sensational description of the lifestyle is not to be taken seriously.

Norman, Philip
 Wild thing / Philip Norman. – London: Heinemann, 1972. – 185p.; 21cm.
 ISBN 0-434-52302-X
With this collection of nine short stories a well-known journalist attempts to satirize a wide range of styles of music and their associated worlds. Rock, soul, country and blues are all explored. Regarded by many as a fine collection of stories, which gets to the heart of the subject, they are on the whole superficial and simplistic, relying heavily on popular images rather than new suggestions.

Parsons, Tony
 Platinum logic / Tony Parsons. – London: Pan Books, 1981. – 509p.; 18cm.
 ISBN 0-330-26457-5 (pbk.)
Written by a former journalist of the *New Musical Express*, the central character is Nathan Chasen, head of MOM Records, a New York company. With the background of the contemporary music industry this lengthy saga is of the effect of a powerful demagogue on his family, employees and artists. He suffers divorce, the alienation of his family and disloyalty of his confidants. The usual rounds of infidelities and exchanging partners cover a weak plot. One would have expected at least a little musical or technical background but it fails to appear.

Pidgeon, John
 Flame / John Pidgeon; based on an original screenplay by Andrew Birkin. – St. Albans: Panther, 1975. – 158p., 8p. of plates: ill.: 18cm.
 ISBN 0-586-04252-0 (pbk.)
The screenplay of a film directed by Richard Loncraine and released in 1974, which provided the author with a good story and strong characterization on which to base his novel. The group Slade play Flame, a pop group who are forced to disband because of their heavy-handed management. Tom Conti played the manager and Slade acted really very well. The author's experience in the music business has helped him embellish his book with some excellent detail and there is a good collection of stills from the film.

Pollock, Bruce
 Playing for change / Bruce Pollock. – Boston, Massachusetts: Houghton Mifflin, 1977. – 204p.; 22cm. ISBN 0-395-25149-4
Written by a freelance journalist and writer on rock music, the central character, Webb, is the songwriter and guitarist of an aspiring rock group, Christie, in New York. An advertisement for a piano player is answered by fifteen-year-old Selena Spry, who auditions but sees Webb as the sole talent of the group and declines to join. After a disastrous concert appearance, Webb and Selena leave for Boston with plans to find an apartment, but the romance is short-lived and Selena returns to her parents in Maine. On his journey back to New York Webb meets a successful rock manager who is impressed by his writing and his hopes of stardom are revived. This is better than some novels centred on the rock world. Basically a teenage romance, it is sympathetically written with some interesting views of teenage mentality.

Shipper, Mark
Paperback writer: the life and times of the Beatles; the spurious chronicle of their rise to stardom, their triumphs and disasters, plus the amazing story of their ultimate reunion; a novel / by Mark Shipper. – London: New English Library; Times Mirror, 1978. – 254p.: ill., ports; 21cm. ISBN 0-450-04085-2 (pbk.)
Originally published: New York: Grosset and Dunlap, 1978.
Also published: New York: Ace Books, 1980.
The author describes it as a 'work of semi fiction . . . with one foot in reality'. The idea is that after an exclusive interview with Ringo Starr the author lost his notes on the way home and proceeded to 'make up his own version' of the Beatles' story. The result is a very funny novel for those with the knowledge of what really happened.

Squire, Robin
The big scene / Robin Squire. – London: New English Library, 1969. – 160p.; 18cm. ISBN 0-4500-0332-9 (pbk.)
Originally published: London: W. H. Allen, 1968.
A struggling young photographer is given the use of a studio to undertake publicity photographs for pop groups. He decides that he would like to get into the pop world and finds a group which he renames the Fancy Free, becoming their manager. They secure a recording contract and travel around the country playing at small-time venues. There is a succession of sexual exploits with their young fans, their first record fails to make it, they have no money and finally the group and their manager go back to their previous careers. The book is singularly lacking in plot, though the disappointment of the characters is a realistic facet of the pop world which is rarely portrayed.

Tabori, Paul
Song of the Scorpions: a novel / by Paul Tabori. – London: New English Library, 1972. – 189p.; 18cm. ISBN 0-450-00768-8 (pbk.)
Originally published: London: New English Library, 1971.
Also published: New York: Tower Publications, 1971.
The Scorpions are an outrageous but very successful rock group whose vast fortune and idle lifestyle lead them into all kinds of excesses of the flesh. After an exposé of the activities published by the *Globe* newspaper, they sue the paper for libel. Eventually the suit is withdrawn. Some explicit description of bizarre sex and drug abuse do not compensate for a weak story and some totally inaccurate observations of the rock world.

Ward, Richard
Rock on speech day / R. Ward; illustrations by Yvonne Poulton. – Amersham, Buckinghamshire: Hulton, 1975. – 91p.: ill., music; 19cm. – (Popswinger 1) ISBN 0-7175-0715-7 (pbk.)
Ward, Richard
First gig / R. Ward; illustrations by Yvonne Poulton. – Amersham, Buckinghamshire: Hulton, 1975. – 89p.: ill., 19cm. – (Popswinger 4) ISBN 0-7175-0732-7 (pbk.)

Ward, Richard
   Flash Band in London / R. Ward; illustrations by Yvonne Poulton. –
   Amersham, Buckinghamshire: Hulton, 1975. – 91p.: ill., 19cm. –
   (Popswinger 3) ISBN 0-7175-0733-5 (pbk.)
Ward, Richard
   The great day / R. Ward; illustrations by Yvonne Poulton. – Amersham,
   Buckinghamshire: Hulton, 1975. – 90p.: ill., 19cm. – (Popswinger 4)
   ISBN 0-7175-0734-3 (pbk.)
Ward, Richard
   Flash Band in the States / R. Ward; illustrations by Yvonne Poulton. –
   Amersham, Buckinghamshire: Hulton, 1976. – 91p.: ill., 19cm. –
   (Popswinger 5) ISBN 0-7175-0735-1 (pbk.)
Ward, Richard
   Flash in the pan / R. Ward; illustrations by Yvonne Poulton. – Amersham,
   Buckinghamshire: Hulton, 1976. – 88p.: ill., 19cm. – (Popswinger 6)
   ISBN 0-7175-0736-X (pbk.)
A controlled-vocabulary series for British schools for a reading age of about
twelve, this is the saga of the Flash Band's rise from school group to an
American tour. Well written, it is easy to relate to the band's ultimate demise
after brief success. It is a realistic, sad little tale.

Woodard, Bronte
   Can't stop the music / by Bronte Woodard and Allan Carr. – Los Angeles:
   Pinnacle Books, 1980. – 142p., 16p. of plates: ill. (some col.); 18cm.
   ISBN 0-523-41177-4 (pbk.)
Published in the photonovel format with stills and comic strip bubbles, this
attempts to represent the film Can't Stop the Music, which was designed to
launch the group Village People. Produced in 1980 by Allan Carr, the producer
of Grease, the film was directed by Nancy Walker. An aspiring young songwriter attempts to break into the pop world with the aid of a very odd group,
Village People. A very poor disco film, it lacked plot, good songs, humour,
good dance sequences and even attractive characters. The resulting photonovel, although beautifully produced, is no more inspiring than the film.

CHAPTER EIGHT

Periodicals

8.1 CURRENT PERIODICALS

One of the most obvious indications of the growth of interest in a subject is the appearance of magazines devoted to it. This is certainly true of popular music and the keeping track of periodicals in the field is a hectic activity.

From the few trade papers which already existed in the fifties, and the long-established *Melody Maker*, there has grown an extensive list. In addition, it is rare to pick up a general newspaper without finding a feature on a rock star or the review of a concert.

Glossy magazines such as *Playboy, Playgirl, Cosmopolitan* and teenage magazines such as *Boyfriend* and *17* all have regular features on the pop scene. In addition, record reviews appear in hi-fi magazines such as *Popular Hi-fi*, *Hi-fi Answers* and the American *Hi-Fidelity*: these are technical magazines but include musical criticism. *Time Out* and *City Limits*, the London entertainment guides, give exceptionally intelligent news coverage of music. It is now established that to be a real star one must appear on the covers of *Time* and *Newsweek*, the American news reviews, as well as perhaps be featured in *The Sunday Times* and *The Observer* colour supplements.

There is, indeed, a vast number of sources of articles, reviews and illustrative material. Included here are the current publications devoted to popular music which are generally available in the UK and North America. They are in a single sequence, partly to avoid confusion and partly because many publications are commonly available on both sides of the Atlantic, and all can be obtained. The overlap of subject coverage is also such that a single sequence rather than an attempt at classification is more appropriate. A notable feature is their volatile nature: their change of format, pagination, publisher, title and aptness to merge. All physical details are current to 1982 and title changes and publication are noted. Equally changeable are the editorial staffs of many of these journals and the total lack of bibliographic control and, in general, indexing. The research required simply to identify the original year of publication is remarkably difficult, even with the help, usually ill-informed, of the current staff.

The publications themselves fall into distinct categories: the trade press, for use within the business; the music press, literally the newspapers focussing on the subject; monthly, or bi-monthly magazines, often glossy, offering in-depth articles; lyric collections; and teenage magazines for the young fan. Each annotation will make evident the category of its particular publication.

Acid Rock. – New York: Stories Layouts & Press, 1977–. Bi-monthly.
  Currently. – 50p.: ill., ports; 30cm.
Featuring the psychedelic rock style of the sixties which faded in the early seventies and has only recently had some revival, the mood is nostalgia. Long, rambling articles, often decidedly esoteric, are presented in a well-designed, attractive format.

Bam: the California music magazine. – Oakland, California: Bam Publications, 1976–. Fortnightly. Currently. – 50p.: ill., ports; 37cm.
  Formerly titled '*Bay Area Music*'.
A high-quality tabloid including excellent features on a wide variety of styles of popular music. There is a good deal of local interest, with club dates and concert advertisements, as well as reviews of local performances, but there is also much of interest for the wider audience.

Billboard. – New York: Billboard Publications, 1894–. Weekly. Currently. – 82p.: ill. (some col.), ports (some col.); 38cm. ISSN 0006-2510
The longest-established of all trade weeklies, *Billboard* is an advertising medium, trade newspaper and detailed business-monitoring service. It carries record reviews, radio schedules and dozens of chart listings for the USA and the rest of the record-consuming world for every kind of popular music. Feature articles are news-orientated on subjects such as legal matters, commercial trends and details of new, emerging artists.

Bim Bam Boom. – New York: Bim Bam Boom Enterprises, 1976–.
  Bi-monthly. Currently. – 40p.: ill., ports; 26cm.
For enthusiasts of fifties rock'n'roll and rhythm & blues and particularly record collectors; the quality of the format and writing is better than for most other magazines devoted to this area.

Black Music and Jazz Review. – London: Napfield Limited, 1978–. Monthly.
  Currently. – 50p.: ill., ports; 30cm.
  Formerly published: Sutton: IPC Specialist and Professional Press.
  Formerly titled '*Black Music*'.
An excellent monthly covering soul, jazz, rhythm & blues and reggae in depth. Record reviews, interviews, letters and historical essays are all of a high standard. American soul singles, soul albums and jazz albums charts as well as British soul singles, soul albums and reggae charts are well presented.

Blues & Soul & Disco Music Review. – London: Napfield Limited, 1966–.
  Fortnightly. Currently. – 48p.: ill., facsims, ports; 28cm.
  Formerly published: London: Contempo International.
  Formerly titled '*Blues and Soul Music Review*'.
Well produced and informative, this fortnightly magazine manages to offer a mixture of serious research and in-depth journalism with a popular presentation and a current appreciation of the disco-music scene. Its evolution from a serious blues and soul magazine to cater for the growing funk, disco market has been shrewdly undertaken. Record reviews, lengthy features, current trends and advertisements for discotheques and clubs are all well presented.

Blues Unlimited. – London: BU Publications, 1963–. Bi-monthly. Currently. –
34p.: ill., facsims, ports; 30cm. ISSN 0006-5153
For the devotee of blues and its associated musical styles, it covers both
historical background and the contemporary scene. Rhythm & blues artists are
included, offering historical background for rock'n'roll fans. There are record
reviews, discographies, historical essays and letters as well as interesting, rare
photographs.

Bomp!. – Burbank, Califormia: Bomp Magazine, 1966–. Bi-monthly.
Currently. – 46p.: ill., facsims, ports; 28cm. ISSN 0039-7873
Formerly titled '*Who Put The Bomp*'.
Originally concerned with the serious historical analysis of rock and pop music,
it has recently included more contemporary coverage. There are lengthy,
intelligent features and interviews, record and book reviews and listings of
fanzines. This is an example of a fanzine which has become more professionally produced, has developed its organization and outgrown the description.
Part of *Bomp!*'s organization includes a rare record-marketing section which
both sells deleted albums and singles and works as an advertising medium for
collectors.

Boogie: Gulf Coast's rock quarterly. – Gulfport, Michigan: John Bialas, 1972–.
Quarterly. Currently. – 80p.: ill., ports; 34cm.
Including very good record, book and film reviews, *Boogie* has grown from a
fanzine into a wide-circulation magazine. Contributions from readers are a
notable feature of this well-produced and intelligent publication which does
feature local musical activities but is generally wide in scope.

Buy Gone Record Sales. – Nottingham: Buy Gone, 1977–. Monthly. Currently.
– 107p.: ill., facsims, ports; 21cm.
For the record collector: this covers a wide range of popular-music styles since
the fifties. There is no editorial, but lists of records for sale and auction. There
are abbreviated annotations of condition and many advertisements for other
magazines and record shops.

Canadian Musician. – Toronto, Ontario: Norris Publications, 1977–.
Bi-monthly. Currently. – 102p.: ill. (some col.), ports (some col.); 28cm.
ISSN 0708-9635
For the professional musician working in the popular-music field, this is rather
more technical than other magazines of its type. Reviews of instruments,
musical analysis of musicians' styles and interviews are all of a high standard.
Full of advertisements and up-to-date business news, this is not for the
interested lay reader. It is distinctly orientated to the Canadian scene.

Cash Box. – New York: Cash Box Publishing, 1942–. Weekly. Currently. –
42p.: ill., ports; 35cm. ISSN 0008-7289

A trade weekly (very similar to *Billboard*) which is an advertising medium, trade newspaper and monitoring service aimed at people working in all parts of the music industry. There are detailed radio-programme schedules, record reviews, dozens of charts, news features and extensive advertisements for new releases.

Cat Talk. – Feltham, Middlesex: Technimedia, 1979–. Quarterly. Currently. – 47p.: ill., facsims, ports; 21cm.
For rock'n'roll and rockabilly enthusiasts, *Cat Talk* has an historical approach but definitely supports the contemporary revival. It is informative, and illustrated with excellent, rare portraits of artists. There are record and book reviews. An important feature is the section of advertisements of rock'n'roll clubs and record shops specializing in the genre. There is a section of readers' letters and an excellent news page.

Chart Songwords. – Hastings, Sussex: Dormbourne, 1978–. Monthly. Currently. – 16p.: ill. (some col.), ports (some col.); 26cm.
Formerly titled '*Discowords*'.
Evolving from the magazine *Disco 45* into the quarterly *Discowords*, this is a collection of lyrics of current pop songs with brief news items and illustrations. There are puzzles and competitions making it an attractive publication for the early teenager.

Chartbusters. – London: JPS Publications, 1980–. Monthly. Currently. – 24p.: ill. (some col.), ports (some col.); 30cm.
Brief articles for a teenage readership on a surprisingly wide range of pop and rock music. It comes with one pull-out poster and the cover can be adapted into another. Not very inspiring but bright and very popular with the age group.

Circus. – New York: Circus Enterprises, 1966–. Fortnightly. Currently. – 74p.: ill. (some col.), ports (some col.); 28cm. ISSN 0009-7365
A glossy competitor of *Creem* and *Rolling Stone*, aimed at a slightly younger group, *Circus* covers not only music but also a range of wider cultural subjects. The format is one of lengthy feature articles, well-presented illustrations, a programme of concert appearances and advertisements of all kinds. Recently *Circus* has emphasized heavy-metal music but it tends to change emphasis towards a particular fashion or trend at regular intervals.

Contemporary Keyboard: the magazine for all keyboard players. – Saratoga, California: G.P.I. Publications, 1975–. Monthly. Currently. – 96p.: ill., ports; 30cm. ISSN 0361-5820
Aimed at keyboard players of all styles and instruments, technique is the dominating theme. Record reviews, analysis of new equipment, interviews with musicians and criticisms of concert performances are all dealt with in an authoritative but except for the initiated, often impenetrable way.

Country Music. – New York: KPO Publications, 1972–. Monthly. Currently. – 68p.: ill. (some col.), ports (some col.); 30cm. ISSN 0010-4007

A well-produced, glossy monthly, this gives an overall survey of the country-music scene including interviews, features, record reviews and reports of concerts. The emphasis is towards the contemporary forms of country music and includes good coverage of country-rock artists.

Country Music People. – Dartford, Kent: Country Music Press, 1969–.
   Monthly. Currently. – 64p.: ill. (some col.), ports (some col.); 28cm.
   ISBN 0591-2237
A well-established British monthly which surveys the contemporary American country-music scene as well as including feature articles on historical background. Record reviews, club advertisements, lists of record˚releases and charts are all well presented. The domestic scene is, strangely, sadly neglected.

Country Music Review. – London: Concorde Distribution, 1971–. Monthly.
   Currently. – 48p.: ill., ports; 30cm.
With a wide scope, featuring contemporary surveys as well as historical analysis, this is regarded by many as the most authoritative and comprehensive journal in its field. Articles, record and book reviews and excellent interviews are complemented by a lively editorial section and interesting illustrations.

Country Music Round Up. – Lincoln: Country Music Round Up Publishing,
   1976–. Monthly. Currently. – 32p.: ill., ports; 42cm. ISSN 0140-5721
With an editorial written by Don Ford, chairman of the Country Music Association of Great Britain, this tabloid is a contemporary guide to the British country-music scene. There is a guide to concerts and club performances, record reviews and gossip.

Country Music World. – Arlington, Virginia: Dobson Publishing, 1972–.
   Monthly. Currently. – 60p.: ill., ports; 28cm. ISSN 0094-1344
Concerned with the more traditional and historical aspects of country music, including bluegrass music, this is an intelligent and well-produced publication. Record and book reviews are an important feature. The approach, in general, is serious but far from dull.

Country Style. – Franklin Park, Illinois: Country Style publications, 1976–.
   Bi-monthly. Currently. – 40p.: ill., ports; 38cm. ISSN 0364-0078
A tabloid with a circulation of 400,000, this gives a popular approach with brief record reviews, interviews and articles. Country rock and outlaw music are widely covered with features on such rock stars as Linda Ronstadt, Elvis Presley and Joe Ely. The design is attractive and the illustrations well produced.

Creem. – Birmingham, Michigan: Creem Magazine, 1969–. Monthly.
   Currently. – 66p.: ill. (some col.), ports (some col.); 28cm. ISSN 0011-1147
A well-produced magazine with the American scene covered in some depth for the younger, serious fan. Less informative than *Feature* and *Circus*, its obvious monthly competitors, it is well illustrated with lengthy, witty features, record reviews and a fascinating range of advertisements covering posters, equipment, back copies of the magazine, special issues, films and records.

Dark Star. – Northolt, Middlesex: Dark Star Publishing, 1975–. Bi-monthly.
Currently. – 64p.: ill., ports; 30cm.
Originating as one of the earlier British fanzines, originally concentrating on American West Coast music, *Dark Star* has developed into a very well-produced, glossy magazine with a more eclectic approach. There are still historical features but with increasingly more pieces on contemporary music. Regular news pages, gossip columns and illustrations make it an often absorbing publication.

Disco & Club News International. – London: Mountain Lion Productions, 1976–. Monthly. Currently. – 86p.: ill. (some col.), facsims (some col.), ports (some col.); 29cm.
Aimed at disc jockeys, would-be disc jockeys and others on the fringe of the world of discothèques, this is a trade magazine with an emphasis on equipment, with a great deal of space devoted to glossy advertisements. There are brief record reviews and international news of the disco scene as well as a more detailed survey of domestic developments.

Disco World. – Buffalo, New York: Transamerican Publishing, 1976–.
Monthly. Currently: 48p.: ill. (some col.), ports (some col.); 30cm.
A survey of the American disco scene, this features the currently in-vogue artists as well as fashionable, new dance routines. Interviews, record and film reviews are the main features, with occasional historical articles on the evolution of contemporary trends.

Disco World. – Leicester, Leicestershire: Petbridge, 1979–. Monthly.
Currently. – 44p.: ill. (some col.), ports (some col.); 30cm.
Aimed at the young disco dancer, this glossy monthly is concerned with disco competitions, stills from disco films and news of the British scene.

Down Beat. – Chicago, Illinois: Maher Publications, 1934–. Monthly.
Currently. – 70p.: ill. (some col.), ports (some col.); 28cm. ISSN 0012-5768
A long-established tradition of good production, a high standard of research and informative journalism make *Down Beat* a leading jazz magazine. Jazz–rock fusion is well covered as are some of the avant-garde movements in the new wave. There are fine record reviews, technical analyses and guides to instruments and instrumental and recording techniques.

Echoes. – London: Black Echoes Ltd, 1976–. Weekly. Currently. – 24p.: ill., ports; 42cm.
Formerly titled '*Black Echoes*'
Covering all styles of black music – soul, disco, two-tone, reggae, funk and, to a lesser extent, jazz – this has become a very popular weekly tabloid for the British fan. Record reviews, concerts and club dates and features are included as well as various charts including US soul albums, US soul singles, US jazz albums, British soul albums, British soul singles, funk, disco, reggae albums and a soul twelve-inch chart.

The Face. – London: Wagadon, 1980–. Monthly. Currently. – 64p.: ill.
  (some col.), ports (some col.); 31cm.
Founded by Nick Logan, former editor of *New Musical Express*, this venture is
independent of the major publishing groups. The result of his experience,
dedication and gamble is an excellent, glossy monthly magazine. Emphasis is
strictly on the contemporary music scene with lengthy, intelligent features and
interviews, analysis of current fashions, record reviews and letters. The quality
of production and the design of the publication give it a unique position among
current British magazines.

Feature. – New York: Feature Publishing, 1966–. Monthly. Currently. – 62p.:
  ill. (some col.), ports (some col.); 29cm. ISSN 0163-9404
  Formerly titled '*Crawdaddy: magazine of rock*'.
Until its takeover by the Feature Publishing Company in 1978, *Crawdaddy* was
an influential magazine which flirted with the American underground culture.
It has now opted for a more popular treatment of rock music and other areas of
popular culture. Well-written features, reviews and news items are interspersed with numerous illustrations and advertisements in a well-produced
format.

Flexipop. – London: Flexipop (Colourgold) Ltd, 1980–. Monthly. Currently. –
  32p.: ill. (some col.), ports (some col.); 30cm. Includes flexidisc
A teenage magazine with very brief articles, comic strips and many coloured
portraits this features a flexidisc reproduction of an unreleased recording of a
major current artist. It is low on information but very popular because of the
disc innovation.

Goldmine: the record collector's marketplace. – Fraser, Michigan: Arena
  Magazines, 1974–. Monthly. Currently. – 48p.: ill., ports; 22cm.
The aim of this magazine, primarily for American consumption, is to offer an
advertising medium for both collector and dealer but it also includes articles,
discographies and reviews of a high standard. A great deal of obscure information can be discovered here.

Gorilla Beat. – Essen, West Germany: I Go Ape Publications, 1979–.
  Quarterly. Currently. – 56p.: ill., facsims, ports; 21cm.
Published in Germany in English, this is a quarterly for record collectors and
those interested in British pop and rock nostalgia, as well as giving space to the
new wave. Informative essays, discographies and rare illustrations make
Gorilla Beat a curiously designed but informative view.

Gramophone Popular Catalogue. – Harrow: General Gramophone
  Publications, 1954–. Quarterly. Currently. – 72p.; 21cm. ISSN 0309-4359
  Formerly titled '*The Long Playing Popular Record Catalogue*'.
Arranged in two alphabetical sequences, artists and collections, this quarterly
covers a wide range of the new album releases of light, popular music and jazz.
Each addition accumulates through the year with full track and discographical

details and an index to record-company addresses. Tapes are included. Useful for its detail, it does not provide the service of *Music Master* or the classification of *New Records* or *New Cassettes*.

Greatest Hits. – Peterborough: EMAP National Publications, 1981–.
   Bi-monthly. Currently. – 63p.: ill. (some col.), facsims (some col.), ports
   (some col.); 30cm.
Pop and rock nostalgia since the mid fifties is the central theme with informative feature articles, record reviews and lengthy, rambling sections of news and gossip. Quizzes and competitions are notable features of this well-designed attempt to offer musical nostalgia in its widest context to a mass market.

Guitar Player: the magazine for professional and amateur guitarists. – Saratoga,
   California: GPI Publications, 1967–. Monthly. Currently. – 80p.: ill., ports;
   30cm. ISSN 0017-5463
With an extraordinarily wide international circulation, underlining the popularity of the instrument, *Guitar Player* is aimed at guitarists of all levels, assuming an interest and basic knowledge of technique. Interviews with musicians, studies of technique, record reviews and reviews of instruments are the main features. This is an excellent, intelligent and informative magazine in its field.

The History of Rock. – London: Orbis, 1982–. Weekly. 1st issue. – 36p.: ill.
   (chiefly col.), facsims (chiefly col.), ports (chiefly col.); 30cm. Projected to
   be in 120 parts
A colourful history of popular music since 1955, essays are included by most of the leading writers in the field. The projected work will reach approaching 4,000 pages and, although well produced and certainly useful, it will have cost the subscriber £80: a somewhat expensive historical source.

Hit Parader. – Derby, Connecticut: Charlton Publications, 1954–. Monthly.
   Currently. – 72p.: ill. (chiefly col.), ports (chiefly col.); 28cm.
   ISSN 0612-0266
Aimed at the teenage fan, *Hit Parader* was for many years the sole publication offering a simple but intelligent contemporary survey. News, record reviews, short extracts of gossip and interviews are included with a collection of over forty song lyrics, which has always been a feature of the magazine along with its coloured portraits.

Hot Press. – Dublin; London: Steady Rolling Publishing, 1977–. Fortnightly.
   Currently. – 32p.: ill., ports; 43cm.
An Irish-based fortnightly tabloid, *Hot Press* established a London office early on but not until 1981 was it widely distributed in Britain. Its coverage is wide, with no emphasis on any particular type of popular music but a definite desire to be current. Interviews, reviews and features are of a high standard. Book reviews are included. It is unlikely that *Hot Press* can seriously compete with the other established tabloids in Britain but it will not be because of its lack of good journalism or quality of production.

Hot Wacks. – Edinburgh: Wackadoo Publications, 1975–. Quarterly.
Currently. – 22p.: ill., ports; 30cm.
Well produced in a bold black and white format, *Hot Wacks* has developed from the basic fanzine style into a rock magazine of wide circulation. Including record-label discographies, interviews, reviews and lengthy, well-researched features, the emphasis is on critically important artists on which there is little generally known, as well as new insights on leading artists. Illustrations are well produced and the editorial notes intelligent.

Impetus. – London: Impetus Publications, 1977–. Bi-monthly. Currently. –
36p.: ill., ports; 30cm.
Devoted to the avant-garde areas of jazz and jazz–rock fusion, *Impetus* is a serious magazine with an editorial board composed of well-known young jazz musicians. Well produced, with good illustrations, it is for the educated enthusiast and not the casual reader. The record reviews and lengthy musical analysis are excellent regular features.

In the City. – London: In the City; Compendium Books, 1978–. Irregular.
Currently. – 27p.: ill., ports; 30cm.
Evolving from the poorly produced fanzine style of format, this is now better produced with a glossy, coloured cover. Articles and reviews have a refreshingly irreverent tone and tend to focus on emerging artists.

International Musician & Recording World. – London: Cover Publications,
1975–. Monthly. Currently. – 210p.: ill., ports; 30cm.
This is aimed at practising or potential musicians, record producers and engineers, and approaches music from a technical viewpoint. Features describe the careers and styles of musicians, recording tecniques and new developments. Selective record reviews are included but a lengthier section is devoted to reviewing musical instruments. Another unique section is devoted to news of recent recording operations, listing studios and artists working in them. There are hundreds of studio and equipment advertisements.

Jazz Journal International. – London: Pitman Periodicals, 1948–. Monthly.
Currently. – 52p.: ill. (some col.), ports (some col.); 30cm. ISSN 0140-2285
Formerly titled '*Jazz Journal*'.
A journal for the jazz enthusiast, often scholarly and always informative, this British monthly is well produced, including historical as well as contemporary feature articles. Record reviews and a diary of British club dates are excellent points. It is aimed at mainstream jazz followers, though jazz–rock fusion is well covered.

Kerrang! – London: Spotlight Publications, 1981–. Monthly. Currently. – 48p.:
ill. (some col.), ports (some col.); 28cm.
A glossy monthly magazine for heavy-metal devotees produced by journalists from *Sounds*. Features articles on leading performers with coloured portraits are mixed with notes on obscure provincial bands: an unusual, refreshing feature. The general attitude is somewhat moronic, reflecting the image heavy metal seems happy to project.

Keyboards and Music Player. – Watford: Fenchurch Designs, 1981–. Monthly.
   Currently. – 82p.: ill. (some col.), ports (some col.); 30cm.
For players of keyboard instruments of all kinds, particularly electronic. There
are reviews of equipment, letters, interviews with musicians, hints on playing
and a great many advertisements. There is considerable information on local
organ societies and articles of historical interest. This is strictly for the enthusiast.

Kicks. – London: Kicks International, 1981–. Monthly. Currently. – 64p.: ill.
   (some col.), ports (some col.); 29cm.
With coverage of the music scene for the teenage reader, there are also features
on a wide range of subjects of interest to the immediately post-adolescent age
group. Fashion, unemployment and advice on youthful relationships are all
included, as are record reviews and many well-produced photographs.

Living Blues. – Chicago, Illinois: Living Blues Publications, 1970–. Quarterly.
   Currently. – 58p.: ill., facsims, ports; 27cm. ISSN 0024-5232
Without the historical or nostalgic emphasis of most serious periodicals, the
theme of *Living Blues* is one of a thriving musical form. Reviews of records,
festival appearances and concerts are included with letters, news and an
editorial. There is coverage of rhythm & blues and the artists involved in the
more popular forms of the music.

Melody Maker. – London: IPC Specialist and Professional Press Ltd, 1926–.
   Weekly. Currently. – 64p.: ill., ports; 33cm. ISSN 0025-9012
The longest-established popular-music journal in the world, *Melody Maker*
was originally a trade paper for musicians, publishers and impressarios. In a
small way it remains a medium within the business and still includes advertisements for 'work' for musicians and equipment for sale. It has on the whole,
however, evolved into a weekly tabloid which treats the whole popular-music
scene with depth although, of late, jazz and folk have played secondary roles to
rock and pop. Lengthy feature articles, gossip, concert and club dates and
record and concert reviews are all of a generally high standard. It is regarded by
the younger element as a staid, traditional publication, though ironically it was
Melody Maker's journalists who supported and treated the new-wave movement with due respect and seriousness.

Music & Video Week. – London: Music Week, 1959–. Weekly. Currently. –
   27p.: ill. (some col.), ports (some col.); 37cm. ISSN 0032-1606
   Formerly titled '*Music Week*' and originally titled '*Record Retailer*'.
This is Britain's leading weekly trade paper with detailed charts, news, advertisements, information on radio airplay and features on the music business.
With the video boom, it is increasingly devoting more space to this side of the
entertainment industry, but is widely subscribed to by retailers, broadcasters
and librarians.

Music City News. – Nashville, Tennessee: Music City News Publishing, 1963–.
   Monthly. Currently. – 32p.: ill. (some col.), ports (some col.); 35cm.
   ISSN 0027-4291

This is a monthly country-music tabloid which is both current and informative. Record reviews, news articles, advertisements and interviews are the main features. It is informative, topical, well illustrated and full of behind-the-scenes Nashville gossip.

Music Express. – Willowdale, Ontario: Wembley Publications, 1977–.
    Monthly. Currently. – 50p.: ill., ports; 35cm. ISSN 0710-6076
This sole Canadian tabloid gives a good coverage of the contemporary Canadian rock and pop scene. Foreign artists touring the country are particularly well covered with criticisms of concert appearances and interviews. There are record reviews, an albums chart, lengthy features and brief news sections. It is far more like the British weekly music papers than any other North American publication.

Music Master. – Hastings, Sussex: John Humphries, 1974–. Monthly.
    Currently. – 48p.; 31cm. ISSN 0308-9347
The monthly supplements to this annual discographical guide offer an excellent, up-to-date selection tool.

Music World. – London: Multi-Language Publications, 1981–. Fortnightly.
    Currently. – 32p.: ill., ports; 38cm.
    Formerly titled '*Country Music World*'.
Originally focussing on the American country-music scene and showing some interest in rock'n'roll and rockabilly, *Music World* retains its original tabloid format and design but with its change of name has come a diversification in coverage. Country music is still well to the fore but, in addition, rock and pop are no longer completely ignored. There are country-music record charts, record reviews and a letters page. This is not a leading British music paper, and with its attempt to change its coverage, it may be difficult for a fortnightly to compete with the established weeklies.

Musician. – Gloucester, Massachussetts: Musician, 1978–. Monthly.
    Currently. – 110p.: ill. (some col.), ports (some col.); 28cm.
This is an excellent magazine which includes lengthy interviews with well-known artists, essays by the best of music writers, information on equipment and a few record reviews. The general approach is to offer a view of the life and business of the modern musician to those who aspire or dream of taking their place. The advertisements will also be of great interest to the initiated.

Musicians Only. – London: IPC Specialist & Professional Press, 1979–.
    Weekly. Currently. – 24p.: ill., ports; 30cm. ISSN 0143-6937
Led by a team of journalists who had previously been the stalwarts of the *Melody Maker*, *Musicians Only* aims to provide a trade paper for aspiring and professional musicians: once *Melody Makers*'s function. It has an impressive advisory board of musicians at the top of their fields. Reviews of performances, notes on new equipment, interviews and an extensive section of advertisements for instruments and engagements are the main features. The esoteric nature of the subject matter and use of language gives it a specialist but enthusiastic readership.

The New Cassettes & Cartridges. – St. Austell, Cornwall: Francis Antony,
   1970–. Monthly. Currently. – 15p.; 21cm.
Classified into eight sections: pop groups, jazz and blues, folk and country,
classical music and so on, like its fellow publication *The New Records*, this is
comprehensive and informative with full track and discographical details. It is a
widely used selection tool within the retail trade and libraries.

New Kommotion. – Wembley, Middlesex: Shazam Promotions, 1974–.
   Quarterly. Currently. – 67p.: ill., facsims, ports; 30cm.
   Originally titled '*Kommotion*'.
Emphatically concerned with fifties rock'n'roll and well produced, its appearance has been somewhat erratic. It is, however, well written, well illustrated
and informative, including work of genuine research but tending towards the
esoteric. Its particular interest is in highlighting lesser-known American artists
of the fifties. Discographical information is meticulously compiled and presented.

New Musical Express. – London: IPC Magazines, 1952–. Weekly. Currently. –
   50p.: ill., ports; 43cm. ISSN 0028-6362
Regarded as the serious weekly tabloid for the younger enthusiast, much of
NME is strongly tinged with an anti-establishment viewpoint. Lengthy
reviews, guides to concerts and club dates and record charts are all well
presented. *NME* covers all styles of pop, rock, black and country music, to a
lesser extent, with no particular bias but a generally provocative approach. It is
well established as Britain's leading weekly tabloid.

The New Records. – St. Austell, Cornwall: Francis Antony, 1951–. Monthly.
   Currently. – 15p.; 21cm.
Classified into eight sections: pop groups, jazz and blues, folk and country,
classical and so on, this little publication is comprehensive and informative with
full track and discographical details. It is widely used as a selection tool within
the retail trade as well as in libraries, along with its fellow publication, *The New
Cassettes & Cartridges*.

New Sounds New Styles. – London: EMAP National Publications, 1981–.
   Monthly. Currently. – 28p.: ill., ports; 28cm.
Published for the new romantic cult, this mixes fashion with music, featuring
the leading futuristic artists but including articles on a surprising range of
subjects. Nightclubs have a special place in the magazine with photographs of
particularly exotic members of their clientele. Pull-out posters are an occasional feature.

New York Rocker. – New York: Over the Hill Productions, 1976–. Monthly.
   Currently. – 56p.: ill., ports; 38cm.
Published monthly except for July and August, this New York-based tabloid
covers mainly new-wave music and its cultural scene. Features, interviews,
record, concert and cinema reviews are all of a very high standard. Although
other forms of popular music are occasionally covered, it is difficult to antici-
pate in which direction *NYR* will evolve.

Noise. – London: Spotlight Publications, 1982–. Fortnightly. Currently. – 48p.:
     ill. (some col.), ports (chiefly col.); 28cm.
Covering the whole range of pop and rock music in a glossy, popular style,
there is a strong emphasis on featuring lesser-known, potential stars. Record
reviews are superficial but the illustrations are well presented and there is a
section featuring the lyrics of selected recent songs and a programme of
forthcoming major tours.

Not Fade Away. – Prescot, Merseyside: Vintage Rock'n'Roll Appreciation ,
     Society, 1976–. Quarterly. Currently. – 52p.: ill., facsims, ports; 30cm.
A serious quarterly, *Not Fade Away* treats the study of rock'n'roll's early
history with a reverence which is often amusing. The features are informative
and intelligent, with rare photographs and reproductions of record sleeves.
There is an almost sinister preoccupation with deceased artists and their
commemoration, but for the real enthusiasts of classic rock'n'roll this is
essential reading.

Pop Pix. – London: Pop Pix, 1981–. Monthly. Currently. – 48p.: ill. (chiefly
     col.), facsims (chiefly col.), ports (chiefly col.); 30cm. Includes flexidisc
A glossy monthly for the young fan filled with coloured portraits and brief non-
critical comment. There are superficial record reviews, a puzzle page, the lyrics
of contemporary songs, brief interviews and advertisements for clothes,
records, posters and magazines. An additional merchandising ploy is the
inclusion of a flexidisc record of unreleased recordings of contemporary pop
artists.

Popular Music Magazine. – Dayton, Ohio: Lorenz Publishing, 1970–.
     Bi-monthly. Currently. – 64p.: ill., ports; 32cm.
     Formerly titled '*Best of Popular Music*'.
With a view to cover all styles of popular music, this is well produced with
features, interviews, record reviews and charts. The articles tend to be informative but lacking serious criticism.

Pow! – London: Scanspeed, 1981–. Monthly. Currently. – 31p.: (some col.),
     ports (some col.); 21cm.
Well produced with a glossy presentation and some excellent colour portraits,
this is aimed at the young fan. The articles, which focus on a small selection of
current stars in each issue, are informative and suitable for the young teenage
age group.

The Record. – Boulder, Colorado: The Record, 1982–. Monthly. Currently. –
     52p.: ill., ports; 35cm.
A highly-regarded new American tabloid, not unlike *Rolling Stone* in its
serious approach but exclusively concerned with music. Well-written features
and record reviews, interviews and critical essays make this a very promising
publication.

Record Business. – London: Record Business Publications, 1977–. Weekly.
     Currently. – 22p.: ill., ports; 33cm.

In the style of American trade papers such as *Billboard* and *Cashbox* and Britain's *Music & Video Week*, this provides up-to-date business news, record reviews, a wide range of charts and features on technical developments as well as airplay schedules and advertisements. *Record Business* is yet to diversify its interest into video.

Record Collector. – London: Record Collector, 1979–. Monthly. Currently. –
  72p.: ill., ports; 21cm. ISSN 0034-1568
A valuable source of information for the collector of mainstream pop and rock records with little information about the more obscure artists. There are lengthy feature articles, complete listings of specific labels and discographies with valuations which often seem rather overestimated. There is a chart of the top five hundred rarest singles, auctions and sales of records. For the first seven issues *Record Collector* included facsimile editions of the original monthly *Beatles Book*.

Record Exchanger. – Orange, California: Vintage Records, 1969–.
  Bi-monthly. Currently. – 52p.: ill., facsims, ports; 28cm. ISSN 0557-9147
Particularly good for its coverage of fifties rhythm & blues and rock'n'roll, as well as unusual illustrations, features and reviews. There are lengthy discographies and price listings. Aimed primarily at record collectors, this is a useful source of obscure information.

Record Mart. – Rayleigh, Essex: Record Mart, 1968–. Monthly. Currently. –
  38p.: ill., facsims, ports; 22cm.
With no text but a selection of portraits and reproductions of posters and record labels, all types of popular music on record are listed for sale and auction. Vaguely classified into styles and arranged by artist, *Record Mart* is possibly the most popular of this type of magazine.

Record Mirror. – London: Spotlight Publications, 1954–. Weekly. Currently. –
  57p.: ill. (chiefly col.), ports (chiefly col.); 30cm. ISSN 0034-1576
  Formerly titled '*Record and Show Mirror*' and '*Stage and Record Mirror*'.
Aimed at readers interested in the more commercial areas of pop and rock music with an unashamed emphasis on the record charts, this weekly magazine has maintained its position over the years. Taking over its main, long-established competitor *Disc and Music Echo* in 1976, it now includes coloured illustrations as well as record reviews, interviews, features and a wide range of record charts. In 1982 its format changed from a newspaper, tabloid design to that of a glossy teenage magazine.

Record Review. – Los Angeles, California, 1976–. Bi-monthly. Currently. –
  64p.: ill., ports; 28cm.
Classified into broad musical categories: classical, rock, country, jazz, folk and so on this comprises nothing but record reviews with occasional features on particular artists. It is an excellent guide to record selection, although reviews tend to be a little belated.

Record World. – New York: Record World Publishing, 1946–. Weekly.
    Currently. – 54p.: ill. (some col.), ports (some col.); 33cm. ISSN 0034-1622
The third American trade weekly, after *Billboard* and *Cashbox*, *Record World*
is an advertising and trade-news medium. There are detailed radio programme
schedules and a wide variety of charts. Articles on current news topics are
included as are record reviews and technical information.

Relix. – New York: Relix Magazine, 1972–. Bi-monthly. Currently. – 64p.: ill.,
    ports; 28cm. ISSN 0146-3489
    Formerly titled '*Dead Relix*'.
A magazine based on nostalgia, originally of the sixties, the seventies are now
included as well as early rock'n'roll. Intelligent articles, reviews and interviews
are well represented with many unusual illustations. Each edition features a
particular band or artist, style or period and develops that theme.

Right On!. – Hollywood, California: Laufer Publishing, 1971–. Monthly.
    Currently. – 70p.: ill., ports; 28cm.
Attractively produced, this focusses on black music with well-written articles
and reviews for teenagers with a more serious approach to their music.

Rock and Soul Songs. – Derby, Connecticut: Charlton Publications, 1956–.
    Monthly. Currently. – 30p.: ill., ports; 28cm. ISSN 0035-743X
    Formerly titled '*Rock and Roll Songs*'.
Apart from illustrations and usually one feature article, this comprises lyrics of
current popular songs. It is similar in format to *Song Hits*.

Rock Legends. – Hastings, Sussex: S B Publications, 1982–. Monthly.
    Currently. – 32p.: ill. (some col.), ports (some col.); 30cm.
Taking a different artist or group each month (number 1 was Elvis Presley and
number 2 the Beatles) the intention is to provide an extensive biographical
encyclopedia. The result is a glossy production with excellent illustrations but
superficial text.

Rock Scene. – Bethany, Connecticut, 1973–. Eight issues per year. Currently. –
    72p.: ill., ports; 30cm. ISSN 0090-3353
A mass-circulation magazine, it is straightforward in approach without the
wider interest or counterculture stance of some of its competitors. The record
reviews, interviews and features are well written, intelligent and lacking
pretentiousness.

Rolling Stone. – New York: Straight Arrow Publishers, 1967–. Fortnightly.
    Currently. – 68p.: ill. (some col.), ports (some col.); 35cm. ISSN 0035-791X
Beginning its life in San Francisco at the height of the flower power period,
Rolling Stone has unquestionably been the most influential journal of popular
culture since its inception. Its list of contributors includes most of the major
names in the journalism of modern popular music. Jann Wenner continues the
editorship with an editing team of Jon Landau, Dave Marsh, Greil Marcus,
Paul Nelson, Robert Palmer and Ben Fong-Torres, to name just a few.

Although lengthy record and concert reviews, analysis of musical trends, biographies and interviews are included, *Rolling Stone* has always treated music as part of a wider popular culture and is often highly political in theme. As with all well-established and successful publications, *Rolling Stone* is regarded by many as too establishment and too pretentious, but as a fortnightly tabloid, it still gives the most intelligent, best-written and comprehensive coverage of today's culture from an American standpoint.

Sailor's Delight. – Mill Hill, London: Sailor Vernon, 1979–. Quarterly.
   Currently. – 64p.: ill., facsims, ports; 26cm.
For collectors of blues and rhythm & blues records, there are informative articles on artists and record labels concerned with these styles of music. Record auction and sales advertisements are an important feature for the collector with reproductions of record labels and some good illustrations of obscure artists. The editorial style is refreshingly humorous with a regular strip cartoon and an elaborate series of in-jokes scattered throughout the text.

SFX. – London: SFX Publications, 1981–. Fortnightly. Currently. – 1 sound
   cassette (60 min.): 1⅞ips, stereo.
First appearing in November 1981, *SFX* is produced by Mel Smith and Griff Rhys Jones of the BBC's Not the Nine O'Clock News television show. It is packaged on an attractive magazine-size board (30cm) with illustrations of artists involved. It includes lengthy interviews, reviews of new releases with comment by guests and extracts from the music together with ten minutes of advertising. It obviously lacks the extensive coverage of a tabloid but it is intelligently written and the production is of a very high standard. *SFX* was initially successful, though it remains to be seen whether a serial in such a format can establish itself.

Sing Out. – New York: Sing Out Magazine, 1950–. Bi-monthly. Currently. –
   62p.: ill., ports; 28cm. ISSN 0037-5624
Born in the early days of the folk protest movement, *Sing Out* remains the premier American journal in the folk field, with record and concert reviews, interviews with leading musicians, scholarly essays and discussions of technique. Singer-songwriters are often covered as part of the American folk scene.

Slash. – Los Angeles, California: Slash, 1980–. Monthly. Currently. – 104p.:
   ill., facsims, ports; 37cm.
A West-Coast-orientated monthly tabloid. *Slash*'s emphasis is on the new-wave scene but included is a wide range of musical and cultural topics. Record, book and concert reviews and essays on current authors as well as musicians are notable features.

Smash Hits. – Peterborough, Cambridgeshire: EMAP National Publications,
   1978–. Fortnightly. Currently. – 40p.: ill. (some col.), ports (some col.);
   28cm.

For the young teenager, there are features, a gossip column, charts, competitions, record reviews and a selection of song lyrics. Well produced, it is informative and has created a place for itself in the British magazine market not far behind the established weeklies and claims to have overtaken them.

Shout. – London: Clive Richardson, 1966–. Monthly. Currently. – 48p.: ill., ports; 28cm. ISSN 0583-1296
Formerly titled '*Soul*', '*Soul Music Monthly*' and '*Soul Music*'.
This privately published magazine has established itself over the years as an authoritative source of information on soul, rhythm & blues and black music in general. It includes well-written, deeply researched articles, as well as exhaustive discographies. It is an excellent publication making a regular contribution to knowledge in its specific field.

Song Hits. – Derby, Connecticut: Charlton Publications, 1942–. Monthly. Currently. – 36p.: ill., ports; 28cm. ISSN 0038-1365
Mainly a monthly collection of current song lyrics, there are some brief features, illustrations and news items. It is very similar in format to *Rock and Soul Songs*.

Soul. – Los Angeles, California: Soul Publications, 1975–. Fortnightly. Currently. – 48p.: ill., ports 26cm.
An intelligently written tabloid, this is the prime source of information on the West Coast soul scene. Features, concert and record reviews, interviews and information on club and concert performances are included. Its coverage of the wider world of soul music is also very good and if obtainable, it is a very useful publication on its particular subject.

Soul Sounds. – New York: Albun Publishing, 1973–. Monthly. Currently. – 50p.: ill., ports; 30cm.
A well-designed and attractively produced magazine; included are regular columns, interviews, record reviews and lengthy features. Advertisements for clubs and concert tours are a significant feature.

Sound International: incorporating Beat Instrumental. – Croydon, Surrey: Link House Publications, 1978–. Monthly. Currently. – 66p.: ill., ports; 29cm. ISSN 0144-6037
Although *Beat Instrumental* was established in 1966, when *Sound International* arrived the two became instant competitors along with *International Musician*. *Sound International* finally took over *Beat Instrumental* at the end of 1980. Its claim is to be a magazine 'written for musicians by musicians' and its list of contributors is indeed impressive. Technical in content, the majority of features discuss types of instruments, amplification and techniques of playing. There are impressive reviews of new equipment, including detailed analysis far above the level of the lay reader. Well designed and produced, it flourished with an obviously constant market.

Soundmaker. – London: Cover Publication, 1982–. Weekly. Currently. – 48p.: ill., ports; 43cm.
Appearing in December 1982, this weekly tabloid attempts to cover both the

news of contemporary music, like the traditional British music press, and, at the same time, provide another magazine for musicians. There are charts, interviews, reviews, concert advertisements, technical articles and an equipment price guide. Exactly how this new venture will fit into the already full market is difficult to see. It is likely that survival will be difficult as this specialist field is well covered by *Musicians Only* and the general approach by the long-established tabloids, *Melody Maker*, *New Musical Express* and *Sounds*.

Sounds. – London: Spotlight Publications, 1970–. Weekly. Currently. – 60p.: ill., ports; 43cm.
A popular tabloid which has changed its interest since its inception from early-seventies progressive rock to current heavy metal. Other styles of popular music are not ignored but are secondary. A range of charts is included: Reggae, Euro-rock, Alternative, Disco, US singles, albums and the charts of five and ten years ago. Record and concert reviews are lengthy. There is a useful guide to club dates and concerts.

Sounds Fan Library. – London: Spotlight Publications, 1982–. Monthly. Currently. – 48p.: chiefly col. ill., ports (chiefly col.); 30cm.
Describing itself as a 'quality fanzine', each month's issue features a different heavy-metal band with little text and well-presented coloured illustrations. It is not a poster magazine, being more substantial and really a lavish complement to *Sounds* and *Kerrang!*.

Swing 51. – Sutton, Surrey: Swing 51 Publications, 1979–. Quarterly. Currently. – 52p.: ill., ports; 30cm.
This covers a wide variety of music in the folk idiom including the folk revival, bluegrass, traditional, some country music and some contemporary writers. Articles are particularly well written. There are features on artists, historical pieces and excellent record reviews. Production is tasteful with well-chosen illustrations and good layout.

Tiger Beat. – Hollywood, California: Laufer, 1977–. Bi-monthly. Currently. – 98p.: ill., ports; 28cm. ISSN 0040-7380
Originally a music magazine featuring teenage idols for very young lady fans, this has deteriorated into a collection of portraits and articles on the prettiest of the young television actors and singers with little about music.

Time Barrier Express. – Yonkers, New York: Time Barrier Express, 1975–. Bi-monthly. Currently. – 72p.: ill., facsims, ports; 29cm, ISSN 0099-0396
For students of the history of rock'n'roll, coverage includes not only rhythm & blues, rockabilly and rock'n'roll in its early forms but also influential artists of the sixties. The editorials are poignant, features intelligent and informative, and illustrations excellent. In addition, there are regular record and book reviews and contributions from readers.

Top Pops. – London: Scanspeed, 1981–. Monthly. Currently. – 12p.: ill. (chiefly col.), ports (chiefly col.); 30cm.
A glossy, coloured monthly for the young fan built around a large pull-out poster. Slightly more than a regular poster magazine. In a competitive market this is not one of the best.

Trax: the London music paper. – London: Girl About Town Magazine Ltd.,
  1981–. Fortnightly. Currently. – 48p.: ill. (some col.), ports (some col.);
  36cm.

Launched in Februrary 1981, the aim of *Trax* was to be a fortnightly tabloid
fusing together a current survey of the British musical scene with a distinct
London bias. The quality of the writing, content and production is very high.
News, reviews, features, interviews and lengthy advertisements of performances are all of an excellent standard. In addition to major clubs and concerts
there is a guide to small venues including pubs, and a guide to London's
cinemas. Whether *Trax* can survive is debatable. Although the editor claims
there is a need for an independent, London-orientated music paper, the fact is
that in a small country like Britain all the music press is London-based and
London-biased.

Trouser Press. – New York: Trans-Oceanic Trouser Press Inc., 1974–.
  Monthly. Currently. – 56p.: ill., facsims, ports; 28cm. ISSN 0164-1883
  Formerly titled '*Trans-Atlantic Trouser Press*'.

A fanzine focussing on the British music scene and aimed at a local New York
circulation, *Trouser Press* has established itself as an important American
magazine with a wide interest and some excellent feature writing. There are
current record reviews as well as historical essays, interviews and analyses of
current trends.

Variety. – New York: Variety inc., 1905–. Weekly. Currently. – 96p.: ill.,
  Ports; 41cm. ISSN 0042-2738

A weekly tabloid bulging with information on all aspects of the entertainment
industry, *Variety* is a trade newpaper with an overall perspective. Cinema,
television and the theatre have as much space as music, but the latter is still well
covered with reviews, international charts of all styles of music, airplay
programme schedules and business news. Emphasis is firmly on the commercial trends in entertainment rather than the artistic.

Vintage Record Mart. – Rayleigh, Essex: Vintage Record Mart, 1970–.
  Bi-monthly. Currently. – 24p.: ill., facsims, ports; 22cm.

A record-collector's magazine listing discs for sale and auction, this is poorly
produced with no additional text or editorial. Coverage is mainly pre-1955 but
some records of around the mid fifties do creep in.

Zigzag. – London: Mentor Bridge, 1969–. Monthly. Currently. – 58p.: ill.,
  ports; 30cm.

Founded by Peter Frame in the style of the American underground magazines
of the late sixties, it is regarded by some as the original British fanzine. It was
always of a high standard of production with excellent photographs, but over
the years it has evolved into a glossy monthly with a wide circulation and
general availability. The *Zigzag* organization has a record label and is a leading
concert-promotion agency. Originally primarily preoccupied with American
West Coast and other underground forms of music, emphasis is now firmly on
the British new wave, although articles appear on a wide range of music with
historical essays and excellent concert and record reviews.

PERIODICALS WHICH HAVE CEASED PUBLICATION IN THE UK

This category of material is elusive indeed. Few publishers keep archives and to discover dates of origin and cessation has required some vigilance.

Aimed as a brief listing, descriptive information is as complete as has been possible.

Beat Instrumental. – London: Campillos, 1966–1980. Monthly. 165th issue. – 62p.: ill., ports; 29cm.
Taken over by *Sound International* in 1980.

Beat Monthly. – London: Beat monthly, 1963–1964. Monthly. ill., ports; 24cm.
A glossy magazine for the fan.

Big Beat. – London: Big Beat 1964–. Monthly. ill., ports; 34cm.

Black Music. – London: IPC Business Press Information Services, 1973–1975.
Monthly. 1st issue. – 64p.: ill. (some col.), ports (some col.); 30cm.
Later evolving into *Black Music and Jazz Review* in 1978.

Country. – London: Hanover Books, 1972–1973. Monthly. 1st issue. – 30p.:
ill., ports; 30cm.
A short-lived publication which failed to estabish itself, being too early for the country-music boom.

Country People. – London: IPC Magazines, 1979–1980. Monthly. 1st issue. –
67p.: ill. (some col.), ports (some col.); 28cm.
A glossy monthly with a popular standpoint.

Cream. – London: IPC Magazines, 1971–1973. Monthly. 1st issue. – 58p.: ill.,
ports; 30cm.
A serious magazine with a team of excellent journalists, it featured high-quality writing and intelligent, critical reviews. It unfortunately could not sustain a stable circulation.

Disc. – London: Go Magazines, 1958–1976. Weekly. ill., ports; 36cm.
In the early sixties *Disc* was one of the leading weekly tabloids. It took over *Music Echo* in 1967 and, for a while, was titled '*Disc and Music Echo*'. It survived with decreasing circluation until it was taken over by *Record Mirror* in 1976.

Disco 45. – St. Leonards, Sussex: Trevor Bolton, 1969–1980. Monthly. 1st
issue. – 16p.: ill., ports; 26cm.
This evolved into *Disco 45 Songwords*.

Easy Listening. – London: Cardfont Publishers, 1973–1974. Monthly. 1st issue.
– 84p.: ill. (some col.), ports (some col.); 30cm.

Fan: your super pin-up album. – London: IPC Magazines, 1972–. Weekly. 1st
   issue. – 32p.: ill. (chiefly col.), ports (chiefly col.); 30cm.
Consisting mainly of colour portraits with poor linking text, this was for the
young fan.

Folk Review. – London: Hanover Books, 1968–1979. Monthly. Vol. 3, No. 5. –
   32p.: ill., music, ports; 30cm.
A scholarly monthly, this featured essays on folk-music research as well as
current revival artists and a few contemporary singers.

Friends. – London: T. F. Much Co. Ltd, 1969–. Monthly. 2nd issue. – 47p.: ill.,
   ports; 28cm.

Fusion. – Boston, Massachusetts: New England Scene Publications; London:
   Fusion, 1970–1971. Fortnightly. 1st issue. – 36p.: ill., ports; 45cm.

Hitsville U.S.A.. – Bexleyheath, Kent: Tamla Motown Appreciation Society,
   1965–1967. Monthly.
A rare publication, this featured exclusively Tamla Motown artists.

Kent Beat. – Rainham, Kent: Kent Beat, 1965–. Monthly.

Let It Rock: the new music review. – London: Hanover Books, 1972–1973.
   Monthly. 1st issue. – 70p.: ill., maps, ports; 30cm.
This was a high-quality attempt to emulate the American monthlies. Sadly it
received a poor following.

Listen Easy. – Hitchin, Hertfordshire: B.B. Enterprises, 1972–1973. Monthly.
   1st issue. – 40p.: ill., ports; 28cm.

Mersey Beat. – Liverpool: Mersey Beat, 1961–1964. Fortnightly. ill., ports;
   33cm.
Billy Harry's classic Liverpudlian music paper, this had much to do with the
promotion of the Beatles and other Liverpool beat groups.

Merseybeating. – Bristol: Merseybeating, 1964–1965. Monthly. ill., ports;
   20cm.

Music Business Weekly. – London: Longacre Press, 1969–. Weekly. 2nd issue.
   – 32p.: ill., ports; 45cm.

Music Echo. – London: Music Echo, 1962–1967. Weekly. ill., ports; 36cm.
A tabloid which could not compete with the mass-circulation weeklies and was
taken over by *Disc* in 1967.

Music Maker. – London: Longacre Press, 1966–1968. Monthly. ill., ports;
   29cm.
Lasting seventeen issues, this fell between a fan magazine and serious monthly.

Music Scene. – London: Fleetway House, 1972–1973. Monthly. 1st issue. –
55p.: ill. (some col.), ports (some col.); 31cm.
Popular in approach and glossy in production.

Music World & Superstar. – London: Surridge, Dawson and Co. Ltd, 1979–.
Monthly. 2nd issue. – 48p. ill. (some col.), ports (some col.); 21cm.

National Rockstar. – London: IPC Magazines, 1976–1977. Weekly. 1st issue. –
40p. ill., ports; 42cm.
A chart-orientated, well-produced weekly, it unfortunately failed to compete
successfully with the established tabloids.

New Music News: the independent rock weekly. – London: Choice Publishers
Ltd., 1980–. Weekly. 1st issue. – 32p. ill., ports; 31cm.
Appearing in May 1980 to fill the vacuum created by an IPC Magazines strike,
this very good substitute for *Melody Maker* and *New Musical Express* lasted
only four issues. It collapsed with the return of the established weekly tabloids.

Pop Records. – London: Pop Records, 1956–. Monthly. ill., ports; 29cm.

Pop Shop and Teenbeat. – Heanor, Derbyshire: Albert Hand Publications,
1964–. Monthly. ill., ports; 29cm.
Formerly titled '*Pop Shop*'.

Pop Show International. – Heanor, Derbyshire: Albert Hand Publications,
1966–1967. Monthly. ill., ports; 28cm.
A chart-orientated pop monthly, this included some excellent illustrations, but
very poor writing.

Pop Star Weekly. – London: Spotlight Publications, 1979–. Weekly. 1st issue. –
40p.: ill. (some col.), ports (some col.); 41cm.

Pop Weekly. – Heanor, Derbyshire: Pop Weekly, 1962–1965. Weekly. 1st
issue. – 20p.: ill., ports; 29cm.
This was a well-produced weekly, packed with photographs. The text makes
amusing reading, very patronizing but informative.

Popster: the new poster magazine. – London: Plant News (Mayfair) Ltd, 1972.
Monthly. ill., ports; 43 × 23cm.

Popswop. – London: Spotlight Publications, 1972–1975. Weekly. 1st issue. –
ill. (some col.), ports (some col.); 30cm.
Featuring the idols of the teenyboppers, it faded with its subject.

The Radio-One Story of Pop: the first encyclopedia of pop. – London: Phoebus,
1973–1974. Weekly. 1st issue. – 34p.: ill. (chiefly col.), ports (chiefly col.);
30cm.
This was a well-produced tie-in, in 26 parts, with a BBC radio series.

Rave. – London: Newnes, 1964–. Monthly. ill., ports; 28cm.

The Record Buyer. – Manchester: World Distributors, 1969–. Monthly. 1st
issue. – 64p.: ill., ports; 28cm.

Record Collector: monthly guide to your kind of music. – London: Hanover
Publications, 1972–. Monthly. 1st issue. – 28p.: ill., ports; 42cm.

Record Review:. – Croydon: Link House, 1970–. Monthly. 1st issue. – 66p.: ill.,
ports; 28cm.

Rhythm & Soul U.S.A.. – Bexleyheath, Kent: FARBS, 1966–. Monthly. ill.,
ports; 22cm.

Rock On!. – London: IPC Magazines, 1978–1980. Monthly. 1st issue. – 32p.:
ill. (some col.), ports (some col.); 30cm. ISSN 0141-7177
A glossy monthly, this neither attracted a purely fan nor a serious readership.

Rock stock. – London: New English Library, 1974–1977. Monthly. ill. (some
col.), ports (some col.); 28cm.
This was colourful, well produced and popular in approach.

Scream: top pop parade of the stars. – London: Brown; Watson, 1964–.
Quarterly. ill., ports; 25cm.

Shout!: Scotland's music and fashion weekly. – Glasgow: Peebles Publications,
1970–. Weekly. 2nd issue. – 16p.: ill., ports; 47cm.

Songsmith. – Stoke on Trent: Dave Wrench and Adrian Crosby, 1977–.
Quarterly. 1st issue. – 14p.: ill., music; 31cm.

Soul Cargo. – Newcastle-under-Lyme, Staffordshire: C. Savory, 1977–.
Bi-monthly. 1st issue. – 2, 24p.: ill., ports; 26cm.

Strange Days: the British rock paper. – London: Top Sellers Ltd., 1970–1971.
Fortnighly. 1st issue. – 32p.: ill., ports; 42cm.
With high-quality writing and presentation, this had a wide approach, not
unlike *Rolling Stone.*

Street Life. – London: Walker-Sheehan Publishing, 1975–1976. Fortnightly. 1st
issue. – 56p.: ill. (some col.), facsims, ports (some col.); 40cm.
Ceasing in early 1976, *Street Life* with its excellent reviews and essays on a wide
range of social topics was a brave attempt to emulate *Rolling Stone.*

Superpop. – London: Superpop, 1979–. Weekly. 1st issue. – 28p.: ill., ports;
42cm.
A colourful, teenage magazine.

Supersonic. – London: IPC Magazines, 1976–1978. Monthly. 1st issue. – 32p.:
ill. (some col.), ports (some col.); 30cm.
A tie-in with a television teenage pop show.

Superstar. – London: Superstar, 1972–1979. Monthly. 1st issue. – 40p.: ill.,
ports; 21cm.
A glossy magazine for the fan, this merged with *Music World* in 1979.

Teen Beat Monthly. – Heanor: Derbyshire: Albert Hand Publications,
1964–1965. Monthly. ill., ports; 19cm.
Merged with *Pop Shop* in 1965.

Thursday: N. Ireland's newspaper for today's generation. – Belfast: Morton
Publications, 1976–. Weekly. ill., ports; 44cm.

Top Boys of the Week Photonews. – London: City Magazines, 1964–. Weekly.
ill., ports; 36cm.

Trick. – London: Wishcastle Ltd., 1977–. Monthly. 1st issue. – 24p.: ill., ports;
42cm.

Words. – London: Felix McGlennon, 1957–1980. Monthly. June 1980. – 16p.:
ill., ports; 26cm.
Formerly titled '*Record Song Book*'.
The first lyric-based British publication, production was poor and, with no
policy of including advertising, it faded in 1980. Its survival had been miracu-
lous.

8.2 FAN MAGAZINES

Devoted to individual artists, these are professionally produced magazines
which have, or had, a wide circulation.

There are examples of one-off publications in magazine format focussing on
a particular artist or group, but the publications listed below have all sustained
a reasonable life.

Arrangement is alphabetical by artist.

ABBA

Abba Magazine. – London: Stafford Pemberton, 1977–. Monthly. Currently. –
32p.: ill. (some col.), ports (some col.); 21cm. ISSN 0141-8394
A well-produced monthly for the Abba fan, full of trivial information, discographies, letters and photographs.

THE BEATLES

Beatlefan. – Decatur, Georgia: The Goody Press, 1977–. Bi-monthly.
  Currently. – 32p.: ill., facsims, ports; 28cm. ISSN 0274-6905
This is an excellent, authoritative, international publication for Beatle fans.
Contributors include: Nicholas Schaffner, Wally Podrazik, Bill Harry, Fred
Lark and other experts on the group. An independent magazine, there are
reviews, letters, recently uncovered facts, essays and a wide range of advertise-
ments for memorabilia, records and publications.

The Beatles Book. – London: Beat Monthly, 1963–1969. Monthly. 1st issue. –
  32p.: ill., ports; 21cm.
Fading out in 1969, *The Beatles Book* was the first of the British small-format
monthlies devoted to a particular British artist or group. Aimed at the young
fan, it was always well produced and illustrated. It is interesting to compare the
style of the early issues with the later and note the evolution in style and
attitude to the readership.

The Beatles Book: appreciation society magazine. – London: Beat
  Publications, 1976–. Monthly. Currently. – viii, 32p, xvp.: ill., ports; 21cm.
  ISSN 0261-1600
A reissue, in facsimile, of the original *Beatles Book* of the sixties with an
additional editorial, features on contemporary Beatle facts, discographies and
advertisements for collectors. Well-reproduced, identical to the original with
the new information surrounding the facsimile nucleus, this is full of information and of good nostalgic value.

Beatles Unlimited. – Alphen aan de Rijn, Holland: Beatles Unlimited, 1974–.
  Bi-monthly. Currently. – 22p, ill., ports; 22cm.
Published in English by the Dutch organization devoted to the maintenance of
the Beatles and their folklore. Interviews, essays, letters, reviews of books and
records and rare photographs are the main features. For the real enthusiast.
The production is unfortunately not at all good.

CASSIDY, DAVID

The Official David Cassidy Magazine. – London: David Cassidy Magazine,
  1971–1975. Monthly. 1st issue. – 32p, ill. (some col.), ports (some col.);
  21cm.
Fading out in 1975, this small-format magazine is full of portraits of the young
singer at his prettiest. The text is suitable for its early-teenage audience, as is
the selective information included.

GERRY AND THE PACEMAKERS

Gerry and the Pacemakers Monthly. – London: Gerry and the Pacemakers
  Magazine, 1964–1965. Monthly. 1st issue. – 32p.: ill., ports; 21cm.

The first magazine to follow the format of *The Beatles Book*, this monthly was well produced and remains the largest body of information on the group. It was aimed at the young fan.

MANILOW, BARRY

The Pure Magic of Barry Manilow. – London: Arlington Press, 1982–.
Monthly. Currently. – 48p.: ill. (some col.), ports (some col.); 21cm.
Well produced with coloured illustrations, interviews, recollections of his career and the loving tributes from fans, this has achieved unaccountably a wide circulation: as unaccountable as the wide appeal of its subject.

THE OSMONDS

Osmonds! World: the official magazine of the Osmonds. – London: IPC
Magazines, 1973–1976. Monthly. 1st issue. – 32p.: ill. (some col.), ports (some col.); 30cm.
Ceasing publication in mid 1976, this large-format monthly for Osmonds fans was well produced with full-page colour portraits and up-to-date news of the family's activities.

THE POLICE

The Police Official File. – London: DPG, 1980–. Monthly. Currently. – 32p.:
ill. (some col.), ports (some col.); 21cm.
Current news on the group's activites, tours, recording schedule, letters and photographs, this is for the young fan in the tradition of the small-format monthlies.

PRESLEY, ELVIS

Always Elvis. – Heanor, Derbyshire: The Official Elvis Presley Fan Club
Worldwide, 1977–. Bi-monthly. Currently. – 20p.: ill., ports; 24cm.
Largely made up of advertisements, descriptions and reviews of Elvis Presley books, records and other merchandise, there are a few brief articles; this is concerned with Elvis's legend, not his music.

Elvis Monthly. – Heanor, Derbyshire: Albert Hand Publications, 1960–.
Monthly. Currently. – 47p.: ill., ports; 18cm.
Remarkably, this continues to be published with a wide circulation, having experienced a revival since the singer's death. Included each month (along with the news items for fans, letters, book and record reviews and advertisements) are a wide range of informative articles by authorities on Presley, as well as memoirs by associates and friends.

Elvis Presley Journal. – London: Elvis Presley Fan Club, 1957–1959. Monthly.
   1st issue. – 32p.: ill., ports; 29cm.
The earliest incarnation of the Elvis Presley Fan Club in Britain produced this
monthly, which was in the form of a tabloid. It seems to have ceased publication by mid 1959 but for its time was informative and well produced.

Elvisly Yours: official photo album and catalogue. – London: Elvisly Yours,
   1980–. Quarterly. Currently. – 35p.: ill., facsims, ports; 30cm.
Including a fine collection of photographs, this is mainly an advertising medium
for a wide range of Elvis merchandise from badges and busts to posters,
clothing and books.

Twenty Five Years the King. – Heanor, Derbyshire: The Official Elvis Presley
   Fan Club Worldwide, 1980–1981. Monthly. 1st issue. – 48p.: ill. (some col.),
   ports (some col.); 28cm.
The last publication appearing in 1981, this was planned to be a well-produced,
regular tribute to Elvis with coloured portraits, quizzes and poorly written
articles. It was also a vehicle for advertisements for Elvis memorabilia.

THE ROLLING STONES

Rolling Stones Book. – London: Beat Publications, 1964–1968. Monthly. 1st
   issue. – 32p.: ill., ports; 21cm.
The third production of Beat Publications in the small format of *The Beatles
Book*, the *Rolling Stones Book* ceased publication in 1968. It contained
portraits, articles by the musicians, letters and general news on the group. It
was claimed to have been edited by the 'Stones for their fans'.

STEVENS, SHAKIN'

Shaky: fanmag. – London: Arlington Press, 1982–. Monthly. Currently. – 48p.:
   ill. (some col.), ports (some col.); 21cm.
Poorly written but well produced with many illustrations, this is a straightforward magazine for the fan. There is little mention of Shakin' Stevens' music
but much trivial background concerning his personal preferences on a variety
of important subjects such as pets and the colour of women's hair.

8.3 FAN CLUB PUBLICATIONS

The vast majority of successful artists in the field of popular music eventually
acquire a fan club. The nucleus of such an organization is usually a small group
of people who wish to be associated, albeit vicariously, with the glamour of the
star and who may even have contact with their idol.
   Such clubs may organize functions, provide badges, T-shirts and other
mementos and also, usually, some kind of newsletter or magazine. Such

publications are generally poorly produced efforts and not commonly available. They may, however, be the biggest sole source of information on an artist.

There are no general collections of this literature and one must attempt to discover the current fan-club secretary: itself a difficult task.

The best approach is to contact the artist's current record company. The clubs of popular stars do advertise in the music press, but this approach will be successful only for a limited number.

8.4 FANZINES

Fanzine is a much misused term which has come to describe a very specific kind of publication. It is not the publication of a fan club or a commercially published magazine.

It is a magazine which is privately published, often with erratic frequency; usually poorly produced; often drawing its copy from its readers; and which has a limited circulation, being available only by post from a private address or from a few record shops, bookshops, stalls and street sellers who deal in such 'alternative' literature. A publication ceases to be a true fanzine when it fails to comply with any of the above criteria.

Nigel Cross in his very good article, 'A survey of fanzines' (*Brio*, autumn / winter, 1981) fails to point out that very often fanzine status is a stage in the evolution of new, emerging magazines. *Blues Unlimited*, *Swing 51*, *Hot Wacks*, *Dark Star*, *In the City*, *Impetus* and *Zigzag*, for example, all regarded by Cross as fanzines, are now well-established wide-circulation magazines which had such humble origins (*see* section 8.1).

Moreover most fanzine editors are not, as widely believed, subversives consciously offering an alternative to the 'straight' music press, but are aspiring, enthusiastic journalists anxious to see their creations in print. They may, however, be enthusiasts with an almost missionary zeal aiming to forward the message of a particular style of music or artist.

When *Zigzag* (*see* section 8.1) began its life in May 1969 it was a true, if rather well-produced fanzine, and stood alone, soon evolving into a magazine proper. It was followed by a few others but it was not until 1976 and the emergence of the punk movement that the form really came into its own with the sudden appearance of hundreds of publications, mostly terribly written and poorly produced. Mark Perry's *Sniffin' Glue* (*see* Chapter 5, Punk: *The bible*), was the leader in the field and set the subversive style of the time, which was soon to fade.

The boom seems now to have passed but a core of publications still survives. Mainly poorly produced and badly written, a few exceptions exist which are seriously edited, well written and thoughtfully produced. There is a curious fraternity between the editors of the likes of the examples cited below. They widely review and advertise each other's publications with no sense of competition and genuine enthusiasm.

There is a useful annotated list of fanzines in Nigel Cross's article which he does not claim to be complete: this would, indeed, be an impossible task. A fuller, current list, *The Fab Fanzine List*, may be obtained from Rough Trade Records, 202 Kensington Park Road, London W11, England. This is poorly produced with no annotations or addresses, but does include American as well as British titles and is by far the most comprehensive available.

Often impossible to track down, varying dramatically in quality, to paraphrase: when fanzines are good they are very good, but when they are bad they are unreadable.

These examples are some of the best.

Bam Balam. – Flat 1, Catellau, Dunbar, East Lothian, Scotland: Brian Hogg, 1975–. Irregular. Currently. – 32p.: ill.,'ports; 30cm.
Originating as an offshoot of *Hot Wacks* magazine, the subject matter focusses on the sixties with excellent articles on the much-neglected or forgotten artists of the time. The tone is literate, almost intellectual, but the production tends to be rather poor and the layout messy. Because of the originality of the research which has gone into many of its issues, it is a noteworthy publication of its kind.

A Bucketful of Brains. – 25b Ridge Road, London N8, England: Bucketful of Brains, 1979–. Irregular. Currently. – 26p.: ill., ports; 30cm.
Edited and published by Nigel Cross, *Bucketful of Brains* is a well-produced, glossy-covered magazine with the editor's strong interest in the West Coast music of the sixties always evident. The articles are intelligent and well researched with interviews which would be regarded as scoops for the big music papers and are certainly real achievements for a small-circulation publication. The new wave is not totally neglected, however, but the bands which are covered have their own musical roots in the sixties with a strong emphasis on the electric guitar and its playing. In general a good fanzine with great expectations.

Comstock Lode. – 51 Bollo Lane, Chiswick, London W4, England: John Platt, 1978–. Quarterly. Currently. – 28p.: ill., ports; 30cm.
A wide-ranging publication which tends to include jazz, poetry, visual arts, West Coast rock, punk and rock'n'roll, often in a single issue. Gathering much of its copy from its literate readership, this is well written and exceptionally well selected and edited by John Platt. The result is a small-circulation, privately published magazine, printed in black and white with well-produced illustrations and a good layout. By the above definitions this is a fanzine but it is quite outstanding in the field.

Omaha Rainbow. – 10 Lesley Court, Harcourt Road, Wallington, Surrey SM6 8AZ, England: Peter O'Brien, 1973–. Quarterly. Currently. – 24p.: ill., ports; 31cm.
One of the longest surviving and most successful of all fanzines, *Omaha Rainbow* is well produced with strong graphics and good, but austere, black and white layout. It concentrates on the styles of music in the country rock, folk-rock area which is neither rock music nor mainstream country and, therefore, touched on but not featured by the wide-circulation music press.

Each issue features a particular artist or band with briefer pieces of news items and record reviews. Well written and illustrated, this is a fine example of an independent journal, just qualifying as a fanzine.

Outlet. – 33 Aintree Crescent, Barkingside, Ilford, Essex, England: T. H. Faull, 1978–. Bi-monthly. Currently. – 38p.: ill., ports; 30cm.
Typewritten and photocopied, each issue of *Outlet* includes a mixture of articles on₁ usually obscure artists and groups as well as a section of discographies. In general the discographies are either listings of the releases of otherwise generally unheard of local or foreign labels or are of little-known artists or bootlegs of the better known. A fanzine in the classic sense, for the aficionado of the esoteric who reject any music with a wider appeal as commercial and therefore unworthy of interest.

INDIVIDUAL ARTISTS

Fanzines focussing on individual artists are another specific kind and are produced by extraordinarily dedicated individuals. Examples have appeared featuring artists from David Bowie to the Stranglers, with *Cosmic Dancer*, begun in 1977, a fanzine featuring Marc Bolan, being one of the longest surviving.

It is Bob Dylan, however, who offers some of the most unusual examples because of the intense interest in that artist's work and the general treatment of him as a serious writer.

Endless Road: a Dylan magazine. – Kingston upon Hull, Humberside: Endless Road Magazine, 1981–. Irregular. Currently. – 38p.: ill., ports; 26cm.
Well produced for a private publication; as well as concert reviews, song analyses and interviews there are some essays written by over-zealous fans who regard their idol as prophet and bard. Nevertheless, this is a fascinating magazine available only from the Wanted Man Office, 23 Winchester Road, Manchester, England.

Occasionally: a magazine about Bob Dylan. – 23 Windsor Road, Pattingham, Wolverhampton, England: BD Occasionally, 1980–. Irregular. Currently. – 50p.: ill., ports; 21cm.
Essays by readers, detailed listings of songs performed on tours, reviews and obscure trivia, some of which is extremely spurious – this is a poorly produced, photocopied effort. Recently it has assumed a poor-quality coloured cover.

The Telegraph. – 23 Winchester Road, Manchester, England: The Bob Dylan Information Office, Wanted Man, 1981–. Monthly. Currently. – 40p.: ill., ports; 21cm.
Packed with answers to the most obscure questions on Bob Dylan, letters from fanatics, essays, song analyses, book and record reviews, this is for the

obsessional fan. Produced by photocopy, it is available only direct from the Wanted Man Office in Manchester. There is a fascinating 'bookshelf' section offering obscure, privately published, usually duplicated, publications and magazines.

Wanted Man: the Bob Dylan information office. – 23 Winchester Road,
     Manchester, England: Wanted Man, 1981–. Quarterly. Currently. – 24p.:
     ill., ports; 21cm.
This is a genuine attempt to act as an information-exchange service for Dylan fanatics. Letters, newly uncovered facts, a book and record sale service, a contact page and bootleg tapes page, all create an atmosphere of exclusiveness for the subscriber. An interesting feature is the listing of privately published pamphlets and fanzines advertised by readers for other readers. The concept of this is unique but the result not so different from some other fanzines, simply a little more esoteric.

8.5 POSTER MAGAZINES

The 'pin-up' portrait of the stars to adorn the walls of doting fans is as old as popular entertainment and, obviously, increased with the likeness made possible by photography. From Lillie Langtry to Rudolph Valentino, through the thirties to Betty Grable, the pin-up was established. Full-page coloured portraits appeared in publications such as *Photoplay* and in annuals, for example, the *Daily Express Film Book*, and such portraits were certainly removed and stuck on walls and in albums.

As popular music took over from film in supplying the majority of idols and sex symbols, the same pattern continued.

In the mid sixties, following the pop-art (op-art) movement during the swinging London period, the full-size wall poster, 100cm × 50cm and sometimes bigger, came into its own. The obligatory wall coverings of every bedsitting room and chic Chelsea mews cottage, not to mention millions of teenagers' bedrooms throughout the world, posters of the period included a range of subjects from Pre-Raphaelite masterpieces and exotic pieces of psychedelia to the classics of Toulouse Lautrec and larger-than-life portraits of rock stars.

Throughout the seventies posters sustained a constant popularity and large fold-out examples occasionally appeared in a wide range of music magazines.

In the late seventies the poster magazine first appeared. Here the aim of the publication is the poster; any biographical narratives or supplementary illustrations are purely incidental. Most publishing houses have produced examples, usually of one-off enterprises to capitalize on the sudden success of a new act.

More recently series have come into existence. *Amazing Magazine, Star-Shots* and *Pop Gallery Magazine* are all published by Time-Scan, Unit 53, Ardleigh Road, London N1 4HZ, England. Here large-format coloured posters of the most popular current stars are folded and stapled into the appearance of a conventional magazine. When the staples are removed, the main poster is 120cm × 80cm and the reverse includes a series of other portraits and text on the artists. This form of magazine appears to be on the increase and is certainly popular with young, early-teenage pop fans.

8.6 PERIODICALS INDEXES

As articles on popular music, artists and their work appear in a wide range of publications, they are naturally indexed by the major indexing services. *British Humanities Index* and the American *Reader's Guide to Periodical Literature* naturally may be used as a general source.

Specialist services, however, are sadly lacking. *Music Index* provides coverage of only the major, established periodicals but is, nevertheless, useful. The scholarly *RILM* abstracts includes no popular-music interest and only *Popular Music Periodicals Index* approaches a useful coverage. An up-to-date edition of this is long overdue.

Annual Index to Popular Music Record Reviews 1972 – . – Metuchen, New
  Jersey; London: Scarecrow Press, 1973–. Annual. 1977 / by Dean Tudor and
  Linda Biesenthal. – 1979. – 604p; 23cm. ISBN 0-8108-1217-7.
  ISSN 0092-3486
Divided into twelve sections: rock, country, jazz, blues and so on, then by performer or anthology title, this cites all published reviews of albums and cassettes. Included are almost 10,000 reviews for around 5,000 recordings. There is an indication of the authority of the reviewer and of the opinion offered. Unfortunately the above-cited edition is the most recent appearance of this excellent annual.

* *The Music Index.* – Detroit, Michigan: Information Coordinators, 1949–.
  Monthly with annual cumulations. Currently. – Vol. 34 – No. 12. December
  1982. – 184p.; 27cm. ISSN 0027-4348
This covers over 300 journals, mainly on serious music but including a number of pop, rock and country-music titles. Book reviews are included and the citations are classified. Coverage is patchy: for example, the American periodical *Crawdaddy* is included but its competitor *Creem* is not. Similarly Britain's *Melody Maker* is included but *New Musical Express*, *Record Mirror* and *Sounds* are not. Another criticism levelled at *Music Index* is its slowness of appearance. Cumulations are up to three years behind.

Noyce, John Leonard
  Rock music index / compiled by John Leonard Noyce and Alison Skinner. –
  Brighton: Noyce, 1977. – 15p.; 30cm. (pbk.)
John Noyce is a leading figure in the British 'librarians for social change' group. This attempt to create a periodicals index is interesting but unsatisfactory in that it includes just nineteen periodical titles and then not all issues are covered. The periodicals are in the most part fanzines and therefore difficult to acquire in any event. Produced itself in a poor, duplicated format, it has failed to reappear.

Popular Music Periodicals Index. – Metuchen, New Jersey; London: Scarecrow Press, 1973–. Annual. Latest edition; 1976/compiled by Dean Tudor and Andrew D. Armitage. – 1976. – xxviii, 349p.; 23cm. ISBN 0-8108-0927-3
A well-produced guide to over fifty of the major English-language periodicals from the whole popular-music field. There is a classified, subject arrangement with an author index. Record reviews are not included.

Glossary

Popular music and its surrounding culture has generated more than a little slang, 'hip' jargon and technical words and phrases since 1955. It has been a direct aim when preparing this bibliographical guide to use such terminology only where it has been impossible to escape it, and then to provide an explanation and context in the introductory notes.

This glossary will provide a further aid for the uninitiated, with additional notes in a convenient alphabetical arrangement.

A & R man. Originally came from the phrase 'artist and repertoire man'. Such a person's function was to match artists to suitable material. Later this role was taken by record producers, many of whom were A & R men. Nowadays A & R men are concerned almost exclusively with finding talent and the commercial logistics of record releases, rarely playing any creative role.

AOR. Adult-orientated rock, a term of the eighties proving the coming of age of the music. It recognizes, at last, that music accepted as part of the rock genre is aimed at an adult market who have grown up with the music. It can describe music of the Eagles, Fleetwood Mac or Dire Straits. Often used as a term of derision by young punks.

A side. The main or most heavily promoted side of a single record. There are exceptions but this tends to be the hit side.

Acid rock. Music of the psychedelic era beginning in 1966 and continuing until the end of the decade. It was aimed to mimic the drug experience of LSD or acid. The Grateful Dead, early Soft Machine and early Pink Floyd are examples. It is also called psychedelic rock.

Afro rock. African rock music, rhythmically complex with much percussion. Osibisa has become the best-known exponent.

Album. Usually a collection of recordings originally issued on a twelve-inch, $33\frac{1}{3}$ revolutions per minute disc, but now also on cassette tape.

Amplifier. A device for magnifying weak electronic signals from a musical instrument or microphone, increasing the original sound and projecting it through a loudspeaker. Amplifiers are used with all electrically amplified and electronic instruments.

Art rock. Until the mid sixties popular music had few pretensions to being an art form. Bob Dylan and the Beatles changed that. The term now refers to

479

musicians who while using electric instruments work in the framework of traditional classical or avant-garde forms. The result is often pretentious. Examples include Emerson, Lake and Palmer, Genesis, King Crimson, Rush, Yes and Sky.

B side. Also known as the flipside, this is the unpromoted side of a single record, regarded as having less commercial potential than the A side.

Ballad. In modern popular music this refers to slow or mid-tempo love songs. 'Ballad singers' generally describes middle-of-the-road artists such as Engelbert Humperdinck, Tom Jones or Barbra Streisand.

Baroque. In popular music, describes over-ornate arrangements.

Beat boom. Period from 1963 to 1966 when, in the wake of the Beatles, British music was dominated by vocal, instrumental groups.

Beat music. The vocal, instrumental groups which included and followed the Beatles after 1963 were described as beat groups. In America beat music was described as the British invasion. Gerry and the Pacemakers, the Dave Clark Five, the Rockin' Berries, the Searchers and the Hollies are notable examples.

Black music. Any music emerging from the black community, including spirituals, gospel, blues, jazz, rhythm & blues, soul, reggae, Tamla Motown, Phillie and disco.

Bluebeat. A West Indian style of popular music which was a forerunner of reggae with basically the same rhythmic pattern.

Blues. A form of black American musical expression, the blues originated in the rural south as a twelve-bar form derived from working songs. By the twenties the blues had reached the cities and the traditional country blues had found a new expression in the urban blues. The electric guitar greatly influenced its development into a driving, exciting form. In many ways the blues is a matter of emotional content and is the basis out of which jazz and rock'n'roll have grown.

Blues revival. In Britain in the mid sixties a number of groups emerged, notably John Mayall's Bluesbreakers, Fleetwood Mac and Chicken Shack, who attempted to reproduce the Chicago style of electric, urban blues.

Boogie. Originating from the jazz form boogie-woogie, boogie bands play debased forms of blues and rhythm & blues. Notable bands include the Allman Brothers, Lynyrd Skynyrd and Status Quo.

Bootlegs. Surreptitiously made or acquired recordings, unofficially produced and sold without the agreement of the artist or recording company. Sometimes of poor quality but often surprisingly well-produced, the recording industry claims to lose millions of pounds of revenue because of such activities.

Break. A solo instrumental passage or a move away from the general structure of the song. Often used with the instrument performing e.g. guitar break, drum break.

British blues. Appearing in the mid sixties, led by John Mayall and the Bluesbreakers and followed by Chicken Shack and the original Fleetwood Mac, this movement developed out of the British rhythm & blues groups of the early sixties. The result was a popularized version of Chicago blues which had become very popular by 1968 and led on to heavy-metal music. Also known as the blues revival.

British invasion. This American phrase describes the period between 1963 and 1966 when the Beatles had broken all previous barriers and led the way for British artists to be commercially successful in the American charts. Groups included the Kinks, the Who, Gerry and the Pacemakers, the Rolling Stones, the Searchers, Freddy and the Dreamers and many more. In Britain this period is called the Beat Boom.

Bubblegum. First coined in the late sixties, this originally described a form of American music which aimed at the lowest common denominator of the record-buying public. Including nasal voices, moronic lyrics and a heavy monotonous beat, the 1910 Fruitgum Company and Ohio Express are good examples. Bubblegum is now a term of derision describing lightweight, commercially orientated pop music.

Burlesque. American variety show, distinct from vaudeville because of its inclusion of striptease and more risqué material.

C & W. Abbreviation for country and western, now generally termed country music.

Cabaret. Originally described music played in a restaurant with dancing. Generally used now to describe the pseudo-sophisticated style of solo vocalists for a middle-aged audience.

Charts. The trade paper or radio station listings of the current week's most popular or bestselling gramophone records. Rated numerically, 'top of the charts' or a 'number one record' is the aim.

Chicago blues. Developed after the Second World War by musicians from Louisiana and Mississippi who travelled north to look for work. Evolving from the rural, Delta blues, it incorporated electric guitars, bass, drums and a heavier beat. Howlin' Wolf, Muddy Waters and Sonny Boy Williamson are important exponents. Current rock band line-ups and instrumentation are derived from this form.

Composer. A writer of music. A composer will often write the tune to match a lyricist's words. Many modern songwriters write both words and music.

Concept album. Describing an album unified by a theme whether instrumental, compositional, narrative or lyrical. The Who's rock operas Tommy and Quadrophenia are obvious examples, as are the Eagles' Desperado and the Kinks' Arthur. The Beatles' Sgt. Pepper's Lonely Hearts Club Band is a less obvious concept but is regarded as such because of its musical cohesion. If popular music aspires to become art, its albums will be conceptual.

Country music. Originally country and western but now simply country, this has become one of the most popular forms of music in the world. Originally based on the white folk music of the southern and southwestern USA, and often said to have emerged as a result of the work of the Carter family and Jimmie Rodgers in the late twenties, country music's popularity was spread by radio shows such as the Grand 'Ole Opry. Over the last fifty years it had increasingly left its folk origins and become a positively commercial form. More recently it has been influenced by rock music.

Country rock. A fusion of the rock'n'roll beat and country accents and themes, this form appeared in the late sixties led by the Byrds, Flying Burrito Brothers and Commander Cody. As with all fusions, it is difficult to know where the rock ends and country begins and vice versa.

Cover version. A recording of a song by a performer other than the original. It was a common practice in the fifties and sixties to issue a cover version when, for example, British artists would copy recordings of successful American songs and capture the sales in the United Kingdom.

Cut. To make a record or, as a noun, cut can be used to describe a recording or track of an album. It can also describe the crucial production of disc pressing from the original tape.

Deleted. A record no longer in the record company's catalogue, equivalent to out-of-print.

Delta blues. Coming from the Mississippi River delta region stretching from Memphis to Louisiana, this region produced many of the greatest bluesmen including Robert Johnson, Charley Patton, Muddy Waters and Howlin' Wolf.

Delta rock. Moody, blues-based rock music from New Orleans and the Mississippi delta area. Notable artists include Dr John and Leon Russell.

Demo. A recording made for demonstration purposes to sell a song or the talents of artists hoping to obtain a recording contract or work.

Detroit sound. In black music, this describes the sound of Tamla Motown, which fused adult rhythm & blues with teenage themes and was a dominant form in the sixties. As a white American sound it refers to heavy rock groups of the seventies such as the MC5, Grand Funk Railroad and Ted Nugent, often thought to be influential in the development of heavy-metal music.

Disc jockey. A radio broadcaster who links the playing of records with comment, gossip and analysis of varying relevance and intelligence. DJs are a very influential factor in the promotion of new records and changing trends. They have had this position of power in the USA for almost fifty years, but only since the mid sixties in Britain.

Disco. An abbreviation of the word discothèque, referring originally to clubs which sprang up during the Twist dance craze of the early sixties. In the seventies this term described records designed to be played in discothèques. It features heavy rhythmic patterns and sophisticated, slick production. In the late seventies this became a dominant form led by such artists as the Bee Gees, Earth, Wind and Fire and Tavares.

Doo-wop. Used to describe a style of black rhythm & blues vocal groups of the fifties who often used vocal arrangements with repeated phrases such as 'doo-wop'. The ornately arranged vocal choruses were popularized by the so-called street-corner groups of New York and Philadelphia. Sh' boom by the Chords is often regarded as the very first rock'n'roll recording and was in the doo-wop style.

Double-track. A studio device of recording the same part more than once on two tracks of the tape. The result is a chorus of sound and may be used for voice or instrument, especially guitar.

Dub. In reggae, instrumental backing tracks with an accentuated bass. Originally vocalists chanted their own improvised words over the recording. Dubs are now popular in their own right.

Easy listening. A phrase used by retailers to classify middle-of-the-road, light music and cabaret and even the blandest of muzak: music which is both undemanding and inoffensive. It is used often as a derogatory term for anything from James Last and Max Bygraves to Neil Diamond.

Electronic music. Not music played on electrically amplified instruments but avant-garde music in which composers work with artificially produced sounds using synthesizers and tone generators. Pioneers include such groups as Kraftwerk and Tangerine Dream but many of the new-wave, futuristic artists can be described as playing electronic music: for example, Gary Numan, the Human League and Ultravox.

EP. A 45 r.p.m., seven-inch disc which includes more than two pieces of music. In the fifties and sixties usually four songs were included. Few EPs appeared during the late sixties and early seventies but there was a renaissance with the new wave.

Europop. The Eurovision Song Contest is an established annual institution in which each country is represented by a popular song and the other countries vote the one they consider to be the best. Often, successful pop singers represent their country: Sandie Shaw and Cliff Richard for Britain, for example. In 1974 Abba won the contest and transformed it by providing their own excellent pop song and modern presentation. Europop was born, led by Abba and followed by hundreds of less successful international pop groups.

Fanzine. A reaction against the established, commercial music press, the fanzine is an independent publication produced by fans for fans. Usually crudely printed in typescript in its early stages, some fanzines have evolved into finely published 'established' periodicals, for example *Zigzag* and *Bomp*. Regularity is no characteristic, however. Some are irregularly produced and some are one-off publications.

Feedback. Howl produced when an instrument's pick-up or microphone comes too near a loudspeaker thus amplifying its own signal. Used as a controlled device by guitarists such as Jimi Hendrix, Brian May and Pete Townshend.

Fender. Leo Fender designed three of the most important electric guitars: the Stratocaster, Telecaster and Precision Bass.

Festival. An outdoor concert, sometimes of several days' duration. The Cambridge Folk Festival and Newport Jazz Festival led to rock festivals like Altamont, Woodstock and Monterey.

Flash. Also known as techno-flash, this is technically complex, very fast playing of any instrument. In the early seventies rock bands such as Yes, with the guitar playing of Steve Howe and keyboard playing of Rick Wakeman, would be described in this way. Such an approach is regarded by many as too contrived and lacking in emotion.

Flipside. Also known as the B side, the unpromoted side of a single record regarded as having less commercial potential.

Folk music. Music of the oral rather than written musical tradition. Since the eighteenth century considerable work has gone into the collection of folk songs by musicologists such as Cecil Sharpe and the Lomax Brothers. In America, more recent singer-songwriters such as Woody Guthrie and even Bob Dylan, singing of contemporary, often political themes, are called folk singers because of the tradition, rather than their style or content.

Folk revival. Beginning around 1958 on American campuses and in city coffee houses, there was a move among the young towards more socially and politically involved music. Civil rights was the significant movement of the day. The Kingston Trio's revival of the song Tom Dooley in 1958 was followed by hundreds of other revived folk songs. Pete Seeger, Bob Dylan, Joan Baez and Judy Collins are just a few artists to emerge from the revival and become singer-songwriters in later styles.

Folk rock. First appeared in 1965 with Bob Dylan's album Bringing It All Back Home, which introduced an electric sound. The Byrds recorded Mr Tambourine Man from that album and it became a massive success and established the form. Songs were lyrically intelligent with political or protest themes using folk-style harmonies and electric instruments. Groups included the Byrds, the Buffalo Springfield, the Turtles and the Fairport Convention. They have been highly influential in singer-songwriters. In Britain Steeleye Span and the Fairport Convention electrified traditional British folk songs and were highly successful during the seventies with their British folk rock.

45. A 45 gramophone record is a seven-inch disc with one recording on each side, revolving at 45 r.p.m. Also known as a single.

Frontman. Usually the singer of a band or group but sometimes the musical centre of the ensemble, often a guitarist and sometimes a keyboard player.

Funk. Originated from the adverb *funky*, descriptive of low-life sights, sounds and smells of black culture. Funk now describes music that is played in a soul-music style with mellow, syncopated rhythm arrangements or more generally black percussion-based instrumental music displaying some complexity.

Fusion. The abbreviated term for jazz–rock, the fusion of jazz and rock forms.

Futuristic. Electronic-based music generally using a series of synthesizers and drum machines. Stage dress is space age with lyrics concerned with machines, computers and the mechanistic aspects of modern life and the anticipated future. Gary Numan and Kraftwerk are the best examples.

Fuzz. A distortion effect operated by a pedal which alters the sound of an electric guitar.

Gibson. A make of guitar including the famous SG and Les Paul models. The latter was designed by the guitarist Les Paul and early models are now treasured collector's terms.

Girl groups. Projecting the classic adolescent fantasies of the early sixties, these (usually black) female vocal groups emerged from gospel and rhythm & blues style traditions. The Shirelles, the Crystals, the Dixie Cups, the Ronettes and the Angels were leading examples produced by Phil Spector with his massive Wall of Sound production system. Later groups evolving from these early examples are the Supremes and even the Three Degrees of the seventies.

Glam rock. An early-seventies trend which included a variety of styles of music. The performers' presentation had a similar highly staged approach. Costumes, make-up and a camp attitude are the cohesive theme. David Bowie, Marc Bolan, Roxy Music and Queen fall into this mode.

Glitter rock. A British pop-music trend of the early seventies aimed at a young teenage audience. The music was simple, featuring heavy droning rhythms and sometimes a twin drum sound, but it was the stage dress of the artists with their sparkling costumes, make-up and enormous, platform-soled boots which made it a cohesive trend. Gary Glitter, the Glitter Band, Sweet and, to some extent Slade, were leading artists.

Gold disc, record. Originally a gold-plated, playable replica of a record selling over one million copies was presented by the record company to its artist. The criterion by which a record is judged to have reached 'gold' status has become confused. One million dollars' value of sales of albums is regarded as 'gold' in the USA. 'Platinum' status is a far newer concept of one million actual album sales.

Gospel. Descending from the spiritual, gospel arose from the upsurge in fundamentalist churchgoing in black urban communities in the twenties. The call-and-response style is a notable feature. It evolved into rhythm & blues and soul music in their purest forms, the gospel roots remaining prominent. Sam Cooke and Aretha Franklin were gospel stars before singing more secular material.

Groupie. Young women, or sometimes men, who offer their sexual favours to members of rock bands. In search of reflected glory, some groupies collect their stars in a competitive fashion.

Gutbucket. Crude rhythm & blues originally played in a cheap saloon or gutbucket, where the music first emerged.

Hammond organ. A revolutionary electric keyboard instrument developed by Laurens Hammond in the thirties. It includes a double keyboard and foot pedals and resembles a conventional organ.

Hard rock. Encompassing most blues-based rock with a driving forceful rhythm.

Harp. Slang term to describe a harmonica or mouth harp.

Hawaiian guitar. A type of steel guitar played with a metal bar or steel. It is tuned differently from the Spanish-style guitar and this enables the musician to play variable-interval notes or quarter tones.

Headbangers. Followers of British heavy-metal groups of the seventies and eighties and also of Status Quo. Young men, dressed in denims, leather jackets and long hair, who take cardboard guitars to concerts to mime to their heroes. The name comes from their dancing style and lunatic antics.

Heavy metal. First coined by Lester Bangs from certain passages in Burrough's *Naked Lunch*, originally this term described sluggishly rhythmic heavy rock of the late sixties and early seventies. Black Sabbath, Grand Funk Railroad and even early Led Zeppelin are good examples. They all basically distorted the blues, using very powerful amplification. Since the late seventies there has been a so-called heavy-metal revival in Britain with such bands as Whitesnake, Rainbow, Motorhead and Gillan. With a following of largely working-class young men, known as headbangers, the style flourishes.

Hit, Hit record. A gramophone record, a single or album, which sells in sufficient quantities to appear in the weekly chart listings of bestsellers.

Hook. A catchy part of a song which sticks in the listener's mind and therefore sells records. A hook can be part of the lyric or melody line.

Hot-rod music. Originating in southern California in the early sixties and made famous by Jan and Dean and the Beach Boys, hot-rod music and its more important partner, surf music, celebrated the middle-class, Californian teenage lifestyle of cars, girls, surfing, beach parties and high school.

Hype. Originating from 'hyperbole' and meaning the excessive salesmanship generally employed in the music business to do anything from launching a new artist to releasing a record.

Improvise. To perform spontaneously, to play music with no written arrangement. It includes the creating of tunes as well as extemporization upon the melody line or chord changes of a known tune.

Instrumental. Music without the inclusion of the human voice.

Jah music. Reggae music specifically involved with Rastafarianism.

Jam, Jam session. Informal, improvised performances. Originally a jazz phrase, it was adopted in the sixties by rock musicians.

Jazz. A twentieth-century form of music originated by black musicians and built around improvisation.

Jazz funk. Not a true jazz form but highly rhythmic, black American dance music of the late seventies appearing during the disco craze. It is associated with a multi-racial following and its fans are known as the Family.

Jazz rock. Although rock music developed from rhythm & blues, which itself had jazz origins, by the mid sixties jazz players were being influenced by rock. Miles Davis, Gary Burton and others began using rock instrumentation. The result of such experimental musical line-ups and improvisatory electrified music by such people as Chick Corea, Larry Coryell and Frank Zappa is now called jazz rock or fusion.

Jesus rock. Rock music first appearing in America in the late sixties with explicitly Christian themes. It was the time of the post-Hippie period when the youth of America's West Coast was searching for new cults. The Children of God and similar extremist Christian groups inspired the movement. The Byrds and Jesus Children are exponents of this short-lived trend.

Ju ju. Term sometimes used for contemporary African rock music.

Keyboards. Traditional keyboard instruments, the piano and organ, have become just part of a current keyboard player's armoury, which will include a range of electric pianos, acoustic piano, mellotron, organ and synthesizers able to repro-duce the full harmonic sounds of an orchestra.

LA sound. Los Angeles possessed no specific style of music until the early sixties and the emergence of the surf music of Jan and Dean and the Beach Boys. Later, folk rock was born in LA with the likes of the Mamas and the Papas and the Byrds. By the seventies singer-songwriters such as Randy Newman, Jackson Browne, Joni Mitchell and Neil Young made it their centre. More recently the soft rock styles of Fleetwood Mac, Bread and the Eagles have evolved in the city's studios.

Lick. A short instrumental phrase usually played between melodic phrases. Usually associated with guitarists.

Light music. Falling somewhere between popular music and serious, classical or art music. Mantovani's swirling string arrangements or James Galway's flute interpretations of popular songs are examples.

Light show. Complex lighting effects including strobe lights and slides to add effect to a band's stage presentation, originally appearing around 1966. Coming at first from the acid-rock trend and attempting to represent the visual effects of hallucinogenic drugs, complex lighting is now an important part of all leading artists' stage shows.

Liner notes. Annotations, often biographical, appearing on record sleeves.

Live. A performance, sometimes recorded, made in a concert situation. Sometimes used to describe a studio recording with no studio effects or overdubs.

Liverpool sound. Including the Beatles, Gerry and the Pacemakers, the Searchers and the Swinging Blue Jeans, this describes the Liverpool groups who came to prominence between 1962 and 1965, playing an anglicized form of rhythm & blues. It is also known as Merseybeat.

Lovers' rock. A form of reggae emerging in the eighties with a heavy, sensuous texture and lyrics relating to the sexual rather than the political aspects of human relationships.

LP. Usually a collection of recordings originally issued on a twelve-inch, 33⅓ r.p.m. disc but now also on a cassette tape.

Lyric. The words to a song.

Lyricist. Writer of the words of songs but not the music, which is the work of the composer.

MOR. Middle-of-the-road music.

Memphis sound. Sam Phillips and his Sun Records made Memphis the key recording centre in the fifties. Recording both black and white artists and a range of styles from country, blues to rhythm & blues and the early rockabilly form. Elvis Presley, Roy Orbison, Charlie Rich and Jerry Lee Lewis all emerged from Sun. Later the Stax label produced such black artists as Otis Redding, Eddie Floyd and Isaac Hayes.

Merseybeat. Including the Beatles, Gerry and the Pacemakers, the Searchers and the Swinging Blue Jeans, this describes the Liverpool groups who came to prominence between 1962 and 1965, playing an anglicized form of rhythm & blues. It is also known as the Liverpool sound.

Miami sound. Two recording studios, Criteria and TK, exist in Miami. Criteria had been used by Crosby, Stills and Nash, Dr John and the Bee Gees. TK focusses on disco groups. There is no really cohesive sound or style.

Middle-of-the-road. In the midstream of popular music with the widest possible following. Often used in a pejorative sense to mean bland, conservative or the lowest common denominator of taste. Barry Manilow is a very good example.

Mix. After a recording is made on more than one track, the producer and engineer arrange the levels of the various recorded tracks. This is known as mixing or mixing down. The result is the mix.

Mod. The Mod subculture with its motor scooters, parka anoraks, Italian-style suits and short hair was a British phenomenon between 1963 and 1966. The mood and attitude of the Mods was portrayed in the music of the Who, the Small Faces and the Creation. During the British new wave of the late seventies several groups revived the feel and image of the mods, as did their fans. Such groups include the Jam, the Step and Eddy and the Hot Rods.

Motown. Berry Gordy created Tamla Motown Records in 1960. Originally based in Detroit, in the seventies the company moved to Los Angeles. Motown combined the intensity of rhythm & blues with a pop-music appeal of innocent teenage-orientated lyrics. The skill in the production of the early records of such artists as Smokey Robinson, the Four Tops, Diana Ross and the Supremes and Marvin Gaye still stands up almost twenty years later.

Multi-tracking. Tape recording on anything from four tracks up to, at present, fifty-six tracks, enabling one or many elements of a recording to by recorded at one time and mixed or edited later. All current recording uses this technique.

Musicals. A mixture of theatre and music, the musical, an established format since the thirties, is the modern description of light opera, operetta or musical comedy. In recent years the rock opera has appeared, being merely an updated version of a by now traditional form.

Music hall. The music-hall tradition – variety entertainment, popular songs, comedy and recitations – reached its height in the later nineteenth and early decades of the twentieth century. The tradition was affected by the cinema and finally killed by television in the mid fifties. Its legacy permeates British popular music from the Kinks through to the melodies of the Beatles.

Muzak. Often described as 'wallpaper' music, not to be listened to but providing a background in, for example, a restaurant or supermarket. Also used as a derogatory term for the blandest of modern popular music. Muzak tapes are produced specifically as background by session musicians but James Last and Bert Kaempfert produce Muzak by default. ('Muzak' is a trade name.)

Nashville sound. Nashville has been the principal country-music centre in the USA since 1925 with the establishment of the WSM radio station. Its first record company appeared in 1945. The Nashville sound evolved as a response to the local musicians adopting electric guitars to work with the rockabilly musicians who came from Memphis. It was the slickest and most professional in the world. By 1963 over half of all records in the USA were produced in Nashville and by the late sixties it had lost its country basis and catered for all styles of popular music.

New Orleans sound. The New Orleans style of rhythm & blues was characterized by a heavily accentuated rhythm section, light piano, brass with strong lead guitar and vocal. It included artists such as Little Richard, Fats Domino and Lee Dorsey, who all emerged from New Orleans, and Ray Charles, who recorded many classics in its studios.

New romantics. A reaction against the austerity of punk, this eighties fashion movement includes vivid-coloured hair, extravagant make-up and flamboyant, 'romantic' dress. Groups presenting themselves in this mode fall into the new wave, generally using electronic synthesizers and drum machines to excess. Spandau Ballet, Duran Duran, Toyah, Dépêche Mode and the Mobiles are good examples.

New wave. This movement, which began to emerge in 1976 as a reaction to the musical establishment, includes a wide range of styles. Punks such as the Clash; futuristic artists such as Ultravox, the Human League and Gary Numan; new-wave pop artists such as the Pretenders, the Tourists and Toyah; and even two-tone groups like the Beat, Selector and the Specials fall into this description. In the USA the definition is different. For example, the Talking Heads, although described there as new wave, are closer in style to the British art-rock concept, and Patti Smith and the Ramones are the American version of punks. In brief, it is the attempt of the artists to work away from what they see as the stagnant state of music and be more creative, contemporary and poignant that is their cohesion.

Novelty records. Records conforming to no pattern or genre, usually humorous in interest. The records of the Scaffold, Tiny Tim and even Benny Hill fall into this category.

Oi!. Appearing in 1980, a later form of British punk rock, with abrasive vocals and driving tuneless guitar. The groups displayed a skinhead image with cropped hair and exaggerated working-class manner. The lyrical themes were nihilistic and decidedly racist. Such groups played at National Front gatherings and at venues in Southall during the riots of summer, 1981, which consisted of provocatively nationalistic audiences. Groups include the 4 Skins, Rose Tattoo and the J J All Stars.

Outlaw music. Heavily influenced by rock'n'roll, this is the latest development in country music emerging in the late seventies in Texas. Leading exponents are Willie Nelson and Waylon Jennings. It is sometimes called redneck rock.

Outtake. A recorded performance not released for sale. Often alternative versions of songs, they may become collectors' items if later released or unofficially bootlegged.

Over-production. The building of the recorded sound of a piece of music which is more ornate or complex than is required or appropriate to that music.

Overdub. To record additional instruments or vocals over a previously-taped recording.

Phasing. A recording effect developed in the sixties involving the splitting of the original sound. Phaser pedals have been availabe since the mid seventies to simulate this effect in live performance.

Philadelphia sound. The Phillie sound of Philadelphia International Records was the seventies equivalent of Motown in the sixties. Formed by Kenneth Gamble and Leon Huff, who had produced dozens of soul hits in the sixties, the company's artists include the O'Jays, Delfonics, Detroit Spinners and Three Degrees. The sound is ornate, heavily orchestrated and although not disco, certainly danceable.

Platinum disc. Awarded by a record company for the sale of one million albums.

Pomp rock. A form of art rock working within the framework of classical musical forms, pomp rock is a grandiose style noted for its pomposity and pretentiousness. Arrangements are complex, using electric instruments, synthesizers and dramatic stage effects. Protagonists include Rick Wakeman, Genesis and Rush.

Pop gospel. Religious-orientated pop music with simple Christian messages and light backing. Cliff Richard is the leading performer to be occasionally involved.

Pop music. Originating from popular music, the term has come to mean the lighter, commercial forms of popular music aimed mainly at selling singles for chart success. Rock, on the other hand, is the more serious end of the spectrum. The problem of definition is that most artists fall between the two extremes. In the sixties pop music described all forms of music aimed at young people.

Power trio. A trio playing blues-based, highly amplified heavy rock with excessively long arrangements and leaden rhythm. Cream was followed by Grand Funk Railroad and hundreds of imitators playing in this format during the late sixties and early seventies. This style was a precursor of heavy metal.

Production. The creation of the sound of a recording and the balancing of the constituent instruments and vocals is done by the producer aided by engineers.

Progressive. During the early seventies this term sometimes described the serious side of rock music, including those musicians experimenting in technological innovation and those using classical forms. Art rock is a preferable term to describe such artists as King Crimson, Yes, Roxy Music and Emerson, Lake and Palmer.

Protest song. Led by Bob Dylan, the protest movement of the early and mid sixties was a direct descendant of the folk revival and in the spirit of such socially conscious singers as Woody Guthrie. Protest songs were the vogue by 1965 and many pop writers such as Jonathan King indulged in the trend. Apart from Dylan, Paul Simon, Art Garfunkel, Joan Baez and Donovan were the most successful artists.

Psychedelic rock. Music of the psychedelic era beginning in 1966 and continuing until the end of the decade. It aimed to mimic the drug experience of LSD. The Grateful Dead, early Soft Machine and early Pink Floyd are examples. It is also called acid rock.

Pub rock. This movement evolved in England during the early seventies when a series of interesting, creative bands built a following by playing pubs, mainly in London. Ducks Deluxe, Brinsley Schwarz, Kilburn and the Highroads and Dr Feelgood were leading examples. Pub rock is an important seminal ingredient in the British new wave.

Punk rock. Emerging in London in 1976, punk is the ultimate reaction against the rock-music establishment. Based on boundless energy, abrasive, politically leftwing lyrics and boasting no musicianship, it is characterized by a relentless guitar and drum rhythm. Most punk is derived from earlier bands such as the New York Dolls, Stooges and MC5. The Sex Pistols and Clash in Britain and the Ramones in America are typical.

R & B. Rhythm & blues.

Race music. Used to describe any form of black music up until the mid fifties.

Raga. An Indian form of music which came into vogue in the mid sixties specifically because of the use of the sitar by George Harrison on Beatles records. The Byrds are often credited with the use of raga-type musical themes described as raga rock, but they never used the sitar on any recording. A stylized electric-guitar-based pseudo form developed, led by Sam Gopal's Dream, and became popular in the London underground.

Record sleeve. The cardboard cover produced as protection for a disc. This has developed as a major marketing medium with much thought and effort being expended on design and production. Song lyrics, portraits and a wide range of gimmick devices may be included. A school of graphic artists has evolved specializing in this growing art form.

Redneck rock. Heavily influenced by rock'n'roll, this is the latest development in country music emerging in the late seventies in Texas. Leading exponents are Willie Nelson and Waylon Jennings. Usually called outlaw music.

Reggae. A style of music that emerged in Jamaica, derived from rhythm & blues but including the syncopated particular rhythms of ska, bluebeat and rock steady. Reggae is characterized by its mobile bass line and odd guitar style. The lyrics tend to concern the themes of the return of black people of Africa as pursued by the Rastafarians. The styles within reggae vary from the smooth and light of Toots and the Maytals to the roughness of Bunny Wailer. Reggae is now a major influence on all forms of popular music.

Release. The placing on the market of a new record. A release may be used to mean a record. Phrases are used such as new release, latest release and the release date of a record.

Rhythm & blues. The American black popular music created in the late forties and fifties, R & B was a synthesis of swing rhythms, blues vocal techniques and gospel intensity. There were regional variations in style and rhythm & blues was seen as a somewhat inferior form to its contemporary jazz form, be-bop. Much of rhythm & blues was transmitted to rock'n'roll and many of the leading artists in the style can be described as major creators of rock'n'roll. Fats Domino, Bo Diddley and Chuck Berry are good examples.

Rhythm guitar. Originally the second guitar part of a group with two guitars in the line-up, simply playing the chords to the rhythm of the piece. More recently many groups claim to have twin lead guitars but essentially the guitar's role was as part of a rhythm section and only with high amplification and the advent of rock'n'roll did it become a substantial front line instrument.

Roadie. Originally the abbreviation of 'road manager', now used to describe a member of the road crew who carry, set up, maintain and transport the equipment of a band.

Rock. Originally rock was used as an abbreviation for rock'n'roll. By 1970, however, a distinction had grown up between what was regarded as the more ephemeral, single record-orientated pop music and the more serious, up-market or heavier album-orientated rock music. This distinction persists and is a completely subjective division: Abba are pop music, Status Quo are rock music.

Rockabilly. Derived in the southern states of America where the country-music guitar style merged with black-music rhythms. Elvis Presley is seen as the catalyst of the style, which includes such artists as Carl Perkins, Buddy Holly and early Johnny Cash. It is the earliest genuine rock'n'roll style.

Rock'n'roll. Although misused as a general term to describe all modern popular music, rock'n'roll is more accurately the basis upon which current popular music has been built. It has influenced all existing styles, including black music, folk, country, jazz, musical shows and ballads. It was born in 1954 with the emergence of Bill Haley and the Comets and was profoundly developed by Elvis Presley. It is a white musical form, fusing black rhythm & blues and white country music with some traces of swing jazz. Rockabilly is a form of rock'n'roll although just where rhythm & blues and rock'n'roll meet is a moot point. Purists claim that rock'n'roll died when Elvis Presley entered the US Army in 1958. In its original form rock'n'roll continues to be enjoyed by the children of its original fans and in addition it continues to evolve throughout modern popular music.

Rock opera. Pete Townshend of the Who is usually credited with the invention of this concept. He changed the idea of the album as a collection of heterogeneous songs into a narrative work with a single theme. Tommy is regarded as the earliest but P. F. Sorrow by the Pretty Things is also cited. Later came works such as Godspell, Jesus Christ Superstar and Evita, which come closer to true operetta but are regarded as part of the genre.

Rock steady. A West Indian style of popular music which followed bluebeat with a louder beat and was the forerunner of reggae.

San Francisco sound. San Francisco had always been a centre for jazz but it was not until 1966, when it became the nucleus of the hippy cult, that rock music began to blossom there. The Fillmore and Avalon ballrooms developed psychedelic dances which produced major artists such as Janis Joplin, the Jefferson Airplane, the Grateful Dead, the Steve Miller Band and dozens more. There is no single style uniting these bands but a general eclecticism and theme of experimentation. Highly influenced by British beat music, it took a great deal from jazz and folk music and later produced music as different as Creedence Clearwater's energetic swamp rock and Sly Stone's revolutionary soul style.

Session musician. A freelance musician. Most often used in the context of a musician hired for a specific recording session.

Singer-songwriter. An artist who both writes and sings his material and who is usually able to perform solo, playing, for example, acoustic guitar or piano. Often the lyrics are highly personal. There was a particularly strong movement in this field in the early seventies including such artists as Joni Mitchell, Neil Young, James Taylor, Jackson Browne and Randy Newman.

Single. A seven-inch gramophone record with one recording on each side revolving at 45 r.p.m., also known as a 45.

Ska. A West Indian style of popular music with a heavy off beat which, like rock steady, was a development of bluebeat and a forerunner of reggae.

Skiffle. A British phenomenon between 1956 and 1958 which incorporated traditional, Dixieland jazz rhythms in country, blues and folk songs. Evolving originally from the rhythm sections of established tradtional jazz bands, Lonnie Donegan, who was with Chris Barber, led the movement. Attractive because of its simplicity and the ease in which amateur groups could be formed, many of the early British beat musicians of the sixties, such as the Beatles and Rolling Stones, learned their guitar playing in skiffle groups.

Soft rock. Emerging in the seventies perhaps with the growing-up of a generation who had been weaned on rock'n'roll and were now mellowing, soft rock includes singer-songwriters, West Coast bands and the more mature, creative elements of pop music. Elton John, the Eagles, Randy Newman, Fleetwood Mac and even Jackson Browne would be examples.

Solo. An instrumental passage performed by one instrument away from the general structure of the song. Also used in the context of a performer who was part of group and has begun a 'solo' career or made a 'solo' album.

Soul. Evolving out of rhythm & blues, soul adapted gospel songs and gospel intensity into a secular form. Ray Charles was a leader in the field, followed notably by Ben E. King and Sam Cooke. Soul arrangements also brought added sophistication to its rhythm & blues base with the complex orchestration of, for example, the Drifters' songs of the late fifties. The record companies Atlantic, Stax and Motown all developed the genre throughout the sixties with artists such as Otis Redding, Wilson Pickett, Aretha Franklin and Curtis Mayfield.

Space rock. Rock music with either lyrical themes concerned with science fiction or a musical sound evoking the atmosphere of space, the cosmos or the unknown. Pink Floyd, David Bowie, Hawkwind and even the Byrds are included.

Spiritual. A folk song usually of the black community with a religious theme. An important influence on gospel music.

Stage show. The presentation of an artist's performance in a live, concert situation. Theatrical effects, lighting, choreography will all be included.

Stringmachine. An electronic synthesizer which enables a keyboard player to create the strings sound of an orchestra. The ARP Stringmachine is the best known.

Surf music. Originating in southern California in the early sixties and made famous by Jan and Dean and the Beach Boys, surf music and its associated, lesser form, hot-rod music, celebrated the middle-class, Californian teenage lifestyle of cars, surfing, girls, beach parties and high school in detail. Its style was based on rock'n'roll chord structures with complex falsetto harmonies which later evolved into some of the most complex music of the sixties. The trend died out in 1966.

Swamp rock. Evoking the atmosphere of the Louisiana bayous both lyrically and in its mysterious sound, this term particularly describes the work of the Creedence Clearwater Revival and Tony Joe White. It is in many ways an artificial form. John Fogerty of the Creedence Clearwater Revival had never even been to Louisiana when he began writing his down home songs.

Synthesizer. An electronic instrument able to create a wide range of musical sounds programmed by the operator.

Take. A single recorded performance in a studio is known as a take. Several takes may be required to perfect the various tracks.

Tamla. Alternative abbreviation of the Tamla Motown record company's sound. Founded by Berry Gordy the company was originally based in Detroit, moving later to Los Angeles. Its artists include Stevie Wonder, Diana Ross and the Supremes, Smokey Robinson and Marvin Gaye.

Techno-flash. Also known as flash, this is technically complex, very fast playing of any instrument. In the early seventies rock bands such as Yes, with the guitar playing of Steve Howe and keyboard playing of Rick Wakeman, would be described in this way. Such an approach is regarded by many as too contrived and lacking in emotion.

Teenybop. Used to describe the music of artists such as the Bay City Rollers, the Osmonds and David Cassidy with a following from a predominantly pre-teenage market, termed teenyboppers. The youthful, pretty appearance of the performers is the significant factor, there is no homogeneous style to the music.

Tex-mex. A term used to describe Latin-influenced rock and country music which has developed in Texas. Ry Cooder is the best-known exponent.

Tin Pan Alley. This described the popular-music industry before the revolutionary changes brought on by rock'n'roll and black music since the fifties.

Tour. A series of concerts undertaken in quick succession. Nowadays touring is a costly and exhausting business and is usually used as an exercise to promote record sales. The costs of road crews, public address equipment, transportation and hotel bills means that only groups like the Rolling Stones playing in enormous stadia can hope to make money from touring.

Trad jazz. British term for traditional New Orleans or Dixieland jazz. In the fifties there were hundreds of bands playing in this style. They included Ken Colyer, Mick Mulligan and Chris Barber. Out of such bands emerged the skiffle craze and artists such as Alexis Korner who pioneered the British blues movement. It was associated with the Campaign for Nuclear Disarmament movement and was regarded as rather more socially acceptable than early rock'n'roll.

Twelve-inch single. Developed for the disco boom to give higher-quality and longer versions of recordings which were usually already hits on standard seven-inch singles.

Two-tone. The name of a record label which appeared in 1978 in Britain. So called because of the racially mixed line-ups of the groups involved. These included the Specials, Bodysnatchers and the Beat. It also describes the style of music which is bluebeat-influenced with British, working-class themes of boredom and unemployment.

Vaudeville. The American form of music hall: variety entertainment, popular songs and comedy. It is less of an influence on American modern popular music than is music hall in Britain.

Voice box. A device by which musicians, usually guitarists, shape an instrument's sound and tone with their mouths. Notably used by Jeff Beck and Peter Frampton.

Wah-wah. An effect operated by the use of a pedal which emerged in 1966. Capable of being used with any amplified instrument, it is most often associated with the guitar. Its operation was perfected by Frank Zappa and Jimi Hendrix.

Wall of sound. A record production style devised by Phil Spector in which the individual musical instruments are merged into an overpowering, massed effect.

Wallpaper music. A colloquialism for muzak. This is not to be listened to but provides a background in, for example, a restaurant or supermarket. The blandest of all popular music, it is usually mechanically produced by session musicians for this express purpose.

West Coast music. The music of Los Angeles and San Francisco, including the styles of surf music, folk rock, acid rock and, more recently, soft rock and many of the singer-songwriters.

Western swing. Country music influenced by jazz as played by country-music bands augmented with brass instruments, originally developed by Bob Wills and his Texas Playboys.

Indexes

The method of alphabetization is word-by-word. References are to page numbers.

Author index

Authors, illustrators, photographers, compilers, editors, translators, designers, and writers of introductions and forewords have all been indexed.

Title index

Subtitles are included only to differentiate between works with identical titles and do not affect the general sequence, merely the order of the specific, identical title.

Subject index

The names of artists, record producers, groups, bands, disc jockeys, songwriters and managers comprise the bulk of entries in this index. The residue consists of forms of literature, forms of music and other subjects along with record companies, festivals, films and musicals. These names are qualified by their contexts; for example: Woodstock (festival), Cats (musical), Help! (film).

Author index

Title index

Subject index